THE O'LEARY SERIES

Microsoft® Access 2000

Introductory Edition

Timothy J. O'Leary
Arizona State University

Linda I. O'Leary

Boston   Burr Ridge, IL   Dubuque, IA   Madison, WI   New York
San Francisco   St. Louis   Bangkok   Bogotá   Caracas   Lisbon
London   Madrid   Mexico City   Milan   New Delhi   Seoul
Singapore   Sydney   Taipei   Toronto

McGraw-Hill Higher Education

*A Division of The **McGraw-Hill** Companies*

MICROSOFT® ACCESS 2000, INTRODUCTORY EDITION

This book is printed on acid-free paper.

domestic   6 7 8 9 0 QPD/QPD 9 0 9 8 7 6 5 4 3 2 1
international 3 4 5 6 7 8 9 0 QPD/QPD 9 0 9 8 7 6 5 4 3 2 1

ISBN 0-07-233749-4

Vice president/Editor-in-chief: *Michael W. Junior*
Publisher: *David Brake*
Sponsoring Editor: *Trisha O'Shea*
Senior project manager: *Beth Cigler*
Manager, new book production: *Melonie Salvati*
Freelance design coordinator: *Gino Cieslik*
Cover design: *Francis Owens*
Cover Illustration: *Paul Wiley*
Supplement coordinator: *Marc Mattson*
Compositor: *Rogondino & Associates*
Typeface: *11/13 Century Book*
Printer: *Quebecor World Dubuque*

Library of Congress Catalog Card Number 99-65256

INTERNATIONAL EDITION ISBN 0-07-116814-1
Copyright © 2000, Exclusive rights by The McGraw-Hill Companies, Inc.
for manufacture and export.
This book cannot be re-exported from the country to which it is consigned
by McGraw-Hill.
The International Edition is not available in North America.

http://www.mhhe.com

Microsoft® Access 2000

Introductory Edition

Timothy J. O'Leary
Arizona State University

Linda I. O'Leary

At McGraw-Hill Higher Education, we publish instructional materials targeted at the higher education market. In an effort to expand the tools of higher learning, we publish texts, lab manuals, study guides, testing materials, software, and multimedia products.

At **Irwin/McGraw-Hill** (a division of McGraw-Hill Higher Education), we realize that technology has created and will continue to create new mediums for professors and students to use in managing resources and communicating information with one another. We strive to provide the most flexible and complete teaching and learning tools available as well as offer solutions to the changing world of teaching and learning.

Irwin/McGraw-Hill is dedicated to providing the tools for today's instructors and students to successfully navigate the world of Information Technology.

- **Seminar series**—Irwin/McGraw-Hill's Technology Connection seminar series offered across the country every year demonstrates the latest technology products and encourages collaboration among teaching professionals.

- **Osborne/McGraw-Hill**—This division of The McGraw-Hill Companies is known for its best-selling Internet titles *Harley Hahn's Internet & Web Yellow Pages* and the *Internet Complete Reference*. Osborne offers an additional resource for certification and has strategic publishing relationships with corporations such as Corel Corporation and America Online. For more information visit Osborne at **www.osborne.com**.

- **Digital solutions**—Irwin/McGraw-Hill is committed to publishing digital solutions. Taking your course online doesn't have to be a solitary venture, nor does it have to be a difficult one. We offer several solutions that will allow you to enjoy all the benefits of having course material online. For more information visit **www.mhhe.com/solutions/index.mhtml**.

- **Packaging options**—For more about our discount options, contact your local Irwin/McGraw-Hill Sales representative at 1-800-338-3987 or visit our Web site at **www.mhhe.com/it**.

Preface

Goals/Philosophy

The goal of *The O'Leary Series* is to give students a basic understanding of computing concepts and to build the skills necessary to ensure that information technology is an advantage in whatever path they choose in life. Because we believe that students learn better and retain more information when concepts are reinforced visually, we feature a unique visual orientation coupled with our trademark "learn by doing" approach.

Approach

The O'Leary Series is the true *step-by-step way to develop computer application skills*. The new Microsoft Office 2000 design emphasizes the step-by-step instructions with full screen captures that illustrate the results of each step performed. Each Tutorial (chapter) follows the "learn by doing" approach in combining conceptual coverage with detailed, software-specific instructions. A running case study that is featured in each tutorial highlights the real-world capabilities of each of the software applications and leads students step by step from problem to solution.

APPROVED MICROSOFT COURSEWARE

Use of the Microsoft Office User Specialist Approved Courseware Logo on this product signifies that it has been independently reviewed and approved in compliance with the following standards: Acceptable coverage of all content related to the Microsoft Office Exam entitled Microsoft Access 2000 and sufficient performance-based exercises that closely apply to all required content, based on sampling of text. For further information on Microsoft's MOUS certification program, please visit Microsoft's Web site at http://www.microsoft.com/office/train_cert/.

About the Book

The O'Leary Series offers 2 *levels* of instruction: Brief and Introductory. Each level builds upon the previous level.

- **Brief**—This level covers the basics of an application and contains two to three chapters.

- **Introductory**—This level includes the material in the Brief textbook plus two to three additional chapters. The Introductory text prepares students for the *Microsoft Office User Specialist Exam (MOUS Certification)*.

Each text features:

- **Common Office 2000 Features**—This section provides a review of several basic procedures and Windows features. Students will also learn about many of the features that are common to all Microsoft Office 2000 applications.

- **Overview**—The Overview contains a "Before You Begin" section which presents both students and professors with all the information they need to know before starting the tutorials, including hardware and software settings. The Overview appears at the beginning of each lab manual and describes (1) what the program is, (2) what the program can do, (3) generic terms the program uses, and (4) the Case Study to be presented.

- **Working Together sections**—These sections provide the same hands-on visual approach found in the tutorials to the integration and new collaboration features of Office 2000.

- **Glossary**—The Glossary appears at the end of each text and defines all key terms that appear in boldface type throughout the tutorials and in the end-of-tutorial Key Terms lists.

- **Index**—The Index appears at the end of each text and provides a quick reference to find specific concepts or terms in the text.

Introductory Edition

The Introductory Edition is divided into six tutorials, and two Working Together sections.

Tutorial 1: You will learn how to design and create the structure for a computerized database and you will enter and edit records in the database. You will also print a table of the records you enter in the database file.

Tutorial 2: You will continue to build, modify, and use the employee database of records. You will learn how to sort the records in a database file to make it easier to locate records. Additionally, you will create a form to make it easier to enter and edit data in the database file.

Tutorial 3: You will learn how to query the database to locate specific information. You will also learn how to create a report and link multiple tables.

Working Together: After querying the database to create a list of all employees who have five years service with the club, you will need to send the query results to Brian, the club owner, along with a brief memo. You will learn how to share information between applications while you create the memo.

Tutorial 4: As you continue to build and enhance the employee database for the Lifestyle Fitness Club you learn about table properties such as input masks, lookup fields, and required property settings that help increase the accuracy of data entry. You also learn more about how to analyze table data by creating calculated fields and using crosstab queries and subdatasheets. Finally, you define relationships between tables and enforce referential integrity as well as learn about the importance of backing up your data.

Tutorial 5: As you have learned, forms make viewing and updating information in tables easier and more efficient. In this tutorial, you will learn how to create a custom form that consists of a main form and a subform which will update multiple tables simultaneously. The addition of command buttons that contain macros will also help automate the process of using the form.

Tutorial 6: Producing meaningful reports from table data and queries is an important aspect of using a database. In this tutorial, you will learn how to group and summarize data in a report and display it in an attractive and organized manner. You will also learn how to create mailing labels. Finally, you will develop macros and a switchboard system that will make it easier for others to use the database and print reports.

Working Together: This tutorial demonstrates how to import and export data between Access and other applications. In addition, you learn how to convert an Access report to a Web page so others using a browser can view it.

Each tutorial features:

- **Step-by-step instructions**—Each tutorial consists of step-by-step instructions along with accompanying screen captures. The screen captures represent how the student's screen should appear after completing a specific step.

- **Competencies**—Listed at the beginning of each tutorial, the Competencies describe what skills will be mastered upon completion of the tutorial.

- **Concept Overview**—Located at the start of each tutorial, the Concept Overviews provide a brief introduction to the concepts to be presented.

- **Concept boxes**—Tied into the Concept Overviews, the Concept boxes appear throughout the tutorial and provide clear, concise explanations of the concepts under discussion, which makes them a valuable study aid.

- **Marginal notes**—Appearing throughout the tutorial, marginal notes provide helpful hints, suggestions, troubleshooting advice, and alternative methods of completing tasks.

- **Case study**—The running case study carried throughout each tutorial and is based on real use of software in a business setting.

- **End-of-tutorial material**—At the end of each tutorial the following are provided:

  Concept Summary—This two-page spread presents a visual summary of the concepts presented in the tutorial and can be used as a study aid for students.

  Key Terms—This page-referenced list is a useful study aid for students.

  Matching/Multiple Choice/True False Questions

  Command Summary—The Command Summary includes keyboard and toolbar shortcuts.

  Screen Identifications—These exercises ask students to demonstrate their understanding of the applications by identifying screen features.

  Discussion Questions—These questions are designed to stimulate in-class discussion.

  Hands-On Practice Exercises—These detailed exercises of increasing difficulty ask students to create Office documents based on the skills learned in the tutorial.

  On Your Own—These problems of increasing difficulty ask students to employ more creativity and independence in creating Office documents based on new case scenarios.

Acknowledgments

The new edition of the Microsoft Office 2000 has been made possible only through the enthusiasm and dedication of a great team of people. Because the team spans the country, literally from coast to coast, we have utilized every means of working together including conference calls, FAX, e-mail, and document collaboration . . . we have truly tested the team approach and it works!

Leading the team from Irwin/McGraw-Hill is Trisha O'Shea, Sponsoring Editor. Her renewed commitment, direction, and support has infused the team with the excitement of a new project.

The production staff is headed by Beth Cigler, Senior Project Manager whose planning and attention to detail has made it possible for us to successfully meet a very challenging schedule. Members of the production team include: Gino Cieslik and Francis Owens, art and design, Pat Rogondino, layout; Susan Defosset, Betsy Blumenthal, and Joan Paterson, copy editing. While all have contributed immensely, I would particularly like to thank Pat and Susan . . . team members for many past editions whom I can always depend on to do a great job. My thanks also go to the project Marketing Manager, Jodi McPherson, for her enthusiastic promotion of this edition.

Finally, I am particularly grateful to a small but very dedicated group of people who helped me develop the manuscript. My deepest appreciation is to my co-author, consultant, and lifelong partner, Tim, for his help and support while I have been working on this edition. Colleen Hayes, who has been assisting me from the beginning, continues to be my right arm, taking on more responsibility with each edition. Susan Demar and Carol Dean have also helped on the last several editions and continue to provide excellent developmental and technical support. New to the project this year are Bill Barth, Kathi Duggan, and Steve Willis, who have provided technical expertise and youthful perspective.

Reviewers

We would also like to thank the reviewers for their insightful input and criticism. Their feedback has helped to make this edition even stronger.

Josephine A. Braneky, *New York City Technical College*
Robert Breshears, *Maryville University*

Gary Buterbaugh, *Indiana University of Pennsylvania*
Mitchell M. Charkiewicz, *Bay Path College*
Seth Hock, *Columbus State Community College*
Katherine S. Hoppe, *Wake Forest University*
Lisa Miller, *University of Central Oklahoma*
Anne Nelson, *High Point University*
Judy Tate, *Tarrant County Junior College*
Dottie Sunio, *Leeward Community College*
Charles Walker, *Harding University*
Mark E. Workman, *Blinn College*

Additionally, each semester I hear from students at Arizona State University who are enrolled in the Introduction to Computers course. They constantly provide great feedback from a student's perspective . . . I thank you all.

Finally, I would like to thank the World Gym of Mesa for their input into the Lifestyle Fitness Club case study.

Features of This Text

Concept 5 Automatic Grammar Check

The automatic grammar-checking feature advises you of incorrect grammar as you create and edit a document, and proposes possible corrections. If Word detects grammatical errors in subject-verb agreements, verb forms, capitalization, or commonly confused words, to name a few, they are identified with a wavy green line. You can correct the grammatical error by editing it or you can display a suggested correction. Not all grammatical errors identified by Word are actual errors. Use discretion when correcting the errors. Grammar checking does not occur until after you enter punctuation or end a line.

2 Right-click on Announcing four to display the Grammar shortcut menu.

Your screen should be similar to Figure 1–10.

Figure 1–10

Additional Information

A dimmed option means it is currently unavailable.

A shortcut menu showing a suggested correction is displayed. The Grammar shortcut menu also includes several related menu options described below.

Option	Effect
Ignore	Instructs Word to ignore the grammatical error in this sentence.
Grammar	Opens the Grammar Checker and displays an explanation of the error.
About this Sentence	If the Office Assistant feature is on, this option is available. It also provides a detailed explanation of the error.

Because you cannot readily identify the reason for the error, you will open the Grammar Checker.

Other Features

Real World Case—Each O'Leary Lab Manual provides students with a fictitious running case study. This case study provides students with the real-world capabilities for each software application. Each tutorial builds upon the gained knowledge of the previous tutorial with a single case study running throughout each Lab Manual.

End-of-Chapter Material—Each tutorial ends with a visual **Concept Summary**. This two-page spread presents a concept summary of the concepts presented in the tutorial and can be used as a study aid for

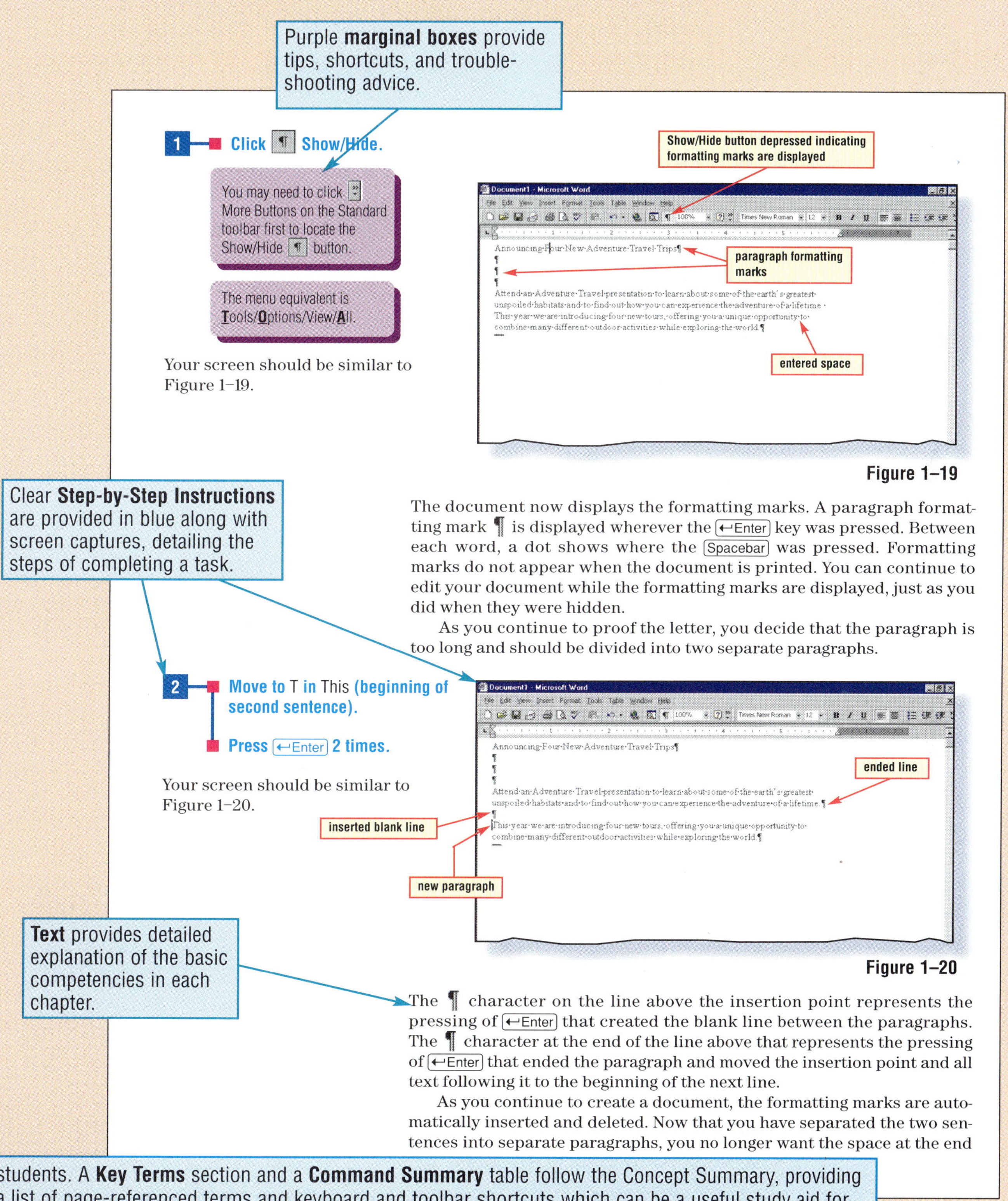

The document now displays the formatting marks. A paragraph formatting mark ¶ is displayed wherever the [←Enter] key was pressed. Between each word, a dot shows where the [Spacebar] was pressed. Formatting marks do not appear when the document is printed. You can continue to edit your document while the formatting marks are displayed, just as you did when they were hidden.

As you continue to proof the letter, you decide that the paragraph is too long and should be divided into two separate paragraphs.

The ¶ character on the line above the insertion point represents the pressing of [←Enter] that created the blank line between the paragraphs. The ¶ character at the end of the line above that represents the pressing of [←Enter] that ended the paragraph and moved the insertion point and all text following it to the beginning of the next line.

As you continue to create a document, the formatting marks are automatically inserted and deleted. Now that you have separated the two sentences into separate paragraphs, you no longer want the space at the end

Teaching Resources

The following is a list of supplemental material that can be used to help teach this course.

Skills Assessment

Irwin/McGraw-Hill offers two innovative systems that can be used with The O'Leary Series, ATLAS and SimNet, which take skills assessment testing beyond the basics with pre- and post-assessment capability.

- **ATLAS (Active Testing and Learning Assessment Software)**— ATLAS is our **live** in-the-application skills assessment tool. ATLAS allows students to perform tasks while working *live* within the Microsoft applications environment. ATLAS is web-enabled and can be customized to meet the needs of your course. ATLAS is available for Office 2000.

- **SimNet (Simulated Network Assessment Product)**—SimNet permits you to test the actual software skills students learn about Microsoft Office applications in a simulated environment. SimNet is web-enabled and is available for Office 97 and Office 2000.

Instructor's Resource Kits

Instructor's Resource Kits provide professors with all of the ancillary material needed to teach a course. Irwin/McGraw-Hill is committed to providing instructors with the most effective instructional resources available. Many of these resources are available at our Information Technology Supersite, found at **www.mhhe.com/it**. Our Instructor's Resource Kits are available on CD-ROM and contain the following:

- **Diploma by Brownstone**—Diploma is the most flexible, powerful, and easy to use computerized testing system available in higher education. The Diploma system allows professors to create an exam as a printed version, as a LAN-based Online version, or as an Internet version. Diploma also includes grade book features, which automate the entire testing process.

- **Instructor's Manual**—The Instructor's Manual includes solutions to all lessons and end of the unit material, teaching tips and strategies, and additional exercises. New to the O'Leary series, all of the figures from the application textbooks are available in PowerPoint slides for presentation purposes.

- **Student Data Files**—Students must have student data files in order to complete practice and test sessions. The instructor and students using this text in classes are granted the right to post student data files on any network or stand-alone computer, or to distribute the files on individual diskettes. The student data files may be downloaded from our IT Supersite at **www.mhhe.com/it**.

- **Series Web site**—Available at **www.mhhe.com/cit/oleary**.

Digital Solutions

- **Pageout Lite**—This software is designed for you if you're just beginning to explore Web site options. Pageout Lite will help you to easily post your own material online. You may choose one of three templates, type in your material, and Pageout Lite will instantly convert it to HTML.

- **Pageout**—Pageout is our Course Web Site Development Center. Pageout offers a syllabus page, Web site address, Online Learning Center content, online exercises and quizzes, gradebook, discussion board, an area for students to build their own Web pages, plus all features of Pageout Lite. For more information please visit the Pageout Web site at **www.mhla.net/pageout**.

- **OLC/Series Web Sites**—Online Learning Centers (OLCs)/series sites are accessible through our Supersite at **www.mhhe.com/it**. Our Online Learning Centers/series sites provide pedagogical features and supplements for our titles online. Students can point and click their way to key terms, learning objectives, chapter overviews, PowerPoint slides, exercises, and Web links.

- **The McGraw-Hill Learning Architecture (MHLA)**—MHLA is a complete course delivery system. MHLA gives professors ownership in the way digital content is presented to the class through online quizzing, student collaboration, course administration, and content management. For a walk-through of MHLA, visit the MHLA Web site at **www.mhla.net**.

Packaging Options

For more about our discount options, contact your local Irwin/McGraw-Hill sales representative at 1-800-338-3987 or visit our Web site at **www.mhhe.com/it**.

Contents

Introducing Common Office 2000 Features

This section will review several basic procedures and windows features. In addition you will learn about many of the features that are common to all Microsoft Office 2000 applications. Although Access 2000 will be used to demonstrate how the features work, only common features will be addressed. The features that are specific to the application itself will be introduced individually in each tutorial.

Turning on the Computer

If necessary, follow the procedure below to turn on your computer.

1 **Turn on the power switch.** The power switch is commonly located on the back or right side of your computer. It may also be a button that you push on the front of your computer.

If necessary, turn your monitor on and adjust the contrast and brightness. Generally, the button to turn on the monitor is located on the front of the monitor. Use the dials (generally located in the panel on the front of the monitor) to adjust the monitor.

If you are on a network, you may be asked to enter your User Name and Password. Type the required information in the boxes. When you are done, press ⏎Enter.

The Windows program is loaded into the main memory of your computer and the Windows desktop is displayed.

Your screen should be similar to Figure 1.

Figure 1

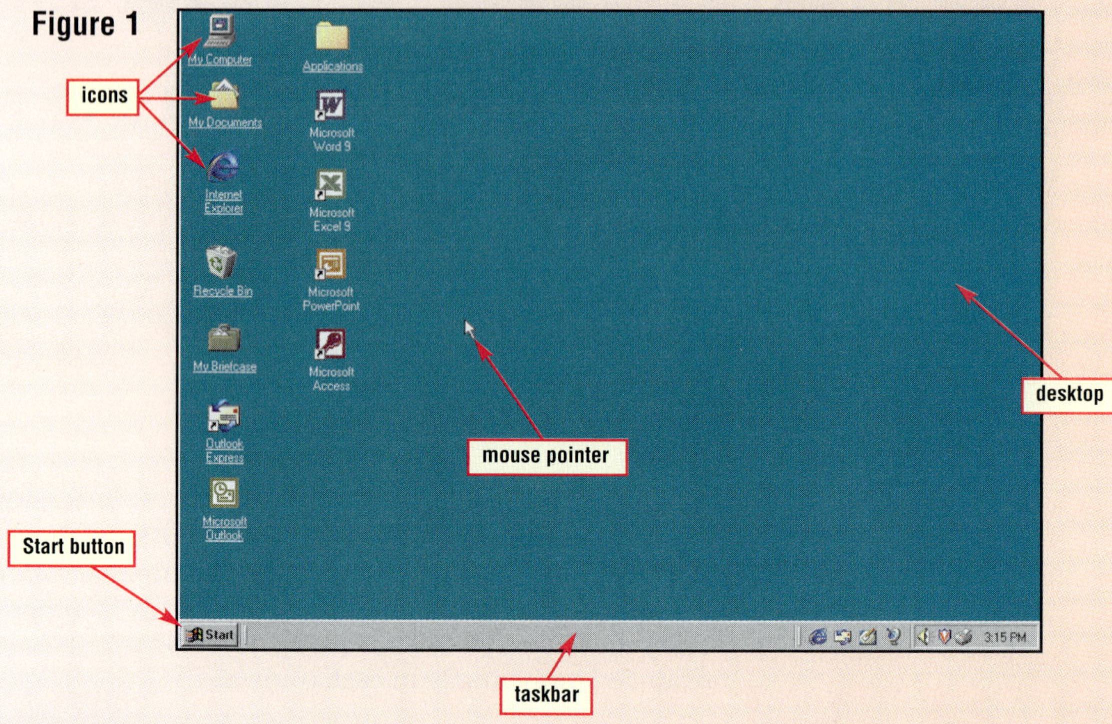

If a Welcome box is displayed, click ▣ (in the upper right corner of the box) to close it.

The **desktop** is the opening screen for Windows and is the place where you begin your work using the computer. Figure 1 shows the Windows 98 desktop. If you are using Windows 95 your screen will look slightly different. Small pictures, called **icons**, represent the objects on the desktop. Your desktop will probably display many different icons than shown here. At the bottom of the desktop screen is the taskbar. It contains buttons that are used to access programs and features. The **Start button** on the left end of the bar is used to start a program, open a document, get help, find information, and change system settings.

If you are already familiar with using a mouse, skip to the section Loading an Office Application.

Using a Mouse

The arrow-shaped symbol on your screen is the **mouse pointer**. It is used to interact with objects on the screen and is controlled by the hardware device called a **mouse** that is attached to your computer.

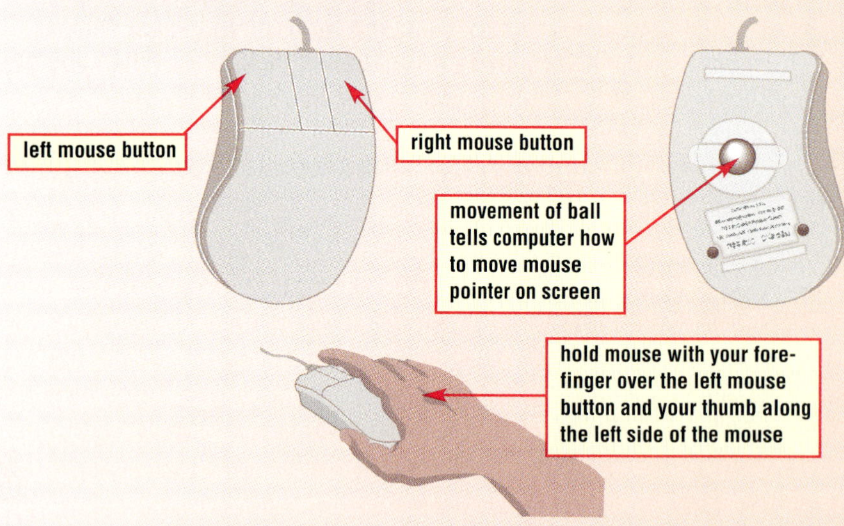

The mouse pointer changes shape on the screen depending on what it is pointing to. Some of the most common shapes are shown in the table below.

Pointer Shape	Meaning
	Normal select
	Link select
	Busy
	Area is not available

On top of the mouse are two or three buttons that are used to choose items on the screen. The mouse actions and descriptions are shown in the table below.

If your system has a stick, ball or touch pad, the buttons are located adjacent to the device.

Action	Description
Point	Move the mouse so the mouse pointer is positioned on the item you want to use.
Click	Press and release a mouse button. The left mouse button is the primary button that is used for most tasks.
Double-click	Quickly press and release the left mouse button twice.
Drag	Move the mouse while holding down the mouse button.

Throughout the labs, click means to use the left mouse button. If the right mouse button is to be used, the directions will tell you to right-click on the item.

1 Move the mouse in all directions (up, down, left, and right) and note the movement of the mouse pointer.

Point to the My Computer.

Your screen should be similar to Figure 2.

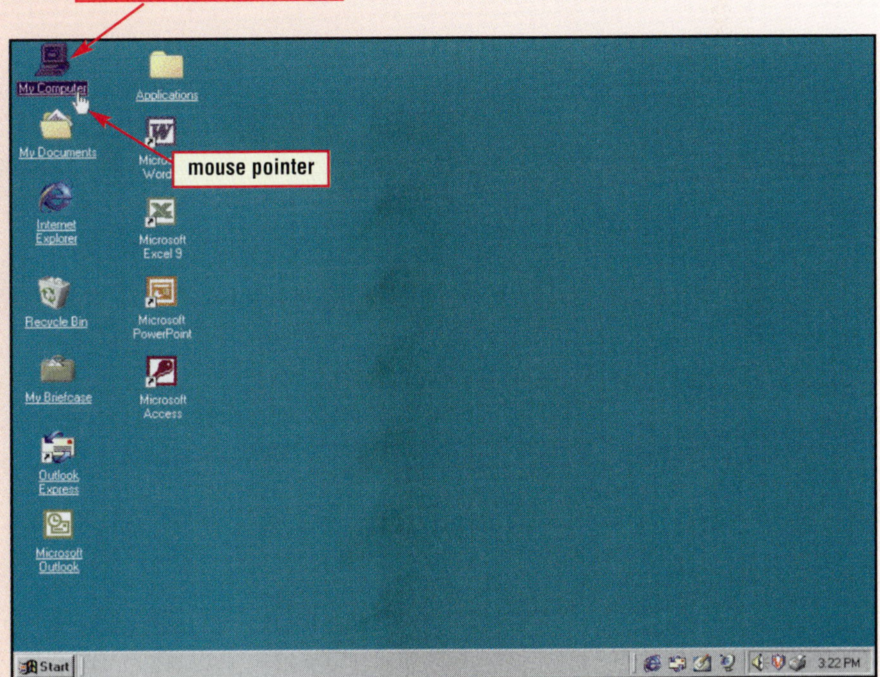

Figure 2

> Depending on the version of Windows you are using and the setup, the mouse pointer may be ↖ and you will need to click on the icon to select it.

The pointer on the screen moved in the direction you moved the mouse and currently appears as a ☝. The icon appears highlighted, indicating it is the selected item and ready to be used. A **ScreenTip** box containing a brief description of the item you are pointing to may be displayed.

Starting an Office Application

There are several ways to start an Office application. One is to use the Start/New Office Document command and select the type of document you want to create. Another is to use Start/Documents and select the document name from the list of recently used documents. This starts the associated application and opens the selected document at the same time. The two most common ways to start an Office 2000 application are by choosing the application name from the Start menu or by clicking a desktop shortcut for the program if it is available.

> Point to a Start menu option to select it; click it to choose it.

> If you are using Windows 98, depending on your setup, you may only need to single-click the shortcut.

1 — **Click Start to display the Start menu.**

Select Programs

Choose Microsoft Access.

or

Double-click the Microsoft Access shortcut.

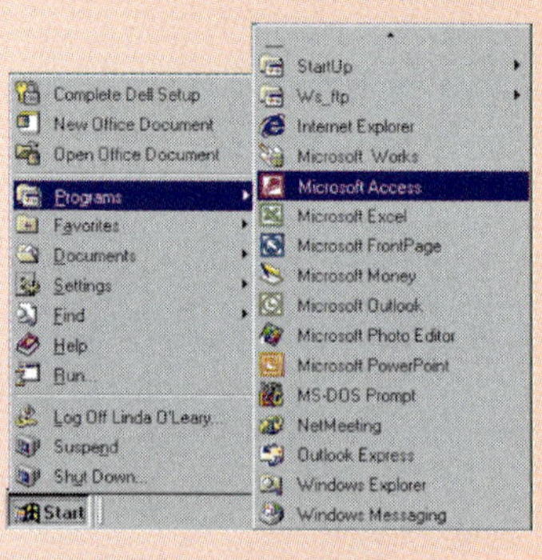

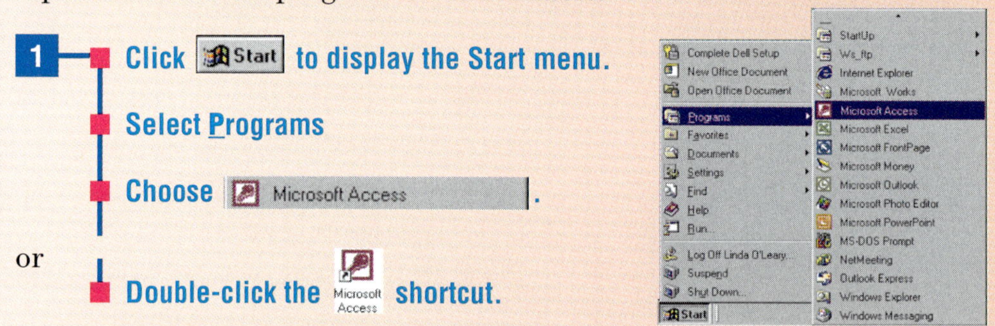

After a few moments, the Access 2000 application window is displayed.

2 — **Click Cancel to close the dialog box.**

Your screen should be similar to Figure 3.

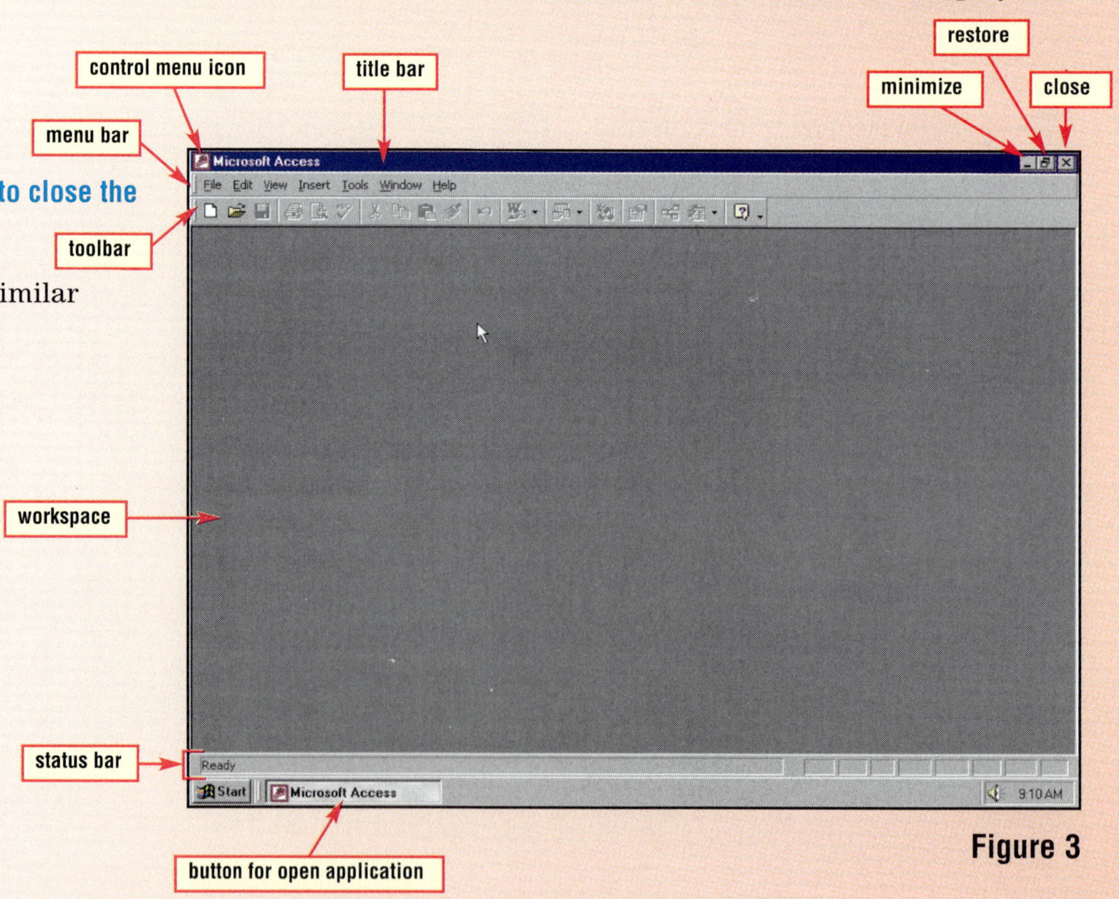

Figure 3

The Access 2000 application is loaded and displayed in a window on the desktop. The taskbar displays a button for the open window.

Basic Windows Features

As you can see, many of the features in the Access window are the same as in other Windows applications. Among those features is a title bar, a menu bar, toolbars, a document window, scroll bars, and mouse compatibility. You can move and size Office application windows, select commands, use Help, and switch between files and programs, just as you can in Windows. The common user interface makes learning and using new applications much easier.

TITLE BAR

The Access window **title bar** displays the program name, Microsoft Access. The left end of the title bar contains the Access application window ▨ Control-menu icon, and the right end displays the ▭ Minimize, ▭ Restore, and ☒ Close buttons. They perform the same functions and operate in the same way as in Windows 95 and Windows 98.

1 ■ If necessary, click ▭ in the title bar to maximize the application window.

MENU BAR

The **menu bar** below the title bar displays the Access program menu, which consists of seven menus. The right end will display the workbook window ☒ Close button when a workbook is open. As you use the Office applications you will see that the menu bar contains many of the same menus, such as File, Edit and Help. You will also see several menus that are specific to each application. You will learn about using the menus in the next section.

TOOLBARS

The **toolbar** located below the menu bar contain buttons that are mouse shortcuts for many of the menu items. Commonly, the Office applications will display two toolbars when the application is first opened; Standard and Formatting. They may appear together on one row or on separate rows. Access 2000 initially displays a single toolbar named Database. You will learn about using the toolbars shortly.

WORKSPACE

The **workspace** is the large center area of the Access application window is where workbook files are displayed in open windows. Currently there is no workbook open.

STATUS BAR

The **status bar** at the bottom of the window displays location information and the status of different settings as they are used. Different information is displayed in the status bar for different applications.

Using Office 2000 Features

MENUS

A **menu** is one of many methods you can use to tell a program what you want it to do. When opened, a menu displays a list of commands. Most menus appear in a menu bar. Other menus pop up when you right-click (click the right mouse button) on an item. This type of menu is called a **shortcut menu**.

1 ■ **Click Tools to open the Tools menu.**

Your screen should be similar to Figure 4.

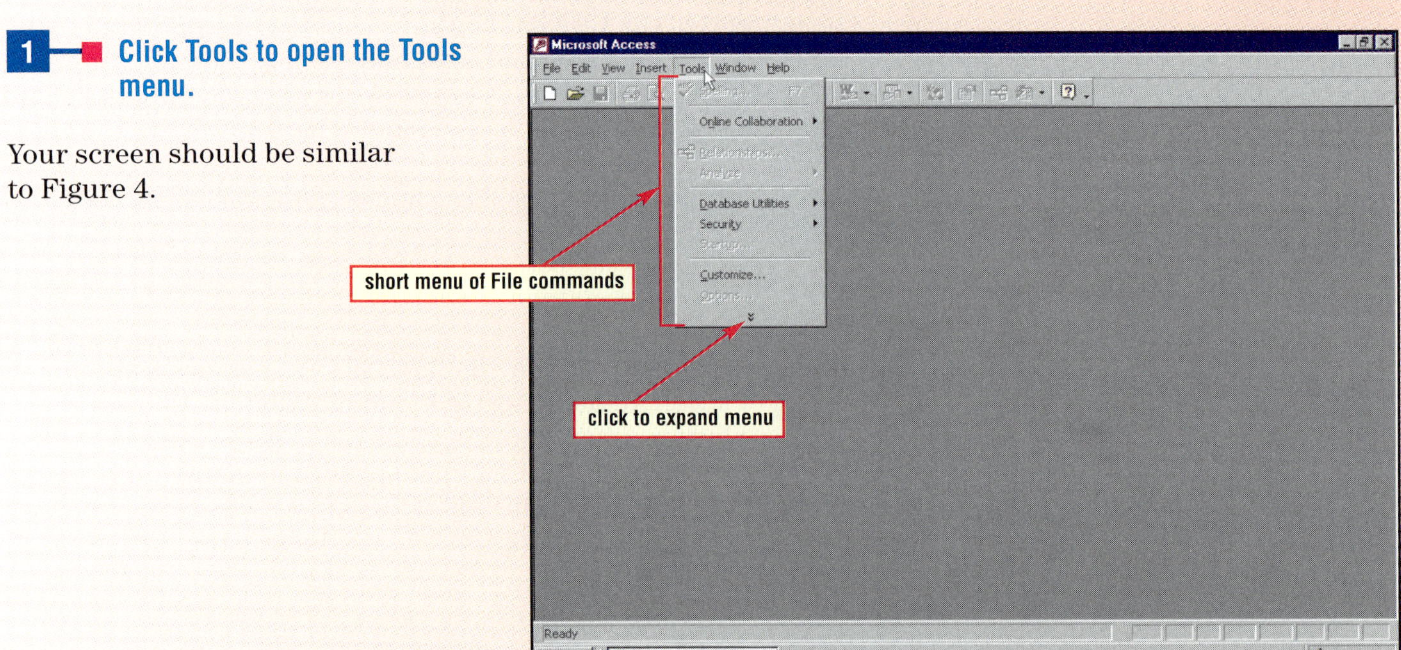

Figure 4

When some menus first open, a short list of commands is displayed. The short menu displays basic commands when the application is first used. As you use the application, those commands you use frequently are listed on the short menu and others are hidden. Because the short menu is personalized automatically to the user's needs different commands may be listed on your Tools menu than appear in Figure 4 above.

An expanded version will display automatically after the menu is opened for a few seconds (see Figure 5). If you do not want to wait for the expanded version to appear, you can click ⌄ at the bottom of the menu and the menu list expands to display all commands.

Additional Information

You can also double-click the menu name to show the expanded menu immediately.

Your screen should be similar to Figure 5.

Figure 5

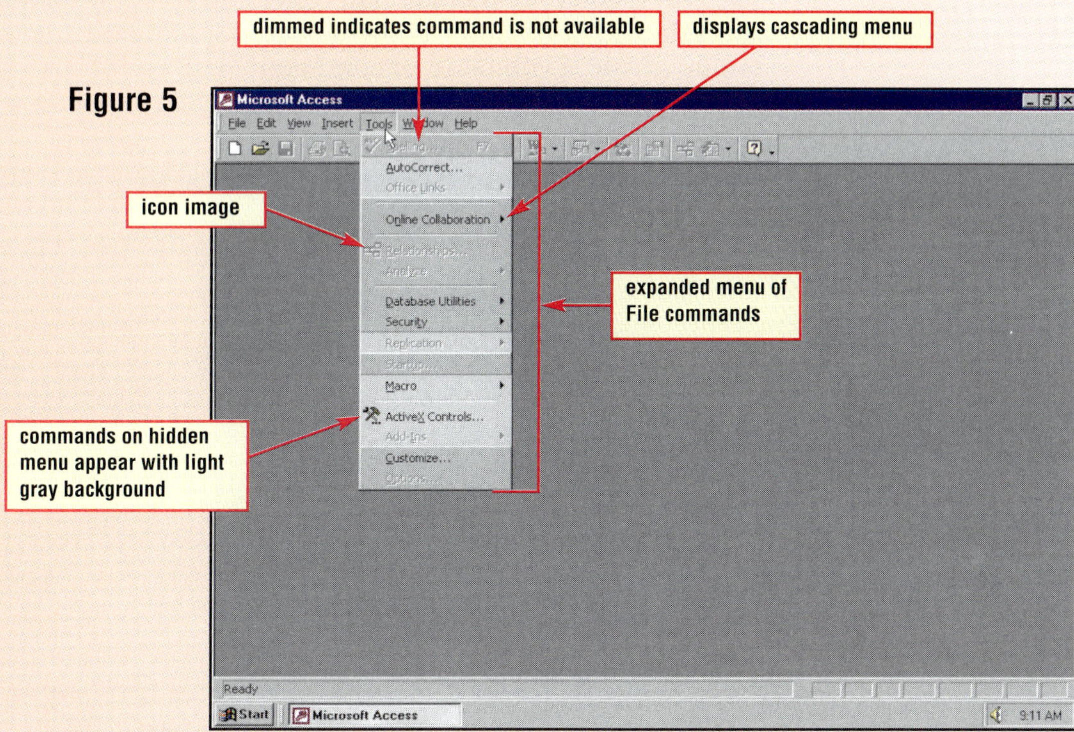

The commands that are in the hidden menu appear on a light gray background. Additionally, because you do not have a document open, many of the commands are not available and appear dimmed. Once one menu is expanded, others are expanded automatically until you choose a command or perform another action.

2 ■ **Point to each menu in the menu bar to see the expanded menu for each.**

■ **Point to the Tools menu again.**

Many commands have images next to them so you can quickly associate the command with the image. The same image appears on the toolbar button for that feature.

Menus may include the following features (not all menus include all features):

Feature	Meaning
Ellipses (...)	Indicates a dialog box will be displayed
▶	Indicates a cascading menu will be displayed
Dimmed	Indicates the command is not available for selection until certain other conditions are met
Shortcut key	A key or key combination that can be used to execute a command without using the menu
Checkmark (✔)	Indicates a toggle type of command. Selecting it turns the feature on or off. A checkmark indicates the feature is on.

Once a menu is open, you can *select* a command from the menu by pointing to it. A colored highlight bar, called the **selection cursor**, appears over the selected command. If the selected command line displays a right-facing arrow, a submenu of commands automatically appears when the command is selected. This is commonly called a **cascading menu**.

3 ■ **Point to the Online Collaboration command to display the cascading menu.**

Your screen should be similar to Figure 6.

You can also type the underlined command letter to choose a command. If the command is already selected, you can press ⟨←Enter⟩ to choose it.

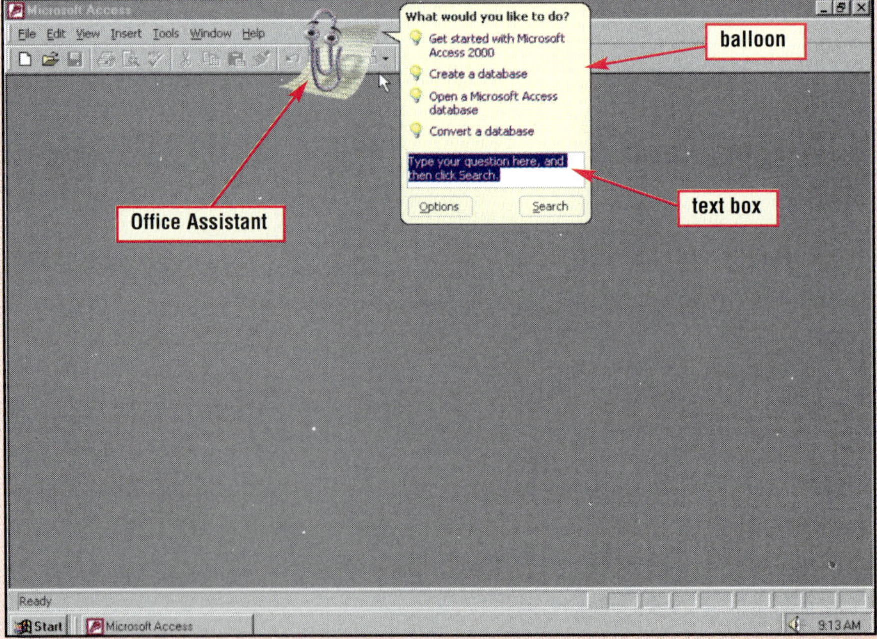

Figure 6

Then to choose a command you click on it. When the command is chosen, the associated action is performed. You will use a command in the Help menu to access the Microsoft Office Assistant and Help feature.

4 ■ **Point to Help.**

   ■ **Choose Show the Office Assistant.**

If the Assistant does not appear, your school has disabled this feature. If this is the case, Choose **H**elp/Microsoft Access **H**elp and skip to the section Using Help.

If the Office Assistant feature is on this command does not appear on the Help menu and the Office Assistant should already be displayed on your screen.

Your screen should be similar to Figure 7.

Figure 7

The command to display the assistant has been executed and the Office Assistant character is displayed. Because there are a variety of Assistant characters, your screen may display a different character than shown here.

Using the Office Assistant

When the Office Assistant is on, it automatically suggests help topics as you work. It anticipates what you are going to do and then makes suggestions on how to perform a task. In addition, you can activate the Assistant at any time to get help on features in the Office application you are using. When active, the Office Assistant balloon appears and displays a prompt and a text box in which you can type the topic you want help on.

1 ━ ■ **If the balloon is not displayed as in Figure 7, click the Office Assistant character to activate it.**

You will ask the Office Assistant to provide information on the different ways you can get help while using the program.

2 ━ ■ **Click in the text box and type How do I get help?**

■ **Click** Search **.**

Your screen should be similar to Figure 8.

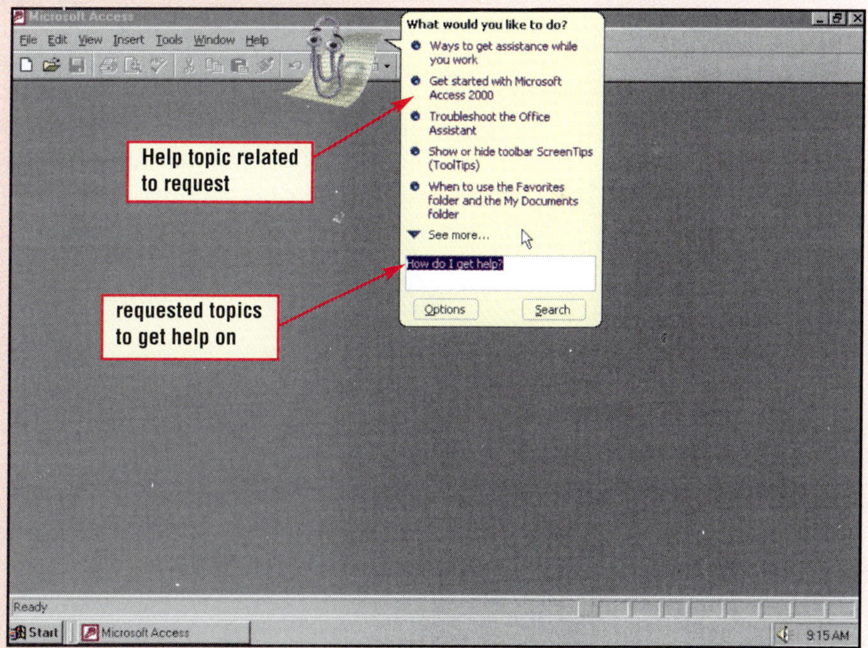

Figure 8

The balloon displays a list of related topics from which you can select.

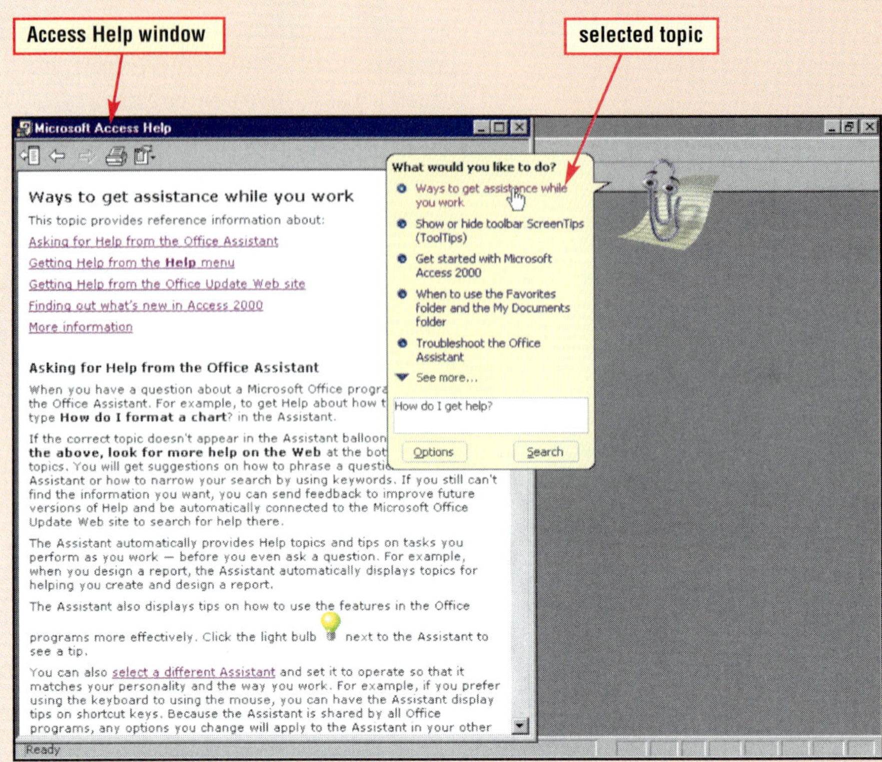

Figure 9

3 **Click** See more….

Click Ways to get more assistance while you work.

Your screen should be similar to Figure 9.

The Help program has been opened and displays the selected topic. Because Help is a separate program it appears in its own window. The taskbar displays a button for both open windows. Now that Help is open, you no longer need to see the Assistant.

Additional Information

You can also press F1 to open Help if the Office Assistant is not on.

Additional Information

The Options button is used to change the Office Assistant settings so it provides different levels of help, or to select a different Assistant character.

4 **Click** Search .

Select Use the Office Assistant to clear the checkmark and turn off this feature.

Click OK .

Click Microsoft Access Help in the taskbar to switch back to the Help window.

Using Help

In the Help window, the toolbar buttons help you use different Help features and navigate within Help. The Show button displays the Help tabs frame.

1   If necessary, click ▣ to maximize the Help window.

   If necessary, click ◁▤ to display the Tabs frame.

   Click the Contents tab to open it and scroll the frame horizontally to the left.

   If necessary, click [+] next to the Getting Help book.

   If necessary, click [+] next to the Displaying and Printing Help Information book.

Your screen should be similar to Figure 10.

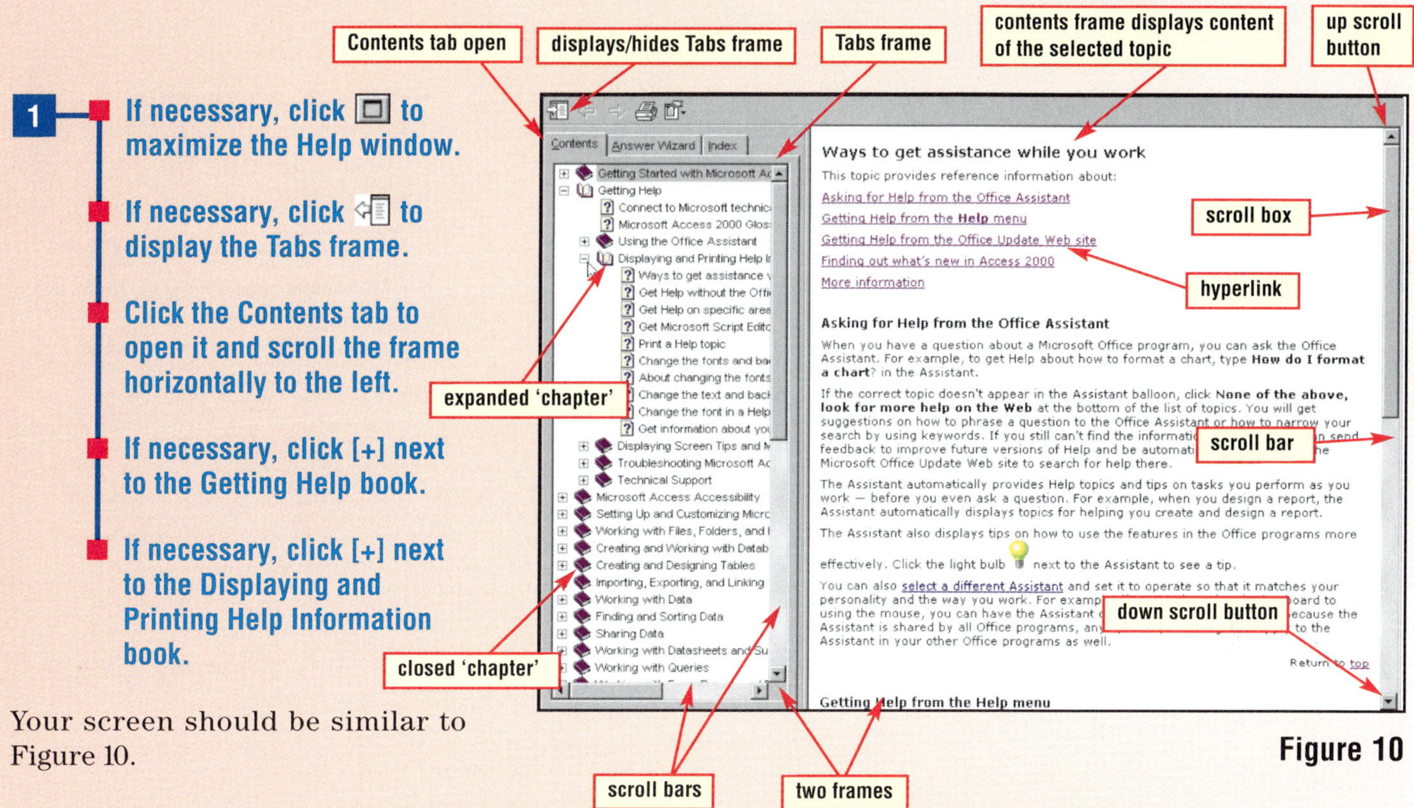

Figure 10

The Help window is divided into two vertical frames. **Frames** divide a window into separate, scrollable areas that can display different information. The left frame in the Help window is the Tabs frame. The three folder-like tabs, Contents, Index and Search, in the left frame are used to access the three different means of getting Help information. The open tab appears in front of the other tabs and displays the available options for the feature.

The Contents tab displays a table of contents listing of topics in Help. Clicking on an item preceded with a 📖 opens a "chapter" which expands to display additional "chapters" or specific Help topics. Chapters are preceded with a 📖 icon and topics with a ❔ icon.

The right frame, commonly called the content frame, displays the located information. It contains more information than can be displayed at one time. A **scroll bar** is used with a mouse to bring additional lines of information into view in a window. It consists of **scroll arrows** and a **scroll box**. Clicking the arrows moves the information in the direction of the arrows, allowing new information to be displayed in the space. You can also move to a general location within the area by dragging the scroll box up or down the scroll bar. The location of the scroll box on the scroll bar indicates your relative position within the area of available information. Scroll bars can run vertically along the right side or horizontally along the bottom of a window. The vertical scroll bar is used to move vertically and the horizontal scroll bar moves horizontally in the space.

2   Use the scroll bar in the content frame to scroll to the bottom of the Help topic.

   Scroll back to the top of the Help topic.

Using a Hyperlink

Another way to move in Help is to click a hyperlink. A **hyperlink** is a connection in the current document, another document, or the World Wide Web. It appears as colored or underlined text. Clicking the hyperlink moves to the location associated with the hyperlink.

1   **Click the** Asking for Help from the Office Assistant **hyperlink.**

The mouse pointer appears as 👆 when pointing to a hyperlink.

Your screen should be similar to Figure 11.

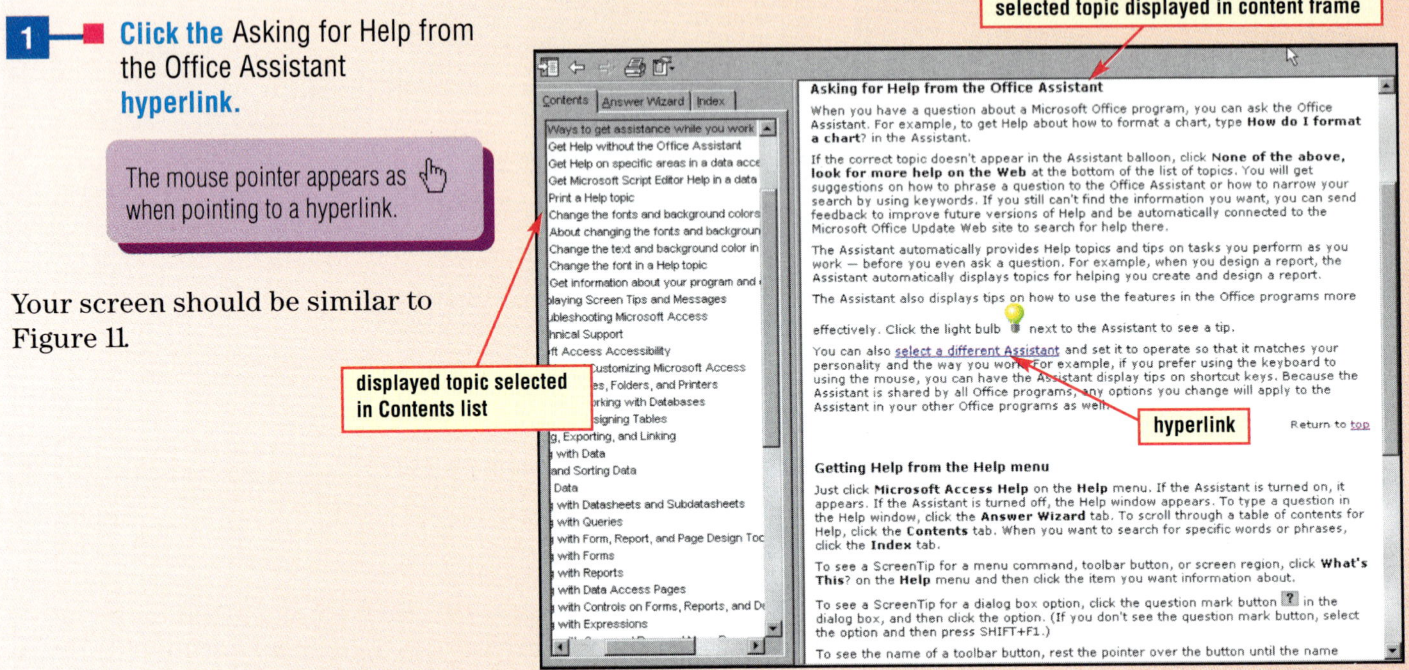

Figure 11

Help quickly jumps to the selected topic and displays the topic heading at the top of the frame. Notice the Contents list now highlights this topic indicating it is the currently selected topic.

2   **Read the information displayed on this topic.**

  Click the select a different Assistant **hyperlink.**

Your screen should be similar to Figure 12.

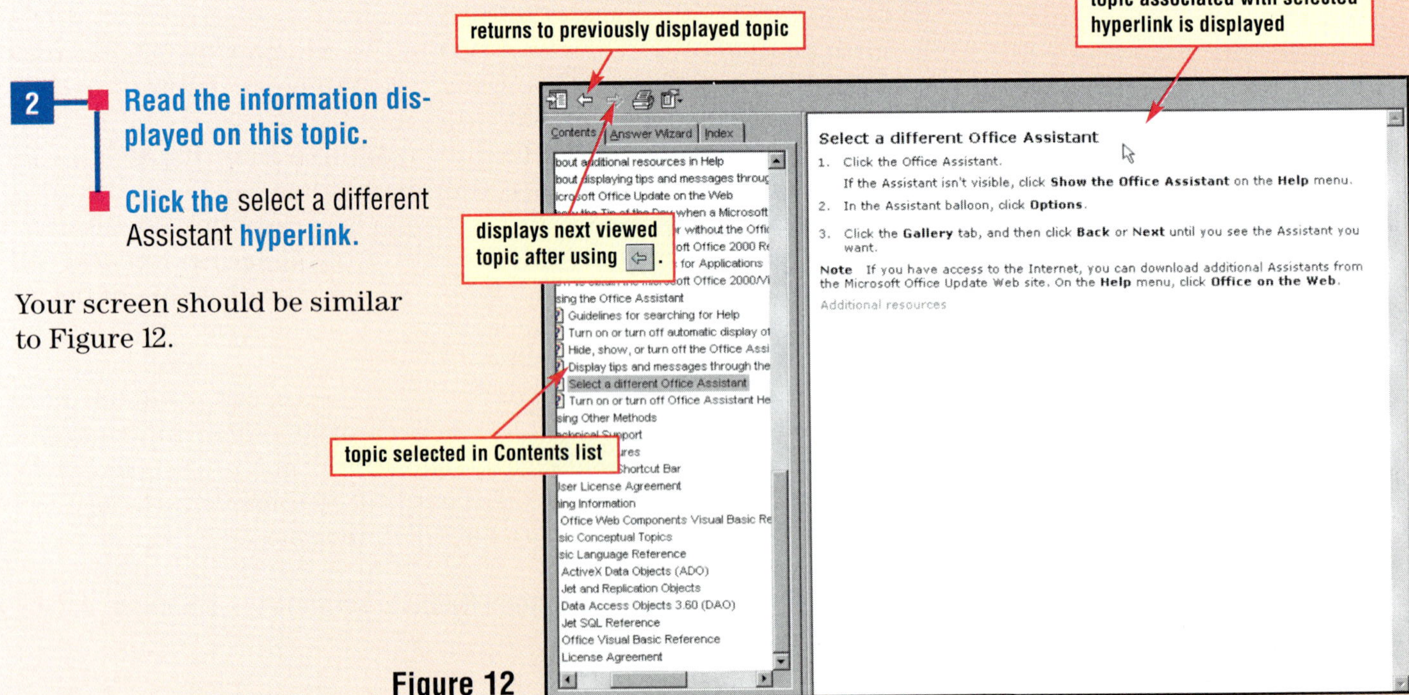

Figure 12

The help topic about selecting a different Assistant is displayed. Other hyperlinks will display a definition of a term in a pop-up box.

To quickly return to the previous topic,

The ⇨ Forward button is available after using ⇦ Back and can be used to move to the next viewed topic.

3 ■ **Click ⇦ Back.**

The previous topic is displayed again.

Using the Index Tab

To search for Help information by entering a word or phrase for a topic, you can use the Index tab.

1 ■ **Open the Index tab.**

Your screen should be similar to Figure 13.

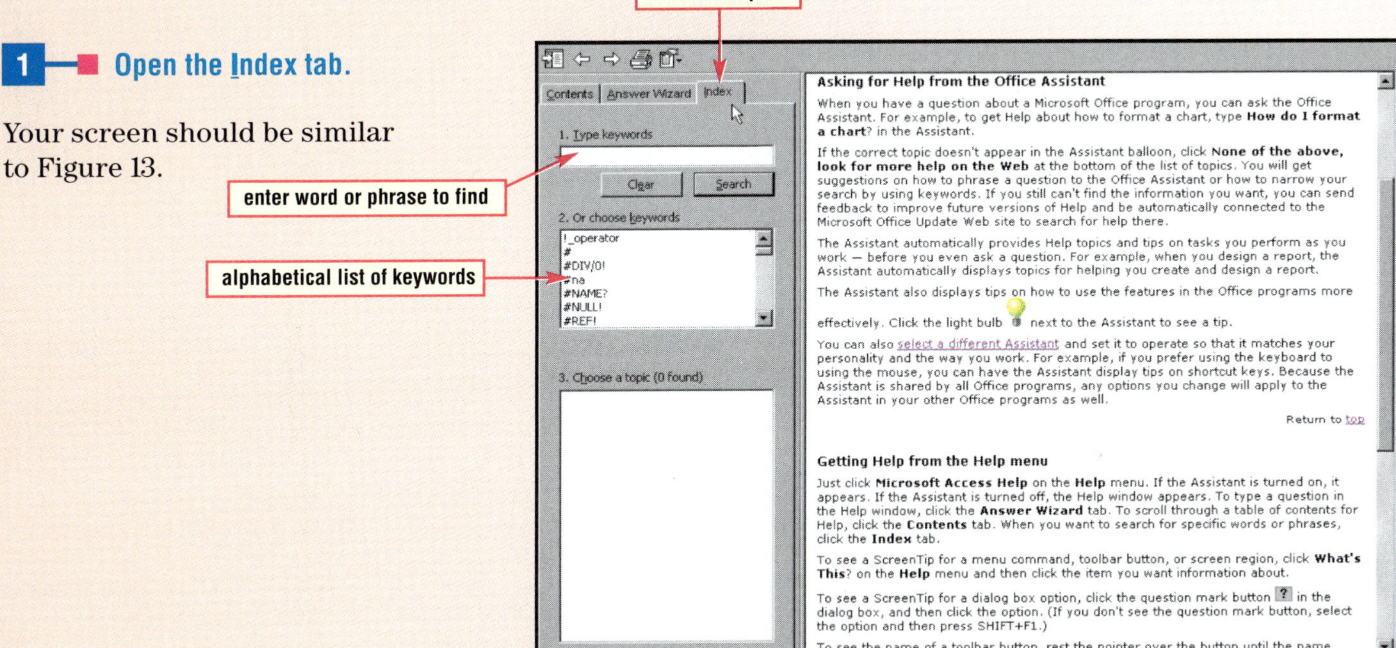

Figure 13

The Index tab consists of a text box where you can type a word or phrase that best describes the topic you want to locate and a list box displaying a complete list of Help keywords in alphabetical order. You want to find information about using the Index tab.

2 ■ **Type index in the text box.**

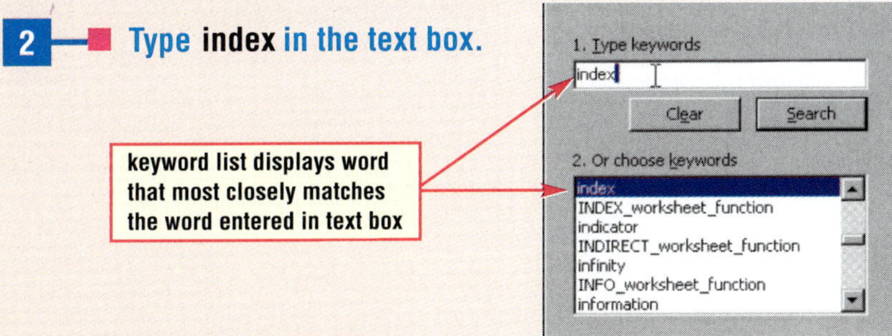

The keyword list jumps to the word index. To locate all Help topics containing this word,

3 — **Click** [Search] .

Your screen should be similar to Figure 14.

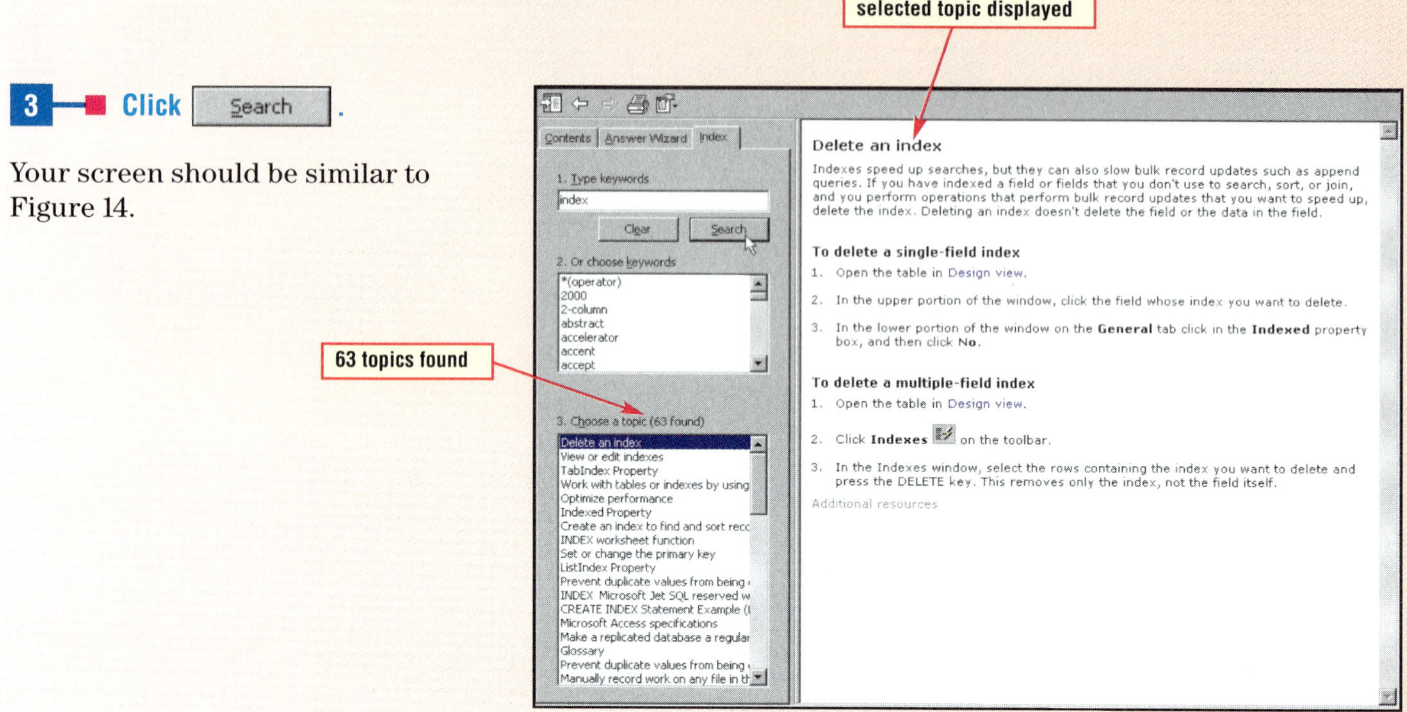

Figure 14

The topic list displays 63 Help topics containing this word and displays the information on the first topic in the content frame. However, many of the located topics are not about the Help Index feature. To narrow the search more, you can add another word to the keyword text box.

4 — **Type help in the keyword text box following the word index.**

Click [Search] .

Your screen should be similar to Figure 15.

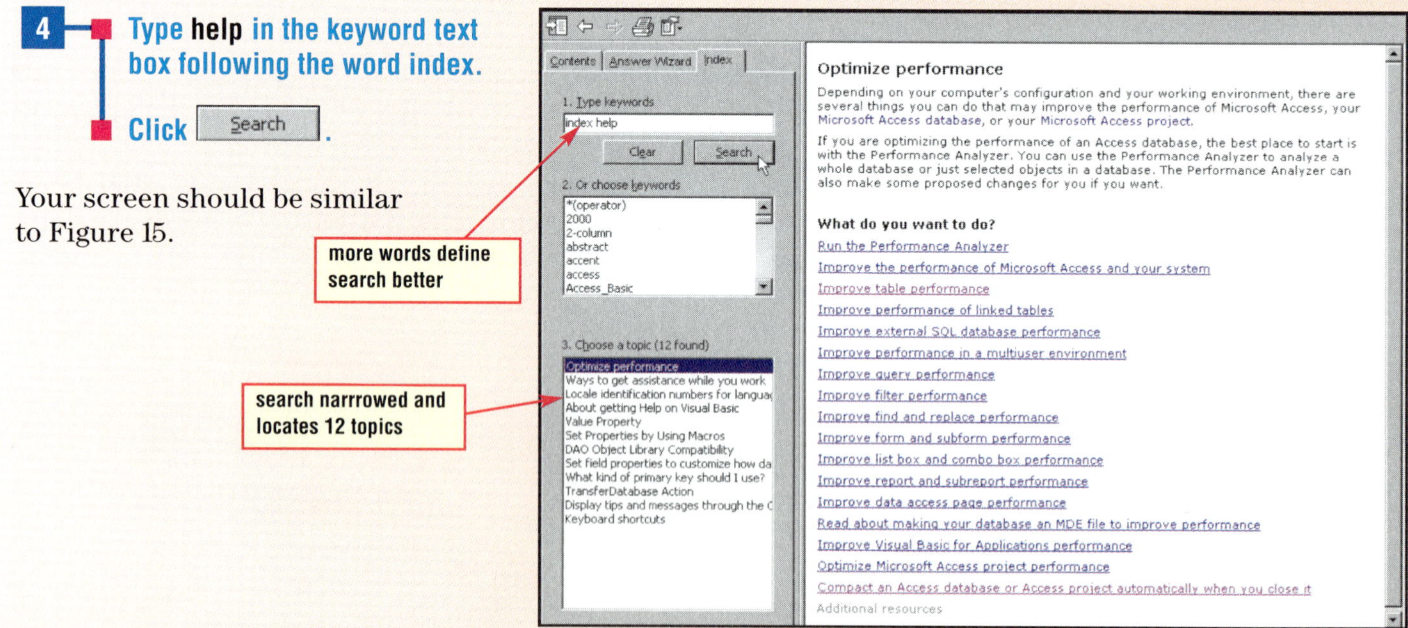

Figure 15

Now only 12 topics were located that contain both keywords. You can then click on a topic to display the information in the contents frame.

Using the Answer Wizard

Another way to locate Help topics is to use the Answer Wizard tab. This feature works just like the Office Assistant to locate topics. You will use this method to locate Help information on toolbars.

1 ■ **Open the Answer Wizard tab.**

■ **Type How do toolbars work? in the text box.**

■ **Click** Search **.**

> The search term does not need to be worded as a question. It can also be a word or phrase.

Your screen should be similar to Figure 16.

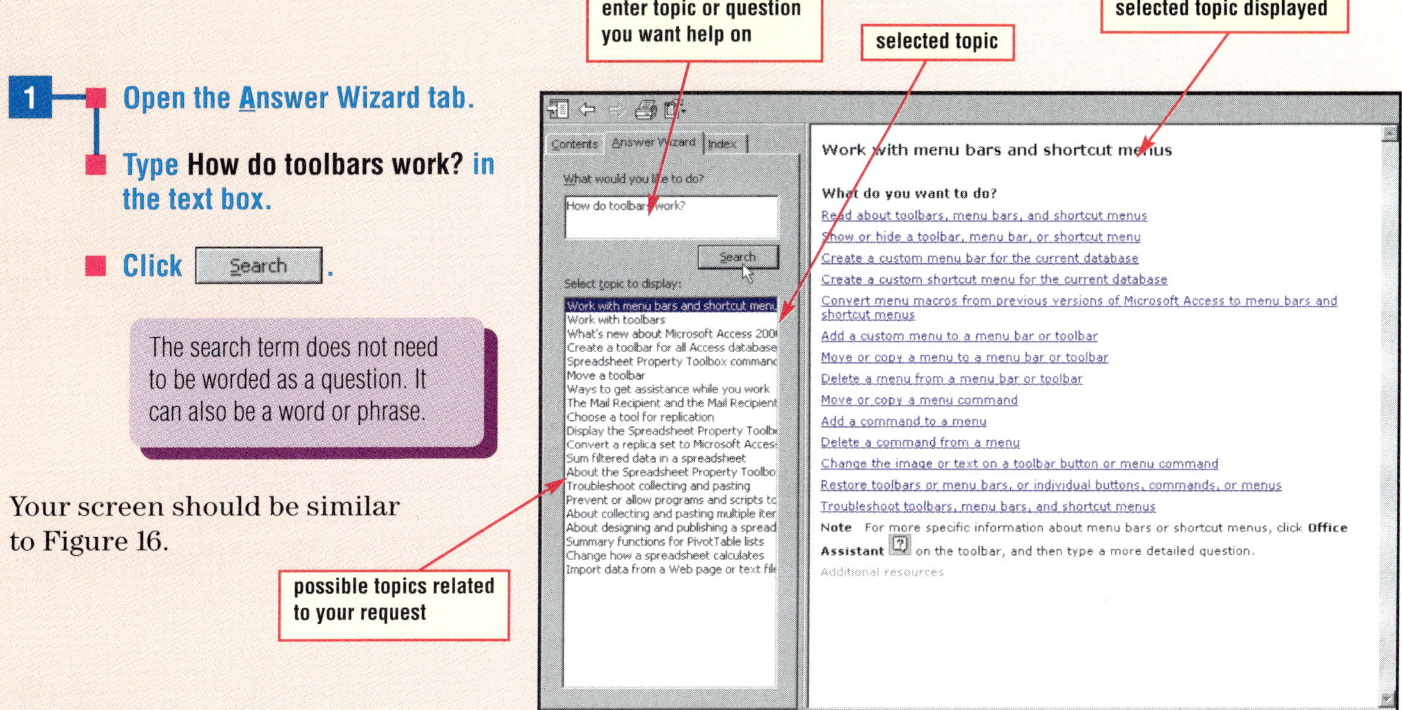

Figure 16

The topic list box displays all topics that the Answer Wizard considers may be related to the question you entered. The first topic is selected and displayed in the content frame.

2 ■ **Click** Read about toolbars, menus, and shortcut menus **from the list of topics in the content frame.**

Your screen should be similar to Figure 17.

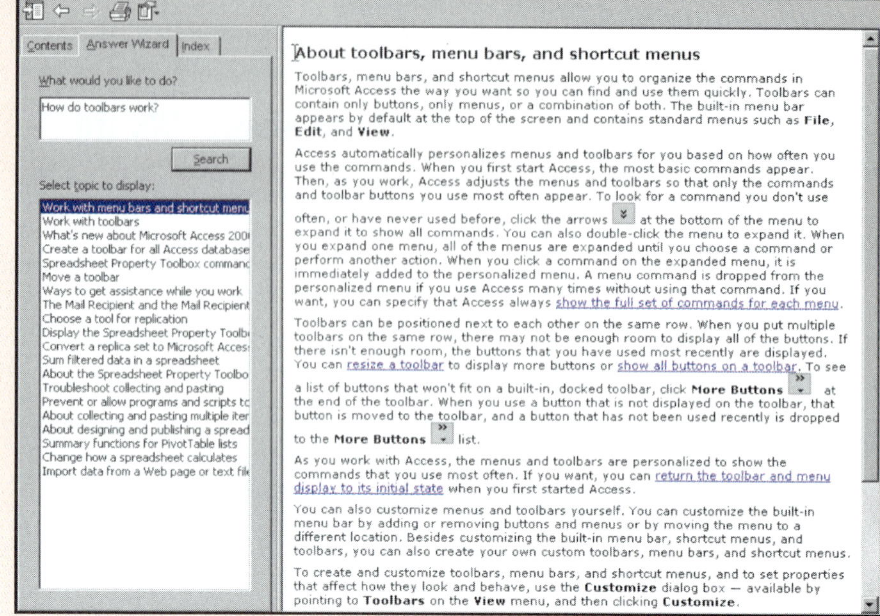

Figure 17

3 ■ **Click** ▣ **to hide the Tabs frame and if necessary, maximize the Help window again.**

■ **Read the information about this topic.**

■ **Read the hyperlink topics** resize a toolbar **and** show all buttons on a toolbar**.**

■ **Click** ☒ **to close Help.**

Your screen should be similar to Figure 18.

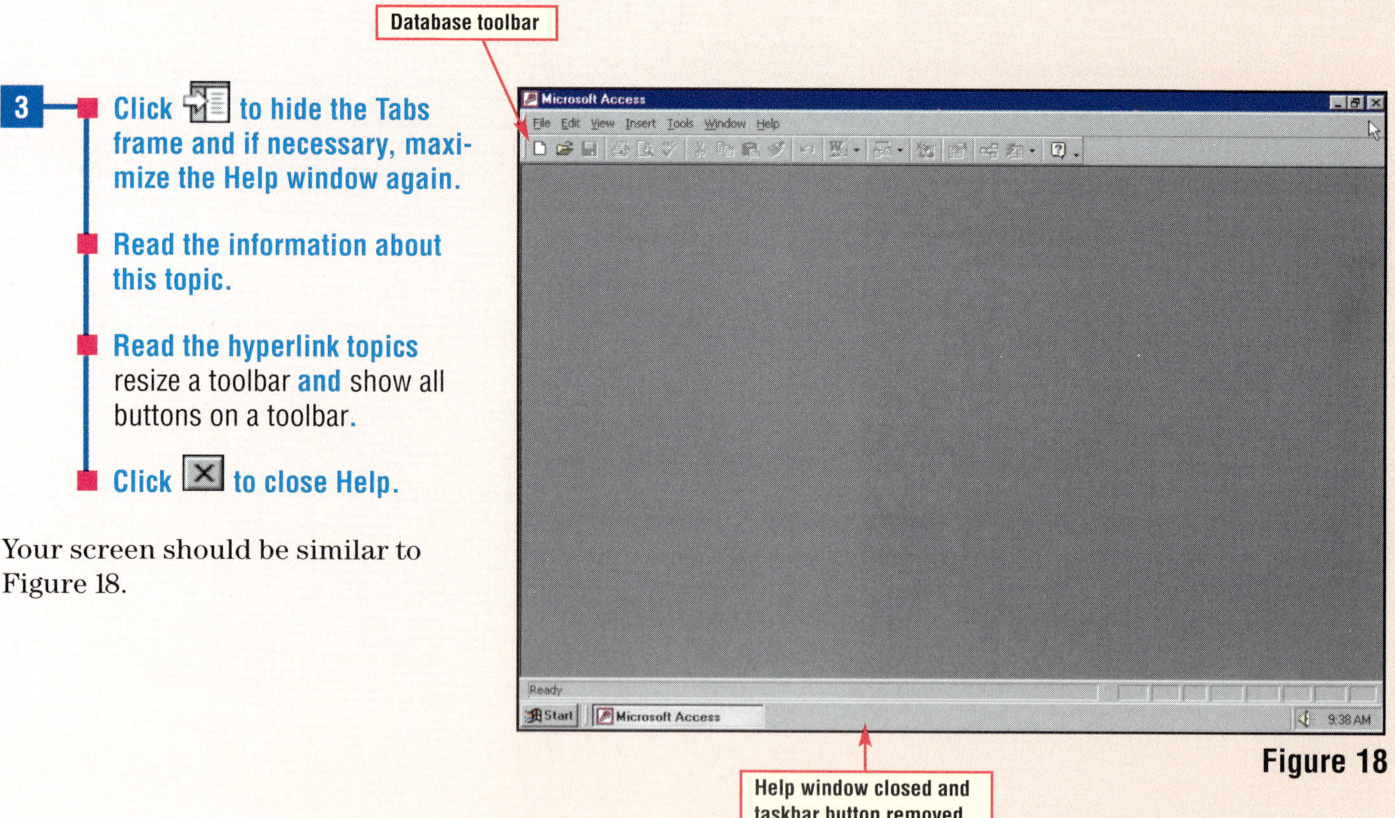

Figure 18

The Help window is closed and the Access window is displayed again.

Using Toolbars

While using Office 2000, you will see that many toolbars open automatically as different tasks are performed. Toolbars initially display the basic buttons. Like menus they are personalized automatically … displaying those buttons you use frequently and hiding others. If there is not enough space to fully display all its buttons, a More Buttons [»] button appears at the end of the toolbar. Clicking it displays a drop-down button list of those buttons that are not displayed. When you use a button from this list, it then is moved to the toolbar and a button that has not been used recently is moved to the More Buttons list.

Initially, Access displays the Database toolbar on one row below the menu bar (see Figure 18). This toolbar contains buttons that are used to complete the most frequently used menu commands. If you right-click on a toolbar, the toolbar shortcut menu is displayed. Using this menu you can see which toolbars are available and select those you want displayed.

Additional Information

Most of the toolbar buttons are dimmed because they are not available for use until a file is open.

1 Right-click on the toolbar.

The menu equivalent is **V**iew/**T**oolbars.

Your screen should be similar to Figure 19.

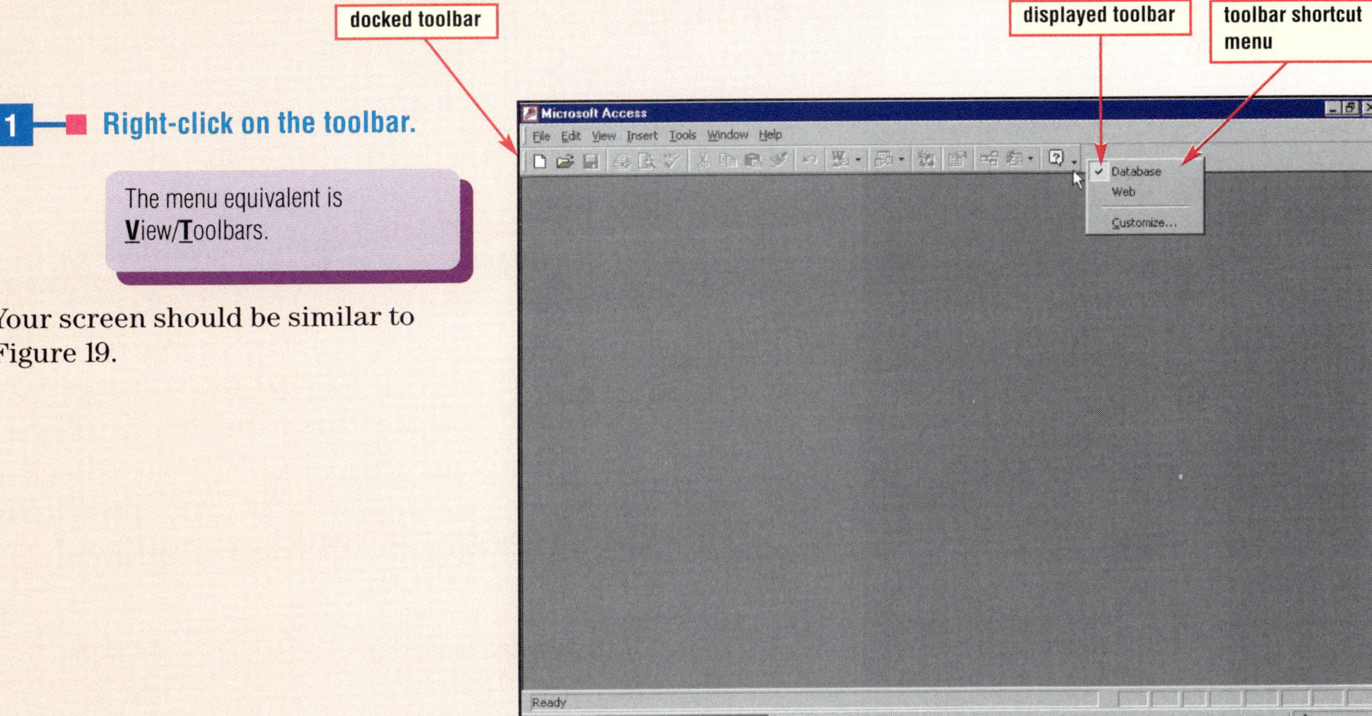

Figure 19

The toolbar shortcut menu lists only two available toolbars. The currently displayed toolbar is checked. Clicking on a toolbar name from the list will display it onscreen. Likewise, clicking on a checked toolbar will hide the toolbar.

2 Press (Esc) to clear the shortcut menu.

When a toolbar is opened, it may appear docked or floating. When **docked** they are fixed to an edge of the window and display the move handle ▯. Dragging this bar up or down allows you to move the toolbar. When docked, multiple toolbars share the same row and dragging the bar left or right adjusts the size of the toolbar. When **floating** they appear in a separate window that can be moved by dragging the title bar.

3 ■ **Drag the move handle of the Database toolbar into the workspace.**

> The mouse pointer appears as ✛ when you can move the toolbar.

Your screen should be similar to Figure 20.

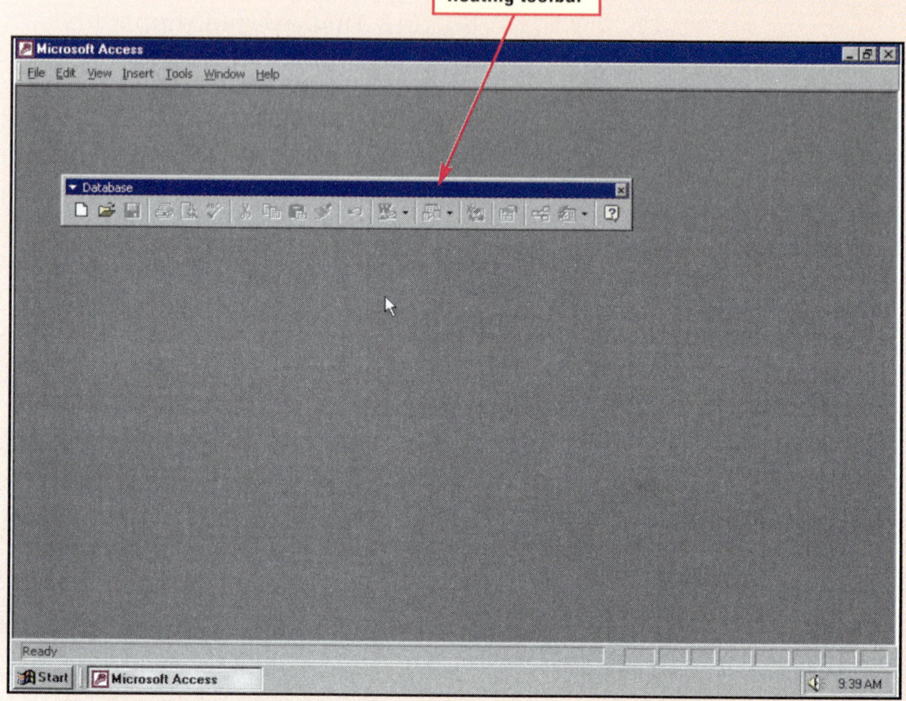

Figure 20

The Database toolbar is now floating and can be moved to any location in the workspace. If you move it to the edge of the window, it will attach to that location and become a docked toolbar. A floating toolbar can also be sized by dragging the edge of the toolbar.

4 ■ **Move the floating toolbar back to the left end of the row below the menu bar.**

To quickly identify the toolbar buttons, you can display the button name by pointing to the button.

5 ■ **Point to any button on the Database toolbar to see the ScreenTip displaying the button name.**

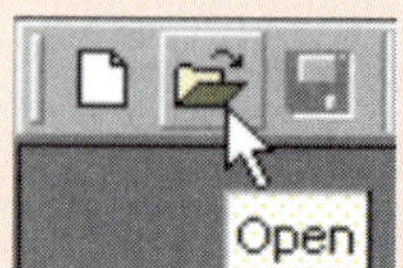

Exiting an Office Application

The Exit command on the File menu can be used to quit most windows programs. In addition, you can click the ⊠ Close button in the application window title bar.

1 ■ Click ⊠ Close.

The application window is closed and the desktop is visible again.

Key Terms

cascading menu xxviii	mouse xxii	status bar xxvi
desktop xxii	mouse pointer xxii	taskbar xxii
docked xxxviii	ScreenTip xxiv	title bar xxv
floating xxxviii	scroll arrows xxxi	toolbar xxv
frame xxxi	scroll bar xxxi	workspace xxv
hyperlink xxxii	scroll box xxxi	
icon xxii	selection cursor xxviii	
menu xxvi	shortcut menu xxvi	
menu bar xxv	Start button xxii	

Command Summary

Command	Shortcut Keys	Button	Action
[Start]/Programs			Opens program menu
File/E**x**it	Alt + F4	⊠	Exits Access program
View/**T**oolbars			Hides or displays toolbars
Help/Microsoft Access **H**elp	F1		Opens Help window
Help/Show the **O**ffice Assistant.			Displays Help's office assistant

Overview of Access 2000

What Is a Database?

Somewhere at home, or maybe in your office, you probably have a file cabinet or desk drawer filled with information. Perhaps you have organized the information into drawers of related information, and further categorized that information into file folders. This is a database.

As organized as you might be, it takes time to locate a specific piece of information by manually opening drawers and searching through the folders. You can just imagine how much time would be required for a large company to manually search through its massive amounts of data. These companies use electronic database management systems. Now you, too, can use electronic database management systems to store, organize, access, manipulate, and present information in a variety of ways.

In this series of tutorials you will learn how to design and create a computerized database using Access 2000, and you will quickly appreciate the many advantages of a computerized database.

Database table

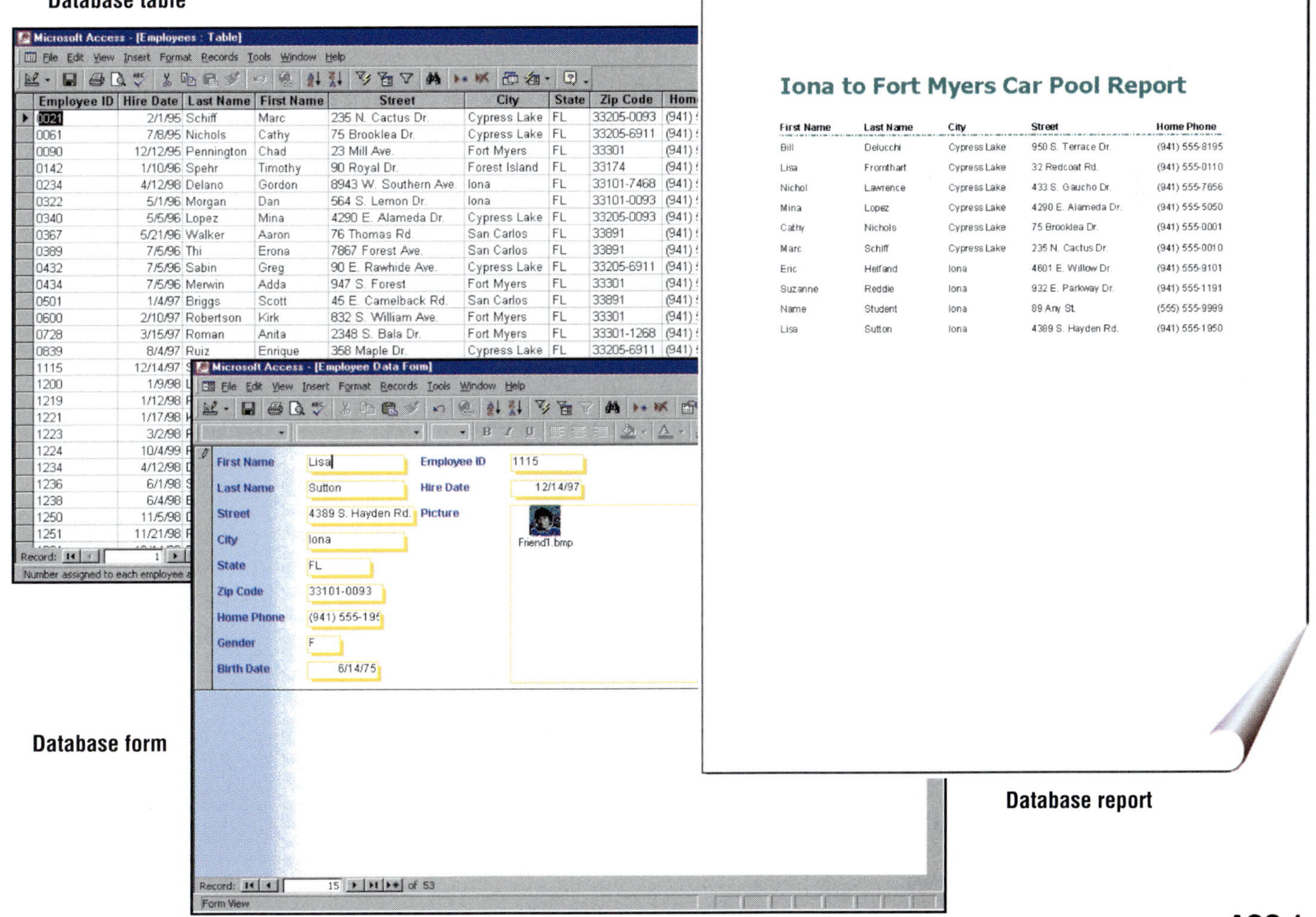

Database form

Database report

Access 2000 Features

Access 2000 is a relational database management system. In relational database systems, data is organized in tables that are related or linked to one another. Each table consists of rows, called records, and columns, called fields.

For example, a state's motor vehicle department database might have an address table. Each row (record) in the table would contain complete address information about one individual. Each column (field) would contain one piece of address information, such as a name. The address table would be linked to other tables in the database by common fields. For example, the address table might be linked to a vehicle owner's table by name and linked to an outstanding citation table by license number (see example below).

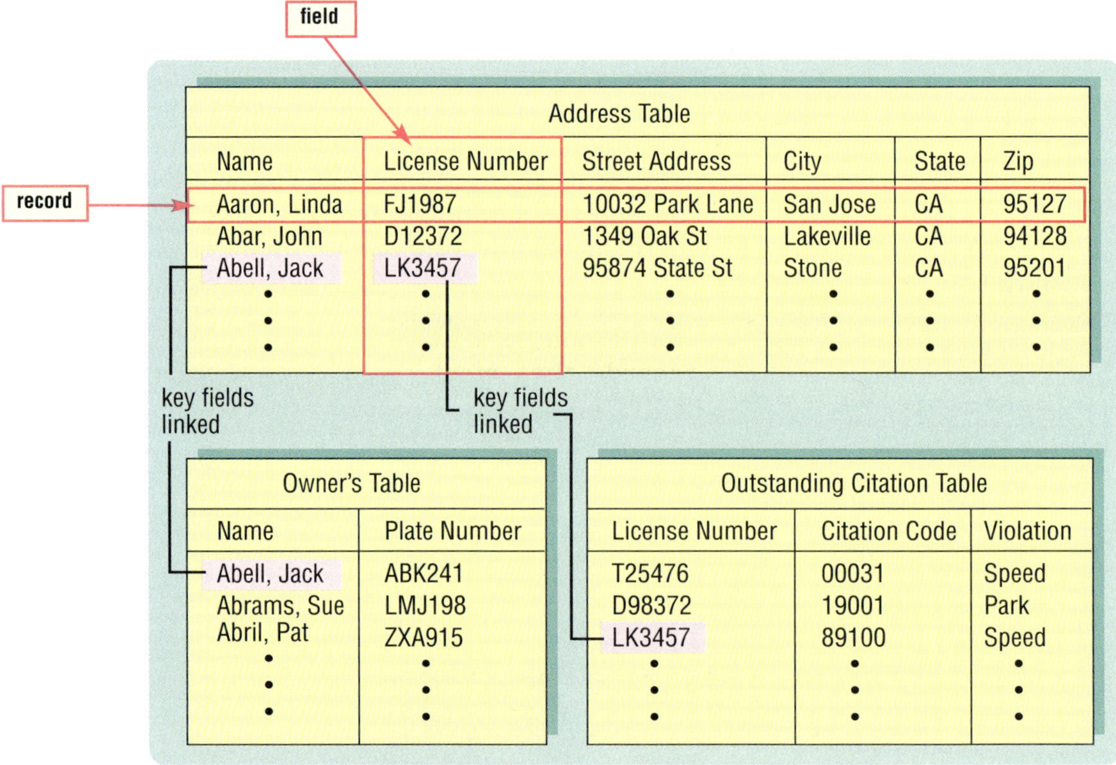

Access 2000 is a powerful program with numerous easy-to-use features, including the ability to quickly locate information, add, delete, and modify records, sort records, analyze data, and produce professional-looking reports. Some of the basic Access 2000 features are described next.

FIND INFORMATION

Once you enter data into the database table, you can quickly search the table to locate a specific record based on the data in a field. In a manual system, you can usually locate a record by knowing one key piece of information. For example, if the records are stored in a file cabinet alphabetically by last name, to quickly find a record you must know the last name.

In a computerized database, even if the records are sorted or organized by last name, you can still quickly locate a record using information in another field.

ADD, DELETE, AND MODIFY RECORDS

Using Access, it is also easy to add and delete records from the table. Once you locate a record, you can edit the contents of the fields to update the record or delete the record entirely from the table. You can also add new records to a table. When you enter a new record, it is automatically placed in the correct organizational location within the table.

SORT RECORDS

The capability to arrange or sort records in the table according to different fields of data helps provide more meaningful information. You can organize records by name, department, pay, class, or any other category you need at a particular time. Sorting the records in different ways can provide information to different departments for different purposes.

ANALYZE DATA

Using Access, you can analyze the data in a table and perform calculations on different fields of data. Instead of pulling each record from a filing cabinet, recording the piece of data you want to use, and then performing the calculation on the recorded data, you can simply have the database program perform the calculation on all the values in the specified field. Additionally, you can ask questions or query the table to find only certain records that meet specific conditions to be used in the analysis. Information that was once costly and time-consuming to get is now quickly and readily available.

GENERATE REPORTS

Access includes many features that help you quickly produce reports ranging from simple listings to complex, professional-looking reports. You can create a simple report by asking for a listing of specified fields of data and restricting the listing to records meeting designated conditions. You can create a more complex, professional report using the same restrictions or conditions as the simple report, but you can display the data in different layout styles, or with titles, headings, subtotals, or totals.

Case Study for Access 2000 Tutorials

You have recently accepted a job as employment administrator for Lifestyle Fitness Club. The Club has recently purchased Microsoft Access 2000, and you are using it to update their manual system for recording employee information.

Before You Begin

To the Student
The following assumptions have been made:

- Microsoft Access 2000 has been properly installed on the hard disk of your computer system.

- The data disk contains the data files needed to complete the series of tutorials and practice exercises. These files are supplied by your instructor.

- You are already familiar with how to use Windows and a mouse.

To the Instructor
By default, Office 2000 installs the most commonly used components and leaves others to be installed when first accessed. It is assumed that these additional features have been installed prior to students' using the tutorials.

Please be aware that the following settings are assumed to be in effect for the Access 2000 program. These assumptions are necessary so that the screens and directions in the manual are accurate.

- The Startup dialog box appears when Access first loads.

- The ScreenTips feature is active. (Use Tools/Customize/Options.)

- The Office Assistant feature is not on. (Click on the Assistant, click Options , and clear the Use the Office Assistant option.)

- The status bar is displayed.

- All default datasheet settings are in effect, including font settings of Arial 10 pt.

- In addition, all figures in the manual reflect the use of a standard VGA display monitor set at 800×600. If another monitor setting is used, there may be more or fewer lines displayed in the windows than in the figures. This setting can be changed using Windows setup.

Microsoft Office Shortcut Bar

The Microsoft Office Shortcut Bar (shown on the next page) may be displayed automatically on the Windows desktop. Commonly, it appears on the right side of the desktop, but it may appear in other locations, depending upon your setup. The Shortcut Bar on your screen may display different buttons. This is because the Shortcut Bar can be customized to display other toolbar buttons.

The Office Shortcut Bar makes it easy to open existing documents or to create new documents using one of the Microsoft Office applications. It can also be used to send e-mail, add a task to a to-do list, schedule appointments using Schedule+, or access Office Help.

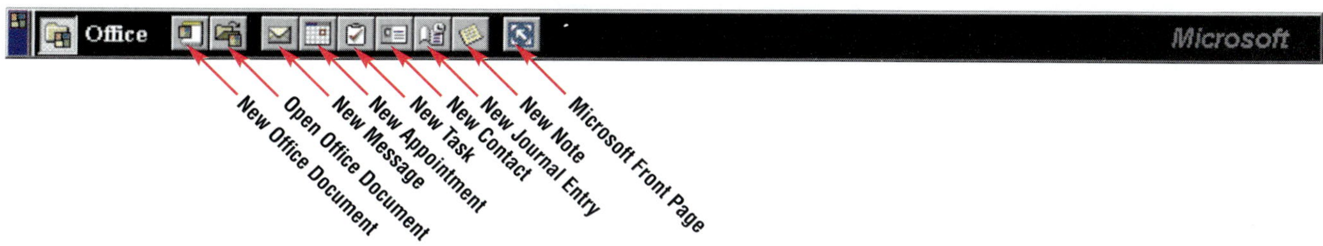

Instructional Conventions

Hands-on instructions you are to perform appear as a sequence of numbered blue steps. Within each step, a series of pink bullets identifies the specific actions that must be performed. Step numbering starts over within each main topic heading throughout the tutorial.

Command sequences you are to issue appear following the word "Choose." Each menu command selection is separated by a /. If the menu command can be selected by typing a letter of the command, the letter will appear underlined and bold. Items that need to be highlighted will follow the word "Select." You can select items with the mouse or directional keys.

EXAMPLE A

1 ■ **Choose File/Open.**

■ **Select** Trip Flyer.

Commands that can be initiated using a button and the mouse appear following the word "Click. " The icon (and the icon name if the icon does not include text) is displayed following Click. The menu equivalent and keyboard shortcut appear in a margin note when the action is first introduced.

EXAMPLE B

The menu equivalent is **File/Open** and the keyboard shortcut is Ctrl + O.

1 ■ **Click**  **Open.**

Black text identifies items you need to select or move to. Information you are asked to type appears in black and bold.

EXAMPLE C

1 ■ **Move to the** A **in** Announcing.

■ **Type Adventure Travel presents four new trips.**

Creating a Database

Competencies

After completing this tutorial, you will know how to:

1. Plan and create a database.
2. Create a table.
3. Save the table structure.
4. Change views.
5. Enter and edit data.
6. Insert a picture.
7. Adjust column widths.
8. Add records in Data Entry.
9. Preview and print a table.
10. Close and open a database.

Case Study

You have recently accepted a new job as employment administrator with Lifestyle Fitness Club. Like many fitness centers, Lifestyle Fitness Club includes exercise equipment, free weights, aerobic classes, tanning and message facilities, swimming pool, steam room and sauna, and child care facilities. In addition, they promote a healthy lifestyle by including educational seminars on good nutrition and proper exercise. They also have a small snack bar that serves healthy drinks, sandwiches, and snacks.

The Lifestyle Fitness Clubs is a franchised chain of clubs that are individually owned. The club you work at is owned by Brian and Cindy

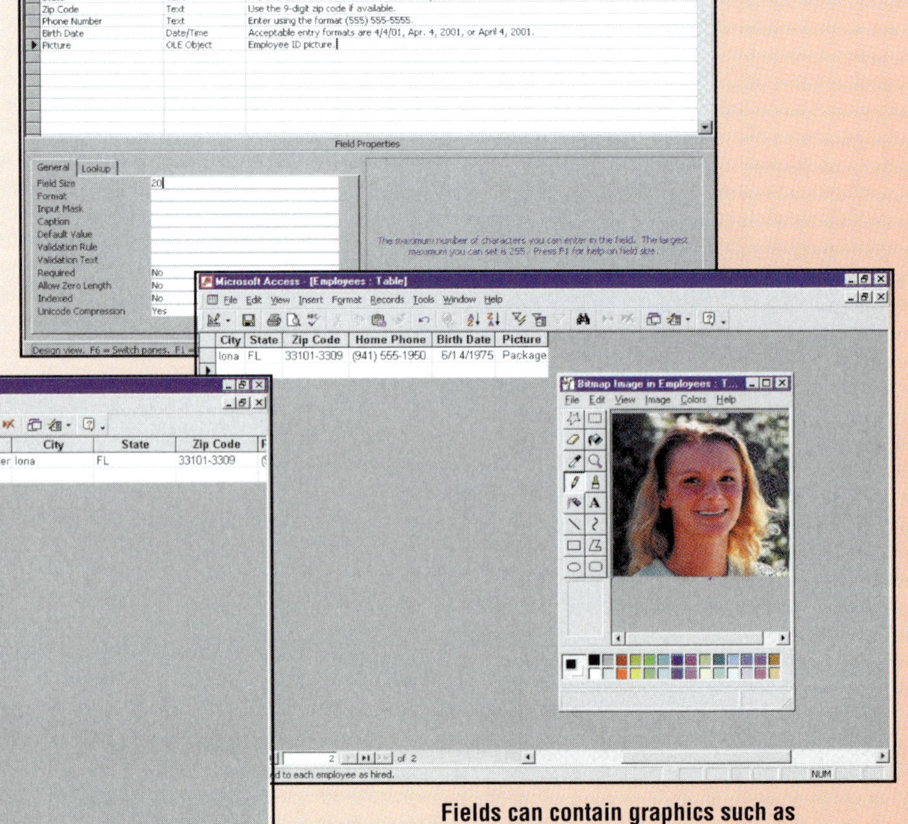

Designing the table structure consists of defining field names, data types, and field properties.

Entering data in a table creates records of information.

Fields can contain graphics such as pictures.

Birch, who also own two others in Florida. Accounting and employment functions for all three clubs are handled centrally at the Fort Myers location.

You are responsible for maintaining the employment records for all employees, as well as traditional employment activities such as hiring and benefits. Currently the Club employment records are maintained on paper forms and stored in file cabinets organized alphabetically by last name. Although the information is well organized, it still takes time to manually leaf through the folders to locate the information you need and to compile reports from this data.

The Club has recently purchased new computers, and the owners want to update the employee record-keeping system to an electronic database management system. The software tool you will use to create the database is the database application Access 2000. In this tutorial, you will learn about entering, editing, previewing, and printing a document while you create the employee database and a table (shown below) of basic employee information.

Employees 1/21/01

Employee ID	Hire Date	Last Name	First Name	Street	City	State
0234	04/12/1998	Delano	Gordon	8943 W. Southern Ave.	Iona	FL
0434	07/05/1996	Merwin	Adda	947 S. Forest St.	Fort Myers	FL
0728	03/15/1997	Roman	Anita	2348 S. Bala Dr.	Fort Myers	FL
0839	08/04/1997	Ruiz	Enrique	358 Maple Dr.	Cypress Lake	FL
1151	10/14/1997	Sutton	Lisa	4389 Hayden Rd.	Iona	FL
9999	02/26/1999	Name	Student	123 N. Fourth St.	Iona	FL

Employees 1/21/01

Zip Code	Phone Number	Birth Date	Picture
33101-8475	(941) 555-8201	08/07/1961	
33301-1268	(941) 555-4494	04/20/1970	
33301-1268	(941) 555-9870	03/15/1961	
33205-6911	(941) 555-0091	12/10/1963	
33101-3309	(941) 555-1950	06/14/1975	Bitmap Image
33101-3309	(941) 555-5555	08/07/1975	

Concept Overview

The following concepts will be introduced in this tutorial:

1   Database   A database is an organized collection of related information.

2   Database Development   The development of a database follows several steps: plan, create, enter and edit data, and preview and print.

3   Object   An item, such as a table, or reports, that can be created, selected, and manipulated as a unit.

4   Field Name   A field name is used to identify the data stored in the field.

5   Data Type   The data type defines the type of data the field will contain.

6   Field Property   Field properties are a set of characteristics that are associated with each field.

7   Primary Key   A primary key is a field that uniquely identifies each record.

8   Edit and Navigation Modes   The Edit and Navigation modes control how you can move through and make changes to data in a table.

9   Graphics   A graphic is a nontext element or object, such as a drawing or picture, that can be added to a table.

10   Column Width   Column width refers to the size of each field column in Datasheet view. It controls the amount of data you can see on the screen.

Exploring the Access 2000 Window

The Fitness Club recently purchased the Office 2000 application software suite and will use the Access 2000 database management program to create several different databases of information.

Concept ① Database

A **database** is an organized collection of related information. Typically, the information in a database is stored in a **table** consisting of vertical columns and horizontal rows. Each row contains a **record**, which is all the information about one person, thing, or place. Each column is a **field**, which is the smallest unit of information about a record. Access databases can contain multiple tables that can be linked to produce combined output from all tables. This type of database is called a **relational database**. See the Overview to Access 2000 for more information about relational databases.

You will begin by creating a database table using Access 2000 to hold the employee data.

1 ■ **Start Access 2000.**

■ **If necessary, maximize the Access application window.**

See Introducing Common Office 2000 Features for information on how to start the application and for a discussion of features that are common to all Office 2000 applications.

Your screen should be similar to Figure 1–1.

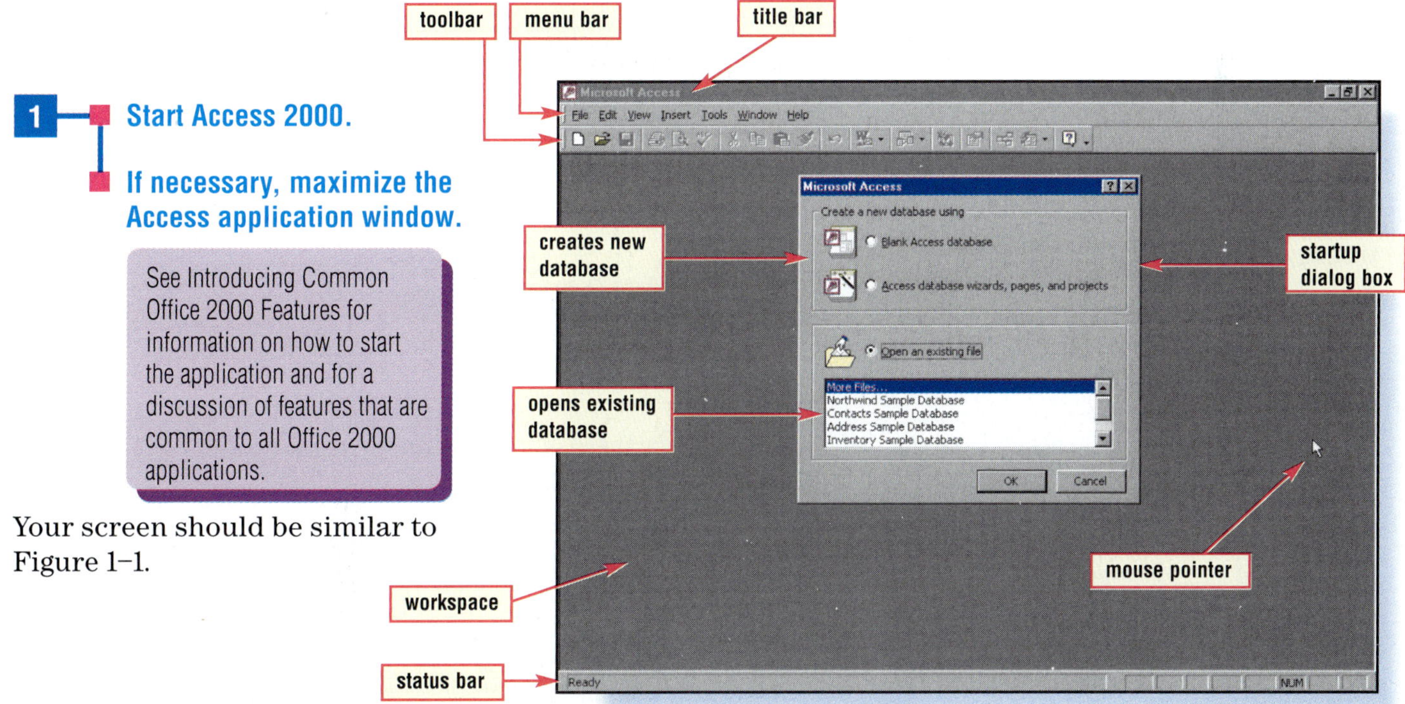

Figure 1–1

Because the Office 2000 applications remember settings that were on when the program was last exited, your screen may look slightly different.

The Microsoft Access 2000 application window with the startup dialog box open in it is displayed. The startup dialog box allows you to create a new database or open an existing database. The menu bar below the title bar displays the Access program menu. It consists of seven menus that provide access to the commands and features you will use to create and modify a database. The menus and commands that are available at any time vary with the task you are performing.

The toolbar, normally located below the menu bar, contains buttons that are mouse shortcuts for many of the menu commands. There are many different toolbars in Access. Most toolbars appear automatically as you perform different tasks and open different windows.

Additional Information

The text assumes the Office Assistant is not activated. See the Introducing Common Features section to learn about this feature and how to turn it off.

The center area of the window is the workspace where different Access windows are displayed as you are using the program. Just below the workspace, the status bar provides information about the task you are working on and the current Access operation. In addition, the status bar displays messages such as button and command descriptions to help you use the program more efficiently.

The mouse pointer appears as a ▱ on your screen. The mouse pointer changes shape depending upon the task you are performing or where the pointer is located on the window.

Finally, your screen may display the Office Assistant. This feature provides quick access to online Help.

Planning a Database

The Lifestyle Fitness Club plans to use Access 2000 to maintain several different types of databases. The database you will create will contain information about each Club employee. Other plans for using Access include keeping track of members and inventory. To keep the different types of information separate, the club plans to create a database for each group. Creating a new database follows several basic steps.

Concept ② Database Development

The development of a database follows several steps: plan, create, enter, and edit data, and preview and print.

Plan   The first step in the development of a database is to understand the purpose of the database and to plan what information it should hold and the output you need from it.

Create   After planning the database, you create tables to hold data by defining the table structure.

Enter and Edit   Once a table has been set up, you enter the data to complete each record. While entering data, you may make typing and entry errors that need to be corrected. This is one type of editing. Another is to revise the structure of the tables by adding, deleting, or redefining information in the table.

Preview and Print   The last step is to print a hard copy of the database or report. This step includes previewing the document onscreen as it will appear when printed. Previewing allows you to check the document's overall appearance and to make any final changes needed before printing.

You will find that you will generally follow these steps in order as you create your database. However, you will probably retrace steps as the final database is developed.

Your first step is to plan the design of your database tables: how many tables, what data they will contain, and how they will be related. You need to decide what information each table in the employee database should contain and how it should be structured or laid out.

You can obtain this information by analyzing the current record-keeping procedures used throughout the company. You need to understand the existing procedures so your database tables will reflect the information that is maintained by different departments. You should be aware of the forms that are the basis for the data entered into the department records, and of the information that is taken from the records to produce periodic reports. You also need to find out what information the department heads would like to be able to obtain from the database that may be too difficult to generate using their current procedures.

After looking over the existing record-keeping procedures and the reports that are created from the information, you decide to create several separate tables of data in the database file. Creating several smaller tables of related data rather than one large table makes it easier to use the tables and faster to process data. This is because you can join several tables together as needed. The main table will include the employee's basic information, such as employee number, name, and address. Another table will contain job-related information, such as department and job title. A third will contain data on pay rate, and another will hold data about the hours worked each week. To clarify the organization of the database, you sketched out the structure for the employee database as shown below.

Employee Database

Employee Table

Emp #	Last Name	First Name	Street	City	State	Zipcode	Phone	Birth Date
7721	Brown	Linda	—	—	—	—	—	—
7823	Duggan	Michael	—	—	—	—	—	—
⋮	⋮	⋮	⋮	⋮	⋮	⋮	⋮	⋮

link on common field

link on common field

Location

Emp #	Location
7721	Iona
7823	Fort Myers
⋮	⋮

Pay Rate

Emp #	Pay	Hours
7721	8.25	30
7823	7.50	20
⋮	⋮	⋮

Creating a Database

Now that you have decided on the information you want to include in the tables, you are ready to create a new database to hold the table information. From the startup dialog box,

1 Select **B**lank Access Database.

  Click [OK] .

Your screen should be similar to Figure 1–2.

> The default location and the folders and files displayed may be different from those shown here.

> You can also start a new database using **F**ile/**N**ew/General/**D**atabase.

Additional Information

Windows documents can have up to 256 characters in the file name. Names can contain letters or numbers. Special symbols cannot be used with the exception of the underscore.

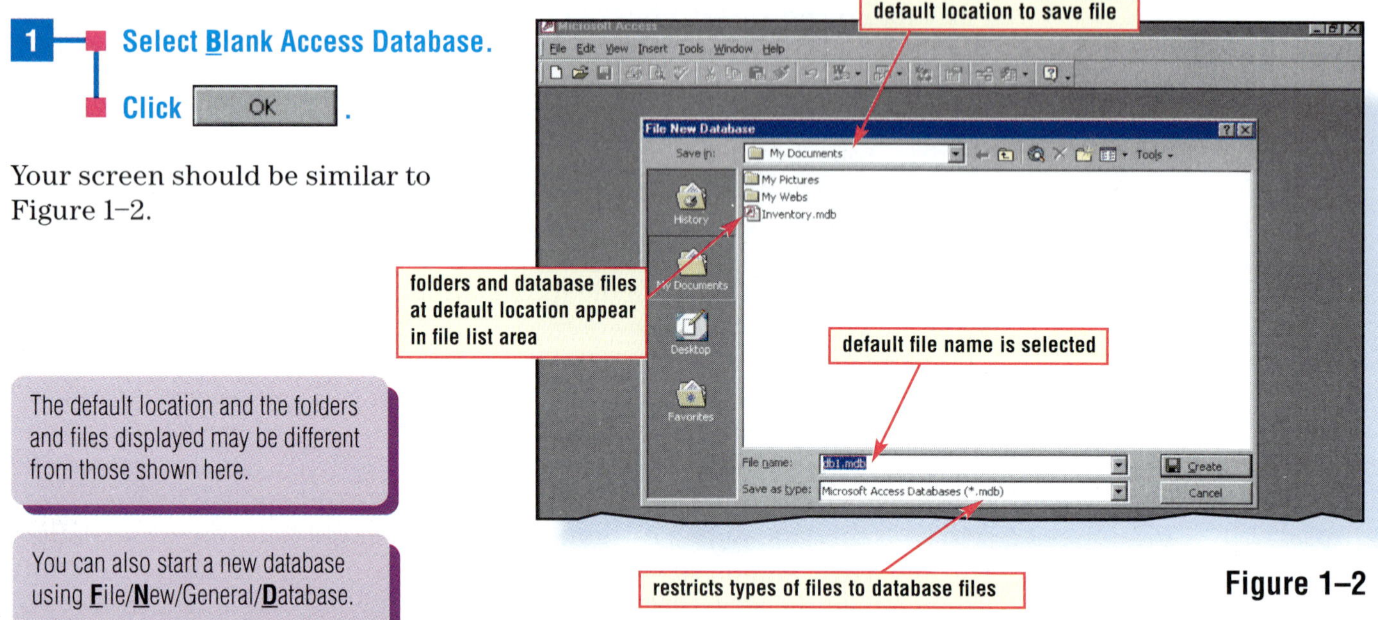

Figure 1–2

The File New Database dialog box is displayed. The first step is to specify a name for the database file and the location where you want the file saved. By default, Access opens the My Documents folder as the location to save the file. The file list section of the dialog box displays the names of folders and database files in the default location. Only database file names are displayed because the file type is restricted to Access Databases in the Save As Type text box. The default file name db1 appears in the File Name text box. You want the program to store the database on your data disk using the name Lifestyle Fitness Employees. Notice the default name is highlighted, indicating it is selected and will be replaced as you type the new name. First you will change the file name.

2 Type **Lifestyle Fitness Employees**.

Your screen should be similar to Figure 1–3.

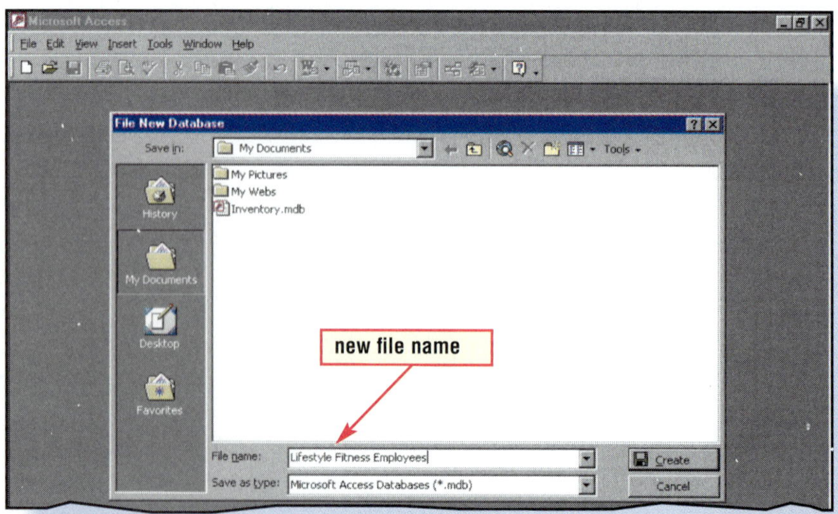

Figure 1–3

The default file name is replaced with the new file name. Next you need to change the location to the drive containing your data disk (A:).

3 **Place your data disk in drive A (or the appropriate drive for your system).**

Open the Save In list box.

Select 3 1/2 Floppy (A:) **from the Save In drop-down list.**

Your screen should be similar to Figure 1–4.

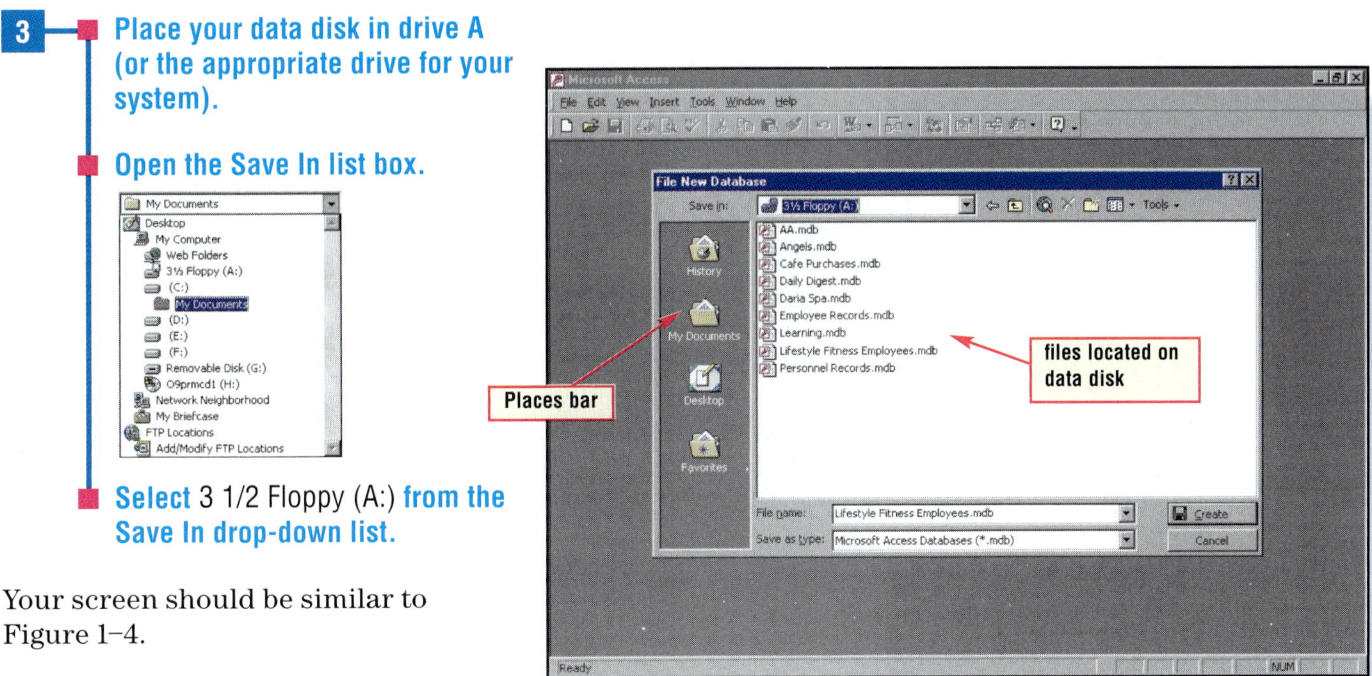

Figure 1–4

Now the file list section displays the names of all Access files on your data disk. You can also select the location to save from the Places bar along the left side of the dialog box. The icons bring up a list of recently accessed files and folders (History), the contents of the My Documents and Favorites folder, and the Windows desktop. Selecting a folder from one of these lists changes to that location. You can also click the ⬅ button in the toolbar to return to folders that were previously opened during the current session.

Notice that the program added the .mdb file extension to the file name. This is the default extension for Access documents.

If your screen does not display file extensions, your Windows program has this option deactivated.

4 ■ Click 🖫 Create .

Your screen should be similar to
Figure 1–5.

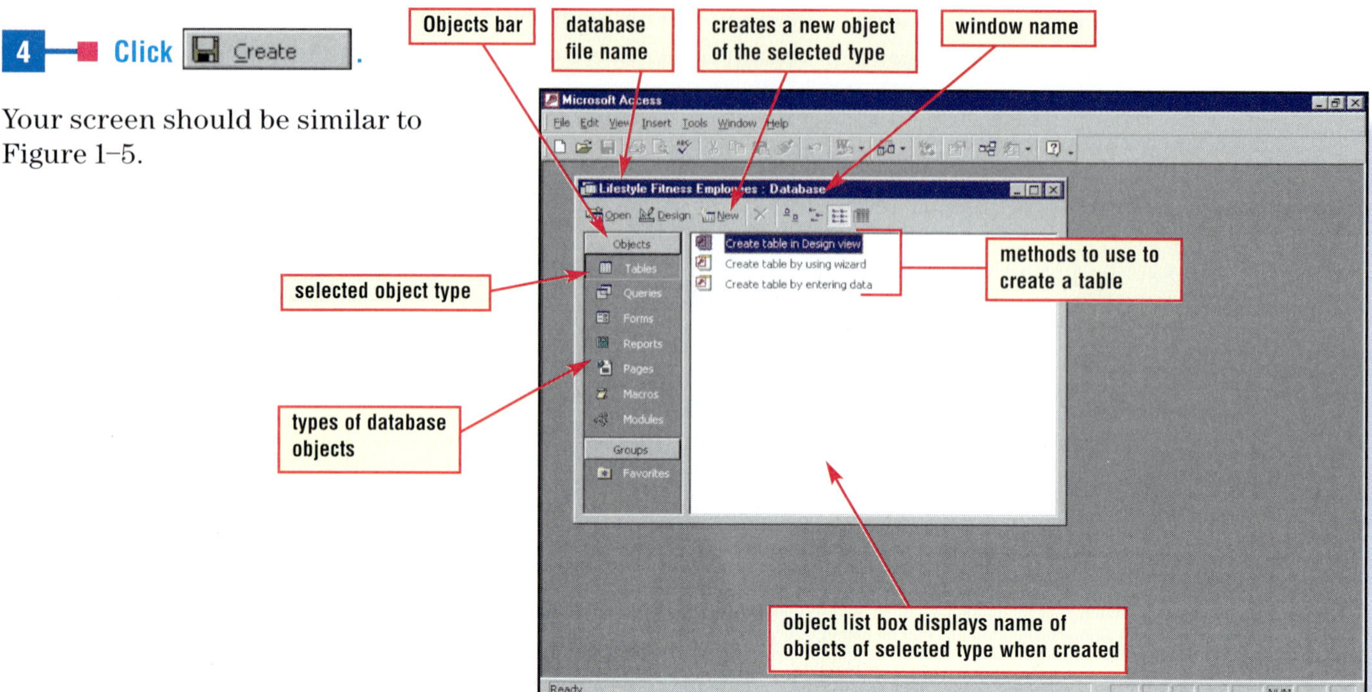

Figure 1–5

Using the Database Window

The Database window displays the name of the database, LifeStyle Fitness
Employees, followed by the name of the window in the window title bar. It
also includes its own toolbar that contains buttons to help you quickly create, open, or manage database objects.

Concept ③ Object

An **object** is an item, such as a table or report, that is made up of many elements and that can be created,
selected, and manipulated as a unit. The **Objects bar** along the left edge of the Database window organizes
the database objects into object types and groups, and is used to quickly access the different database objects. The currently selected object is Tables. The table object is the basic unit of a database and must be
created first, before any other types of objects are created. The **object list box** to the right of the object bar
normally displays a list of objects associated with the selected object type. The Tables object list box displays
three ways you can create a table. It will also display the names of objects of the selected object type once
they are created.

Access displays each different type of object in its own window. You can display multiple object windows
in the workspace; however, you cannot open more than one database file at a time.

Creating a Table

After naming the database, your next step is to create the new table to hold the employee information by defining the structure of the table.

1 ■ Click  .

Your screen should be similar to Figure 1–6.

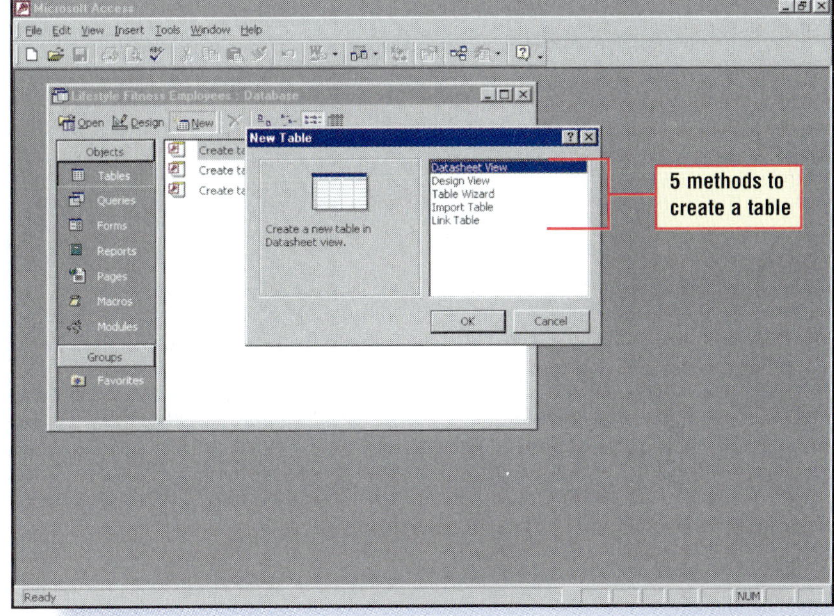

Figure 1–6

Additional Information

Access includes many different Wizards that can be used to create different Access objects.

You will learn more about views later in the tutorial.

The New Table dialog box provides five different ways to create a table. The first three, Datasheet View, Design View, and Table Wizard, are the most commonly used. They are the same three methods that are listed in the object list box. The Table Wizard option starts the Table Wizard feature, which lets you select from 45 predesigned database tables. The Wizard then guides you through the steps to create a table based upon your selections. The Datasheet and Design View options open different windows in which you can create a new custom table from scratch.

You will use the Design View option to create the table.

2

- **Select Design View.**

- **Click** OK **.**

- **If necessary, maximize the Table window.**

Your screen should be similar to Figure 1–7.

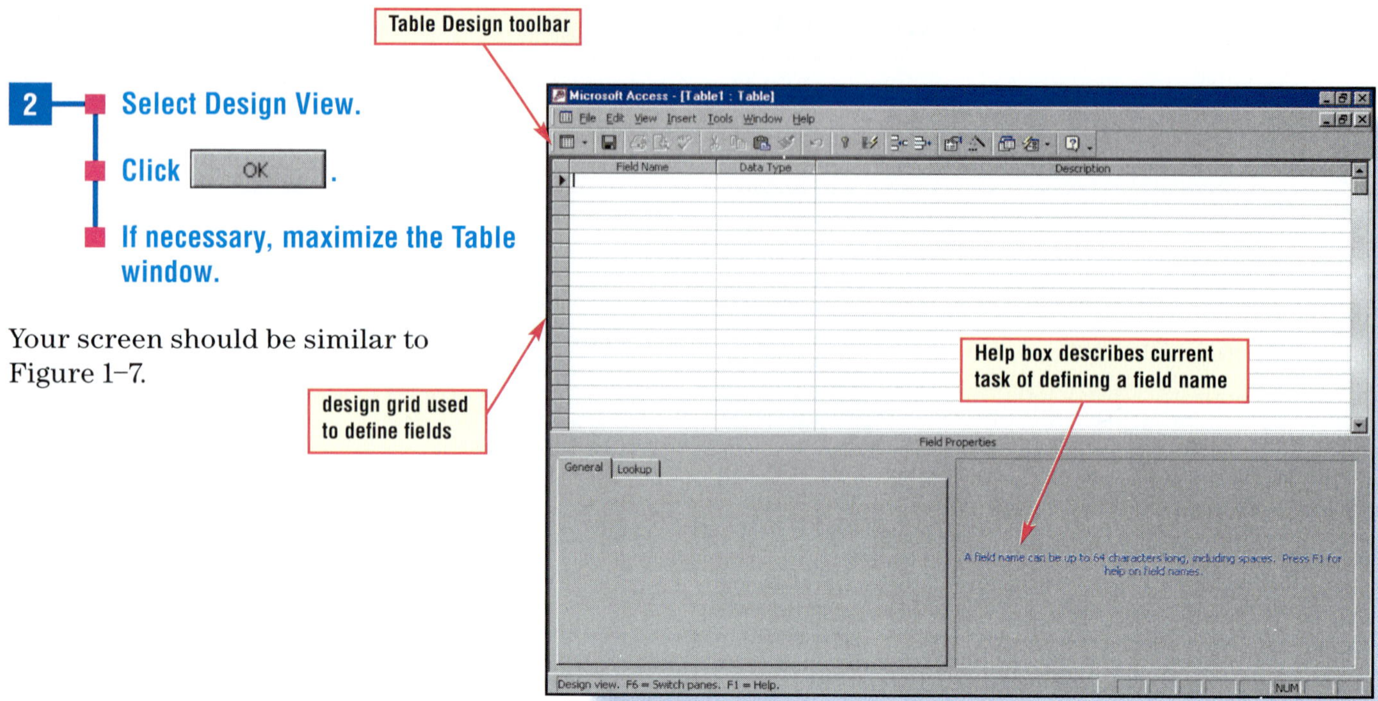

Figure 1–7

The Table Design window is opened and displayed over the Database window in the workspace. This window also has its own toolbar, the Table Design toolbar, which contains the standard buttons as well as buttons (identified below) that are specific to this window.

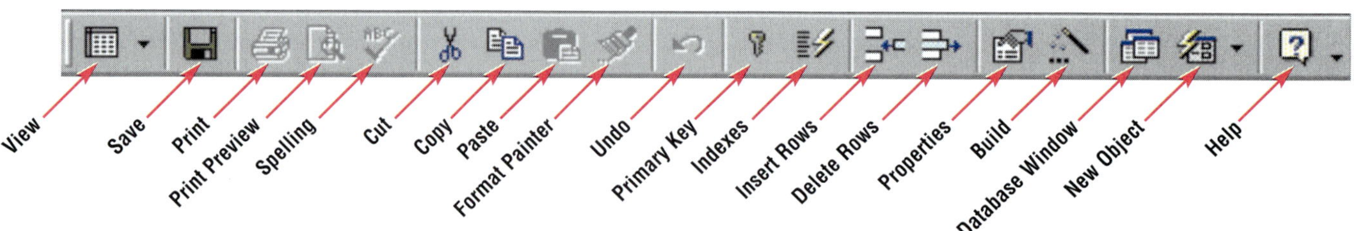

The upper section of the Table Design window consists of a **design grid** where you define each field to include in the table. Each row in the grid is where a field is defined by entering the required information in each of the columns. You decide to include the data currently maintained in the personnel folder on each employee in one table using the following 11 fields: Employee Number, Date Hired, Last Name, First Name, Street, City, State, Zip Code, Phone Number, Birth Date, and Picture.

Defining Field Names

The first step is to give each field a field name.

Concept 4 Field Name

A **field name** is used to identify the data stored in the field. A field name should be descriptive of the contents of the data to be entered in the field. It can be up to 64 characters long and can consist of letters, numbers, spaces, and special characters, except a period, an exclamation point, an accent grave (`` ` ``), and brackets ([]). You also cannot start a field name with a space. Examples of field names are: Last Name, First Name, Address, Phone Number, Department, Hire Date, or other words that describe the data. It is best to use short field names to make the tables easier to manage.

In the lower right section of the dialog box, a Help box provides information on the task you are performing in the window. Since the insertion point is positioned in the Field Name text box, the Help box displays a brief description of the rules for entering a valid field name.

The first field of data you will enter in the table is the employee number, which is assigned to each employee when hired. Each new employee is given the next consecutive number, so no two employees can have the same number. It is a maximum of four digits. The ▶ to the left of the first row indicates the current field.

The field name can be typed in uppercase or lowercase letters, and will be displayed exactly as entered.

1 ■ **Type Employee Number.**

Your screen should be similar to Figure 1–8.

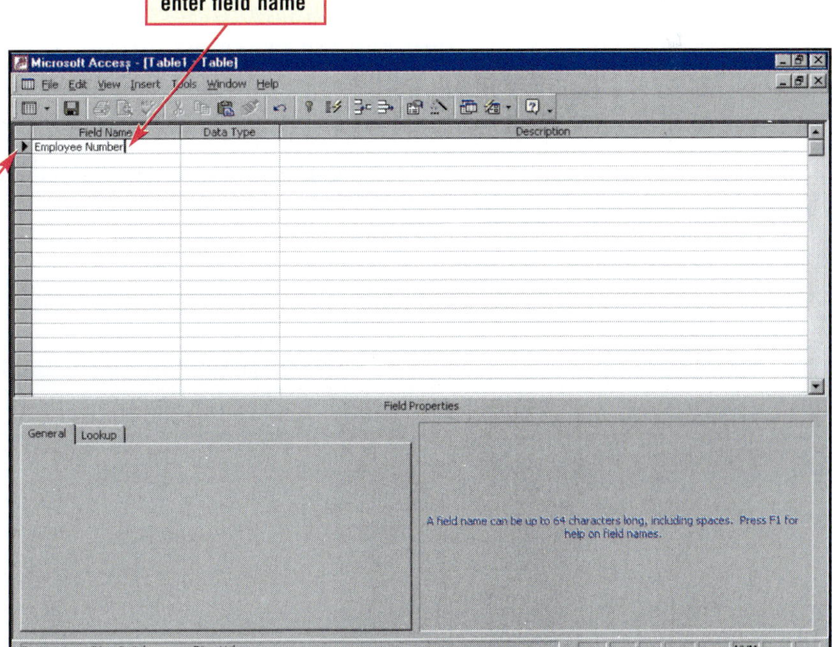

Figure 1–8

Since the data you will enter in this field is a maximum of four characters, you decide to change the field name to Employee ID, so the field name is closer in size to the data that will be entered in the field.

To edit the entry,

2 ■ **Press** Backspace **(6 times).**

> The Backspace key deletes characters to the left of the insertion point, and the Delete key deletes characters to the right.

■ **Type ID.**

■ **Press** ←Enter**.**

Your screen should be similar to Figure 1–9.

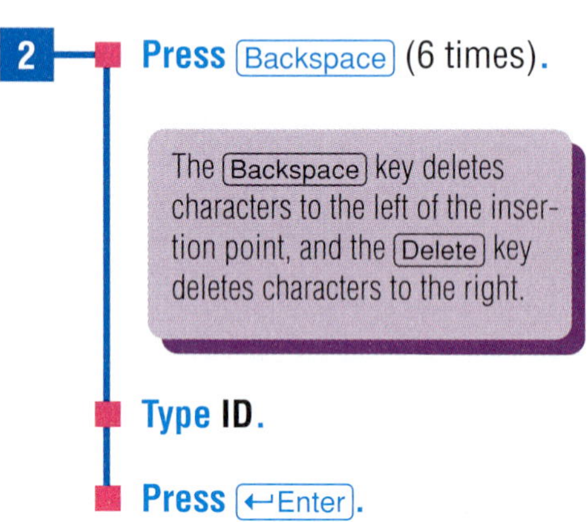

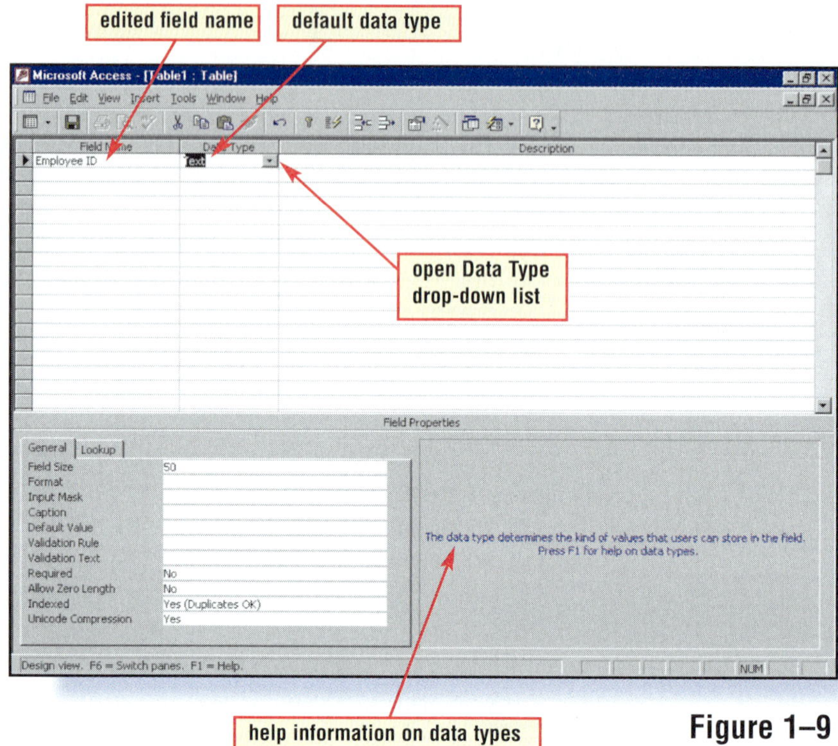

Figure 1–9

The insertion point has moved to the Data Type column, where the default data type of "Text" is automatically entered. The Help box provides a definition of what defining a data type does.

Defining Data Type and Field Properties

To specify the data type for the Employee ID field,

1 ■ **Open the Data Type drop-down list.**

Your screen should be similar to Figure 1–10.

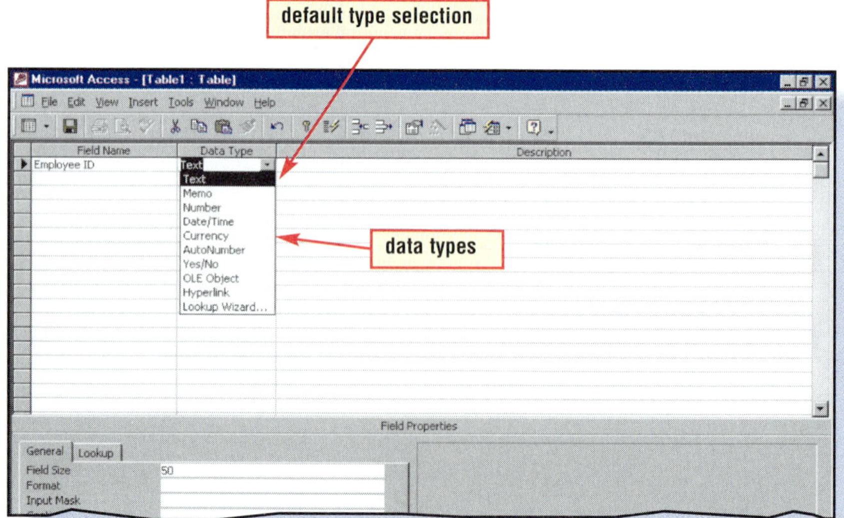

Figure 1–10

Concept (5) Data Type

The **data type** defines the type of data the field will contain. Access uses the data type to ensure that the right kind of data is entered in a field. It is important to choose the right data type for a field before you start entering data in the table. You can change a data type after the field contains data, but if the data types are not compatible, such as a text entry in a field whose data type accepts numbers only, you may lose data. The data types are described below.

Data Type	Description
Text	Text entries (words, combinations of words and numbers, numbers that are not used in calculations) up to 255 characters in length (this is the default). Names and phone numbers are examples of Text field entries. Text is the default data type.
Memo	Text that is variable in length and usually too long to be stored in a Text field. A maximum of 65,535 characters can be entered in a Memo field.
Number	Digits only. Number fields are used when you want to perform calculations on the values in the field. Number of Units Ordered is an example of a Number field entry.
Date/Time	Any valid date. Access allows dates from January 1, 100 to December 31, 9999. Access correctly handles leap years and checks all dates for validity.
Currency	Exactly like the Number field, but formatted to display decimal places and a currency symbol.
AutoNumber	A unique, sequential number that is automatically incremented by one whenever a new record is added to a table.
Yes/No	Accepts only Yes/No, True/False, or On/Off entries.
OLE Object	An object, such as a graphic (picture), sound, document, or spreadsheet, that is linked to or embedded in a table.
Hyperlink	Accepts hyperlink entries that are paths to an object, document, Web page, or other destinations.
Lookup Wizard	Displays a list of options you choose from another table in the database. Choosing this data type starts the Lookup Wizard.

Even though a field such as the Employee ID field may contain numeric entries, unless the numbers are used in calculations, the field should be assigned the Text data type. This allows other characters, such as the parentheses or hyphens in a telephone number, to be included in the entry. Also, by specifying the type as Text, any leading zeros (for example, in the zip code 07739) will be preserved, whereas leading zeros in a Number type field are dropped (which would make this zip code incorrectly 7739).

To close the Data Type drop-down menu without changing the selection,

2 ■ Press Esc.

Your screen should be similar to
Figure 1–11.

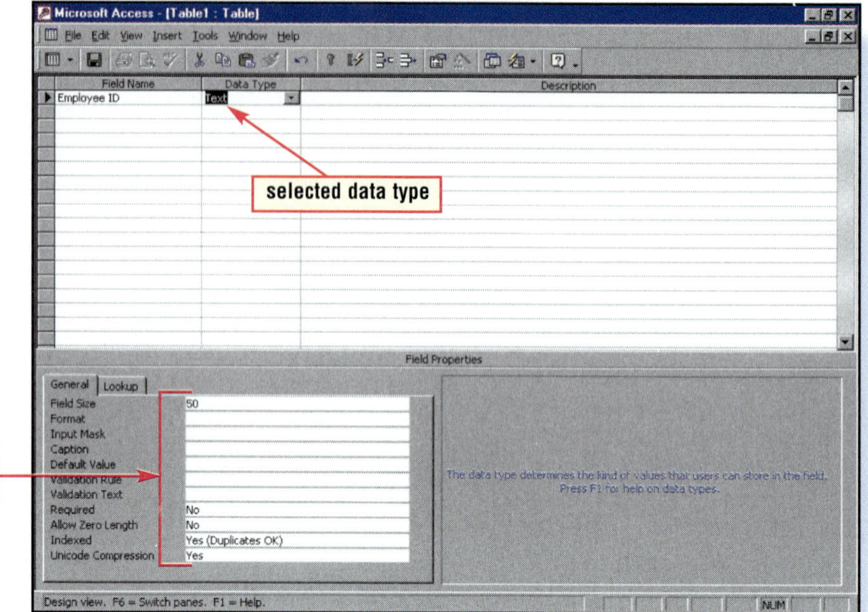

Figure 1–11

Notice in the Field Properties area of the dialog box that the General tab displays the default field property settings associated with a Text data type.

Concept ⑥ Field Property

Field properties are a set of characteristics that are associated with each field. Each data type has a different set of field properties. Setting field properties enhances the way your table works. Some of the more commonly used properties and their functions are described below.

Field Property	Description
Field Size	Sets the maximum number of characters that can be entered in the field.
Format	Specifies how data displays in a table and prints.
Input Mask	Simplifies data entry by controlling what data is required in a field and how the data is to be displayed.
Caption	Specifies a field label other than the field name.
Default Value	Automatically fills in a certain value for this field in new records as you add to the table. You can override a default value by typing a new value into the field.
Validation Rule	Limits data entered in a field to values that meet certain requirements.
Validation Text	Specifies the message to be displayed when the associated Validation Rule is not satisfied.
Required	Specifies whether or not a value must be entered in a field.
Allow Zero Length	Specifies whether or not an entry containing no characters is valid.
Indexed	Sets a field as an index field (a field that controls the order of records). Speeds up searches on fields that are searched frequently.

You need to set the **field size** for the Employee ID field. By default, Access sets a Text field size to 50. Although Access uses only the amount of storage space necessary for the text you actually store in a Text field, setting the field size to the smallest possible size can decrease the processing time required by the program. Additionally, if the field data to be entered is a specific size, setting the field size to that number restricts the entry to the maximum number. Since the Employee ID field will contain a maximum of four characters, you want to change the field size from the default of 50 to 4.

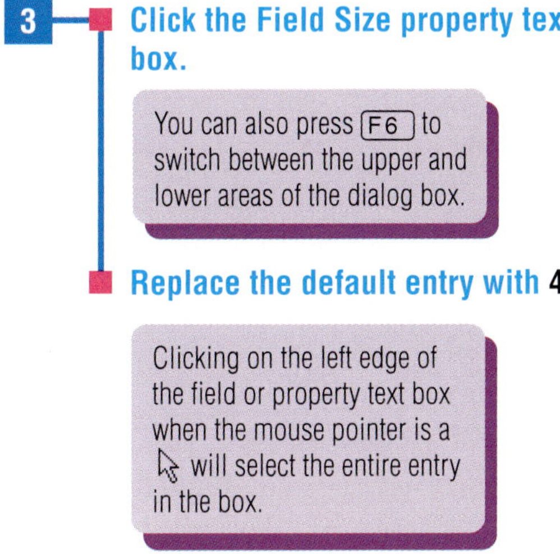

3 **Click the Field Size property text box.**

You can also press F6 to switch between the upper and lower areas of the dialog box.

Replace the default entry with 4.

Clicking on the left edge of the field or property text box when the mouse pointer is a ⬚ will select the entire entry in the box.

Your screen should be similar to Figure 1–12.

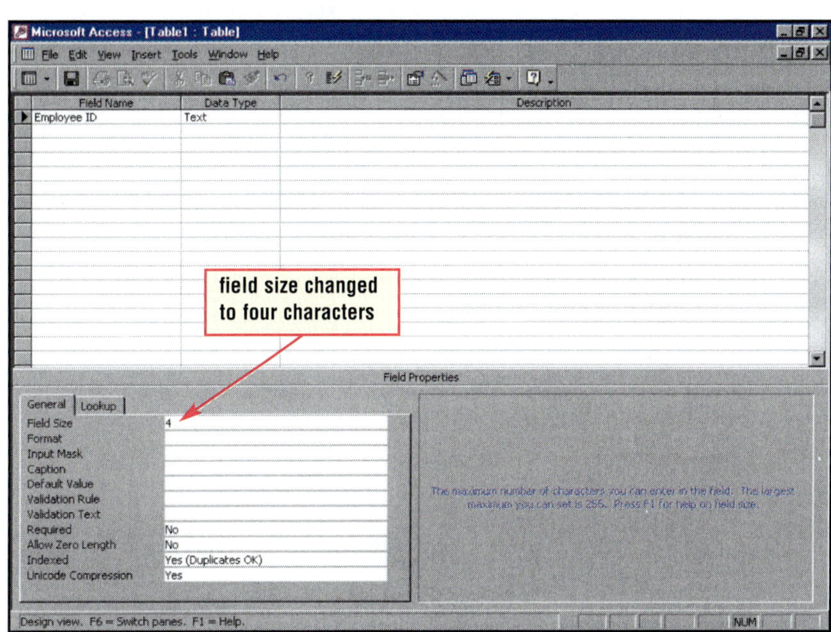

Figure 1–12

Entering a Field Description

To continue defining the Employee ID field, you will enter a description of the field in the Description text box. Although it is optional, a field description makes the table easier to understand and update because the description is displayed in the status bar when you enter data into the table.

1 ■ **Click the Description text box for the Employee ID field.**

■ **Type A unique 4-digit number assigned to each employee when hired.**

> Text in the Description box scrolls horizontally as needed.

Your screen should be similar to Figure 1–13.

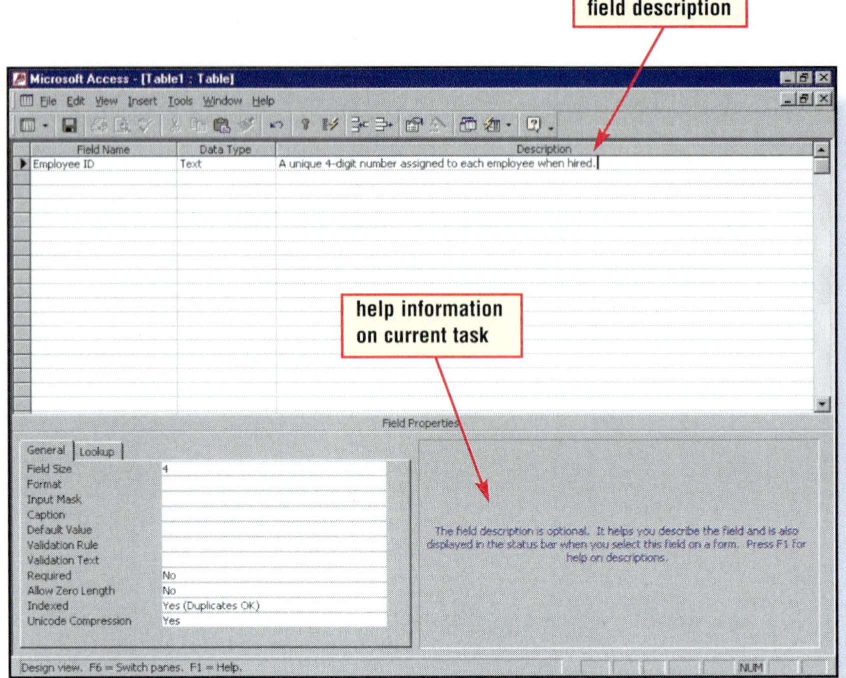

Figure 1–13

Defining a Primary Key Field

Next you want to make the Employee ID field a primary key field.

Concept ⑦ Primary Key

A **primary key** is a field that uniquely identifies each record. Most tables have at least one field that is selected as the primary key. The data in the primary key field must be unique for each record. For example, a Social Security number field could be selected as the primary key because the data in that field is unique for each employee. Other examples of a primary key field are parts numbers or catalog numbers.

A primary key prevents duplicate records from being entered in the table and is used to control the order in which records display in the table. This makes it faster for databases to locate records in the table and to process other operations. The primary key is also used to create a link between tables in a database.

Although any field can be the primary key, traditionally the first field or group of fields in the table is the primary key field.

To define the field as a primary key,

1 Click 🔑 **Primary Key.**

The menu equivalent is **E**dit/Primary **K**ey.

Your screen should be similar to Figure 1–14.

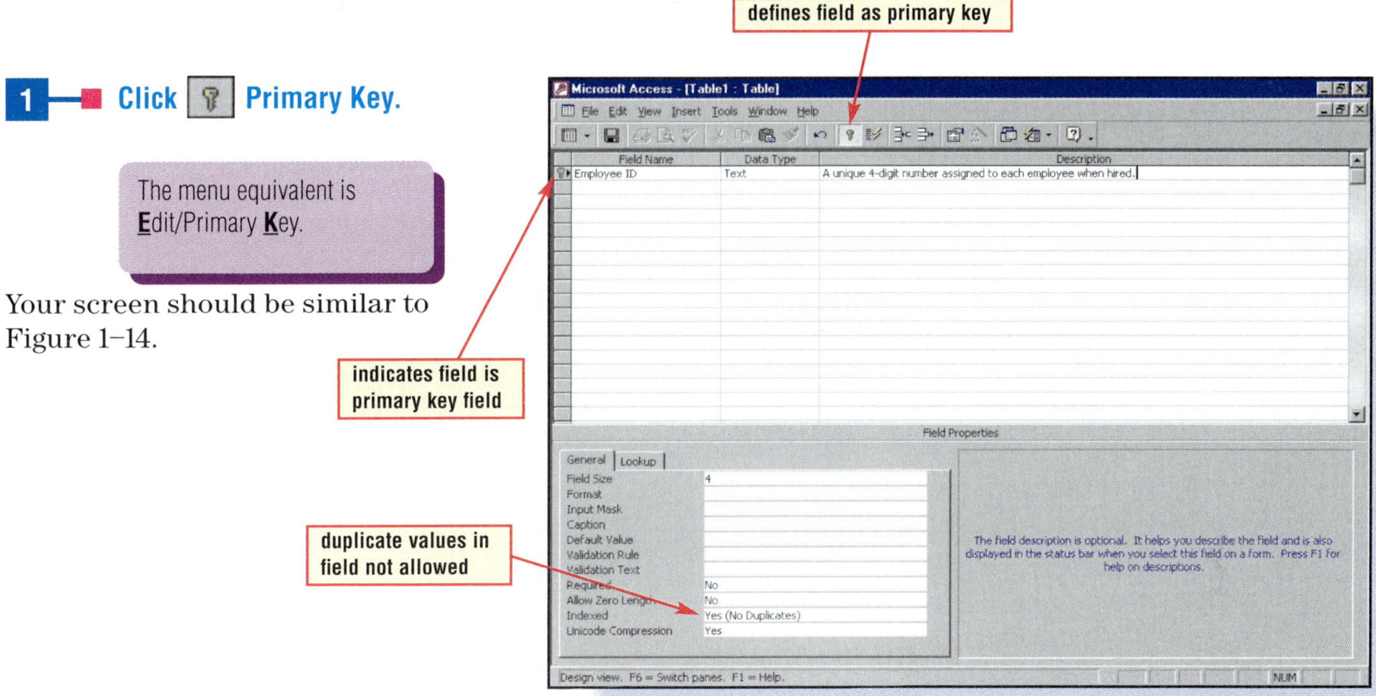

Figure 1–14

The 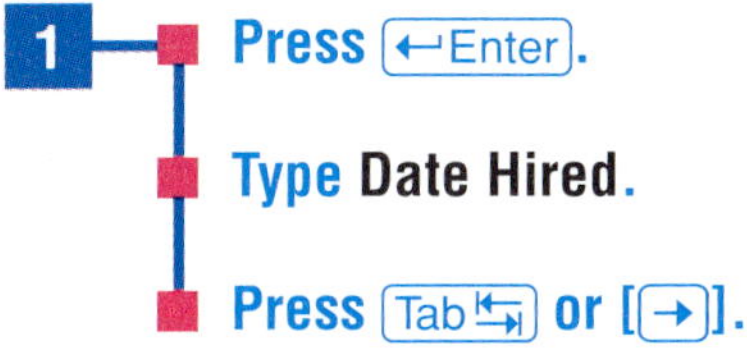 icon appears in the column to the left of the field name, showing that this field is a primary key field. Now that this is the primary key field, the Indexed property setting has changed to Yes (No Duplicates). This setting prohibits duplicate values in a field.

Defining Additional Fields

The second field will display the date the employee started working at Lifestyle Fitness Club in the form of month/day/year. To enter the second field name,

Additional Information

Using [Tab ⇆] or [→] has the same effect as pressing [←Enter]; it moves the insertion point to the next column to the right. [⇧Shift] + [Tab ⇆] or [←] moves the insertion point to the left one column.

1 Press [←Enter].

Type **Date Hired.**

Press [Tab ⇆] or [[→]].

2 Select the Date/Time data type.

Additional Information

You can also enter the data type by typing the first character of the data type option. For example, you can enter "d" for Date/Time.

Your screen should be similar to Figure 1–15.

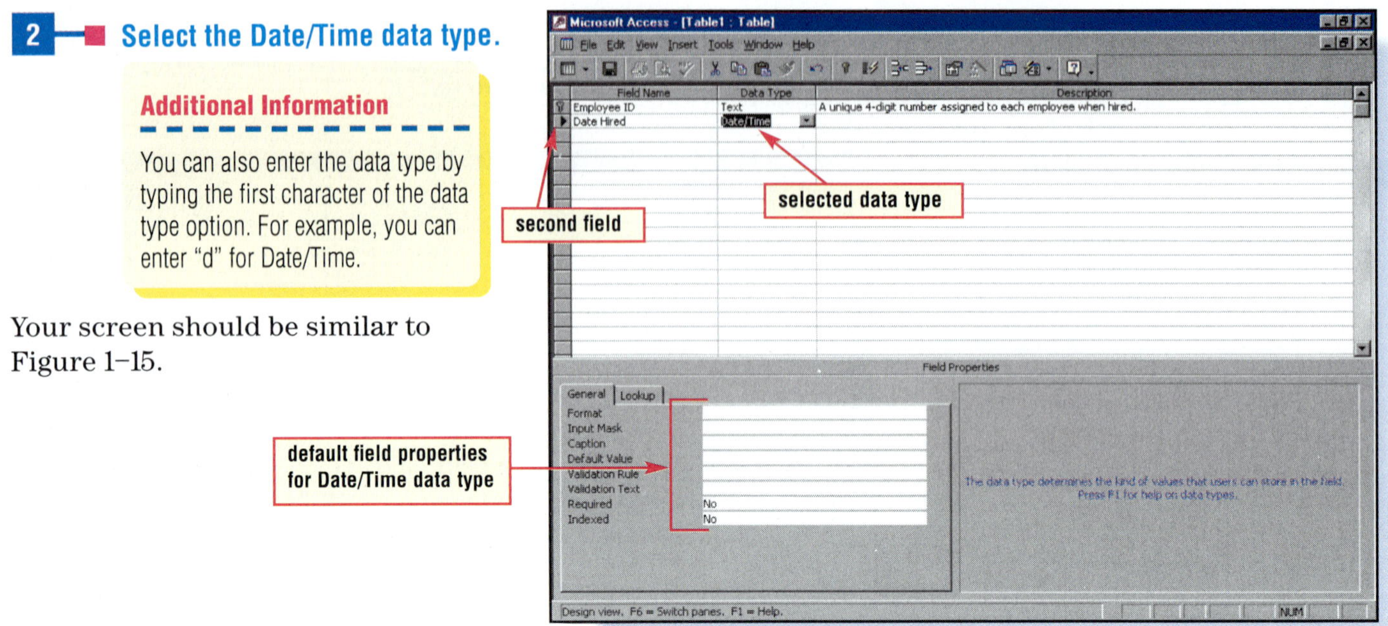

Figure 1–15

You cannot set the field size in Date/Time fields.

The default field properties for the selected data type are displayed. This time you want to change the format of the field so that the date will display as mm/dd/yy, regardless of how it is entered.

3 Select the Format property box.

Open the drop-down list of Format options.

Your screen should be similar to Figure 1–16.

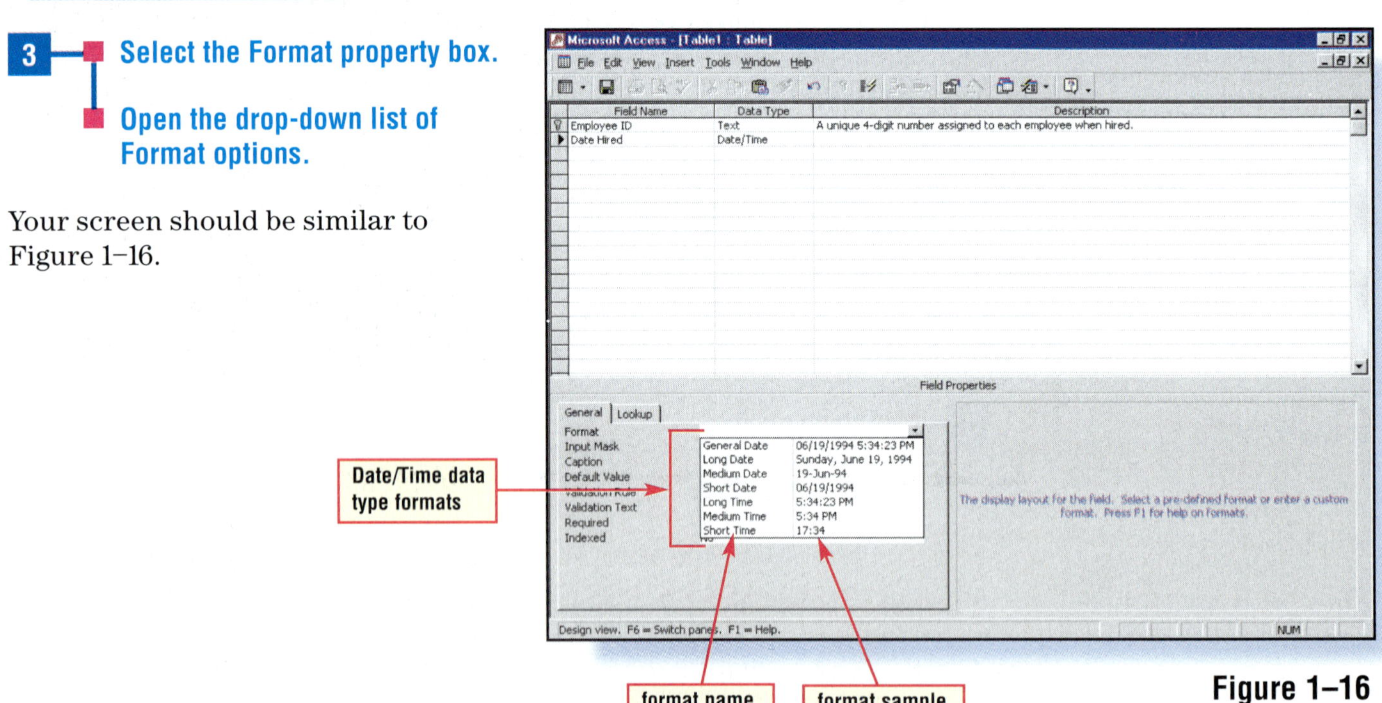

Figure 1–16

The names of the seven predefined layouts for the Date/Time field type are displayed in the list. An example of each layout appears to the right of the name.

4 Choose Short Date.

In the Description text box of the Date Hired field, enter the description: **Acceptable entry formats are 4/4/01, Apr. 4, 2001, or April 4, 2001.**

Your screen should be similar to Figure 1–17.

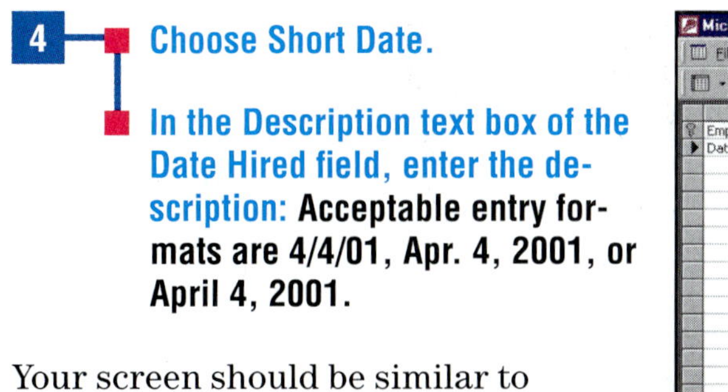
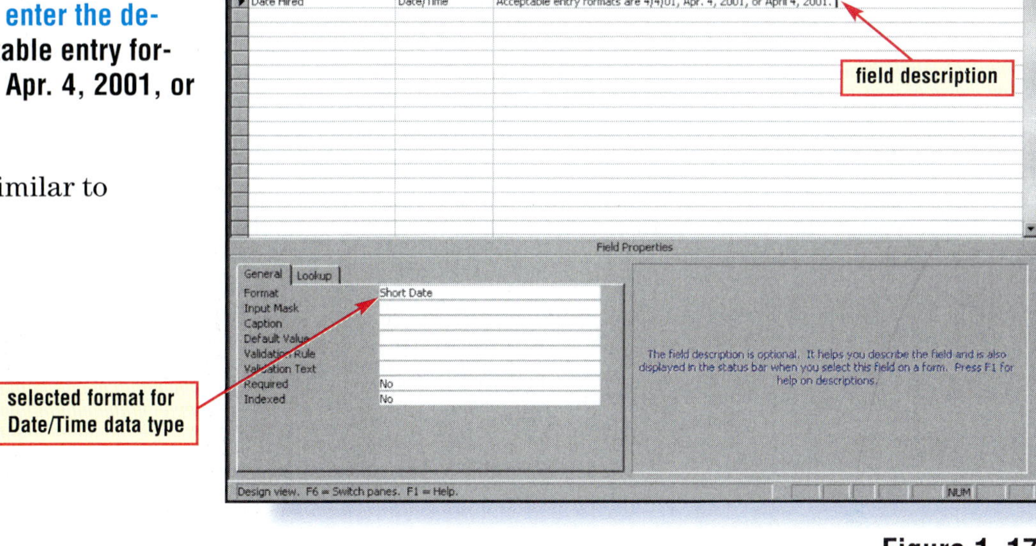

Figure 1–17

The third field is a Text field type that will contain the employee's last name. Because the field name is descriptive of the field contents, a description is not needed.

5 Press ↵Enter.

Type **Last Name**.

Press ↵Enter (3 times).

Your screen should be similar to Figure 1–18.

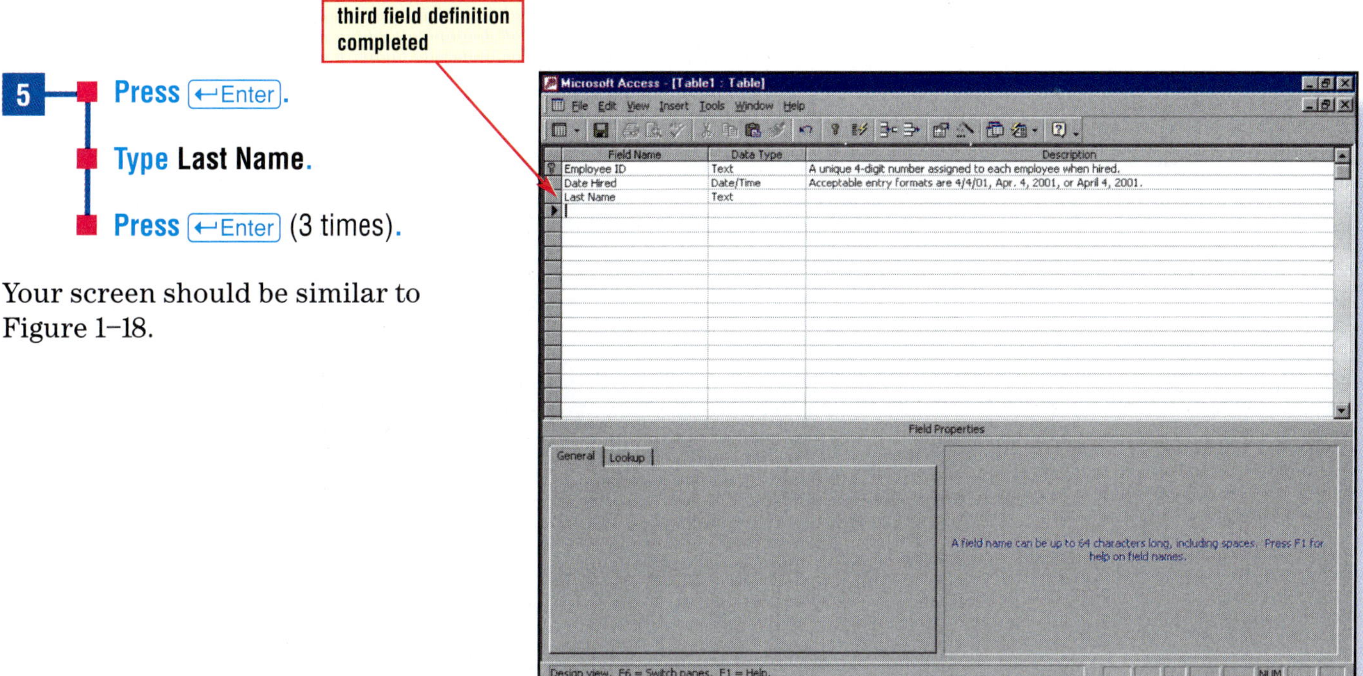

Figure 1–18

6 In the same manner, enter the information shown on the next page for the next seven fields. If you make a typing mistake, use Backspace and Delete to correct errors.

Field Name	Data Type	Description	Field Size/Format
First Name	Text		50
Street	Text		50
City	Text		50
State	Text	A 2-character abbreviation entered in all capital letters.	2
Zip Code	Text	Use the 9-digit zip code if available.	10
Phone Number	Text	Enter using the format (555) 555-5555.	15
Birth Date	Date/Time	Acceptable entry formats are 4/4/01, Apr. 4, 2001, or April 4, 2001.	Short Date
Picture	OLE object	Employee ID picture.	

You can copy the description from the Date Hired field to the Birth Date field.

When you have completed the seven additional fields, your field definition grid should be similar to Figure 1–19.

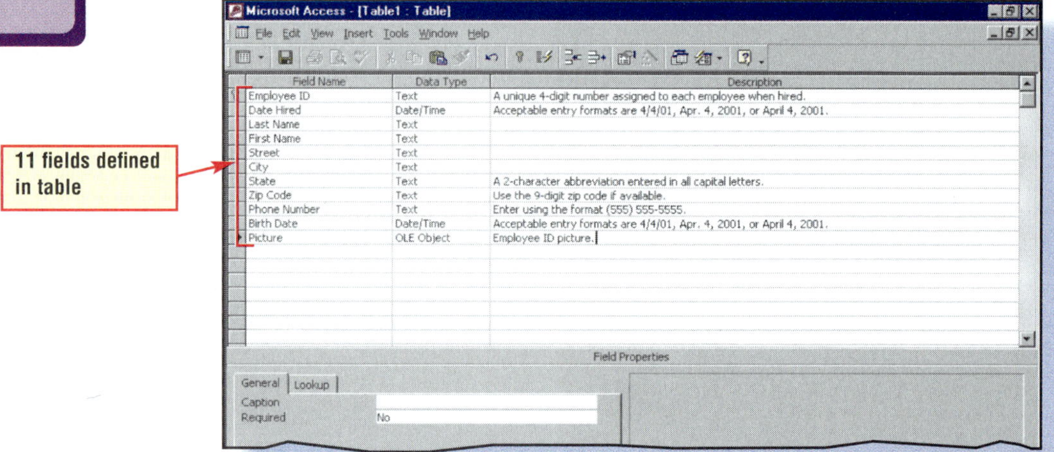

Figure 1–19

Editing Field Definitions

After looking over the fields, you decide to change the field sizes of the Last Name, First Name, and City fields to 20 character entries. Positioning the insertion point in any column of a field will display the properties for that field.

1 Move to any column in the Last Name field.

Change the field size to 20.

In a similar manner, change the field size for the First Name and City fields to 20.

Carefully check your screen to ensure that each field name and field type was entered accurately and make any necessary corrections.

> To delete an entire field, move to the field and choose **E**dit/Delete **R**ows or click 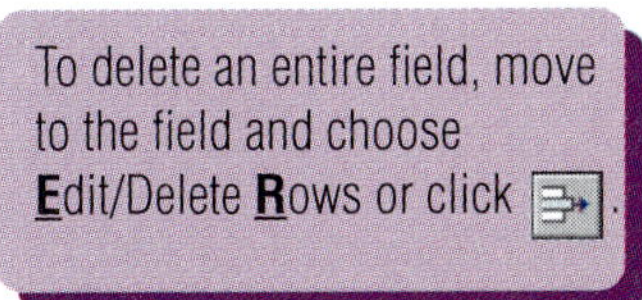.

Your screen should be similar to Figure 1–20.

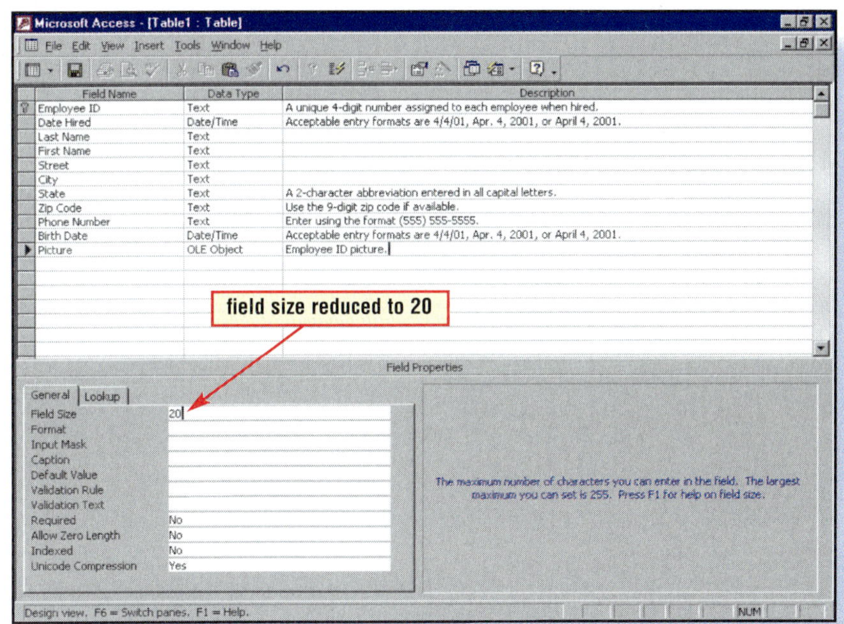

Figure 1–20

Saving the Table Structure

Once you are satisfied that your field definitions are correct, you can save the table design by naming it.

1 Click 🖫 Save.

> The menu equivalent is **F**ile/**S**ave, and the keyboard shortcut is Ctrl + S.

Your screen should be similar to Figure 1–21.

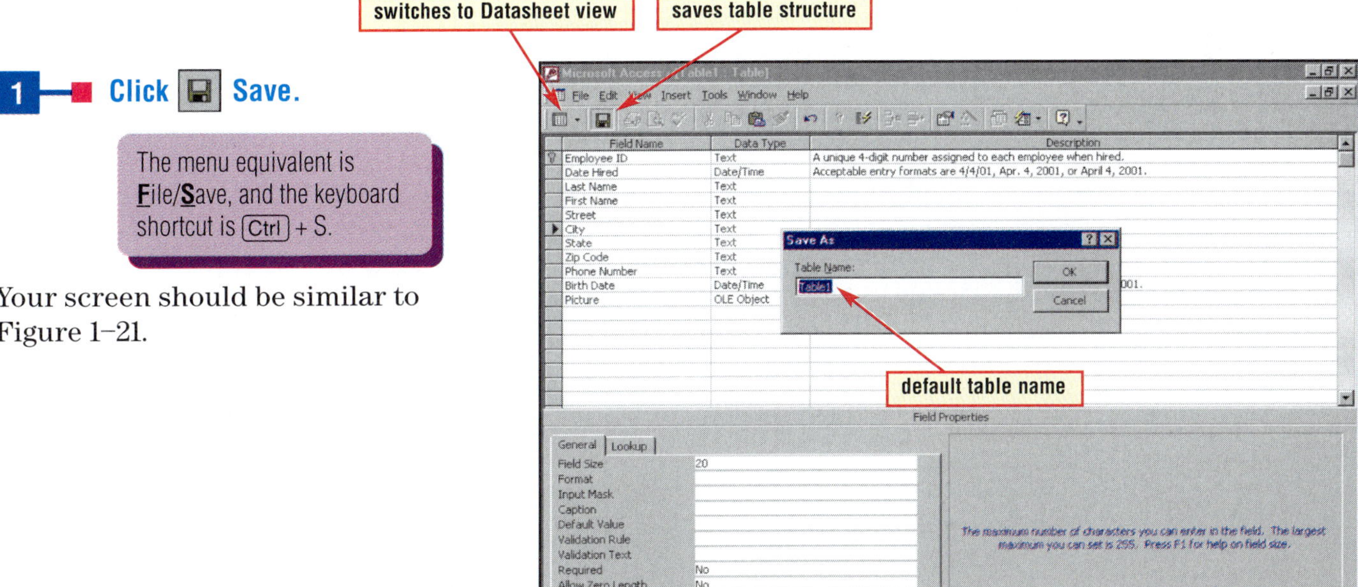

Figure 1–21

In the Save As dialog box, you want to replace the default name, Table 1, with a more descriptive name. A table name follows the same set of standard naming conventions or rules that you use when naming fields. It is acceptable to use the same name for both a table and the database, although each table in a database must have a unique name. You will save the table using the table name Employees.

The table structure is saved with the database file. You have created a table named Employees in the Lifestyle Fitness Employees database file.

Switching Views

Now that the table structure is defined and saved, you can enter the employee data into the new table. You enter and display data in the table in Datasheet view. Access allows you to view the objects in your database in several different window formats, called **views**. Each view includes its own menu and toolbar designed to work with the object in the window. The views that are available change depending on the type of object you are working with. The basic views are described in the table below.

View	Use
Design view	Used to create a table, form, query, or report.
Datasheet view	Provides a row-and-column view of the data in tables, forms, and queries.
Form view	Displays the records in a form.
Preview	Displays a form, report, table, or query as it will appear when printed.

Opening the ▦▾ View button displays a drop-down list of available views.

The ▦▾ View button is a toggle button that switches between the different available views. The graphic in the button changes to indicate the view that will be displayed when selected. The View button appears as ☒▾ for Design view and ▦▾ for Datasheet view.

1   **Click** [image] **Datasheet View.**

If necessary, maximize the window.

The menu equivalent is View/Datasheet View.

Your screen should be similar to Figure 1–22.

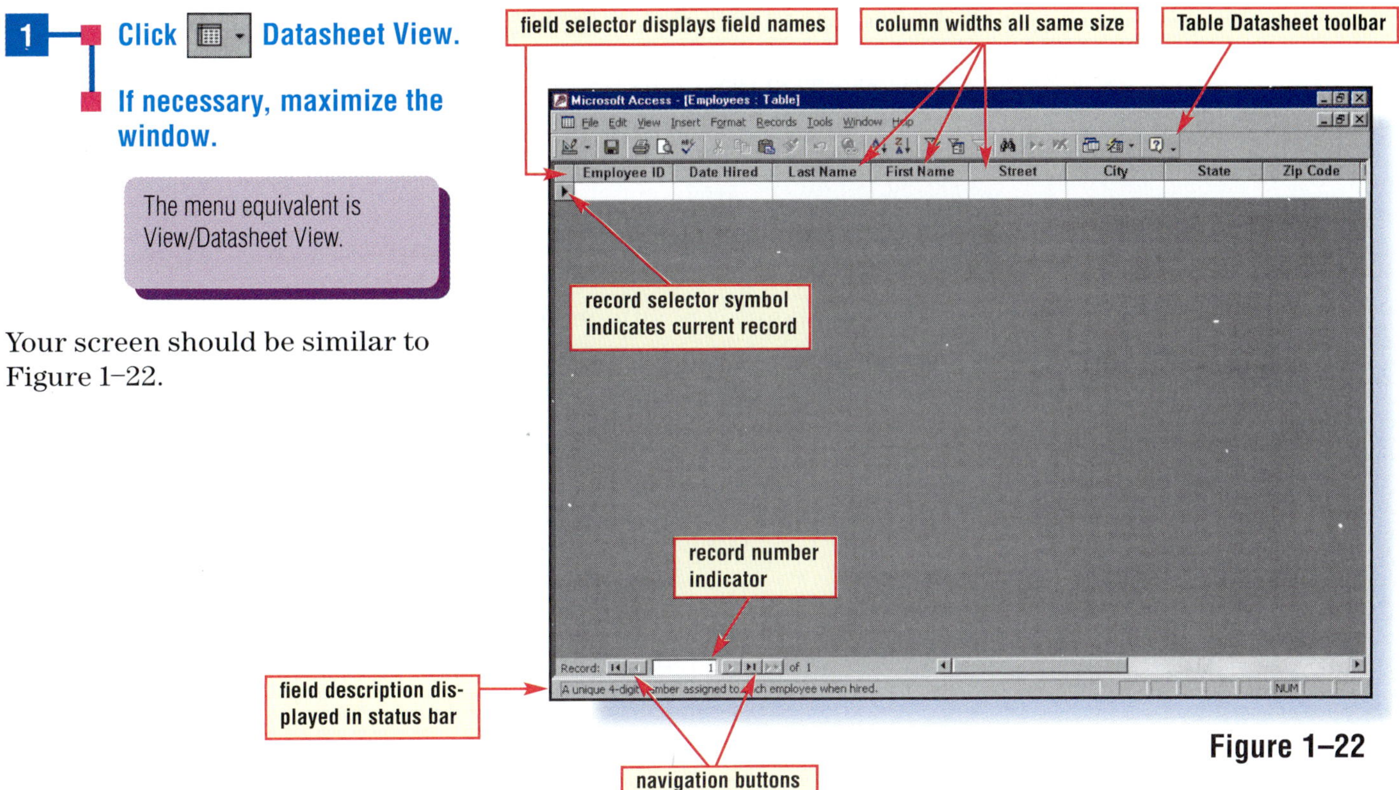

Figure 1–22

In Table Datasheet view, you can enter and delete records and edit field data in existing records. This view displays the table data in a row-and-column format. Each field is a column of the table, and the field names you entered in Design view are displayed as column headings. The column heading area is called the **field selector** for each column. Below the field selector is a blank row where you will enter the data for a record. To the left of the row is the **record selector** symbol ▶, which indicates which record is the **current record**.

The bottom of the window displays a horizontal scroll bar, navigation buttons, and a record number indicator. The **record number indicator** shows the number of the current record as well as the total number of records in the table. Because the table does not yet contain records, the indicator displays "Record: 1 of 1" in anticipation of your first entry. On both sides of the record number are the **navigation buttons**, which are used to move through records with a mouse.

In addition, this view displays a Table Datasheet toolbar containing the standard buttons as well as buttons (identified below) that are specific to the Table Datasheet view window.

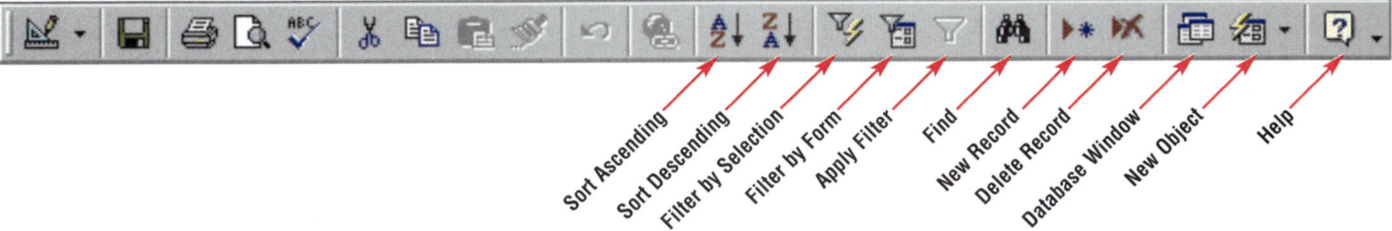

Notice also in this view that the column widths are all the same, even though you set different field sizes in the Table Design window. This is because the Table Datasheet view window has its own default column width setting. You will learn how to change the column width later in this tutorial.

Entering and Editing Data

The insertion point is positioned in the Employee ID field, indicating the program is ready to accept data in this field. The status bar displays the description you entered for the field. The data you will enter in the following steps for the first record is:

Field Name	Data
Employee ID	1151
Date Hired	October 14,1997
Last Name	Sutton
First Name	Lisa
Street	4389 S. Hayden Rd.
City	Iona
State	FL
Zip Code	33101-3309
Phone Number	(941) 555-1950
Birth Date	June 14, 1975
Picture	friend1.bmp

When you enter data in a record, it should be entered accurately and consistently. The data you enter in a field should be typed exactly as you want it to appear. This is important because any printouts of the data will display the information exactly as entered. It is also important to enter data in a consistent form. For example, if you decide to abbreviate the word "Street" as "St." in the Street field, then it should be abbreviated the same way in every record where it appears. Also be careful not to enter a blank space before or after a field entry. This can cause problems when using the table to locate information.

You will try to enter an Employee ID number that is larger than the field size of 4 that you defined in Table Design view.

1 ▪ **Type 11510.**

▪ **Press** ⟨←Enter⟩.

Your screen should be similar to Figure 1–23.

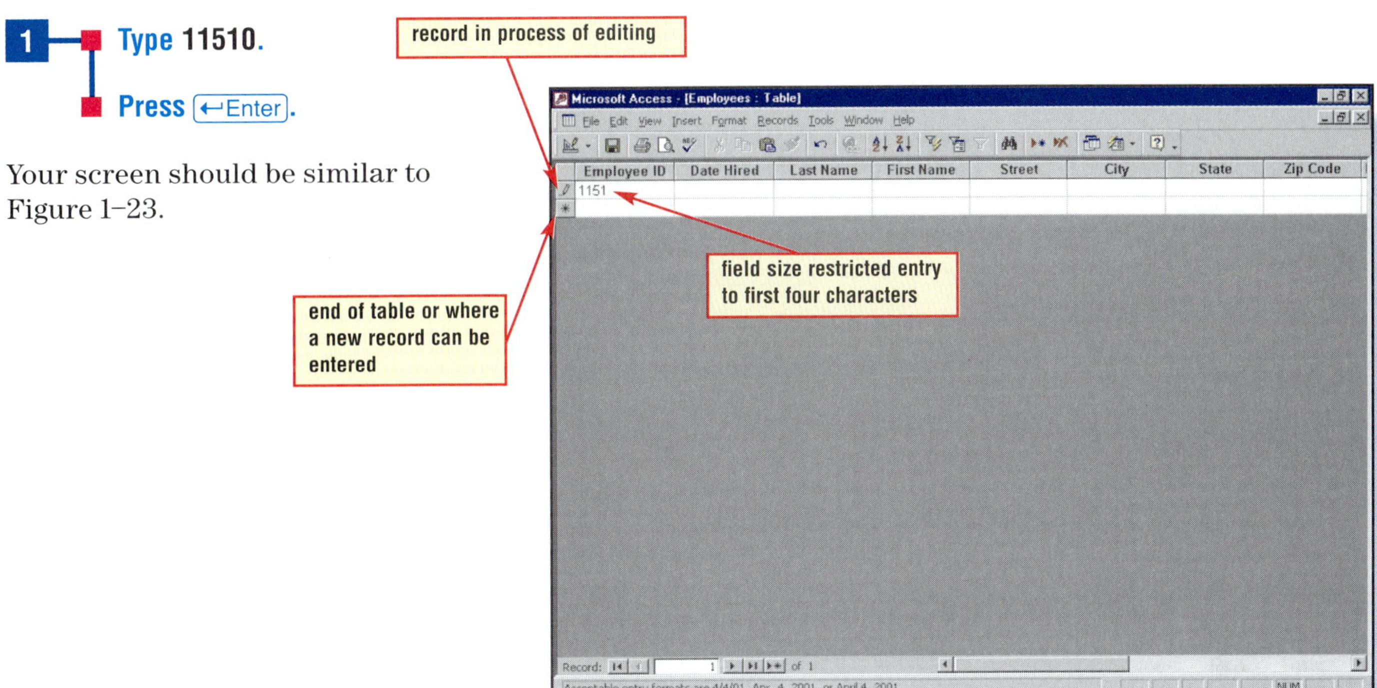

Figure 1–23

The program accepted only the first four digits you typed. The field size restriction helps control the accuracy of data by not allowing an entry larger than specified. Also notice that a second row has appeared in the table. The * symbol in the record selector column indicates the end of the table or where a new record can be entered. In addition, the current record symbol has changed to a ⟨ 🖉 ⟩. This symbol means the record is in the process of being entered or edited and has not yet been saved.

To enter the date hired (it is intentionally incorrect) for this record,

2 ▪ **Type 10/41/97.**

▪ **Press** ⟨←Enter⟩.

Your screen should be similar to Figure 1–24.

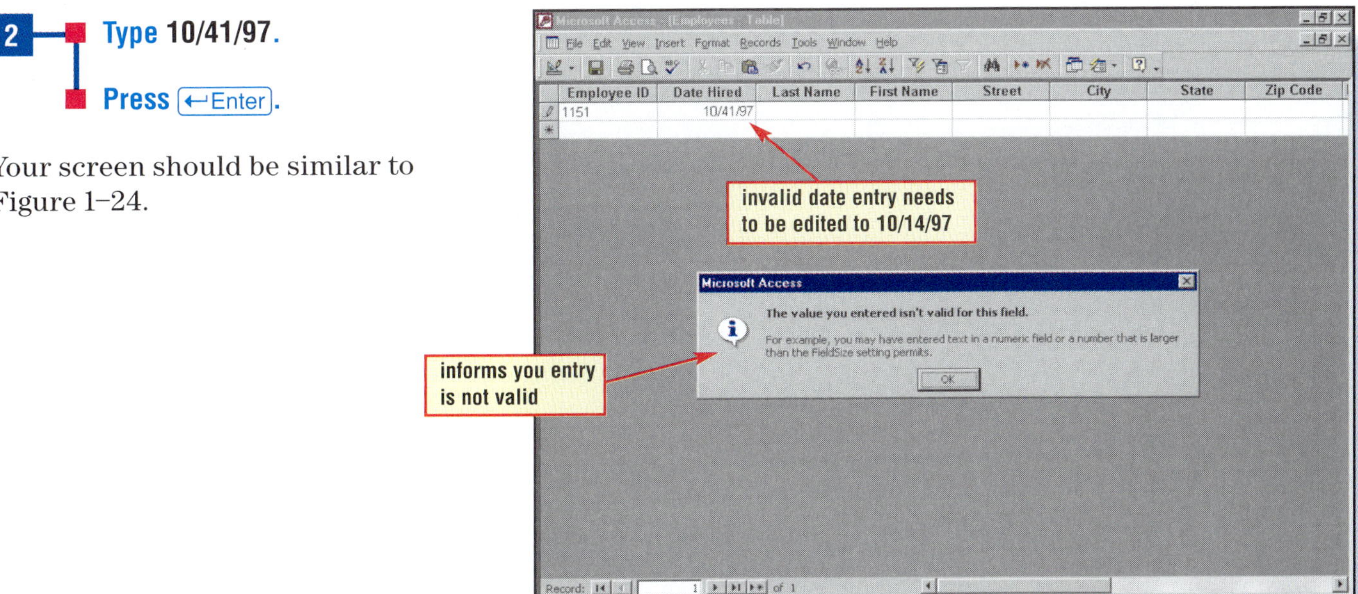

Figure 1–24

An informational message box is displayed. Access automatically performs some basic validity checks on the data as it is entered based upon the field type specified in the table design. This is another way Access helps you control data entry to ensure the accuracy of the data. In this case the date entered (10/41/97) could not be correct because there cannot be 41 days in a month. To close the message box,

3 ■ Click  .

Next you need to edit the entry to correct it. How you edit data in Access depends on which mode of operation is active.

Concept ⑧ Edit and Navigation Modes

The Edit and Navigation modes control how you can move through and make changes to data in a table. **Edit mode** is used to enter or edit data in a field. In Edit mode the insertion point is displayed in the field so you can edit existing data or enter new data. To position the insertion point in the field entry, click at the location where you want it to appear. The keyboard keys shown in the table below can also be used to move the insertion point in Edit mode and to make changes to individual characters in the entry.

Navigation mode is used to move from field to field and to delete an entire field entry. In Navigation mode the entire field entry is selected (highlighted), and the insertion point is not displayed. You move from field to field using the keyboard keys shown in the table below.

Key	Edit Mode
← or →	Moves insertion point left or right one character.
Ctrl + ← or →	Moves insertion point left or right one word.
↓	Moves insertion point to current field in next record.
Home or End	Moves insertion point to beginning or end of field in single-line field.
Ctrl + Home or End	Moves insertion point to beginning or end of field in multiple-line field.
Delete	Deletes character to right of insertion point.
Backspace	Deletes character to left of insertion point.
Tab or ⇧ Shift + Tab	Ends Edit mode and highlights next or previous field.

Key	Navigation Mode
→ or Tab	Moves highlight to next field.
← or ⇧ Shift + Tab	Moves highlight to previous field.
↓	Moves highlight to current field in next record.
Home or End	Moves highlight to first or last field in current record.
Delete or Backspace	Deletes highlighted field contents.

To activate Navigation mode, point to the left edge of a field and click when the pointer is a ✚. To activate Edit mode, click on the field when the mouse pointer is an I-beam. To switch between modes using the keyboard, press F2.

Because you are entering data in a new record, Edit mode is automatically active.

4 ■ **Edit the entry to be 10/14/97.**

■ **Press ⏎Enter.**

> You can also press Tab to move to the next field. → will move to the next field if the insertion point is at the end of the entry or you are in Navigation mode.

Your screen should be similar to Figure 1–25.

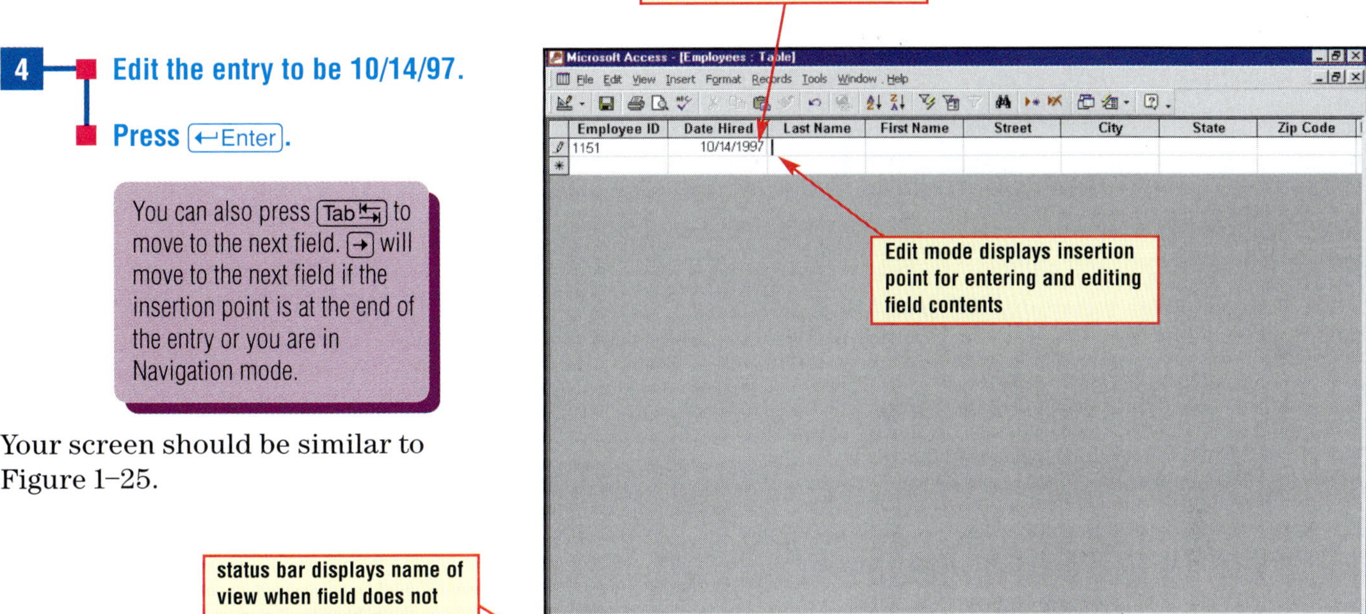

Figure 1–25

Additional Information

You can cancel changes you are making in the current field at any time by pressing Esc, and the original entry is restored.

The corrected date is accepted, and the insertion point moves to the Last Name field. Because no description was entered for this field, the status bar displays "Datasheet View," the name of the current view, instead of a field description.

5 ■ **Enter the data shown below for the remaining fields, typing the information exactly as it appears.**

> The fields will scroll on the screen as you move to the right in the record.

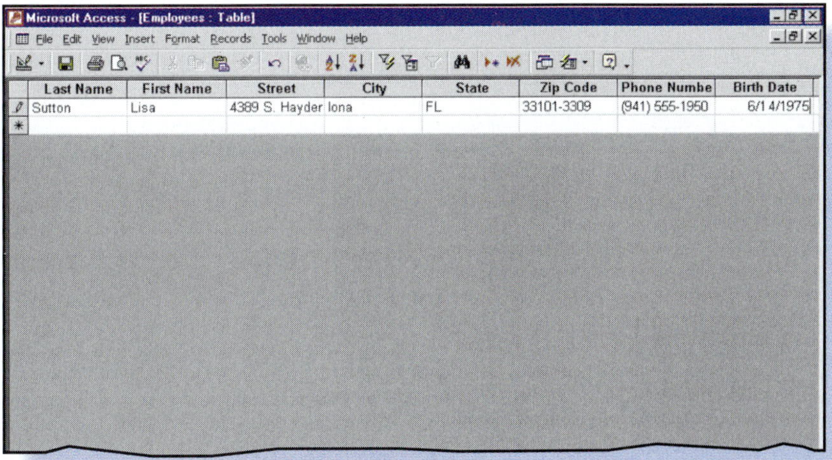

Field Name	Data
Last Name	Sutton
First Name	Lisa
Street	4389 S. Hayden Rd.
City	Iona
State	FL
Zip Code	33101-3309
Phone Number	(941) 555-1950
Birth Date	6/14/75

Figure 1–26

Your screen should be similar to Figure 1–26.

Inserting a Picture

To complete the information for this record, you need to insert a picture of Lisa in the picture field. A picture is one of several different types of graphic objects that can be added to a database table.

Concept 9 Graphics

A **graphic** is a nontext element or object, such as a drawing or picture, that can be added to a table. A graphic can be a simple **drawing object** consisting of shapes such as lines and boxes that can be created using a drawing program such as Paint. A **picture** is an illustration such as a scanned photograph. Most images that are scanned and inserted into documents are stored as Windows bitmap files (.bmp). Other types of objects that can be added are a worksheet created in Excel or a Word document.

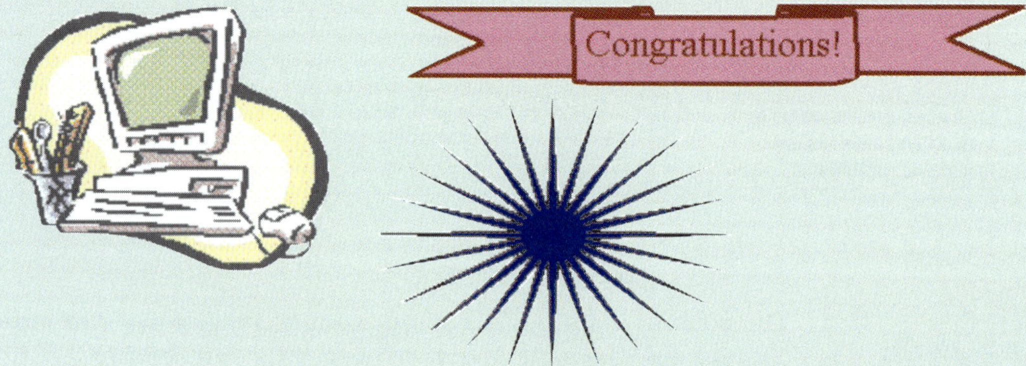

Picture files can be obtained from a variety of sources. Many simple drawings, called **Clip art**, are available in the Clip Gallery that comes with Office 2000. You can also create graphic files using a scanner to convert any printed document, including photographs, to an electronic format. All types of graphics, including clip art, photographs, and other types of images can be found on the Internet. These files are commonly stored as .jpg or .pcx files. Keep in mind that any images you locate on the Internet may be protected by copyright and should be used only with permission. You can also purchase CDs containing graphics for your use.

Since you do not have employee pictures yet, you will insert a picture of a friend to demonstrate to the owners how this feature works. Then after the database design is completed, you will arrange to have all employee pictures taken and inserted into the appropriate field. You have a recent photograph of your friend that you scanned and saved as Friend1.jpg. You will insert the picture in the Picture field for Lisa.

1 ▪ **Move to the Picture field.**

▪ **Choose Insert/Object.**

Your screen should be similar to Figure 1–27.

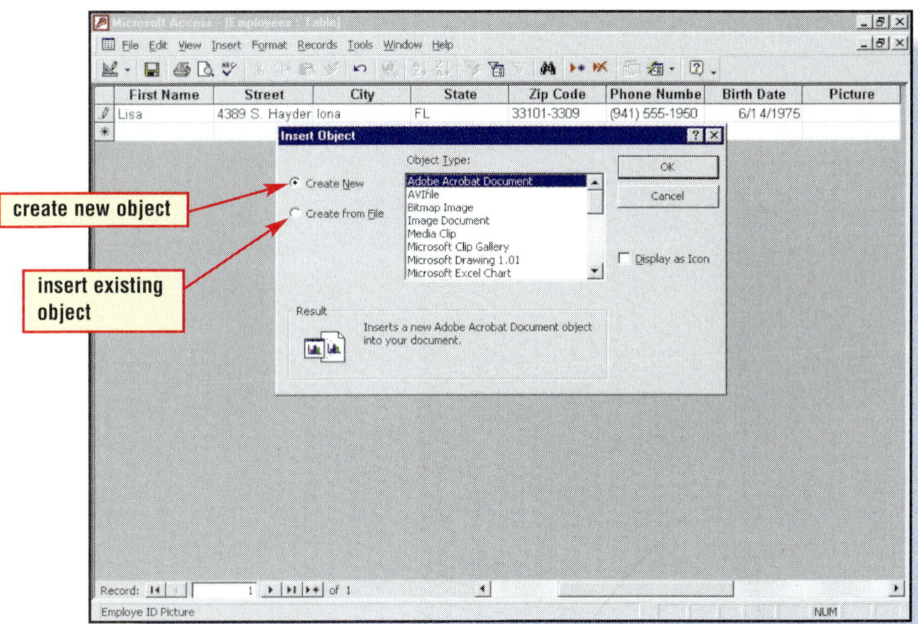

Figure 1–27

From the Insert Object dialog box you specify whether you want to create a new object or insert an existing object. Since the picture is already created and stored on your data disk, you will use the Create from File option and specify the location of the file.

2 ▪ **Select Create from File.**

▪ **Click** Browse... **.**

Your screen should be similar to Figure 1–28.

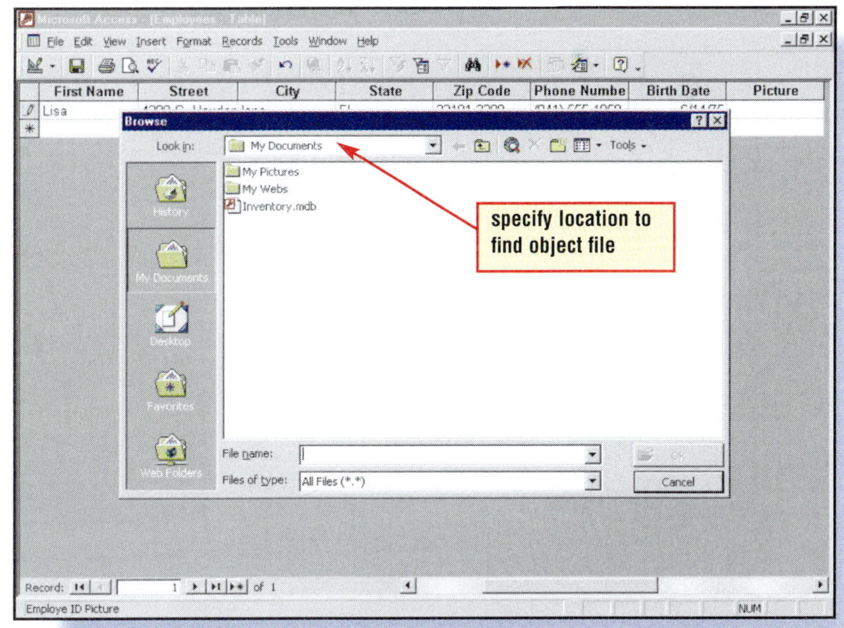

Figure 1–28

This Browse dialog box is used to locate and select the name of the file you want to insert. The Look In drop-down list box displays the default folder as the location where the program will look for files, and the file list box displays the names of all files at that location. First you need to change the location to the drive containing your data disk.

3 ▪ **Open the Look In drop-down list box.**

▪ **Choose** 3 1/2 Floppy (A:) **or the drive containing your data disk.**

If a system error message appears, check that your disk is properly inserted in the drive.

Your screen should be similar to Figure 1–29.

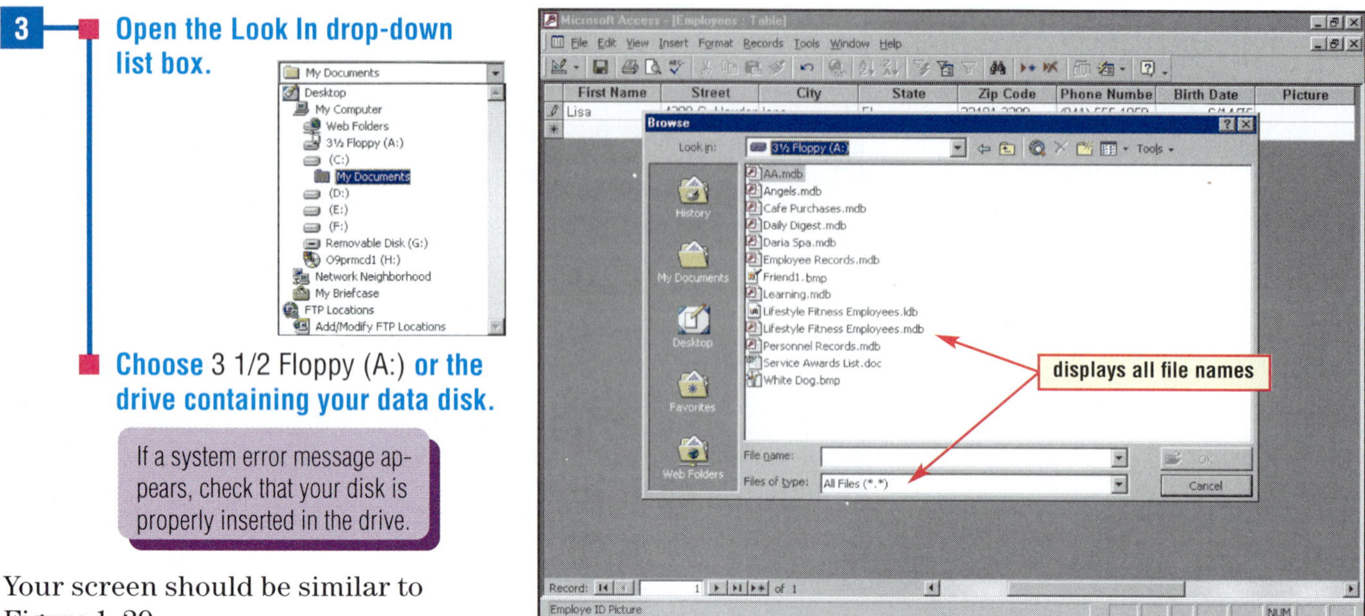

Figure 1–29

Now the file list box displays the names of all files on your data disk. When selecting a file to insert, it may be helpful to see a preview of the file first. To do this you can change the dialog box view.

4 ▪ **Select** Friend1.

If necessary, scroll the list box until the file name Friend1 is visible. If the file name is not displayed, ask your instructor for help.

▪ **Open the** ▦ **Views drop-down list.**

List
Details
Properties
Preview

Arrange Icons ▸

▪ **Choose Pre̲view.**

Your screen should be similar to Figure 1–30.

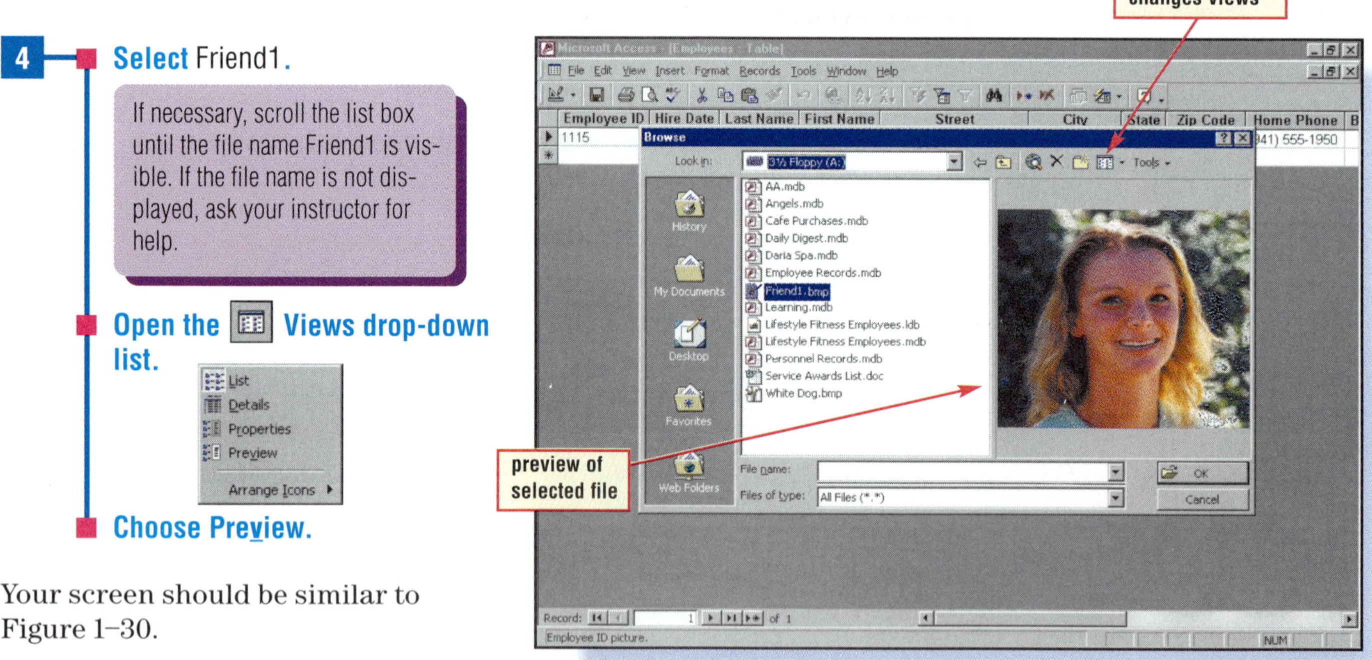

Figure 1–30

A preview of the selected file is displayed in the right side of the dialog box. To return the view to the list of file names and open this file,

5 — **Click** 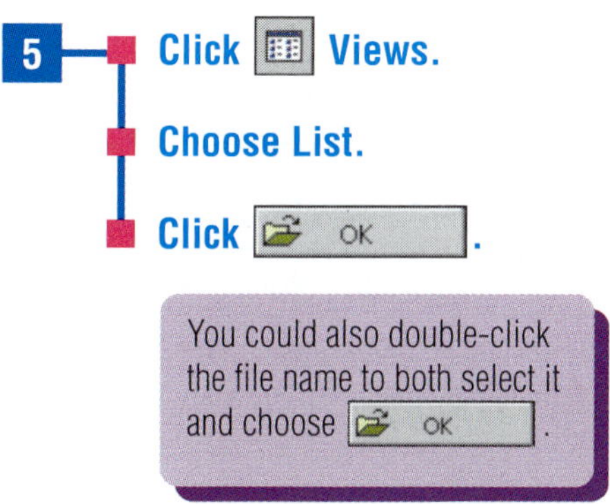 **Views.**

Choose List.

Click OK .

You could also double-click the file name to both select it and choose OK .

Your screen should be similar to Figure 1–31.

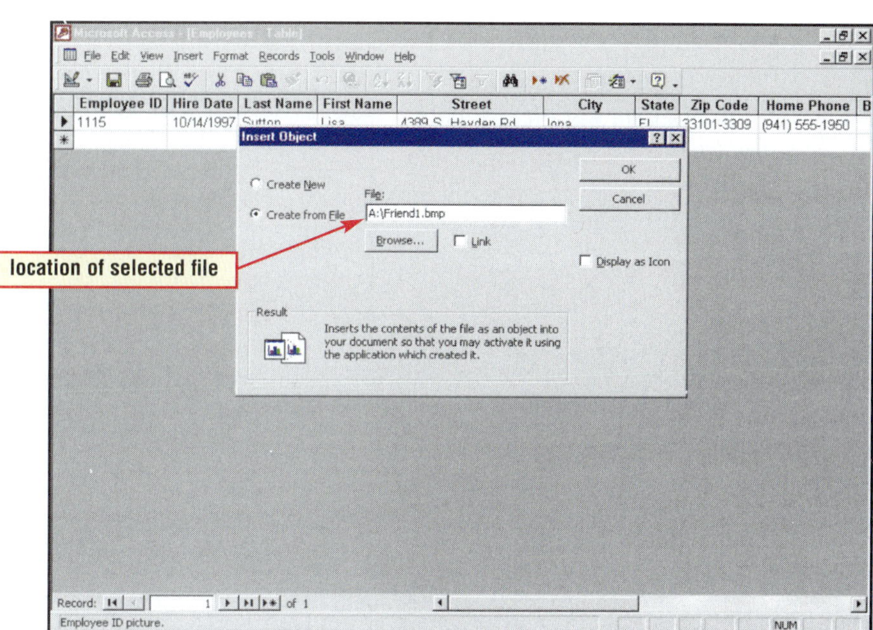

Figure 1–31

You could also type the path and file name directly in the File text box.

The Insert Object dialog box is displayed again with the path to the selected object displayed in the File text box. When inserting an object, you can specify if you want to display the object as an icon instead of the picture. Using this setting saves a lot of disk space because only an icon appears for the object rather than the complete object. Although the future plan is to include a picture for each employee and display it as an icon, for the test picture you will display the picture.

6 — **Click** OK .

Your screen should be similar to Figure 1–32.

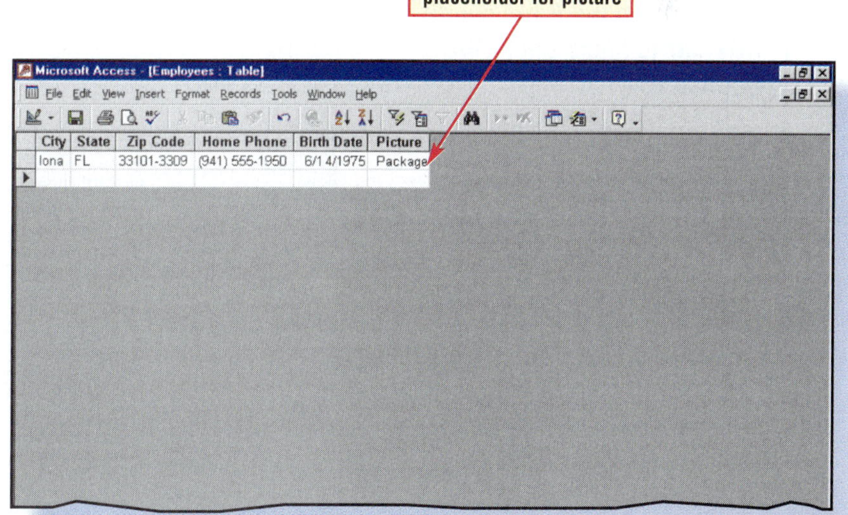

Figure 1–32

In Table Datasheet view, the field displays a text placeholder such as "Package" or "Bitmap Image" instead of the picture. The actual placeholder you will see will depend upon the software your computer used to import the image into Access. Then, to see the picture,

7 ■ **Double-click on the Picture field entry.**

Your screen should be similar to Figure 1–33.

Figure 1–33

The picture object is opened and displayed in the associated graphics program, in this case, Paint. Yours may have opened and be displayed in a different graphics program. It can be further manipulated using the program features.

8 ■ **Click** ☒ **in the Paint window title bar to close the Paint application.**

■ **Press** ⏎Enter.

Your screen should be similar to Figure 1–34.

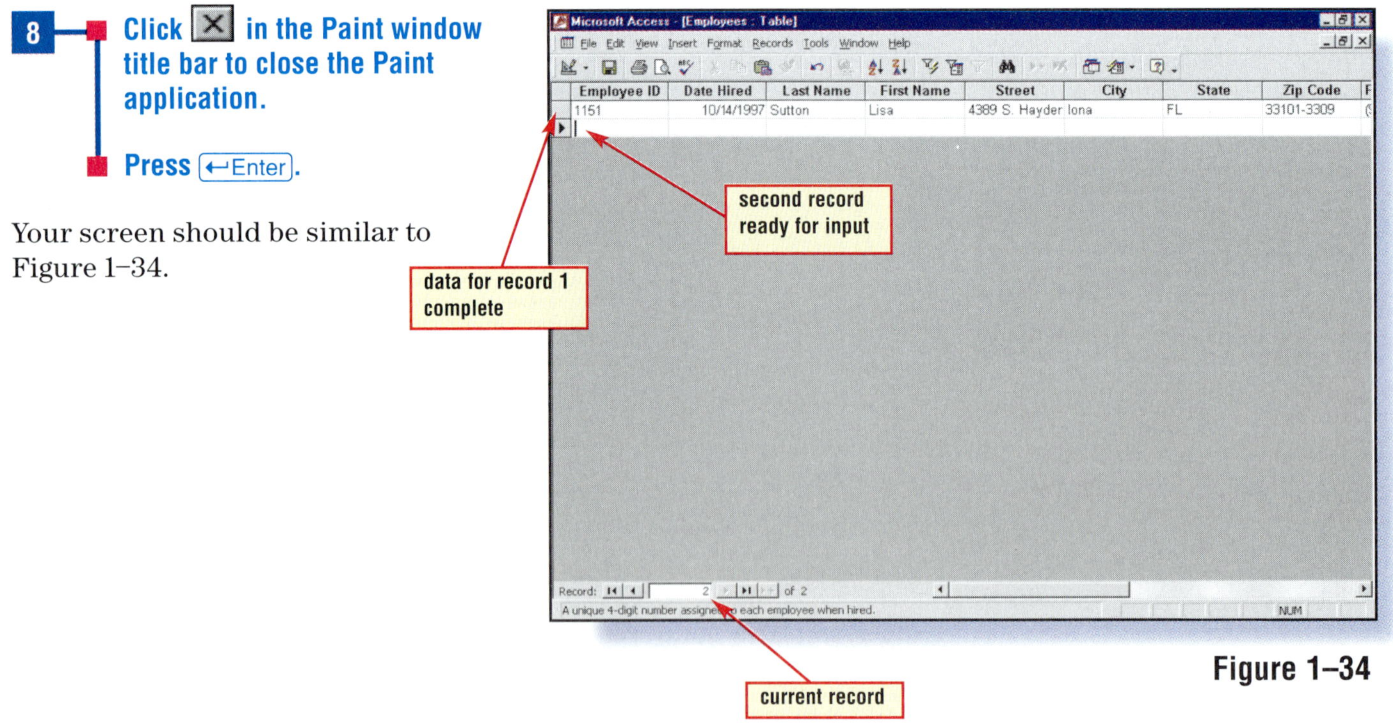

Figure 1–34

Using Navigation Mode

The data for the first record is now complete. The insertion point moves to the first field on the next row and waits for input of the employee number for the next record. As soon as the insertion point moves to another record, the data is saved on the disk and the number of the new record appears in the status bar. The second record was automatically assigned the record number 2.

Next you will check the first record for accuracy.

1 **Point to the left end of the Employee ID field for the first record. When the mouse pointer appears as ✛, click the mouse button.**

Your screen should be similar to Figure 1–35.

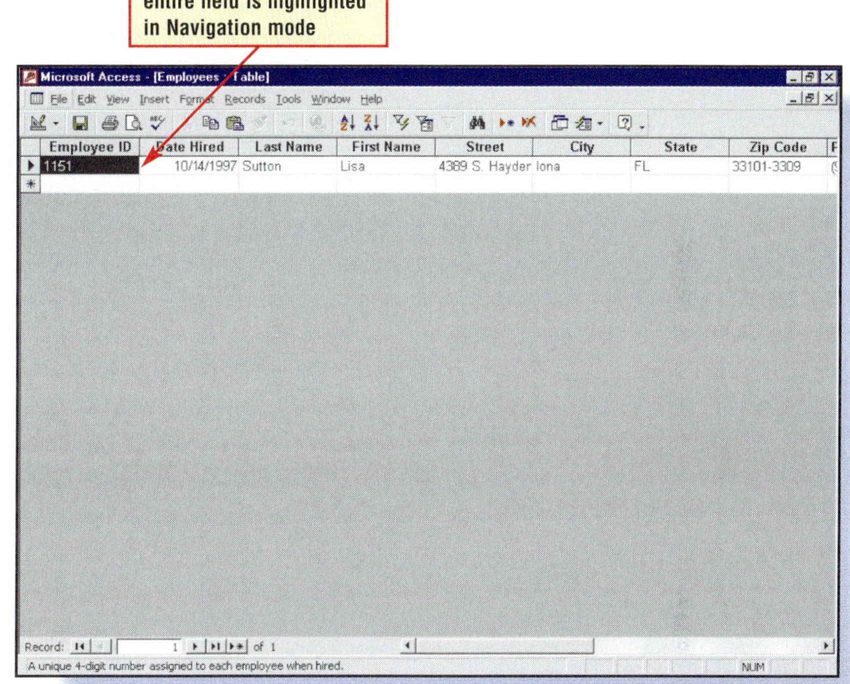

Figure 1–35

The entire field is selected (highlighted), and you have activated Navigation mode. If you type, the entire selection will be replaced with the new text. To select the Street field to check the field contents,

2 **Press → (4 times).**

Click the Street field with the mouse pointer shape as an I-beam.

The insertion point is positioned in the field, and you have activated the Edit mode. Now you can edit the field contents if necessary. To move the insertion point to the end of the address so that you can check the rest of the entry,

3 **Press End.**

The text scrolled in the field, and the insertion point is positioned at the end of the entry. However, now you cannot see the beginning of the entry. To expand the field box to view the entire entry in the field,

4 ■ Press ⇧Shift + F2 .

Your screen should be similar to Figure 1–36.

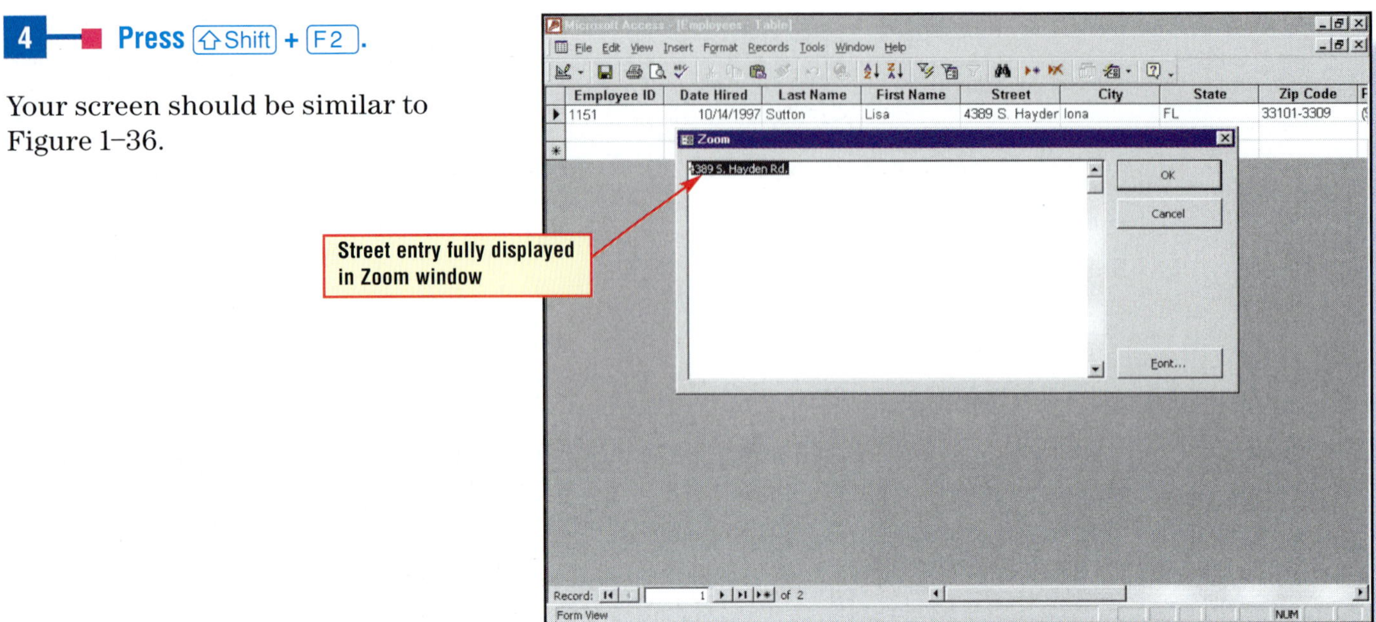

Figure 1–36

The entry is fully displayed in a separate Zoom window. You can edit in the window just as you would in the field box.

> You can also expand a text box in the same way to make it easier to edit.

5 ■ If the entry contains an error, correct it.

■ Click OK .

■ Press Tab.

■ Continue to check the first record for accuracy and edit as needed.

■ Enter the following data for the second record.

> You can also use the horizontal scroll bar to scroll the window to check fields that are not visible.

> Notice that the date format changed automatically to the format set in the date property field.

Field Name	Data
Employee ID	0434
Date Hired	July 5, 1996
Last Name	Merwin
First Name	Adda
Street	947 S. Forest St.
City	Fort Myers
State	FL
Zip Code	33301-1268
Phone Number	(941) 555-4494
Birth Date	April 20, 1970

6 **Press** ⬅Enter **twice.**

Check the second record for accuracy and edit it if necessary.

Your screen should be similar to Figure 1–37.

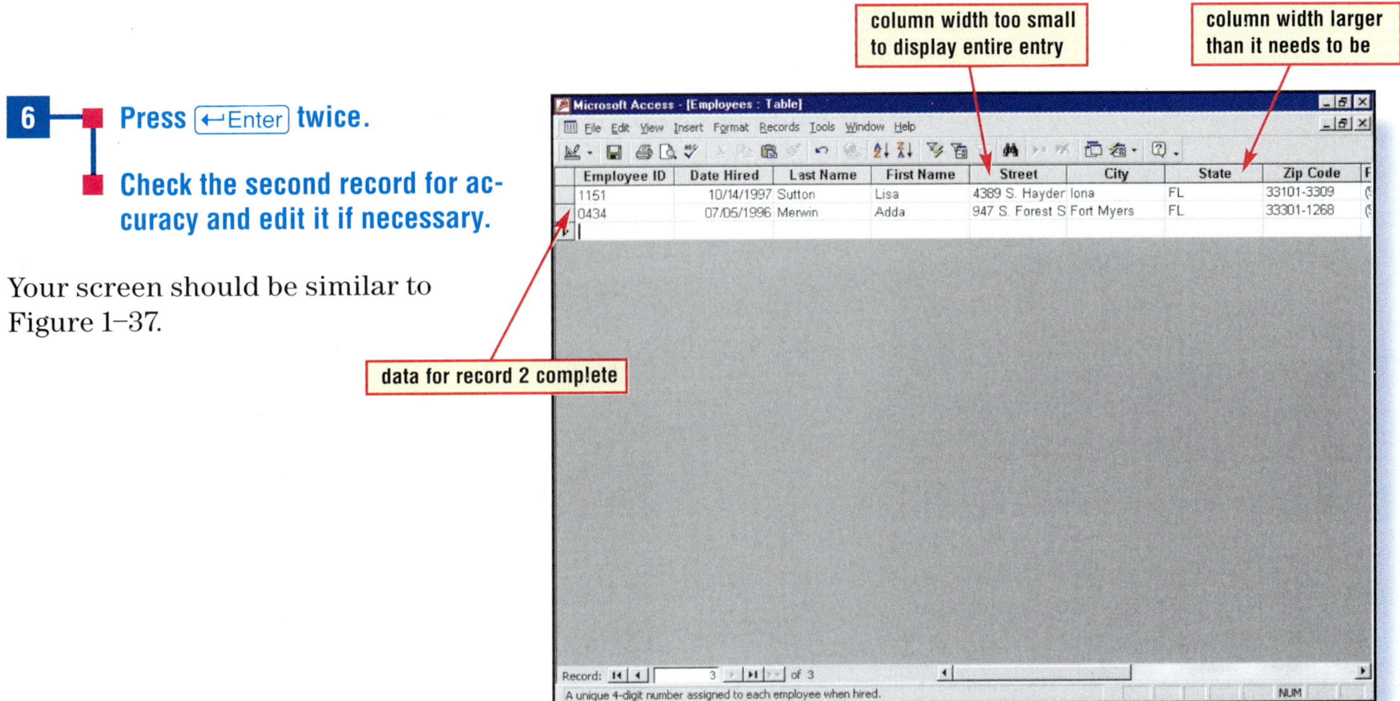

Figure 1–37

Adjusting Column Widths

As you have noticed, some of the fields (such as the Street field) do not display the entire entry, while other fields (such as the State field) are much larger than the field's column heading or contents. This is because the default column width in Datasheet view is not the same size as the field sizes you specified in Design view.

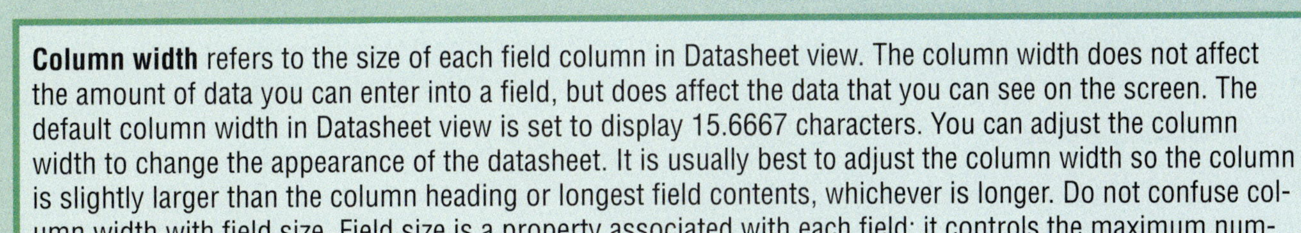

Concept 10 Column Width

Column width refers to the size of each field column in Datasheet view. The column width does not affect the amount of data you can enter into a field, but does affect the data that you can see on the screen. The default column width in Datasheet view is set to display 15.6667 characters. You can adjust the column width to change the appearance of the datasheet. It is usually best to adjust the column width so the column is slightly larger than the column heading or longest field contents, whichever is longer. Do not confuse column width with field size. Field size is a property associated with each field; it controls the maximum number of characters that you can enter in the field. If you shorten the field size, you can lose data already entered in the field.

To quickly modify the column width, simply drag the right column border line in the field selector in either direction to increase or decrease the column width. The mouse pointer shape is ↔ when you can drag to size the column. As you drag, a column line appears to show you the new column border. When you release the mouse button, the column width will be set. First you will increase the width of the Street field so the entire address will be visible.

1 ■ **Point to the right column border line in the field selector for the Street field name.**

■ **When the mouse pointer is ↔, drag the border to the right until you think the column width will be long enough to display the field contents.**

■ **Adjust the column width again if it is too wide or not wide enough.**

> You can also adjust the column width to a specific number of characters using Fo**r**mat/**C**olumn Width.

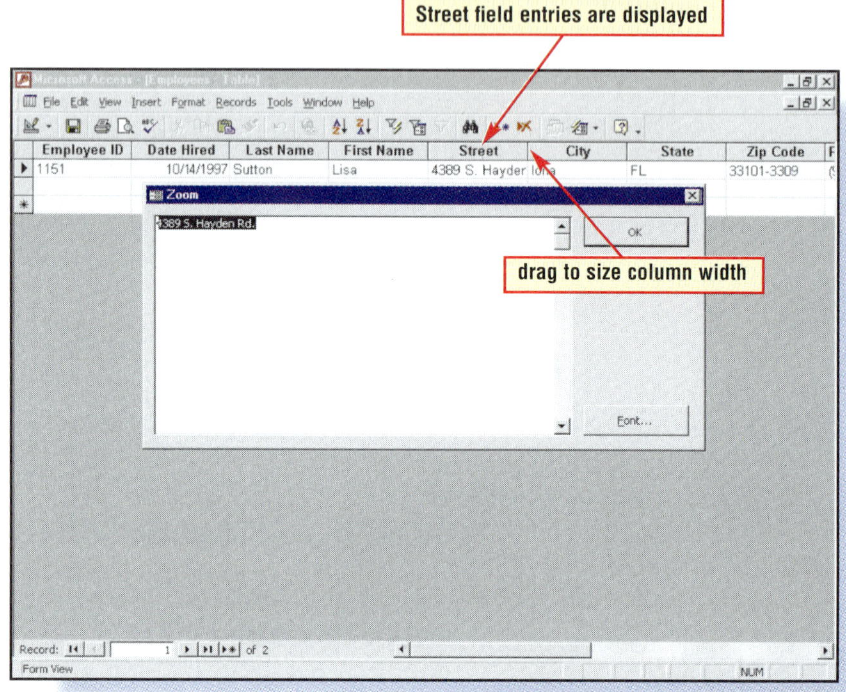

Your screen should be similar to Figure 1–38.

Figure 1–38

> The keyboard equivalent for selecting columns is to select a field entry in the first column, press Ctrl + Spacebar, then press ⇧Shift + the appropriate arrow key to select multiple columns.

> To clear a selection, click anywhere in the table.

Rather than change the widths of all the other columns individually, you can select all columns and change their widths at the same time. To select multiple columns, point to the column heading in the field selector area of the first or last column you want to select. Then, when the mouse pointer changes to ↓, click, and without releasing the mouse button, drag in either direction across the column headings.

2   **Point to the Employee ID field name.**

When the mouse pointer is ↓, drag to the right across all column headings.

The fields will scroll horizontally in the window as you drag to select the columns.

Use the horizontal scroll bar to bring the first field column back into view in the window.

Your screen should be similar to Figure 1–39.

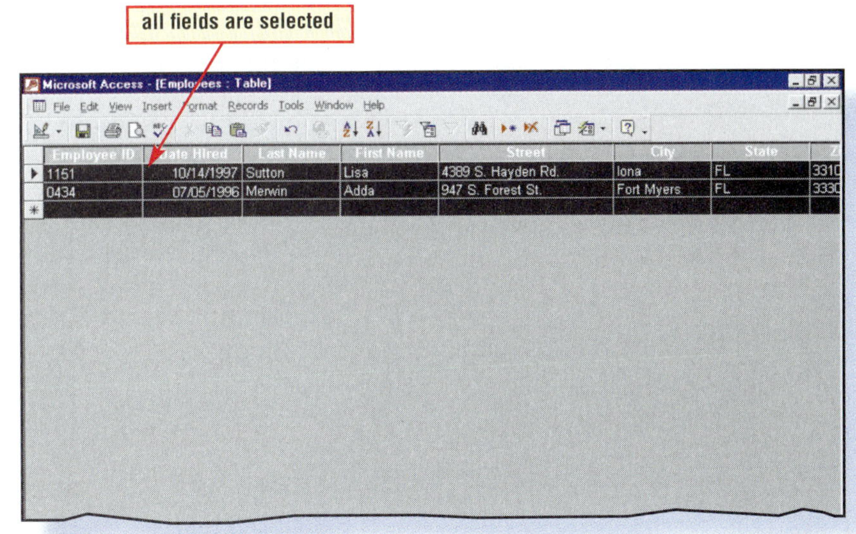

Figure 1–39

Clicking the box to the left of the first field name will also select the entire table; however, you cannot use Best Fit when the entire table is selected in this manner.

The menu equivalent is Format/Column Width. The Column Width command is also on the shortcut menu when an entire column is selected.

Multiple columns are highlighted. Now, if you were to drag the column border of any selected column, all the selected columns would change to the same size. However, you want the column widths to be adjusted appropriately to fit the data in each column. To do this you can double-click the column border to activate the Best Fit feature. The **Best Fit** feature automatically adjusts the column widths of all selected columns to accommodate the longest entry or column heading in each of the selected columns.

3   **Double-click any column border line (in the field selector) within the selection when the mouse pointer is ↔.**

Your screen should be similar to Figure 1–40.

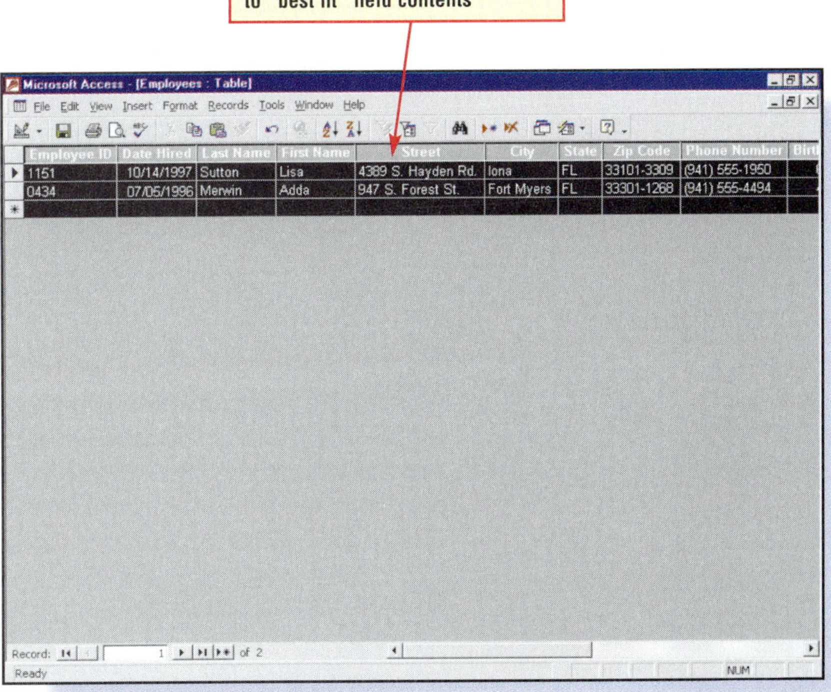

Figure 1–40

ACCESS 2000

Clicking anywhere in the table will clear the section.

4 Now that you can see the complete contents of each field, check each of the records again and edit any entries that are incorrect.

Add the following record to the table as record 3.

Field Name	Data
Employee ID	0434
Date Hired	April 12, 1998
Last Name	Delano
First Name	Gordon
Street	8943 W. Southern Ave.
City	Iona
State	FL
Zip Code	33101-8475
Phone Number	(941) 555-8201
Birth Date	August 7, 1961

5 Press ⏎Enter twice.

Your screen should be similar to Figure 1–41.

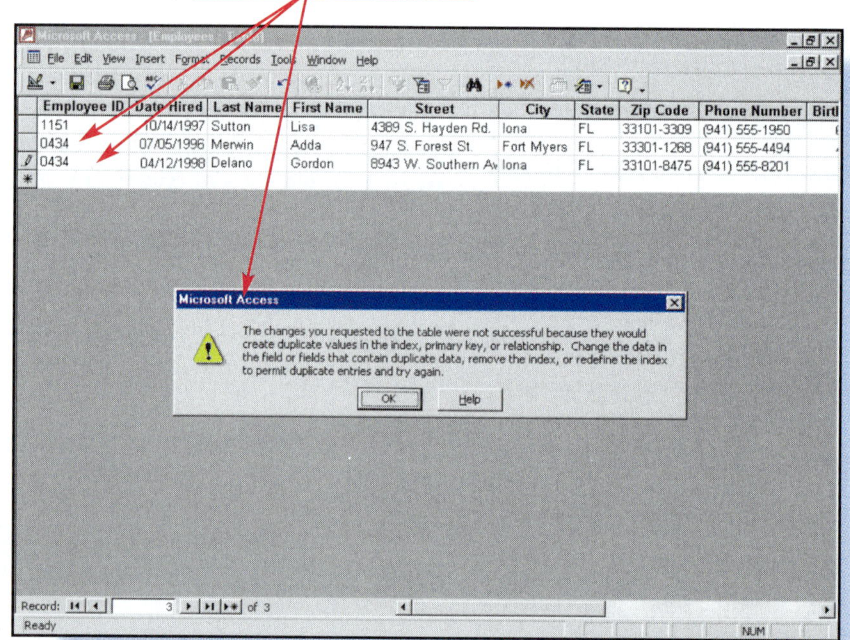

Figure 1–41

As soon as you complete the record, an error message dialog box appears indicating that Access has located a duplicate value in a key field. The key field is Employee ID. You realize you were looking at the employee number from the previous record when you entered the employee number for this record. To clear the message and enter the correct number,

6 Click  OK .

Change the Employee ID for record 3 to **0234**.

Press ↓.

The record is accepted with the new employee number. Notice that the address for this record does not fully display in the Street field. It has a longer address than either of the other two records.

7 ■ **Double-click the right border of the Street field to best fit the field column.**

When you add new records in Datasheet view, the records are displayed in the order you enter them. However, they are stored on disk in order by the primary key field. You can change the display on the screen to reflect the correct order by using the ⇧Shift + F9 key combination.

8 ■ **Press ⇧Shift + F9 .**

Your screen should be similar to Figure 1–42.

records in order by
employee number

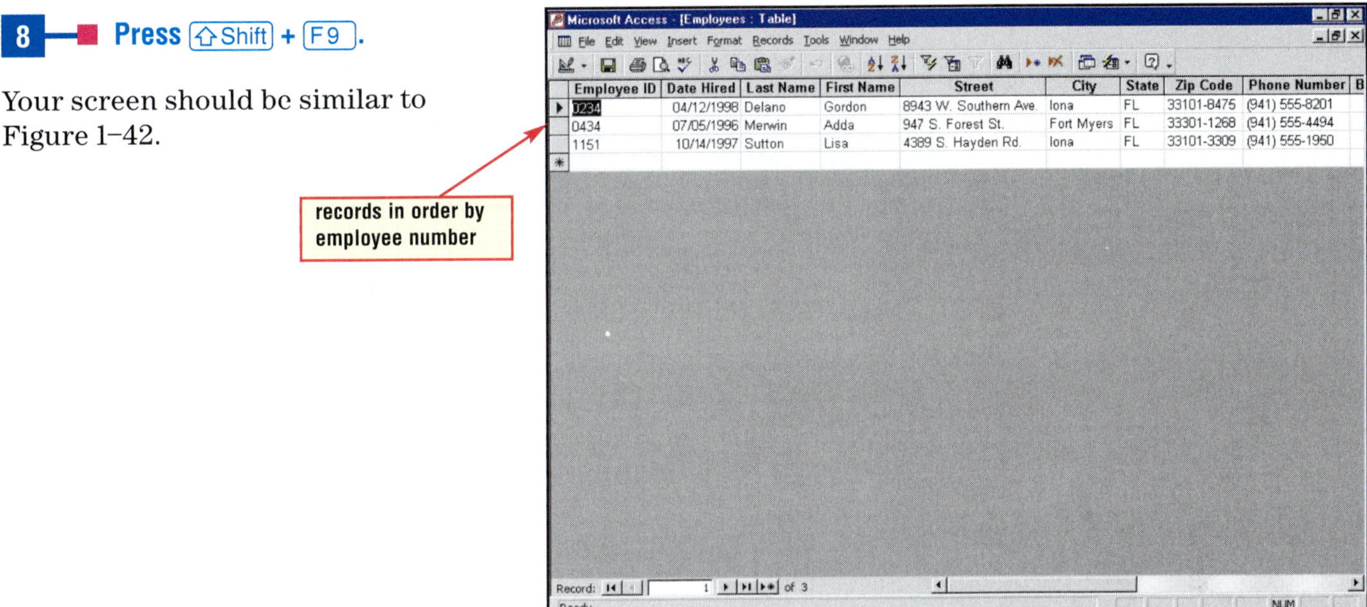

Figure 1–42

The records are now in order by employee number. This is the order determined by the primary key field.

Adding Records in Data Entry

Next you want to add several more employee records to the table. Another way to add records is to use the Data Entry command on the Records menu. This command does not display existing records, which prevents accidental changes to the table data.

1 ━━ **Choose** **R**ecords/**D**ata Entry.

Your screen should be similar to Figure 1–43.

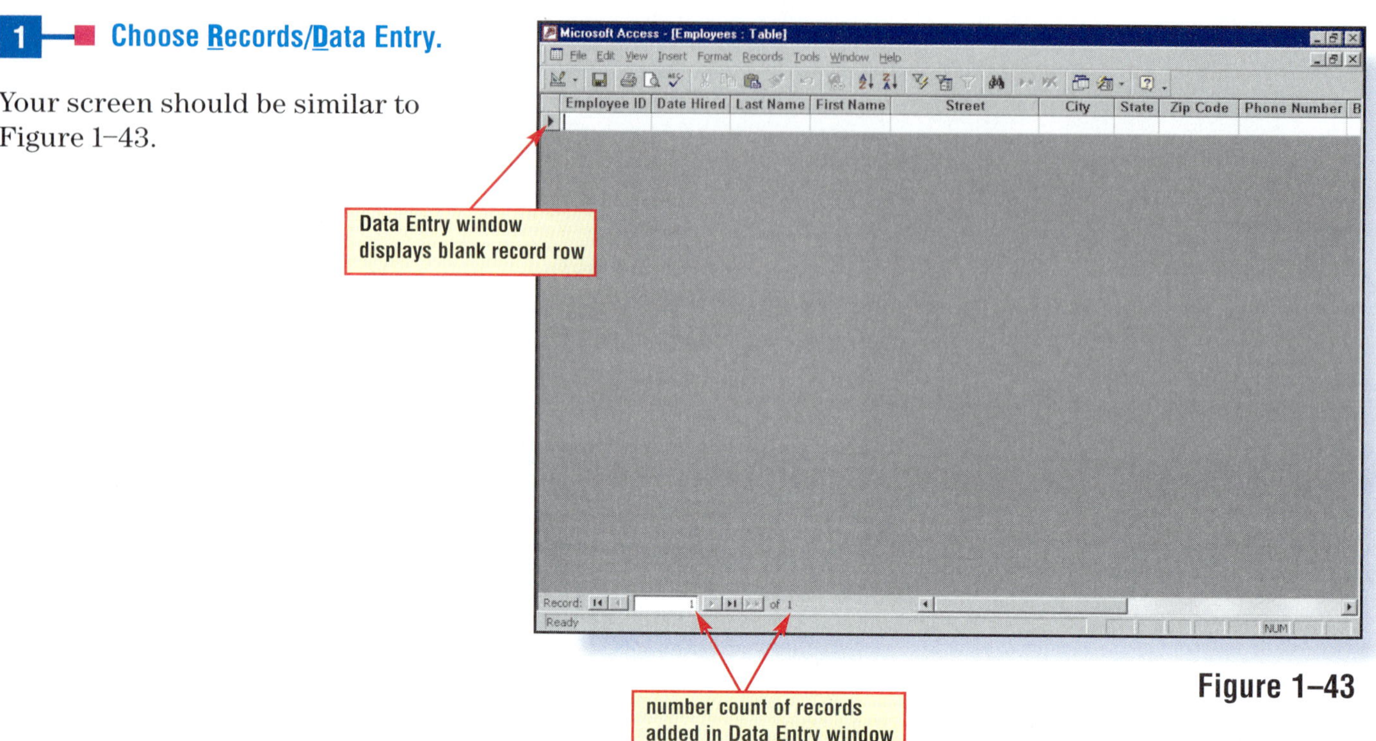

Figure 1–43

The existing records are hidden, and the only row displayed is a blank row where you can enter a new record. The status bar displays "1 of 1." This number reflects the number of new records as they are added in Data Entry rather than all records in the table.

2 ■ Enter the data for the two records shown below.

Field	Record 1	Record 2
Employee ID	0839	0728
Hire Date	August 14, 1997	March 15, 1997
Last Name	Ruiz	Roman
First Name	Enrique	Anita
Street	358 Maple Dr.	2348 S. Bala Dr.
City	Cypress Lake	Fort Myers
State	FL	FL
Zip Code	33205-6911	33301-1268
Phone Number	(941) 555-0091	(941) 555-9870
Birth Date	December 10, 1963	March 15, 1961

Your screen should be similar to Figure 1–44.

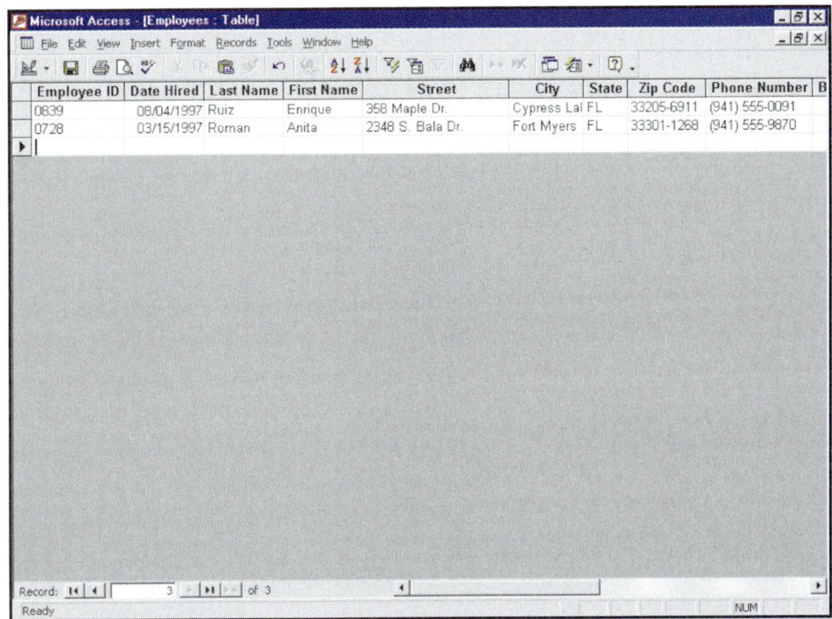

Figure 1–44

3 ■ Enter a final record using your first and last names. Enter 9999 as your employee number and the current date as your date hired. The information you enter in all other fields can be fictitious.

■ Best fit the City column and any other columns that do not fully display the field contents.

■ Check each of the records and correct any entry errors.

Now that you have entered the new records, you can redisplay all the records in the table. To do this,

4 ■ Choose **R**ecords/**R**emove Filter/Sort.

Your screen should be similar to Figure 1–45.

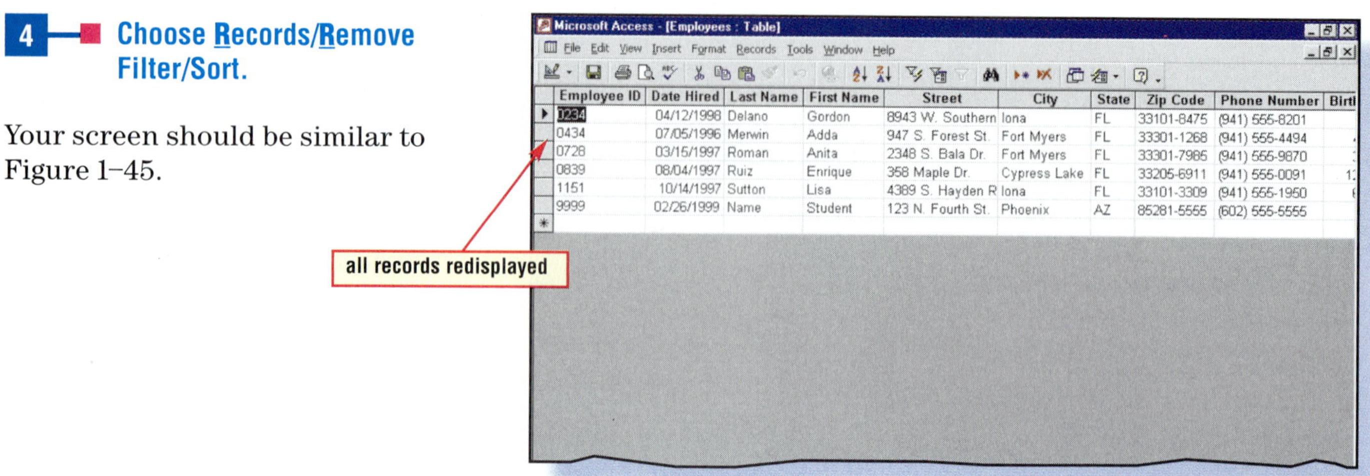

Figure 1–45

The new records are added to the table in order by employee number. If you had added these records in Datasheet view, they would not appear in primary key field order until you updated the table display. This is another advantage of using Data Entry.

Previewing and Printing the Table

If you have printer capability, you can print a copy of the records in this table. Before printing the table, you will preview how it will look when printed using Print Preview view. Previewing the document displays each page of your document in a reduced size so you can see the layout. Then, if necessary, you can make changes to the layout before printing to both save time and avoid wasting paper.

To preview the Employees table,

1 ■ Click ◻ **Print Preview.**

> The menu equivalent is **F**ile/Print Pre**v**iew.

Your screen should be similar to Figure 1–46.

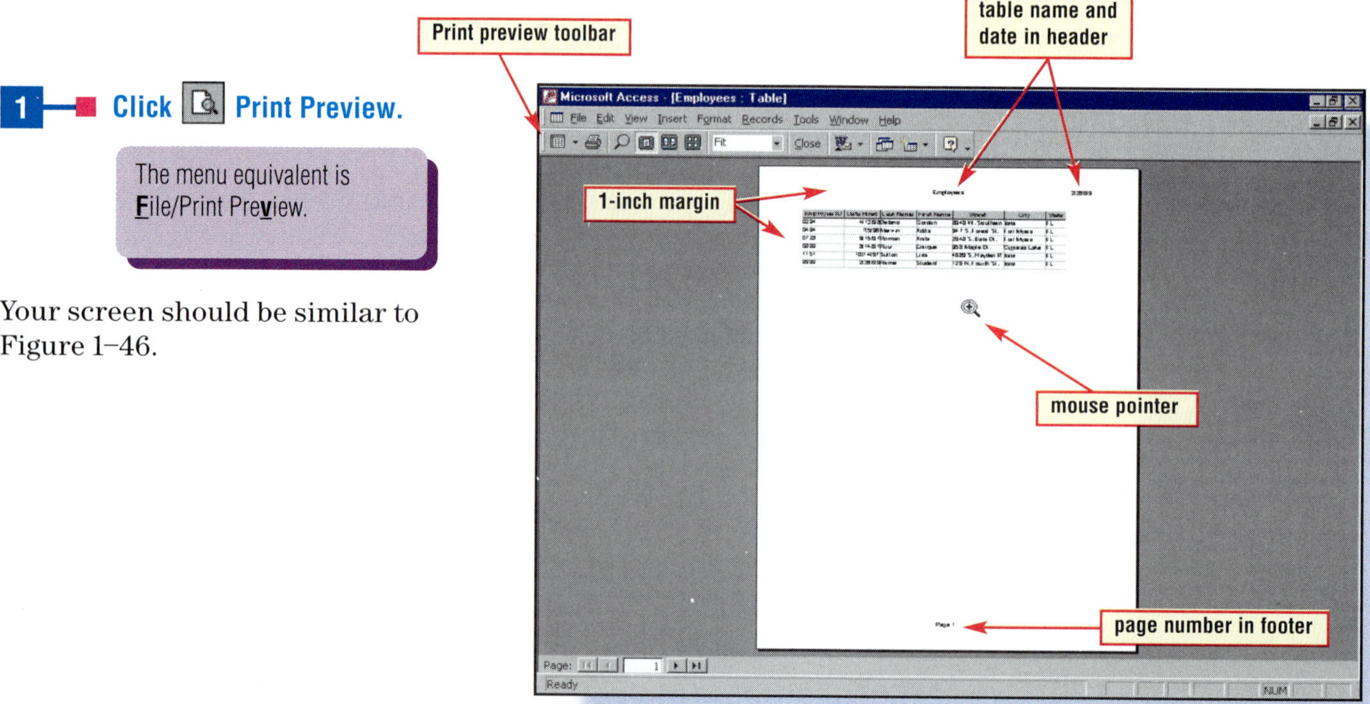

Figure 1–46

The Print Preview window displays a reduced view of how the table will appear when printed. The window also includes its own toolbar. The document will be printed using the default report and page layout settings, which include such items as 1-inch margins, the table name and date displayed in a header, and the page number in a footer.

To better see the information in the table, you can change the magnification level of the Preview window. The current magnification level is Fit as displayed in the [Fit ▾] button in the toolbar. This setting adjusts the magnification of the page to best fit in the size of the window. Notice that the mouse pointer is a 🔍 magnifying glass when it is positioned on the page. This indicates that you can click on the page to switch between the Fit magnification level and the last used level.

> Use the [Fit ▾] Zoom button on the Print Preview toolbar to select a magnification percentage or type.

2 ■ **Click on the file name in the header.**

> Clicking [🔍] Zoom will also toggle between the magnification levels.

> The location where you click determines the area that is displayed initially.

Your screen should be similar to Figure 1–47.

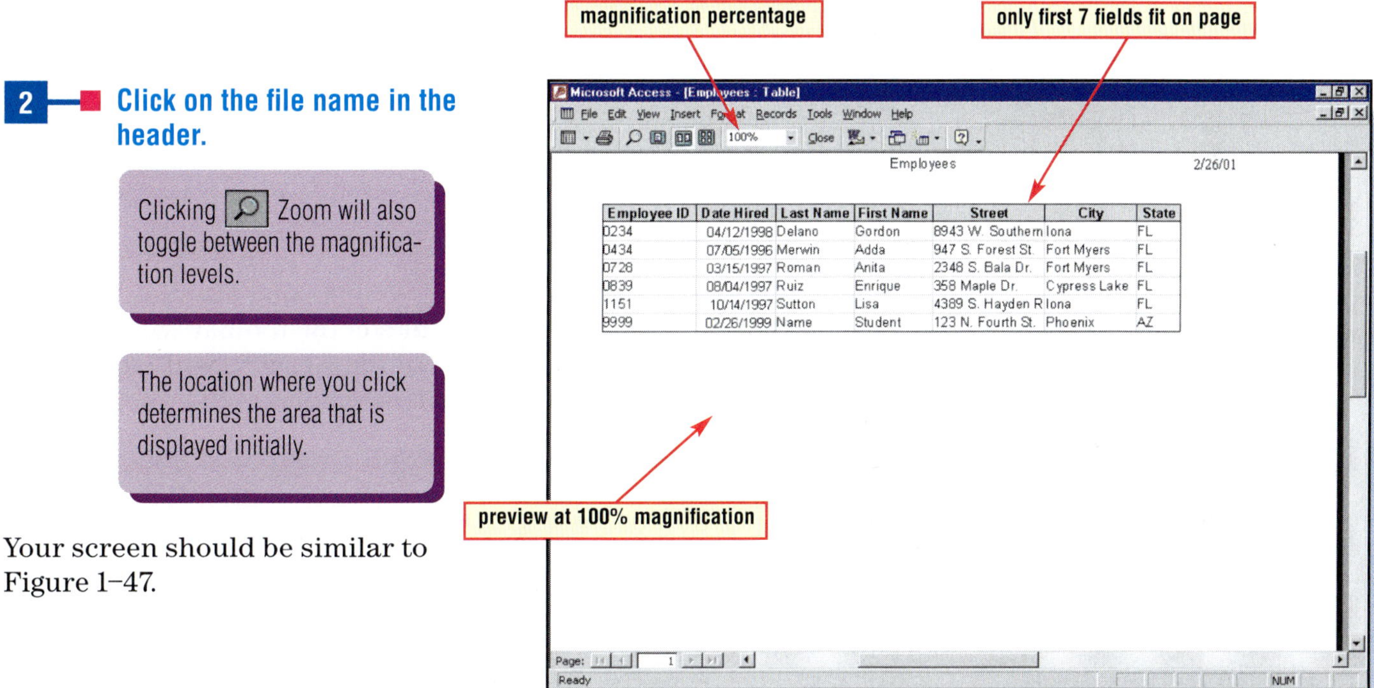

Figure 1–47

> Because Access remembers the last zoom percentage, your zoom percentage may be different. Use the Zoom button to change your percentage to 100%.

The table appears in 100% magnification. This is the size it will appear when printed. Notice, however, that because the table is too wide to fit across the width of a page, only the first seven fields are displayed on the page. The rest of the table will be printed on a second page. To see both pages,

3 ■ Click  Two Pages.

Your screen should be similar to Figure 1–48.

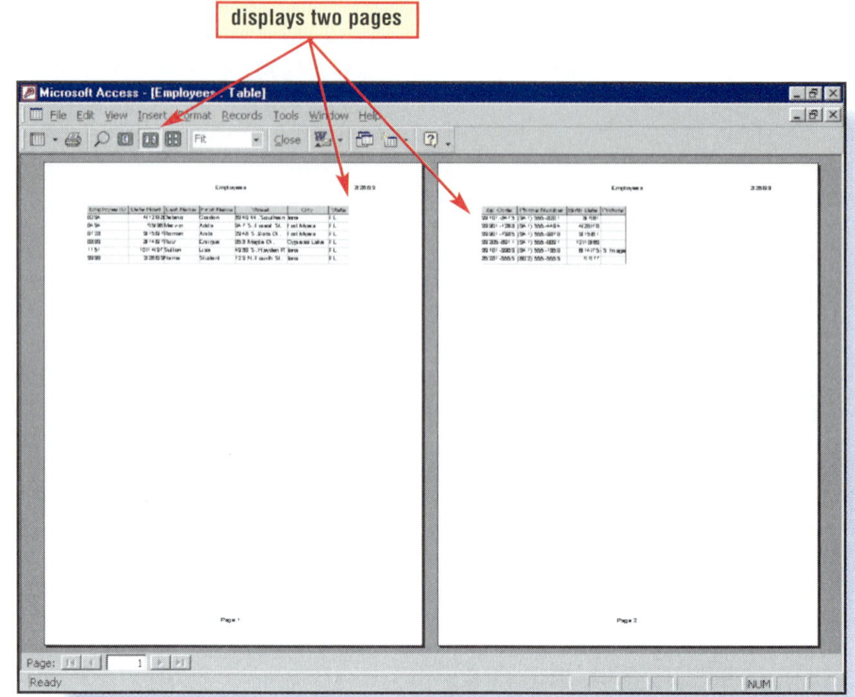

Figure 1–48

The last four field columns are displayed on the second page. Now you are ready to print the table. The 🖨 Print button on the toolbar will immediately start printing the report using the default print settings. To check the print settings first, you need to use the Print command.

4 ■ Click One Page to return the display to a single page.

■ If necessary, make sure your printer is on and ready to print.

■ Choose **File/Print**.

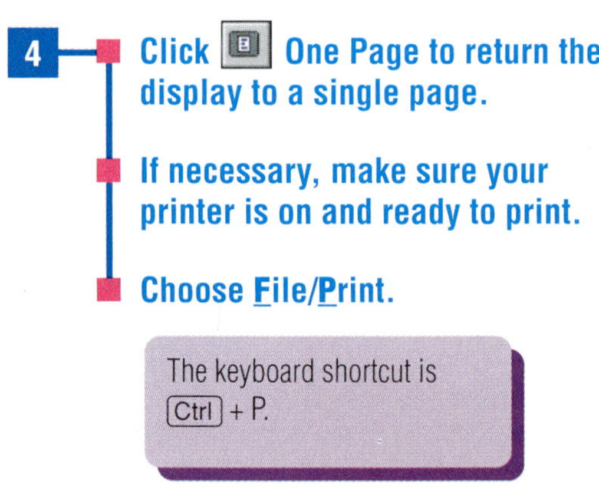

Your screen should be similar to Figure 1–49.

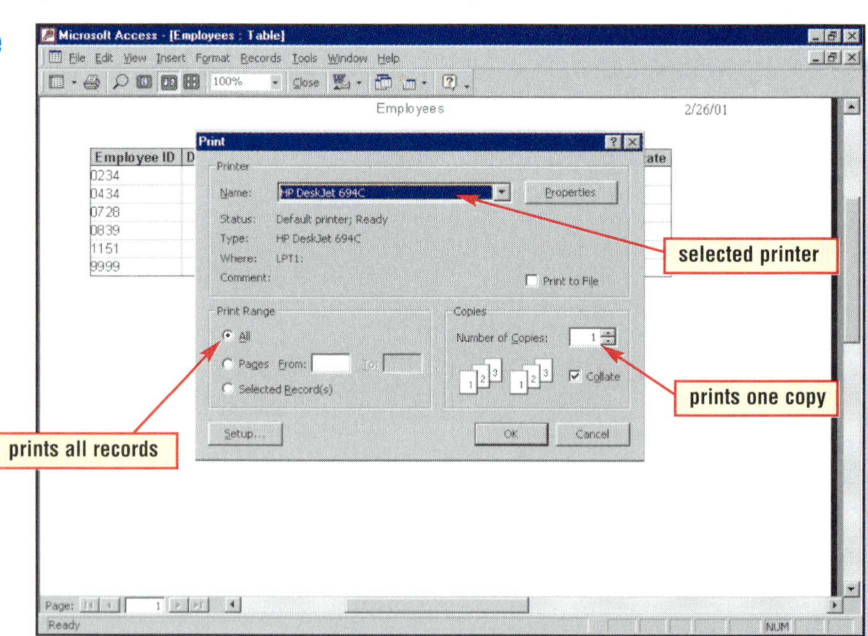

Figure 1–49

Please consult your instructor for printing procedures that may differ from the directions here.

From the Print dialog box, you need to specify the printer you will be using and the document settings. The printer that is currently selected is displayed in the Name drop-down list box in the Printer section of the dialog box.

5 If you need to change the selected printer to another printer, open the Name drop-down list box and select the appropriate printer (your instructor will tell you which printer to select).

The Page Range area of the Print dialog box lets you specify how much of the document you want printed. The range options are described in the following table:

Option	Action
All	Prints the entire document.
Pages	Prints pages you specify by typing page numbers in the text box.
Selected Records	Prints selected records only.

The default range setting, All, is the correct setting. In the Copies section, the default setting of one copy of the document is acceptable. To begin printing using the settings in the Print dialog box,

6 Click .

Your printer should be printing out the database table report. The printed copy should be similar to the final product shown in the opening case study of this tutorial.

To close the Print Preview window and return to the Datasheet view,

The menu equivalent is **V**iew/Data**s**heet View.

7 Click .

Closing and Opening a Database

To close the table,

The menu equivalent is **F**ile/Close.

1 Click ☒ (in the Table window).

Because you changed the column widths of the table in Datasheet view, you are prompted to save the layout changes you made before the table is closed. If you do not save the table, your column width settings will be lost.

2 ■ Click Yes .

Your screen should be similar to Figure 1–50.

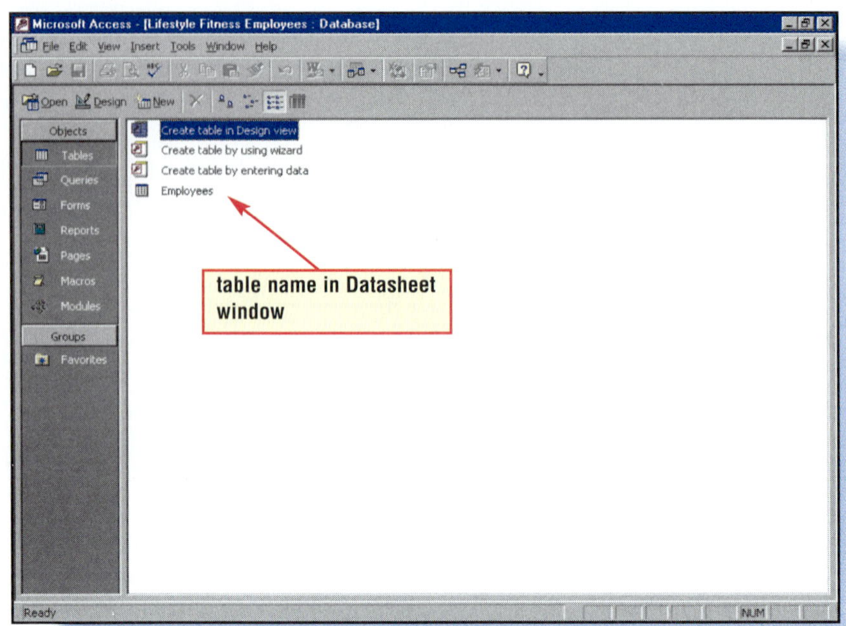

Figure 1–50

The Database window is displayed again. The name of the table you created appears in the Table object list. Now the Open and Design command buttons can be used to modify the selected table in the list box. To close the database file,

3 ■ Click X (on the menu bar).

Then to open and redisplay the table of employee records,

4 ■ Click 📂 Open.

■ If necessary, display the Look In drop-down list and select the location of your data disk.

> The menu equivalent is **F**ile/**O**pen and the keyboard shortcut is Ctrl + O. You can also select "Open an existing database" from the startup dialog box when Access is first loaded.

Your screen should be similar to Figure 1–51.

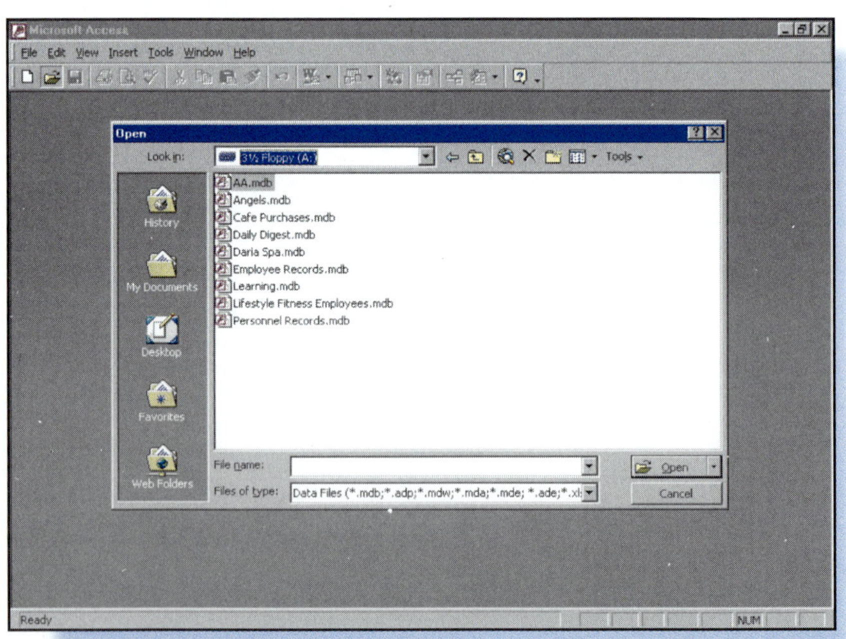

Figure 1–51

Now the name of the database file you just created, as well as others you will use in the labs, is displayed in the list box. To open the database file and the table of employee records,

5 ■ **Select Lifestyle Fitness Employees.**

■ **Click**  .

■ **If necessary, select Employees.**

■ **Click**  .

> You can also double-click the table name to open it.

The table of employee records is displayed in Datasheet view again, just as it was before you saved and closed the table.

6 ■ **Close the table again.**

Notice that this time you were not prompted to save the table because you did not make any changes.

Exiting Access

You will continue to build and use the table of employee records in the next tutorial. To exit Access and return to the Windows desktop,

> The menu equivalent is File/Exit, and the keyboard shortcut is [Alt] + [F4].

1 ■ **Click** ☒ (in the Access window title bar).

Warning: Do not remove your data disk from the drive until you close the Access application window.

Concept Summary

Tutorial 1: Creating a Database

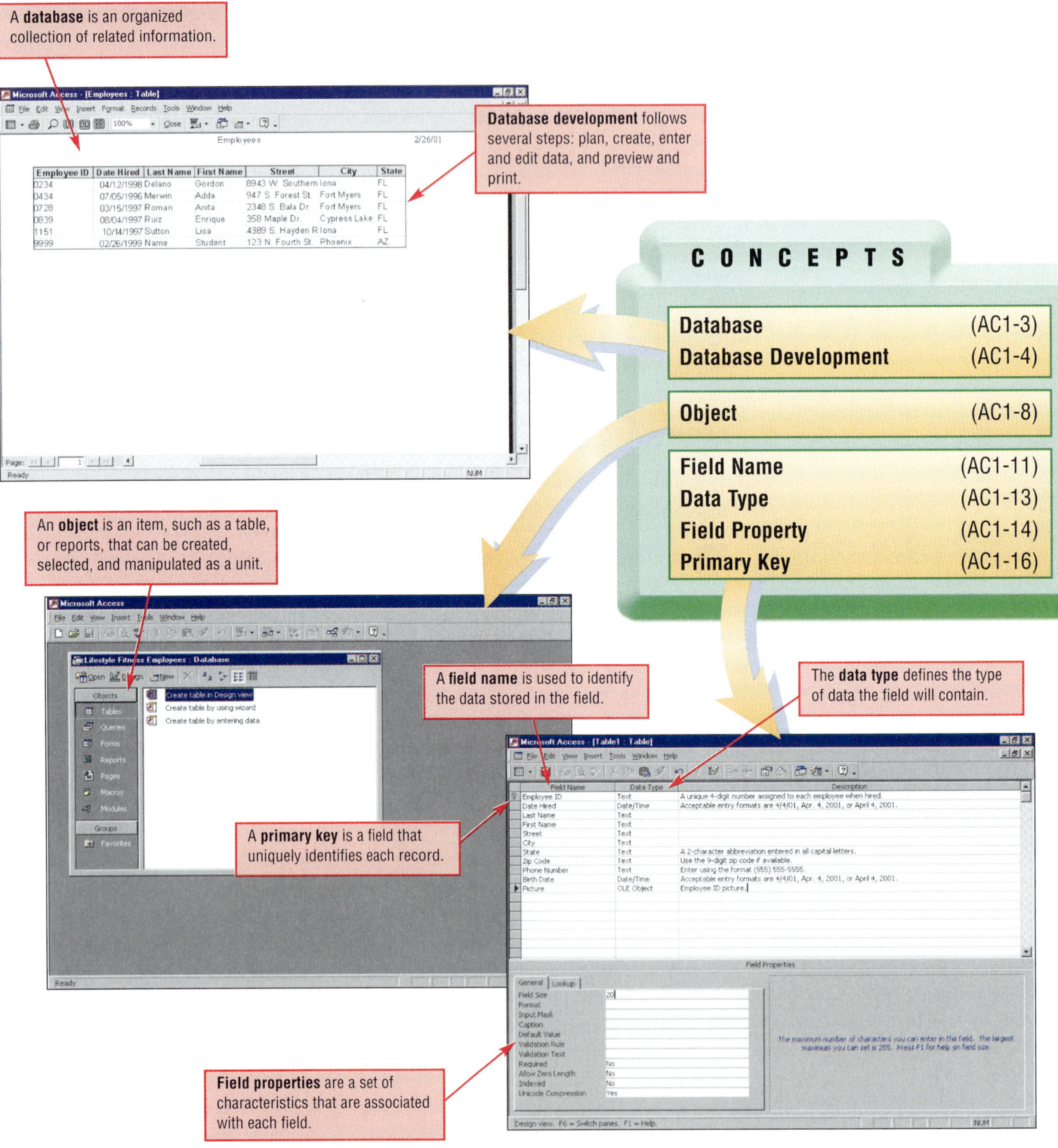

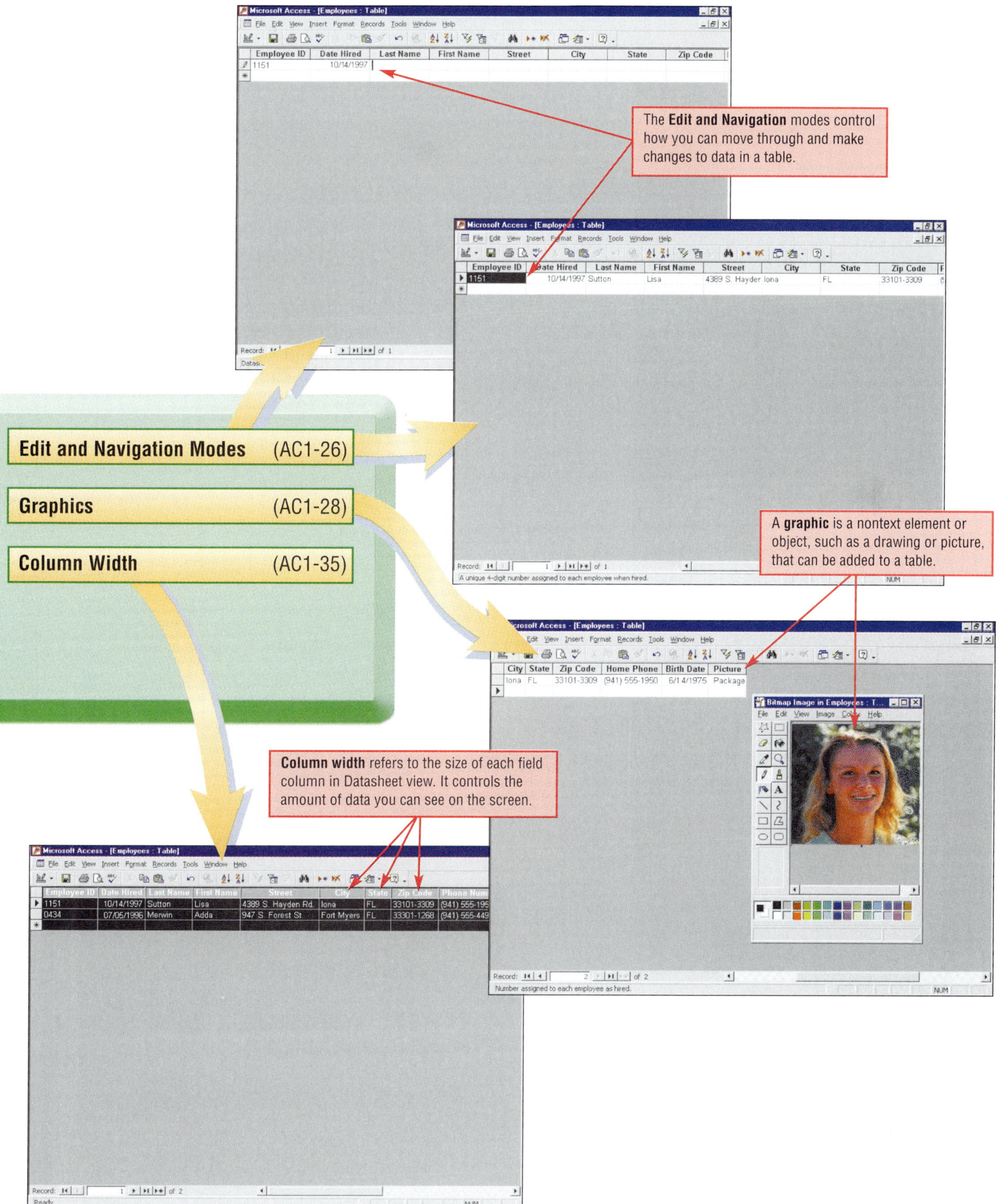

Edit and Navigation Modes   (AC1-26)

Graphics   (AC1-28)

Column Width   (AC1-35)

The **Edit and Navigation** modes control how you can move through and make changes to data in a table.

A **graphic** is a nontext element or object, such as a drawing or picture, that can be added to a table.

Column width refers to the size of each field column in Datasheet view. It controls the amount of data you can see on the screen.

Tutorial Review

Key Terms

Best Fit   AC1-37
Clip art   AC1-28
column width   AC1-35
current record   AC1-23
database   AC1-3
data type   AC1-13
design grid   AC1-10
drawing object   AC1-28
Edit mode   AC1-26
field   AC1-3
field name   AC1-11
field property   AC1-14
field selector   AC1-23
field size   AC1-15
graphic   AC1-28
navigation buttons   AC1-23
Navigation mode   AC1-26
object   AC1-8
Objects bar   AC1-8
object list box   AC1-8
picture   AC1-28
primary key   AC1-16
record   AC1-3
record number indicator   AC1-23
record selector   AC1-23
relational database   AC1-3
table   AC1-3
view   AC1-22

Command Summary

Command	Shortcut Keys	Button	Action
File/**N**ew	Ctrl + N		Creates a new database
File/**O**pen	Ctrl + O		Opens an existing database
File/**C**lose			Closes open window
File/**S**ave	Ctrl + S		Saves table
File/Print Pre**v**iew			Displays file as it will appear when printed
File/**P**rint	Ctrl + P		Prints contents of file
File/E**x**it			Closes Access and returns to Windows desktop
Edit/Delete **R**ows			Deletes selected field in Design view
Edit/Primary **K**ey			Defines a field as a primary key field
View/Data**s**heet View			Displays table in Datasheet view
Insert/**O**bject/Create from **F**ile			Inserts an existing object into current field.
Format/**C**olumn Width			Changes width of table columns in Datasheet view
Format/**C**olumn Width/**B**est Fit			Sizes selected columns to accommodate longest entry or column header
Records/**R**emove Filter/Sort			Displays all records in table
Records/**D**ata Entry			Hides existing records and displays Data Entry window mode

Screen Identification

In the following screen, several items are identified by letters. Enter the correct term for each item in the spaces that follow.

a. ______________________

b. ______________________

c. ______________________

d. ______________________

e. ______________________

f. ______________________

g. ______________________

h. ______________________

i. ______________________

j. ______________________

k. ______________________

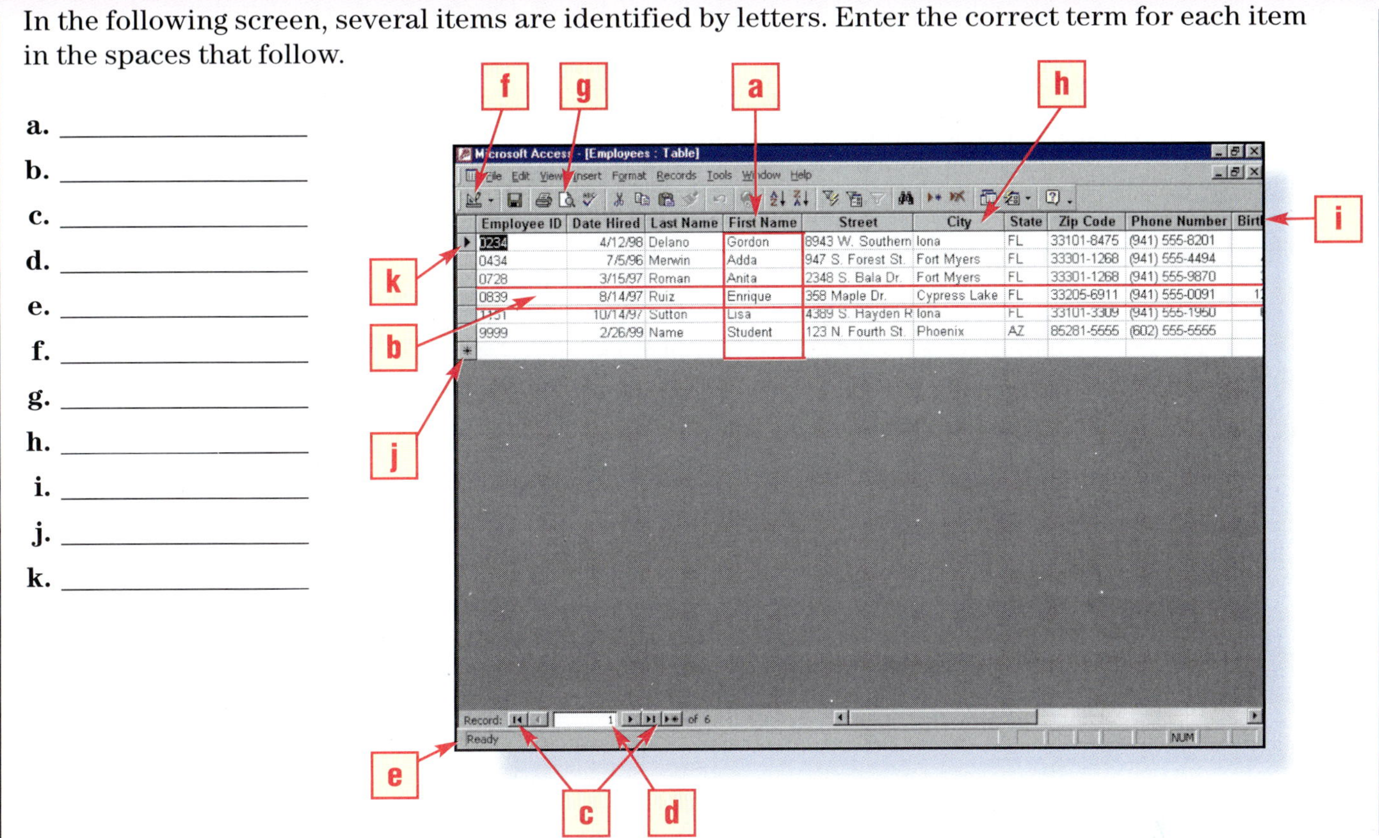

Matching

Match the letter to the correct item in the numbered list.

1. record	______	**a.**	specific item of information contained in a record
2. database	______	**b.**	collection of related fields
3. field property	______	**c.**	an organized collection of related information
4. primary key	______	**d.**	used to define the table structure
5. Best Fit	______	**e.**	feature used to adjust column width to largest entry
6. field size	______	**f.**	controls the type of data a field can contain
7. data type	______	**g.**	field used to order records
8. Design view	______	**h.**	displays table in row and column format
9. Datasheet view	______	**i.**	characteristics associated with a field
10. field	______	**j.**	controls the maximum number of characters that can be entered in a field

True/False

Circle the correct answer to the following statements.

1. A database is an organized collection of related properties. True False
2. The first step in database development is planning. True False
3. Tables, forms, and reports are objects. True False
4. Field names are used to define properties for a database. True False
5. Text, memo, number, and date/time are data types. True False
6. Data properties are a set of characteristics that are associated with each field. True False
7. A person's first name is often used as the primary key. True False
8. The Edit and Database modes control how you can move through and make changes to data in a table. True False
9. Drawings and pictures can be added to a database. True False
10. While column width does not affect the amount of data that you can see on the screen, it does affect the amount of data that you can enter into a field. True False

Multiple Choice

Circle the correct answer to the following statements.

1. A(n) _______ is an organized collection of related information.

   a. object
   b. database
   c. property
   d. document

2. The steps of database development include planning, creating, and _________ data.

   a. entering
   b. graphing
   c. developing
   d. organizing

3. Located at the left of the Database window, the Objects _______ is used to select the type of object you want to work with.

   a. bar
   b. buttons
   c. properties
   d. tabs

4. A field name is used to identify the _________ stored in a field.

   a. characters
   b. keys
   c. data
   d. graphics

5. The _______ type defines the type of data the field contains.

   a. property
   b. entry
   c. data
   d. specification

6. Field size, format, input mask, caption, and default value are:

   a. key elements
   b. field properties
   c. navigating modes
   d. data types

7. The ___________ key uniquely identifies each record.

   a. primary
   b. database
   c. object
   d. premier

8. The ___________ mode is used to move from field to field and to delete an entire field entry.

   a. Edit
   b. Browser
   c. Entry
   d. Navigation

9. A _________ is a nontext element or object that can be added to a database.

   a. graphic
   b. data element
   c. property
   d. medium

10. In Datasheet view, ________ refers to the size of each field column.

   a. maximum
   b. content capacity
   c. data range
   d. column width

Fill-In Questions

Complete the following statements by filling in the blanks with the correct terms.

1. A(n)___________ is a collection of organized information. The information is stored in __________.

2. Relational databases define ________________ between tables by having common data in the tables.

3. The first step in developing a database is ________________.

4. The __________________ defines the type of data that can be entered in a field.

5. A(n) ___________________ is an item made up of different elements.

6. The set of characteristics associated with a field are the _____________________.

7. A descriptive label called a(n) __________________ is used to identify the data stored in a field.

8. The _________________ data type is used to format numbers with dollar signs and decimal places.

9. A(n) ________________ is a field that uniquely identifies each record in a table.

10. ___________________ view allows the user to enter, edit, and delete records in a table.

Discussion Questions

1. Discuss several uses you may have for a relational database. Then explain the steps you would follow to create the first table.

2. Discuss why it is important to plan a database before creating it. How can proper planning save you time later?

3. Discuss the difference between Edit mode and Navigation mode.

4. Design view and Datasheet view are two of the Access views. Discuss when it would be appropriate to use each of these views.

5. Discuss why it is important to choose the correct data type for a field. What may happen to the data if you change the data type?

Hands-On Practice Exercises

Step by Step

Rating System ☆ Easy
☆☆ Moderate
☆☆☆ Difficult

1. After being open for only two months, Daria's Day Spa is quickly becoming recognized for its excellent service to the Madison community. The spa's owner, Daria O'Dell, originally delayed computerizing the spa's operations; however, she now recognizes the numerous benefits she will receive from using a database management system. Ms. O'Dell has asked you to build a database that will enable her to keep information about her clients. When you are finished, your completed database table should look like the table shown here.

Client ID	First Name	Last Name	Home Phone	Work Phone	Street Address	City	State	Zip Code
001	Elaine	Grace	(217) 555-4215	(217) 555-4557	718 North Coltrane	Madison	TX	75380
002	Polly	Trawe	(217) 555-0091	(217) 555-2831	619 Portland Drive	Alison	TX	76890
003	Nadine	Richmond	(217) 555-1748	(217) 555-4279	1248 Trammell Avenue	Alison	TX	76890
004	[Your first name]	[Your last name]	(217) 555-1212	(217) 555-9335	987 Hyde Park	Bakersville	TX	76987

To create the client database, follow these steps:

a. Create a database named Spa. Design a table using the following field information:

Field Data	Type	Description	Field Size
Client ID	Text	A unique 3-digit number	3
First Name	Text		25
Last Name	Text		25
Home Phone	Text		15
Work Phone	Text		15
Street Address	Text		30
City	Text		25
State	Text	2-letter abbreviation	2
Zip Code	Text		10

b. Make the Client ID field the primary key field.

c. Save the table as Clients.

d. Switch to Datasheet view and enter the following records into the table:

Record 1	Record 2	Record 3	Record 4
001	002	003	004
Elaine	Polly	Nadine	[Your first name]
Grace	Trawe	Richmond	[Your last name]
(217) 555-4215	(217) 555-0091	(217) 555-1748	(217) 555-1212
(217) 555-4557	(217) 555-2831	(217) 555-4279	(217) 555-9335
718 North Coltrane	619 Portland Drive	1248 Trammell Avenue	987 Hyde Park
Madison	Alison	Alison	Bakersville
TX	TX	TX	TX
75380	76890	76890	76987

e. Adjust the column widths appropriately.

f. Print, save, and close the table.

2. You work for the Daily Digest, a small, startup publication that is distributed door-to-door in your local town and relies solely on advertising income from local businesses. Your managing editor has asked you to create a database to keep track of advertiser contact information. When you are finished, your completed database table should look like the table shown here.

Advertisers : Table

Advertiser ID	Business Name	Business Type	Contact Name	Phone Number	Billing Street	Billing City	Billing State	Billing Zip
A003	Paper and Pencil	Office Supplies	Sharon Smith	(650) 555-5050	1021 Lakeland Dr.	Middlefield	CA	95054
A340	Fix It Up	Auto Repair	Karen Little	(650) 555-3903	59 Main St.	Temple	CA	95056
B299	Happy Feet	Shoe Repair	[Your name]	(650) 555-3589	344 Park Ave.	Beacon Shores	CA	95055
C101	Discount Drugs	Pharmacy	Dan O'Donald	(650) 555-2233	142 Poppin Ave.	Beacon Shores	CA	95055

To create the advertiser database, follow these steps:

a. Create a database named Digest. Design a table using the following field information:

Field Data	Type	Description	Field Size
Advertiser ID	Text	A unique 4-digit number	4
Business Name	Text		25
Business Type	Text		15
Contact Name	Text		30
Phone Number	Text		15
Billing Street	Text		30
Billing City	Text		25
Billing State	Text		2
Billing Zip	Text		10

b. Make the Advertiser ID field the primary key field.

c. Save the table as Advertisers.

d. Switch to Datasheet view and enter the following records into the table:

Record 1	Record 2	Record 3	Record 4
C101	A340	A003	B299
Discount Drugs	Fix It Up	Paper and Pencil	Happy Feet
Pharmacy	Auto Repair	Office Supplies	Shoe Repair
Dan O'Donald	Karen Little	Sharon Smith	[Your Name]
(650) 555-2233	(650) 555-3903	(650) 555-5050	(650) 555-3589
142 Poppin Ave.	59 Main St.	1021 Lakeland Dr.	344 Park Ave.
Beacon Shores	Temple	Middlefield	Beacon Shores
CA	CA	CA	CA
95055	95056	95054	95055

e. Adjust the column widths appropriately.

f. Display the records in primary key order.

g. Print, save, and close the table.

3. The Downtown Internet Café, which you helped the owner, Evan, get off the ground, is an over-whelming success. The clientele is growing every day, as is the demand for the beverages you serve. Up until now, the information about the vendors has been kept in an alphabetical card file and a vendor contacted whenever you needed something. This has become quite unwieldy, how-ever, and Evan would like a more sophisticated tracking system. For starters, he would like you to create a database containing each purchase item and the contact information for the vendor that sells that item. When you are finished, your completed database table should look like the table

Item #	Description	Vendor Name	Contact	Address	City	State	Zip Code	Phone
1100	Coffee filters	Restaurant Supply	[Your Name]	13990 N. Central Ave.	Phoenix	AZ	84137-7214	(602) 555-0037
1723	Decaf Colombian	Pure Processing	Nancy Young	1124 Mariner Rd.	Half Moon Bay	CA	94019	(640) 555-5689
3527	Kona coffee	Quality Coffee	Fred Wilmington	772 First Street	Seattle	WA	73210-7214	(206) 555-9090
7926	Darjeeling tea	The Beverage Co.	Mae Yung	12 Main Street	Pacifica	CA	94044-3322	(415) 555-1122

shown here.

To create the database, follow these steps:

a. Create a database named Purchases. Design a table using the following field information:

Field Data	Type	Description	Field Size
Item #	Text	Unique 4-digit product number	4
Description	Text	Name of product	50
Vendor Name	Text	Name of supplier	50
Contact	Text	First & Last Name of contact person	50
Address	Text		50
City	Text		50
State	Text	2-letter abbreviation	2
Zip Code	Text	Include the 4-digit extension number if possible	10
Phone	Text	Include the area code in parentheses: (999) 123-4567	15

b. Make the Item # field the primary key field.

c. Save the table as Vendors.

d. Enter the following records into the table in Datasheet view:

Record 1

3527
Kona coffee
Quality Coffee
Fred Wilmington
772 First Street
Seattle
WA
93210-7214
(206) 555-9090

Record 2

1723
Decaf Colombian
Pure Processing
Nancy Young
1124 Mariner Rd.
Half Moon Bay
CA
94019
(650) 555-5689

e. Add the following records into the table in Data Entry:

Record 1

7926
Darjeeling tea
The Beverage Co.
Mae Yung
12 Main Street
Pacifica
CA
94044-3213
(415) 555-1122

Record 2

1100
Coffee filters
Restaurant Supply
Manny Smith
13990 N. Central Ave.
Phoenix
AZ
84137-7214
(602) 555-0037

f. Return to Datasheet view and display the records in primary key order.

g. Adjust the column widths appropriately.

h. Edit the record for Item # 7926 to change the four-digit zip code extension from 3213 to 3322.

i. Edit the record for Item # 1100 to replace the current Contact name with your name.

j. Preview the table. Print, save, and close the table.

4. You have just been hired by Adventure Travel tours to create and maintain a database containing information about the tours they offer and the clients who have purchased those tours. When you are finished, your completed database table should look like the table shown here.

	Client #	Last Name	First Name	Address	City	State	Zip Code	Phone	Tour Name	Tour Date
▶	009	Crane	Lauren	727 N. Hayden Rd.	Mesa	AZ	85205-9999	(602) 555-0932	Dude Ranch	01/23/1998
	023	[Your name]	[Your name]	12 Central Ave.	Phoenix	AZ	89472-8141	(602) 555-7321	Mountain Magic	07/17/1998
	090	McMahon	Cynthia	95 Chandler Blvd.	Chandler	AZ	85601-3144	(602) 555-1122	Capital Sites	10/04/1998
	101	Van Duesen	Mark	2421 Forest St.	Tempe	AZ	85301-7985	(602) 555-3956	Hawaiian Islands	02/25/1999
*										

Clients : Table

To create the database, follow these steps:

a. Create a database named Adventure. Design a table using the following field information:

Field Data	Data Type	Description	Field Size/Format
Client #	Text	Unique 3-digit number	3
Last Name	Text		50
First Name	Text		50
Address	Text		50
City	Text		50
State	Text	2-letter abbreviation	2
Zip Code	Text	Include the 4-digit extension number if possible	10
Phone	Text	Include the area code in parentheses: (999) 123-4567	15
Tour Name	Text		50
Tour Date	Date/Time		Short Date

b. Make the Client # field the primary key field.

c. Change the Last and First Name fields sizes to 15, the Address field size to 25, and the Tour Name field size to 30.

d. Save the table as Clients.

e. Enter the following records into the table in Table Datasheet view:

Record 1	Record 2
101	009
Van Duesen	Crane
Mark	Lauren
2421 Forest St.	727 N. Hayden Rd.
Tempe	Mesa
AZ	AZ
85301-7985	85205-0346
(602) 555-3956	(602) 555-0932
Hawaiian Islands	Dude Ranch
2/25/99	1/23/98

f. Add the following records into the table in Data Entry:

Record 1	Record 2
023	090
Frazier	McMahon
Barry	Cynthia
12 Central Ave.	95 Chandler Blvd.
Phoenix	Chandler
AZ	AZ
89472-8141	85601-3144
(602) 555-7521	(602) 555-1122
Mountain Magic	Capital Sites
7/17/98	10/4/98

g. Return to Datasheet view and display the records in primary key order.

h. Adjust the column widths appropriately.

i. Edit the record for Client # 023 to replace Barry Frazier's name with your name.

j. Change the four-digit zip code extension in Lauren Crane's record to 9999.

k. Preview and print the table. Save and close the table.

5. As a volunteer at the Animal Angels charity organization, you offer to create an Access database for them, to help them keep track of the animals that are picked up from local shelters. It needs to show which animals were boarded at Animal Angels by ID#; type of animal, name, and gender; when they were boarded; when they were placed in foster homes; and finally, when placed in adoptive homes. When you are finished, your completed database table should look like the table shown here.

ID #	Type	Gender	Name	Boarded Date	Foster Date	Adoption Date	Photo
012	Dog	F	Erin	03/02/1998	04/01/1998		
062	Dog	M	Max	12/09/1998			Package
123	Cat	M	Puddy	03/23/1998		04/15/1998	
199	Cat	F		01/15/1999		02/01/1999	
345	Rabbit	M	Bunny	05/01/1998	12/15/1998		
752	Horse	F	[your name's] Pet	02/07/1999			

To create the database, follow these steps:

a. Create a database named Animal Angels. Design a table using the following field information:

Field Data	Data Type	Description	Field Size/Format
ID #	Text	Unique 3-digit number given to animal when picked up from shelter	3
Type	Text	Type of animal (cat, dog, horse, etc.)	50
Gender	Text	Enter M (male) or F (female)	1
Name	Text	Name of animal, if any	50
Boarded Date	Date/Time	Date animal was boarded	Short Date
Foster Date	Date/Time	Date animal was placed in foster home	Short Date
Adoption Date	Date/Time	Date animal was adopted	Short Date
Photo	OLE object		

b. Change the field size of Type to 10 and Name to 30.

c. Make the ID # field the primary key field, and save the table as Tracking.

d. Enter six records: two for animals that are still being boarded (make one of these a dog), another two for animals in foster homes, and another two for animals that have been adopted. Enter [your name]'s Pet in the Name field of the last new record you add.

e. In Datasheet View select the Photo field in a record you entered for a dog that is still being boarded. Insert the Whitedog.bmp picture file as an object in the selected field. View the inserted picture.

f. Display the records in primary key order. Adjust the column widths appropriately.

g. Preview and print the table, and then save and close the table.

On Your Own

6. After creating the Adventure Travel database (in Practice Exercise 4), you realize that it does not accommodate clients who have taken more than one tour through your agency. Open the Adventure database and Clients table, change the existing Tour fields to include the number 1, and add four more fields for Tour 2 and Tour 3 names and dates. Adjust the field sizes as appropriate. Edit the existing records to include one or two more tours, and enter two new records. Adjust the column widths as necessary and display the table in primary key order. Preview and print the table. Close the table, saving any changes.

7. When you first started working at Lewis & Lewis, Inc., as an administrative assistant, you knew everyone by name and had no problems taking and transferring calls. However, the company has grown quite a bit and you no longer have everyone's phone extension memorized. Since you are on the computer most of the day, you decide that having this information online would be quite helpful, not only when you receive calls, but also to print out and distribute phone lists within the office. Create a database table that contains employees' last and first names, positions, and extension numbers, with the last name field as the primary key. Enter at least ten records, including one with your name as the employee and a phone extension of 0. Preview and print the table when you are finished.

8. You have been hired to create a patient database by a dentist who just opened his own office. The database table you set up should contain patient identification numbers, last and first names, addresses, phone numbers, "referred by" information, "patient since" dates, and insurance company information. Use appropriate field sizes and make the ID number field the primary key. Enter at least ten records, using both Data Entry and Datasheet view, adjusting the column widths as necessary. Display the table in primary key order. To practice editing data, change two of the records. Add a record that contains your name as the patient. Preview and print the table.

9. National Packing is a nationwide company that sells packing materials to mailing service chains and to businesses that do their own shipping. Based on your excellent reputation as a freelance database developer, the owner of the company has contacted you to create an Access database for tracking sales territories and representatives. First you need to design a table that includes the sales representatives' names, territories, and their customers' company name, contact, and address information. You should enter more than one field for the territory and client information, as the sales representative may cover multiple territories (e.g., Territory 1, Customer 1, Contact 1 . . . and Territory 2, Customer 2, Contact 2 . . .). Assign a primary key and appropriately size the fields. After designing the table, enter at least ten records using both Data Entry and Datasheet view, and adjust the column widths as necessary. Display the table in primary key order, and then edit one of these records so it contains your name as the sales representative or customer contact. Preview and print the table.

10. You work for Oldies But Goodies, a small company that locates and sells vintage record albums. The current method used to keep track of on-hand inventory is a notebook taped to the storeroom wall with a typewritten list where employees check records in and out. The business and inventory has grown large enough now to warrant an online database. Create a database with a table that contains stock identification numbers, record titles, artist, category (such as rock, R&B, and classical), cost, and inventory on hand. Size the fields as appropriate and assign a primary key to one of them. To obtain title, category, and artist information for records you might sell in this type of company, search for "vintage record albums" on the Web and select an appropriate site. Use this information to enter records into your table, adjusting column widths as necessary. Display the table in primary key order, change the artist's name in one of the records to your name, and then preview and print the table.

Modifying a Table and Creating a Form

Case Study

The Lifestyle Fitness Club owners, Brian and Cindy, are very pleased with your plans for the organization of the database and on your progress in creating the first table of basic employee data. As you have seen, creating a database takes planning and a lot of time to set up the structure and enter the

Competencies

After completing this tutorial, you will know how to:

1. Navigate a large table.
2. Change field properties.
3. Find and replace data.
4. Use Undo.
5. Insert a field.
6. Add validity checks.
7. Hide and redisplay fields.
8. Sort records.
9. Delete records.
10. Create and enter records into a form.
11. Preview, print, close, and save a form.

Field properties make a table easier to use and more accurate.

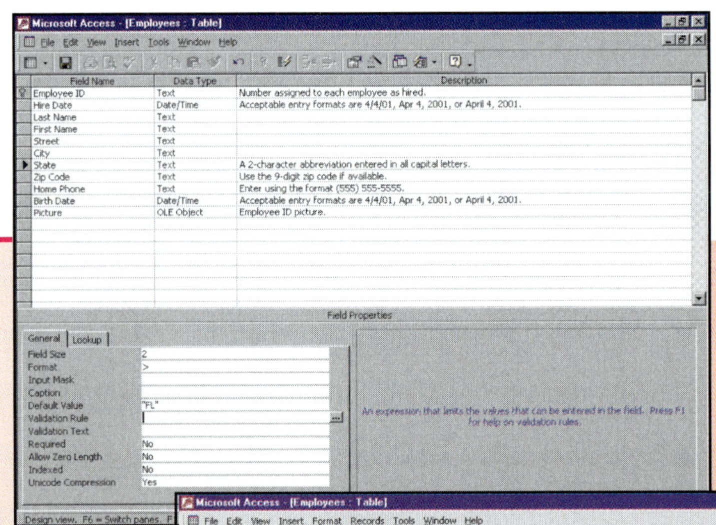

Forms can be used to display information in an easy-to-read manner and make data entry easier.

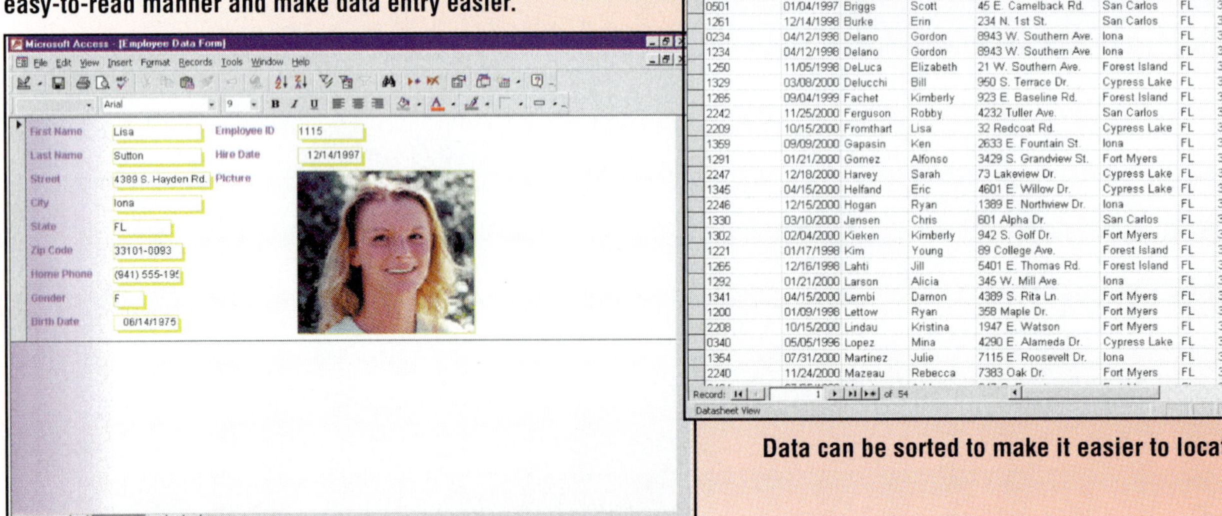

Data can be sorted to make it easier to locate information.

data. As you have continued to add more employee records to the table, you have noticed several errors. You also realize that you forgot to include a field for the employee's sex. Even with the best of planning and care, errors occur and the information may change. You will see how easy it is to modify the database structure and to customize field properties to provide more control over how and what data is entered in a field.

Even more impressive, as you will see in this tutorial, is the program's ability to locate information in the database. This is where all the hard work of entering data pays off. With a click of a button you can find data that might otherwise take hours to locate. The end result both saves time and improves the accuracy of the output.

You will also see how you can make the data you are looking at onscreen more pleasing by creating a form (shown here).

Printed form of employee record.

Concept Overview

The following concepts will be introduced in this tutorial:

1   **Format Property**   You can use the Format property to create custom formats that change the way numbers, dates, times, and text display and print.

2   **Default Value Property**   The Default Value property is used to specify a value to be automatically entered in a field when a new record is created.

3   **Find and Replace**   The Find and Replace feature helps you quickly find specific information and automatically replace it with new information.

4   **Validity Check**   Access automatically performs certain checks, called validity checks, on values entered in a field to make sure that the values are valid for the field type.

5   **Sort**   You can quickly reorder records in a table by sorting the table to display in a different record order.

6   **Form**   A form is a database object used primarily to display records onscreen to make it easier to enter new records and to make changes to existing records.

Navigating a Large Table

The database file that contains the additional employee records is on your data disk and is named Employee Records. To open this file,

1   ■ Load Access 2000. Put your data disk in drive A (or the appropriate drive for your system).

■ Select Open an Existing Database.

■ Click   OK   .

■ From the Look In drop-down list box, change the location to the drive containing your data disk.

■ Select Employee Records.

■ Click   Open   ▾ .

The Database window for the Employee Records file is displayed. To open the currently selected table with the additional employee records, Employees,

2 — **Click** [Open].

Maximize the Datasheet window.

Your screen should be similar to
Figure 2–1.

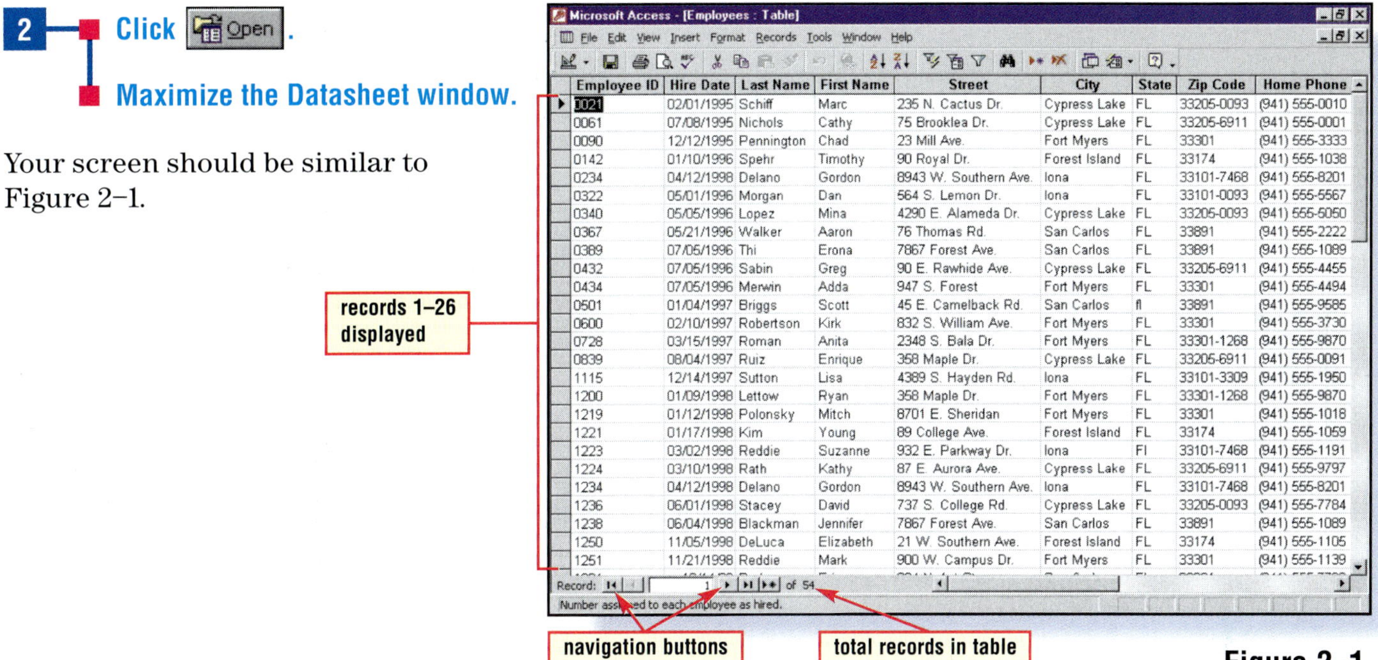

Figure 2–1

By default, the Datasheet view of the Table window is displayed. As you
can see from the record number indicator, there are now 54 records in the
table.

In a large table, there are many methods you can use to quickly navigate, or move, through records in Datasheet view. You can always use the
mouse to move from one field or record to another. However, if the information is not visible in the window, you must scroll the window first. The
table below presents several keyboard methods that make moving around
a table faster in Navigation mode.

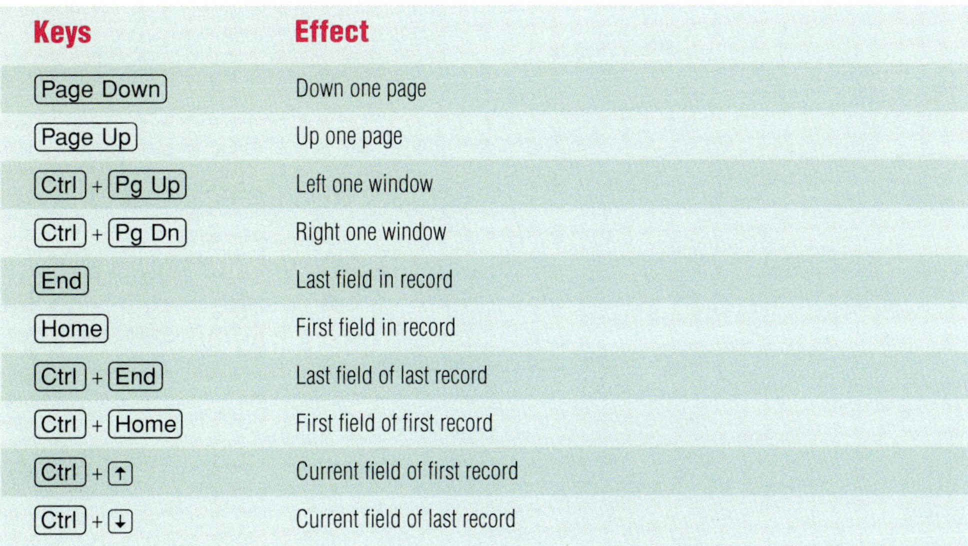

Keys	Effect
Page Down	Down one page
Page Up	Up one page
Ctrl + Pg Up	Left one window
Ctrl + Pg Dn	Right one window
End	Last field in record
Home	First field in record
Ctrl + End	Last field of last record
Ctrl + Home	First field of first record
Ctrl + ↑	Current field of first record
Ctrl + ↓	Current field of last record

The Navigation buttons in the status bar also provide navigation shortcuts. These buttons are described on the next page.

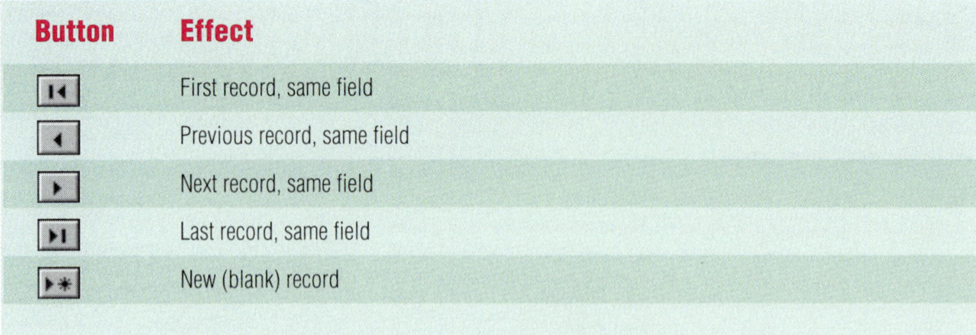

Button	Effect
◄◄	First record, same field
◄	Previous record, same field
►	Next record, same field
►►	Last record, same field
►*	New (blank) record

Currently, records 1 through 26 are displayed in the window. To see the next full window of records,

3 ■ **Press** Pg Dn.

Your screen should be similar to Figure 2–2.

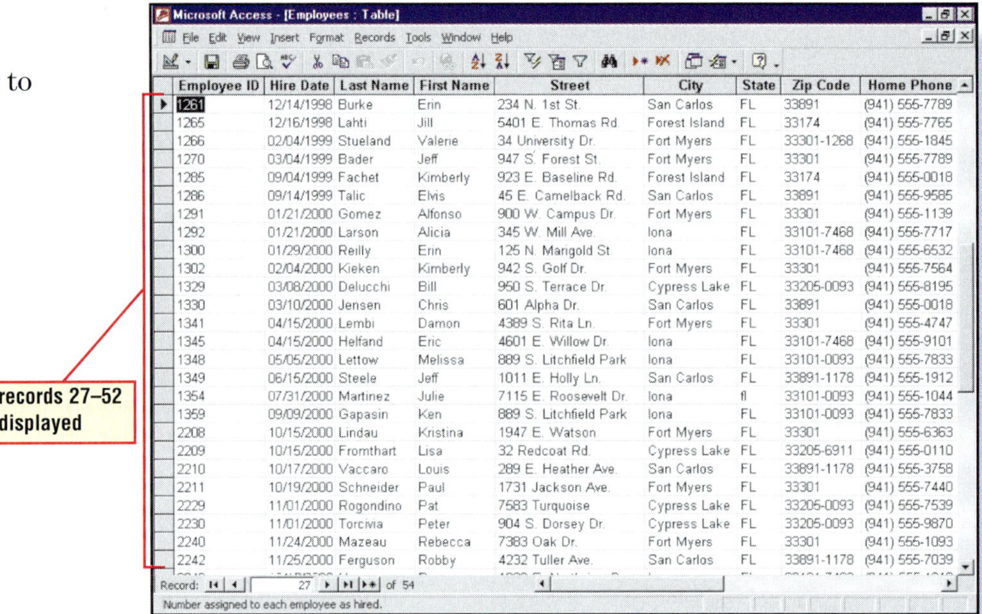

Figure 2–2

Now records 27 through 52 are displayed in the window. The first record in the window is now the current record.

Due to the number and width of the fields, not all fields can be displayed in the window at the same time. Rather than scrolling the window horizontally to see the additional fields, you can quickly move to the right a window at a time.

 **4** ■ **Press** [End].

Your screen should be similar to Figure 2–3.

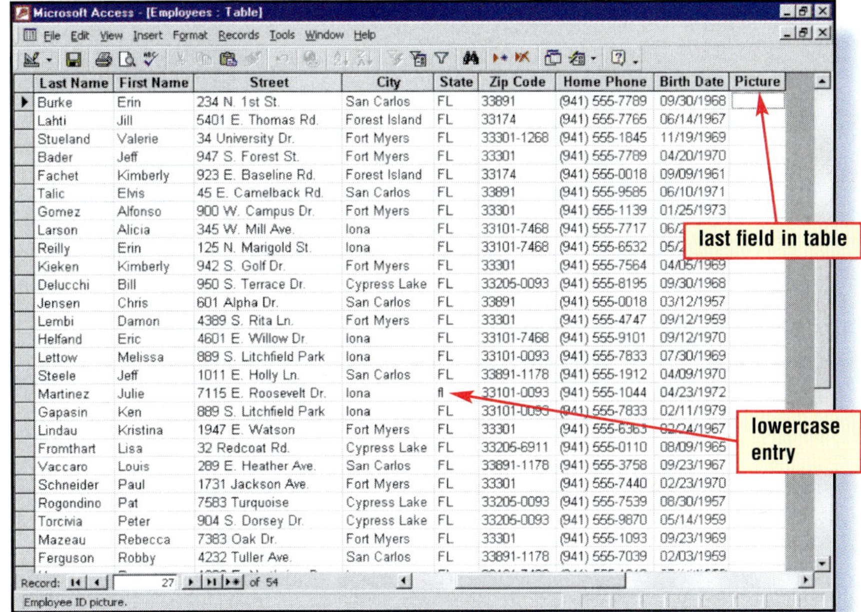

Last Name	First Name	Street	City	State	Zip Code	Home Phone	Birth Date	Picture
Burke	Erin	234 N. 1st St.	San Carlos	FL	33891	(941) 555-7789	09/30/1968	
Lahti	Jill	5401 E. Thomas Rd.	Forest Island	FL	33174	(941) 555-7765	06/14/1967	
Stueland	Valerie	34 University Dr.	Fort Myers	FL	33301-1268	(941) 555-1845	11/19/1969	
Bader	Jeff	947 S. Forest St.	Fort Myers	FL	33301	(941) 555-7789	04/20/1970	
Fachet	Kimberly	923 E. Baseline Rd.	Forest Island	FL	33174	(941) 555-0018	09/09/1961	
Talic	Elvis	45 E. Camelback Rd.	San Carlos	FL	33891	(941) 555-9585	06/10/1971	
Gomez	Alfonso	900 W. Campus Dr.	Fort Myers	FL	33301	(941) 555-1139	01/25/1973	
Larson	Alicia	345 W. Mill Ave.	Iona	FL	33101-7468	(941) 555-7717	06/2	
Reilly	Erin	125 N. Marigold St.	Iona	FL	33101-7468	(941) 555-6532	05/2	
Kieken	Kimberly	942 S. Golf Dr.	Fort Myers	FL	33301	(941) 555-7564	04/05/1969	
Delucchi	Bill	950 S. Terrace Dr.	Cypress Lake	FL	33205-0093	(941) 555-8195	09/30/1968	
Jensen	Chris	601 Alpha Dr.	San Carlos	FL	33891	(941) 555-0018	03/12/1957	
Lembi	Damon	4389 S. Rita Ln.	Fort Myers	FL	33301	(941) 555-4747	09/12/1959	
Helfand	Eric	4601 E. Willow Dr.	Iona	FL	33101-7468	(941) 555-9101	09/12/1970	
Lettow	Melissa	889 S. Litchfield Park	Iona	FL	33101-0093	(941) 555-7833	07/30/1969	
Steele	Jeff	1011 E. Holly Ln.	San Carlos	FL	33891-1178	(941) 555-1912	04/09/1970	
Martinez	Julie	7115 E. Roosevelt Dr.	Iona	fl	33101-0093	(941) 555-1044	04/23/1972	
Gapasin	Ken	889 S. Litchfield Park	Iona	FL	33101-0093	(941) 555-7833	02/11/1979	
Lindau	Kristina	1947 E. Watson	Fort Myers	FL	33301	(941) 555-6363	02/24/1967	
Fromthart	Lisa	32 Redcoat Rd.	Cypress Lake	FL	33205-6911	(941) 555-0110	08/09/1965	
Vaccaro	Louis	289 E. Heather Ave.	San Carlos	FL	33891-1178	(941) 555-3758	09/23/1967	
Schneider	Paul	1731 Jackson Ave.	Fort Myers	FL	33301	(941) 555-7440	02/23/1970	
Rogondino	Pat	7583 Turquoise	Cypress Lake	FL	33205-0093	(941) 555-7539	08/30/1957	
Torcivia	Peter	904 S. Dorsey Dr.	Cypress Lake	FL	33205-0093	(941) 555-9870	05/14/1959	
Mazeau	Rebecca	7383 Oak Dr.	Fort Myers	FL	33301	(941) 555-1093	09/23/1969	
Ferguson	Robby	4232 Tuller Ave.	San Carlos	FL	33891-1178	(941) 555-7039	02/03/1959	

Record: 14 ◀ 27 ▶ ▶I ▶* of 54

Employee ID picture.

Figure 2–3

The last field in the table is now visible in the window. To quickly move to the same field of the last record and then back to the first field of the first record,

 **5** ■ **Click** ▶I .

■ **Press** [Ctrl] + [Home].

Changing Field Properties

As you looked through the records, you noticed that records 12, 22, and 43 have mixed-case entries in the State field. You would like all the State field entries to be in all uppercase letters. Also, rather than having to enter the same state for each record, you want the field to display the state FL automatically. This will make data entry faster because all the stores are located in Florida and it is unlikely that the employees will live in another state.

In Tutorial 1 you set the field properties of several fields. For example, you set the Employee ID field size to 4 so that a larger number could not be entered into the field. In addition, you set the format of the Hire Date field to display a date using the Short Date style. You can also set a field's property to automatically change the entry to uppercase characters. To change the properties of a field, you use Design view.

1 Click 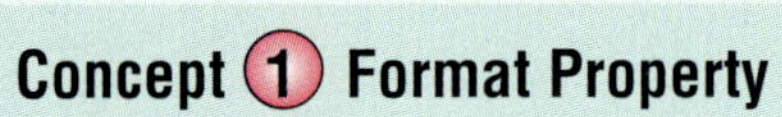 ▾ Design View.

Make the State field the current field.

> The menu equivalent is **V**iew/**D**esign View.

Your screen should be similar to Figure 2–4.

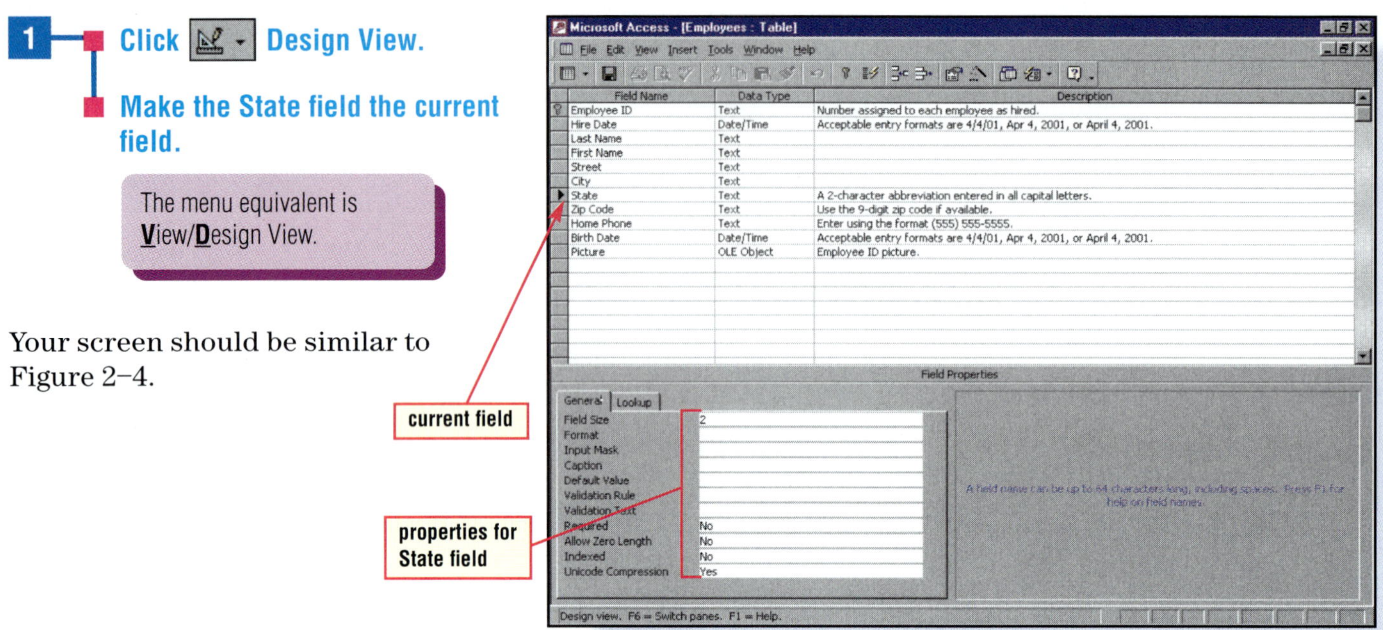

Figure 2–4

The properties associated with the State field are displayed in the General tab. The Format property is used to customize the way an entry is displayed.

Concept ① Format Property

You can use the Format property to create custom formats that change the way numbers, dates, times, and text display and print. Format properties do not change the way Access stores data, only how the data is displayed. To change the format of a field, different symbols are entered in the Format text box. Text and Memo Data Types can use any of the four symbols below:

Symbol	Meaning	Example
@	A required text character or space	@@@-@@-@@@@ would display 123456789 as 123–45–6789. Nine characters or spaces are required.
>	Forces all characters to uppercase	> would display SMITH whether you entered SMITH, smith, or Smith.
<	Forces all characters to lowercase	< would display smith whether you entered SMITH, smith, or Smith.
&	An optional text character	@@-@@& would display 12345 as 12–345 and 12.34 as 12–34. Four out of five characters are required, and a fifth is optional.

To enter the symbol to change all entries in the field to uppercase,

2 ∎ **Move to the Format field property text box.**

∎ **Type >**

Your screen should be similar to Figure 2–5.

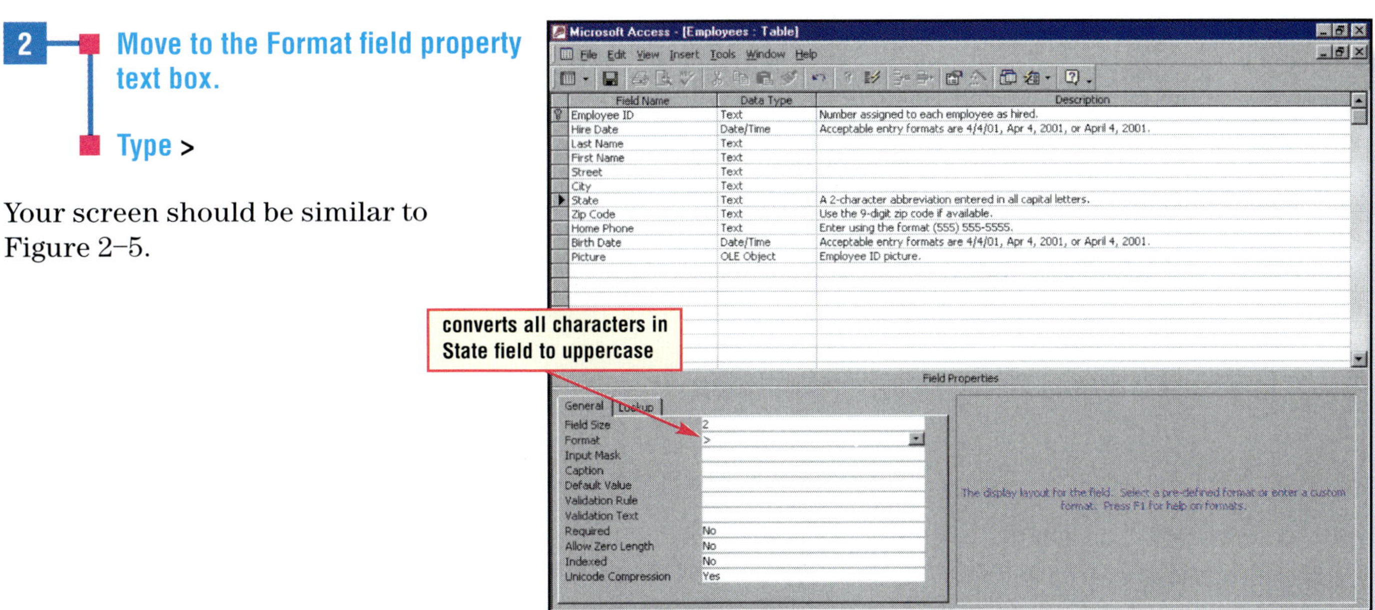

Figure 2–5

Next you want to change the State field property to automatically display the default value of FL.

Concept ② Default Value Property

The Default Value property is used to specify a value that is automatically entered in a field when a new record is created. This property is commonly used when most of the entries in a field will be the same for the entire table. That default value is then displayed automatically in the field. When users add a record to the table, they can either accept this value or enter another value. This saves time while entering data.

3 ∎ **Move to the Default Value property text box.**

∎ **Type FL**

∎ **Press ←Enter.**

Your screen should be similar to Figure 2–6.

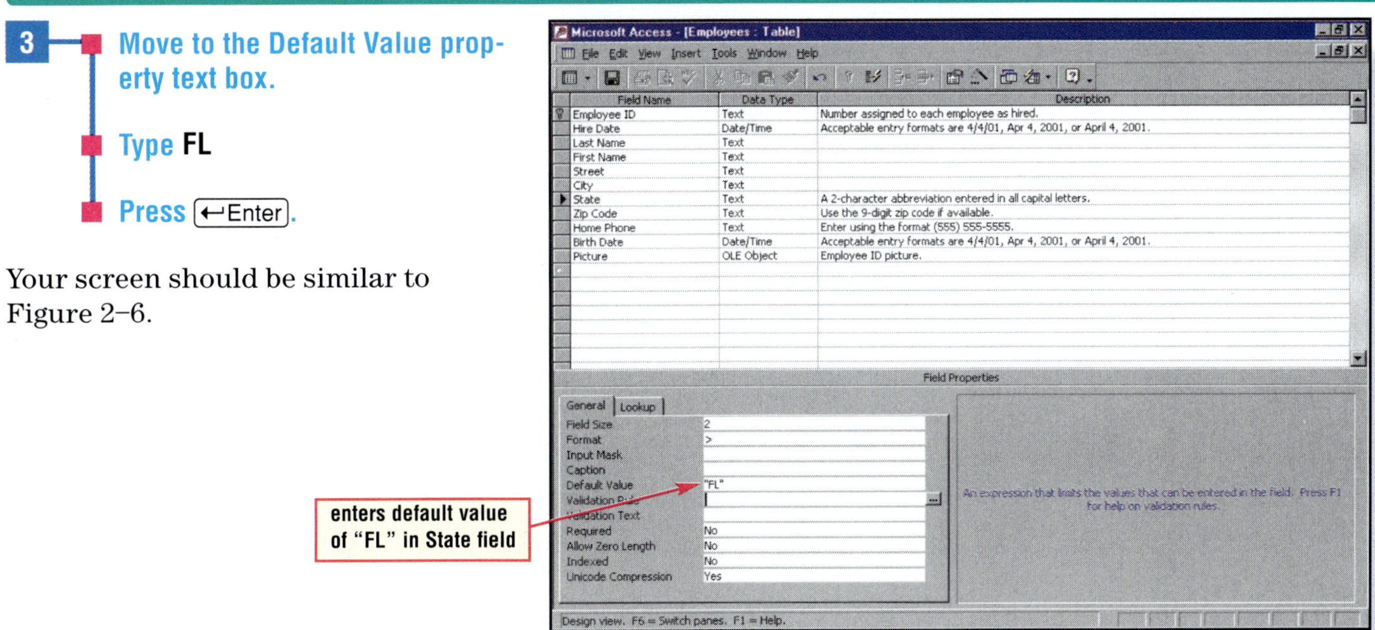

Figure 2–6

The default value is automatically enclosed in quotes to identify the entry as a group of characters called a **character string**.

4 ■ **Click** 🔲 ▾ **Datasheet view.**

■ **Click** [Yes] **to save the table.**

Your screen should be similar to Figure 2–7.

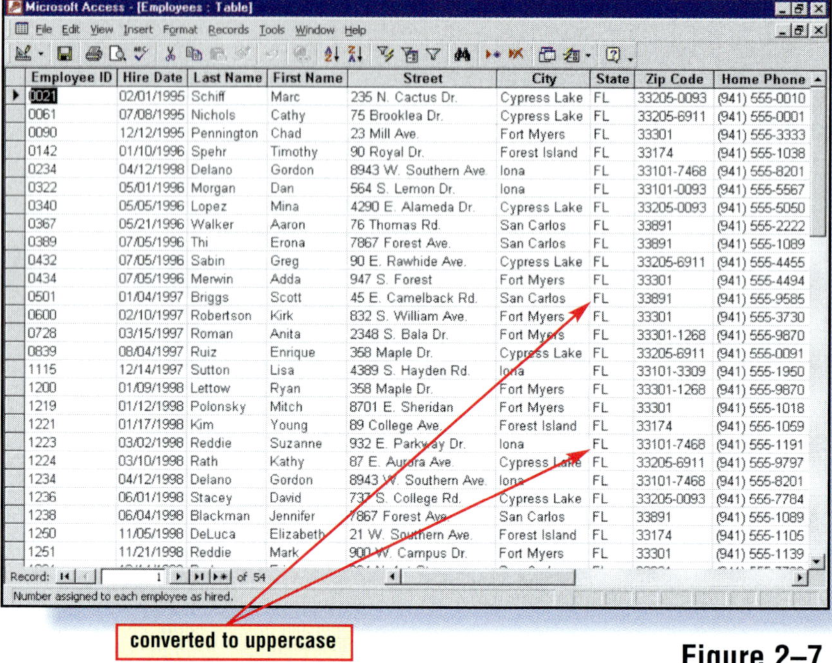

Figure 2–7

You can now see that records 12 (Scott Briggs) and 22 (Suzanne Reddie) correctly display the state in capital letters as a result of the format property setting you entered for the State field. To see the default value of FL displayed in a new blank record,

5 ■ **Click** ▶✱ .

Your screen should be similar to Figure 2–8.

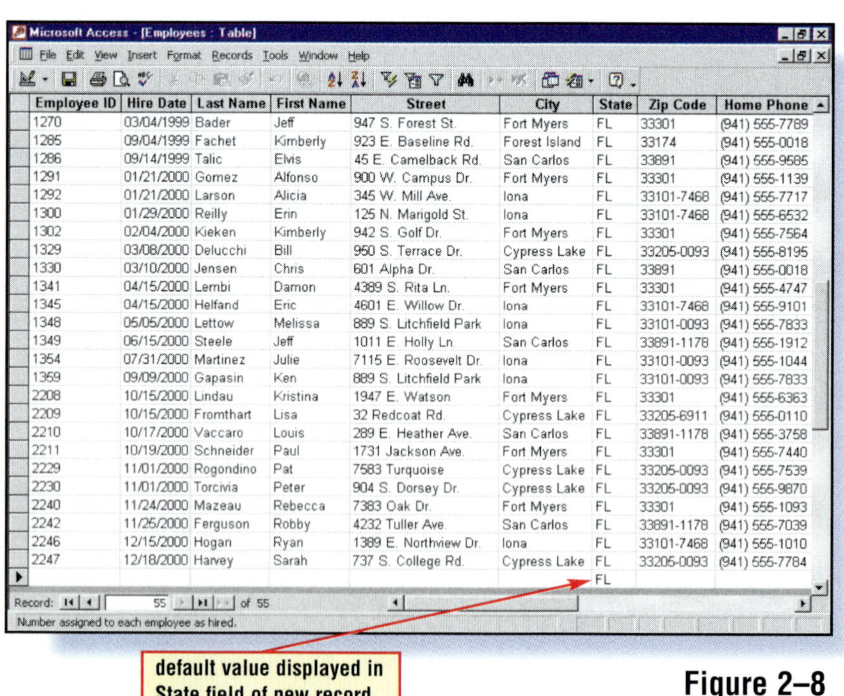

Figure 2–8

The new blank record at the end of the table displays FL as the default value for the State field.

Finding and Replacing Data

Next you want to update the Zip Code field for the existing records. You have checked with the U.S. Postal Service and found that all zip codes of 33891 have a four-digit extension of 1605. To locate all the records with this zip code, you could look at the Zip Code field for each record to find the match and then edit the field to add the extension. If the table is small, this method would be acceptable. For large tables, however, this method could be quite time consuming and more prone to errors. A more efficient way is to search the table to find specific values in records and then replace the entry with another.

Concept 3 Find and Replace

The Find and Replace feature helps you quickly find specific information and automatically replace it with new information. The Find command will locate all specified values in a field, and the Replace command will both find a value and automatically replace it with another. For example, in a table containing supplier and item prices, you may need to increase the price of all items supplied by one manufacturer. To quickly locate these items, you would use the Find command to locate all records with the name of the manufacturer and then update the price appropriately. Alternatively, you could use the Replace command if you knew that all items priced at $9.95 were increasing to $11.89. This command would locate all values matching the original price and replace them with the new price. Finding and replacing data is fast and accurate, but you need to be careful when replacing not to replace unintended matches.

The Replace command will search the current field to find the specified data and replace it with other data.

1 **Move to the Zip Code field of record 1.**

Choose Edit/Replace.

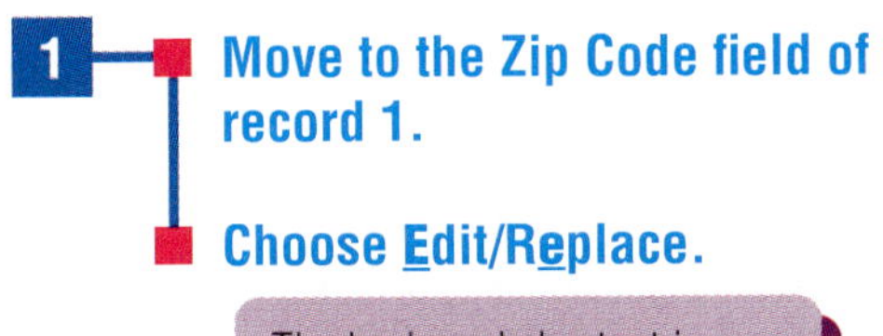

Your screen should be similar to Figure 2–9.

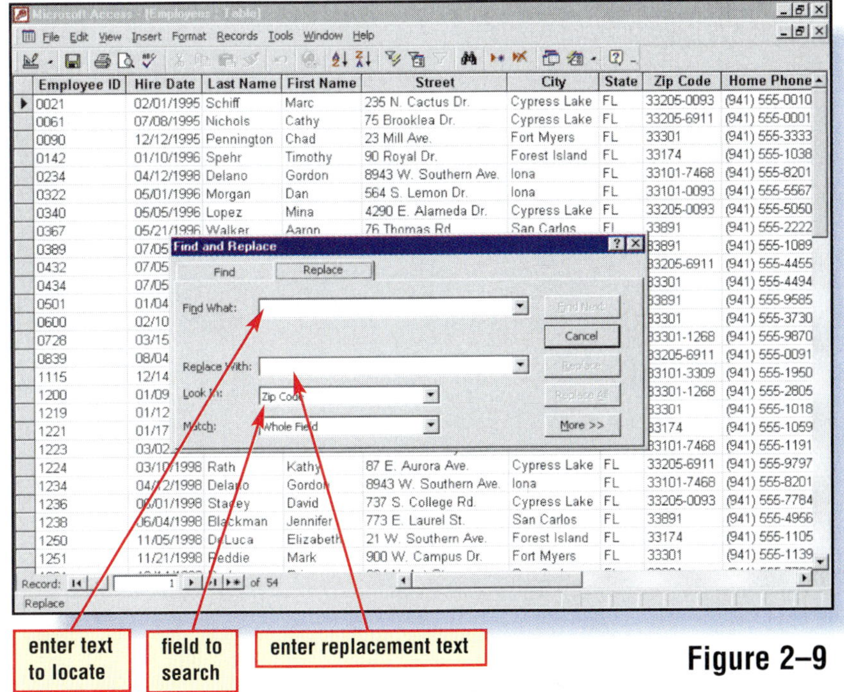

Figure 2–9

The Find and Replace dialog box shows the name of the field it will search in the Look In text box. In the Find What text box, you enter the text you want to locate, and in the Replace With text box, you enter the replacement text exactly as you want it to appear in your document. In addition, you can use the advanced search options to refine the search. To see these options,

2 ▬ **Click** More >> .

Your screen should be similar to Figure 2–10.

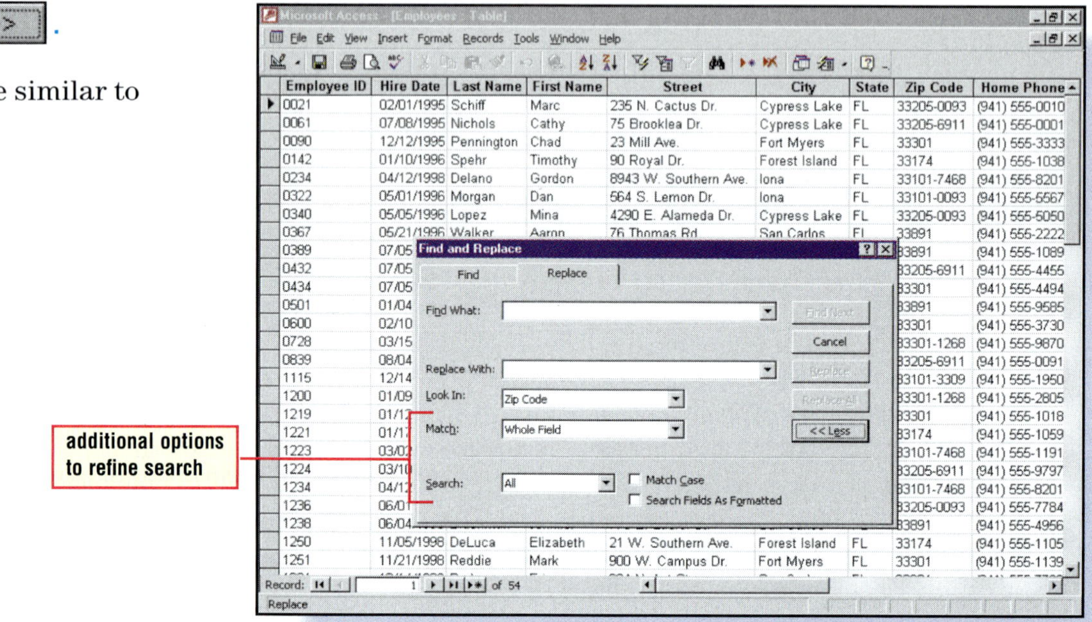

Figure 2–10

The additional options in the Find and Replace dialog box can be combined in many ways to help you find and replace text in documents. They are described in the table below.

Option	Effect on Text
Match	Refines area in field to locate match to the whole field, any part of the field, or the start of the field.
Search	Specifies direction in table to search: All (search all records), Down or Up (search down or up from the current insertion point location in the field).
Match Case	Finds words that have the same pattern of uppercase letters as entered in the Find What text box. Using this option makes the search case sensitive.
Search Fields as Formatted	Finds data based on its display format.

To enter the zip code to find and the replacement zip code, and to search using the default options,

3 ● **Click in the Find What text box.**

● **Type 33891**

● **Press** Tab.

● **Type 33891-1605**

● **Click** Find Next .

If necessary, move the dialog box so you can see the located entry.

Your screen should be similar to Figure 2–11.

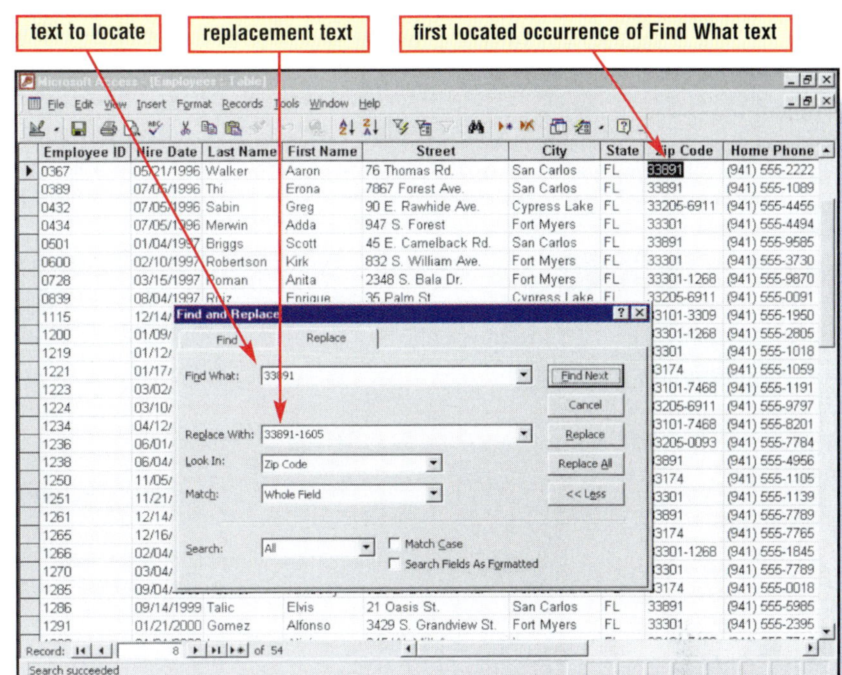

Figure 2–11

Immediately the highlight moves to the first occurrence of text in the document that matches the Find What text and highlights it. To replace the highlighted text,

4 ● **Click** Replace .

Your screen should be similar to Figure 2–12.

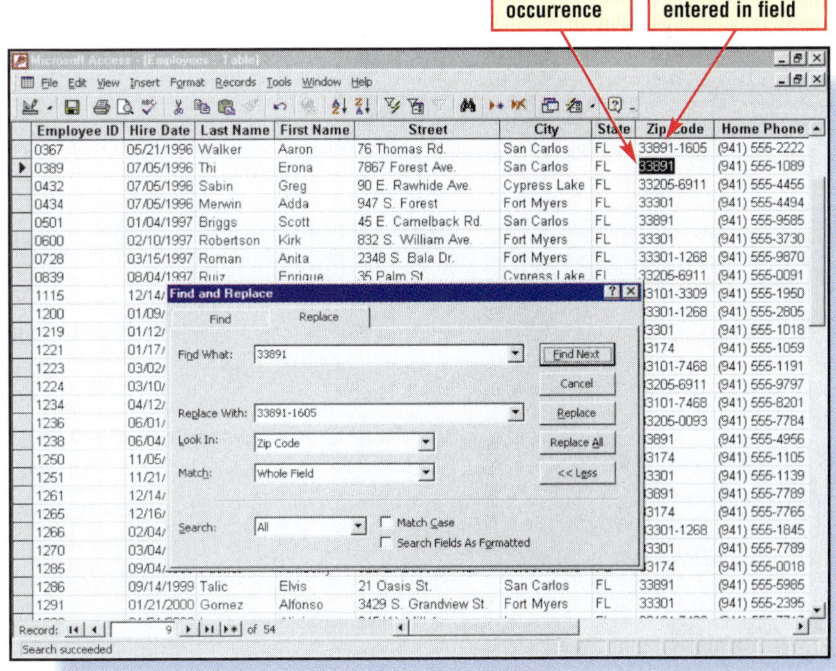

Figure 2–12

The original zip code entry is replaced with the new zip code. The program immediately continues searching and locates a second occurrence of the entry. You decide the program is locating the values accurately, and it will be safe to replace all finds with the replacement value. To do this,

5 — ● **Click** Replace All .

● **Click** Yes **in response to the advisory message.**

Your screen should be similar to Figure 2–13.

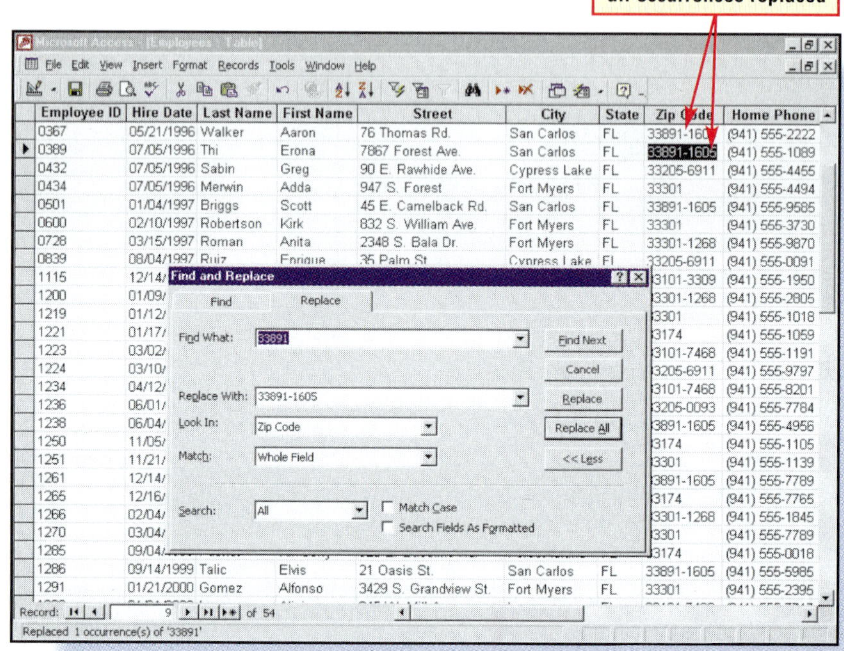

Figure 2–13

All matches are replaced with the replacement text. It is much faster to use Replace All than to confirm each match separately. However, exercise care when using Replace All, because the search text you specify might be part of another field and you may accidentally replace text you want to keep.

6 — ● **In the same manner, update the zip code for 33301 to include the extension 1268.**

● **Click the** << Less **button to close the other options portion of the dialog box.**

The menu equivalent is **E**dit/**F**ind, the toolbar button is 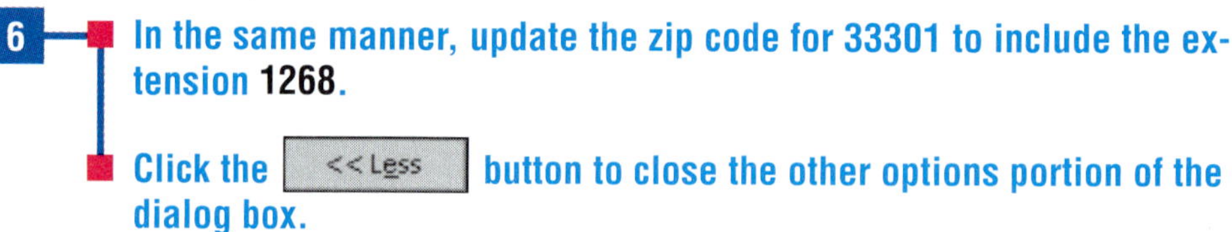, and the keyboard shortcut is Ctrl + F.

Over the past few days you have received several change request forms to update the employee records. The first change request is for Melissa Lettow, who recently married and has both a name and address change. To quickly locate this record you will use the Find command. This command works just like the Find and Replace command, except it does not enter a replacement.

7 **Move to the Last Name field of record 1.**

Open the Find tab.

Replace the Find What text with lettow.

Click Find Next **.**

Because the Match Case option is not selected, Find will look for an exact match regardless of uppercase or lowercase characters.

Your screen should be similar to Figure 2–14.

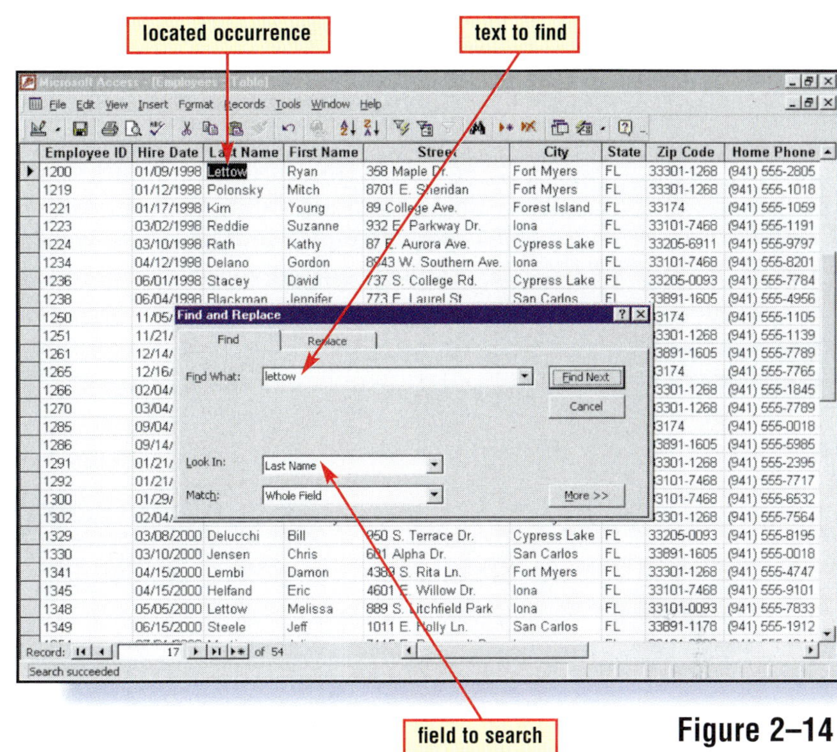

Figure 2–14

If the Find command did not locate this record, reissue the command and make sure you enter the name Lettow exactly as shown and you are searching the Last Name field.

Access searches the table and moves to the first occurrence of the entry. The Last Name field is highlighted in record 17. To change the last name to Richards,

8 **Double-click on Lettow in the Last Name field of record 17.**

Type Richards

Press ←Enter **.**

Your screen should be similar to Figure 2–15.

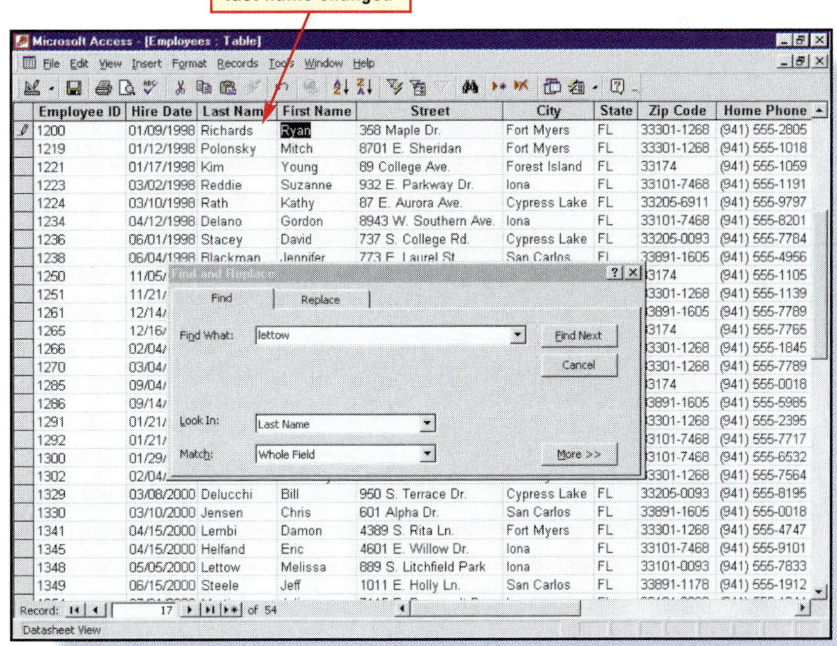

Figure 2–15

Using Undo

Now that the highlight is on the First Name field, you notice this is the record for Ryan Lettow, not Melissa. You changed the wrong record. You can use the Undo command to quickly undo this change. Undo will cancel your last action as long as you have not made any further changes to the table. Even if you save the record or the table, you can undo changes to the last edited record by using the Undo Saved Record command on the Edit menu or by clicking 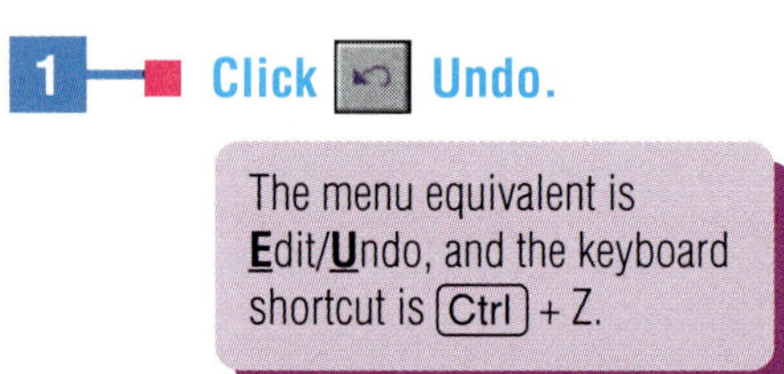. Once you have changed another record or moved to another window, however, the earlier change cannot be undone. To quickly undo the change made to this record,

You can also press [Esc] before leaving the field you are editing to cancel changes you have made.

1 Click ↶ Undo.

The menu equivalent is **E**dit/**U**ndo, and the keyboard shortcut is [Ctrl] + Z.

Your screen should be similar to Figure 2–16.

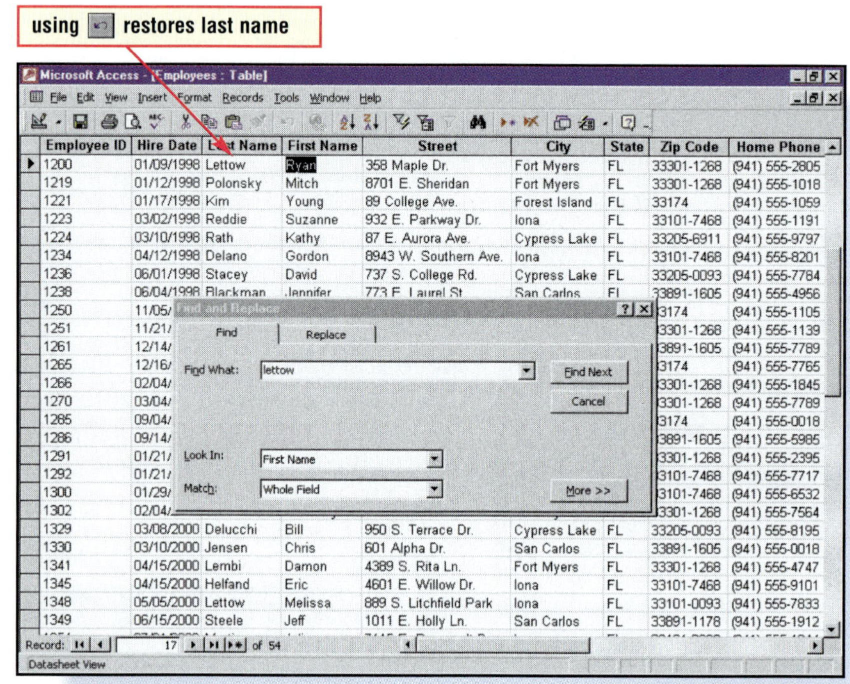

Figure 2–16

The original field value of Lettow is restored. Now you want to continue the search to locate the next record with the last name of Lettow.

Reminder: The insertion point must be on the field you want to search before clicking Find Next.

2 Move back to the Last Name field of record 17.

Click Find Next.

Change the last name to **Richards** and the street to **5401 E. Thomas Rd.**

Use the Find command to search the table for the following records and correct the entries.

Employee Name	Field	Correction
Peter Torcivia	Street	**4290 E. Alameda Dr.**
Eric Helfand	City, Zip Code	**Cypress Lake 33205-0093**
Jennifer Blackman	Last Name	**Thomas**
Lisa Sutton	Zip Code	**33101-0093**

3 ■ **When you are done, close the Find and Replace dialog box and return to the first field of record 1.**

Inserting a Field

Additional Information

If you remove a field, Access permanently deletes the field definition and any data in the field. Click 🖭 or use **E**dit/Delete **R**ows to remove a field.

While continuing to use the table, you have realized that you need to include a field of information to hold each employee's gender. Although it is better to include all the necessary fields when creating the table structure, it is possible to add or remove fields from a table at a later time. After looking at the order of the fields, you decide to add the new field, Gender, between the Home Phone and Birth Date fields. To insert the new field in the table and define its properties,

1 ■ Click 🖉 ▾ Design view.

> You can also add or delete fields in Datasheet view.

■ **Make the Birth Date field current.**

■ Click 🖳 **Insert Rows.**

> The menu equivalent is **I**nsert/**R**ows. You can also use the Insert Row command on the shortcut menu.

Your screen should be similar to Figure 2–17.

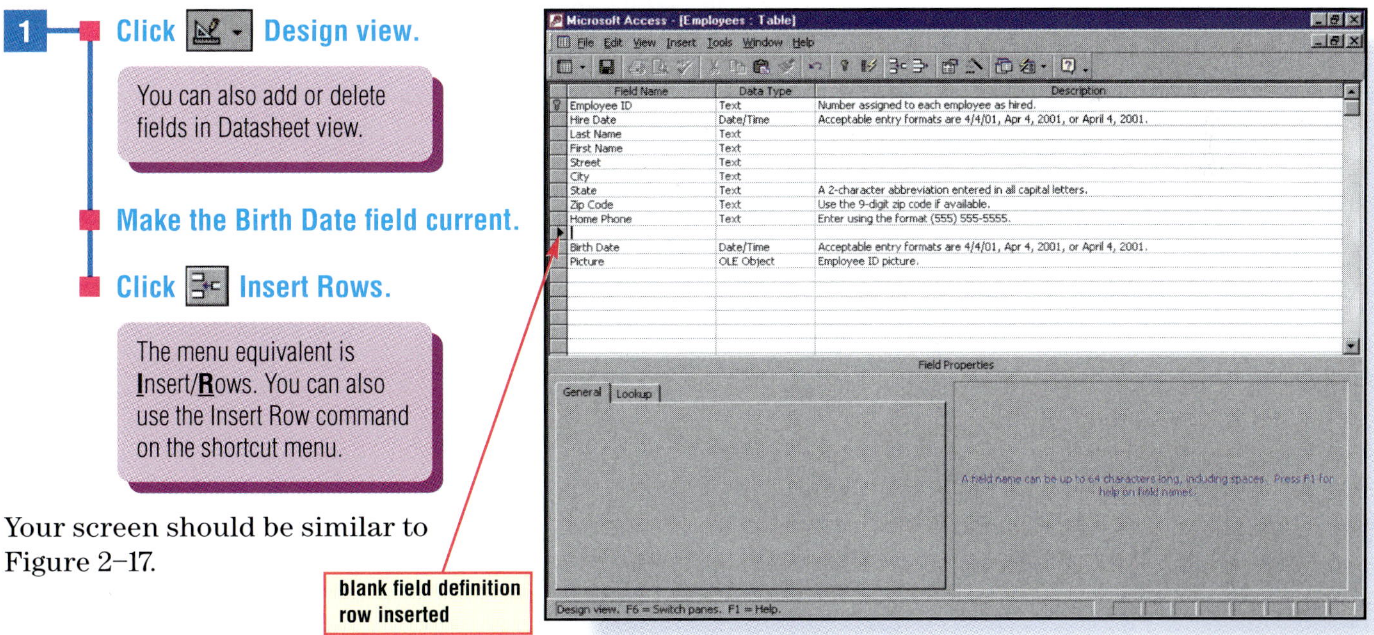

blank field definition row inserted

Figure 2–17

2 ■ **Enter the new field information as follows:**

Field Name: **Gender**

Data Type: **Text**

Description: **Enter M for male or F for female.**

Field Size: **1**

Format: **>**

Your screen should be similar to Figure 2–18.

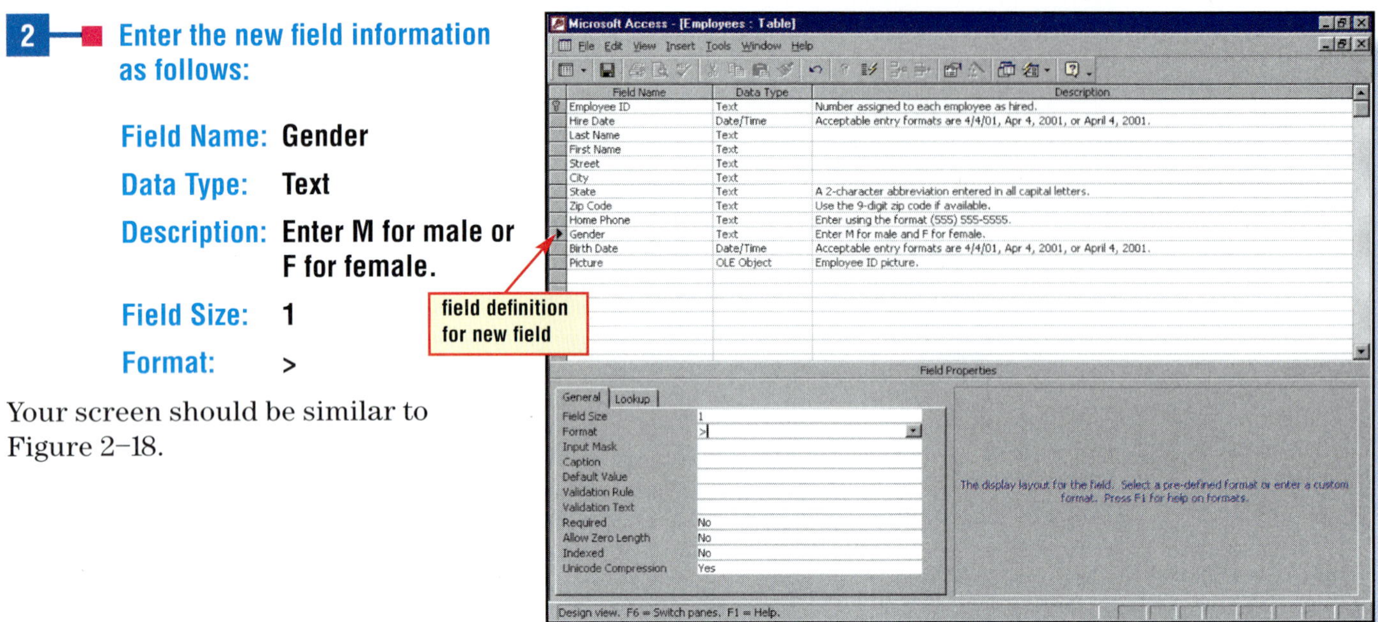

Figure 2–18

Adding Validity Checks

The only two characters you want the Gender field to accept are M for male and F for female. To specify that these two characters are the only entries acceptable in the field, you will include a validity check.

Concept ④ Validity Check

Access automatically performs certain checks, called **validity checks**, on values entered in a field to make sure that the values are valid for the field type. A Text field type has few restrictions, but you can create your own validity checks for a field, which Access will apply during data entry.

A validity check is set by entering an expression to describe acceptable values. An **expression** is a combination of symbols that produces specific results. Expressions are used throughout Access to create validity checks, queries, forms, and reports. These are examples of possible expressions:

Expression	Result
=[Sales Amount] + [Sales Tax]	Sums value in two fields.
="M" OR "F"	Includes M or F entries only.
>--#1/1/95# AND <=#12/31/95#	Includes entries greater than or equal to 1/1/95, and less than or equal to 12/31/95.
="Tennis Rackets"	Includes Tennis Rackets entries only.

You create an expression by combining identifiers, operators, and values to produce the desired result. An **identifier** is an element that refers to the value of a field, a graphical object, or property. In the expression =[Sales Amount] + [Sales Tax], [Sales Amount] and [Sales Tax] are identifiers that refer to the values in the Sales Amount and Sales Tax fields.

An **operator** is a symbol or word that indicates that an operation is to be performed. The Access operators include = (equal to), <> (not equal to), >= (greater than or equal to), <= (less than or equal to), LIKE, OR, and AND. In the expression ="M" OR "F," the = sign and OR are operators. The = operator is assumed if no other operator is specified.

Values are numbers, dates, or character strings. Character strings such as "M," "F," or "Tennis Rackets" are enclosed in quotation marks. Dates are enclosed in pound signs (#), as in >=#1/1/95# AND <=#12/31/95#.

When you add a validity check, you can also add validation text in the Validation Text property box. **Validation text** is an explanatory message that appears if a user attempts to enter invalid information in a text field for which there is a validity check. For example, if you added a validity check to a field to allow only the numbers 1 through 10, you might create validation text that would display the message, "The only valid entries for this field are numbers 1 through 10." If you do not specify a message, Access will display a default error message, which will not clearly describe the reason for the error.

You want to add a validity check to allow only M or F to be entered in the field. You also want to include a validation text message that will be displayed if the wrong character is entered in the Gender field.

1

■ **Move to the Validation Rule field property text box.**

■ **Type M or F**

You do not need to type the = as it is assumed if no operator is entered.

■ **Press ←Enter.**

■ **For the validation text, type The only valid entries are M or F.**

Your screen should be similar to Figure 2–19.

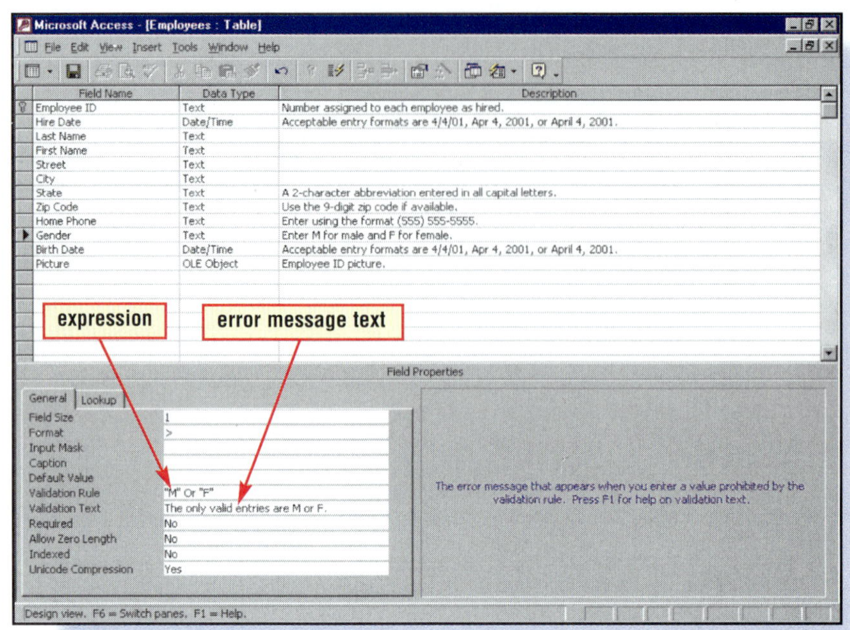

Figure 2–19

The expression states that the acceptable values can only be equal to an M or an F. Notice that Access automatically added quotation marks around the two character strings and changed the "o" in "or" to uppercase. Because the Format property has been set to convert all entries to uppercase, an entry of m or f is also acceptable.

Next you want to add the data for the Gender field to the table.

2

■ **Click ▦ ▾ Datasheet.**

■ **Click Yes to save the table.**

Your screen should be similar to Figure 2–20.

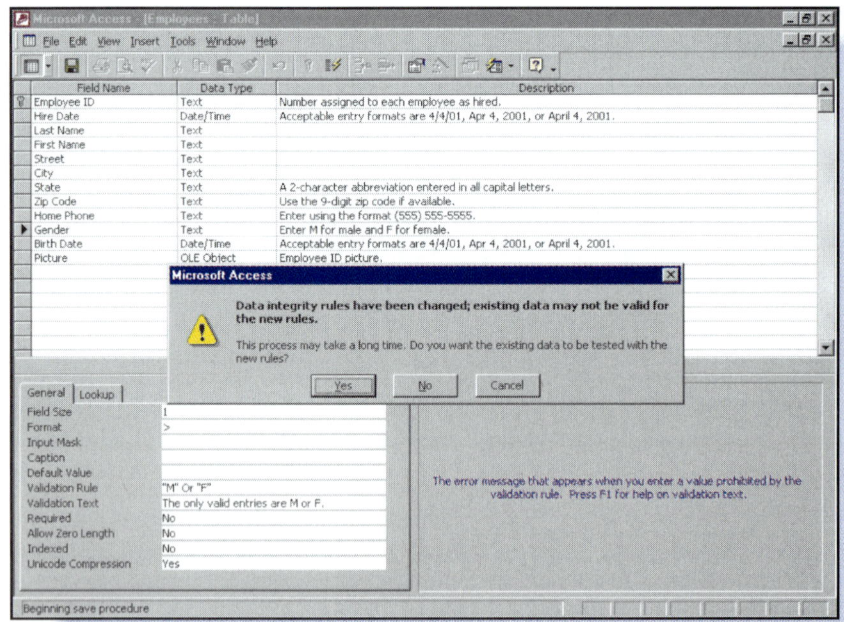

Figure 2–20

A message box advises you that data integrity rules have been changed. When you restructure a table, you often make changes that could result in a loss of data. Changes such as shortening field sizes, creating validity checks, or changing field types can cause existing data to become invalid. Because the field is new, there are no data values to verify, and a validation check is unnecessary. To continue,

3 **Click** 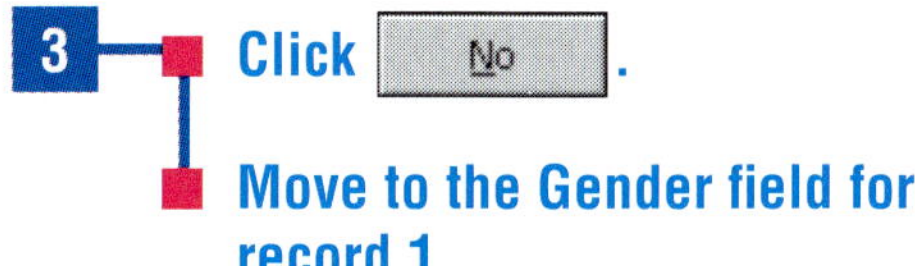 .

Move to the Gender field for record 1.

Your screen should be similar to Figure 2–21.

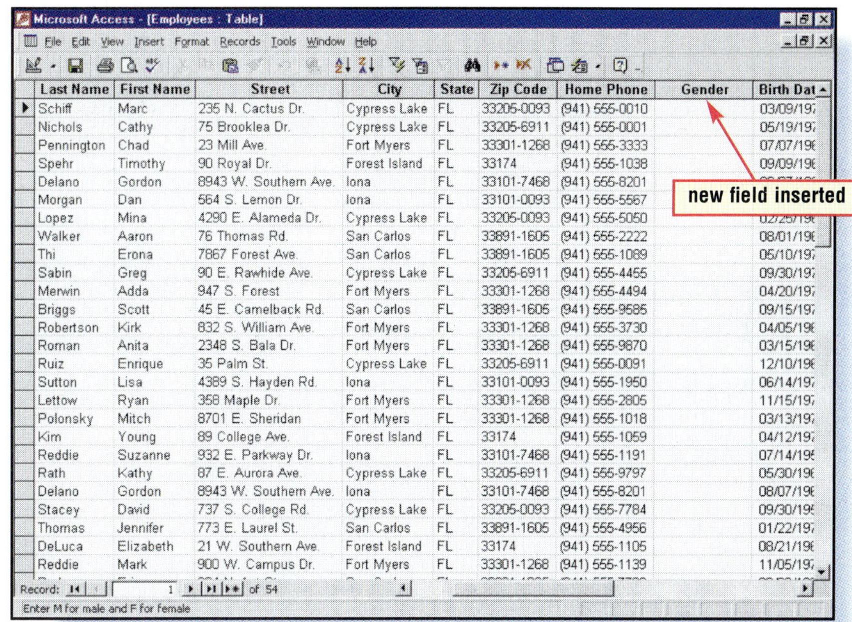

Figure 2–21

The new field was added to the table between the Home Phone and Birth Date fields.

Hiding and Redisplaying Fields

You can most likely tell the gender for each record by looking at the employee's first name. Unfortunately, the First Name field is on the opposite side of the screen from the Gender field. A quick way to view the fields side by side is to hide the fields that are in between.

1 **Select the Street field through the Home Phone field.**

Drag in the column heads to select the fields.

Choose Format/Hide Columns.

Your screen should be similar to Figure 2–22.

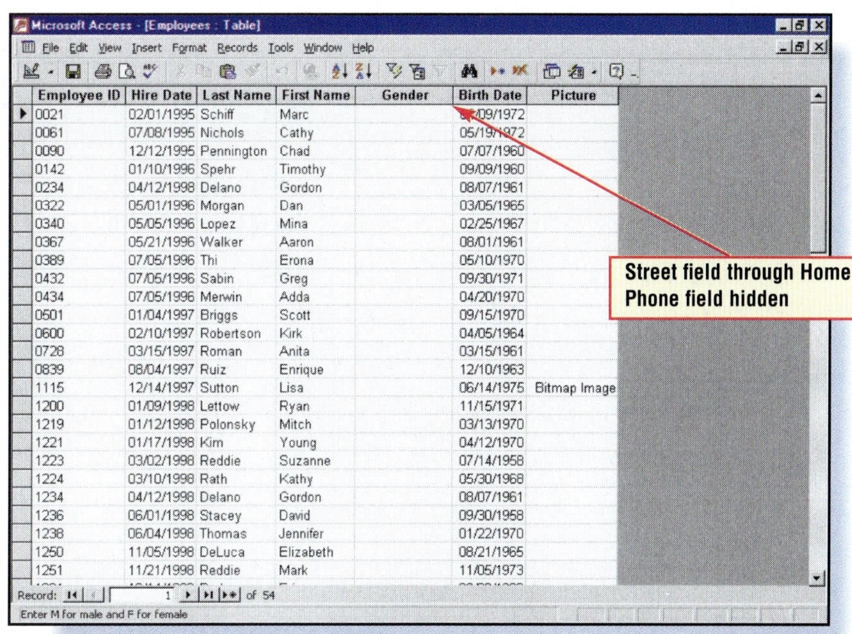

Figure 2–22

Now both the First Name and Gender columns are next to each other, and you can see the first name for record 1 is Marc. Therefore the Gender field for record 1 should be M. To verify that the validity check works, you will enter an invalid field value in the Gender field for this record.

2 Move to the Gender field of record 1.

Type **g**

Press ⏎Enter.

Your screen should be similar to Figure 2–23.

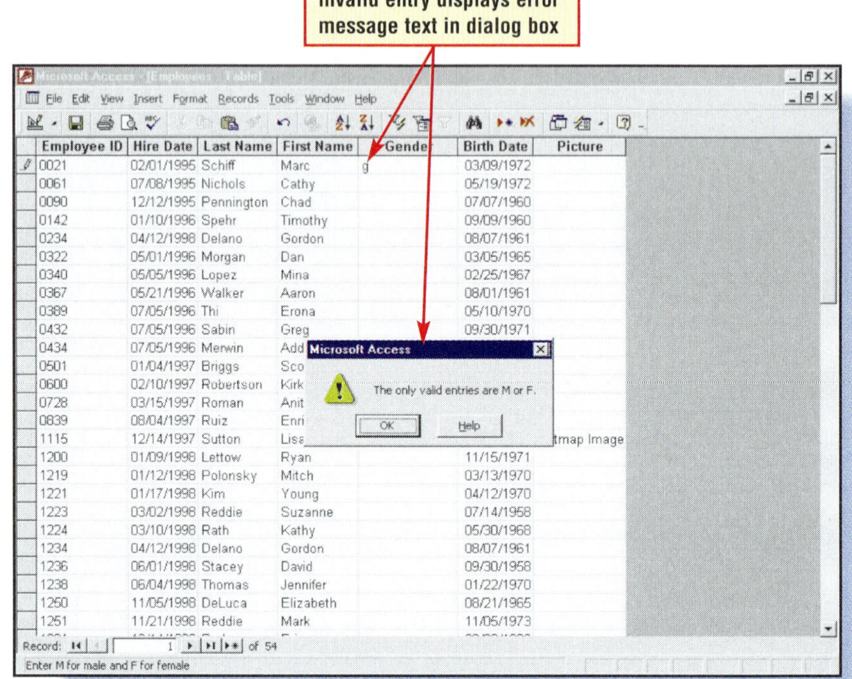

Figure 2–23

Access displays the error message you entered in the Validation Text box of Design view. To clear the error message and correct the entry,

3 Click OK.

Press Backspace.

Type **m**

Press ↓.

Your screen should be similar to Figure 2–24.

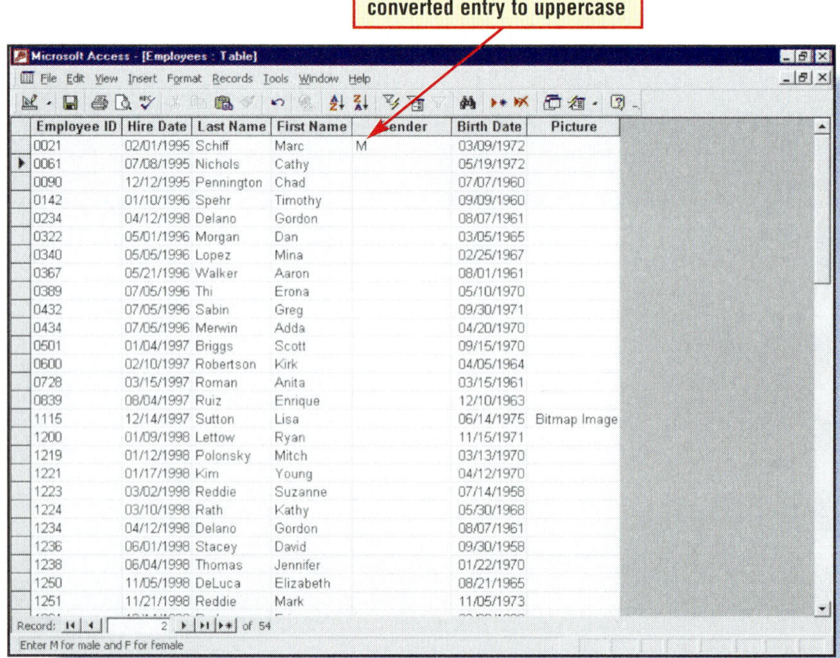

Figure 2–24

The entry for the first record is displayed as an uppercase M. Next you will enter the gender for each record and then redisplay the hidden fields.

4 ▪ **Enter the Gender field values for the remaining records by looking at the First Name field to determine whether the employee is male or female.**

▪ **Reduce the size of the Gender field using the Best Fit command.**

> Reminder: Double-click on the right column border to best fit the field.

▪ **Choose Format/Unhide Columns.**

Your screen should be similar to Figure 2–25.

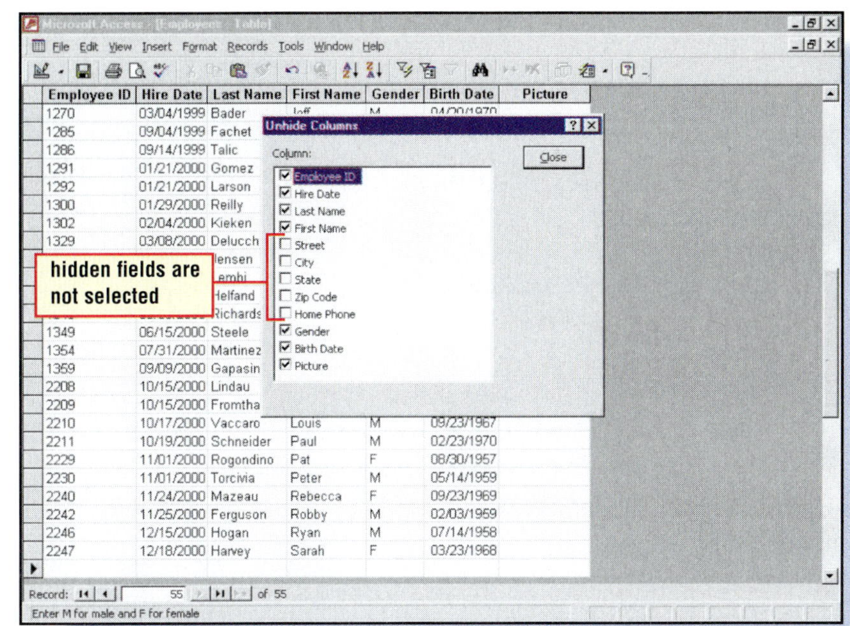

Figure 2–25

5 ▪ **Select the five fields that do not display checkmarks.**

▪ **Click** Close .

Sorting on a Single Field

As you may recall from Tutorial 1, the records are ordered by the primary key field, Employee ID. The Accounting department manager, however, has asked you for an alphabetical list of all employees. To do this you can sort the records in the table.

Concept ⑤ Sort

You can quickly reorder records in a table by **sorting** a table to display in a different record order. Sorting data often helps you find specific information quickly. In Access you can sort data in ascending order (A to Z or 0 to 9) or descending order (Z to A or 9 to 0). You can sort all records in a table by a single field, such as State, or you can select adjacent columns and sort by more than one field, such as State and then City. When you select multiple columns to sort, Access sorts records starting with the column farthest left, then moves to the right across the columns. For example, if you want to quickly sort by State, then by City, the State field must be to the left of the City field. Access saves the new sort order with your table data and reapplies it automatically each time you open the table. To return to the primary key sort order, you must remove the temporary sort.

For the first sort, you want the records arranged in ascending alphabetical order by last name.

1 ■ **Move to the Employee ID field of record 1.**

■ **Move to the Last Name field of any record.**

■ **Click** [A↓] **Sort Ascending.**

> The menu equivalent is **R**ecords/**S**ort/Sort **A**scending.

Your screen should be similar to Figure 2–26.

> Use [Z↓] or **R**ecords/**S**ort/Sort Des**c**ending to sort in descending alphabetical order.

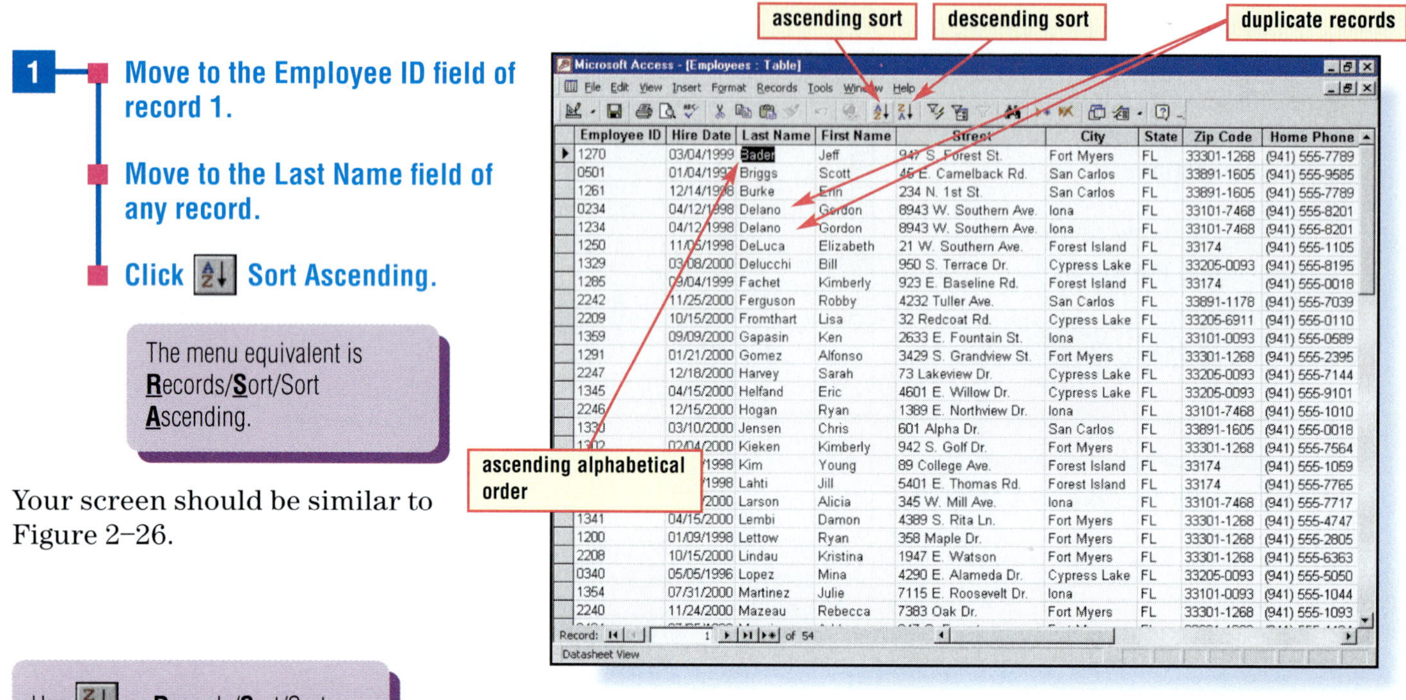

Figure 2–26

The employee records are displayed in alphabetical order by last name.

Deleting Records

> You cannot use Undo to restore deleted records.

Now that the records are alphabetically arranged, you immediately notice that Gordon Delano's record has been entered into the table twice. The records contain identical information in all the fields except for the Employee ID field. By checking the employee card, you determine that the record with the employee number of 0234 is incorrect. You need to delete the duplicate record.

> Records are selected using **E**dit/Se**l**ect Record or by clicking in the row selector when the mouse pointer shape is ➡. In Navigation mode, ⇧Shift + Spacebar selects the current record.

Records can be removed from a table by selecting the entire record and pressing [Del] or clicking [✂] Cut. This method is useful when you have multiple records to be deleted that you can select and delete as a group. It is quicker, however, to use the [✕] Delete Record button when you want to remove records individually. This is because the record is both selected and deleted at the same time.

1. ■ **Move to any field in record 4.**

   ■ **Click** ✖ **Delete Record.**

   ■ **Click** [Yes] **to confirm that you want to delete the record.**

> The menu equivalent is **E**dit/Cu**t**, and the keyboard shortcut is (Ctrl) + X. The Cut command is also on the shortcut menu when a record is selected.

Your screen should be similar to Figure 2–27.

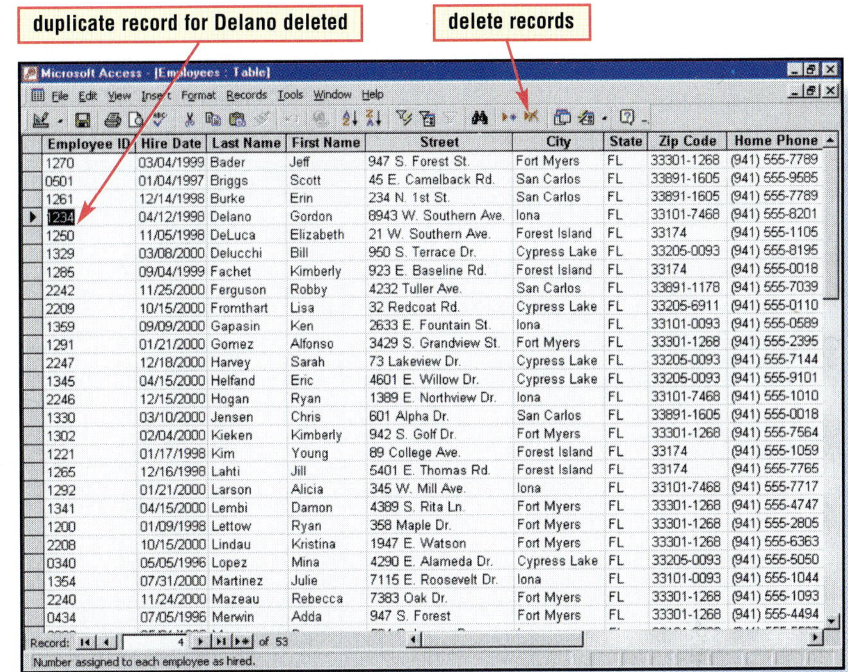

Employee ID	Hire Date	Last Name	First Name	Street	City	State	Zip Code	Home Phone
1270	03/04/1999	Bader	Jeff	947 S. Forest St.	Fort Myers	FL	33301-1268	(941) 555-7789
0501	01/04/1997	Briggs	Scott	45 E. Camelback Rd.	San Carlos	FL	33891-1605	(941) 555-9585
1261	12/14/1998	Burke	Erin	234 N. 1st St.	San Carlos	FL	33891-1605	(941) 555-7789
1234	04/12/1998	Delano	Gordon	8943 W. Southern Ave.	Iona	FL	33101-7468	(941) 555-8201
1250	11/05/1998	DeLuca	Elizabeth	21 W. Southern Ave.	Forest Island	FL	33174	(941) 555-1105
1329	03/08/2000	Delucchi	Bill	950 S. Terrace Dr.	Cypress Lake	FL	33205-0093	(941) 555-8195
1285	09/04/1999	Fachet	Kimberly	923 E. Baseline Rd.	Forest Island	FL	33174	(941) 555-0018
2242	11/25/2000	Ferguson	Robby	4232 Tuller Ave.	San Carlos	FL	33891-1178	(941) 555-7039
2209	10/15/2000	Fromthart	Lisa	32 Redcoat Rd.	Cypress Lake	FL	33205-6911	(941) 555-0110
1359	09/09/2000	Gapasin	Ken	2633 E. Fountain St.	Iona	FL	33101-0093	(941) 555-0589
1291	01/21/2000	Gomez	Alfonso	3429 S. Grandview St.	Fort Myers	FL	33301-1268	(941) 555-2395
2247	12/18/2000	Harvey	Sarah	73 Lakeview Dr.	Cypress Lake	FL	33205-0093	(941) 555-7144
1345	04/15/2000	Helfand	Eric	4601 E. Willow Dr.	Cypress Lake	FL	33205-0093	(941) 555-9101
2246	12/15/2000	Hogan	Ryan	1389 E. Northview Dr.	Iona	FL	33101-7468	(941) 555-1010
1330	03/10/2000	Jensen	Chris	601 Alpha Dr.	San Carlos	FL	33891-1605	(941) 555-0018
1302	02/04/2000	Kieken	Kimberly	942 S. Golf Dr.	Fort Myers	FL	33301-1268	(941) 555-7564
1221	01/17/1998	Kim	Young	89 College Ave.	Forest Island	FL	33174	(941) 555-1059
1265	12/16/1998	Lahti	Jill	5401 E. Thomas Rd.	Forest Island	FL	33174	(941) 555-7765
1292	01/21/2000	Larson	Alicia	345 W. Mill Ave.	Iona	FL	33101-7468	(941) 555-7717
1341	04/15/2000	Lembi	Damon	4389 S. Rita Ln.	Fort Myers	FL	33301-1268	(941) 555-4747
1200	01/09/1998	Lettow	Ryan	358 Maple Dr.	Fort Myers	FL	33301-1268	(941) 555-2805
2208	10/15/2000	Lindau	Kristina	1947 E. Watson	Fort Myers	FL	33301-1268	(941) 555-6363
0340	05/05/1996	Lopez	Mina	4290 E. Alameda Dr.	Cypress Lake	FL	33205-0093	(941) 555-5050
1354	07/31/2000	Martinez	Julie	7115 E. Roosevelt Dr.	Iona	FL	33101-0093	(941) 555-1044
2240	11/24/2000	Mazeau	Rebecca	7383 Oak Dr.	Fort Myers	FL	33301-1268	(941) 555-1093
0434	07/05/1996	Merwin	Adda	947 S. Forest	Fort Myers	FL	33301-1268	(941) 555-4494

Record: ◄ ◄ 4 ► ►► ►* of 53
Number assigned to each employee as hired.

Figure 2–27

Next you want to check the rest of the table to see if you see any other problems.

> As you drag the scroll box, the record location is displayed in the scrolltips box [Record: 32 of 53].

2. ■ **Use the scroll box to scroll down to record 32.**

Now you can see that the records for Suzanne and Mark Reddie are sorted by last name but not by first name. You want all records that have the same last name to be further sorted by first name.

Sorting on Multiple Fields

> If the columns are not adjacent, you can hide the columns that are in between. If they are not in the correct order, you can move the columns. You will learn how to do this in Tutorial 3.

To sort first names within same last names, you need to sort using multiple sort fields. When sorting on multiple fields, the fields must be adjacent to each other, and the most important field in the sort must be to the left of the secondary field. The Last Name and First Name fields are already in the correct locations for the sort you want to perform. To specify the fields to sort on, both columns must be selected.

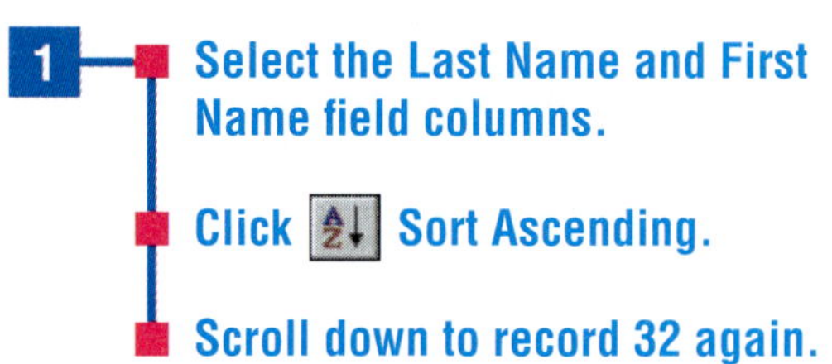

1 Select the Last Name and First Name field columns.

Click ![A-Z Sort Ascending] Sort Ascending.

Scroll down to record 32 again.

Your screen should be similar to Figure 2–28.

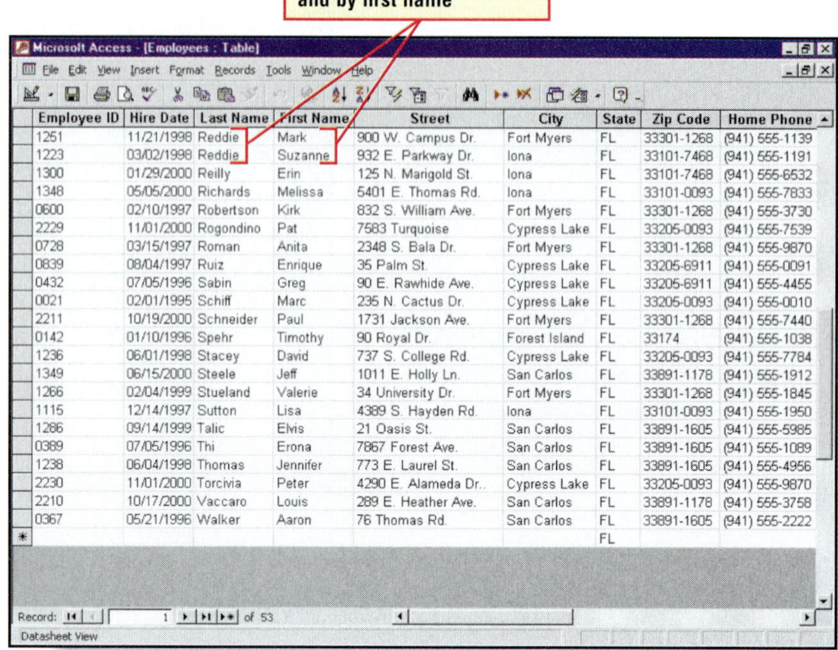

Figure 2–28

The record for Mark Reddie is now before the record for Suzanne. As you can see, sorting is a fast, useful tool. The sort order remains in effect until you remove the sort or replace it with a new sort order. Although Access remembers your sort order even when you exit the program, it does not actually change the table records. You can remove the sort at any time to restore the records to the primary key sort order. To do this,

2 Choose **R**ecords/**R**emove Filter/Sort.

Close the table and save your design changes.

Note: If you are ending your session now, close the database file and exit Access. When you begin again, load Access and open the Employee Records database.

Creating a Form

One of your objectives is to make the database easy to use. You know from experience that long hours of viewing large tables can be tiring. Therefore you want to create an onscreen form to make this table easier to view and use.

Concept ⑥ Forms

A **form** is a database object used primarily to display records onscreen to make it easier to enter new records and to make changes to existing records. Forms are based on an underlying table, and include design control elements such as descriptive text, titles, labels, lines, boxes, and pictures. Forms often use calculations as well, to summarize data that is not listed on the actual table, such as a sales total. Forms make working with long lists of data easier. They enable people to use the data in the tables without having to sift through many lines of data to find the exact record.

You want the onscreen form to be similar to the paper form that is completed by each new employee when hired. The information from that form is used as the source of input for the new record that will be added to the table for the new employee.

As when creating a table, there are several different methods that can be used to create a form. You will use the Form Wizard to guide you through the steps to create a form.

1 ● **To create a form, click** [⊞ Forms] **to open the Forms object.**

● **Double-click** Create form by using wizard**.**

Your screen should be similar to Figure 2–29.

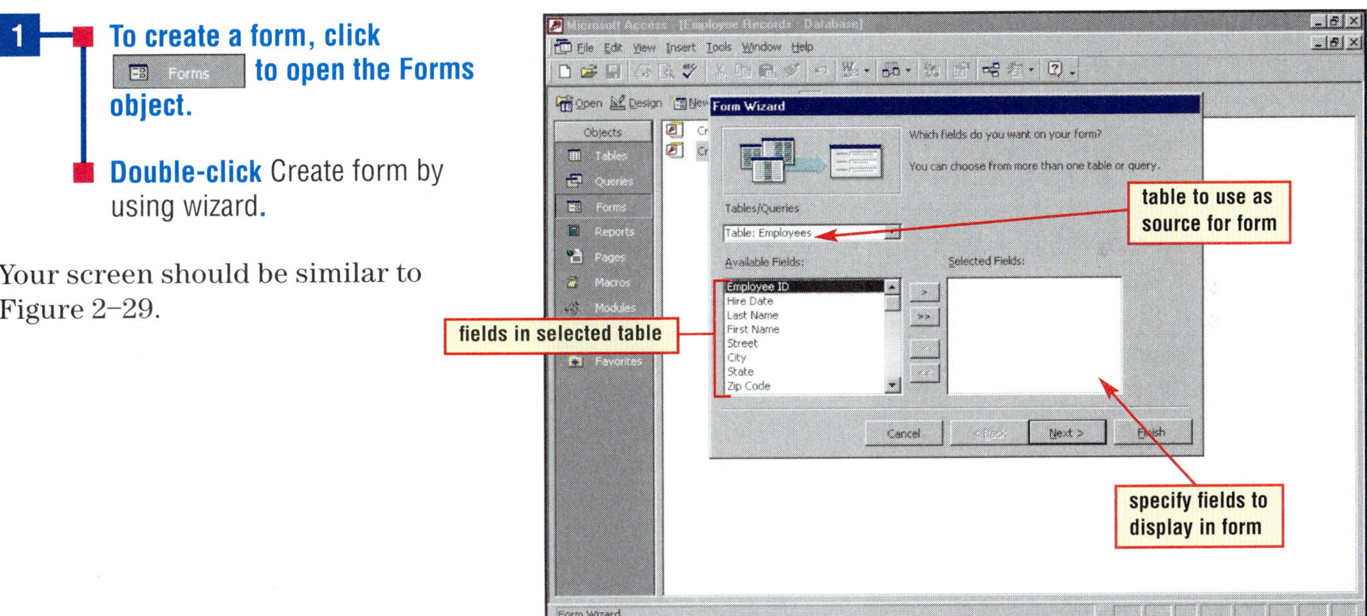

Figure 2–29

The Form Wizard dialog box displays the name of the current table, Employees, in the Tables/Queries list box. This is the underlying table that will be used when creating the form. If your database contained multiple tables, you could open the Tables/Queries drop-down list to select the appropriate underlying table to use for the form.

After selecting the table, you select the fields to include in the form. The fields from the selected table will appear in the Available Fields list box. The order in which you select the fields is the **tab order**, or the order in which the highlight will move through the fields on the form when you press [Tab] during data entry. You would like the order to be the same as the order on the paper form. To add the First Name field to the form first, from the Available Fields list box,

2 ■ **Select** First Name.

■ **Click** > .

You can also double-click on each field name in the Available Fields list box to move the field name to the Selected Fields list box.

The >> button adds all available fields to the Selected Fields list.

Your screen should be similar to Figure 2–30.

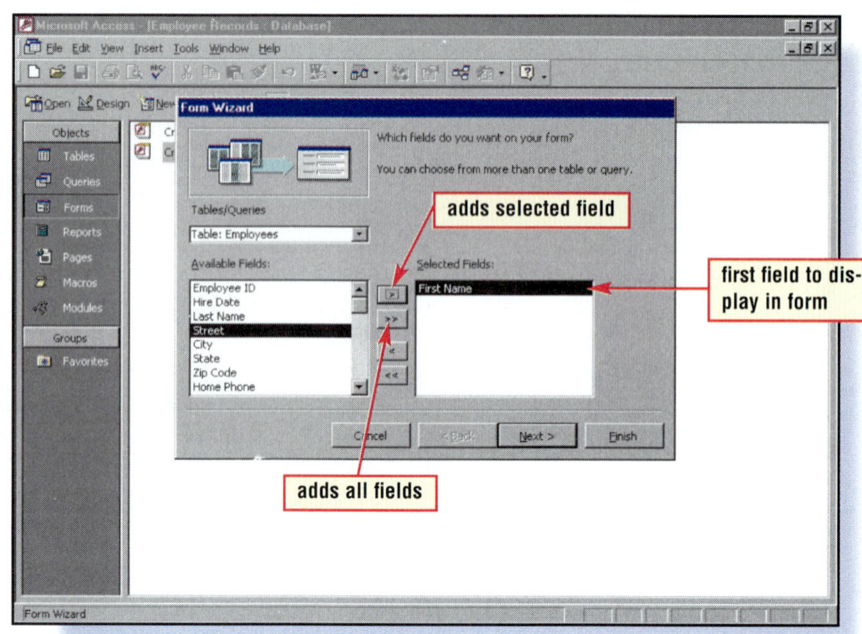

Figure 2–30

The First Name field is removed from the Available Fields list and added to the top of the Selected Fields list box.

3 ■ **In the same manner, select the fields in the order shown below and add them to the Selected Fields list.**

Last Name
Street
City
State
Zip Code
Home Phone
Gender
Birth Date
Employee ID
Hire Date
Picture

Your screen should be similar to Figure 2–31.

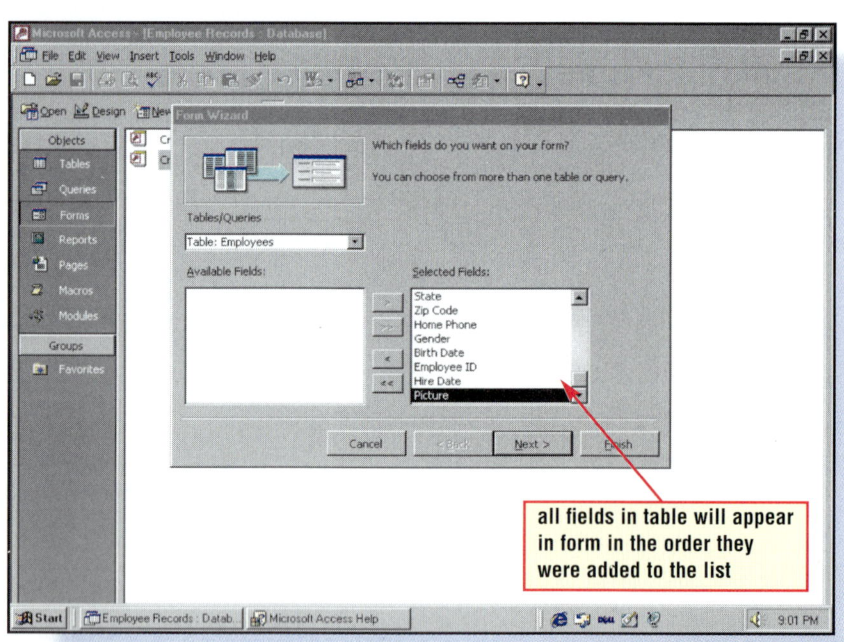

Figure 2–31

When you are done, the Available Fields list box is empty, and the Selected Fields list box lists the fields in the selected order. To move to the next Form Wizard screen,

4 Click Next >.

Your screen should be similar to Figure 2–32.

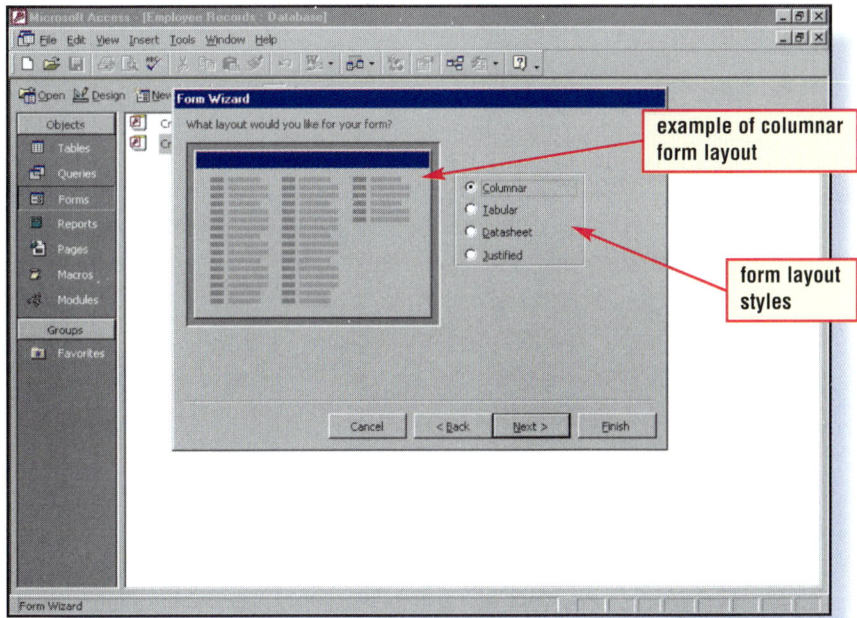

Figure 2–32

In this Wizard dialog box you are asked to select the layout for the form. Four form layouts are available: Columnar, Tabular, Datasheet, and Justified. They are described in the table below.

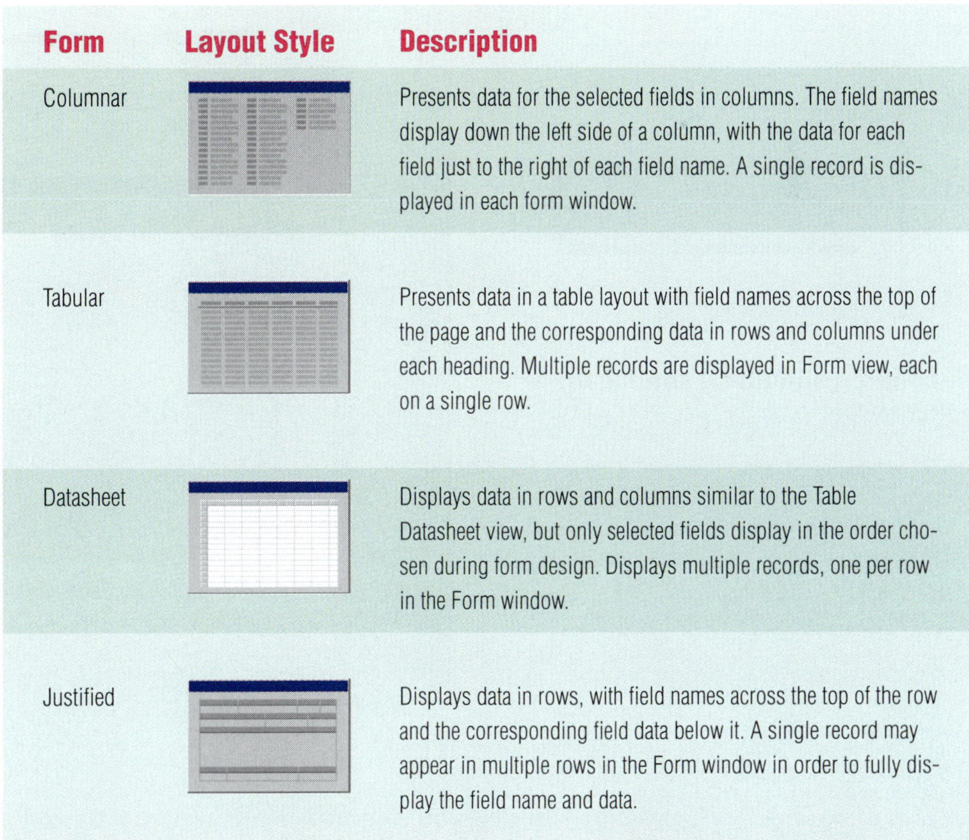

Form	Layout Style	Description
Columnar		Presents data for the selected fields in columns. The field names display down the left side of a column, with the data for each field just to the right of each field name. A single record is displayed in each form window.
Tabular		Presents data in a table layout with field names across the top of the page and the corresponding data in rows and columns under each heading. Multiple records are displayed in Form view, each on a single row.
Datasheet		Displays data in rows and columns similar to the Table Datasheet view, but only selected fields display in the order chosen during form design. Displays multiple records, one per row in the Form window.
Justified		Displays data in rows, with field names across the top of the row and the corresponding field data below it. A single record may appear in multiple rows in the Form window in order to fully display the field name and data.

The columnar layout would appear most similar to the paper form currently in use by the personnel department.

5 ■ **If necessary, select** Columnar.

■ **Click** [Next >] .

Your screen should be similar to
Figure 2–33.

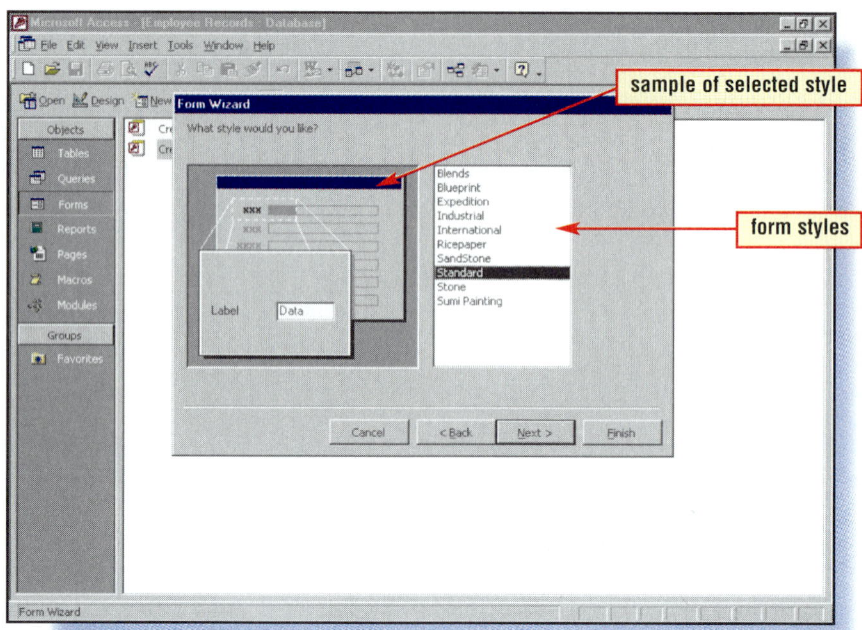

Figure 2–33

From the next dialog box, you select from ten different styles for your
form. A sample of each style as it is selected is displayed on the left side of
the dialog box. Standard is the default selection. You will create the form
using the Blends style.

6 ■ **Select** Blends.

■ **Click** [Next >] .

Your screen should be similar to
Figure 2–34.

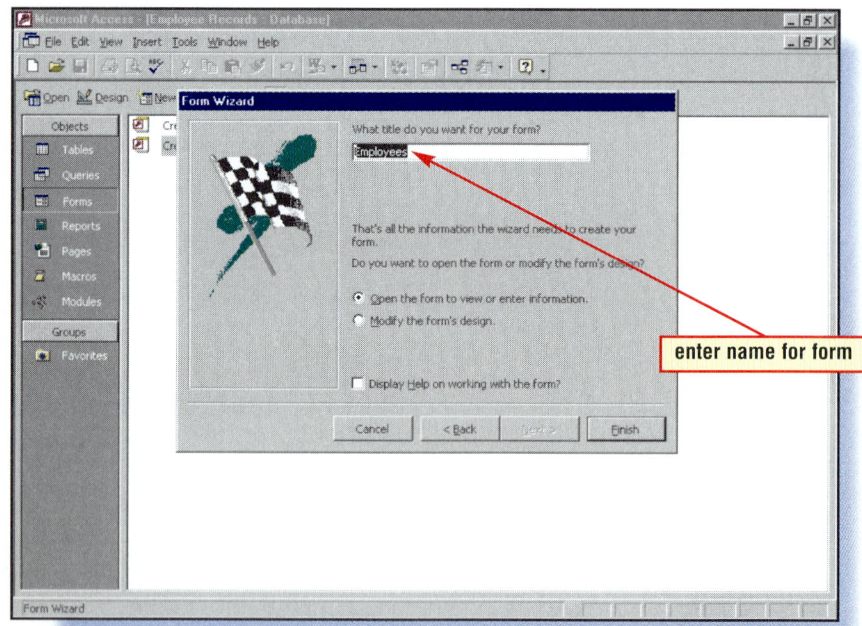

Figure 2–34

Finally, you need to enter a form title to be used as the name of the form,
and you need to specify whether the form should open with data displayed
in it. The Wizard uses the name of the table as the default form title. You
want the form to display data, but you want to change the form's title. To
do this,

7 Type **Employee Data Form**.

Click [Finish].

If necessary, maximize the Form window.

Your screen should be similar to Figure 2–35.

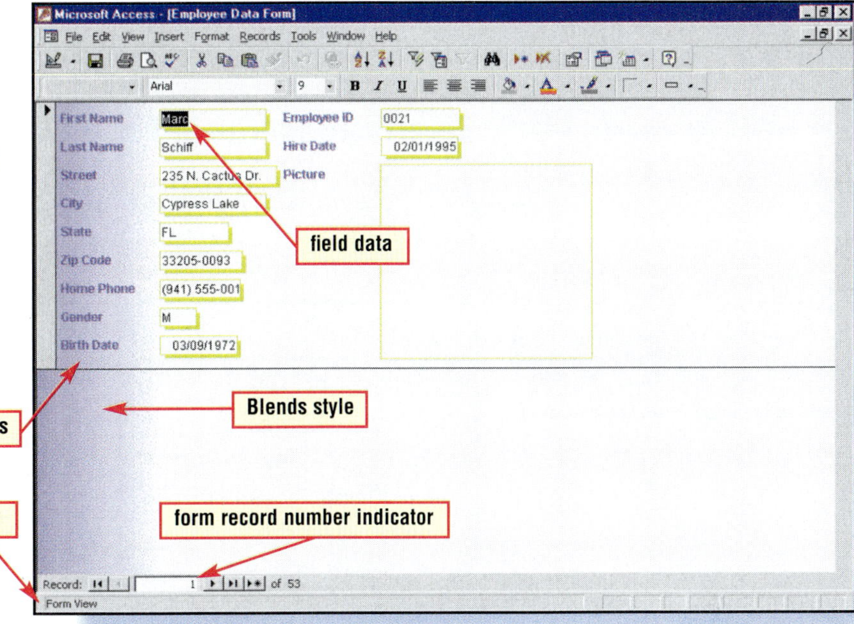

Figure 2–35

The completed form is displayed in the Form view window. The form displays the selected fields in columnar layout using the Blends style. The field name labels are in two columns with the field data text boxes in adjacent columns to the right. The employee information for Marc Schiff, the current record in the table, is displayed in the text boxes.

You use the same navigation keys in Form view that you used in Datasheet view. You can move between fields in the form by using the [Tab], [←Enter], [⇧Shift] + [Tab], and directional arrow keys on the keyboard (the navigation buttons at the bottom of the form). The [Page Up] and [Page Down] keys allow you to move between records in Form view. You can also use the Find command to locate and display specific records.

8 Display the record for Lisa Sutton.

> If you use the Find command, you can select the name from the Find drop-down list.

Your screen should be similar to Figure 2–36.

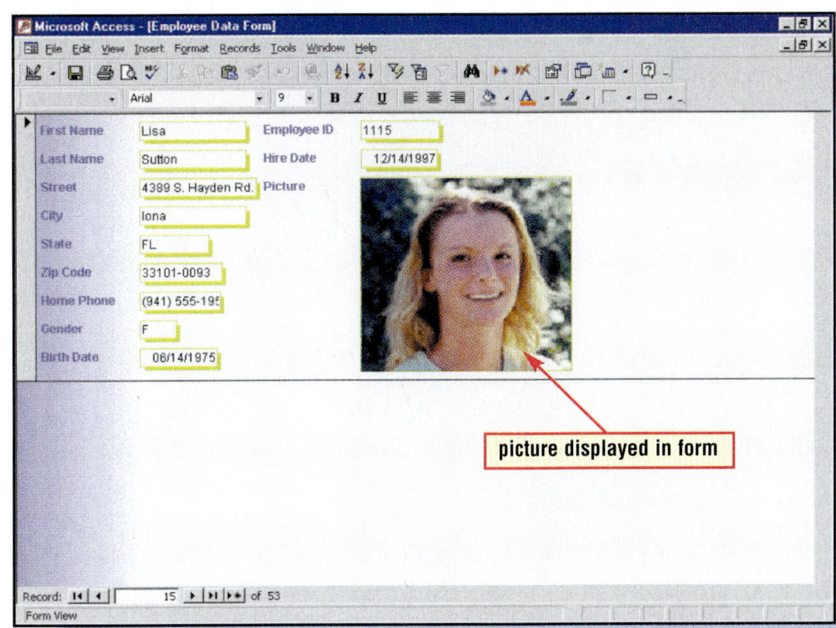

Figure 2–36

Reminder: You would double-click on the picture to see an enlarged view and modify the object.

Lisa Sutton's record is displayed in the form. Because this record contains the inserted picture in the Picture field, the photo is displayed.

Entering Records in Form View

Now you want to add a few new employee records from data on the paper form shown below to the table.

Use ▶* New Record in the Form toolbar or the ▶* navigation button to display a blank form.

EMPLOYEE DATA

First Name	Kevin	Last Name	Tillman
Street	89 E. Southern Dr.		
City	Fort Myers	State FL	Zip Code 33301-2316
Home Phone	(941) 555-3434		
Gender	M	Birth Date	April 13, 1971

For Personnel Use Only:

Employee ID   2295

Hire Date   Jan. 12, 2001

1 — Move to a new blank entry form and enter the data shown in the paper form for a new record.

Press (Tab) to move to the next field.

Your screen should be similar to Figure 2–37.

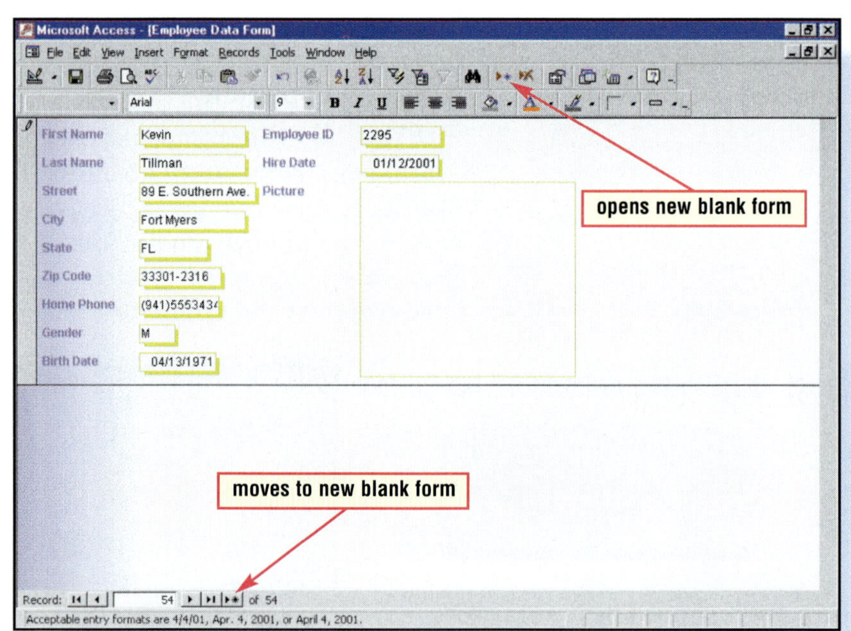

Figure 2–37

You will learn how to enhance forms in Tutorial 3.

Using the form makes entering the new employee data much faster because the fields are in the same order as the information in the paper Employee Data form used by the personnel department.

When using the Form Wizard most of the field text boxes are appropriately sized to display the data in the field. You probably noticed, however, that the Home Phone field is not quite large enough. You will learn how to fix this problem by sizing the object in the next tutorial.

2 Enter another record using your special Employee ID 9999 and your first and last name. Enter the current date as your Hire Date. The data in all other fields can be fictitious.

To see the records you entered in Form Datasheet view, open the 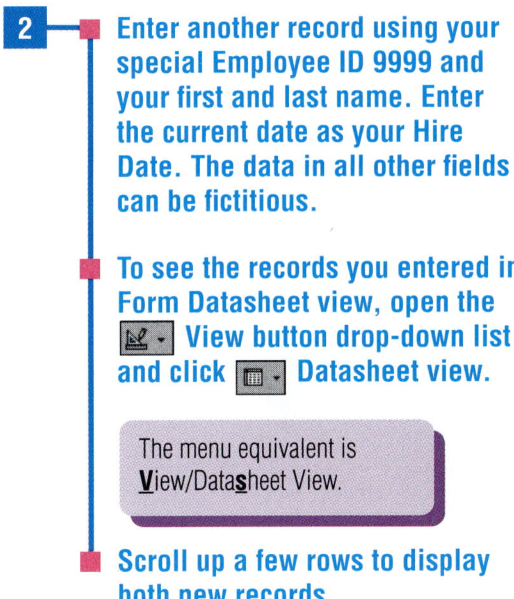 View button drop-down list and click 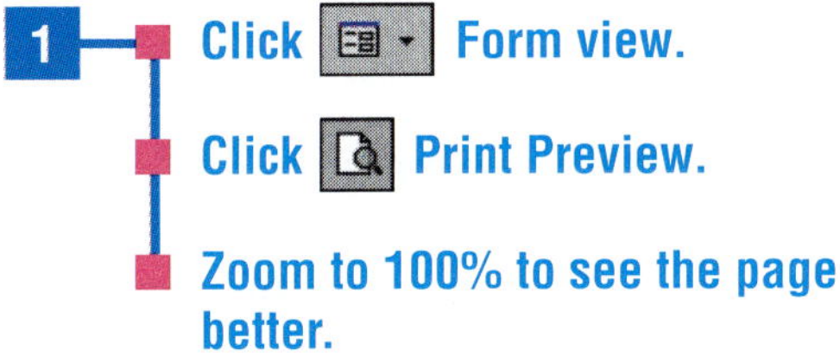 Datasheet view.

> The menu equivalent is **V**iew/Data**s**heet View.

Scroll up a few rows to display both new records.

Your screen should be similar to Figure 2–38.

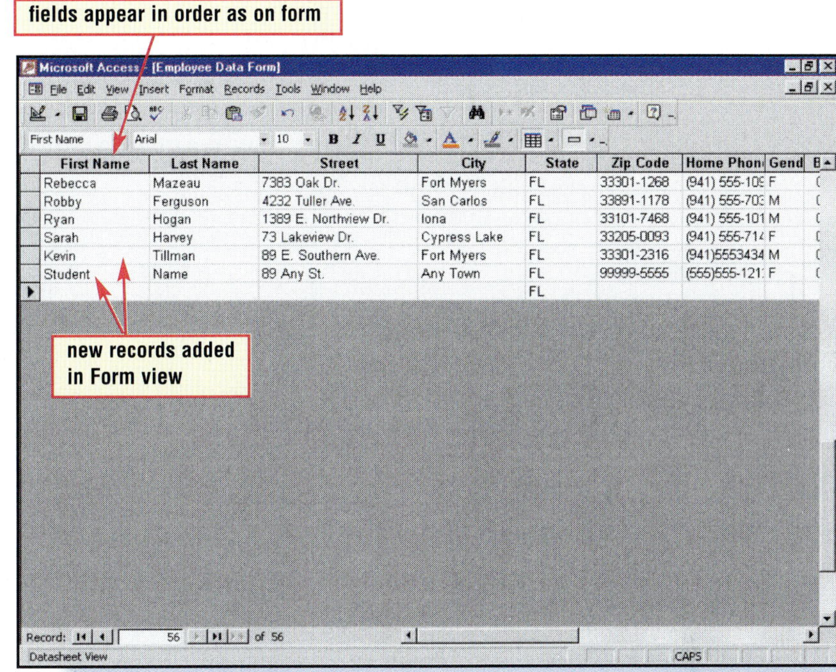

Figure 2–38

Form Datasheet view provides a datasheet view of the form data. Notice that the field columns are in the same order as in the form. Also notice that the new records are not in primary key order by employee number. When you open the table in Datasheet view, the new records will appear in primary key order.

Previewing and Printing a Form

You want to preview, then print just the form displaying your record.

1 Click 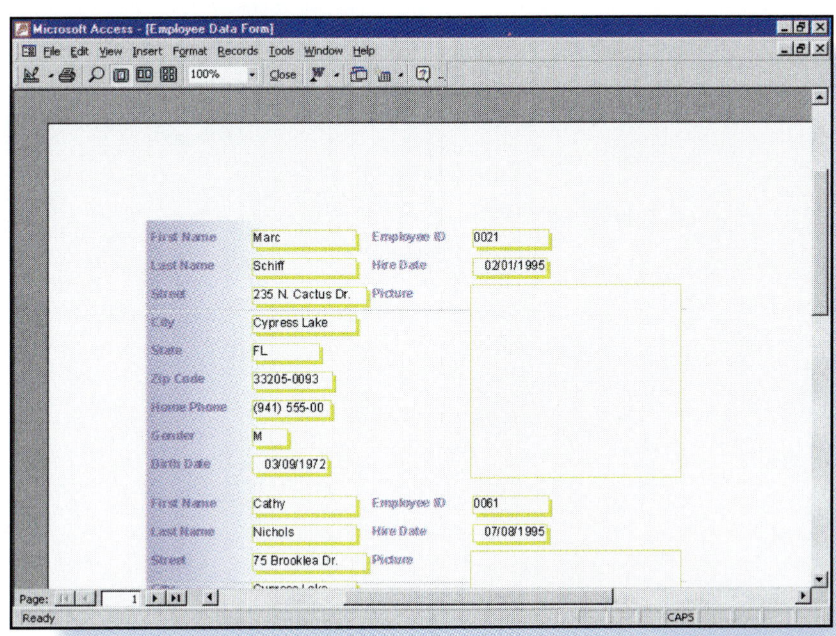 Form view.

Click Print Preview.

Zoom to 100% to see the page better.

Your screen should be similar to Figure 2–39.

Figure 2–39

Print Preview displays whatever view you were last using. In this case, because you were last in Form view, the form is displayed in the Preview window. Access prints as many records as can be printed on a page in the Form layout. You want to print only the form displaying your record. To do this,

2 — **Click** Close .

Display your record in the form.

Click the gray bar along the left side of the form to select the entire record.

The menu equivalent is **E**dit/S**e**lect Record.

Choose File/Print.

Select Selected Record(s).

Click OK .

Your printed output should be similar to Figure 2–40.

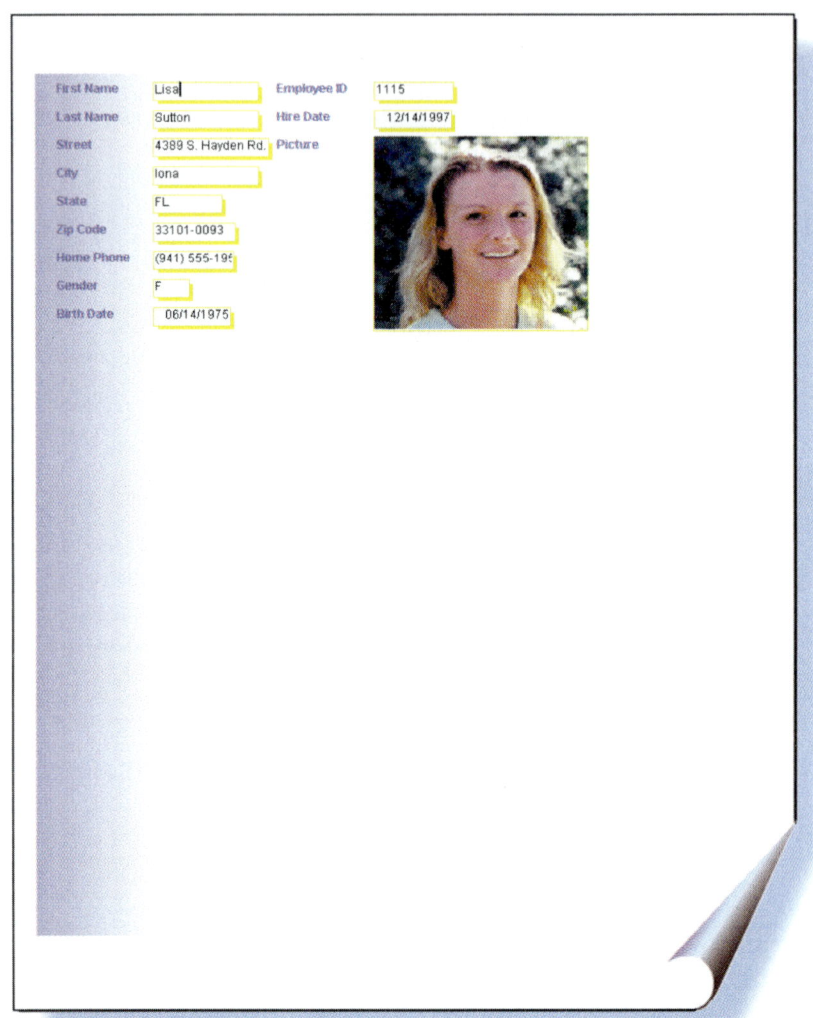

Figure 2–40

Closing and Saving a Form

Next you will close and save the form.

1 ■ **Close the Form window.**

The Database window is displayed, showing the new form object name in the Forms tab object list.

2 ■ **Exit Access.**

Warning: Do not remove your data disk from the drive until you exit Access.

Tutorial 2: Modifying a Table and Creating a Form

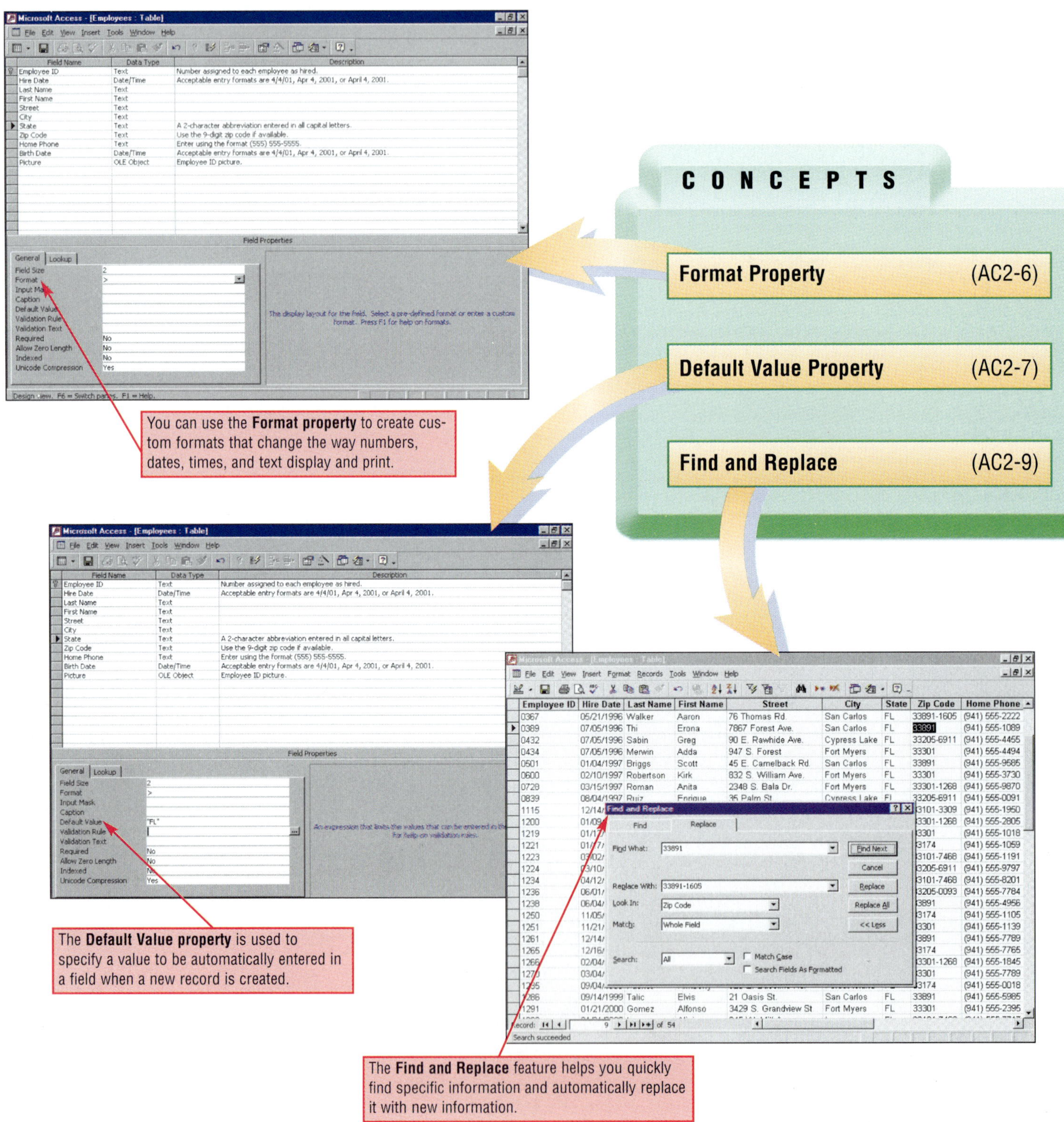

You can use the **Format property** to create custom formats that change the way numbers, dates, times, and text display and print.

The **Default Value property** is used to specify a value to be automatically entered in a field when a new record is created.

The **Find and Replace** feature helps you quickly find specific information and automatically replace it with new information.

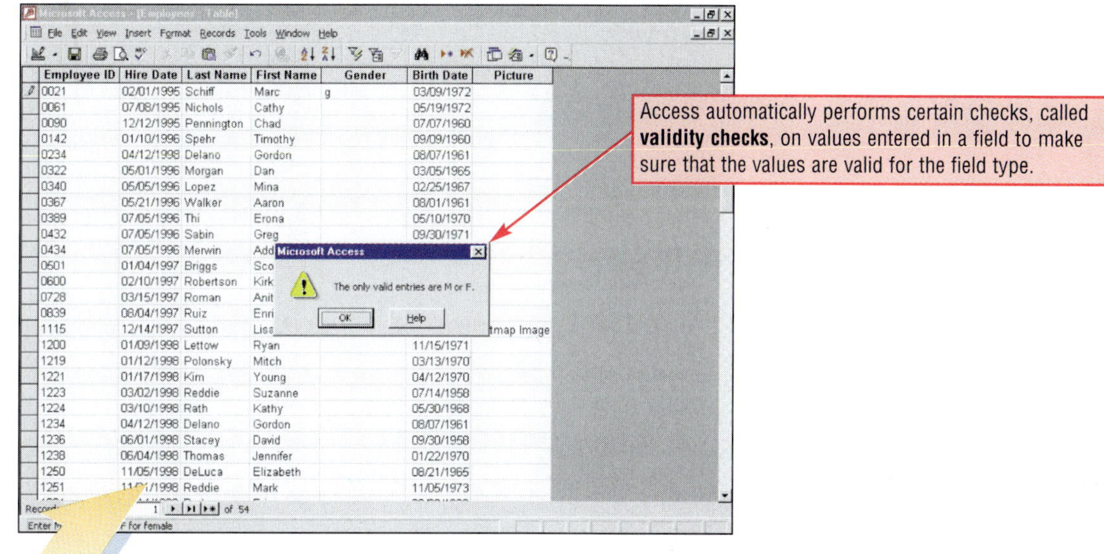

You can quickly reorder records in a table by **sorting** a table to display in a different record order.

Validity Check   (AC2-17)

Sort   (AC2-21)

Form   (AC2-25)

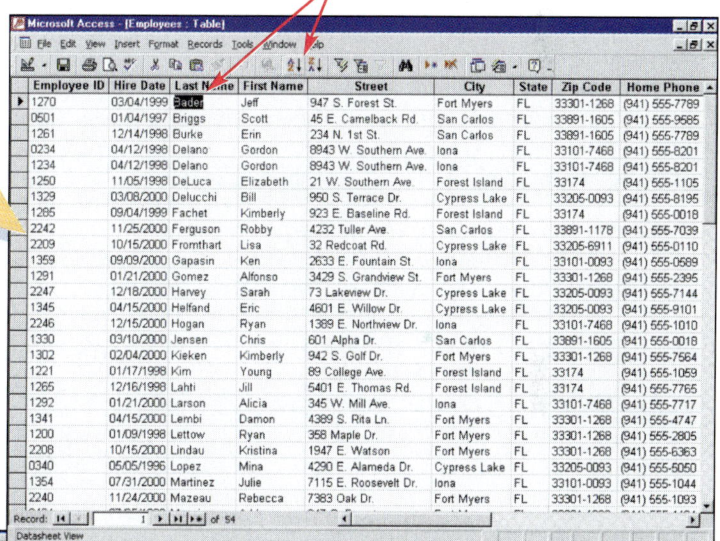

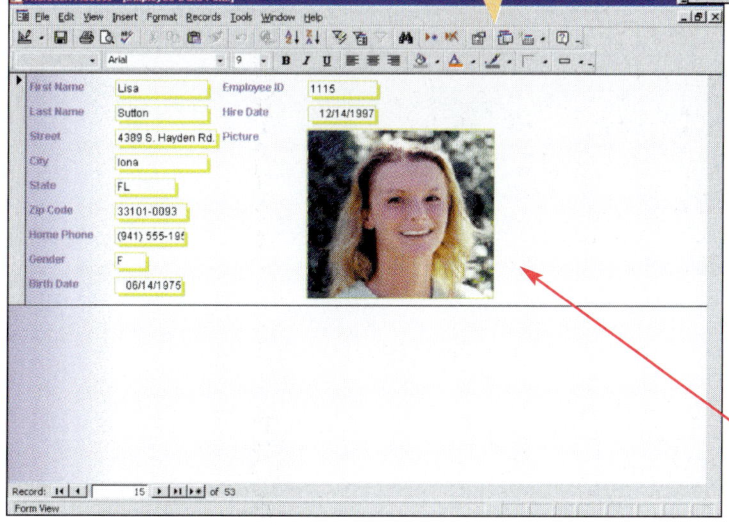

Tutorial Review

Key Terms

character string AC2-8	operator AC2-17	validity check AC2-17
expression AC2-17	sort AC2-21	value AC2-17
form AC2-25	tab order AC2-25	
identifier AC2-17	validation text AC2-17	

Command Summary

Command	Shortcut Keys	Button	Action
Edit/**U**ndo	Ctrl + Z		Cancels last action
Edit/**Cut**	Ctrl + X or Del	or	Deletes selected record
Edit/Se**l**ect Record	Shift + Spacebar		Selects current record
Edit/**F**ind	Ctrl + F		Locates specified data
Edit/**R**eplace	Ctrl + H		Locates and replaces specified data
View/**D**esign View			Display Design view
View/**F**orm View			Displays a form in Form view
Insert/**R**ows			Inserts a new field in table in Design view
Format/**H**ide Columns			Hides columns in Datasheet view
Format/**U**nhide Columns			Redisplays hidden columns in Datasheet view
Records/**S**ort/Sort **A**scending			Reorders records in ascending alphabetical order

Screen Identification

In the following screen, several items are identified by letters. Enter the correct term for each item in the spaces that follow.

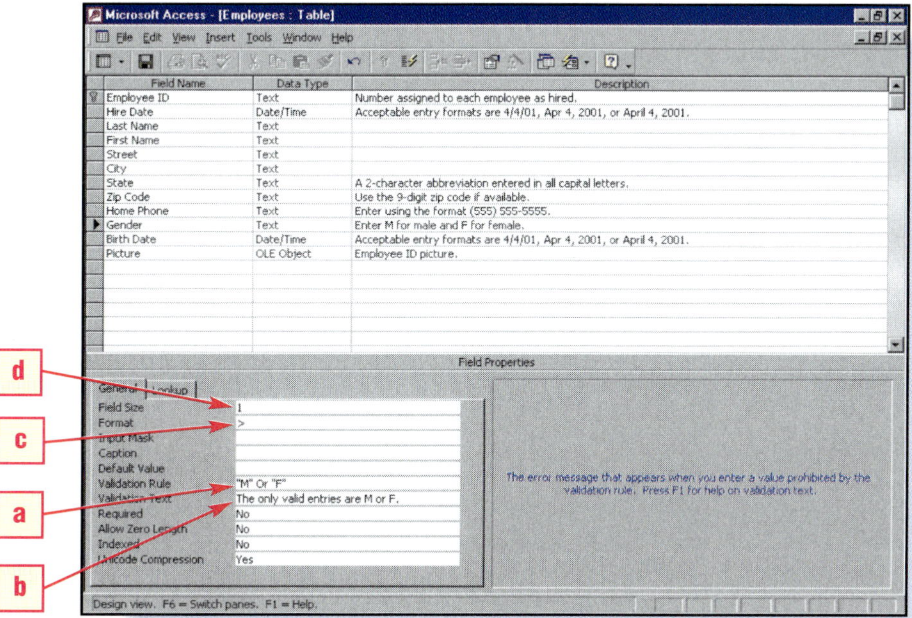

a. _________________ b. _________________ c. _________________ d. _________________

Matching

Match the letter to the correct item in the numbered list.

1. match case	_______ **a.**	cancels your last action
2. [Ctrl] + [Home]	_______ **b.**	used to check that a value entered in a field is valid for the field type
3. ↶	_______ **c.**	database object used primarily for onscreen display
4. character string	_______ **d.**	moves to the first field of the first record
5. tab order	_______ **e.**	makes the find case sensitive
6. >	_______ **f.**	displays Design view
7. sort	_______ **g.**	order in which pressing [Tab] moves through fields in a form
8. validity check	_______ **h.**	a group of characters
9.	_______ **i.**	changes display order of a table
10. form	_______ **j.**	format character that forces all data in field to uppercase

True/False

Circle the correct answer to the following statements.

1. Format properties do not change the way Access stores data.   True   False

2. The Format property determines the value automatically entered into a field of a new record.   True   False

3. An identifier is a symbol or word that indicates that an operation is to be performed.   True   False

4. The Find command will locate specific values in a field and automatically replace them.   True   False

5. Format properties change the way data is displayed.   True   False

6. The Default Value property is commonly used when most of the entries in a field will be the same for the entire table.   True   False

7. Values are numbers, dates, or pictures.   True   False

8. The Replace command will automatically restore properties to an object.   True   False

9. Sorting reorders records in a table.   True   False

10. Forms are database objects used primarily for report generation.   True   False

Multiple Choice

Circle the correct answer to the following statements.

1. Format ________ is used to create custom formats that change the way numbers, dates, times, and text display and print.

   a. specification
   b. alignment
   c. range
   d. property

2. Values to be automatically entered into a field are specified in the ________ Value property.

   a. Auto
   b. Initial
   c. Default
   d. Assumed

3. ________ are automatically performed on values entered in a field to make sure that the values are valid for the field type.

   a. Object validations
   b. Security specifications
   c. Form searches
   d. Validity checks

4. You can quickly reorder ________ in a table by sorting.

   a. fields
   b. properties
   c. records
   d. forms

5. Forms are based on the underlying table by using design _________ elements.

   a. control
   b. default
   c. property
   d. object

6. To change the format of a field, different ________ are entered in the Format text box.

   a. symbols
   b. buttons
   c. objects
   d. graphics

7. When users add a record to a table, they can either accept the ________ value or enter another value.

   a. default
   b. initial
   c. last
   d. null

8. Expressions are combinations of ________ that are used to create validity checks, queries, forms, and reports.

   a. symbols
   b. objects
   c. functions
   d. values

9. Data sorted in ________ order is arrange alphabetically A to Z or numerically 0 to 9.

   a. increasing
   b. descending
   c. ascending
   d. decreasing

10. Forms are database objects used primarily to display records ________ to make it easier to enter new records and to make changes to existing records.

   a. numerically
   b. onscreen
   c. in reports
   d. alphabetically

Fill-In Questions

Complete the following statements by filling in the blanks with the correct terms.

1. A(n) _________ is a combination of symbols that produces specific results.

2. The _________ property is used to specify a value that is automatically entered in a field when a new record is created.

3. When _________ are performed, Access makes sure that the entry is acceptable in the field.

4. Records can be temporarily displayed in a different order by using the _________ feature.

5. Forms are primarily used for _________ and making changes to existing records.

6. The _________ property changes the way data appears in a field.

7. The four form layouts are _________ , _________ , _________ , and _________ .

8. Use _________ to cancel your last action.

9. The _________ layout creates a form that displays records with field names across the top of the page and records in rows.

10. To return to _________ order, you must remove the temporary sort.

Discussion Questions

1. Discuss several different format properties and how they are used in a database.

2. Discuss the different types of form layouts and why you would use one layout type over another.

3. Discuss how validity checks work. What are some advantages of adding validity checks to a field? Include several examples.

4. Discuss the different ways records can be sorted. What are some advantages of sorting records?

Hands-On Practice Exercises

Step by Step

1. Daria O'Dell is very impressed with the work you have done on the spa's database. After an initial review of the database, Ms. O'Dell realizes that the inclusion of additional data in the database can help her with other administrative functions. For example, as part of her future advertising campaigns, she would like to send birthday cards to each of her clients and wonders if it is possible to include birth date information in the database. Also, she would like you to modify some client records, create a form to ease data entry, and print a copy of the form. Your completed form is shown here.

To make the requested changes to the database and create the form, follow these steps:

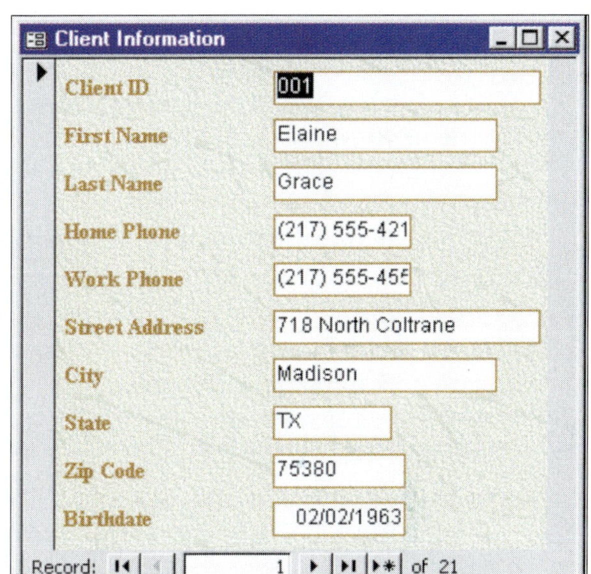

a. Open the database on your data disk named Spa and the table named Clients.

b. In Design view, add the following field to the end of the table:

Field name: **Birthdate**

Data type: **Date/Time**

Description: **Identifies client's birthday**

Field format: **Short date**

c. Make the First Name and Last Name required fields. Hint: Set the Required property to Yes.

d. Save the table design changes and return to Datasheet view. Update the table by filling in the new field for each record with appropriate data. Include several birthdates before 01/01/64.

e. Edit the appropriate records to reflect the client changes that Ms. O'Dell gave you:

- Sally Grimes has moved to 1499 Parkview. The city, state, and zip code will remain the same.

- Mr. Lin Chen has a new home telephone number. It is now (217) 555-9076.

- Debbie Linderson just called and said that she is moving to San Francisco, California. She has asked that her record be deleted from the spa's database.

f. Close the table.

g. Use the Form Wizard to create a form for the Clients table. Include all fields as listed. Use the columnar layout and Expedition style. Title the form **Client Information**.

h. Use the new form to enter the following records:

Record 1	Record 2
023	024
Georgia	[Your first name]
Kendall	[Your last name]
(217) 555-5522	(217) 555-0091
(217) 555-3434	[no work phone]
243 May Avenue	1234 Timber
Bakersville	Alison
TX	TX
75380	76890
3/21/73	8/14/74

i. Preview and print the form for the second new record you added.

2. Your managing editor at the Daily Digest has asked you to expand the advertiser database to include the ad size, rate, and frequency that the client has contracted for. He would also like you to create a data-entry form when you're finished with the basic design. Your completed form is shown here.

To add the new fields to the database and create the form, follow these steps:

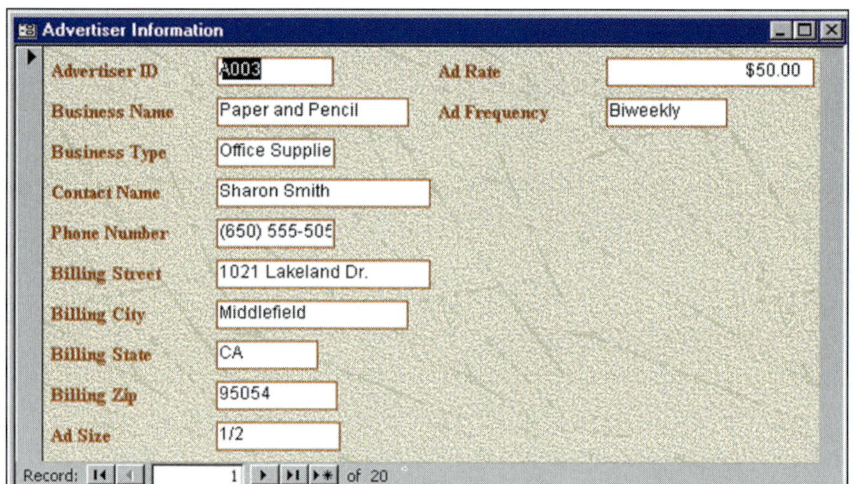

a. Open the database on your data disk named Daily Digest and the table named Advertisers.

b. In Design view, add the following three fields to the table:

Field name:	Ad Size
Data type:	Text
Description:	Enter one of the following: ¼, ½, or Full
Field size:	5

Field name:	Ad Rate
Data type:	Currency
Description:	Contracted rate per ad

Field name:	Ad Frequency
Data type:	Text
Description:	Enter one of the following: Daily, Weekly, Biweekly, or Monthly
Field size:	10

c. Save the table design changes and return to Datasheet View. Update the table by filling in the new fields for each record. Readjust the column widths as necessary.

d. Close the table.

e. Use the Form Wizard to create a form for the Advertisers table. Include all the table fields in their current order. Use the columnar layout and Expedition style. Title the form **Advertiser Information**.

f.   Use the new form to enter the following records:

Record 1	**Record 2**
E592	A437
Hearth & Home	Fun Stuff
Furniture Store	Toy Store
Doris Francis	[Your Name]
(650) 555-0022	(650) 555-1221
1002 Lincoln Rd.	802 Trenton Way
Temple	Beacon Shores
CA	CA
95056	95055
1/2	Full
50	100
Biweekly	Monthly

g. Preview and print the form for the second new record you added.

3. You and other employees of the Downtown Internet Café have been sharing the task of entering product and vendor information into the purchase items database. You are now ready to add fields that show the inventory on hand and to indicate special orders so Evan, the cafe owner, knows when to place an order. However, when you open the database, you noticed that some of the information for the existing fields is missing, incorrect, or inconsistent. You realize that besides adding the new fields, you need to change some of the field properties, specify required fields, correct some errors, and create a form that reflects the cafe's Vendor Information Sheet to make data entry easier. When you are finished, you will end up with an easy-to-use data entry form shown here.

To make the changes and create the form, follow these steps:

a.   Open the database on your data disk named Cafe Purchases and the table named Inventory.

b.   Item #6983 was a holiday season special and the cafe is no longer carrying it, so delete that item from the table.

c.   Use the Replace command to replace item #2579 with the correct item number, 2575. Use the same command to replace The Beverage Co. with their new name, Better Beverages, Inc. Adjust the Vendor Name column to fit the new name.

d.   In Design view, make the Item #, Description, and Vendor Name required fields. Add a Format property to the State field to force the data in that field to display in all capital letters.

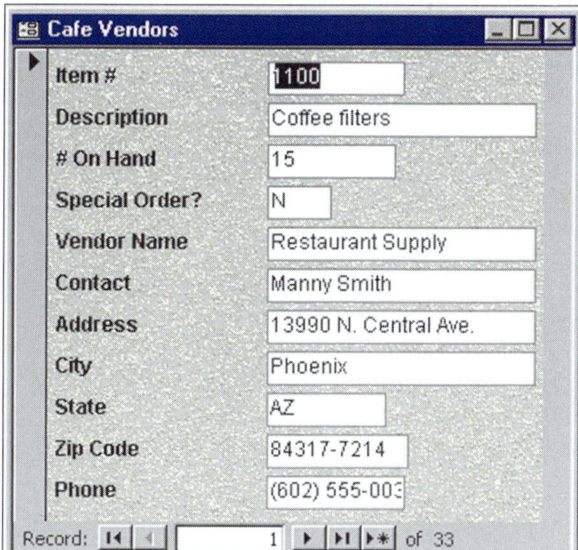

e. Add a field before the Vendor Name to specify the inventory on hand for each item:

Field name: # On Hand

Data type: Number

Description: Number of individual units (bags, boxes, etc.) in stock

Field size: Integer

f. Add another field before the Vendor Name to specify whether the item is a special order (not regularly stocked):

Field name: Special Order?

Data type: Text

Description: Is this a special order item?

Field size: 1

Default value: N

Validation rule: Y or N

Validation text: The only valid entry is Y (yes) or N (no)

g. Return to Datasheet View and update the table by filling in the new fields for each record with data of your choice.

h. Use the Form Wizard to create a columnar form with the SandStone style and include all the table fields in their current order. Title the form Cafe Vendors.

i. Use the new form to add the following purchase items to the table:

Record 1	Record 2
1102	2924
Napkins	Coffee mugs
50	12
N	Y
Restaurant Supply	Central Ceramics
Manny Smith	[your name]
13990 N. Central Ave.	772 Hayden Road
Phoenix	Scottsdale
AZ	AZ
84137-7214	85254
(602) 555-0037	(602) 555-1924

j. Preview and print the form for the second new record you added.

4. The EduSoft Company, which develops computer curriculums for grades K–8, has just hired you to update and maintain their software database. Some of the tasks your manager asks you to accomplish involve correcting some known errors and applying some validation rules. She would also like you to create a form, shown here, which will make it easier to enter new software titles. To update the database and create the form, follow these steps:

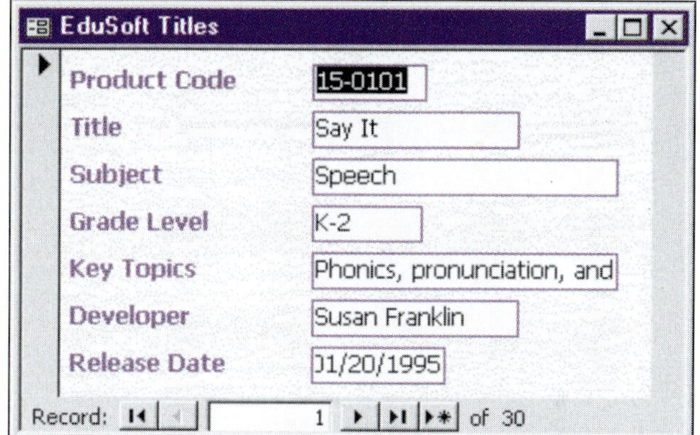

a. Open the database on your data disk named Learning and the table named Software.

b. The corrections you need to make to the table are related to the software titles. Sort the table in ascending order by Title so it will be easier to see the names you need to correct.

c. You have a note that the name of the Figure It series has been changed to Solve It. Use the Replace command (match the Start of Field to retain the numbers) or navigate through the table to find the three records with this title and change them.

d. The program called Reading & Writing was never released and has been replaced by separate reading and writing programs. Find and delete this record.

e. Switch to Design view and add a validity rule and text to the Grade Level field so that it only allows an entry of K–2, 3–5, or 6–8 (all three valid entries must be in quotes).

f. Add a field above Release Date to specify the name of the lead program developer for each title.

Field name:	Developer
Data type:	Text
Description:	Name of lead program developer
Field size:	20

g. Return to Datasheet view and hide the Title through Key Topic columns. Next you need to update the table by filling in the new field for each record. Each lead programmer has a unique two-digit prefix on their product numbers. Using Teri O'Neill and the other names of your choice, complete the Developer field for each record. For example, Teri O'Neill worked on products with the 36 prefix. Unhide the columns when you are done.

h. Create a columnar form using the Form Wizard. Use the Sumi Painting style and include all the fields in their current order. Name the form EduSoft Titles.

i. Use the form to enter a new record for a software program called Web Wise, Product Code 90–0103, which is currently in development for grades 6–8 to help them learn to use the Internet and do research. Enter your name as the developer. Preview and print the form for this new record.

5. You have continued to add records to the database for tracking the animals that come into and go out of Animal Angels. Now you need to modify the database structure and customize field properties to control the data entered by the Animal Angels volunteers who are assigned this task. You also want to create a form to make it easier for the volunteers to enter the necessary information, as shown here.

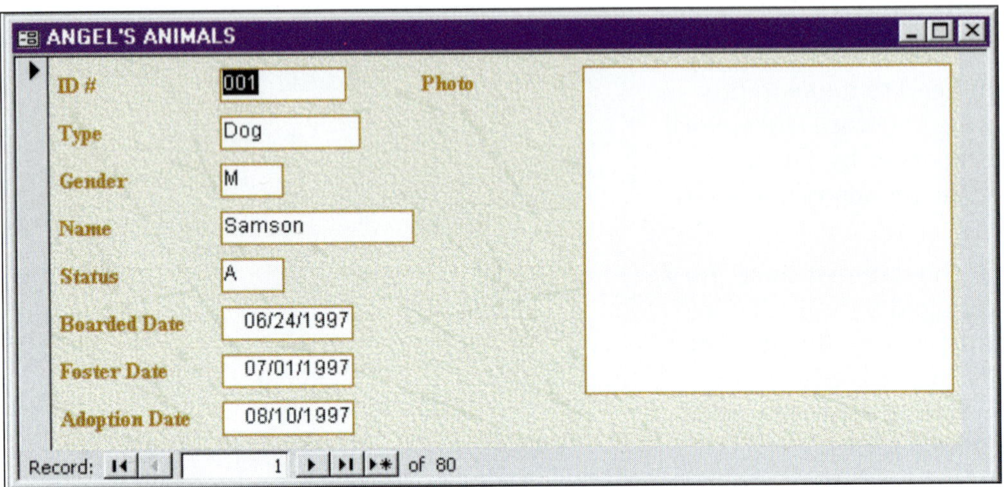

To enhance the Animal Angels database and create the form, follow these steps:

a.   Open the database named AA and the table named Animals.

b.   In Design view, insert the following field above the Boarded Date field:

Field name:	Status
Data type:	Text
Description:	Enter B (boarded), F (in foster home), or A (adopted)
Field size:	1
Format:	>

c.   Make the following additional changes to the database structure:

- Add a validation rule and appropriate validation text to the Gender field to accept only M or F (male or female). Also format the field to display the information uppercase.

- Add a validation rule and appropriate validation text to the Status field to accept only B, F, or A (boarded, foster home, or adopted).

d.   Return to Datasheet view and update the table by filling in the new Status field for each record with the data of your choice.

e.   So you can easily see the current status of the animals to ascertain which still need homes, sort the table in descending order by the Status, Boarded Date, Foster Date, and Adoption Date fields (hold down the ⇧Shift key and click the Status column and then the Adoption Date column). Change the status of Lemon to A and enter today's date as the Adoption Date. Remove the sort filter.

f.   Use the Form wizard to create a columnar form. Use the Expedition style and include all the fields in their current order. Title the form ANGEL'S ANIMALS.

g.   Add two records using the new form. Enter [your name]'s Pet in the Name field of the second record you add, and then select, preview, and print it.

On Your Own

6. You have heard from the employees of Adventure Travel that the database table you created is a bit unwieldy for them to enter the necessary data, because it now contains so many fields that it requires scrolling across the screen to locate them. You decide to create a form that will make entering data not only easier, but more attractive as well. Open the Adventure database you modified in Practice Exercise 6 of Tutorial 1 and use the Form Wizard to create a form for the Clients table. Use the form to enter one new record with a fictitious client name and another with your name as the client. Select and print the second new record.

7. While creating the basic database table for National Packing, you find out that the sales representatives sell from different product lines: packing cartons, insulation materials, and shipment tracking services. You need to add a field to accommodate this information before creating the final data entry form that you intend to submit to the company as part of your final database package. Open the database and table that you created in Practice Exercise 9 of Tutorial 1. Add a one-character product line field and enter the description **Enter 1 (packing cartons), 2 (insulation materials), or 3 (shipment tracking services)**. Add a corresponding validation rule and message. Update the table to include appropriate values in this new field in the existing records. Close the table, saving the changes. Then use the Form Wizard to create a data entry form for this table. To test the form, enter a new record with your name as the contact and then select and print the record.

8. The single-dentist office for which you created a patient database has now expanded to include a second dentist and receptionist, requiring you to identify required fields and to add more fields that identify which patient is assigned to which dentist. You also decide that creating a form for the database would make it easier for both you and the other receptionist to enter and locate patient information. Open the database and table you created in Practice Exercise 8 of Tutorial 1 and make the patient identification number, name, and phone number required fields. Add a Dentist Name field, with the two dentist's names in the field description and an appropriate validation rule and message. Update the table to "assign" some of the patients to one of the dentists and some patients to the other dentist. Sort the table by dentist name to see the results of your new assignments. "Reassign" one of the displayed patients and then remove the sort filter. Close the table, saving the changes. Create a form for the table using the Form Wizard. Enter two new records, one for each of the dentists. Use the Find command to locate the record form that has your name as the patient, and then select and print the displayed record.

9. The management at Lewis & Lewis, Inc., is quite impressed with the employee database you created. However, they would like you to include home phone numbers and addresses so the database can be used to send mail (such as Christmas cards, 401K information, and tax forms) to employees. Also, you have been asked to create a form that will make it easier for other administrative assistants to enter employee data into the database as well. Open the database and table you created in Practice Exercise 7 of Tutorial 1 and add home address and phone number fields to it. Update the table to include information in the new fields for the existing records. Sort the table by employee last name and use the Replace command or table navigation to locate and change the last name of a female employee who has gotten married since you first created the database. Use the same technique to locate and delete a record for an employee who has left the company. Remove the sort filter and close the table, saving the changes. Create a form for the table using the Form Wizard. Enter two new records. Use the Find command to locate the record form that has your name as the employee, and then select and print the displayed record.

10. You realize that you have left out some very important fields in the database table you created for the Oldies But Goodies company in Practice Exercise 10 of Tutorial 1—fields that identify the sources where you can obtain the vintage records your customers are looking for. Repeat your Web search for vintage record albums and note the resources (e.g., a company, such as Borders, or an individual collector who is offering these items online) for the titles you have included in your table. Add source name and address fields to the table and update it to include this information in the existing records. Sort the records according to the source name field and adjust the column widths to accommodate the new information. Remove the sort filter and close the table, saving the changes. Now, to make data entry easier for the company's employees, create a data entry form using the Form Wizard. Use the form to enter a new record with your name as the source, and then print it.

Analyzing Tables and Creating Reports

Competencies

After completing this tutorial, you will know how to:

1. Filter table records.
2. Create a query.
3. Move columns.
4. Query two tables.
5. Create a report.
6. Modify a report design.
7. Print a selected page.

Case Study

After modifying the structure of the table of employee records, you have continued to enter many more records. You have also created a second table in the database that contains employee information about location and job titles.

Filtered data displaying only records of employees living in Iona.

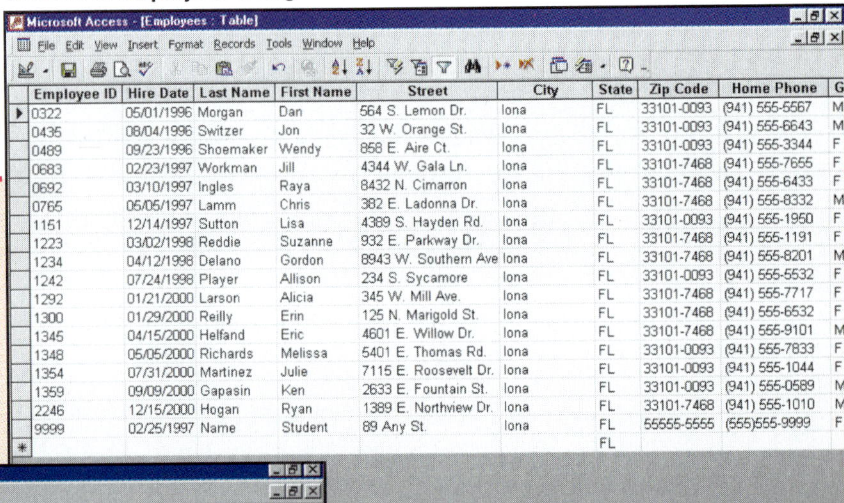

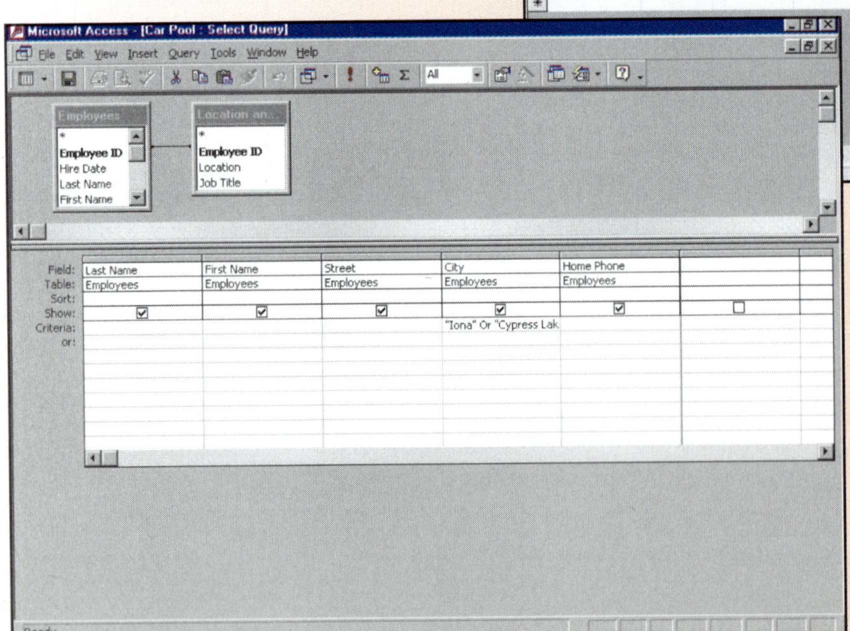

Query design view used to limit information in query results.

Again, the owners are very impressed with the database. They are anxious to see next how the information in the database can be used.

As you have seen, compiling, storing, and updating information in your database is very useful. The real strength of a database program, however, is how it can be used to find the information you need quickly and to manipulate and analyze it to answer specific questions. You will use the information in the tables to provide the answers to several inquiries about the Club employees. As you learn about the analytical features, think what it would be like to do the same task by hand. How long would it take? Would it be as accurate or as well presented? In addition, you will create several reports that present the information from the database attractively.

Employee Address Report

First Name	Last Name	Street	City	State	Zip Code	Home Phone
Jeff	Bader	947 S. Forest St.	Fort Myers	FL	33301-1268	(941) 555-7789
Andrew	Beinbrink	45 Burr Rd.	Fort Myers	FL	33301-1268	(941) 555-5322
Brian	Birch	742 W. Lemon Dr.	Fort Myers	FL	33301-1268	(941) 555-4321
Cindy	Birch	742 W. Lemon Dr.	Fort Myers	FL	33301-1268	(941) 555-4321
William	Bloomquist	43 Kings Rd.	Forest Island	FL	33174	(941) 555-6432
Anna	Brett	23 Suffolk Ln.	Fort Myers	FL	33301-1268	(941) 55
Scott	Briggs	45 E. Camelback Rd.	San Carlos	FL	33891-1605	(941) 55
Erin	Burke	234 N. 1st St.	San Carlos	FL	33891-1605	(941) 55
Gordon	Delano	8943 W. Southern Ave.	Iona	FL	33101-7468	(941) 55
Elizabeth	DeLuca	21 W. Southern Ave.	Forest Island	FL	33174	(941) 55
Bill	Delucchi	950 S. Terrace Dr.	Cypress Lake	FL	33205-0093	(941) 55
Barbara	Ernster	1153 S. Wilson	San Carlos	FL	33891-1605	(941) 55
Kimberly	Fachet	923 E. Baseline Rd.	Forest Island	FL	33174	(941) 55
Daniel	Facqur	5832 Fremont St.	Forest Island	FL	33174	(941) 55
Nancy	Falk	9483 W. Island Dr.	San Carlos	FL	33891-1605	(941) 55
Robby	Ferguson	4232 Tuller Ave.	San Carlos	FL	33891-1178	(941) 55
Lisa	Fromthart	32 Redcoat Rd.	Cypress Lake	FL	33205-6911	(941) 55

Sunday, March 04, 2001   Page

Basic report of all data in table.

Iona to Fort Myers Car Pool Report

First Name	Last Name	City	Street	Home Phone
Bill	Delucchi	Cypress Lake	950 S. Terrace Dr.	(941) 555-8195
Lisa	Fromthart	Cypress Lake	32 Redcoat Rd.	(941) 555-0110
Nichol	Lawrence	Cypress Lake	433 S. Gaucho Dr.	(941) 555-7656
Mina	Lopez	Cypress Lake	4290 E. Alameda Dr.	(941) 555-5050
Cathy	Nichols	Cypress Lake	75 Brooklea Dr.	(941) 555-0001
Marc	Schiff	Cypress Lake	235 N. Cactus Dr.	(941) 555-0010
Eric	Helfand	Iona	4601 E. Willow Dr.	(941) 555-9101
Suzanne	Reddie	Iona	932 E. Parkway Dr.	(941) 555-1191
Name	Student	Iona	89 Any St.	(555) 555-9999
Lisa	Sutton	Iona	4389 S. Hayden Rd.	(941) 555-1950

Report created from query displaying only selected fields.

Concept Overview

The following concepts will be introduced in this tutorial:

1   **Filter**   A filter is a restriction you place on records in the open datasheet or form to temporarily isolate and display a subset of records.

2   **AND and OR Operators**   The AND and OR operators are used to specify multiple conditions that must be met for the records to display in the datasheet.

3   **Query**   A query is a question you ask of the data contained in a database. You use queries to view data in different ways, to analyze data, and even to change existing data.

4   **Joins and Relationships**   A join is an association that tells Access how data between tables is related. A relationship is established between tables usually through at least one common field.

5   **Report**   Reports are the printed output you generate from tables or queries.

6   **Control**   Reports and forms are linked to the underlying table by using controls. Controls are graphical objects that can be selected and modified.

Using Filter by Selection

You have continued to enter employee records into the Employees table. The updated table has been saved for you as Employees in the Personnel Records database on your data disk.

1

Start Access 2000. Put your data disk in the appropriate drive for your system.

Open the Personnel Records database file.

Your screen should be similar to Figure 3–1.

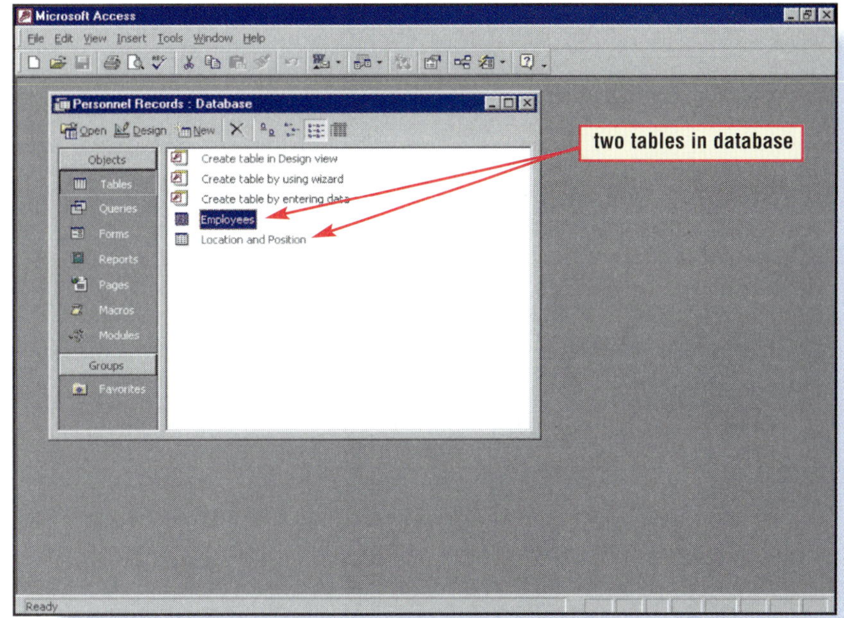

Figure 3–1

The Tables list box of the Database window displays the names of two tables in this database: Employees, and Location and Position. These tables will be used throughout the tutorial.

2

Open the Employees table.

If necessary, maximize the Table Datasheet window.

Add your information as record number 81 using your special ID number 9999 and the date 2/25/97 as your hire date. Enter your city as Iona.

Return to the first field of the first record.

Your screen should be similar to Figure 3–2.

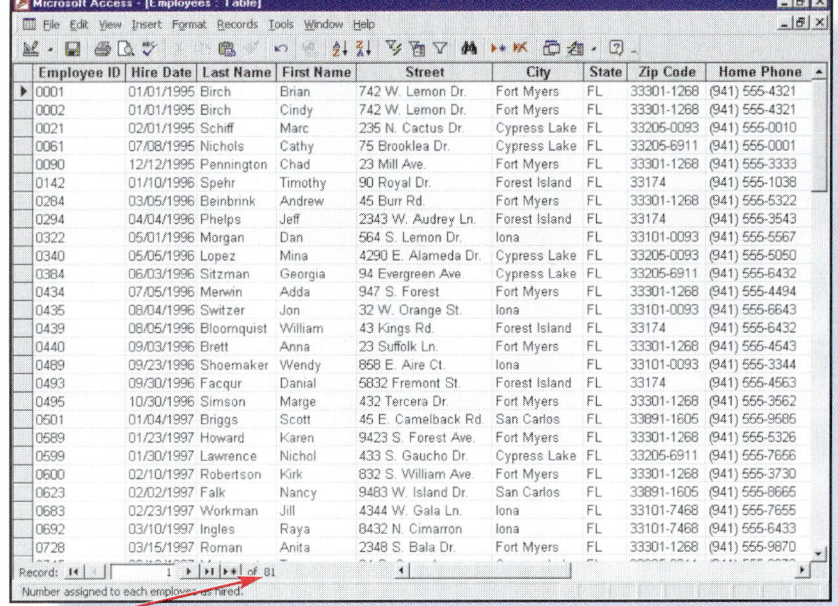

Figure 3–2

Julie Martinez, an employee at the Fort Myers location, is interested in forming a car pool. She recently approached you about finding others who may also be interested. You decide this would be a great opportunity to see how you can use the employee table to find this information. To find the employees, you could sort the table and then write down the needed information. This could be time consuming, however, if you had hundreds of employees in the table. A faster way is to apply a filter to the table records to locate this information.

Concept ① Filter

A **filter** is a restriction you place on records in the open datasheet or form to quickly isolate and display a subset of records. A filter is created by specifying a set of limiting conditions, or criteria, you want records to meet in order to be displayed. A filter is ideal when you want to display the subset for only a brief time, then return immediately to the full set of records. You can print the filtered records as you would any form or table. A filter is only temporary and all records are redisplayed when you remove the filter or close and reopen the table or form. The filter results cannot be saved. However, the last filter criteria you specify are saved with the table, and the results can be quickly redisplayed.

Julie lives in Iona, and wants to find others who work at the same location and live in Iona. To do this, you can quickly filter out all the other records using the Filter by Selection method. Filter by Selection is used when you can easily find and select an instance of the value in the table that you want the filter to use as the criterion to meet.

How the value is selected determines what results will be displayed. Placing the insertion point in a field selects the entire field contents. The filtered subset will include all records containing an exact match. Selecting part of a value in a field (by highlighting it) displays all records containing the selection. For example, in a table for a book collection, you could position the mouse pointer anywhere in a field containing the name of the author Stephen King, choose the Filter by Selection command, and only records for books whose author matches the selected name, "Stephen King," would be displayed. Selecting the last name "King" would include all records for authors Stephen King, Martin Luther King, and Barbara Kingsolver.

If the selected part of a value starts with the first character in the field, the subset displays all records whose values begin with the same selected characters.

You want to filter the table to display only those records with a City field entry of Iona. To specify the city to locate, you need to select an example of the data in the table.

3 ▸ **Move to the City field of record 9.**

▸ **Click** ⬛ **Filter by Selection**

> The menu equivalent is
> **R**ecords/**F**ilter/Filter by
> **S**election.

Your screen should be similar to
Figure 3–3.

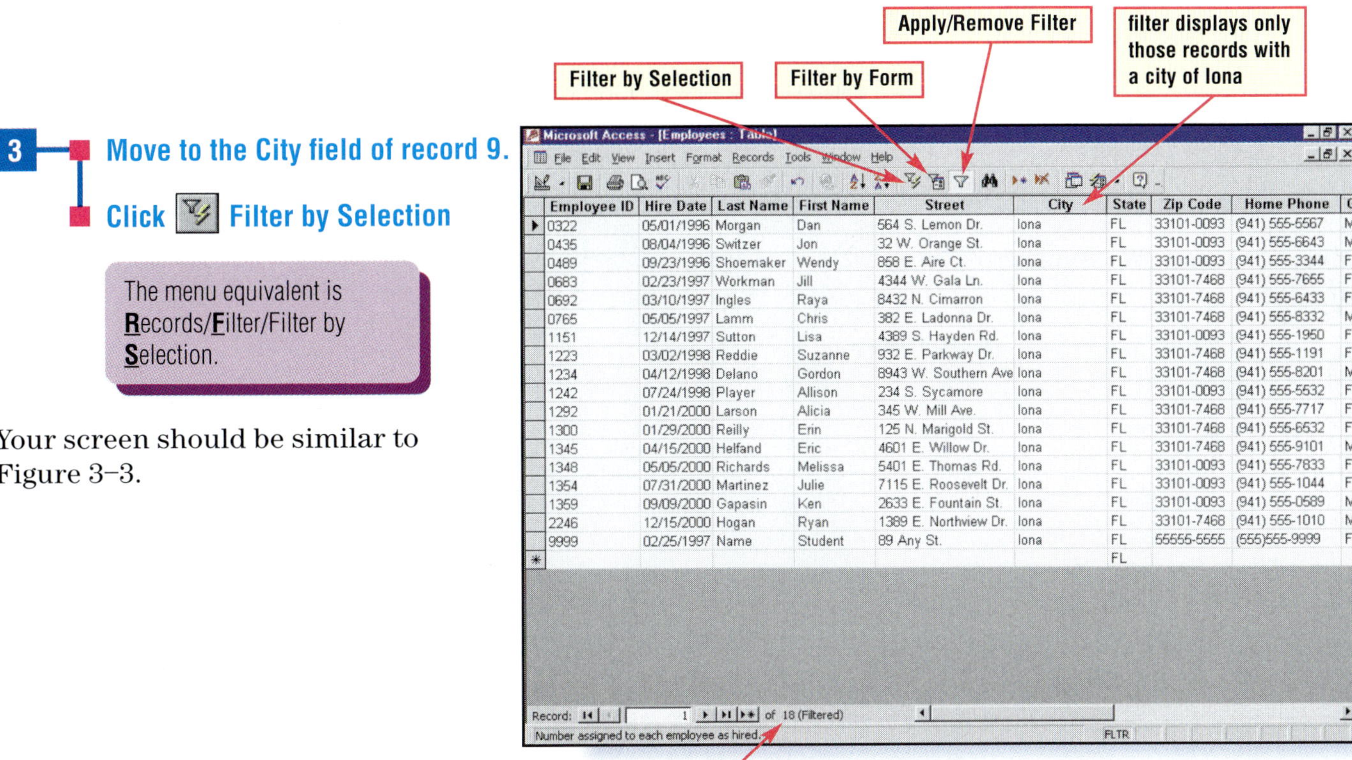

Figure 3–3

> You can print the filtered
> datasheet like any other
> datasheet.

The datasheet displays only those records that contain the selected city.
All other records are temporarily hidden. The status bar indicates the
total number of filtered records (18) and shows that the datasheet is filtered. To remove the filter,

> The menu equivalent is
> **R**ecords/**R**emove Filter/Sort.

4 ▸ **Click** ⬛ **Remove Filter.**

Using Filter by Form

After seeing how easy it was to locate this information, you want to locate
employees who live in the city of Cypress Lake. This information may help
in setting up the car pool, because the people traveling from the city of
Iona pass through Cypress Lake on the way to the Fort Myers location. To
find out this additional information, you need to use the Filter by Form
method. This method allows you to perform filters on multiple criteria.

1 ▪ **Click** 📋 **Filter by Form.**

The menu equivalent is
Records/**F**ilter/**F**ilter By
Form.

Your screen should be similar to
Figure 3–4.

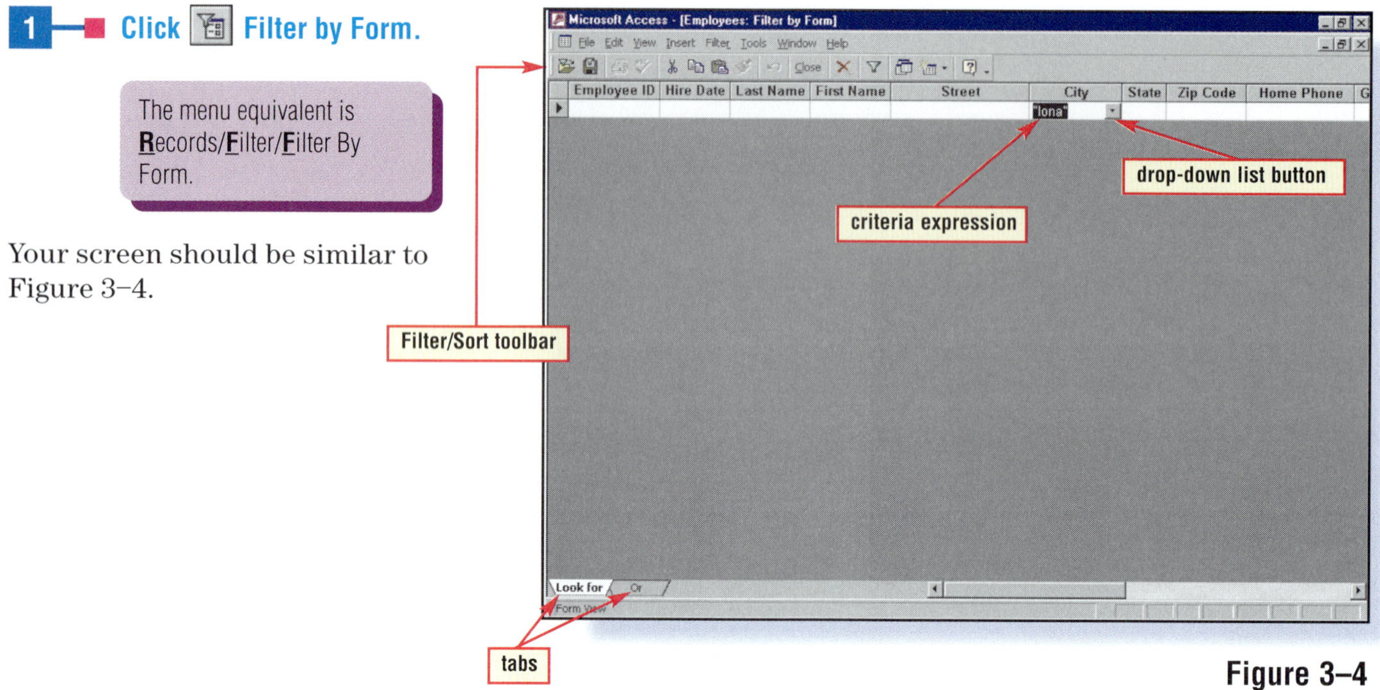

Figure 3–4

The Filter by Form window displays a blank version of the current
datasheet with empty fields in which you specify the criteria. This window automatically displays a Filter/Sort toolbar that contains the standard buttons as well as buttons (identified below) that are specific to the
Filter by Form window.

The window also includes two tabs, Look For and Or, where you enter
the filter criteria. The criteria are entered in the blank field space of the
record row as an expression. A **criteria expression** specifies the criteria
for the filter to use. You can either type values or choose values from a
drop-down list in the desired field to create the criteria expression.

Currently the City field displays the criterion you last specified using
Filter by Selection as the criteria expression. Notice that the field displays
a drop-down list button. Each field will display a drop-down button when
the field is selected. Clicking the button displays a list of values that are
available in that field from which you can select to help you enter the criteria expression. Since the City field already contains the correct criterion, you do not need to enter a different one.

Next you need to add the second criterion to the filter to include all records with a City field value of Cypress Lake. To instruct the filter to locate records meeting multiple criteria, you use the AND or OR operators.

Concept ② AND and OR Operators

The AND and OR operators are used to specify multiple conditions that must be met for the records to display in the filter datasheet. The AND operator narrows the search, because a record must meet both conditions to be included. The OR operator broadens the search, because any record meeting either condition is included in the output.

The AND operator is assumed when you enter criteria in multiple fields. Within a field, typing the word "AND" between criteria in the same field establishes the AND condition. For example, in the book table you could enter "Stephen King" in the author name field, then you could enter "Horror" in the category field to display records where the author's name is Stephen King and the category is Horror.

The OR operator is established by entering the criterion in the Or tab, or by typing "OR" between criteria in the same field. For example, you could enter "Stephen King" in the author name field, select the Or tab, then enter "Horror" in the category field. This filter would display those records where the author's name is Stephen King or where the category is Horror.

In this filter you will use an OR operator so that records meeting either city criterion will be included in the output. To include the city as an OR criterion, you enter the criterion in the Or tab.

2 ■ **Open the Or tab.**

A value must be entered in the Look For tab before the Or tab is available.

Your screen should be similar to Figure 3–5.

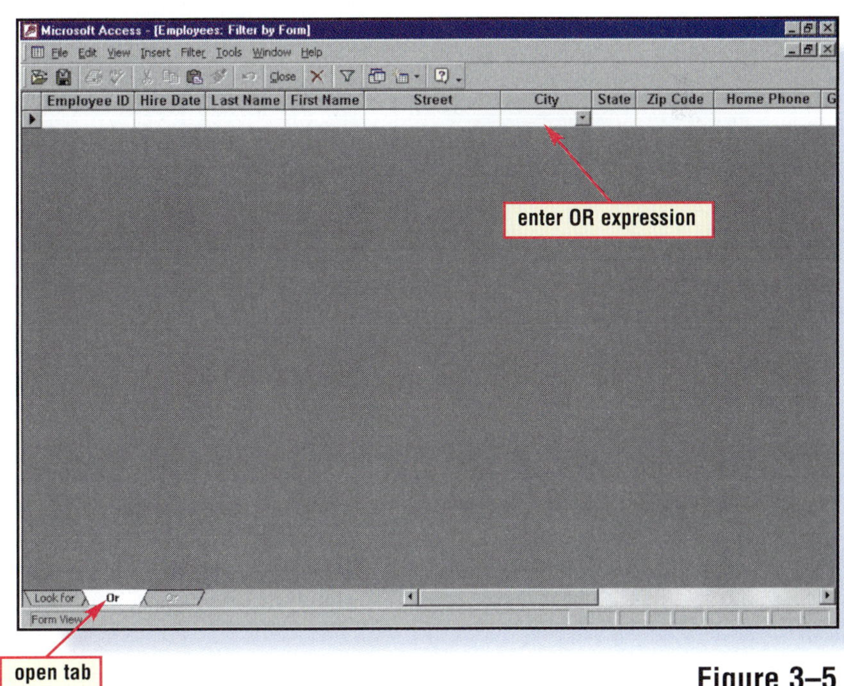

Figure 3–5

The Or tab is opened, and a new blank row is displayed. You will enter the expression specifying the criterion by selecting the criterion from the City drop-down list.

3 ■ **Click** ▼ **(in the City field).**

■ **Choose** Cypress Lake.

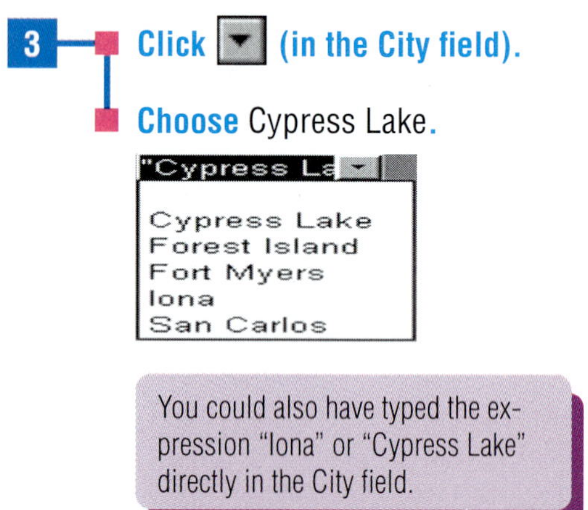

You could also have typed the expression "Iona" or "Cypress Lake" directly in the City field.

Your screen should be similar to Figure 3–6.

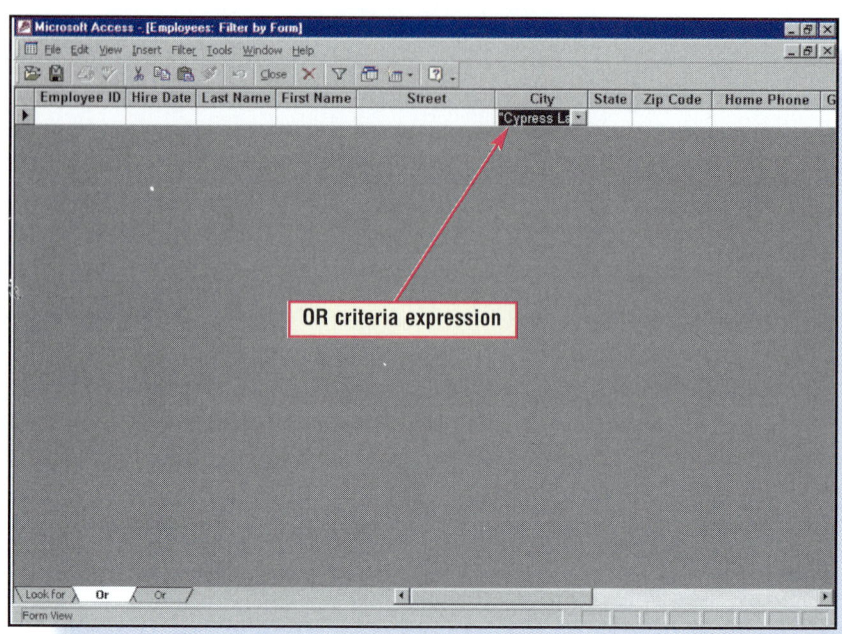

Figure 3–6

The selected criterion is displayed in the City field. It is surrounded by quotes as required of all text entries used in an expression. The Look For tab still contains the criterion for the city of Iona. To apply the filter,

4 ■ **Click** ▼ **Apply Filter.**

The menu equivalent is Filter/Apply Filter/Sort.

Your screen should be similar to Figure 3–7.

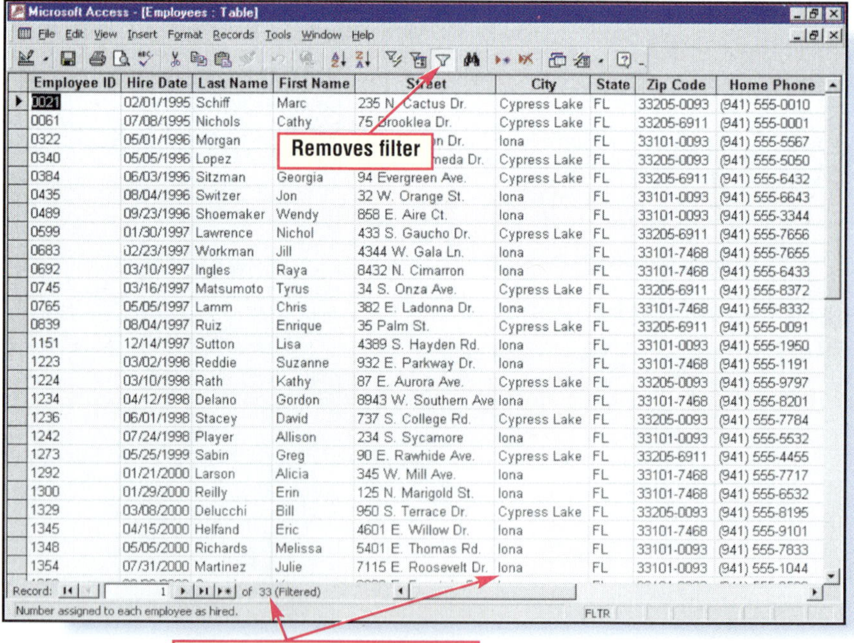

Figure 3–7

The filtered datasheet displays the records for all 33 employees who live in the city of Iona or Cypress Lake. To redisplay all records in the table,

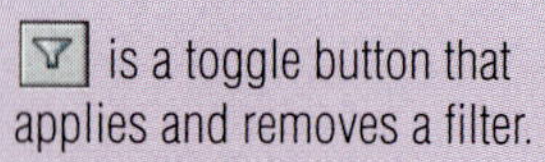 is a toggle button that applies and removes a filter.

5 ■ **Click** ▼ **Remove Filter.**

The filter criteria you last specified are stored with the table, and the results can be redisplayed simply by applying the filter. To see the results again,

6 ● Click  **Apply Filter.**

● **Redisplay all records.**

● **Close the Employees table and save your changes.**

Creating a Query

Using the filters does not help you determine which employees travel to the Fort Myers location from Iona or Cypress Lake. You also do not need all the employee information for the car pool. To obtain exactly what information you need, you will use a query.

Concept ③ Query

A **query** is a question you ask of the data contained in a database. You use queries to view data in different ways, to analyze data, and even to change existing data. Since queries are based on tables, you can also use a query as the source for forms and reports. The five types of queries are described in the table below.

Query Type	Description
Select query	Retrieves the specific data you request from one or more tables, then displays the data in a query datasheet in the order you specify. This is the most common type of query.
Crosstab query	Summarizes large amounts of data in an easy-to-read, row-and-column format.
Parameter query	Displays a dialog box prompting you for information, such as criteria for locating data. For example, a parameter query might request the beginning and ending dates, then display all records matching dates between the two specified values.
Action query	Makes changes to many records in one operation. There are four types of action queries: a make-table query creates a new table from selected data in one or more tables; an update query makes update changes to records, such as when you need to raise salaries of all sales staff by 7 percent; an append query adds records from one or more tables to the end of other tables; and a delete query deletes records from a table or tables.
SQL query	Created using SQL (Structured Query Language), an advanced programming language used in Access.

To create a new query,

1 **Click** 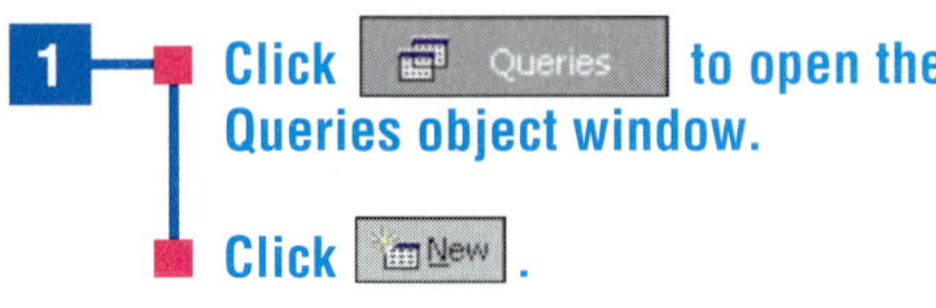 **to open the Queries object window.**

Click New .

Your screen should be similar to Figure 3–8.

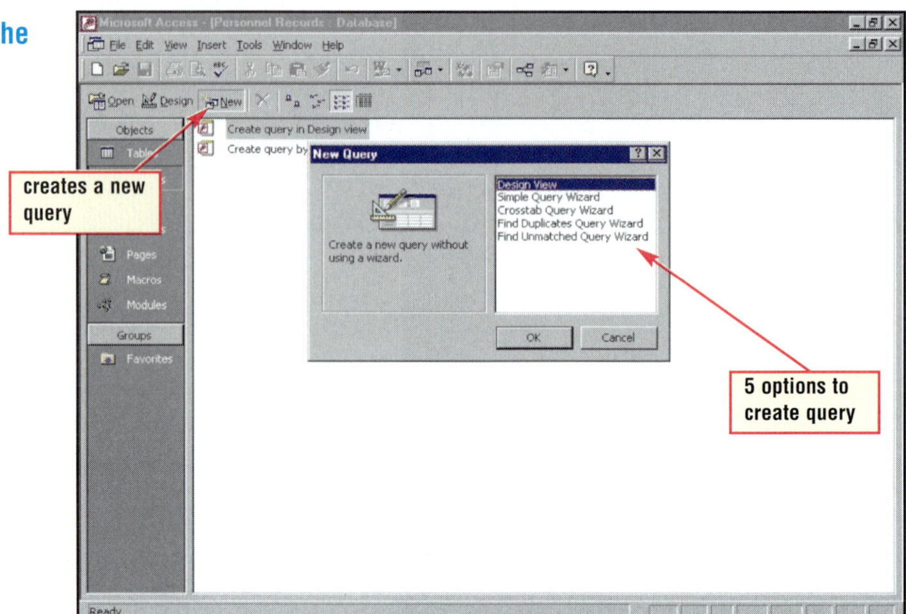

Figure 3–8

The New Query dialog box contains five options for creating queries. You can create a query from scratch in Query Design view or by using one of the four Query Wizards. The table below explains the type of query each of the four Wizards creates.

Query Wizard	Type of Query Created
Simple	Select query
Crosstab	Crosstab query
Find Duplicates	Locates all records that contain duplicate values in one or more fields in the specified tables.
Find Unmatched	Locates records in one table that do not have records in another. For example, you could locate all employees in one table who have no hours worked in another table.

To create a select query using the Simple Query Wizard,

2   **Select** Simple Query Wizard.

   Click OK .

The dialog box on your screen should be similar to Figure 3–9.

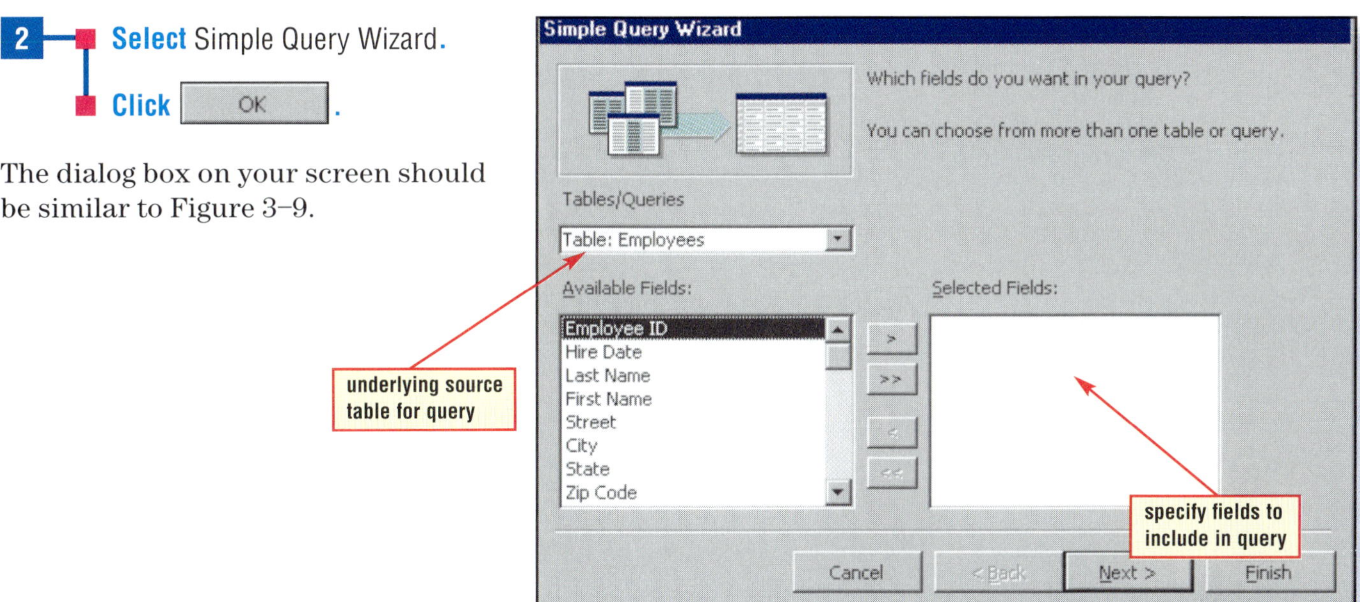

Figure 3–9

In the first Simple Query Wizard window, you specify the underlying table and the fields from the table that will give you the desired query result, just as you did when creating a form. You will use data from the Employees table, which is already selected. You need to select the fields you want displayed in the query output.

3   **Add the Last Name, First Name, Street, City, and Home Phone fields to the Selected Fields list.**

> Double-click the field name in the Available Fields list to add it to the Selected Fields list.

The dialog box on your screen should be similar to Figure 3–10.

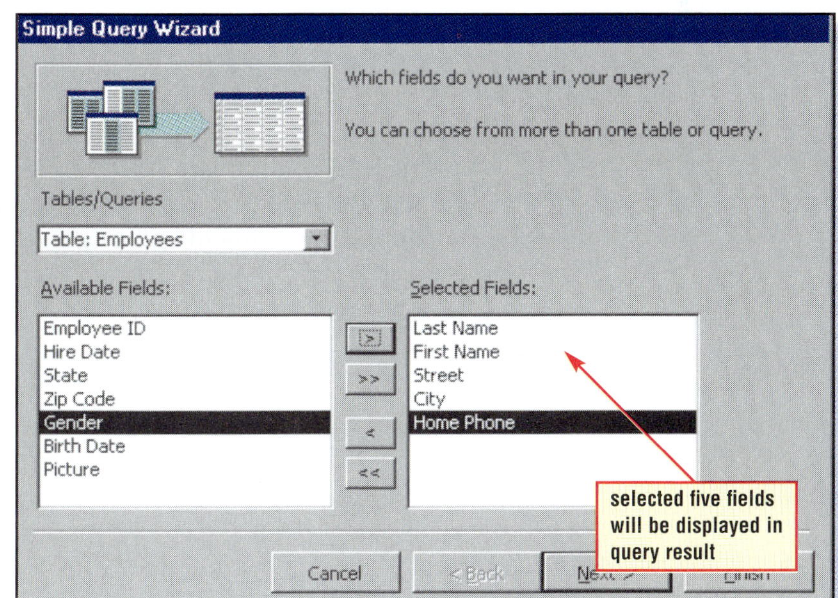

Figure 3–10

4 ▪ Click [Next >] .

▪ Replace the suggested title in the text box with **Car Pool**.

▪ Click [Finish] .

After a few moments, your screen should be similar to Figure 3–11.

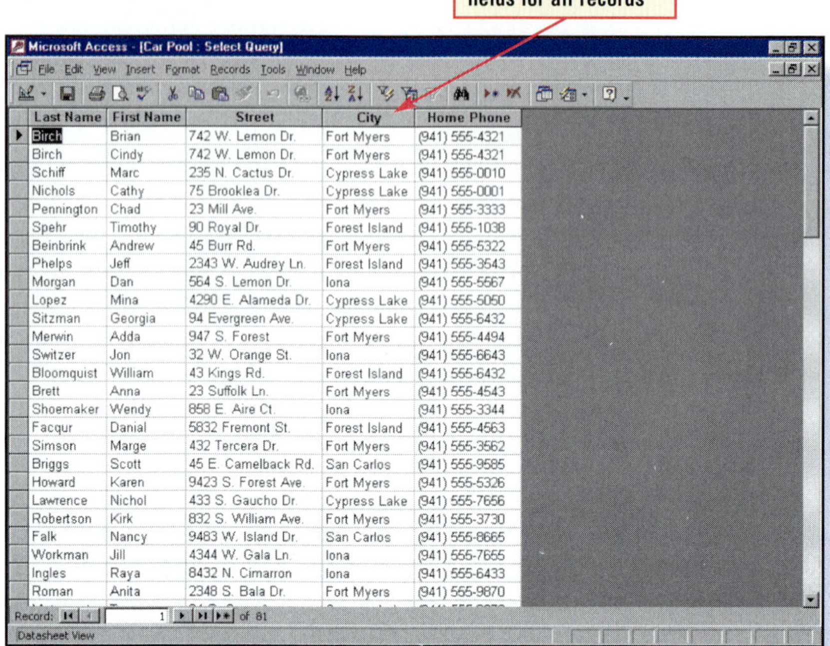

Figure 3–11

The result or answer to the query is displayed in a **query datasheet.** The query datasheet displays only the five specified fields for all records in the table. Query Datasheet view includes the same menus and toolbar buttons as in Table Datasheet view.

Moving Columns

The order of the fields in the query datasheet reflects the order they were placed in the Selected Fields list. You want the list of names to be organized with the first name before the last name. You can change the display order of the fields by moving the columns. To reorder columns, first select the column you want to move and then drag the selection to its new location. You want to move the Last Name column to the right of the First Name column.

1 **Select the Last Name column.**

> Reminder: Click on the Last Name column heading when the mouse pointer is a ↓ to select it.

Click and hold the mouse button on the Last Name column heading.

> When the mouse pointer is a ⬚, it indicates you can drag to move the selection.

Drag the Last Name column to the right until a thick black line is displayed between the First Name and Street columns. Release the mouse button.

Clear the selection.

> You can also press [Ctrl] + [F8] to turn on Move mode. Then press [←] or [→] to move the column in the desired direction, then press [Esc].

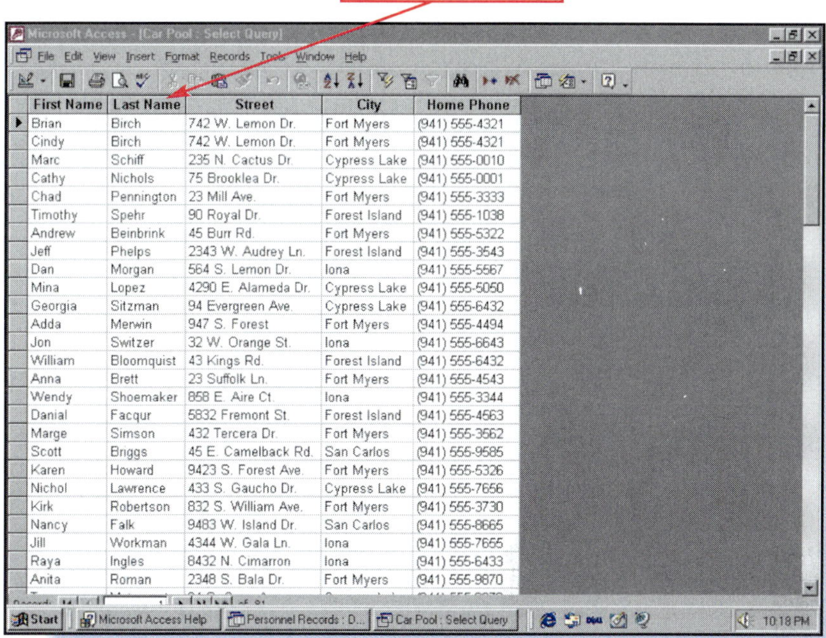

Figure 3–12

Your screen should be similar to Figure 3–12.

Additional Information

You can move fields in Table Datasheet view in the same manner.

Changing the column order in the query datasheet does not affect the field order in the table, which is controlled by the table design.

Specifying Multiple Criteria in a Query

Although the query result displays only the fields you want to see, it displays all the records in the database. To refine the query to display only selected records, you need to specify the criteria in the Query Design view window.

1 ■ **Click [icon] ▾ View to switch to the Query Design view.**

Your screen should be similar to Figure 3–13.

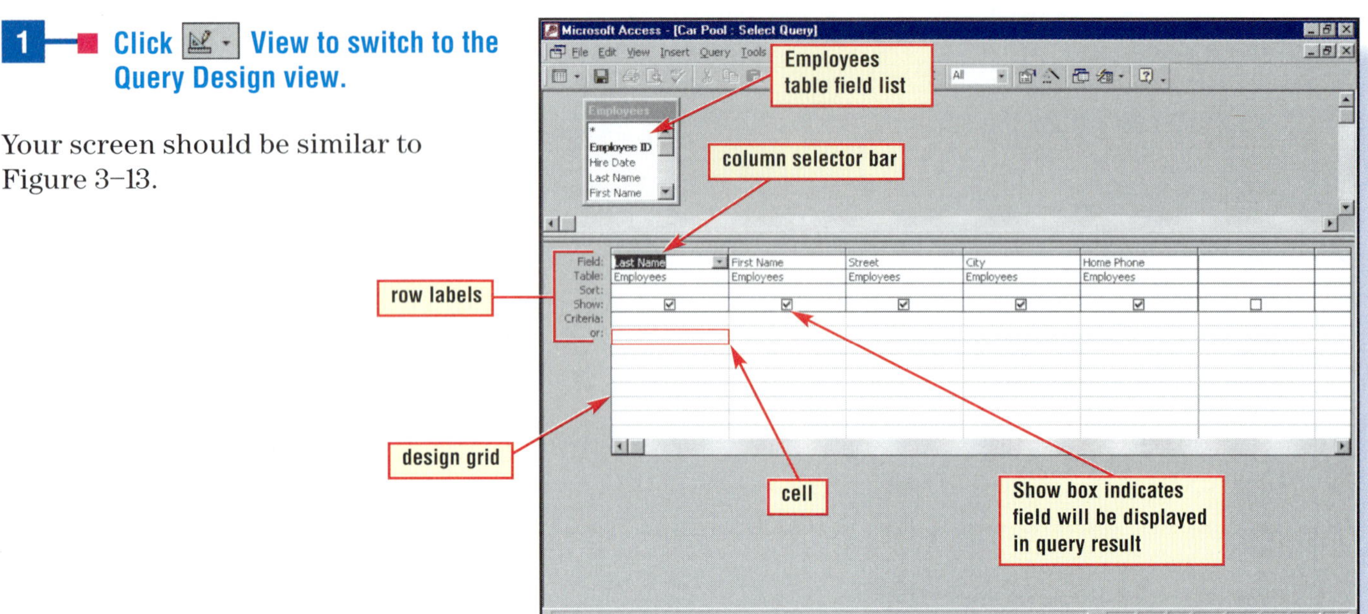

Figure 3–13

The Query Design view is used to create and modify the structure of the query. This view automatically displays a Query Design toolbar that contains the standard buttons as well as buttons (identified below) that are specific to the Query Design view window.

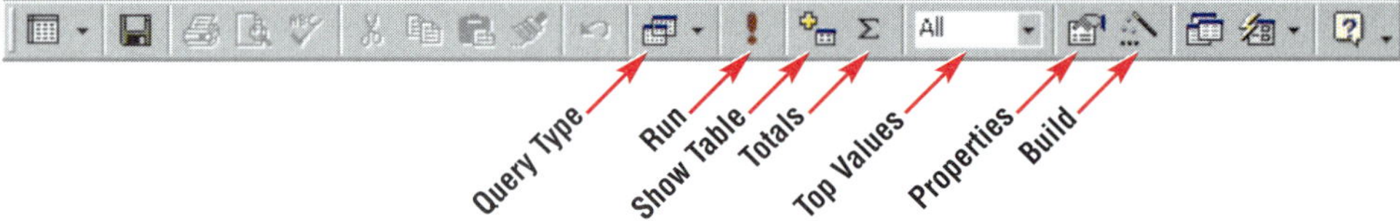

The Query Design window is divided into two areas. The upper area displays a list box of all the fields in the selected table. This is called the **field list.** The lower portion of the window displays the design grid, where the settings you enter to define the query are displayed. Each column in the grid holds the information about each field to be included in the query datasheet. The design grid currently displays the fields you specified in the Query Wizard. Above the field names is a narrow bar called the **column selector bar.** It is used to select an entire column. Each row label identifies the type of information that can be entered. The intersection of a column and row creates a **cell.** This is where you enter expressions to obtain the query results you need. Notice the boxes, called Show boxes, in the Show row. The Show box is checked for each field. This indicates that the query result will display the field column.

In the Criteria row of the City column, you first need to enter a criteria expression to locate only those records where the city is Iona. To specify the criterion, you will enter an expression that contains a comparison operator. A **comparison operator** is used to compare two values. The comparison operators are = (equal to) <> (not equal to), < (less than), >

(greater than), <= (less than or equal to), and >= (greater than or equal to). You will use the equal to comparison operator to find all records with a city of Iona. You do not need to enter the = sign for the equal to comparison, as this is the assumed comparison if none is entered.

2 **Move to the City Criteria cell.**

Type Iona.

Press ⏎Enter.

> The criteria expression is not case sensitive.

Your screen should be similar to Figure 3–14.

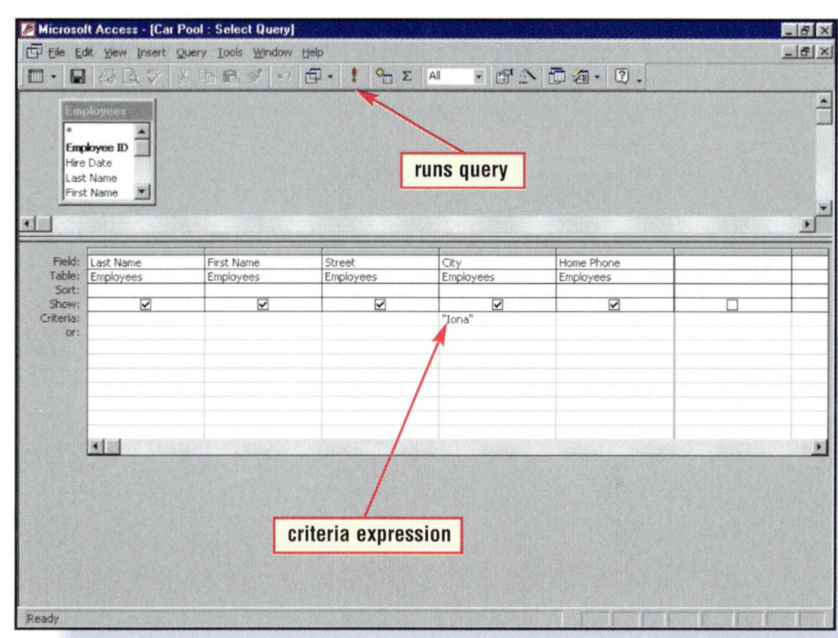

Figure 3–14

The expression is enclosed in quotes because it is a string. To display the query results, you run the query.

3 **Click** ❗ **Run.**

Your screen should be similar to Figure 3–15.

> The menu equivalent is **Q**uery/**R**un. You can also click ▦ ▾ Datasheet View to run the query and display the query datasheet.

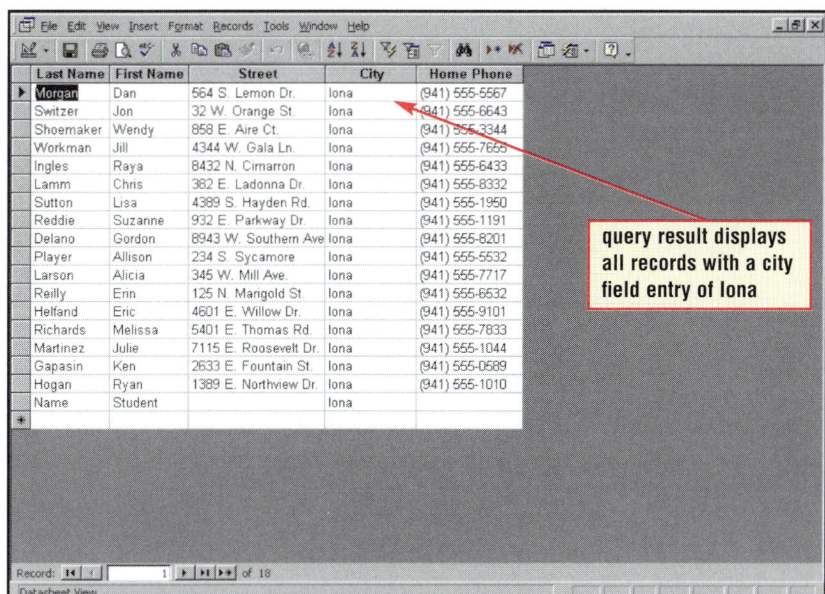

Figure 3–15

The query datasheet displays only those records meeting the city criterion. This is the same result as the first filter except that it displays only the specified fields.

Next you will add a second criterion to include the city of Cypress Lake in the result. In the Query Datasheet, the AND condition is established by typing the AND operator in the Criteria cell as part of the expression. An OR condition in a single field is established by entering the second criterion in the Or row cell of the same field. To see how this works, you will add Cypress Lake as the Or criteria.

4 ■ Switch to Query Design view.

■ Type **Cypress Lake** in the Or cell of the City column.

■ Press ⏎Enter.

Your screen should be similar to Figure 3–16.

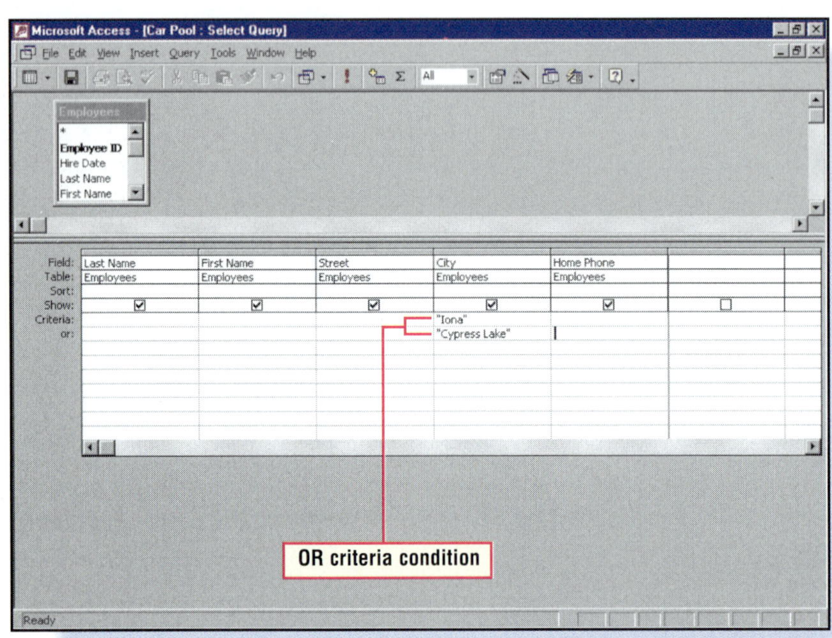

Figure 3–16

5 ■ Run the query.

If an expression is entered incorrectly, an informational box will be displayed indicating the source of the error.

Your screen should be similar to Figure 3–17.

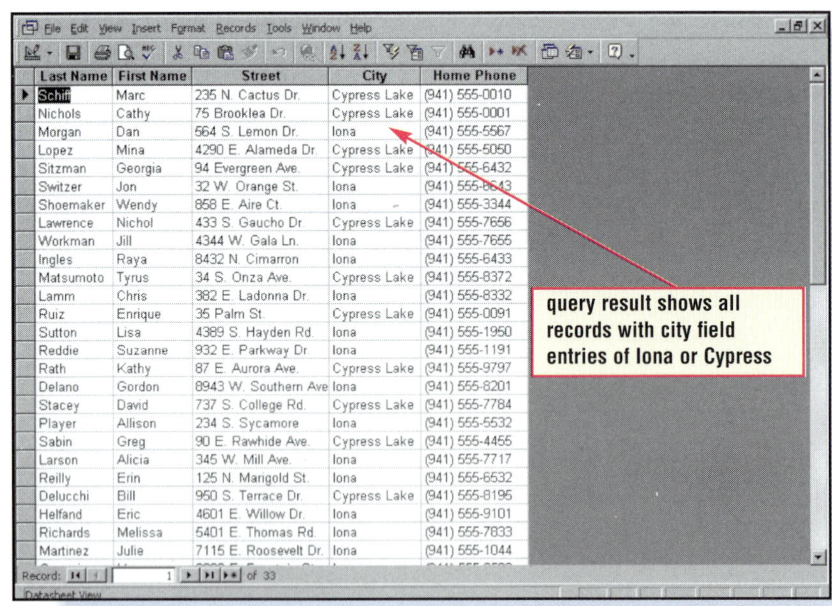

Figure 3–17

Thirty-three records were located in which the employee met the specified criteria. Notice that the fields are again in the order in which they appear in the Design grid.

6 ▬ **Move the Last Name column after the First Name column.**

While you are working on the carpool query, Brian, the owner, stops in and asks if you can find some information quickly for him. Because you plan to continue working on the carpool query, you will save the query so you do not have to re-create it. This is another advantage of queries over filters. Filters are temporary, whereas queries can be permanently saved with the database.

7 ▬ **Click** 🖬 **Save.**

▪ **Close the Query Datasheet window.**

Your screen should be similar to Figure 3–18.

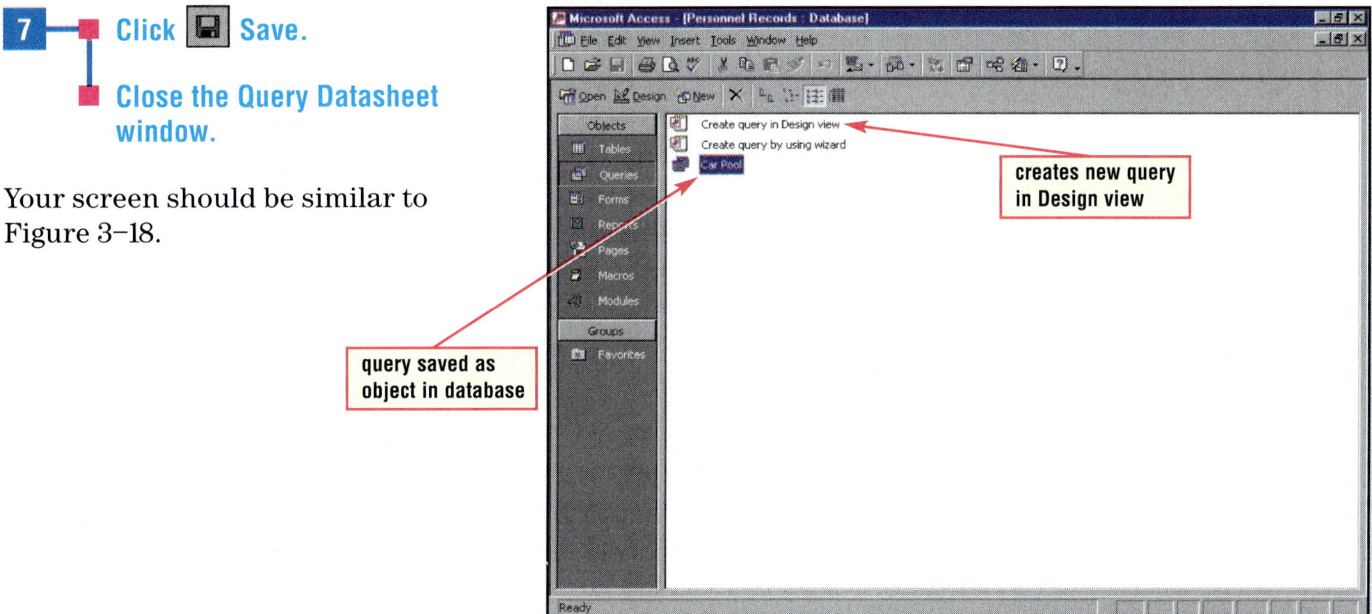

Figure 3–18

The query name, Car Pool, is displayed in the Queries object list.

Creating a Query in Design View

Brian is planning a ten-year anniversary celebration party and plans to recognize those employees who have worked with Lifestyle Fitness Club for 3, 5, or more years. He needs to know how many people are in each category so that he can order the correct number of awards. To help Brian locate these employees, you will create a new query using the Query Design view.

1 ■ **Double-click** Create query in Design view.

Your screen should be similar to Figure 3–19.

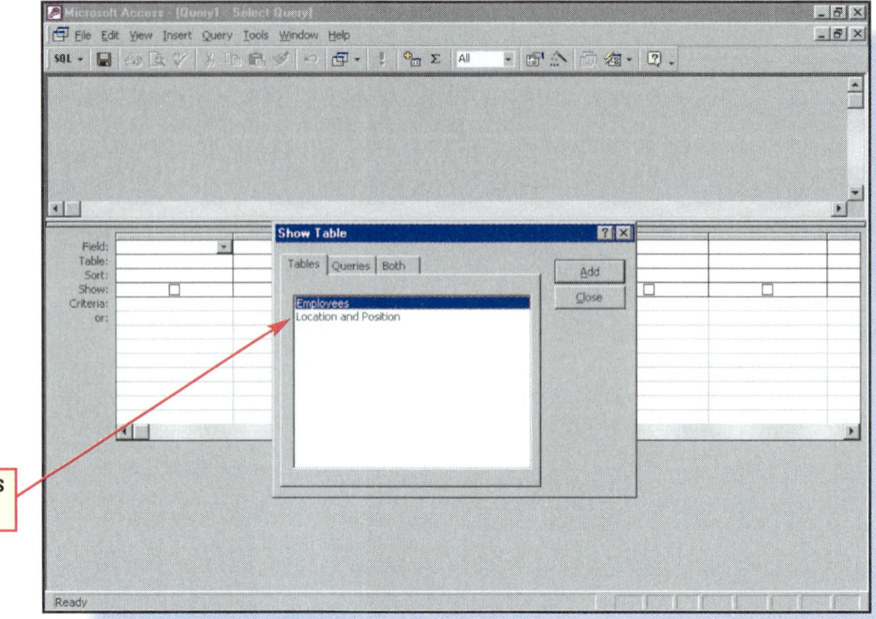

Figure 3–19

The Query Design window is open with the Show Table dialog box open on top of it. The dialog box is used to specify the underlying table or query to use to create the new query. The three tabs—Tables, Queries, and Both—contain the names of the existing tables and queries that can be used as the information source for the query. You need to add the Employees table to the query design.

2 ■ **If necessary, open the Tables tab and select the Employees table.**

■ **Click** Add .

> You can also double-click the table name to add it to the query design.

■ **Click** Close .

■ **If necessary, maximize the Query Design window.**

Your screen should be similar to Figure 3–20.

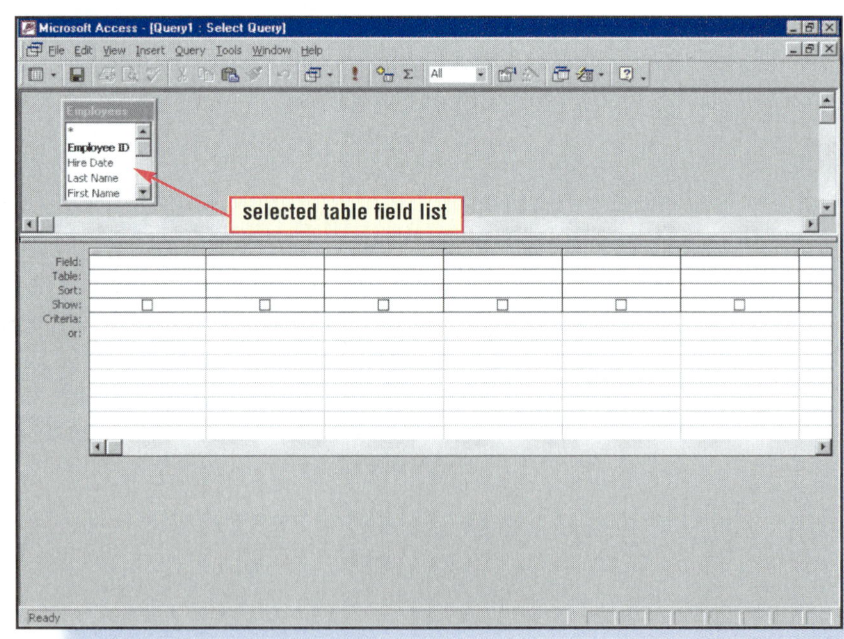

Figure 3–20

A field list for the selected table appears above the design grid. From the field list, you need to add the fields to the grid that you want to use in the query. The methods you can use to add fields to the design grid are described below.

■ Drag the field name from the field list to the grid. You can add several fields at once by pressing ⇧Shift and clicking to select adjacent fields, or by pressing Ctrl and clicking to select non-adjacent fields. When you drag multiple fields at a time, Access places each field in a separate column.

■ Double-click on the field name. The field is added to the next available column in the grid.

To select all fields, double-click the field list title bar.

■ Select the Field cell drop-down arrow in the grid, then choose the field name.

In addition, if you select the asterisk in the field list and add it to the grid, Access displays the table or query name in the field row followed by a period and asterisk; all fields in the table will be included in the query results. Using this feature also will automatically include any new fields that may later be added to the table, and will exclude deleted fields. You cannot sort records or specify criteria for fields, however, unless you also add those fields individually to the design grid.

3 ■ **Double-click** Hire Date **in the field list to add it to the grid.**

■ **Add the** First Name **and** Last Name **fields to the grid next.**

Your screen should be similar to Figure 3–21.

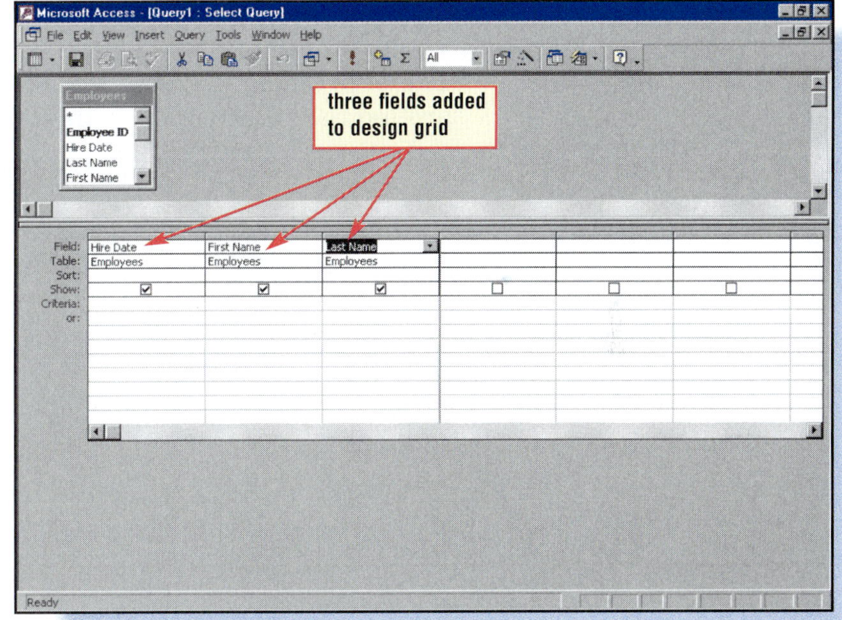

Figure 3–21

First you want to locate all employees who have at least 3 years with the club. To do this you will use the < operator to locate all records with a hire date less than 1/1/98. To specify the criterion,

4 ■ **In the Hire Date Criteria cell, type <1/1/98**

■ **Press** Enter.

Your screen should be similar to Figure 3–22.

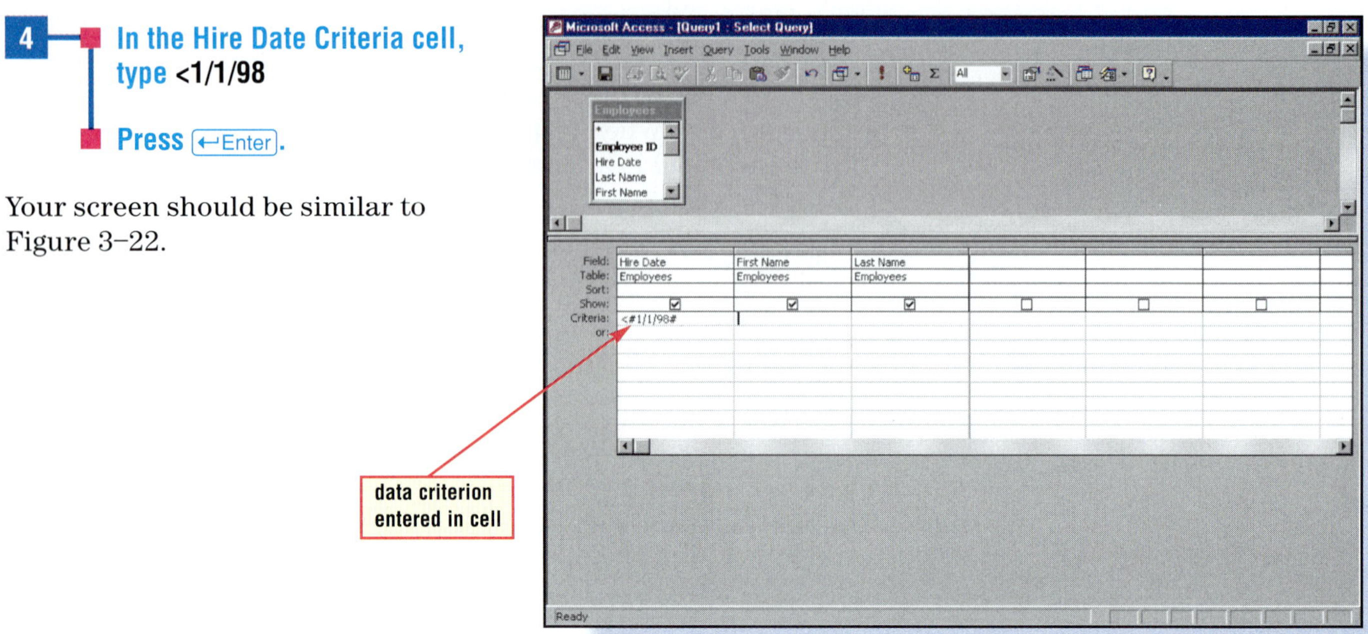

Figure 3–22

The expression appears in the cell as <#1/1/98#. Access adds # signs around the date to identify the values in the expression as a date.

5 ■ **Click**  **Run.**

Your screen should be similar to Figure 3–23.

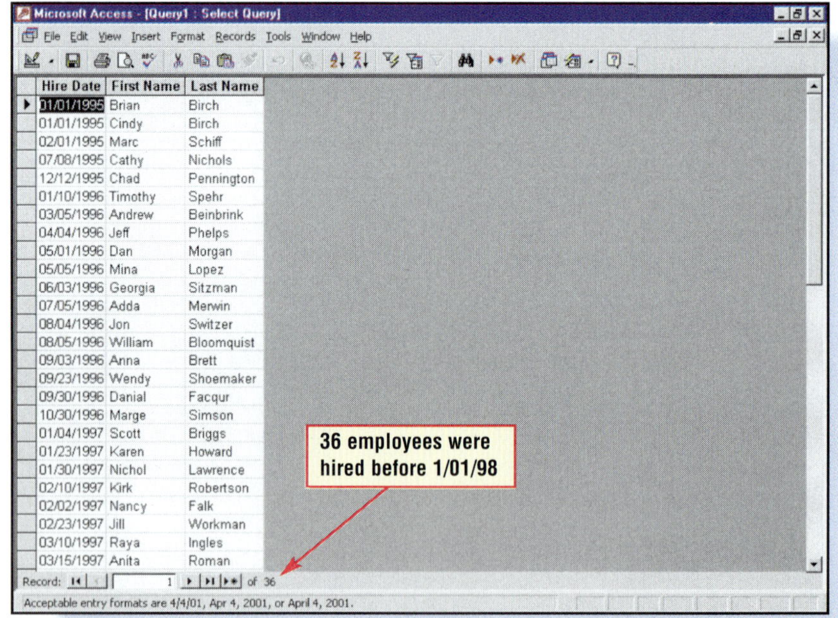

Figure 3–23

The query datasheet displays only those records meeting the date criterion. The record number indicator of the query datasheet shows that 36 employees were hired before January 1998. Next you will refine the search to locate employees with more than 3 years service, but less than 5 years.

6 **Return to Query Design view.**

Enter >1/1/96 and <1/1/98 in the Hire Date Criteria cell.

Click Run.

Your screen should be similar to Figure 3–24.

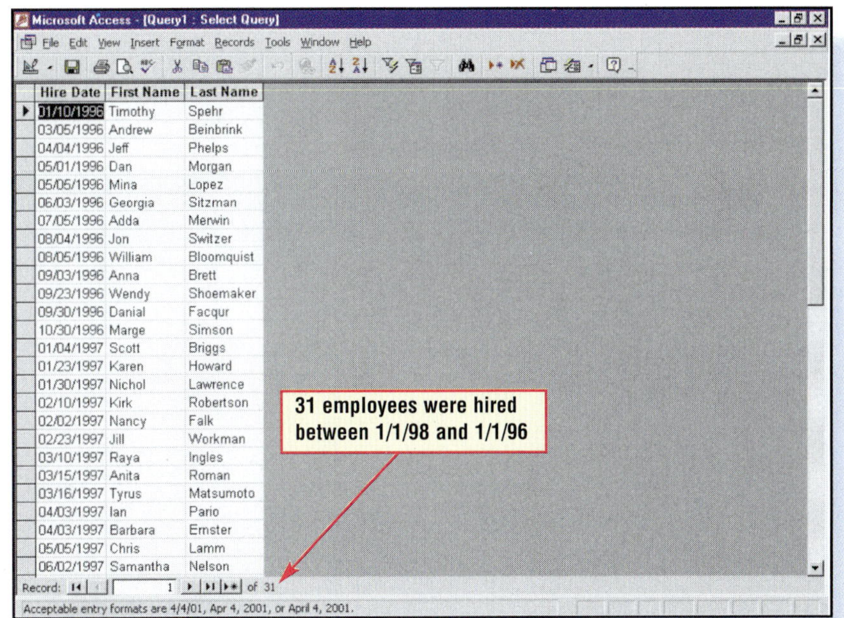

Figure 3–24

The number of employees with between 3 and 5 years with the Club is 31. Brian also wants a printed list of these employees. And just in case Brian wants this information again, you will save the query.

Click Print or use **F**ile/**P**rint if you need to specify printer settings.

7 **Print the query datasheet.**

Click Save.

In the Save As dialog box, enter Service Awards.

Click OK .

Knowing the total with over 3 years was 36 means there are 5 employees with more than 5 years. To verify this,

You can quickly clear the entire grid using **E**dit/Cle**a**r Grid.

8 **Return to Query Design view and enter <1/1/96 in the Hire Date Criteria cell.**

Run the query.

Print the query datasheet.

Close the Query Datasheet without saving the changes.

The query result confirms your calculation.

Querying Two Tables

Now that you have provided Brian with the answers he needed, you can get back to work on the car pool query. The car pool list would be more helpful if it had only the people that work at the Fort Myers location.

Unfortunately, the Employees table does not contain this information. This information, however, is available in the Location and Position table.

1 Click ⊞ Tables and open the Location and Position table.

Your screen should be similar to Figure 3–25.

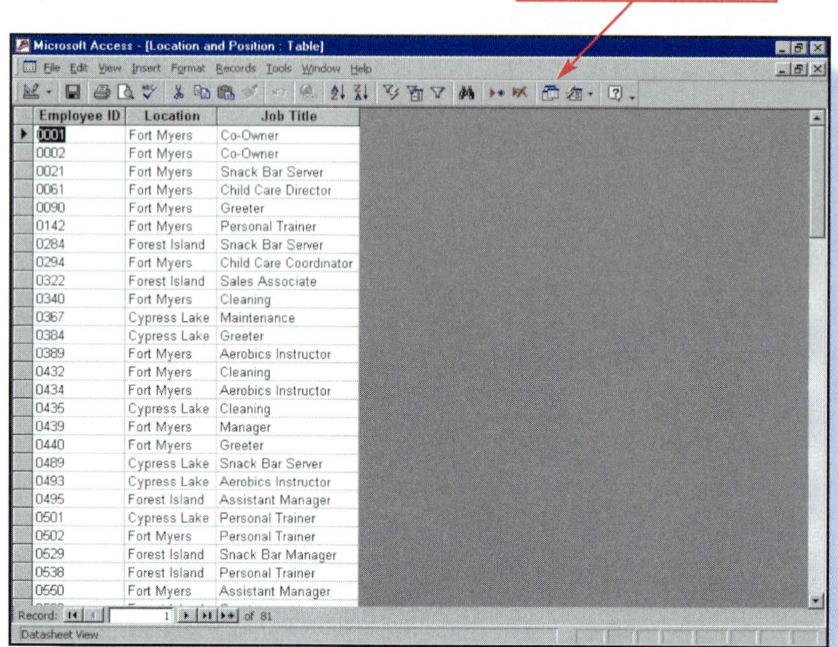

Figure 3–25

The Location and Position table contains three fields of data for each employee: Employee ID, Club Location, and Job Title. The Employee ID field is the key field and is the common field between the two tables. To display the information on the Fort Myers employees, you need to create a query using information from this table and from the Employees table. A query that uses more than one table is called a **multitable query.**

To open the Car Pool query you saved,

2

Click 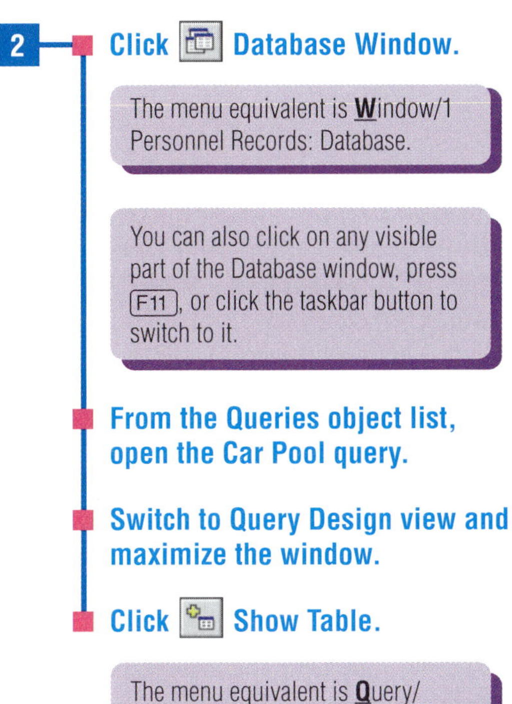 **Database Window.**

The menu equivalent is **W**indow/1 Personnel Records: Database.

You can also click on any visible part of the Database window, press F11, or click the taskbar button to switch to it.

From the Queries object list, open the Car Pool query.

Switch to Query Design view and maximize the window.

Click **Show Table.**

The menu equivalent is **Q**uery/ Show **T**able.

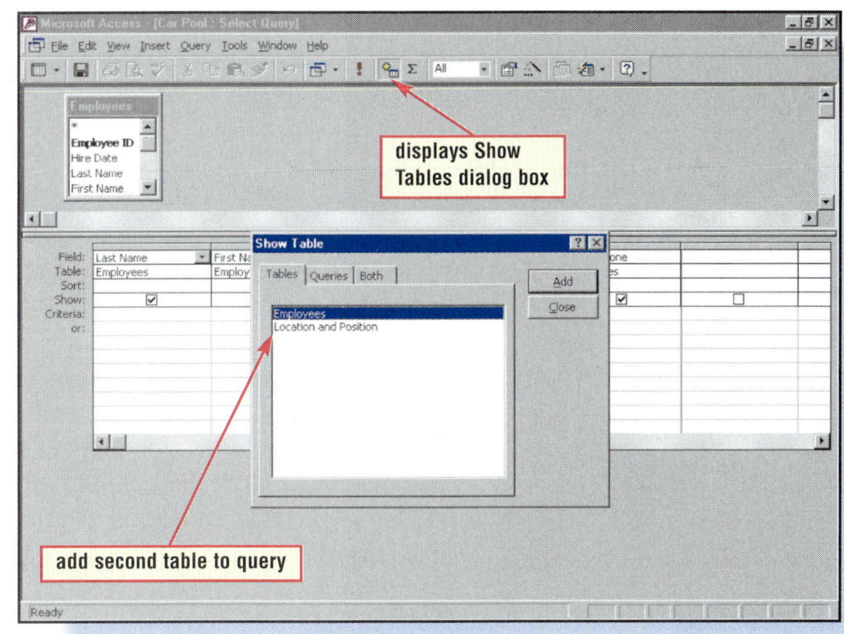

Figure 3–26

Your screen should be similar to Figure 3–26.

From the Query Design window, you need to select the name of the table you want to add to the query.

3

If necessary, open the Tables tab and select Location and Position.

Click Add **.**

Close the Show Table dialog box.

Your screen should be similar to Figure 3–27.

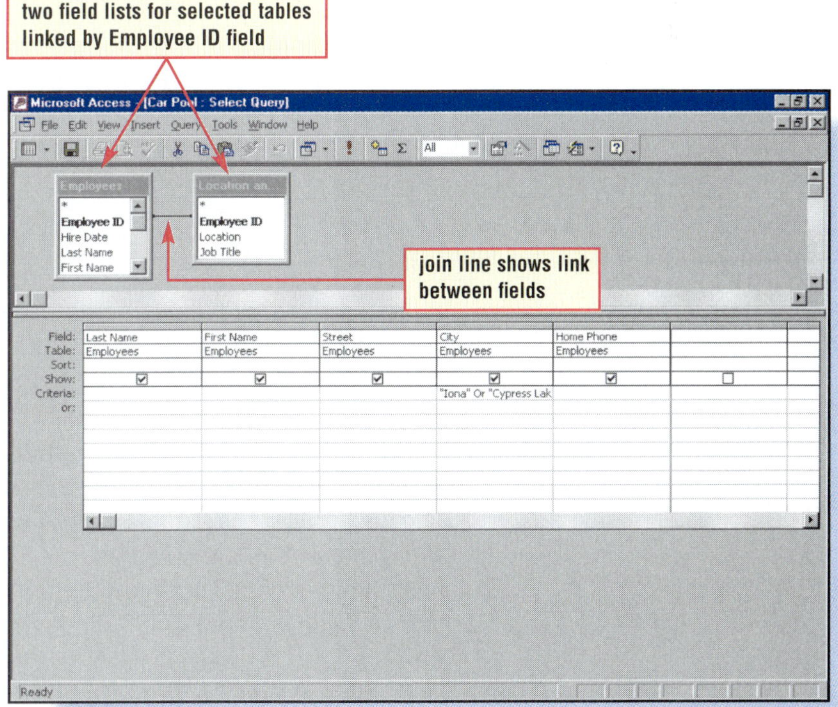

Figure 3–27

The field list for the second table is added to the Query Design window. The line between the two field lists indicates that the two tables have been temporarily joined.

Concept ④ Joins and Relationships

More information and examples of relationships are available through the Office Assistant.

Use **T**ools/**R**elationships to define permanent relationships between tables.

A **join** is an association that tells Access how data between tables is related. Joining tables allows you to bring information from different tables in your database together. A **relationship** is established between tables usually through at least one common field. The common fields must be of the same data type and contain the same kind of information, but can have different field names. When you add multiple tables to a query, Access automatically joins tables based on the common fields if one of the common fields is a primary key. This is called the default join or **inner join.** If the common fields have different names, Access does not automatically insert the line and create the join. You can create the join manually by dragging from one common field to the other. The join instructs the query to check for matching values in the joined fields. When matches are found, the matching data is added to the query datasheet as a single record.

The three types of relationships, one-to-many, many-to-many, and one-to-one, are described in the table below. The most common type is a one-to-many relationship.

Relationship Type	Description
One-to-many	A record in table A can have many matching records in table B, but a record in table B has only one matching record in table A.
Many-to-many	A record in table A can have many matching records in table B, and a record in table B can have many matching records in table A. This requires a third table in the relationship, known as a junction table, that serves as a bridge between the two tables.
One-to-one	A record in table A has only one matching record in table B, and a record in table B has only one matching record in table A.

In a one-to-many relationship, there is a primary table and a related or foreign table. The primary table is usually the "one" side of two related tables in a one-to-many relationship, and the related table is usually on the "many" side of a one-to-many relationship.

Using Tools/Relationships, you can also define permanent relationships between tables that will enforce the rules of referential integrity. These rules help ensure that the database always contains accurate and complete data. When these rules are enforced, you cannot add records to a related table when there is no associated record in the primary table. You also cannot change values in the primary table that would result in records that do not have a match in a related table, or delete records from the primary table when there are matching related records in a related table.

The diagram below shows that when the Employee ID fields of the two tables are joined, a query can be created using data from both tables to provide the requested information.

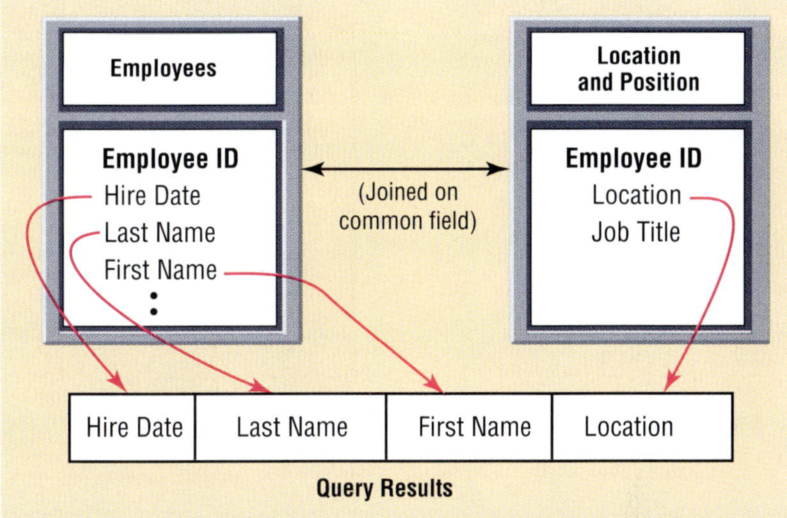

The type of relationship created using these two tables is a one-to-one relationship. This is because each record in the first table has one matching record in the second table.

Next you need to add the fields to the grid that you want to use in the query.

4 ■ **Add the Location field to the design grid.**

■ **To specify the location criterion, enter the expression Fort Myers in the Location Criteria cell.**

Your screen should be similar to Figure 3–28.

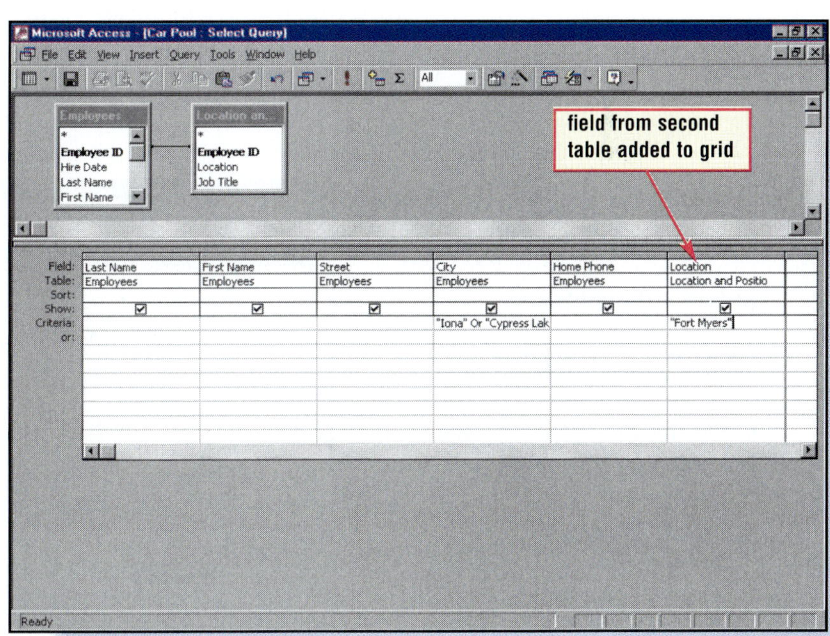

Figure 3–28

5 ▪ **Run the query.**

Your screen should be similar to
Figure 3–29.

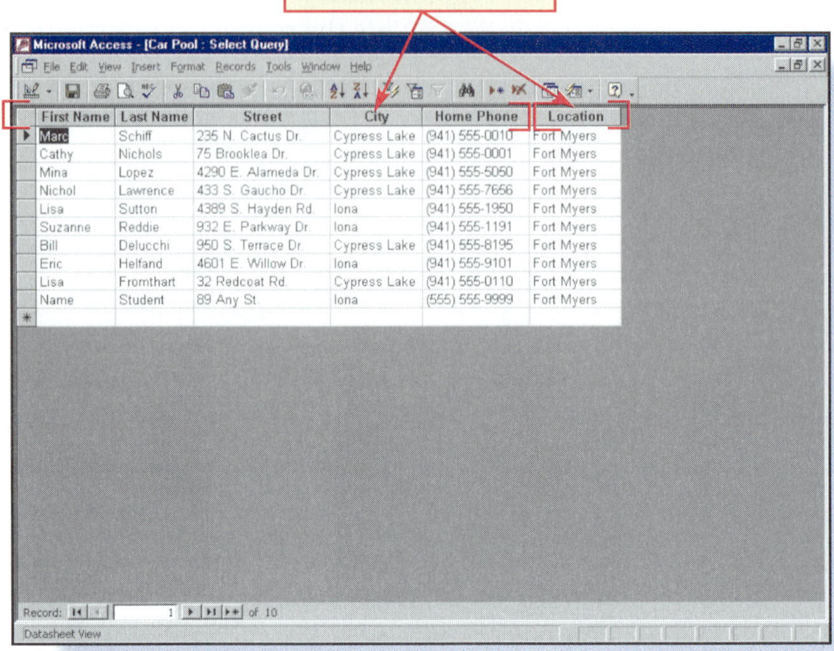

Figure 3–29

The query result shows there are ten employees who live in either Iona or
Cypress Lake and work at the Fort Myers location. Each record consists
of information from both tables. Both tables must contain matching
records in order for a record to appear in the query's result.

Next you want to sort the query datasheet by City and Last Name.

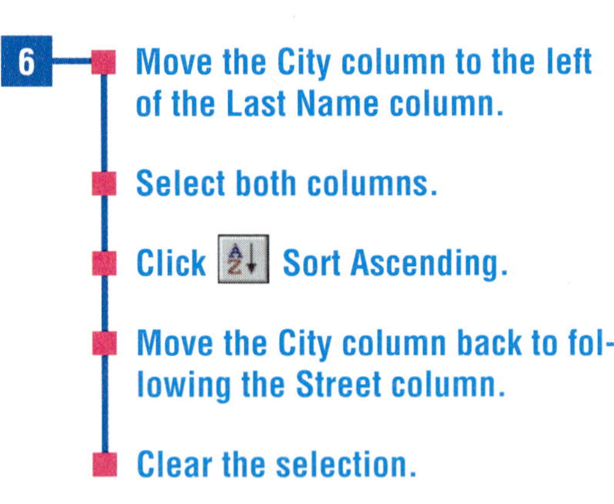

6 ▪ **Move the City column to the left
of the Last Name column.**

▪ **Select both columns.**

▪ **Click** [Sort Ascending icon] **Sort Ascending.**

▪ **Move the City column back to following the Street column.**

▪ **Clear the selection.**

Your screen should be similar to
Figure 3–30.

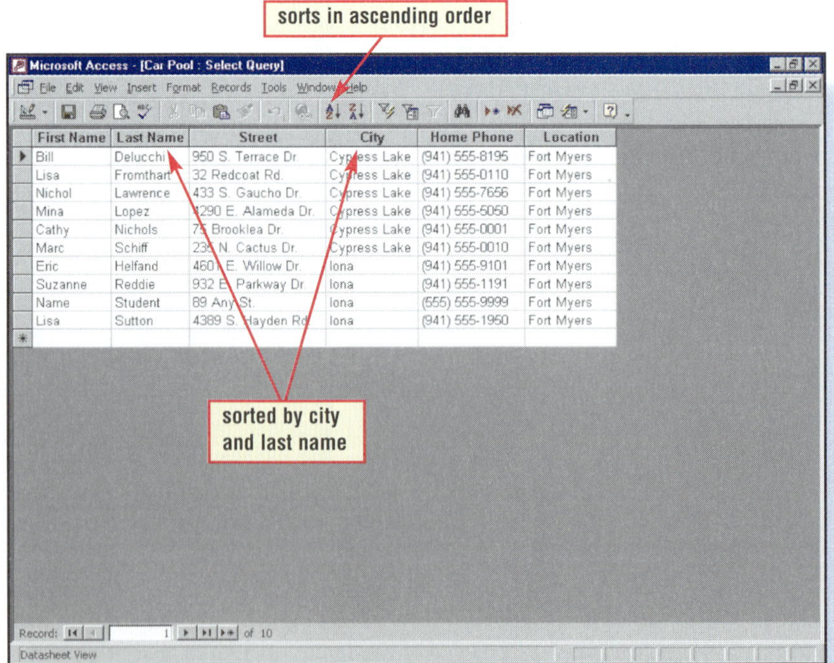

Figure 3–30

7 ■ **Close the query, saving your changes.**

Note: If you are running short on time, this is an appropriate point to end this session. When you begin again, open the Personnel Records database.

Using the AutoReport Wizard

Brian showed Cindy the printout you gave him of the employees that will get service awards. She sees many uses for the information generated by Access, including the ability to quickly analyze information in the database. As a starter, she has asked you to create an address report for all employees sorted by name. You have already created and printed several simple reports using the Print command on the File menu. This time, however, you want to create a custom report of this information.

Concept ⑤ Report

Reports are the printed output you generate from tables or queries. A report might be a simple listing of all the fields in a table, or it might be a list of selected fields based on a query.

Access also includes a custom report feature that allows you to create professional-appearing reports. The custom report is a document that includes text formats, styles, and layouts that enhance the display of information. In addition, you can group data in reports to achieve specific results. You can then display summary information, such as totals, by group to allow the reader to further analyze the data. Creating a custom report displays the information from your database in a more attractive and meaningful format.

You will create the address list report using the data in the Employees table.

1 **Open the Reports Object window.**

Click New .

The menu equivalent is
Insert/**R**eport.

Your screen should be similar to
Figure 3–31.

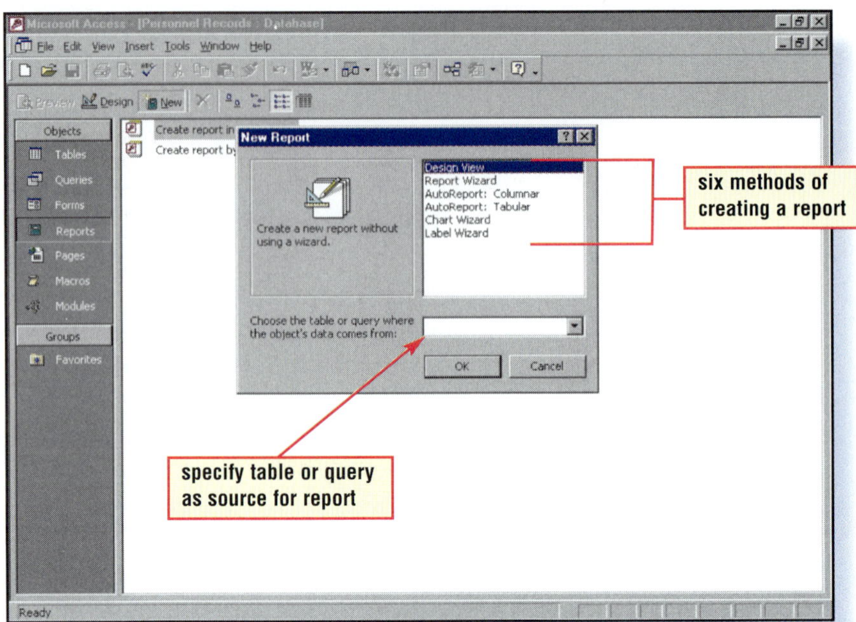

Figure 3–31

The New Report dialog box presents six ways to create a report. You can
create a report from scratch in Design view, or by using the Report Wizard
or one of the AutoReport Wizards. The Report Wizard lets you choose the
fields to include in the report and helps you quickly format and lay out the
new report. The AutoReport Wizard creates a report that displays all
fields and records from the underlying table or query in a predesigned report layout and style.

You decide to use the AutoReport Wizard to create a columnar report
using data in the Employees table.

2 **Select** AutoReport: Columnar.

Select Employees **from the
Choose the Table or Query drop-
down list.**

Click OK .

Your screen should be similar to
Figure 3–32.

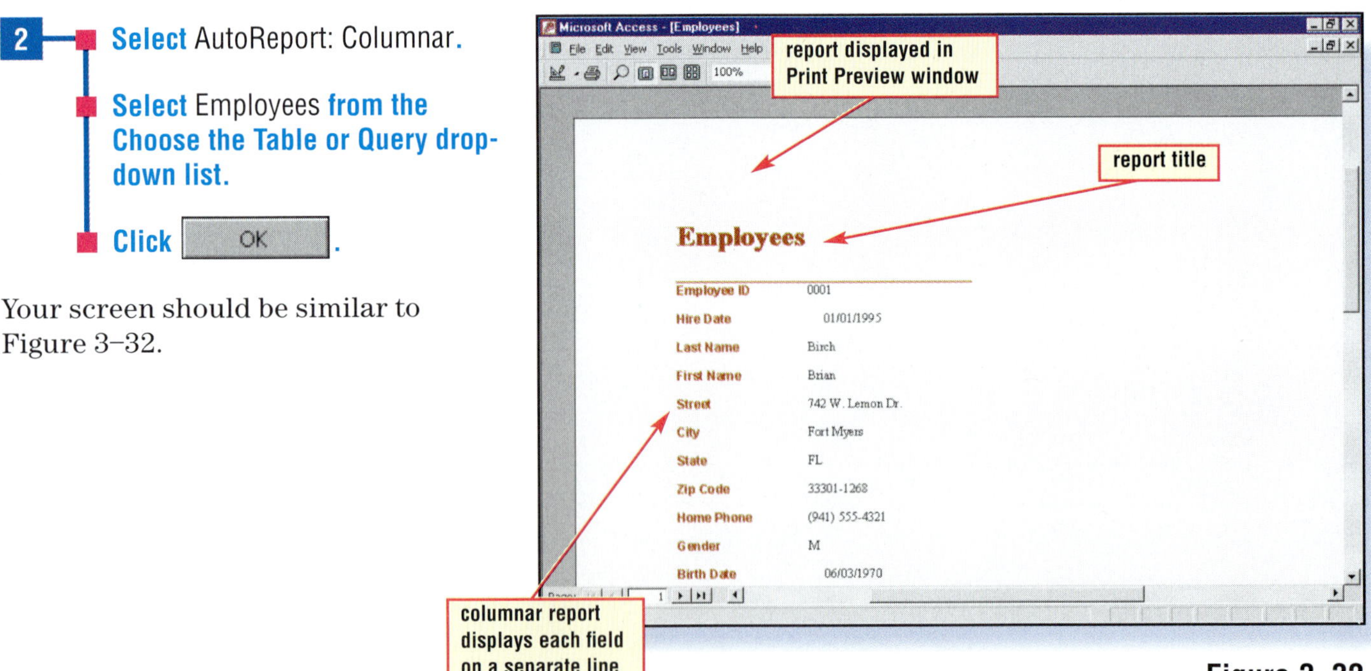

Figure 3–32

After a few moments, the report is created and displayed in the Print Preview window. The AutoReport Wizard creates a columnar report that displays each field on a separate line in a single column for each record. The fields are in the order they appear in the table. The report appears in a predefined report style and layout. The report style shown in Figure 3–32 uses the table name as the report title and includes the use of text colors, typefaces and sizes, and horizontal lines and boxes.

Your report may be displayed with a different style. This is because when creating an AutoReport, Access remembers the last autoformat report style used to create a report on your machine, then applies that same style to the new report. If the Autoformat command has not been used, the report will use the basic style.

Zooming the Window

Only the upper part of the first page of the report is visible in the window. To see more of the report in the window at one time, you can toggle between 100% and Fit by clicking on the window, or you can decrease the on-screen character size by specifying a smaller magnification percentage using the Zoom command. You can increase the character size up to two times normal display (200%) or reduce it to 10%.

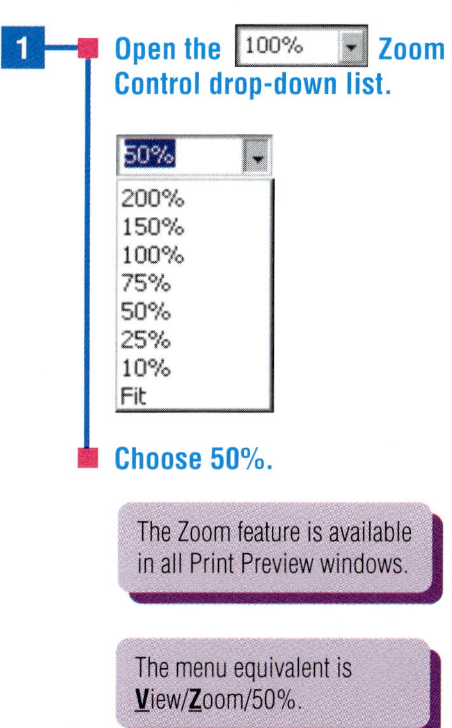

1 ■ **Open the** `100%` **Zoom Control drop-down list.**

■ **Choose 50%.**

> The Zoom feature is available in all Print Preview windows.

> The menu equivalent is **V**iew/**Z**oom/50%.

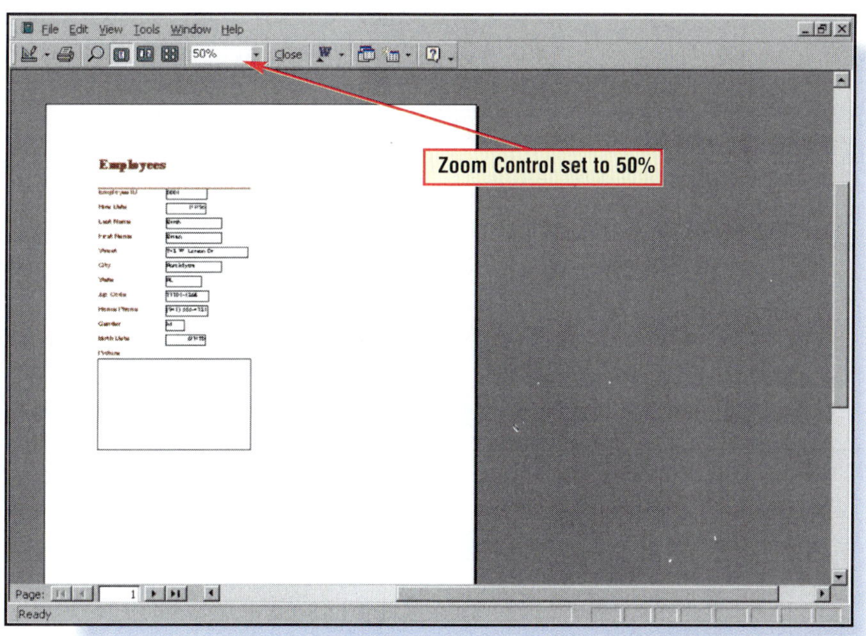

Figure 3–33

Your screen should be similar to Figure 3–33.

The text is reduced in size by half, allowing you to view more of the page in the window. You can now see three sides of the page. This is very close to the magnification level you get using the Fit option.

2 ■ **Click on the page to change the magnification to Fit.**

> The menu equivalent is **V**iew/**Z**oom/**F**it to Window.

Your screen should be similar to Figure 3–34.

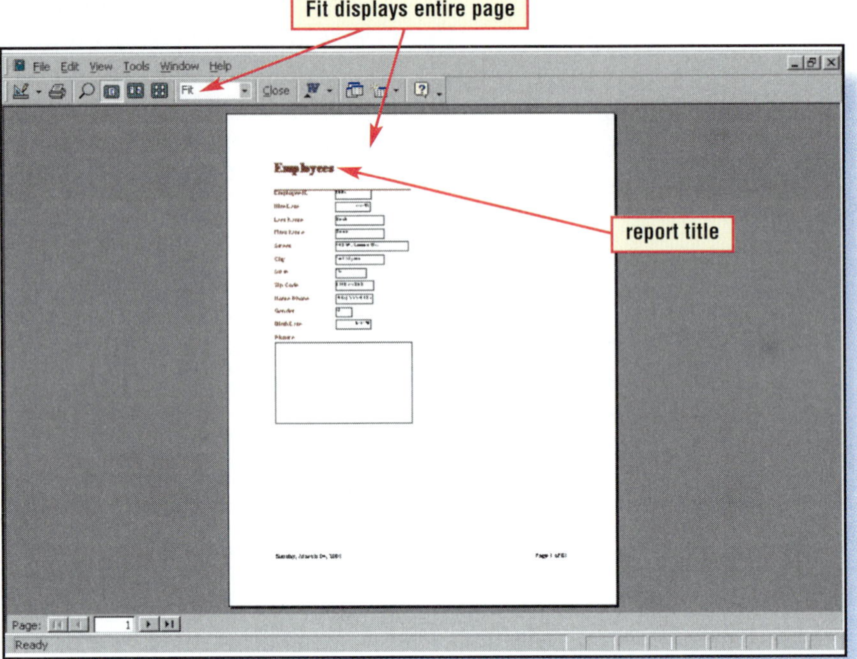

Figure 3–34

Now the entire page is visible, and although most of the text is too small to read, you can now see the entire page layout. The report title appears at the top of the page, and each field of information is displayed on a separate line in a single column for each record. The current date and page number appear at the bottom of the page in the footer. The first record from the Employees table is displayed on the first page of the report.

Now, because the last magnification level you used was 50%, clicking on the page again will switch between the last-used magnification level and the Fit magnification. The location of the pointer on the report when you click indicates the area of the report that will appear in the window.

3 ■ **With the mouse pointer as** 🔍 **, click on the report title.**

The page is displayed at 50% magnification again.

4 ■ **Return the magnification level to 100%.**

You can also view multiple report pages at the same time in Print Preview. To view six pages,

5 **Click**  **Multiple Pages.**

The **V**iew/P**a**ges command can be used to display up to 12 pages, and the [ ] button can be used to display up to 20 pages of a report in the window.

Select six pages 2x3.

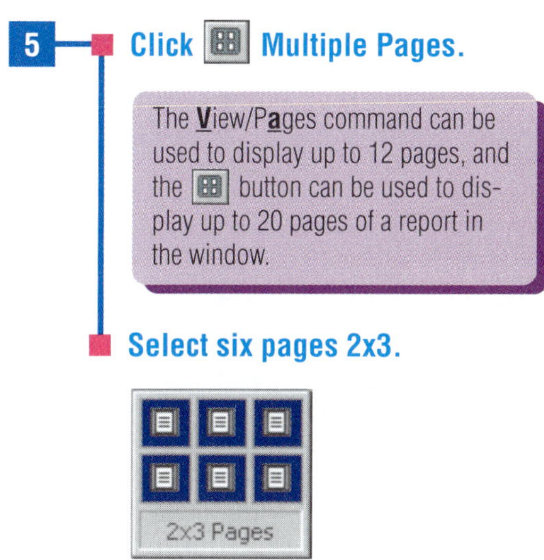

Your screen should be similar to Figure 3–35.

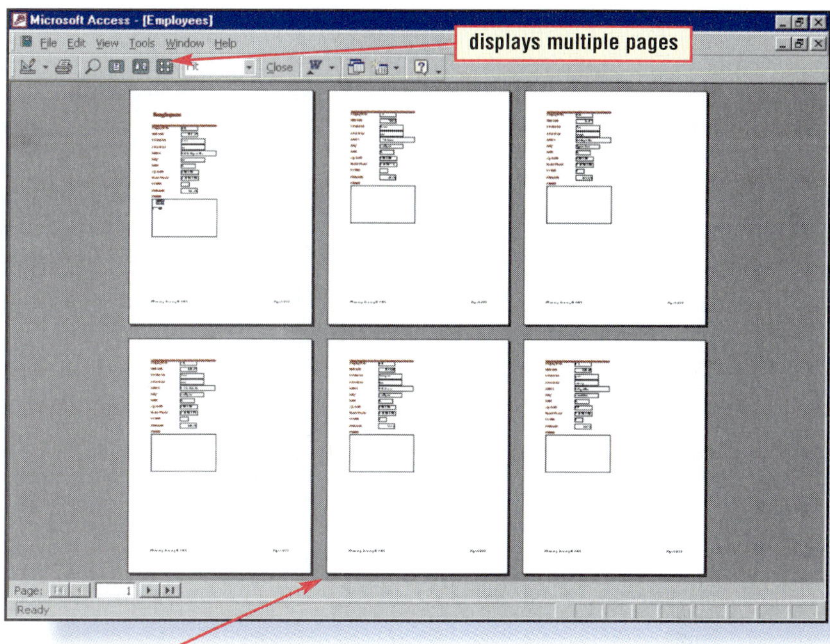

Figure 3–35

After looking over the columnar report, you decide the layout is inappropriate for your report because only one record is printed per page. In addition, you do not want the report to include all the fields from the table. To close the report file without saving it,

Do not click Close on the toolbar. This closes the Print Preview window, but does not close the report file.

6 **Click** ✕ .

Click No

Using the Report Wizard

You want the report to display the field contents for each record on a line rather than in a column. The Report Wizard will create this type of report. From the Reports tab,

1 **Double-click** Create report by using wizard.

Fields are added just as in Form Wizard.

The Report Wizard consists of a series of dialog boxes, much like the Form Wizard. In the first dialog box (see Figure 3–36) you specify the table or query to be used in the report and select the fields.

2 Select Table: Employees from the Tables/Queries drop-down list.

Add the First Name field to the Selected Fields list.

Then add the Last Name, Street, City, State, Zip Code, and Home Phone fields in that order.

You do not have to include all the fields in the table or query on a report.

Your screen should be similar to Figure 3–36.

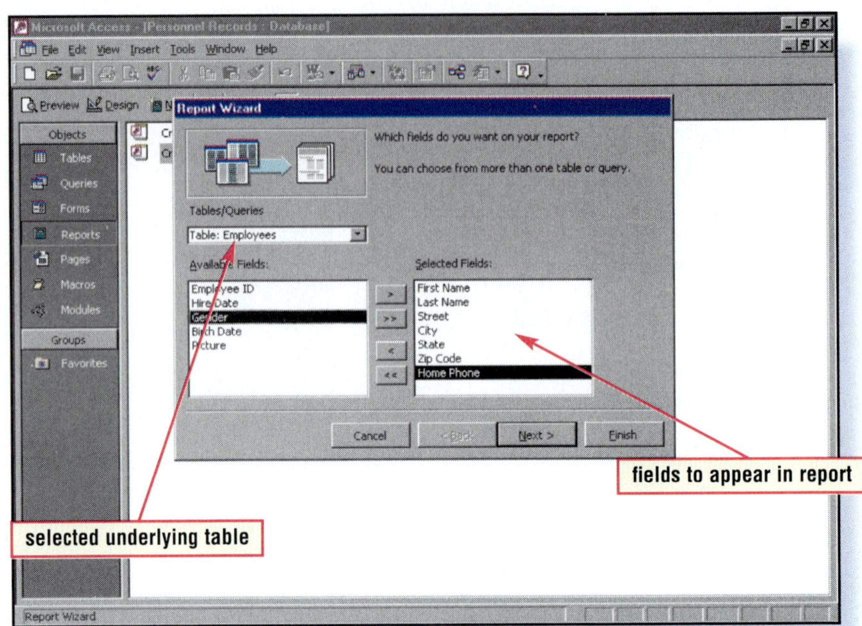

Figure 3–36

3 Click   Next > .

In the second Report Wizard dialog box, you specify how to group the data in the report. Cindy does not want the report grouped by any category. To move to the next dialog box,

4 Click   Next > .

The next dialog box (see Figure 3–37) is used to specify a sort order for the records. A report can be sorted on up to four fields. Again, you want the report sorted in ascending order by last name and first name within same last names.

5 **Select the** Last Name **field from the number 1 drop-down list and the** First Name **field from the number 2 drop-down list.**

Clicking ⬇ toggles between ascending and descending sort order.

Your screen should be similar to Figure 3–37.

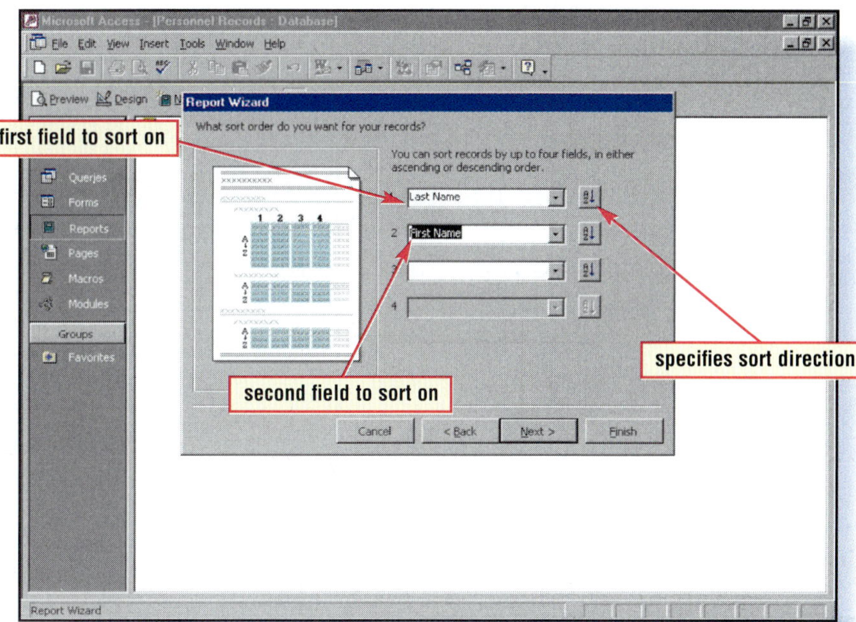

Figure 3–37

6 **Click** Next > .

Your screen should be similar to Figure 3–38.

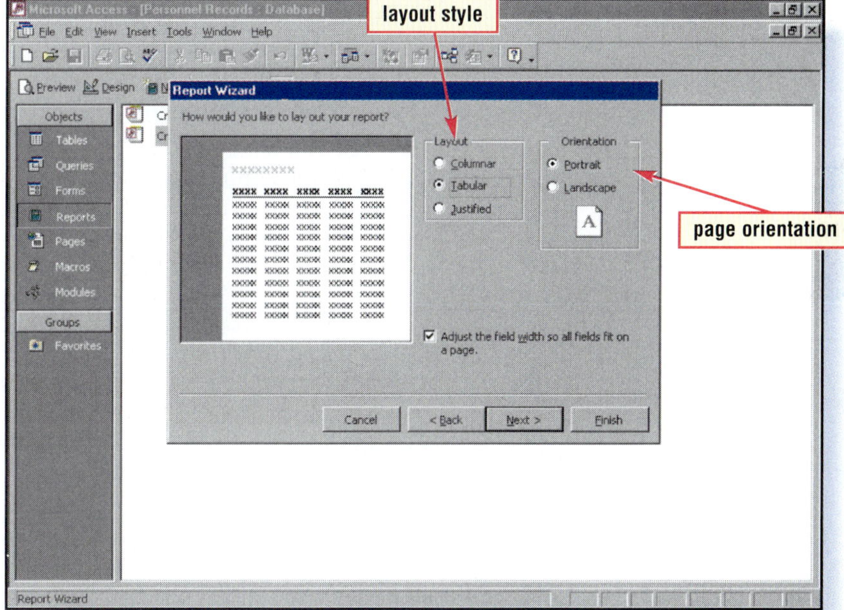

Figure 3–38

The next dialog box is used to change the report layout and orientation. **Orientation** refers to the direction text prints on a page. Normal orientation is to print across the width of an 8½-inch page. This is called **portrait** orientation. You can change the orientation to print across the length of the paper. This is called **landscape** orientation. The default report settings create a tabular layout using portrait orientation. In addition, the option to adjust the field width so all fields fit on one page is selected. Because this report is only five columns, the default settings are acceptable.

7 ■ **Click** Next > .

Your screen should be similar to
Figure 3–39.

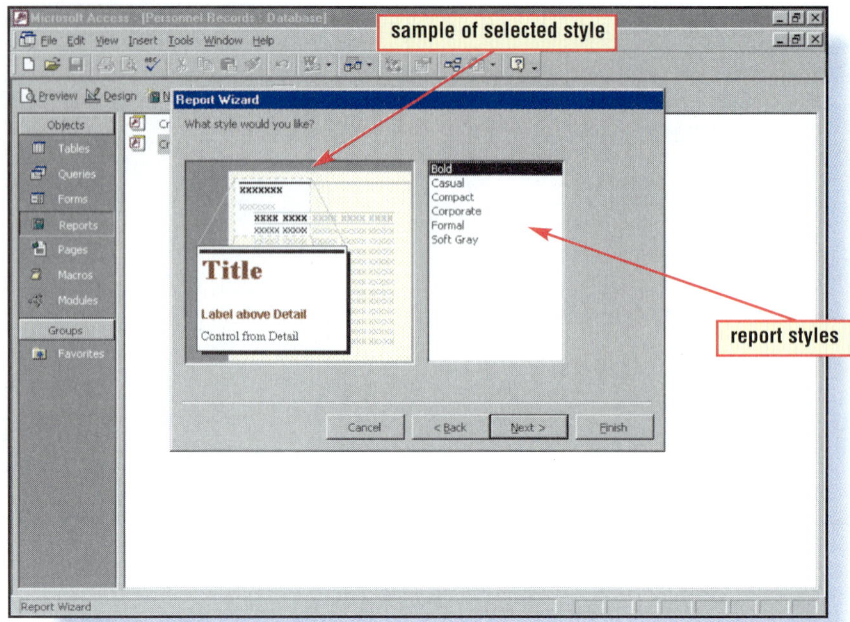

Figure 3–39

From this dialog box you select a style for the report. The preview area displays a sample of each style as it is selected.

8 ■ **Select each style to preview the style options.**

■ **You believe the Bold style is most appropriate for this report.**

■ **Select** Bold.

■ **Click** Next > .

The last Report Wizard dialog box is used to add a title to the report and
to specify how the report should be displayed after it is created. The only
change you want to make is to replace the table name with a more descriptive report title.

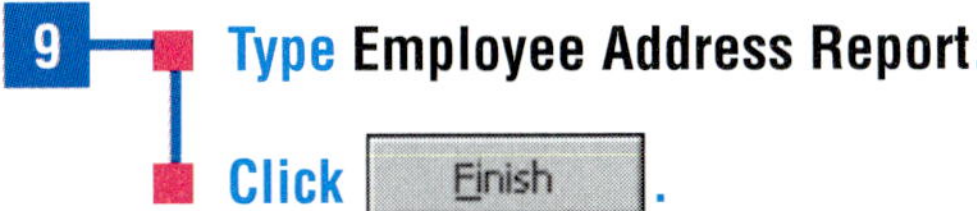

9 **Type Employee Address Report.**

Click Finish .

Your screen should be similar to Figure 3–40.

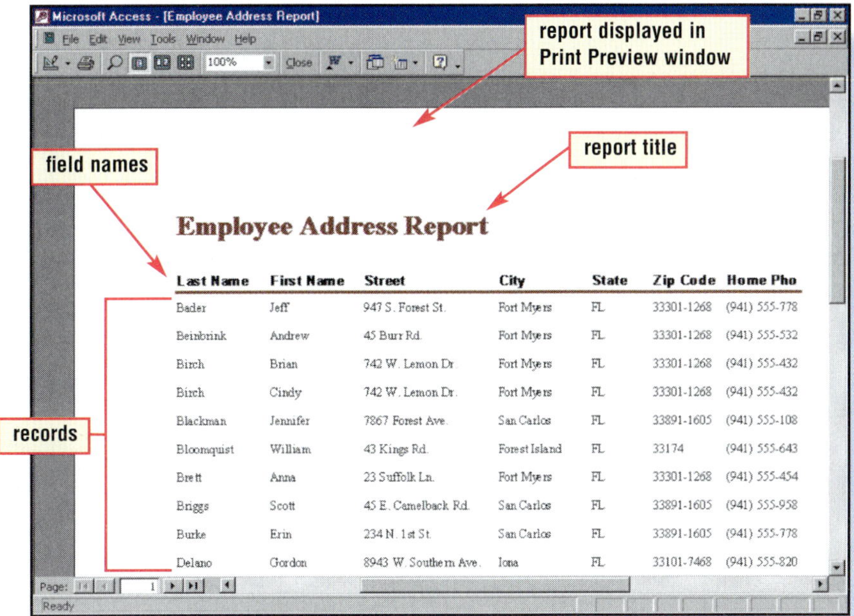

Figure 3–40

The program takes a minute to generate the report, during which time Report Design view is briefly displayed. In a few moments, the completed report with the data from the underlying table is displayed in the Print Preview window.

The Print Preview window displays the report using the selected Bold report style. The report title reflects the title you specified using the Wizard. The names of the selected fields are displayed on the first line of the report, and each record appears on a separate row below the field names. Notice that the Last Name field is the first field, even though you selected it as the second field. This is because the sort order overrides the selected field order.

10 **Change the magnification to Fit.**

Your screen should be similar to Figure 3–41.

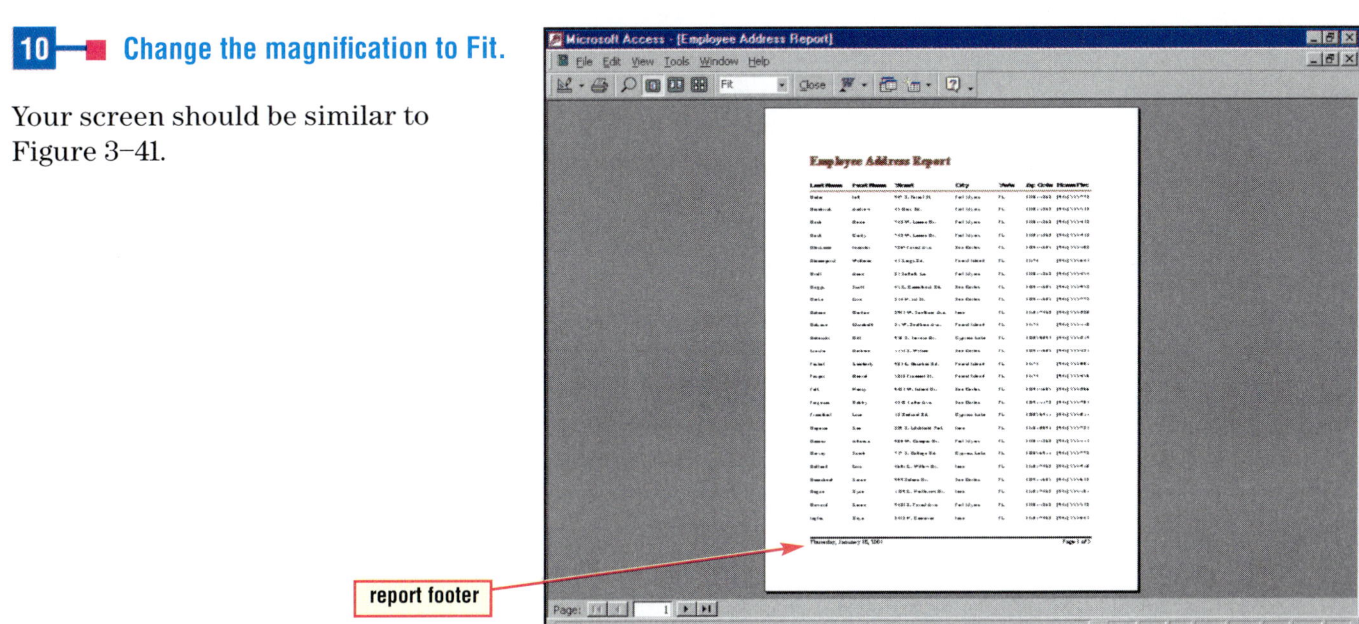

Figure 3–41

You can now see the layout of the report on the entire page. The report information easily fits across the page with the orientation set to portrait.

Modifying the Report Design

You like the layout of this report, but you still want the Last Name field to follow the First Name field. You also notice that you need to fix the Home Phone field label so that it displays the label fully. To make these changes, you need to modify the report design.

1 — ■ Click 🖉 ▾ **Design View.**

Your screen should be similar to Figure 3–42.

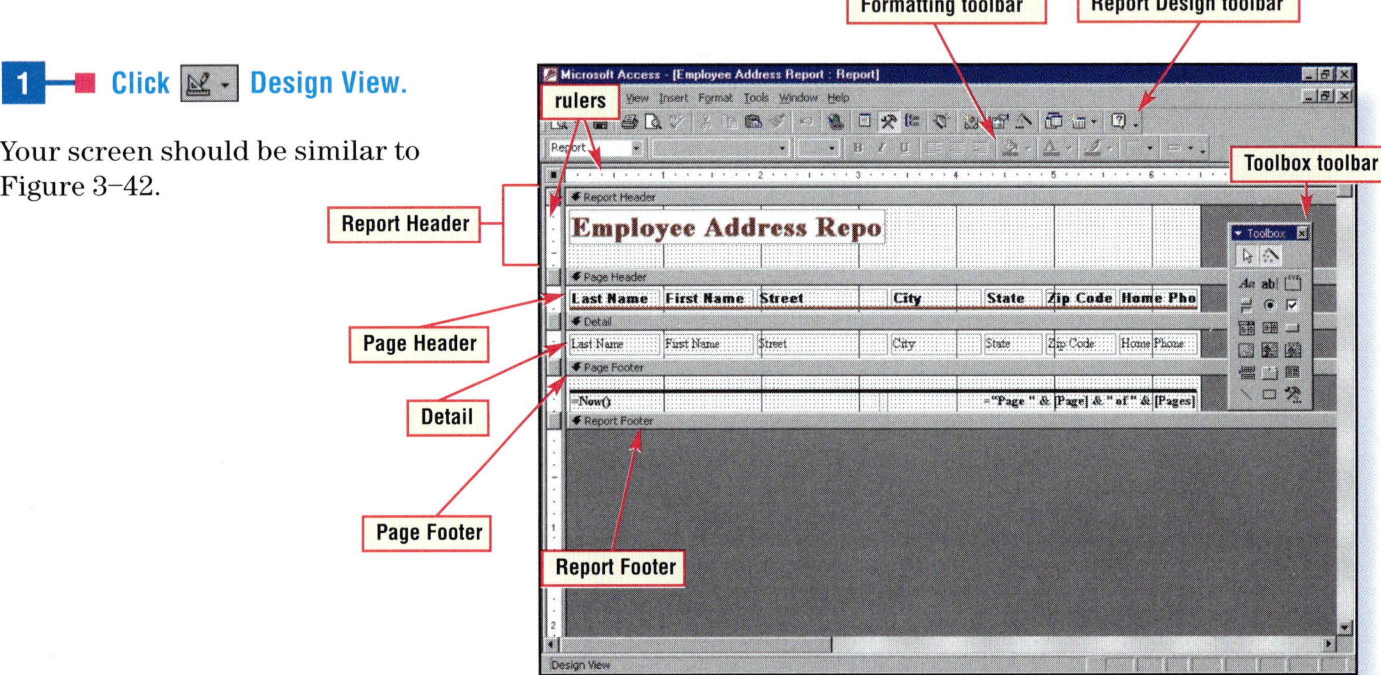

Figure 3–42

Report Design view displays the report in a window that is bordered along the top by a horizontal ruler and along the left by a vertical ruler. The rulers help you correctly place items in the Report Design window.

The Report Design view automatically displays three toolbars: Report Design, Formatting, and Toolbox. The Report Design toolbar contains the standard buttons as well as buttons that are specific to the Report Design view window. The Formatting toolbar displayed below the Report Design toolbar contains buttons that allow you to make text enhancements. The Toolbox toolbar contains buttons that are used to add and modify report design objects.

> If the Toolbox is not displayed use **V**iew/T**o**olbox or click 🔧 to display it.

2 ■ **If necessary, move the Toolbox toolbar to the right side of the window.**

The Report Design window is divided into five areas: Report Header, Page Header, Detail, Page Footer, and Report Footer. The contents of each section appear below the horizontal bar containing the name. The sections are described in the table below.

Section	Description
Report Header	Contains information to be printed once at the beginning of the report. The report title is displayed in this area.
Page Header	Contains information to be printed at the top of each page. The column headings are displayed in this section.
Detail	Contains the records of the table. The field column widths are the same as the column widths set in the table design.
Page Footer	Contains information to be printed at the bottom of each page, such as the date and page number.
Report Footer	Contains information to be printed at the end of the report. The Report Footer section currently contains no data.

Selecting, Moving, and Sizing Controls

Every object in a report is contained in a control.

Concept  6 Control

Reports and forms are linked to the underlying table by using controls. **Controls** are graphical objects that can be selected and modified. Once a control is selected, it can be sized, moved, or enhanced in other ways.

The most common type of control is a text box. A **text box control** creates a link to the underlying source, usually a field from a table, and displays the field entry in the report or form. This type of control is called a **bound control** because it is tied to a field in an underlying table.

The report or form usually also includes a label with each text box control. A **label control** initially displays the field name from the underlying table associated with the text box control. Label controls can also display custom names you specify instead of the field name, or other descriptive text entries such as a title or instructions for the user. These controls are **unbound controls** because they are not connected to a field. Other unbound controls contain elements that enhance the appearance of the form, such as lines, boxes, and pictures.

A third type of control is a **calculated control,** which displays the results of a calculation in the form or report. It contains an expression that uses data from the underlying table or another control as its source of data.

Finally, some text box and label controls are connected and act as one when manipulated. These controls are called **compound controls.**

You select, size and move controls in Form Design view just like in Report Design view.

In this report design, the label controls are displayed in the Page Header section, and the text box controls are in the Detail section. You need to select controls to modify them. To select the Last Name control,

1 **Click on the Last Name label control in the Page Header section.**

The mouse pointer must be when selecting controls.

Your screen should be similar to Figure 3–43.

When you first click on a control, the shape appears and will display as long as you hold down the mouse button.

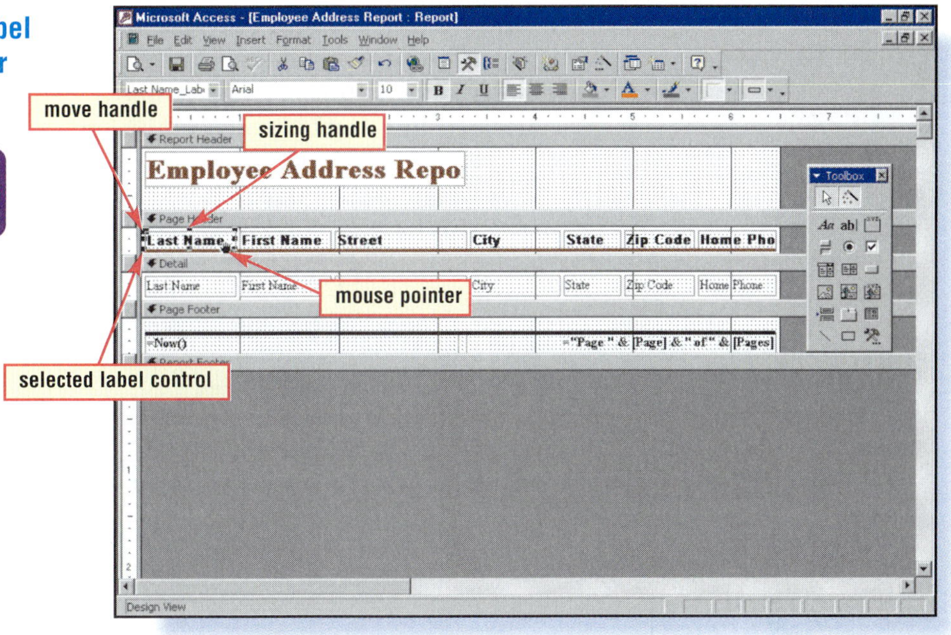

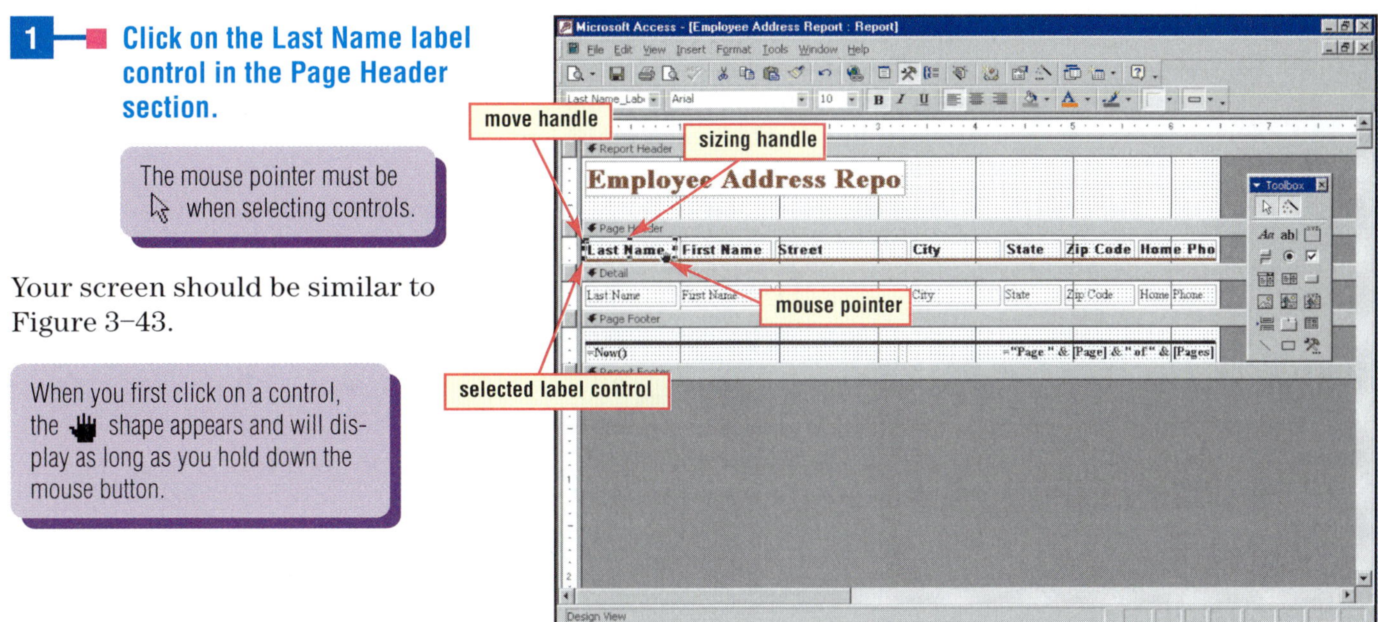

Figure 3–43

The Last Name label control is surrounded by eight small boxes called **sizing handles** that indicate the label control is selected. The sizing handles are used to size the control. In addition, a large box in the upper left corner is displayed. This is a **move handle** that is used to move the selected control.

You also want to select the Last Name text box control.

2 **Hold down Shift and click on the Last Name text box control in the Detail section.**

You can also delete controls by selecting them and pressing Delete.

Your screen should be similar to Figure 3–44.

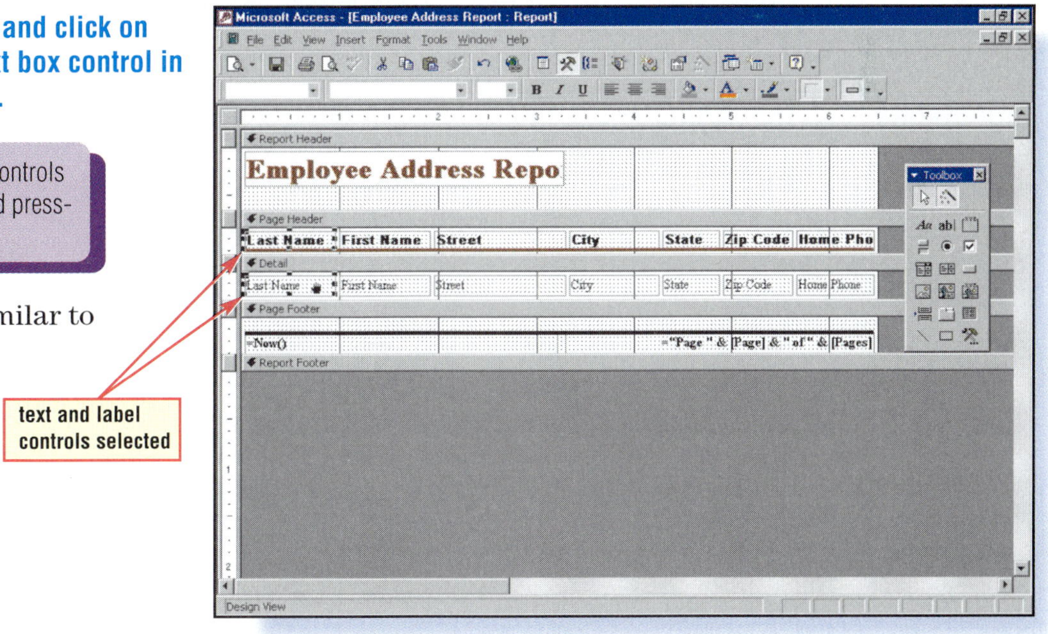

Figure 3–44

Now both controls are selected. Once controls are selected, they can be modified. In this case, you want to move the Last Name controls to the right of the First Name controls. Controls are moved by dragging them to the new location. When you can move a selected control, the mouse

You can also move controls using [Ctrl] + the directional arrow keys.

pointer shape appears as 🖐. You can then drag the control to any location in the report design. The grid of dots helps you position the controls on the form. It not only provides a visual guide to positioning and sizing controls, but controls are "snapped" to the grid, or automatically positioned on the nearest grid line.

Because you need to swap positions of the two fields, you will first move the Last Name controls to the right, then you will move the First Name controls to the left.

3 ▪ **Drag the Last Name controls to the right until they overlap part of the Street controls.**

Do not point to a sizing or move handle.

▪ **Select the First Name controls and drag them to the left edge of the grid.**

▪ **Select the Last Name controls again and drag them to between the First Name and Street controls.**

Your screen should be similar to Figure 3–45.

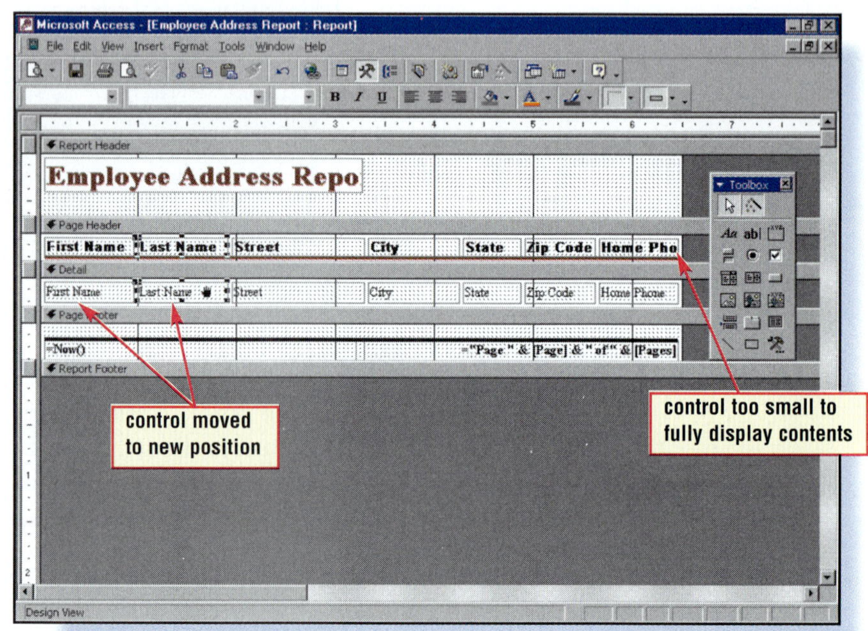

Figure 3–45

Next you will increase the size of the Home Phone control. When you position the mouse pointer on a sizing handle, it changes to a ↔. The direction of the arrow indicates in which direction dragging the mouse will alter the shape of the object. This is similar to sizing a window.

4 ■ **Select the Home Phone text box and label controls.**

■ **Point to the middle handle on the right end of either selected control.**

■ **When the mouse pointer appears as ↔, drag the control to the right until the entire field label is displayed.**

The right edge of the form will automatically increase as you increase the size of the control.

Your screen should be similar to Figure 3–46.

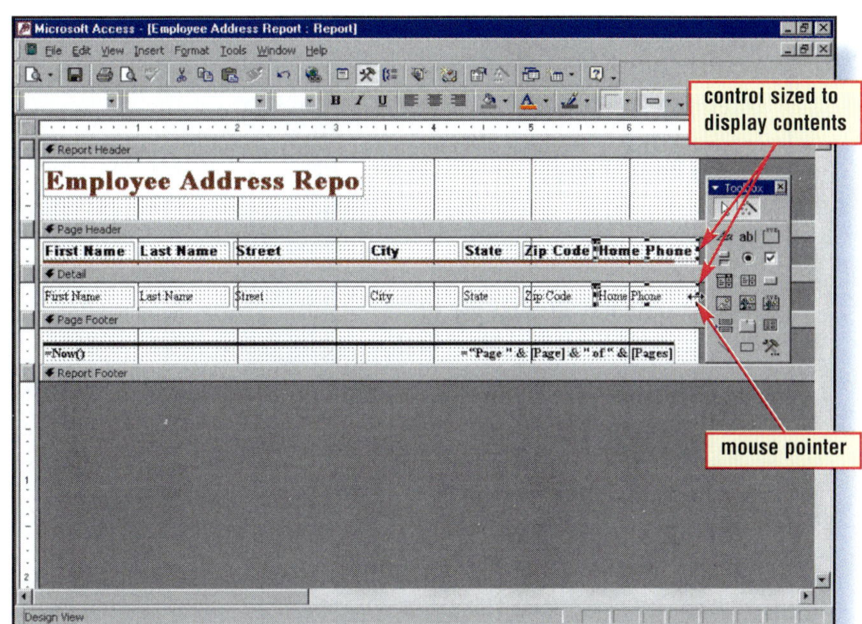

Figure 3–46

Then to see the change in the report,

5 ■ **Click** 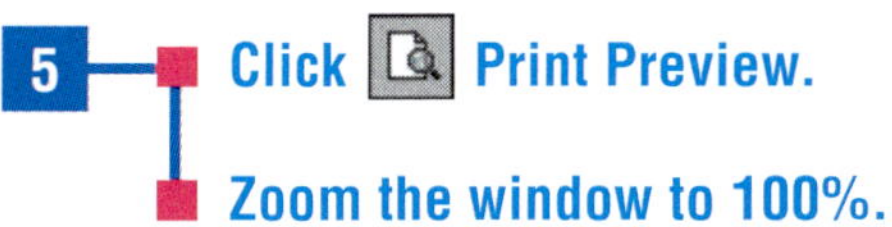 **Print Preview.**

■ **Zoom the window to 100%.**

Your screen should be similar to Figure 3–47.

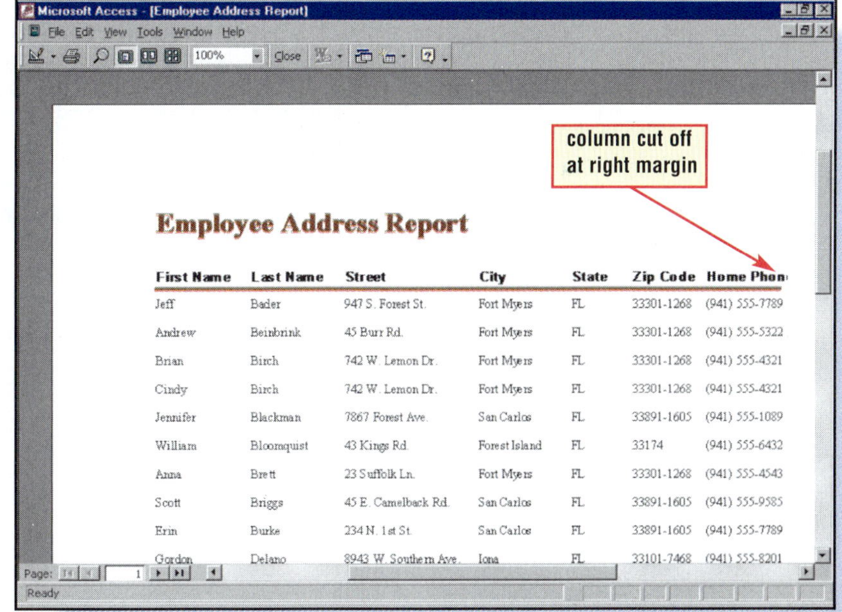

Figure 3--47

The Home Phone label is still cut off because it extends beyond the right margin. To change the page orientation to landscape so the entire width of the report will print on the page,

6 ■ **Choose File/Page Setup.**

■ **Open the Page tab.**

■ **Select Landscape.**

■ **Choose** OK **.**

■ **Zoom the preview window to Fit.**

Your screen should be similar to
Figure 3–48.

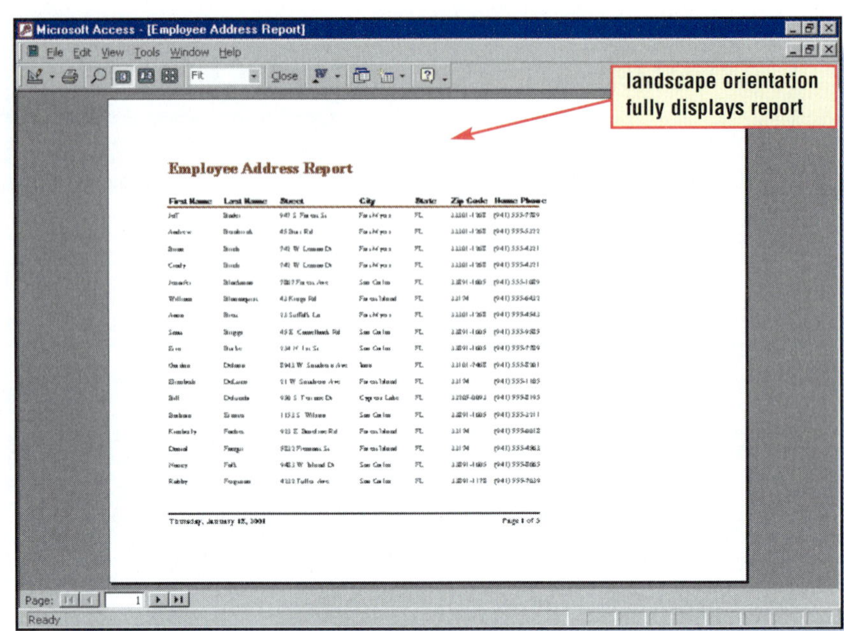

Figure 3–48

Printing a Selected Page

The report is now in the order you want it to appear. Now you will print
the page containing your record.

1 ■ **Move to the page of the report
that contains your name.**

Increase the magnification
to locate your record more easily.

■ **Choose File/Print.**

The ⎙ Print button prints the entire report.

■ **If necessary, select the appropriate printer for your system.**

■ **Select Pages.**

The page number is displayed in
the page indicator box.

■ **Type the page number containing
your record in the From and To
text boxes.**

Your screen should be similar to
Figure 3–49.

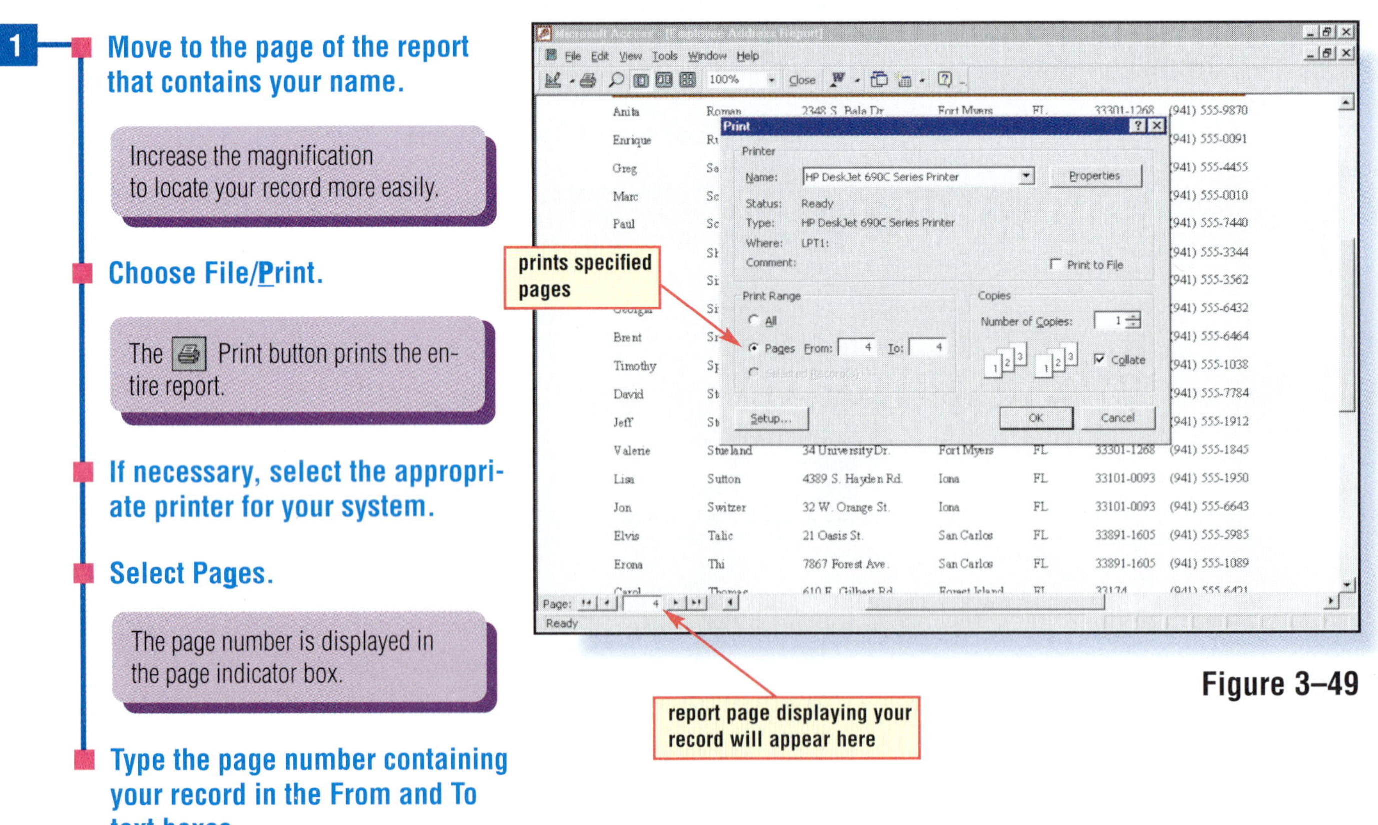

Figure 3–49

2 — Click  OK .

Close the Report window, saving the changes you have made.

The Database window is displayed again, and the report object name is listed in the Reports object list. The Report Wizard automatically saves the report using the report title as the object name.

Creating a Report from a Query

You have seen how easy it is to create a report from a table, so you would like to create a report from the car pool query.

1 — Use the Report Wizard to create a tabular report based on the car pool query using the following specifications:

Include all fields except Club Location.

Sort on City **first, then** Last Name and First Name. **Use the casual style.**

Title the report **Iona to Fort Myers Car Pool Report.**

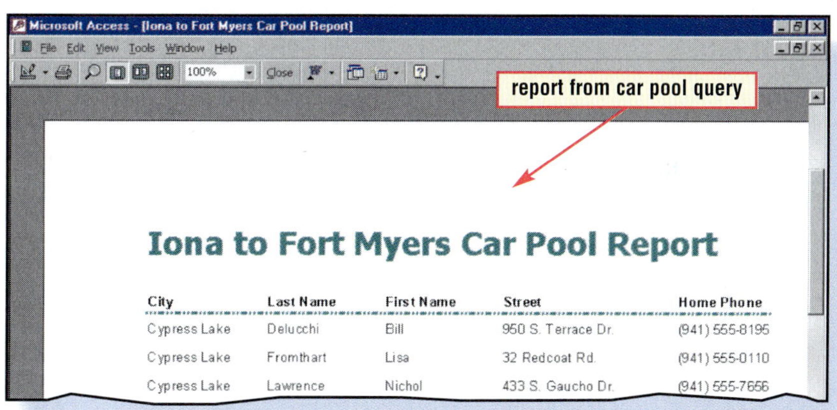

Figure 3–50

When the Wizard finishes, your screen should be similar to Figure 3–50.

2 — Use Report Design view to move the fields into First Name, Last Name, Street, City, and Home Phone order.

Print the report.

Your completed report should look like the report shown in the Case Study at the beginning of the tutorial.

Compacting the Database

Additional Information

A file is fragmented when it becomes too large for your computer to store in a single location on your disk. When this happens, the file is split up and stored in pieces in different locations on the disk, making it slower to access.

As you modify a database the changes are saved to your disk. When you delete data or objects the database file can become fragmented and use disk space inefficiently. To make the database perform optimally, you should compact the database on a regular basis. Compacting makes a copy of the file and rearranges how the file is stored on your disk. To compact the database,

1 — Choose **T**ools/**D**atabase Utilities/**C**ompact and Repair Database.

Close the Database file and exit Access.

Tutorial 3: Analyzing Tables and Creating Reports

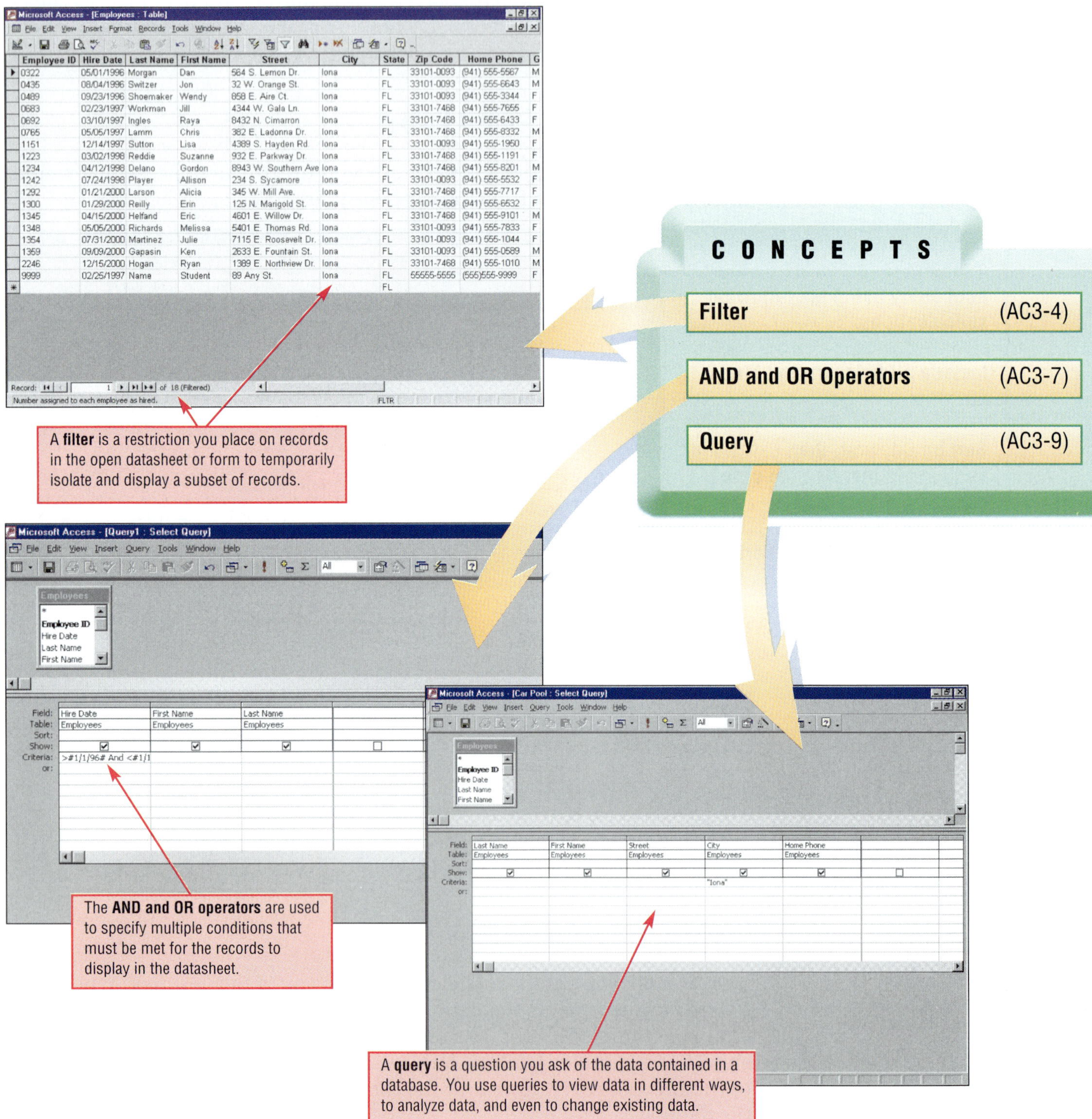

A **filter** is a restriction you place on records in the open datasheet or form to temporarily isolate and display a subset of records.

The **AND and OR operators** are used to specify multiple conditions that must be met for the records to display in the datasheet.

A **query** is a question you ask of the data contained in a database. You use queries to view data in different ways, to analyze data, and even to change existing data.

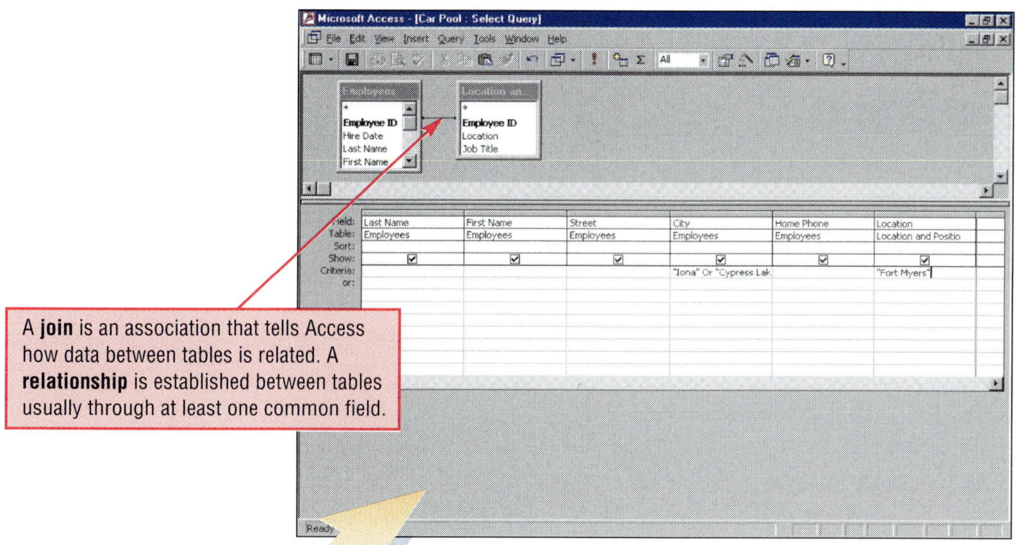

A **join** is an association that tells Access how data between tables is related. A **relationship** is established between tables usually through at least one common field.

Joins and Relationships (AC3-24)

Report (AC3-27)

Control (AC3-38)

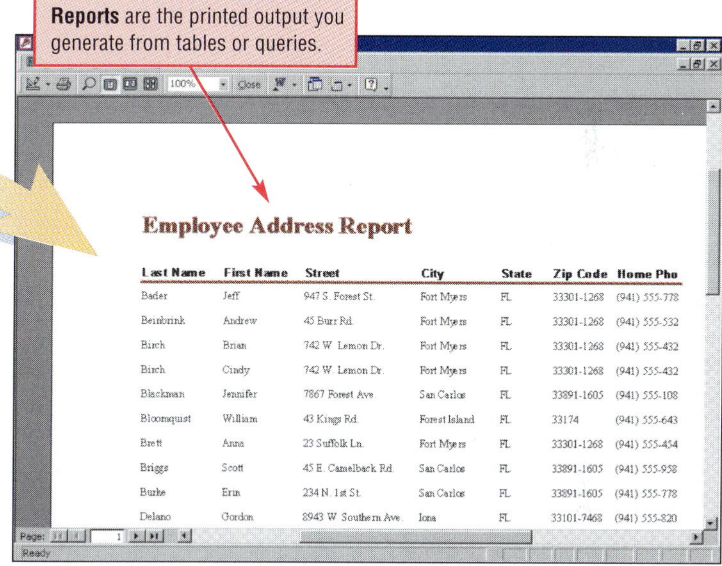

Reports are the printed output you generate from tables or queries.

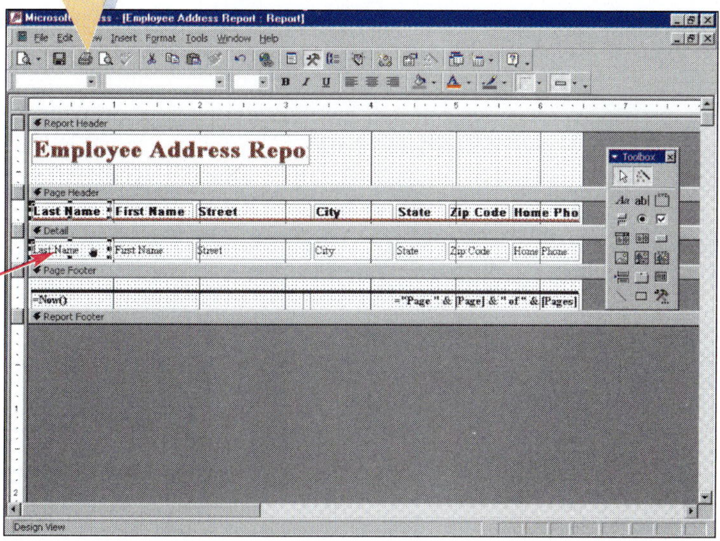

Reports and forms are linked to the underlying table by using **controls**. Controls are graphical objects that can be selected and modified.

Tutorial Review

Key Terms

bound control   AC3-38
calculated control   AC3-38
cell   AC3-14
column selector bar   AC3-14
comparison operator   AC3-14
compound control   AC3-38
control   AC3-38
criteria expression   AC3-6
field list   AC3-14

filter   AC3-4
inner join   AC3-24
join   AC3-24
label control   AC3-38
landscape   AC3-33
move handle   AC3-39
multitable query   AC3-22
orientation   AC3-33

portrait   AC3-33
query   AC3-9
query datasheet   AC3-12
relationship   AC3-24
report   AC3-27
sizing handles   AC3-39
text box control   AC3-38
unbound control   AC3-38

Command Summary

Command	Button	Action
File/Page Set**u**p/Page/**L**andscape		Changes page orientation to landscape
File/**P**rint/Pa**g**es/**F**rom		Prints selected pages
Edit/Cle**a**r Grid		Clears query grid
Insert/**R**eport		Creates a new report object
View/**Z**oom/%.		Displays previewed document at specified percentage
View/**Z**oom/**F**it to Window		Displays entire previewed document page
View/**Pa**ges		Displays specified number of pages of previewed document
Records/**F**ilter/**F**ilter by Form		Displays blank datasheet for entering criteria to display specific information
Records/**F**ilter/Filter by **S**election		Displays only records that contain a specific value
Records/Appl**y** Filter/Sort		Applies filter to table
Records/**R**emove Filter/Sort		Removes filter from table
Tools/**R**elationships		Defines permanent relationship between tables
Tools/**D**atabase Utilities/**C**ompact and Repair Database		Compacts and repairs database file
Filte**r**/Appl**y** Filter/Sort		Applies filter to table
Query/**R**un		Displays query results in Query Datasheet view
Query/Show **T**able		Displays Show Table dialog box
Window/**1** <name>		Displays Database window

Screen Identification

In the following screen, several items are identified by letters. Enter the correct term for each item in the spaces that follow.

a. _______________________________   f. _______________________________

b. _______________________________   g. _______________________________

c. _______________________________   h. _______________________________

d. _______________________________   i. _______________________________

e. _______________________________

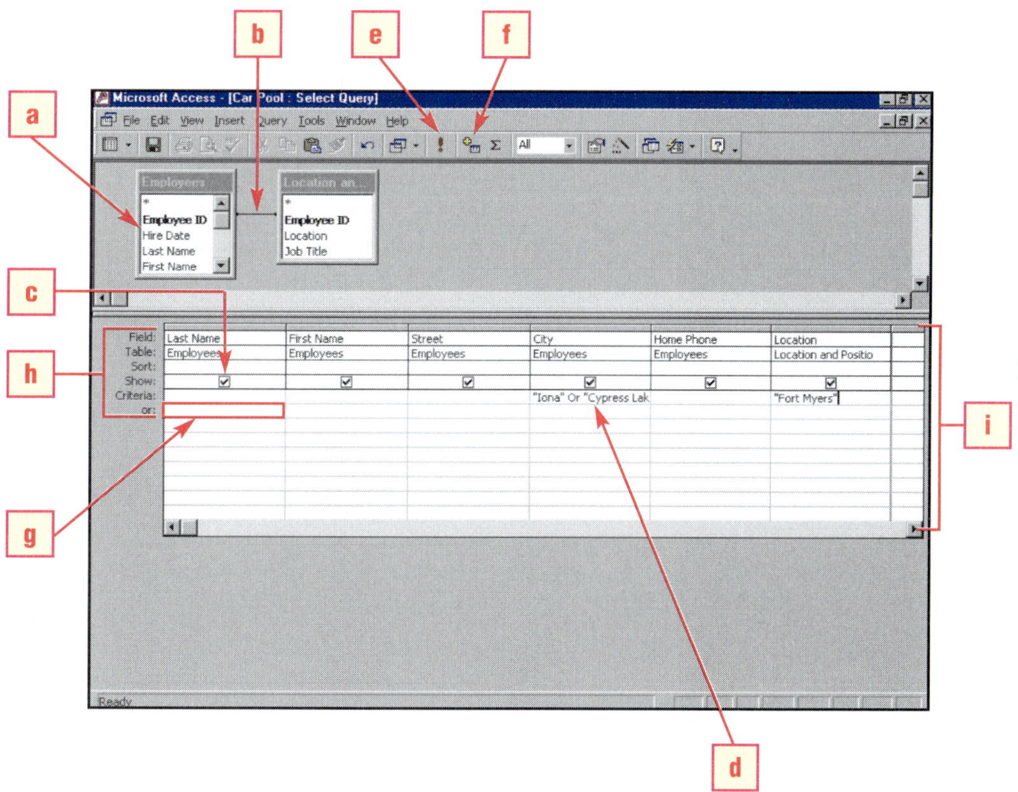

Matching

Match the letter to the correct item in the numbered list.

1. [icon]   ______ **a.** intersection of a column and row

2. query   ______ **b.** a control that is tied to a field in an underlying table

3. multitable query   ______ **c.** temporary restriction placed on displayed data to isolate specific records

4. criteria   ______ **d.** includes any records containing either condition

5. [icon]   ______ **e.** object that links a form or report to the underlying table

6. filter   ______ **f.** runs a query and displays query datasheet

7. OR   ______ **g.** used to ask questions about database tables

8. bound   ______ **h.** query that uses data from more than one table

9. control   ______ **i.** set of limiting conditions

10. cell   ______ **j.** accesses Filter By Form feature

True/False

Circle correct answer to the following statements.

1. Multiple filter results can be saved.   True   False

2. The OR operator narrows a search.   True   False

3. Queries are used to view data in different ways, to analyze data, and to change existing data.   True   False

4. Outer join is the default join in Access.   True   False

5. Access includes a custom report feature to assist in creating professional-appearing reports.   True   False

6. Filters use reports to set limiting conditions.   True   False

7. The AND operator is assumed when you enter criteria in multiple fields.   True   False

8. The most common type of relationship is many-to-many.   True   False

9. Reports are printed output generated from tables and queries.   True   False

10. Controls are text objects.   True   False

Multiple Choice

Circle the letter of the correct answer to the following statements.

1. A ______________ is a restriction placed on records in the open datasheet or form to quickly isolate and display a subset of records.

    a. filter

    b. query

    c. join

    d. property

2. AND and OR are ______________.

    a. criteria

    b. operators

    c. elements

    d. properties

3. Select, crosstab, parameter, action, and SQL are different types of ______________.

    a. action elements

    b. formats

    c. queries

    d. property elements

4. One-to-many, many-to-many, and one-to-one are different types of ______________.

    a. relationships

    b. queries

    c. filters

    d. reports

5. Reports and forms are linked to the underlying table by using _______________.

   a. filters

   b. criteria

   c. controls

   d. keys

6. A filter is created by specifying a set of limiting conditions or _______________.

   a. forms

   b. controls

   c. criteria

   d. objects

7. The operator that broadens a search, because any record meeting either condition is included in the output, is _______________.

   a. AND

   b. OR

   c. MOST

   d. ALL

8. A(n) _______________ is a question asked of the data contained in a database.

   a. form

   b. inquiry

   c. request

   d. query

9. A(n) _______________ is an association that tells Access how data between tables is related.

   a. join

   b. criteria

   c. query

   d. object

10. Text box, bound, unbound, label, and calculated are _______________.

    a. buttons

    b. forms

    c. properties

    d. controls

Fill-In Questions

Complete the following statements by filling in the blanks with the correct terms.

1. A(n) _______________ is used to isolate and display a specific group of records.

2. The _______________ operator narrows the search for records that meet both conditions.

3. The _______________ operator narrows the search for records that meet either condition.

4. A(n) _______________ is an association that shows how data between tables is related.

5. A(n) _______________ retrieves specific data from one or more tables and displays the results in a query datasheet.

6. The _______________ of the Query window is where the fields to be displayed in the query datasheet are placed.

7. Tables are joined by defining a(n) _______________ between the tables.

8. _______________ are used to link the underlying table or query to the report.

9. Custom names in a report are _______________ because they are not connected to a field.

10. The _______________ comparison operator is used to find values that are less than or equal to another value.

Discussion Questions

1. Discuss what filters are and how they can be used in a database. When would it be appropriate to use a filter?

2. Discuss the differences between the AND and OR filter conditions.

3. Discuss what a query can do and some advantages of using queries.

4. Discuss the three types of relationships. Give an example of how an inner join could be created in a database.

Hands-On Practice Exercises

Step by Step

1. Daria O'Dell, the owner of Daria's Day Spa, is thinking of offering a "Young Again" spa package that would include various skin treatments and massages. To get an idea of how much interest there would be in this package among her current clientele, Ms. O'Dell has asked you for a list of clients who are over the age of 35. (She does not need anything as formal as a report.) You decide that the simplest way to do this is to filter the table and print the filtered datasheet (which you completed in Practice Exercise 1 of Tutorial 2). The printed datasheet is shown here.

Clients								1/22/01	

Client ID	First Name	Last Name	Home Phone	Work Phone	Street Address	City	State	Zip Code	Birthdate
001	Elaine	Grace	(217) 555-4215	(217) 555-4557	718 North Coltrane	Madison	TX	75380	02/02/1963
017	Pauline	Kelly	(217) 555-3822	(217) 555-8989	1723 Edwards Drive	Madison	TX	75380	05/11/1954
002	Polly	Trawe	(217) 555-0091	(217) 555-2831	619 Portland Drive	Alison	TX	76890	11/27/1954
003	Nadine	Richmond	(217) 555-1748	(217) 555-4279	1248 Trammell Avenue	Alison	TX	76890	09/10/1950
009	Bobbi	Miller	(217) 555-3844		7435 Red Robin Lane	Madison	TX	75380	02/21/1957
010	Charlene	Riley	(217) 555-0975	(217) 555-2499	2424 Eastern	Murray	TX	75377	03/16/1958
011	Fen	Woo	(217) 555-5380	(217) 555-1441	8547 Lindsey Avenue	Murray	TX	75377	01/25/1954

To filter the table, follow these steps:

a. Open the Daria Spa database and the Clients table. Best Fit the columns.

b. Select Filter by Form and enter **<1/1/64** in the Birthdate field. Apply the filter.

c. Enter your name in the last of the displayed fields and print the filtered datasheet in landscape orientation.

d. Remove the filter. Close the table, saving the changes.

e. Compact and repair the database.

2. The managing editor of the Daily Digest periodically contacts businesses that are currently advertising in the publication only once a month to see if they would like to increase the frequency of their ads. To do this, he needs a datasheet from you that contains the contact information for these businesses, as shown here.

	Monthly Advertisers									1/22/01	

Advertiser ID	Business Name	Business Type	Contact Name	Phone Number	Billing Street	Billing City	Billing State	Billing Zip	Ad Size	Ad Rate	Ad Frequency
E233	Prints	Print Shop	Richard Jones	(650) 555-4217	58 Lantana Ln.	Beacon Shores	CA	95055	1/4	$50.00	Monthly
A437	Fun Stuff	Toy Store	[Your Name]	(650) 555-1221	802 Trenton Way	Beacon Shores	CA	95055	Full	$100.00	Monthly
D504	Little Feet	Daycare	Joanne Kramer	(650) 555-3008	29B Roake Ct.	Beacon Shores	CA	95055	Full	$100.00	Monthly
B121	Fancy Pants	Clothing Store	Lucy Stevens	(650) 555-1938	222 Redwood Ln.	Beacon Shores	CA	95055	Full	$100.00	Monthly

To produce this datasheet, you will perform a query on the Advertisers table (which you completed in Practice Exercise 2 in Tutorial 2).

a. Open the Daily Digest database and select the Queries tab.

b. Use the Query Wizard to run a detail query on the Advertisers table. Include all the fields in the order listed. Title the query **Monthly Advertisers**.

c. In Query Design view, enter **Monthly** in the Ad Frequency criteria field. Run the query. Sort the Ad Rate field in ascending sort order. Print the query using landscape orientation.

d. Close the query, saving the changes.

e. Compact and repair the database.

3. Now that you have your Café Purchases database set up for the Downtown Internet Cafe (which you completed in Practice Exercise 3 of Tutorial 2), you are ready to actually use it to track inventory. In addition to performing your daily query of the database for low-quantity items, Evan, the owner, has asked you for a datasheet that shows all special-order items. He would also like a report (shown here) by the end of the day that shows the results of your low-quantity query so he can place the necessary orders.

To create the datasheet, query, and report, follow these steps:

a. Open the Cafe Purchases database and the Inventory table. Filter the table to display only those records where the Special Order? field is Y. Hide the address columns. Print the filtered datasheet to give to Evan. Unhide the hidden columns and remove the filter.

Cafe Items To Be Ordered

Vendor Name	Better Beverages, Inc.
Contact	Mae Yung
Phone	(415) 555-1122
Description	Darjeeling tea
# On Hand	39
Special Order?	N
Vendor Name	Better Beverages, Inc.
Contact	Mae Yung
Phone	(415) 555-1122
Description	Orange Pekoe tea
# On Hand	21
Special Order?	N
Vendor Name	Better Beverages, Inc.
Contact	Mae Yung
Phone	(415) 555-1122
Description	Earl Grey tea
# On Hand	17
Special Order?	N

Monday, January 22, 2001

b. Use the Query Wizard to create a query based on the Inventory table. Include all fields except Item # in their current order. Name the query **To Be Ordered**. In Design view, enter the criteria to display only those records with an On-Hand # that is less than 25, and run the query. Review the resulting datasheet.

c. Upon reviewing the datasheet, you realize that it is not in a very useful order. Also, since Evan typically places orders by phone, the address information is not really necessary. Return to Design view and do the following:

■ Apply an ascending sort to the Vendor Name column.

■ Delete the four address columns.

■ Move the Vendor Name, Contact, and Phone columns to the left of the Description column.

d. Run the query and review the resulting datasheet. Since the query now looks satisfactory enough to create a report from it, close the query window, saving the changes.

e. Use the Report Wizard to create a report based on the To Be Ordered query you just saved. Include the listed fields in the following order:

■ Vendor Name

■ Contact

■ Phone

■ Description

■ # On Hand

■ Special Order?

f. Select Vendor Name as the only sort field. Select the Columnar layout and Bold style. Name the report **Cafe Items To Be Ordered**.

g. Preview and print the page of the report that contains your name in the Contact field, and then close the Report window, saving the changes.

h. Compact and repair the database.

4. As the database manager for the EduSoft curriculum software company, you need to periodically submit reports to the head of marketing so she can use them to canvass school systems for potential customers. You just received a memo from her requesting a report, shown here, on titles for grades 3–8.

To create the requested report, follow these steps:

a. Open the database named Learning, which you completed in Practice Exercise 4 of Tutorial 2.

b. Use the Query Wizard to create a query based on the Software table. Include the following fields in this order: Grade Level, Title, Subject, Key Topics. Name the query **Marketing**.

c. In Query Design view, enter **3-5** in the first Grade Level criteria cell, and **6-8** in the second (Or) cell. Run the query and review the resulting datasheet. Close the query window, saving the changes.

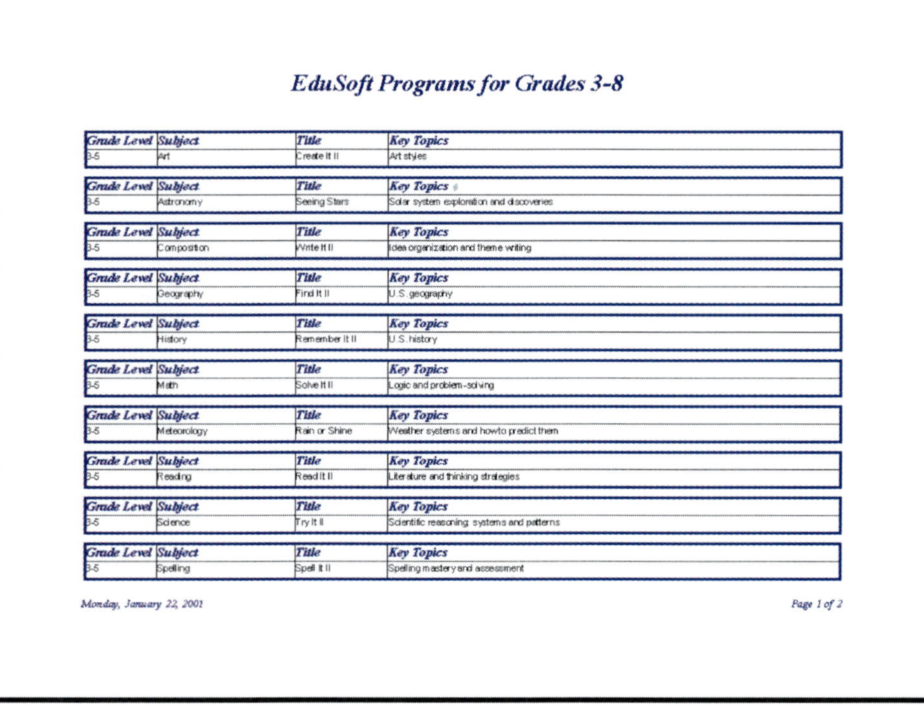

EduSoft Programs for Grades 3-8

Grade Level	Subject	Title	Key Topics
3-5	Art	Create It II	Art styles
3-5	Astronomy	Seeing Stars	Solar system exploration and discoveries
3-5	Composition	Write It II	Idea organization and theme writing
3-5	Geography	Find It II	U.S. geography
3-5	History	Remember It II	U.S. history
3-5	Math	Solve It II	Logic and problem-solving
3-5	Meteorology	Rain or Shine	Weather systems and how to predict them
3-5	Reading	Read It II	Literature and thinking strategies
3-5	Science	Try It II	Scientific reasoning, systems and patterns
3-5	Spelling	Spell It II	Spelling mastery and assessment

Monday, January 22, 2001 — Page 1 of 2

d. Use the Report Wizard to create a report based on the Marketing query you just saved. Include all the fields in the order listed. Select Grade Level as the first sort field and Subject as the second sort field. Select the Justified layout, landscape orientation, and Corporate style. Name the report **EduSoft Programs for Grades 3–8**.

e. Center the Report Header control at the top of the page.

f. Preview and then print the report. Close the Report window, saving the changes you made.

g. Compact and repair the database.

5. The Animal Angels volunteers are successfully using the database you created to enter information for all the animals picked up by the organization and boarded, placed in foster care, and/or adopted. Meanwhile, you created another table containing information about the adoptive homes (including names, addresses, and phone numbers). The Animal Angels owners have now asked you for a report, shown below, of all animals adopted in the past six months and by whom so the appropriate thank you notes can be sent.

To create the requested report, follow these steps:

a. Open the database named Angels.

b. Open the Queries tab and create a query in Design view. Join the Animals and Adopters tables, and add the following fields to the design grid in the order listed below:

- Animal Type
- Status
- Adoption Date
- Adopter First Name
- Adopter Last Name
- Adopter Street
- Adopter City
- Adopter State
- Adopter Zip

Animal Angels Adoption Report

Adopter First Name	Adopter Last Name	Adopter Street	Adopter City	Adopter State	Adopter Zip	Type
Blair	Castillo	382 E. Meadow Ave.	Chandler	AZ	83174-2311	Cat
Craig	Nelson	77 E. Lincoln Dr.	Mesa	AZ	84101-8475	Iguana
Daniel	Klinger	289 E. Heather Ave.	Phoenix	AZ	82891-1605	Cat
Dianne	Trenton	899 High St.	Mesa	AZ	84101-8475	Horse
Erica	Snider	234 N. 1st St	Tempe	AZ	86301-1268	Cat
Helen	Cady	34 University Dr.	Tempe	AZ	86301-1268	Dog
Kate	Broeker	23 Price Rd.	Tempe	AZ	86301-1268	Dog
Kevin	Hanson	235 W. Camelback Rd.	Tempe	AZ	86301-1268	Dog
Kurt	Ehmann	7867 Forest Ave.	Phoenix	AZ	82891-1605	Cat
Scott	Briggs	45 E. Camelback Rd.	Phoenix	AZ	82891-1605	Dog

Monday, January 22, 2001

Page 1 of 2

c. Specify A as the Status criteria and >9/1/98 as the Adoption Date criteria. Run the query and review the resulting datasheet. Select an ascending sort in the Adopter Last Name column. Save the query as Adoptees and close the Query window.

d. Use the Report Wizard to create a report based on the **Adoptees** query you just saved. Include the following fields in the order listed below:

- Adopter First Name
- Adopter Last Name
- Adopter Street
- Adopter City
- Adopter State
- Adopter Zip
- Type

e. Select Adopter First Name as the first sort field and Adopter Last Name as the second sort field. Select the Justified layout, landscape orientation, and the Casual style. Name the report **Animal Angels Adoption Report**.

f. Center the Report Header control at the top of the page.

g. Preview and then print the report. Close the report window, saving the changes you made.

On Your Own

6. The program manager for the EduSoft Company is requesting a list of software titles that were worked on by Teri O'Neill so he can use it for Teri's review. Open the database named Learning and the Software table you updated in Practice Exercise 4 of Tutorial 2. Filter the table to include only those records that have Teri O'Neill in the Developer field. Add your name to one of the software titles (e.g., "[Your Name]'s Solve It") and print the filtered datasheet.

7. As an administrative assistant at Lewis & Lewis, Inc., you are responsible for sending out W2 forms to all of the employees. Use the employee database that you updated in Practice Exercise 9 of Tutorial 2 and create a query that includes only the employee name and home address fields. Run and print the resulting query datasheet.

8. Based on the overwhelming positive response from the Hawaiian Islands tour, Adventure Travel is planning a reunion trip and would like to contact the clients who took the first trip. Open the Adventure database that you updated in Practice Exercise 6 of Tutorial 2 and create a query that includes the client name, address, and phone fields as well as the tour name fields. Enter query sort criteria to find only those records that have Hawaiian Islands in one of the tour name fields, and apply an ascending sort to the Last Name field. Save the query and then use the Report Wizard to create a report based on the query. Include all the fields except the Client # field, and reverse the order of the Last Name and First Name fields. Sort the report by the Last Name and then First Name fields. Preview and print the report.

9. The Animal Angels owners have finished sending thank you cards to those who adopted animals in the last six months, and would now like to send cards to those who have provided foster care in the same time period. Using the same techniques you used in Practice Exercise 5 of this tutorial, create a query in the Angels database that joins the Animals and Fosters tables; includes the animal type, status, and foster home information; and specifies F and >9/1/98 as the Status and Foster Date criteria. Save and close the query, and then use the Report Wizard to create a report based on this query. Include all fields except the status field, with the foster home name and address information fields first and the type field last. Preview and print the report.

10. Oldies But Goodies has expanded to include out-of-print books as well as vintage record albums. Revisit the Web to obtain some book titles and resources and add the appropriate fields to the table you updated in Practice Exercise 10 of Tutorial 2. To create a list of only the new products, filter the table to include the client and book fields (not the record album fields), and print the filtered datasheet. Then create a query that includes the records for both product types (record and book), sorted by category. Use the Report Wizard to create a report that is based on the query; include the customer name, product type, category, and source fields; and sort it by customer last name. Preview and print the report.

Working Together: Linking Access and Word

Case Study Brian, the Club owner, recently asked you to provide him with a list of all employees who have 3 years service with the Club. He also wanted the same information for all employees with over 5 years service. You queried the Employee table in the Personnel Records database and were quickly able to obtain this information. Now you want to include the query results with a brief memo to Brian.

All Microsoft Office applications have a common user interface such as similar commands and menu structures. In addition to these obvious features, they have been designed to work together, making it easy to share and exchange information between applications. You will learn how to share information between applications while you create the memo. Your memo containing the query results generated by Access will look like that shown here.

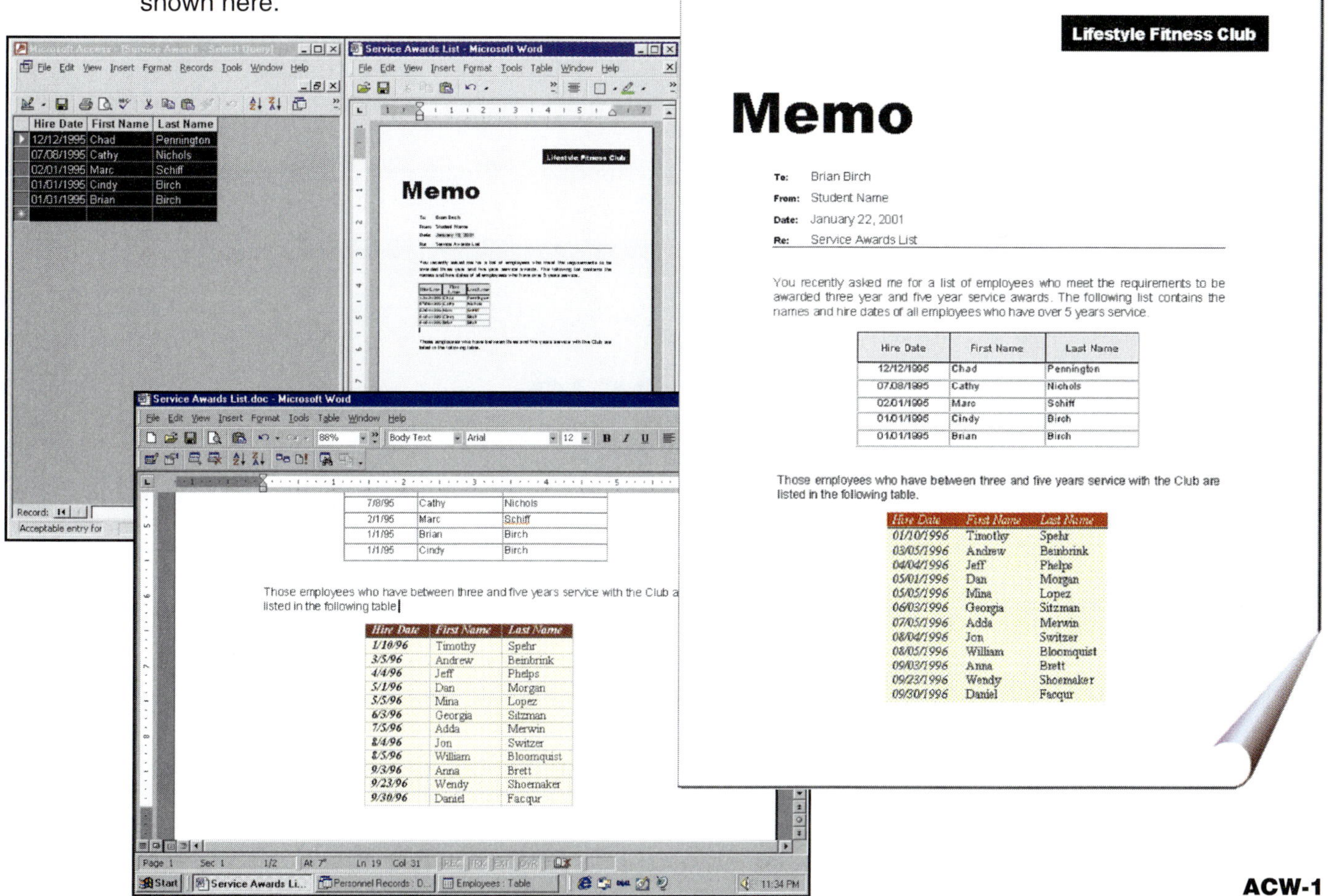

Note: This tutorial assumes that you already know how to use Word 2000 and that you have completed Tutorial 3 of Access. You will need the data file Personnel Records you saved at the end of Tutorial 3.

Copying between Applications

You have already created the memo to the owner of the Club, and just need to add the information from Access to the memo. To see the memo,

1 ■ **Start Word 2000 and open the document Service Awards List from your data disk.**

■ **If necessary, maximize the application and document windows.**

Your screen should be similar to Figure 1.

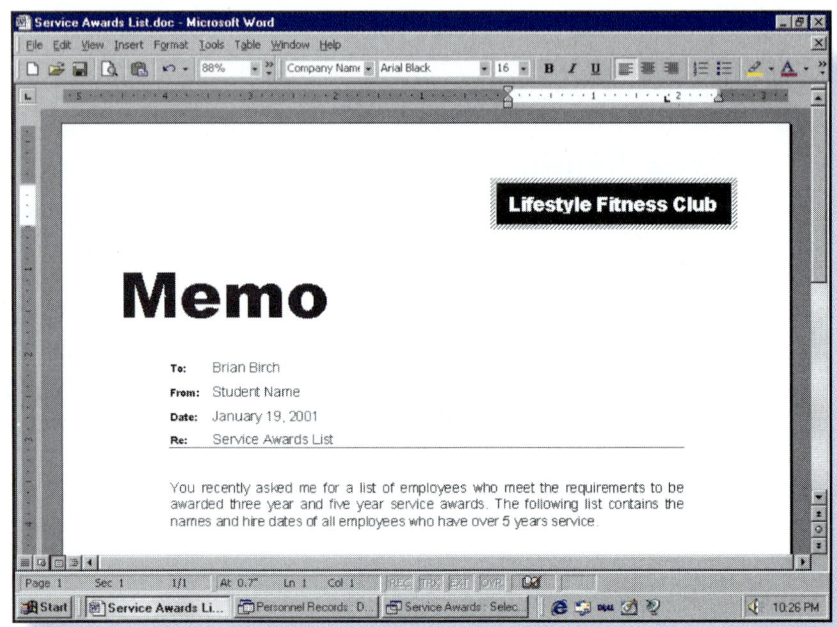

Figure 1

This document contains the text of the memo to the owner.

2 ■ **Replace "Student Name" in the memo header with your name.**

■ **Scroll the memo so you can see the two paragraphs in the body of the memo.**

Your screen should be similar to Figure 2.

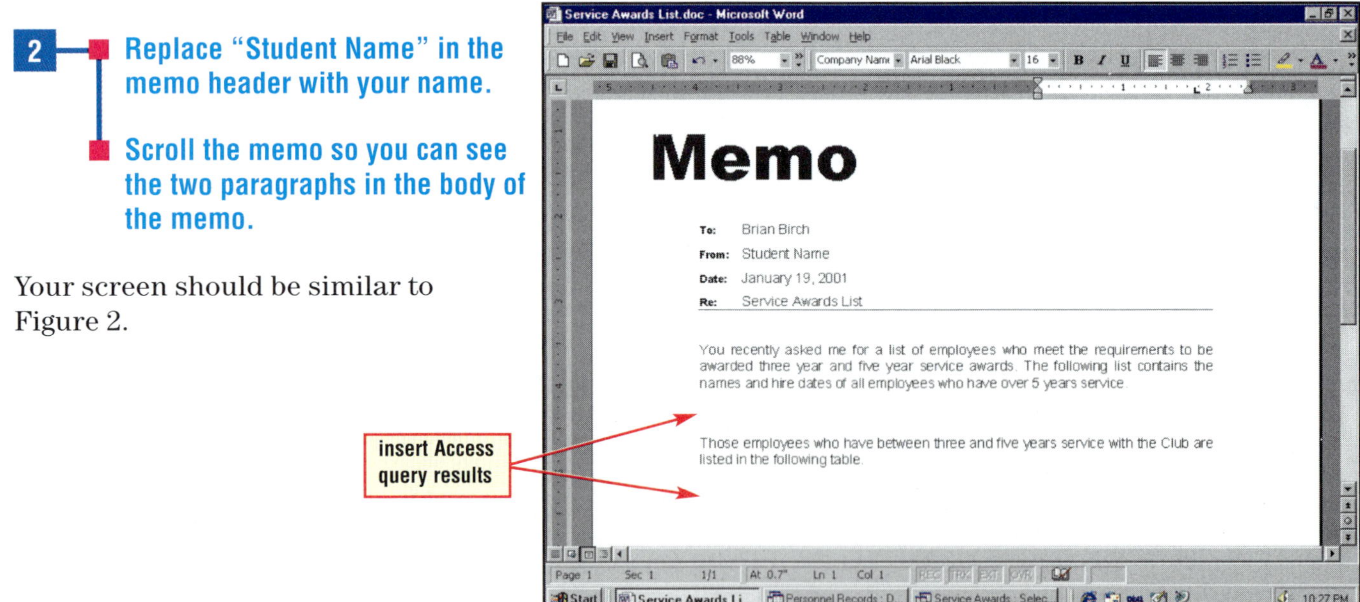

Figure 2

Below each of the paragraphs, you want to display the appropriate list of employees. This information is available in the Personnel Records database file and can be obtained using the Service Awards query you created and saved.

3 ■ **Start Access 2000.**

■ **Open the Personnel Records database from your data disk.**

■ **Open the Service Awards query.**

■ **If necessary, maximize the query datasheet window.**

Your screen should be similar to Figure 3.

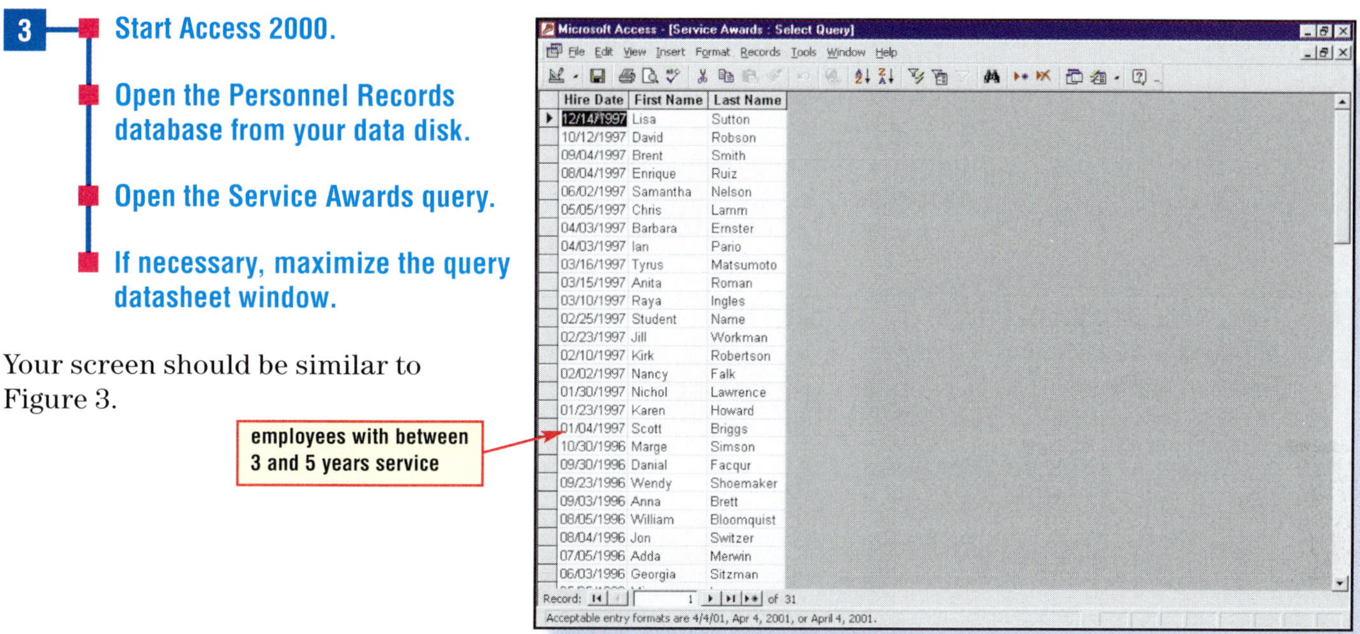

Figure 3

There are now two open applications, Word and Access. Word is open in a window behind the Access application window. Application buttons for all open windows are displayed in the taskbar. Access is the active application, and Service Awards: Select Query is the active file.

The 31 employees who have between 3 and 5 years service with the Club are listed in the query datasheet. Below the first paragraph of the memo, you want to display those employees with 5 years or more of service. To obtain this information, you need to modify the query.

4 ■ **Display Design view.**

■ **Change the criteria in the Hire Date cell to <1/1/96**

■ **Run the query.**

Your screen should be similar to Figure 4.

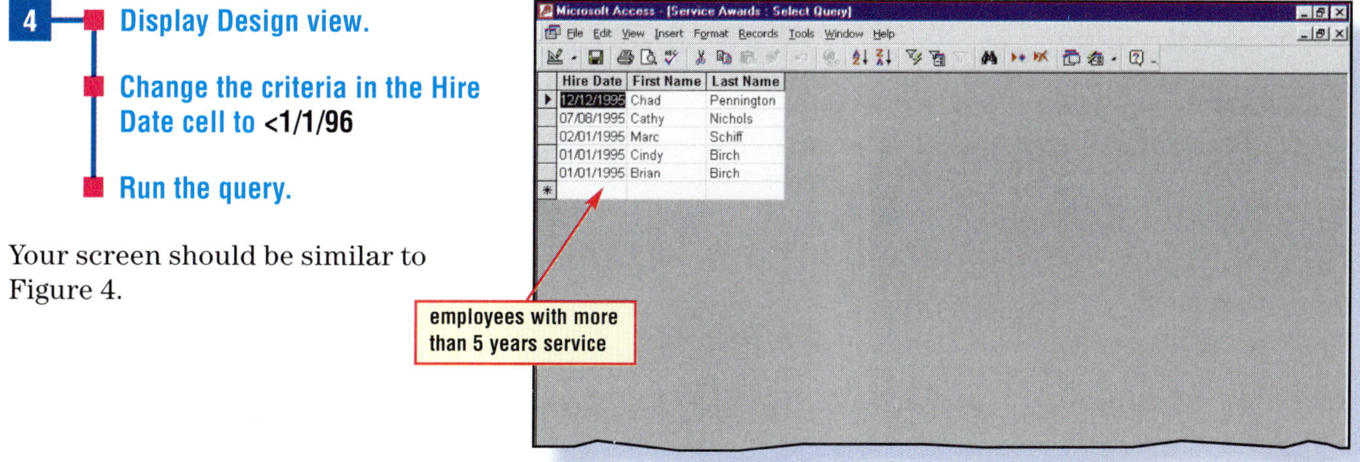

Figure 4

You want to copy the output from the query below the first paragraph of the memo. As with all Office applications, you can cut, copy, and paste selections within and between tables and objects in an Access database. You can also perform these operations between Access databases and other applications. For example, you can copy a database object or selection into a Word document. The information is inserted in a format the application can edit, if possible.

To do this, you can use Copy and Paste or drag and drop between applications to copy the database object. To use drag and drop, both applications must be open and visible in the window. To display both applications at the same time on the desktop, you will tile the two open applications vertically in the window.

5 **Right-click on a blank area of the taskbar to open the Shortcut menu.**

Select Tile Windows Vertically.

Your screen should be similar to Figure 5.

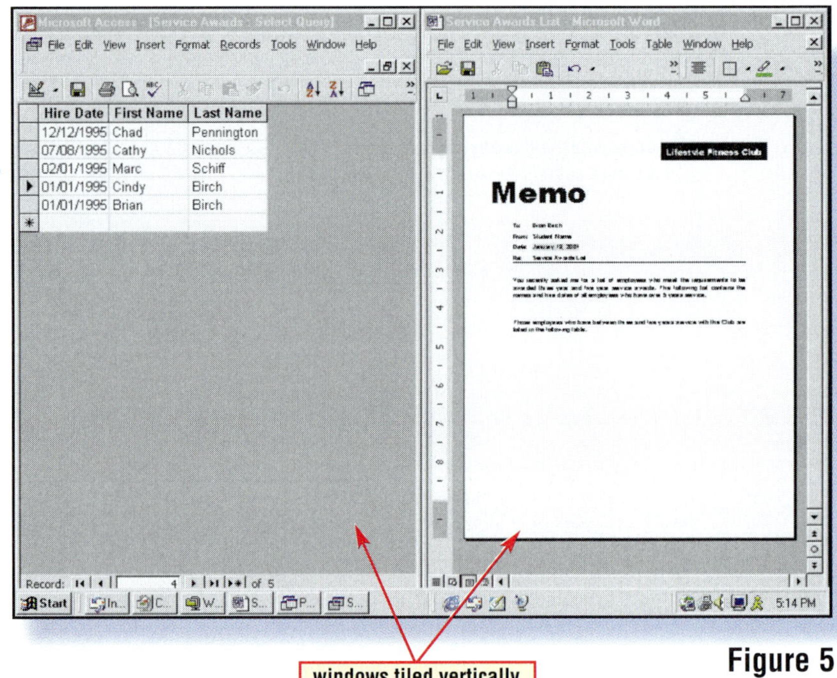

Figure 5

6 — Click in the Access application window to make it active.

Use **E**dit/Select **A**ll Records to select the query datasheet table.

Copy and Paste the selected table to the space below the first paragraph of the memo in the document.

Your screen should be similar to Figure 6.

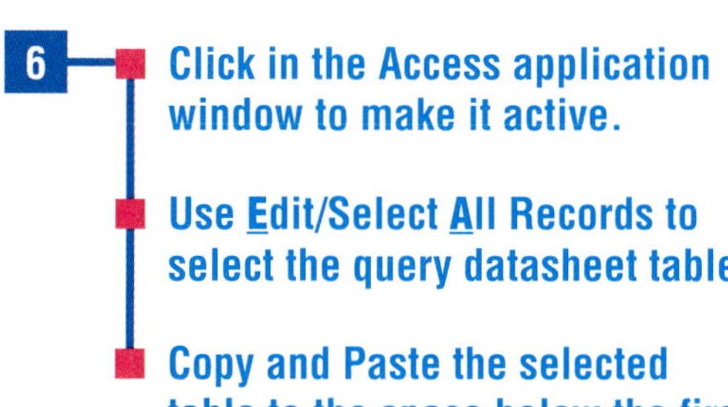
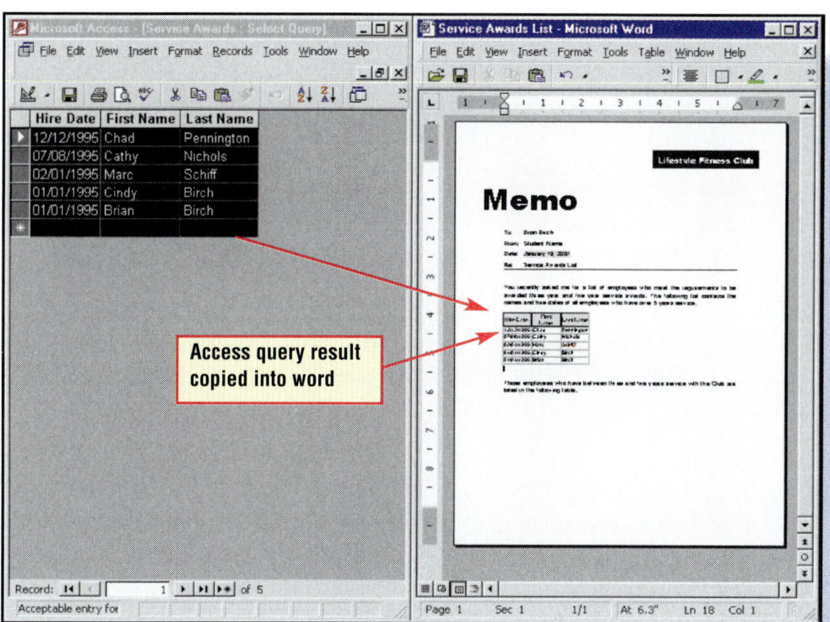

Figure 6

The query results have been copied into the Word document as a table that can be edited and manipulated within Word. Much of the formatting associated with the copied information is also pasted into the document. You think the memo would look better if it was larger and centered between the margins.

7 — Choose **U**ndo Tile from the taskbar Shortcut menu.

Select the table and increase the size of the table by dragging the lower right sizing handle.

Select the entire table.

Click ■.

Center the Hire Date column.

Clear the selection.

Your screen should be similar to Figure 7.

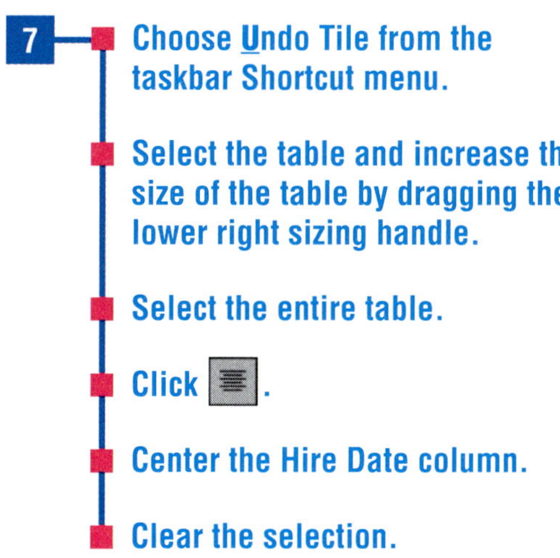
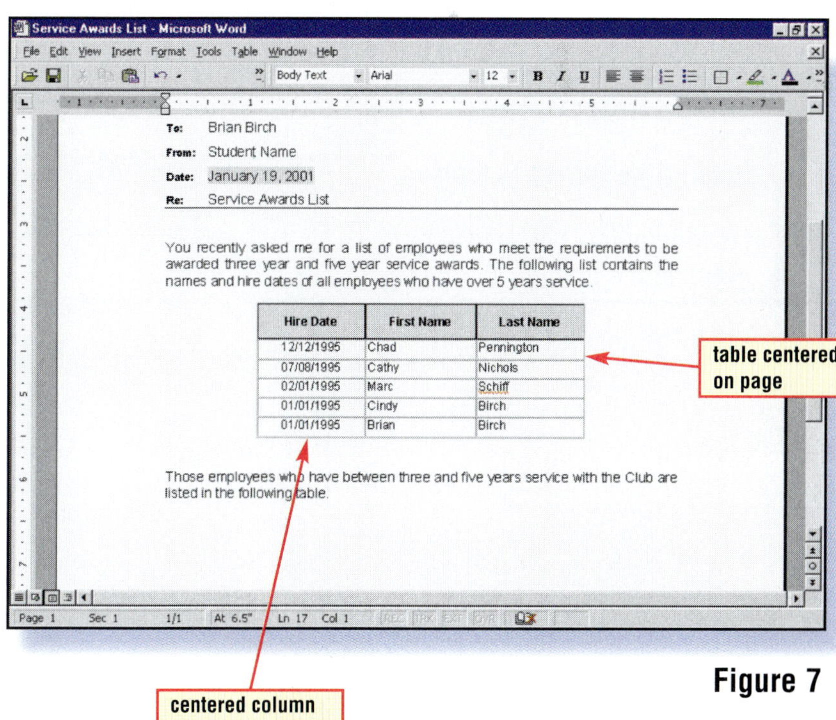

Figure 7

Linking an Access Object to Another Application

Next you need to insert the query results showing all employees who have more than 3 years and less than 5 years with the Club. As you consider the memo, you are concerned that Brian, when he sees the large number of employees meeting the criteria, may ask you to modify the query to provide a different analysis. If this request is made, you want the memo to be automatically updated when you modify the query. To do this you will link the query object to the memo.

You will insert the query result into the memo as a **linked object**. Information created in one application can also be inserted as a linked object into a document created by another application. When an object is linked, the data is stored in the **source file** (the document it was created in). A graphic representation or picture of the data is displayed in the **destination file** (the document in which the object is inserted). A connection between the information in the destination file to the source file is established by the creation of a link. The link contains references to the location of the source file and the selection within the document that is linked to the destination file.

When changes are made in the source file that affect the linked object, the changes are automatically reflected in the destination file when it is opened. This is called a **live link**. When you create linked objects, the date and time on your machine should be accurate, because the program refers to the date of the source file to determine whether updates are needed when you open the destination file.

To create a link to the query, you use the Insert Database button on the Database toolbar of Word.

1   **Display the Database toolbar.**

   Move to below the second paragraph of the memo.

   Click Insert Database.

Your screen should be similar to Figure 8.

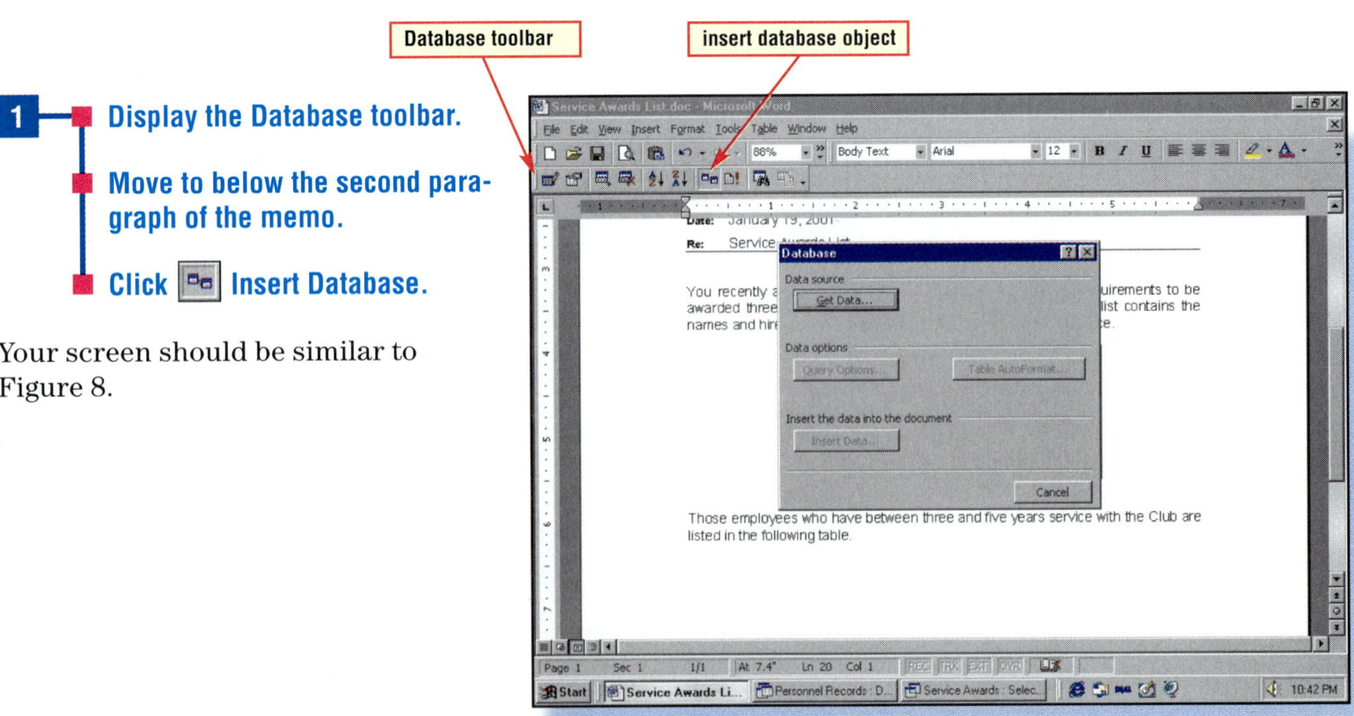

Figure 8

From the Database dialog box, you need to first select the database file to be inserted into the memo.

2 — **Click** Get Data... .

If necessary, select the drive containing your data disk from the Look In drop-down list.

To display Microsoft Access file types, select MS Access Databases **from the Files of Type drop-down list.**

Select the file Personnel Records.

Click Open .

Your screen should be similar to Figure 9.

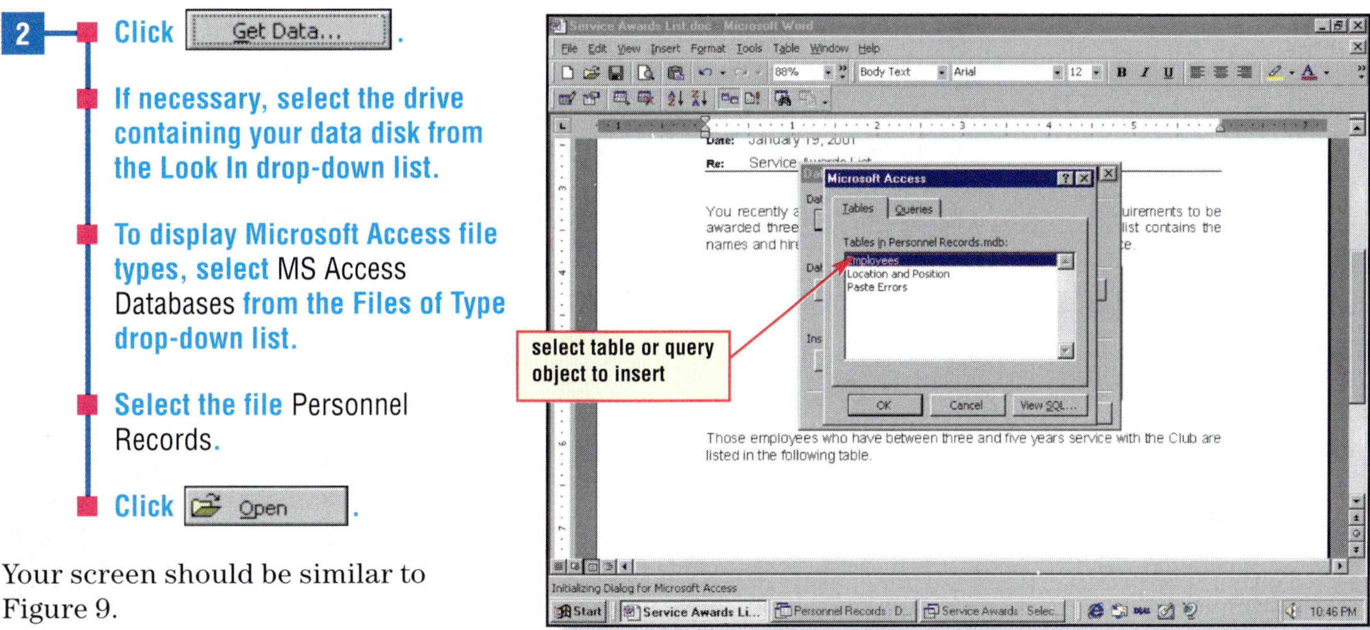

Figure 9

In the Microsoft Access dialog box, you select the table or query you want to insert in the Word document.

3 — **Open the Queries tab and select** Service Awards.

Your screen should be similar to Figure 10.

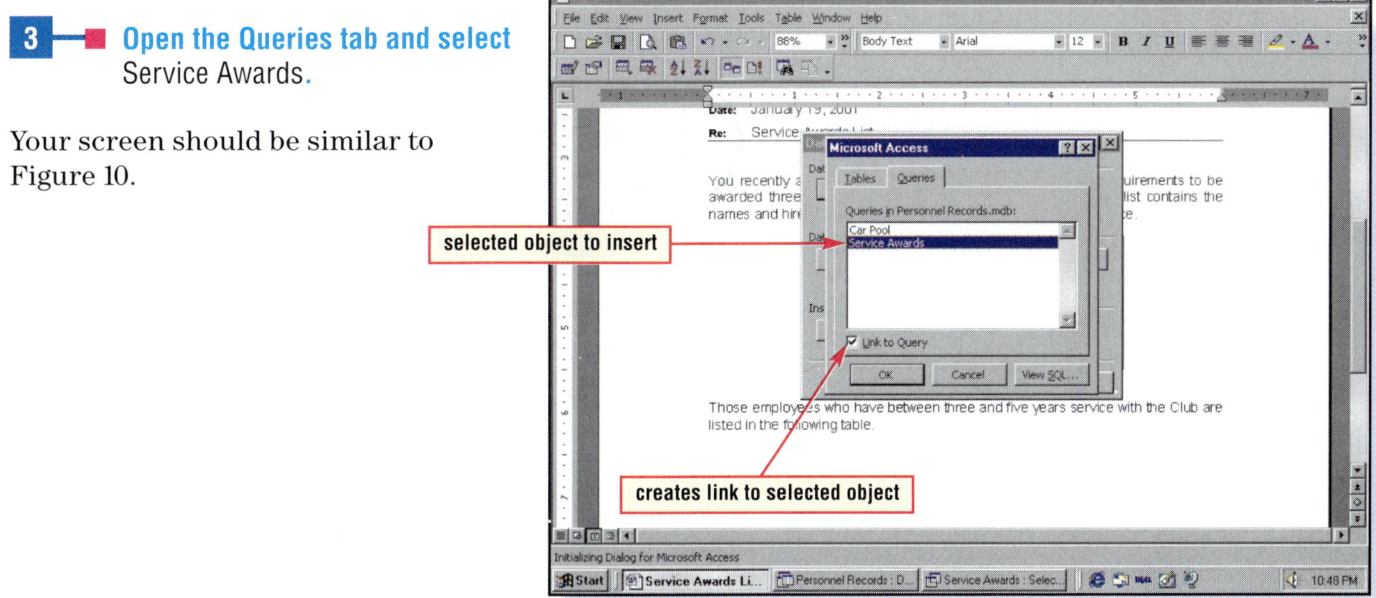

Figure 10

Notice that the Link to Query option is preselected. This option establishes the link between the query object and the Word document.

4 ■ **Click** [OK] .

The Database dialog box is displayed again. The Query Options button allows you to modify the query settings. Since you want it to appear as it is, you do not need to use this option. The AutoFormat button lets you select a format to apply to the table. If you do not select a format style, the datasheet is copied into the document as an unformatted table.

5 ■ **Click** [<u>T</u>able AutoFormat...] .

Your screen should be similar to Figure 11.

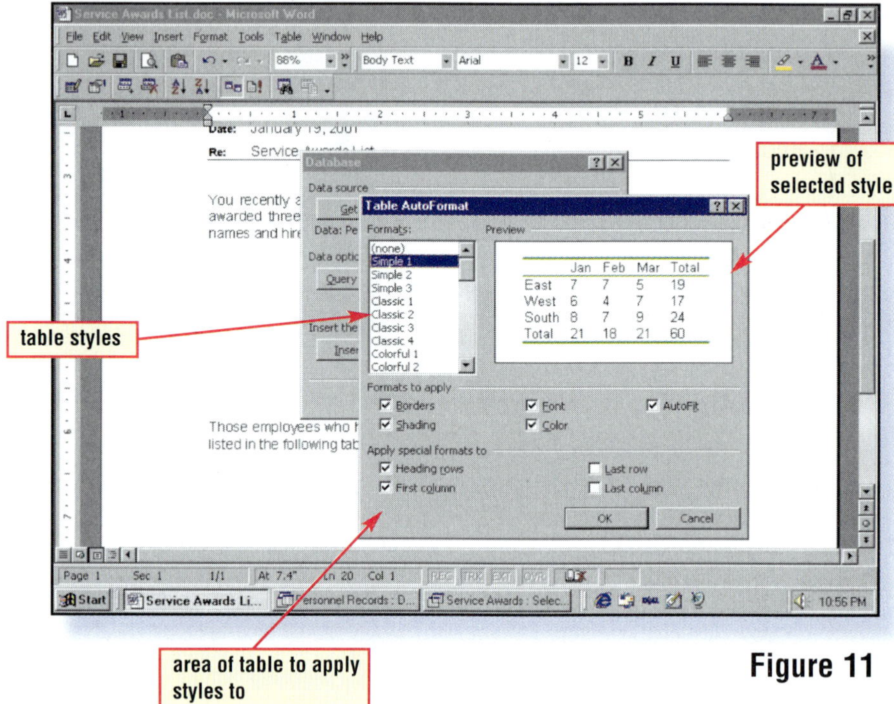

Figure 11

From the Table Autoformat dialog box, you select the style you want to use and the parts of the table you want to apply it to. You want the formats applied to the heading rows and first column.

6 ■ **If necessary, select the Heading rows and First column options as the only two areas to apply special formats.**

■ **Select a style of your choice.**

■ **Click** [OK] .

The Database dialog box is displayed again. Finally, to insert the data into the document,

7 — Click [Insert Data...] .

Your screen should be similar to Figure 12.

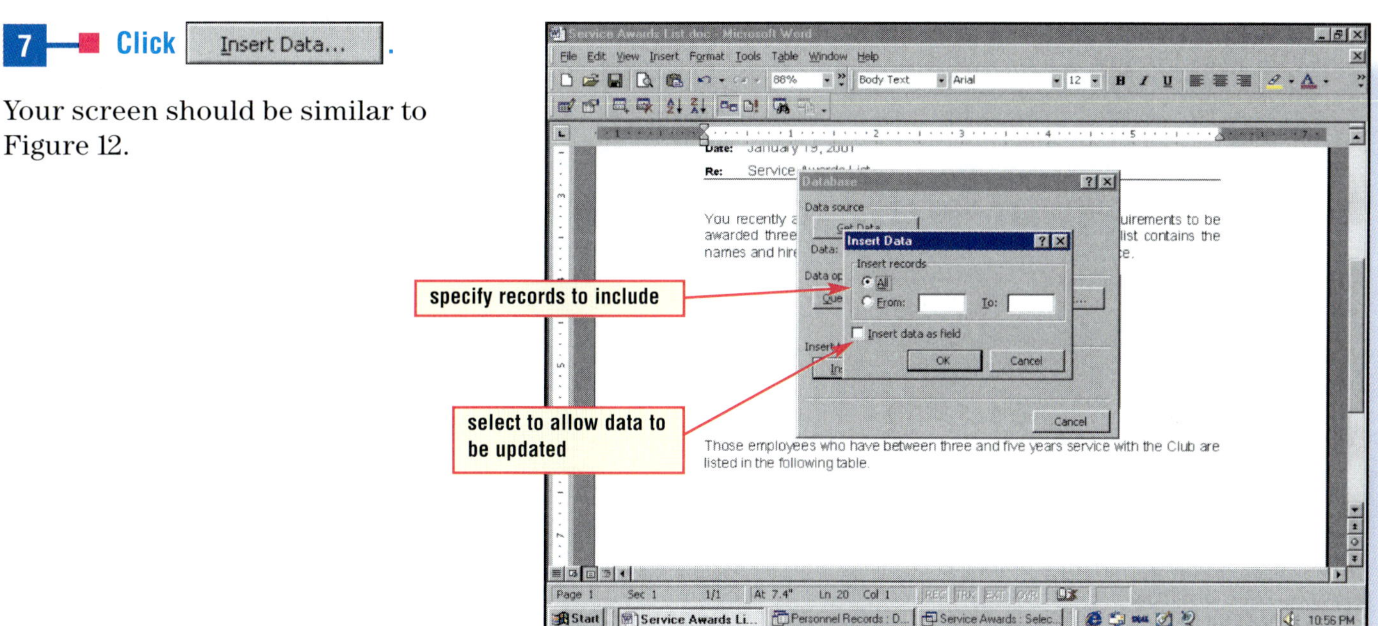

Figure 12

From the Insert Data dialog box, you specify what records to include in the inserted table and whether to insert the data as a field. Inserting it as a field allows the data to be updated whenever the source changes.

8 — If necessary, select **A**ll.

Select **I**nsert data as field.

Click [OK] .

Scroll the memo to see more of the inserted table.

> The table continues on the second page of the memo.

Your screen should be similar to Figure 13.

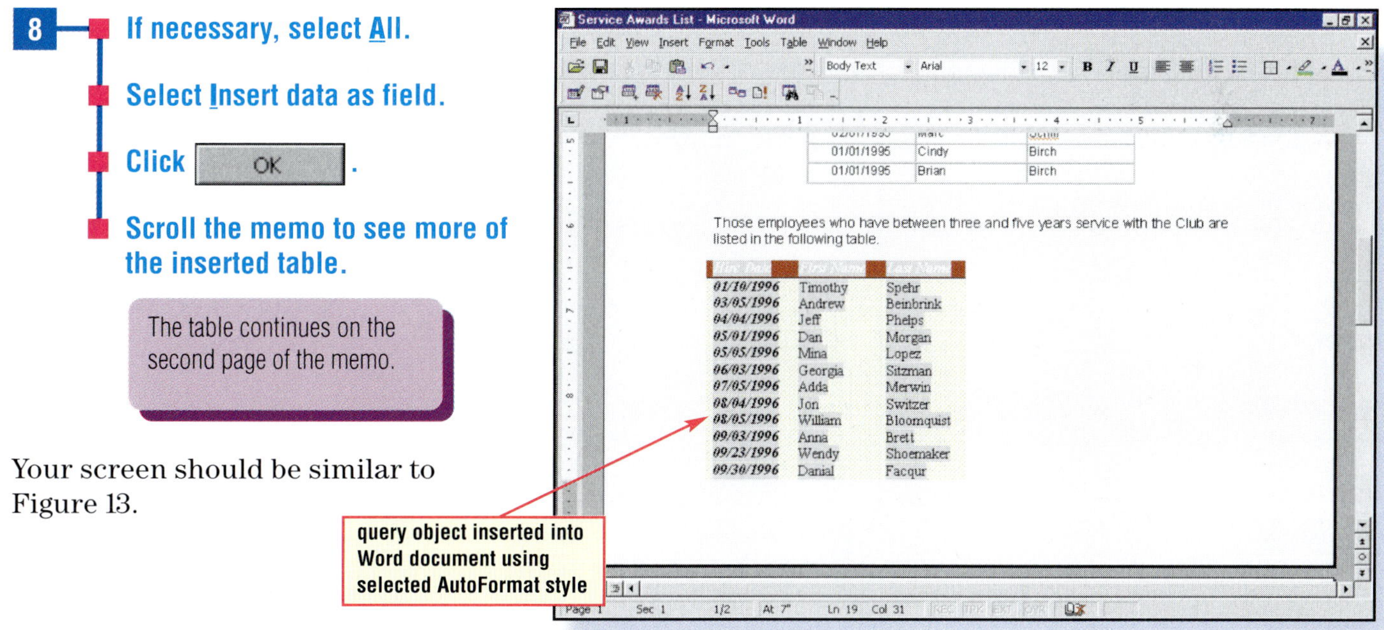

Figure 13

The link to the database file and to the query object is established, and the database table is inserted into the document in the selected format style. The table lists the 31 employees who have between 3 and 5 years with the Club. Even though you modified the query earlier, the original query results are displayed. This is because you did not save the changes you made to the query. Consequently, the inserted table reflects the results of the original query.

9 ■ **Center the table on the page.**

■ **Click above the table to clear the selection.**

■ **If necessary, insert a blank line between the paragraph and the table.**

Your screen should be similar to Figure 14.

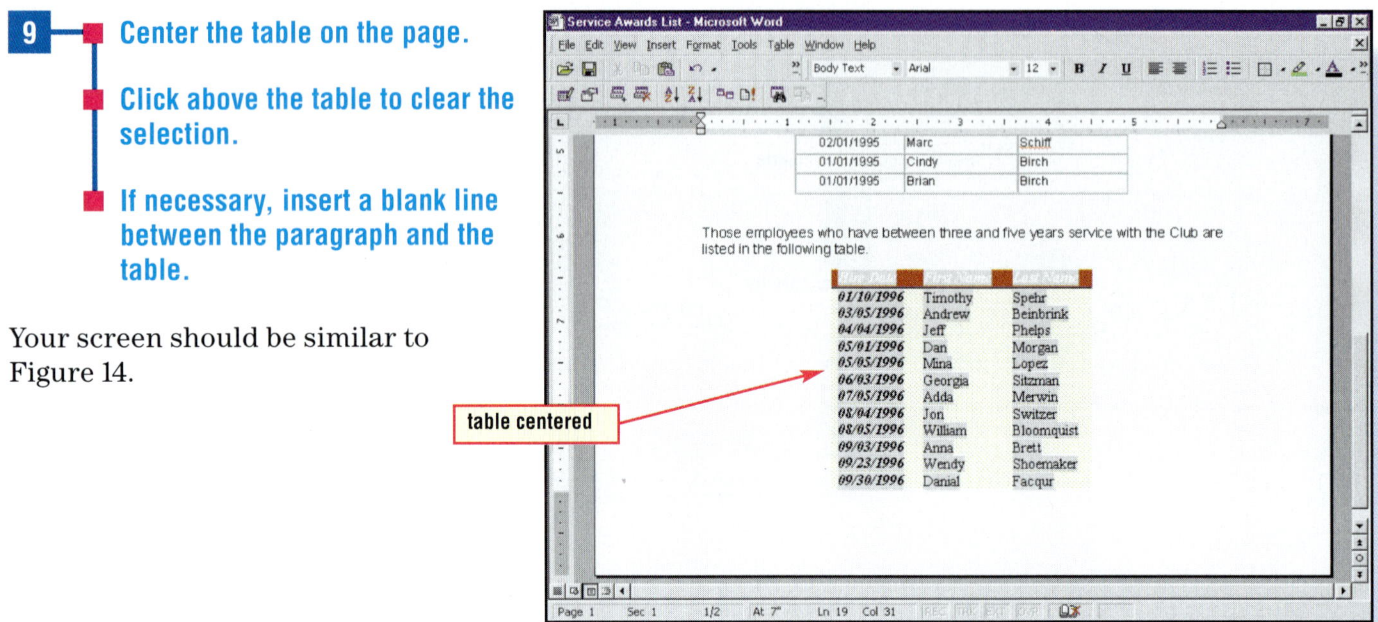

Figure 14

You think the information in the table should be sorted by last name. To make this change to the table,

10 ■ **Select the Last Name column.**

■ **Click** ⧉ **Sort Ascending.**

Your screen should be similar to Figure 15.

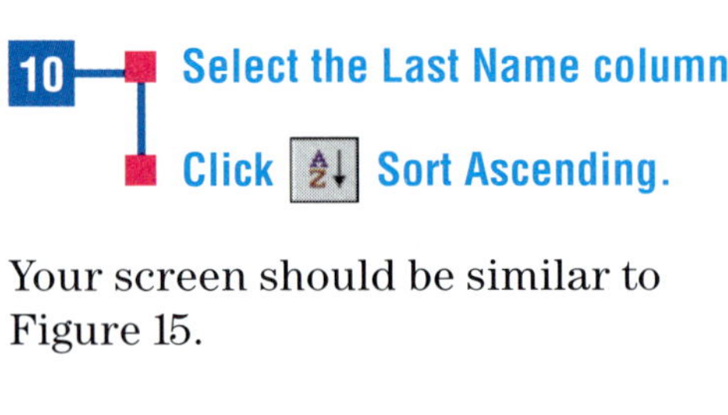

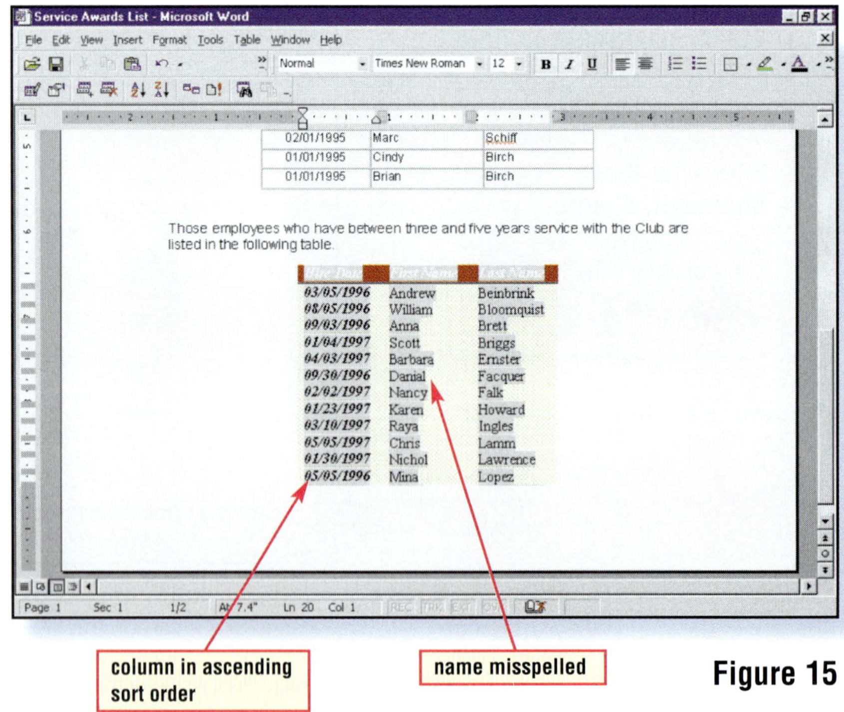

Figure 15

Updating a Linked Object

Now you notice that Daniel Facquer's first name is misspelled. You want to correct this in both the table in Access and in the memo. By making the change in Access, you can then update the memo to reflect the change because it is a linked object.

1
- **Switch to the Access Query datasheet window.**
- **If necessary, maximize the Access window.**
- **Close the query without saving the changes.**
- **Open the Employees table.**
- **Change the spelling of Danial Facquer's first name to Daniel (record 17).**

Your screen should be similar to Figure 16.

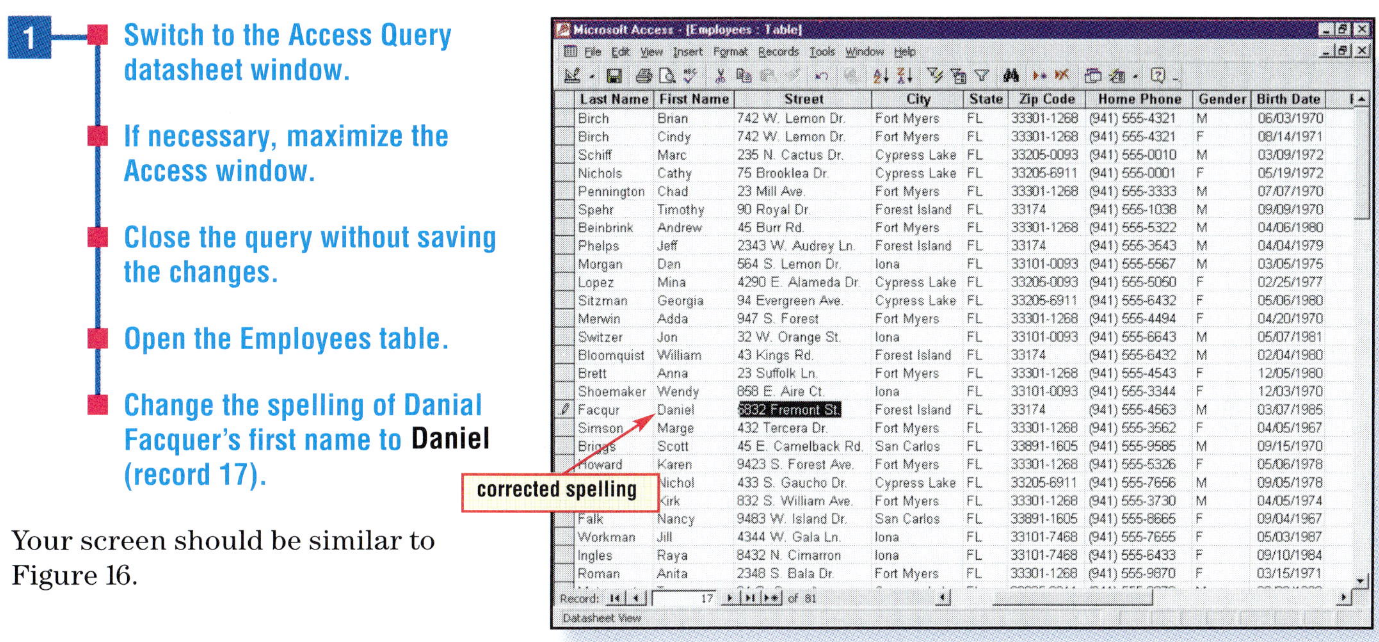

Figure 16

2
- **Switch to the Word memo.**
- **Click Update Field to update the table contents.**

Your screen should be similar to Figure 17.

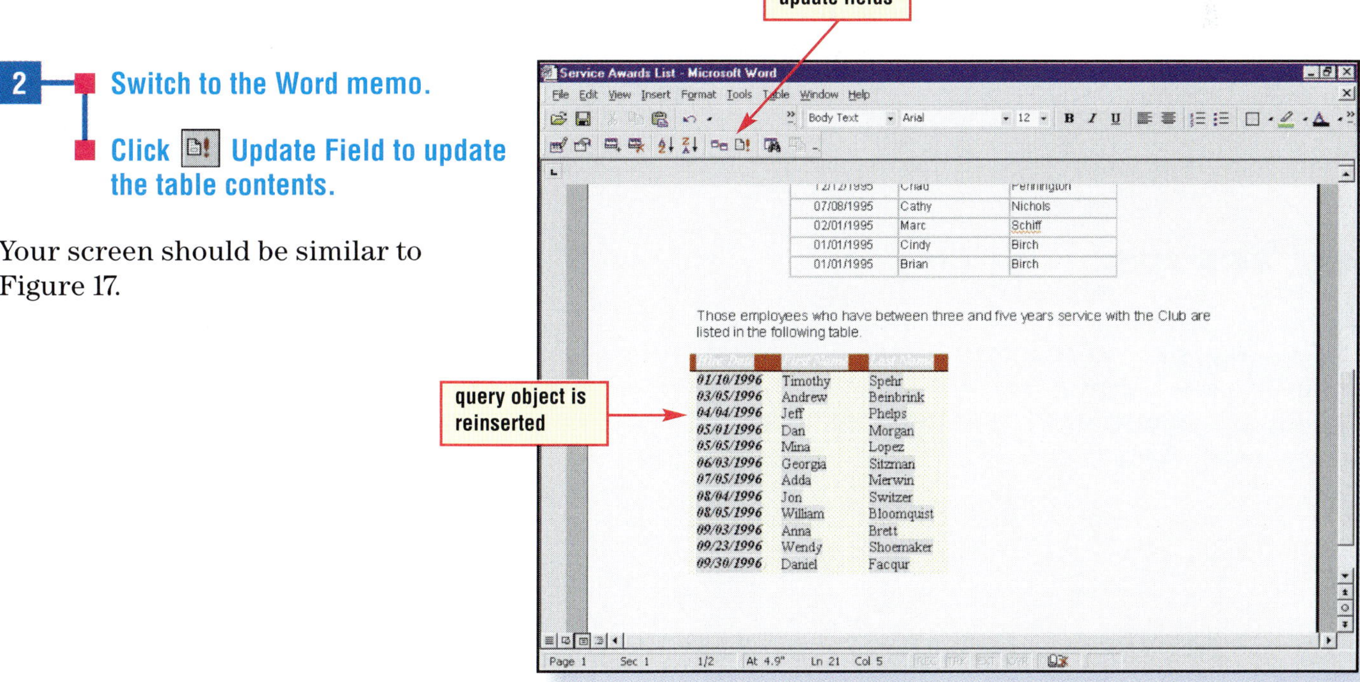

Figure 17

The query results are regenerated and inserted into the document again.

3 ■ **Confirm that Daniel's name is now corrected in the table.**

■ **Center the table on the page.**

Your screen should be similar to Figure 18.

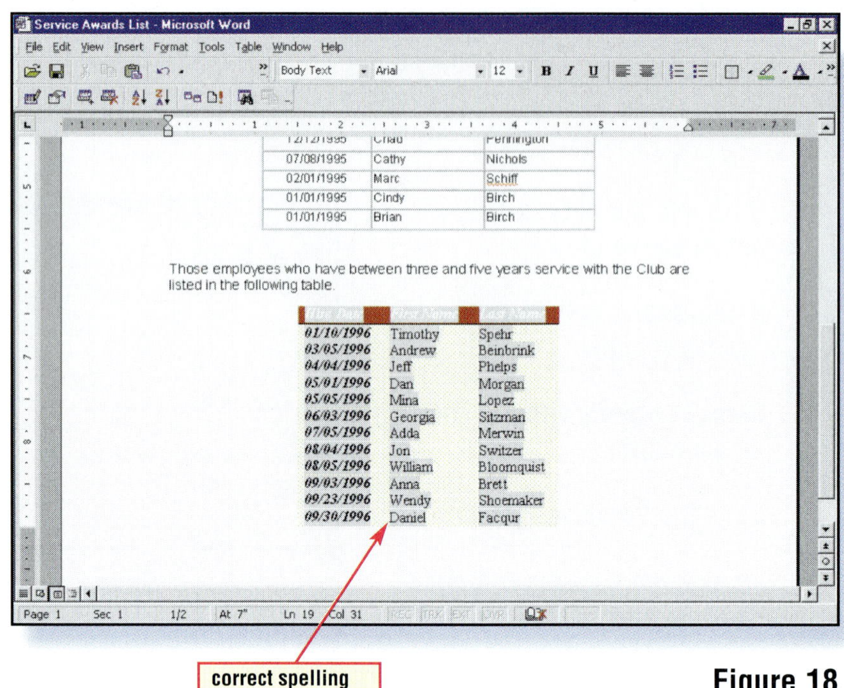

Figure 18

4 ■ **Save the memo as Service Awards Linked.**

■ **Close the Database toolbar.**

■ **Print the memo and exit Word.**

■ **Close the Personnel Records database.**

Key Terms

Destination file   ACW-6
Linked object   ACW-6
Live link   ACW-6
Source file   ACW-6

Hands-On Practice Exercises

Step by Step

Rating System   ☆ Easy
☆☆ Moderate
☆☆☆ Difficult

1. This problem is a continuation of Practice Exercise 1 in Tutorial 3. Daria O'Dell, the owner of Daria's Day Spa, has asked you for a list of clients who are over the age of 35 to get an idea of how much interest there would be in a "Young Again" spa package she is considering offering. You already filtered the Clients table to locate this information and now want to include the results in a memo to Daria.

  a. Open the Daria Spa database and the Clients table. Apply the filter. (If you did not save the table with the filter, create the filter again by following the instructions in Hands-On Practice Exercise 1 of Tutorial 3.)

  b. Hide the Client ID, Home Phone, and Work Phone fields.

  c. Open Word and enter the following text in a new document.

> **TO: Daria O'Dell**
> **FROM: [your name]**
> **DATE: [current date]**
>
> **Below is the information you requested on clients over the age of 35.**

  d. Copy the query results into the Word document.

  e. Save the memo as Daria Clients. Print the document. Close the document and exit Word.

  f. Unhide the three fields. Remove the filter. Close the table and database.

2. This problem is a continuation of Practice Exercise 2 in Tutorial 3. You have queried the Daily Digest database to locate all businesses that are currently advertising in the publication only once a month. Now you want to send this information in a memo to the managing editor. You want to link the database query results to the memo, as this information is periodically requested. Then each time this request is made, all you would need to do is rerun the query to get the updated results and update the memo.

  a. Open the Daily Digest database and the Monthly Advertisers query.

  b. Modify the query to display the following fields only: Business Name, Business Type, Contact Name, Phone Number, Ad Size, and Ad Frequency. *Hint:* Clear the Show box of the fields you do not want displayed. Run the query. Save the query.

  c. Open Word, and enter the following text in a new document.

> **TO: Dan Lenz, Managing Editor**
> **FROM: [your name]**
> **DATE: [current date]**
>
> **Below is the information you requested on monthly advertisers.**

   d. Copy the query results into the Word document as a linked object using an autoformat of your choice.

   e. Change the Ad Frequency of one of the Biweekly ads to Monthly. Run the query again.

   f. Update the memo. Size the table appropriately.

   g. Save the memo as Daily Digest Memo. Print the document. Exit Word

   h. Save the query changes. Close the table and database.

3. This problem is a continuation of Practice Exercise 4 in Tutorial 3. EduSoft's marketing director has asked you to locate the same information for grade levels K–2. You will quickly modify the marketing query to get this information and include it in a memo to the director.

   a. Open the Learning database and the Marketing query.

   b. Modify the query to display the grade levels K–2 only. Best fit the fields. Save the modified query as **Marketing K2**.

   c. Open Word and enter the following text in a new document.

       TO: Marketing Director, Valerie McLaughlin
       FROM: [your name]
       DATE: [current date]

       Below is the information you requested on grade levels K–2.

   d. Copy the query results into the Word document as a linked object using an autoformat of your choice.

   e. Add a new record to the database using the following information: **90-0102; Tell It; Speech; K–2; Story Telling; your name; current date**.

   f. Run the query again.

   g. Update the memo.

   h. Save the memo as EduSoft. Print the document.

   i. Save the query changes. Close the table and database.

Controlling Data Input, Using Advanced Queries, and Enforcing Referential Integrity

Competencies

After completing this tutorial, you will know how to:

1. Create a table using the Table Wizard.
2. Create an input mask.
3. Create a lookup field.
4. Set required properties.
5. Add a calculated field to a query.
6. Create a crosstab query.
7. Insert a subdatasheet in a table.
8. Define table relationships and enforce referential integrity.
9. Print a database relationships report.
10. Back up and restore your database.

Case Study

You have created an employee database and several queries and reports related to this database for the Lifestyle Fitness Club; this has made recordkeeping at the club much easier than it used to be when everything was done manually. Based on the success of this database, the club owners would like you to use Access to store the employees' salary information. They would like this information kept in a separate data table, and they want to be able to use it along with the other employee data tables to calculate gross weekly salaries.

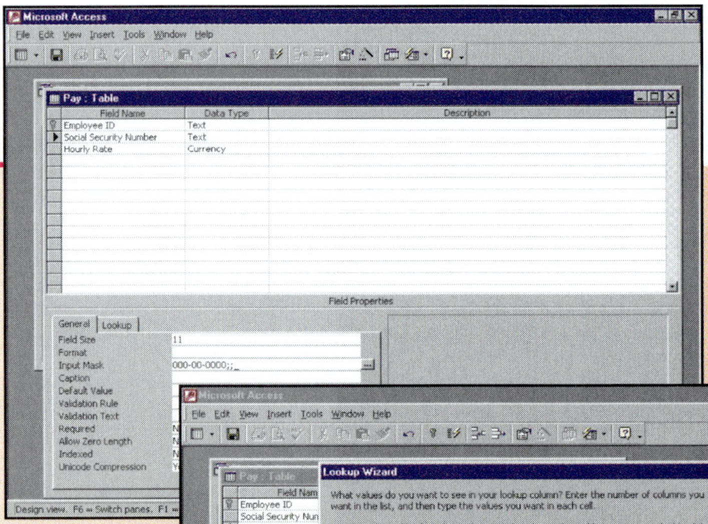

Using an input mask makes data entry easier and more accurate.

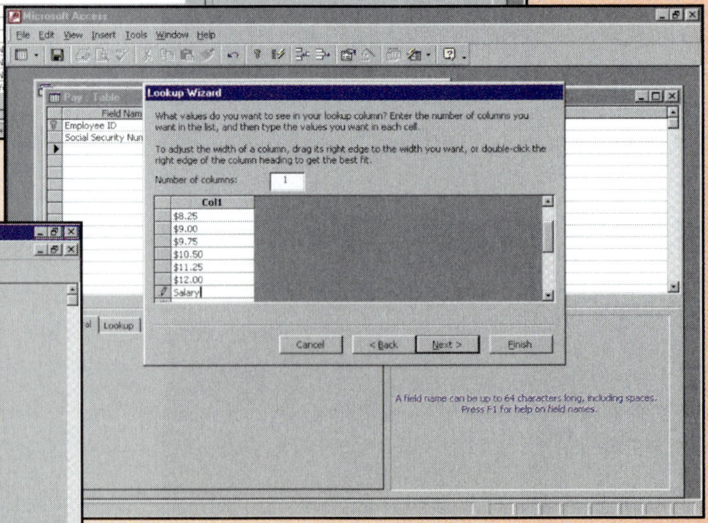

Restricting a field entry to values from a lookup list is another way to ensure data accuracy.

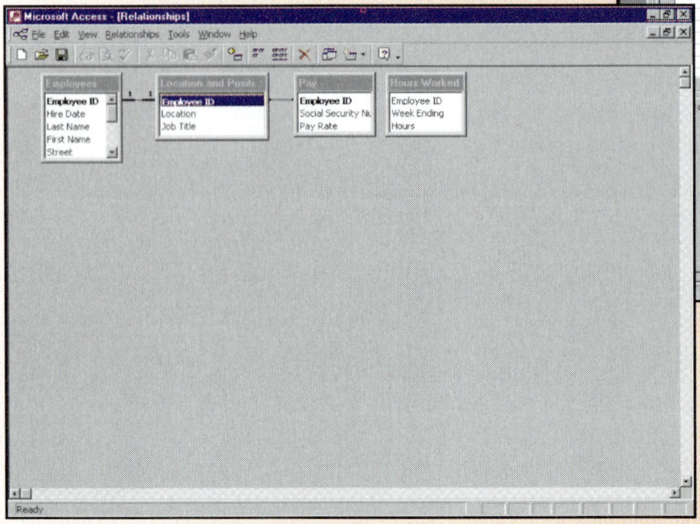

The table relationship report shows how tables are related.

In creating the new table and queries, you'll learn about features, such as applying input mask and required properties to fields to ensure the correct information is entered. You'll also learn how to run one query that shows table data in tabular format and another that includes a field to calculate your numerical data. Since you will be sharing employee information between data tables, you'll also learn how to create subdatasheets, enforce referential integrity between data, and print a report that shows the database relationships.

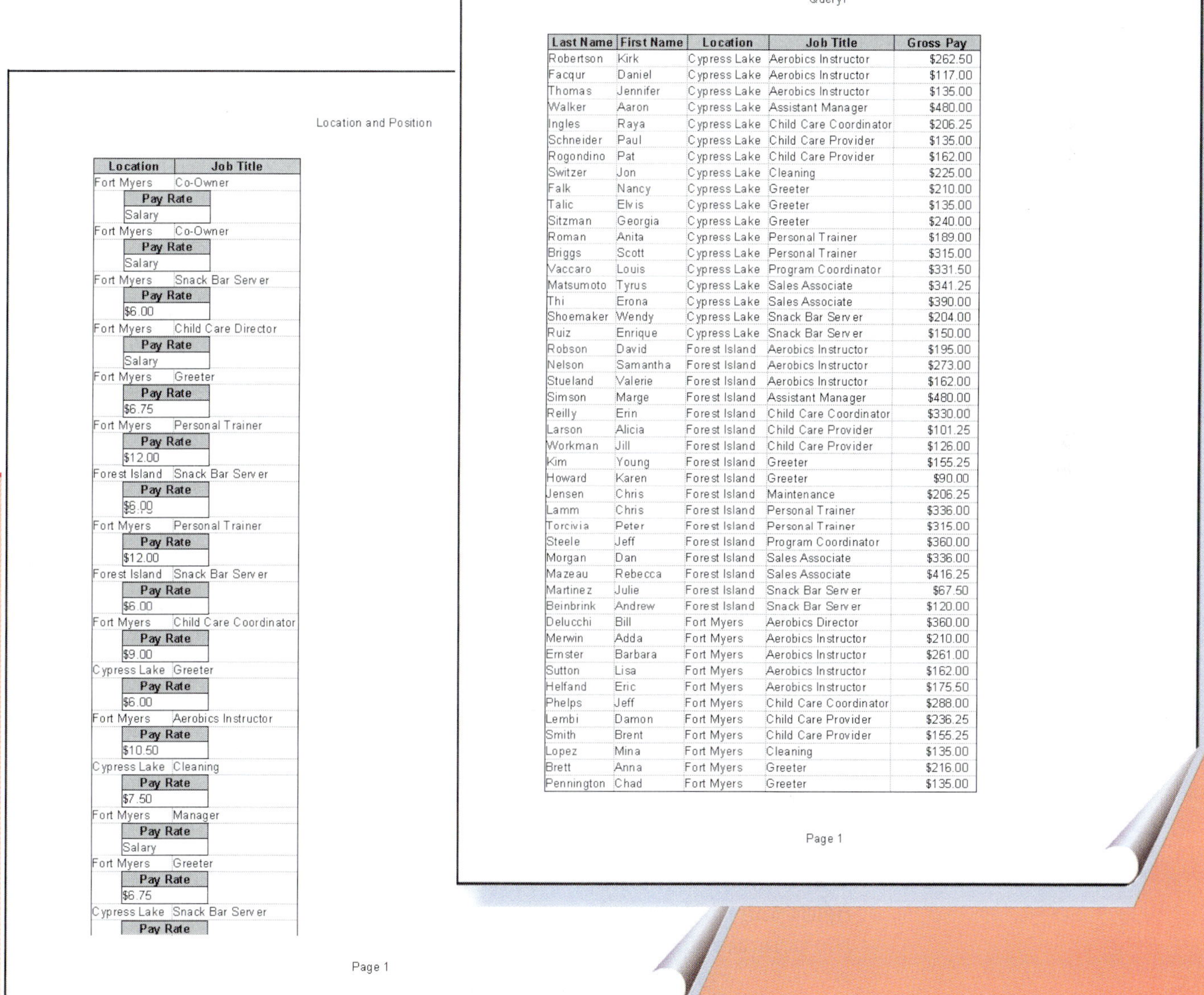

Location and Position

Location	Job Title
Fort Myers	Co-Owner
Pay Rate	
Salary	
Fort Myers	Co-Owner
Pay Rate	
Salary	
Fort Myers	Snack Bar Server
Pay Rate	
$6.00	
Fort Myers	Child Care Director
Pay Rate	
Salary	
Fort Myers	Greeter
Pay Rate	
$6.75	
Fort Myers	Personal Trainer
Pay Rate	
$12.00	
Forest Island	Snack Bar Server
Pay Rate	
$6.00	
Fort Myers	Personal Trainer
Pay Rate	
$12.00	
Forest Island	Snack Bar Server
Pay Rate	
$6.00	
Fort Myers	Child Care Coordinator
Pay Rate	
$9.00	
Cypress Lake	Greeter
Pay Rate	
$6.00	
Fort Myers	Aerobics Instructor
Pay Rate	
$10.50	
Cypress Lake	Cleaning
Pay Rate	
$7.50	
Fort Myers	Manager
Pay Rate	
Salary	
Fort Myers	Greeter
Pay Rate	
$6.75	
Cypress Lake	Snack Bar Server
Pay Rate	

Query1

Last Name	First Name	Location	Job Title	Gross Pay
Robertson	Kirk	Cypress Lake	Aerobics Instructor	$262.50
Facqur	Daniel	Cypress Lake	Aerobics Instructor	$117.00
Thomas	Jennifer	Cypress Lake	Aerobics Instructor	$135.00
Walker	Aaron	Cypress Lake	Assistant Manager	$480.00
Ingles	Raya	Cypress Lake	Child Care Coordinator	$206.25
Schneider	Paul	Cypress Lake	Child Care Provider	$135.00
Rogondino	Pat	Cypress Lake	Child Care Provider	$162.00
Switzer	Jon	Cypress Lake	Cleaning	$225.00
Falk	Nancy	Cypress Lake	Greeter	$210.00
Talic	Elvis	Cypress Lake	Greeter	$135.00
Sitzman	Georgia	Cypress Lake	Greeter	$240.00
Roman	Anita	Cypress Lake	Personal Trainer	$189.00
Briggs	Scott	Cypress Lake	Personal Trainer	$315.00
Vaccaro	Louis	Cypress Lake	Program Coordinator	$331.50
Matsumoto	Tyrus	Cypress Lake	Sales Associate	$341.25
Thi	Erona	Cypress Lake	Sales Associate	$390.00
Shoemaker	Wendy	Cypress Lake	Snack Bar Server	$204.00
Ruiz	Enrique	Cypress Lake	Snack Bar Server	$150.00
Robson	David	Forest Island	Aerobics Instructor	$195.00
Nelson	Samantha	Forest Island	Aerobics Instructor	$273.00
Stueland	Valerie	Forest Island	Aerobics Instructor	$162.00
Simson	Marge	Forest Island	Assistant Manager	$480.00
Reilly	Erin	Forest Island	Child Care Coordinator	$330.00
Larson	Alicia	Forest Island	Child Care Provider	$101.25
Workman	Jill	Forest Island	Child Care Provider	$126.00
Kim	Young	Forest Island	Greeter	$155.25
Howard	Karen	Forest Island	Greeter	$90.00
Jensen	Chris	Forest Island	Maintenance	$206.25
Lamm	Chris	Forest Island	Personal Trainer	$336.00
Torcivia	Peter	Forest Island	Personal Trainer	$315.00
Steele	Jeff	Forest Island	Program Coordinator	$360.00
Morgan	Dan	Forest Island	Sales Associate	$336.00
Mazeau	Rebecca	Forest Island	Sales Associate	$416.25
Martinez	Julie	Forest Island	Snack Bar Server	$67.50
Beinbrink	Andrew	Forest Island	Snack Bar Server	$120.00
Delucchi	Bill	Fort Myers	Aerobics Director	$360.00
Merwin	Adda	Fort Myers	Aerobics Instructor	$210.00
Ernster	Barbara	Fort Myers	Aerobics Instructor	$261.00
Sutton	Lisa	Fort Myers	Aerobics Instructor	$162.00
Helfand	Eric	Fort Myers	Aerobics Instructor	$175.50
Phelps	Jeff	Fort Myers	Child Care Coordinator	$288.00
Lembi	Damon	Fort Myers	Child Care Provider	$236.25
Smith	Brent	Fort Myers	Child Care Provider	$155.25
Lopez	Mina	Fort Myers	Cleaning	$135.00
Brett	Anna	Fort Myers	Greeter	$216.00
Pennington	Chad	Fort Myers	Greeter	$135.00

Concept Overview

The following concepts will be introduced in this lab:

1 **Input Mask**   An input mask controls how data is entered in a field of a table, query, or form.

2 **Lookup Field**   A lookup field provides a list of values from which the user can choose to enter data into that field.

3 **Required Property**   The Required property specifies whether a value is required in a field.

4 **Calculated Field**   A calculated field displays the result of a calculation in a query.

5 **Crosstab Query**   A crosstab query summarizes table data and displays it in a tabular format.

6 **Subdatasheet**   A subdatasheet is a data table nested in another data table that contains data related or joined to the table where it resides.

7 **Referential Integrity**   Referential integrity is a set of rules used by Access to ensure that relationships between tables are valid and that related data is not accidentally changed or deleted.

Using the Table Wizard to Create a Table

The owners of the Lifestyle Fitness Club have asked you to create a new data table that will hold the employees' pay rate information. You know that the Table Wizard contains a sample data table that is very similar to what you need, so you decide to use it to create your new table.

The **Table Wizard** is an Access wizard that automatically creates a new data table with predefined fields. It leads you step-by-step through selecting the type, or category, of table you want to create (personal or business), the sample table you want to use from a list of 45 predesigned tables, and the fields from that sample that you want to include. You can select fields from more than one sample table, and you can delete the fields you don't want once the table is created. The wizard will also assign the primary key field for you and create a related data-entry form, if desired.

You will create the employee salary table using the Table Wizard in the Club Employees database.

1 Start Access 2000.

Open the Club Employees data-base.

In the Database window, double-click the Create table by using wizard option.

Alternatively, you can click New at the top of the Club Employees: Database dialog box, and then choose Table Wizard from the New Table dialog box.

Your screen should be similar to Figure 4–1.

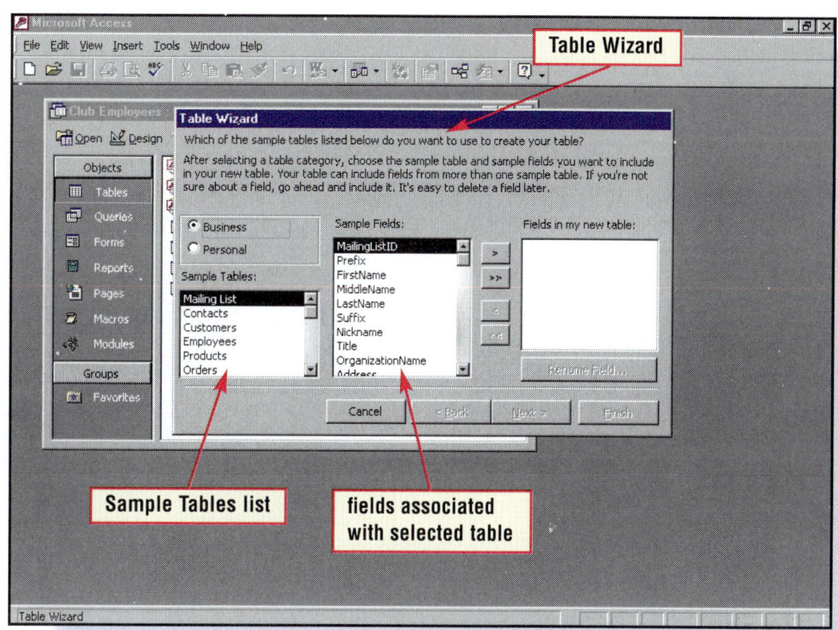

Figure 4–1

The first screen of the Table Wizard is displayed. On this screen, you select the table category, sample table, and sample fields you want to use. The Business category is already selected, which is the appropriate category for the database you are creating. The sample table you want to use for your database is called Time Billed.

2 Select Time Billed from the Sample Tables list.

Now the sample fields reflect field names that would be used in the selected type of table. You want to use two of the fields from the sample table in your new Pay data table: EmployeeID and HourlyRate.

3 Add the EmployeeID and HourlyRate fields to the Fields in my new table list.

Double-click the field name to add it to the list.

Your screen should be similar to Figure 4–2.

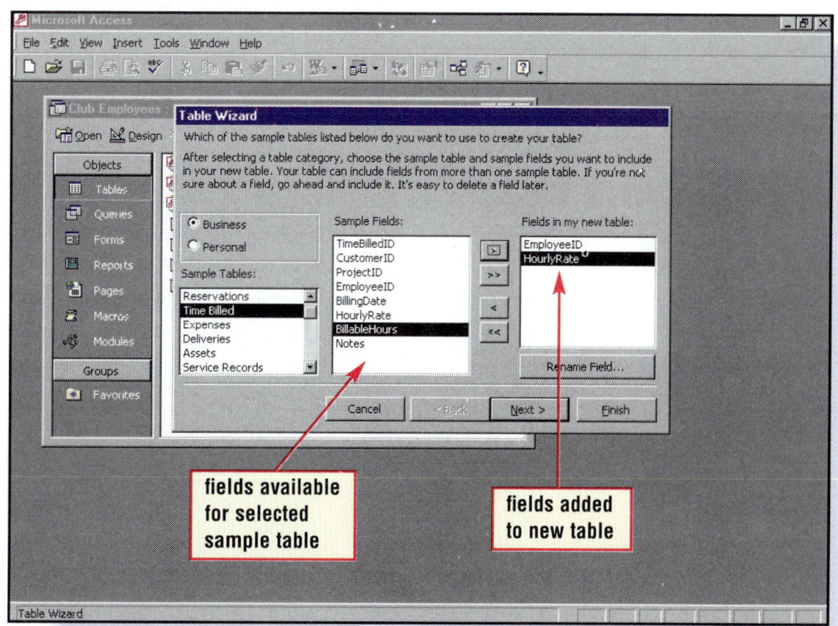

Figure 4–2

If you add a field in the wrong order or add the wrong field, you can remove it from the list of fields in your new table by selecting it and clicking [<]. If you want to remove all fields from this list and start over, click [<<].

Now that the fields are specified for the new table, you want to rename the fields. The EmployeeID field name needs to be changed to Employee ID so that it is exactly the same as the corresponding field name in the employee data tables you created earlier. You will also change the name of the HourlyRate field to Hourly Rate.

4 ▪ **Select** EmployeeID.

▪ **Click** [Rename Field...].

▪ **Insert a blank space before ID in the field name.**

▪ **Click** [OK].

▪ **In a similar manner, rename the** HourlyRate **field Hourly Rate.**

Your screen should be similar to Figure 4–3.

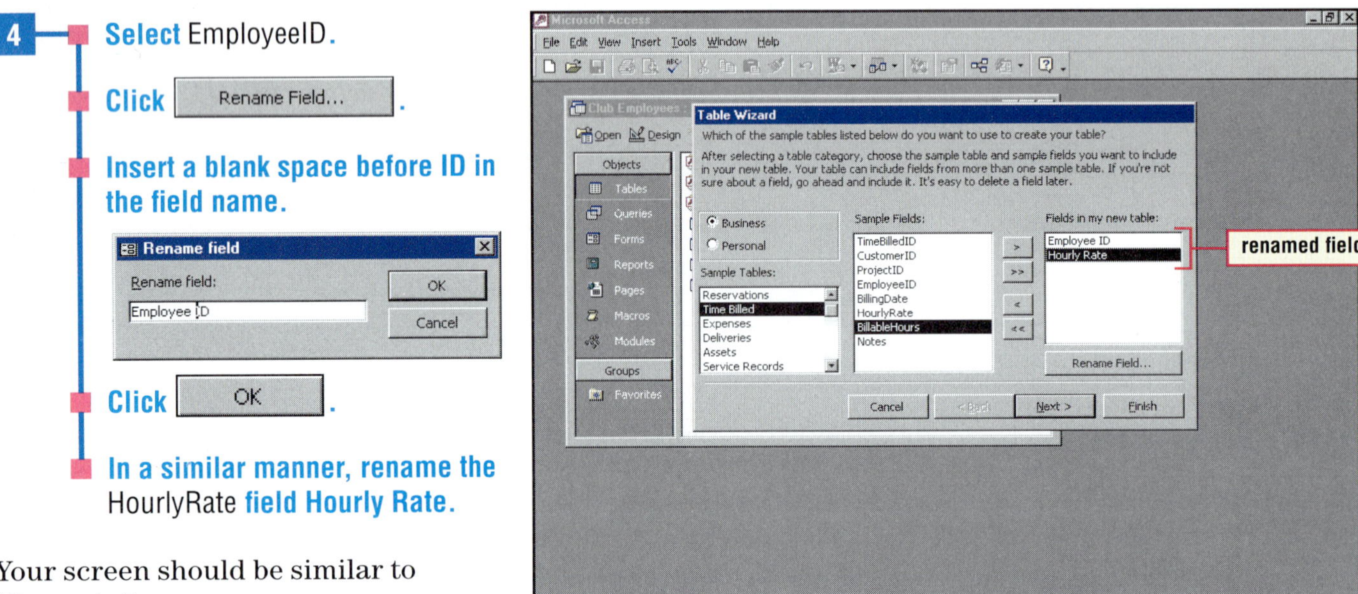

Figure 4–3

The fields you want included in the new table are now specified and you are ready to go to the next step in the Table Wizard.

5 ▪ **Click** [Next >].

Your screen should be similar to Figure 4–4.

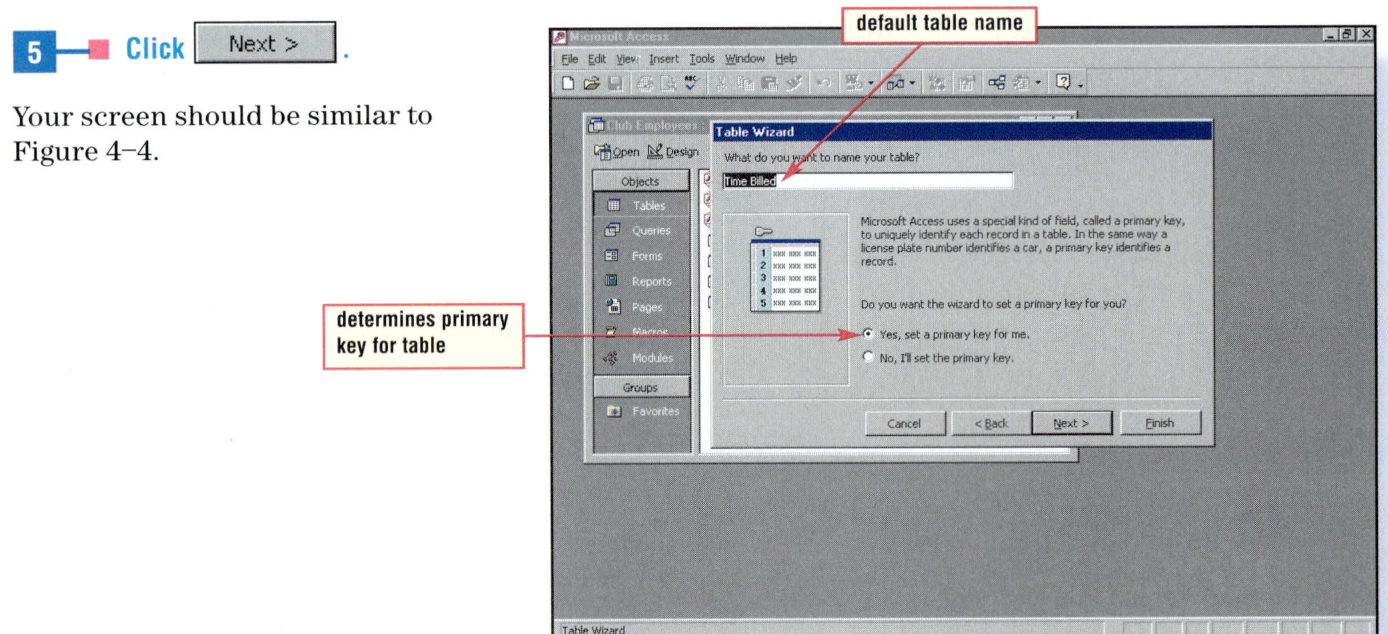

Figure 4–4

In this dialog box you specify the name for the new table and a primary key field. The Table Wizard automatically displays the sample table name as the name for your new table. You want to rename the table to Pay and let the Table Wizard set the primary key (which is the default).

6 ■ Type **Pay** as the new table name.

■ Click Next > .

Your screen should be similar to Figure 4–5.

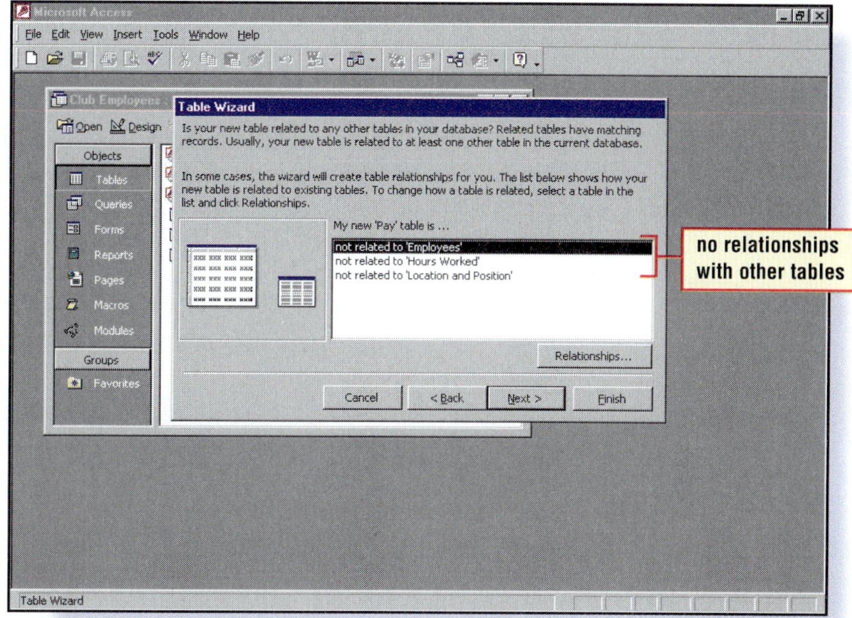

Figure 4–5

In the next Wizard dialog box you specify how the new table is related to other tables in the database. For now you will not establish a relationship between the tables.

7 ■ Click Next > .

Your screen should be similar to Figure 4–6.

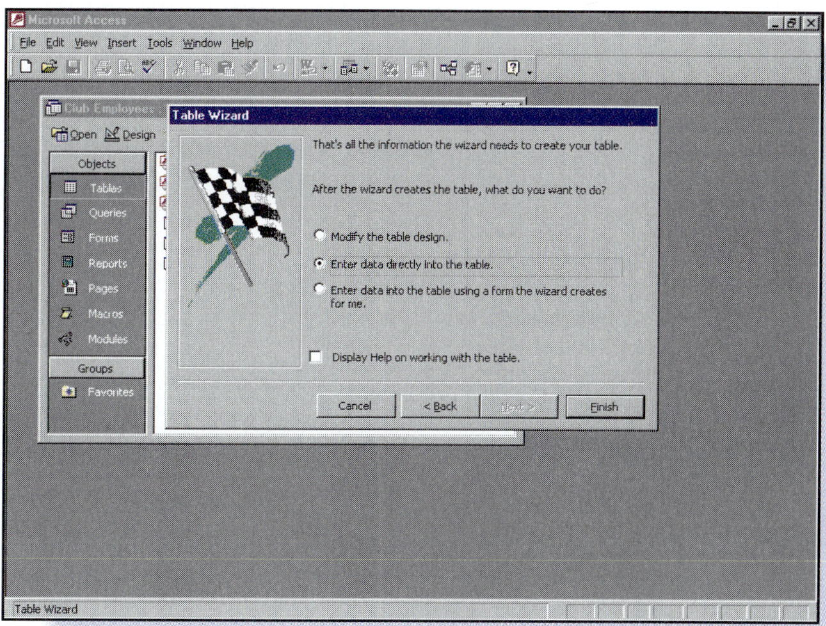

Figure 4–6

In the final Table Wizard dialog box, you specify what action you want to do after the table is created. Your selection will determine in what view the Wizard opens your table. You want to check the field properties and modify them if necessary, and you will create the data-entry form yourself after you've got the table set up the way you want it.

8 — **Select** Modify the table design.

Click Finish .

Your screen should be similar to Figure 4–7.

primary key field

design window for Pay table

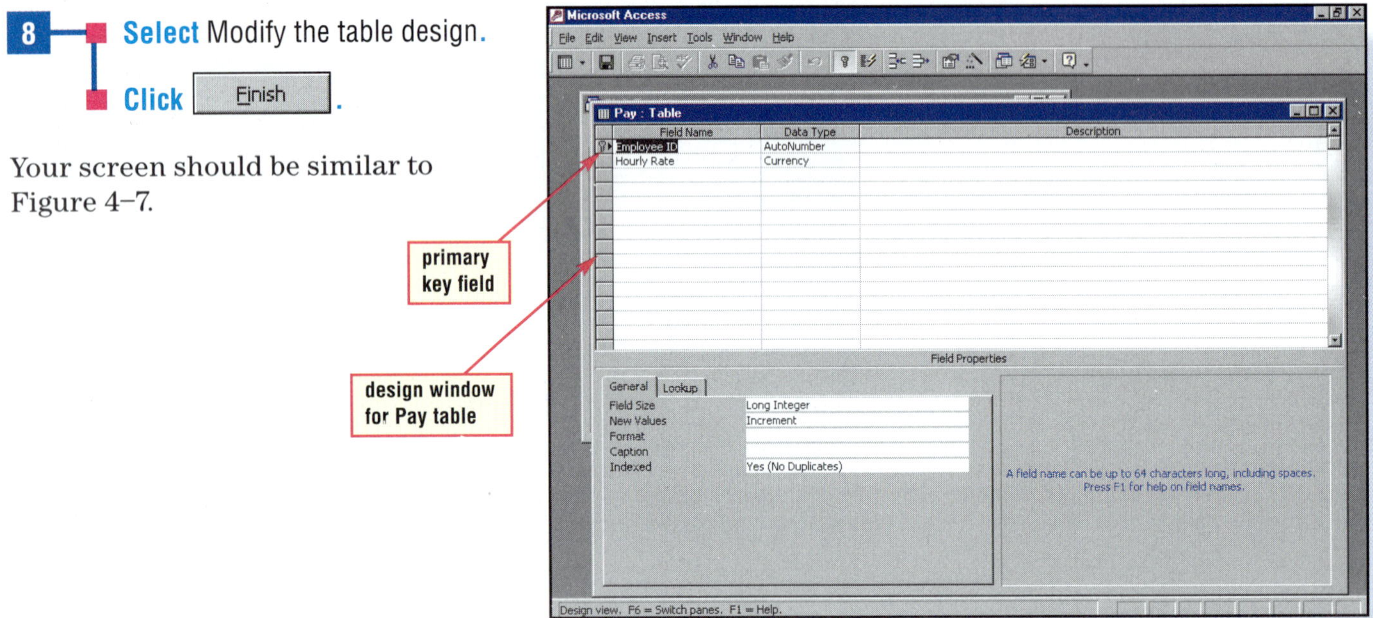

Figure 4–7

Your new Pay table is created and displayed in Design view. Notice that the Hourly Rate has been automatically assigned the Currency data type. Also, the Employee ID field has been assigned the primary key, which is what you want. However, its data type has been set to Autonumber, which will automatically increment the data entries in this field. Because the employee numbers are not necessarily in exact numerical order, you want to change the Employee ID field property to Text and the field size to 4, as it is in the other employee tables.

9 Change the Employee ID data type to **Text** and the field size to **4**.

Your screen should be similar to Figure 4–8.

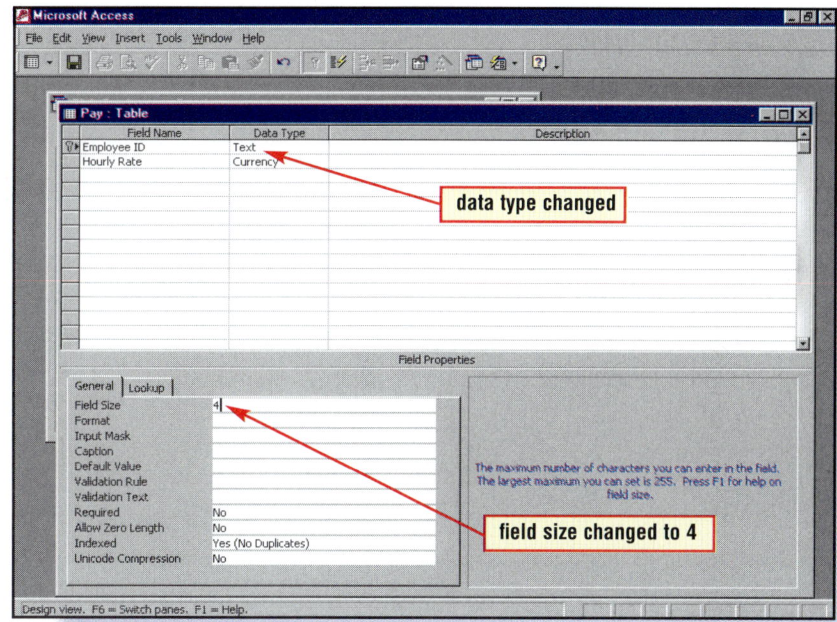

Figure 4–8

Next, you want to include the employees' social security numbers in this data table for payroll purposes. To add a new field where this information can be entered,

10 Insert a row between Employee ID and Hourly Rate.

Name the new field **Social Security Number** and select the Text **data type.**

Change the Field Size property to 11.

Your screen should be similar to Figure 4–9.

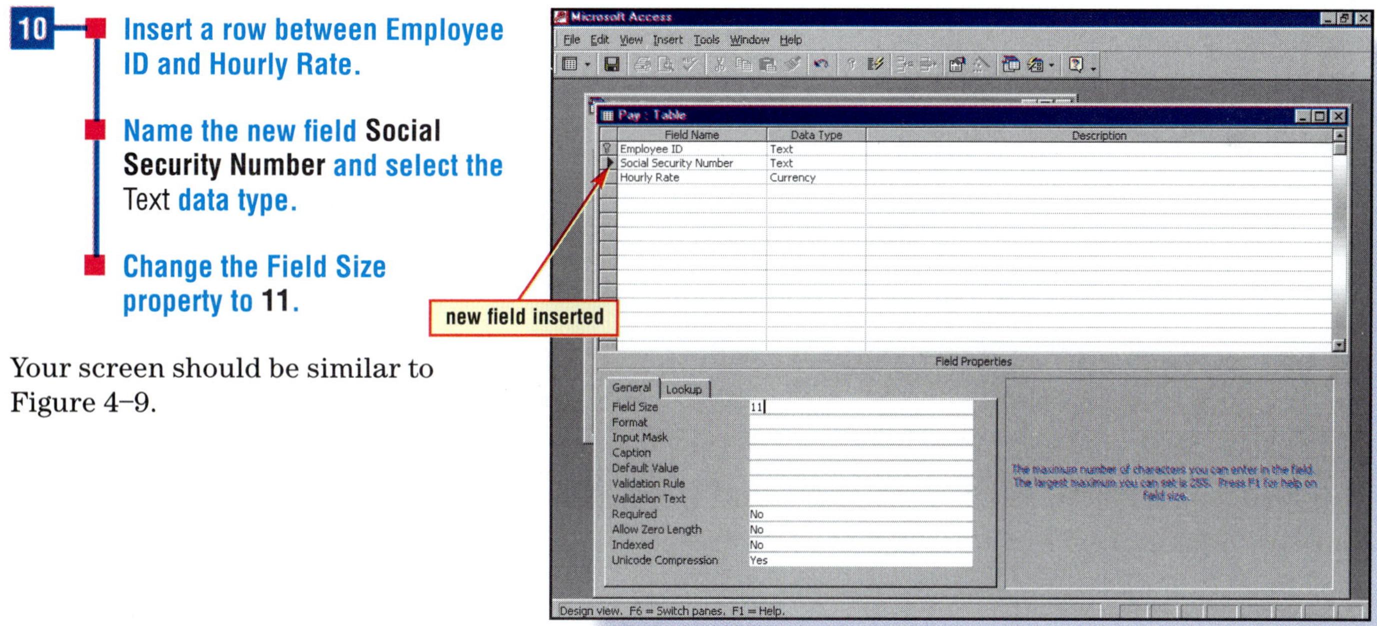

Figure 4–9

Creating an Input Mask

Most people know that a social security number is always 9 digits, typically in the format ###-##-####. However, when someone has to enter several records in one sitting, it's very easy to make a mistake and enter a letter or punctuation mark instead of a digit, the wrong number of digits, or the hyphens in the wrong place. To make the task of entering each club employee's social security number a bit easier, as well as to ensure that the entry is made in the proper format, you decide to apply an input mask to the Social Security Number field.

Concept  Input Mask

An **input mask** controls how data is entered in a field of a table, query, or form. For example, you could create an input mask for a phone number field that will display a new number as (###) ###-####, even if the user enters only a series of 10 numbers with no punctuation.

You set up an input mask for a field in the General Tab of a field's properties box, either by manually typing it in or by letting the InputMask Wizard set the property for you.

Access uses the following characters to define an input mask:

Character	Description
0	Requires that a digit from 0–9 be entered.
9	An entry is not required, but if an entry is made, it must be a digit or space.
#	An entry is not required, but if an entry is made, it must be a digit, space, + (plus sign), or – (minus sign).
L	Requires that a letter from A–Z be entered.
?	An entry is not required, but if an entry is made, it must be a letter from A–Z.
A	Requires that a letter or digit be entered.
a	An entry is not required, but if an entry is made, it must be a letter or digit.
&	An entry is required, and it can be any character or a space.
C	An entry is not required, but if an entry is made, it can be any character or a space.
. , : ; - /	A decimal placeholder and thousand, date, and time separators.
<	Converts entries to all lowercase.
>	Converts entries to all uppercase
!	Displays the input mask from right to left at the point where the ! is inserted, rather than from left to right.
\	Displays the character that follows as a literal character (for example, \A is displayed as just A).

To create an input mask for the Social Security Number field,

1 ➡ **Click the Input Mask property box.**

If the Input Mask wizard is not installed on your system, type 000-00-0000;;_ in the Input mask text box and skip to below Figure 4–11.

To avoid the Save warning message, you can save the table design by clicking 🖫 before clicking the Input Mask property box.

Additional Information

You can also create your own custom Input masks for the Input Mask Wizard to display.

3 ■ **Select** Social Security Number.

■ **Click in the Try It box.**

Your screen should look similar to Figure 4–10.

A 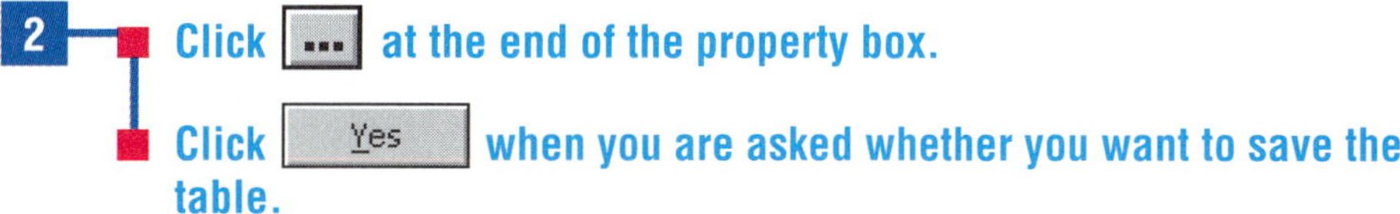 button appears at the end of the box, signifying that there is a wizard connected to this property. You can use the wizard to define the input mask or you can type it in directly in the text box. Because input masks are sometimes complicated, it is easier to use the wizard.

2 ■ **Click** ••• **at the end of the property box.**

■ **Click** Yes **when you are asked whether you want to save the table.**

The Input Mask Wizard dialog box lists 10 predefined masks. You can also use this dialog box to try out one of the masks or create your own. For your purposes, the Social Security input mask is exactly what you want.

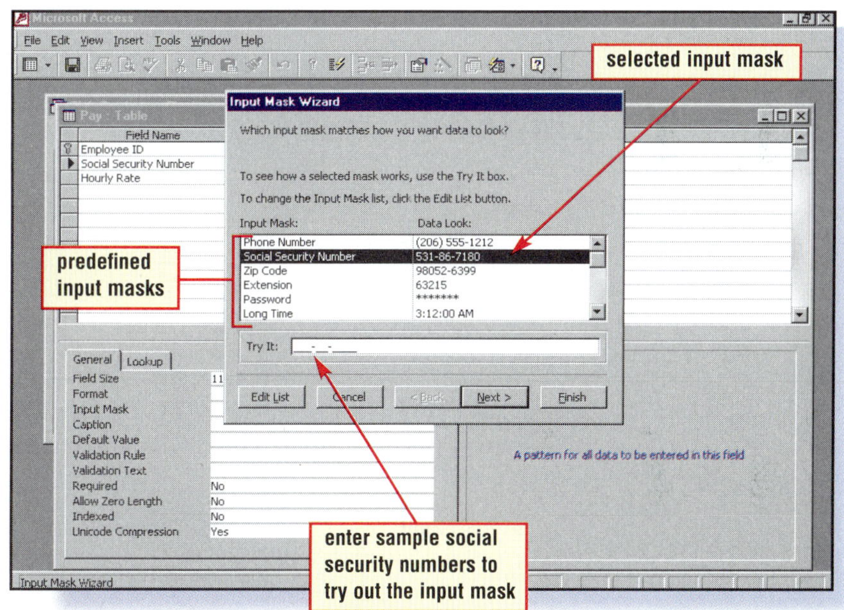

Figure 4–10

Notice that the input mask automatically inserted hyphens in the correct locations for a social security number. This means that the person who is entering the employee social security numbers in this table can just enter the digits without having to worry about entering the hyphens as well. If, however, they do enter the hyphens or enter the hyphens in the wrong place, that's okay, too. To test this,

4 ■ **Position the cursor at the beginning of the Try It box.**

■ **Type 123456789.**

■ **Clear the entry and type 123-45-6789.**

■ **Clear the entry and type 12-345-6789.**

Press (Esc) to clear the entry.

In each case, the hyphens were automatically entered in the proper location. Now you want to see what happens when you make an incorrect entry.

5 ■ **Clear the entry and type 12345678.**

■ **Press** ⏎Enter .

Your screen should be similar to Figure 4–11.

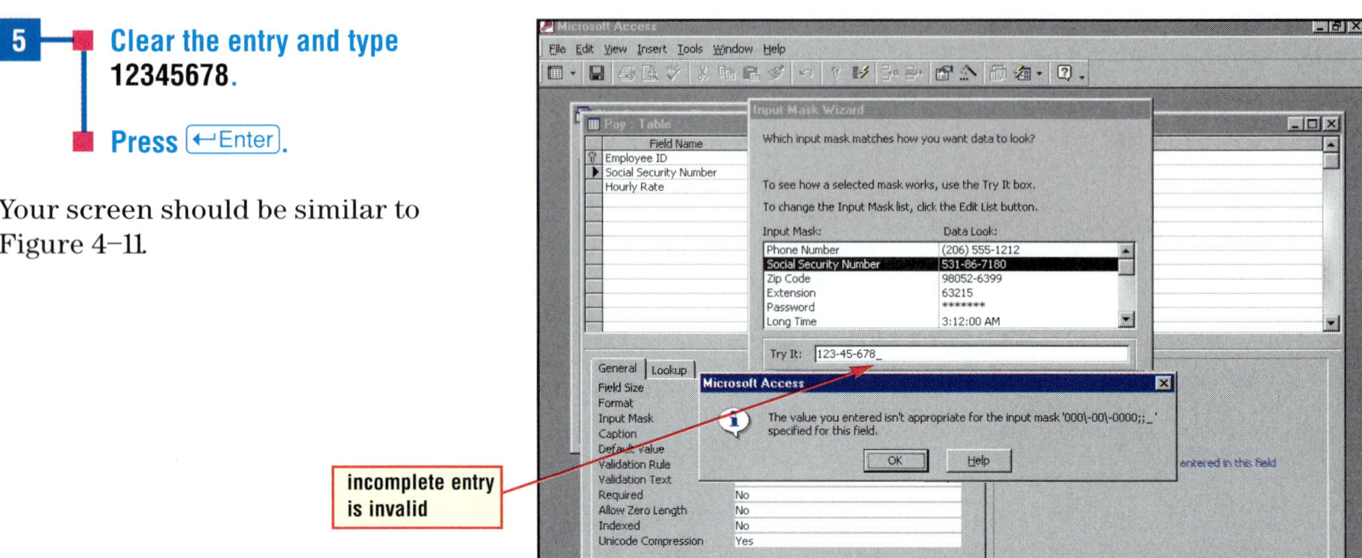

incomplete entry is invalid

Figure 4–11

A validation error message is displayed advising you that you have made an invalid entry. To return to the Input Mask dialog box, clear the incorrect entry and continue with your input mask creation,

6 ■ **Click** 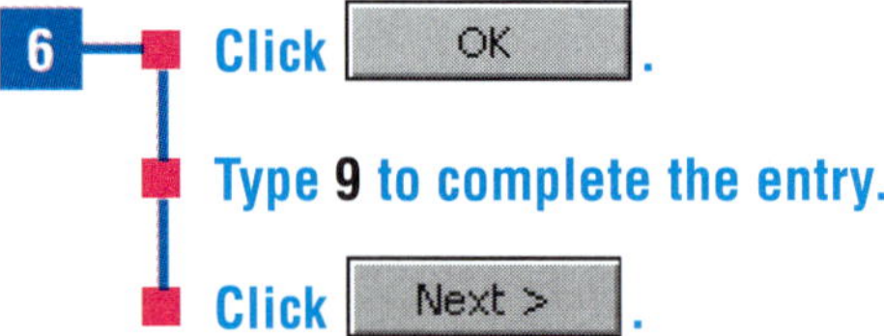 OK .

■ **Type 9 to complete the entry.**

■ **Click** Next > .

The sample entry is accepted and the next Input Mask Wizard dialog box is displayed. Next you need to specify the placeholder character you want to display as data is entered into the field. The default is the standard flashing underline, which is acceptable, so you can proceed to the next step.

7 ■ **Click**  Next > .

The Wizard now asks you how you want to store the data that is entered in this field. The default, storing the data without the hyphens, takes up less data storage space and is fine with you. To accept the default and proceed to the final Wizard dialog box and finish the process,

Your screen should look similar to Figure 4–12.

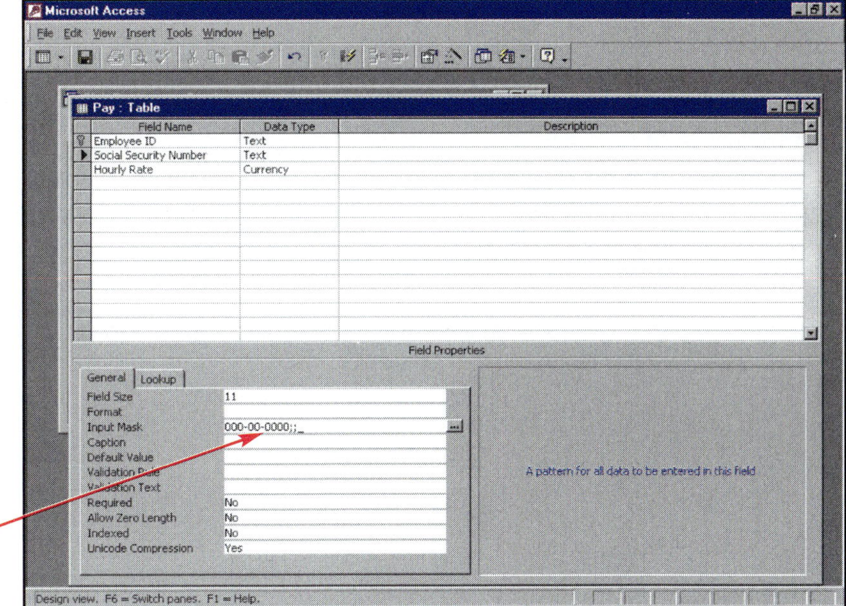

Figure 4–12

The input mask for the Social Security Number field is added to the General properties. The first part of the input mask 000-00-0000 specifies a required number entry consisting of 9 numbers. The hyphens are literal characters used to separate the parts of the entry. The first semicolon indicates the end of the mask definition. The second semicolon indicates the end of the second part of the input mask definition. Because there is nothing entered between the semicolons, this means that only the characters that are typed will be stored. Finally, the _ identifies the selected placeholder character.

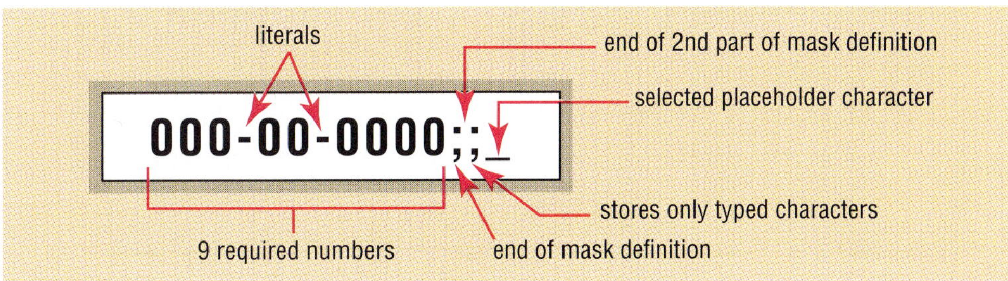

Creating a Lookup Field

Next, you decide to replace the current Hourly Rate field with a lookup field that will make entering hourly pay rates easier, faster, and less prone to errors. The hourly pay rates at the club range from $6 to $12. In addition, if the employee is on salary, the field entry is salary rather than an hourly pay rate. By creating a lookup field, you can list only the valid pay rates, so that anyone entering a new employee record in the Pay table will merely have to choose from this list to enter it as the rate for that employee.

Concept ❷ Lookup Field

A **lookup field** provides a list of values from which the user can choose to make entering data into that field simpler. The lookup field can get the values from an existing table or a fixed set of values that are defined when the lookup field is created. The lookup field that uses another table as the source for values is called a **lookup list** and one that uses fixed values is called a **value list**.

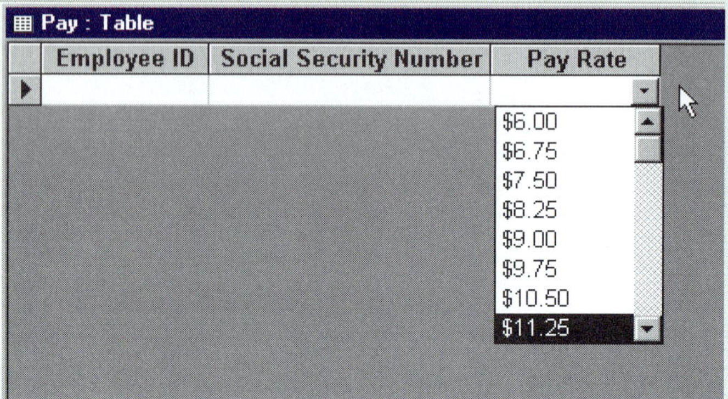

When the lookup field uses a table for the values it displays, an association is created between the two tables. Picking a value from the lookup list sets the **foreign key value** (a field that refers to the primary key field in another table to show how the tables are related, data must match although field names do not need to) in the current record to the primary key value of the corresponding record in the related table. The related table displays but does not store the data in the record. The foreign key is stored but does not display. For this reason, any updates made to the data in the related table will be reflected in both the list and records in the table containing the lookup field. You must define a lookup list field from the table that will contain the foreign key and display the lookup list.

A lookup field that uses a fixed list of values looks the same as a lookup field that uses a table. However, the fixed set of values is entered when the lookup field is created. A value list should only be used for values that will not change very often and don't need to be stored in a table. For example, a list for a Salutation field containing Mr., Mrs., or Ms. would be a good candidate for a value list. Choosing a value from a value list will store that value in the record—it doesn't create an association to a related table. For this reason, if you change any of the original values in the value list later, they will not be reflected in records added before this change was made.

The Lookup Wizard is used to create a lookup field. Because it creates a new field for you, you will need to first delete the existing Hourly Rate field.

1 **Select the** Hourly Rate **row.**

Click 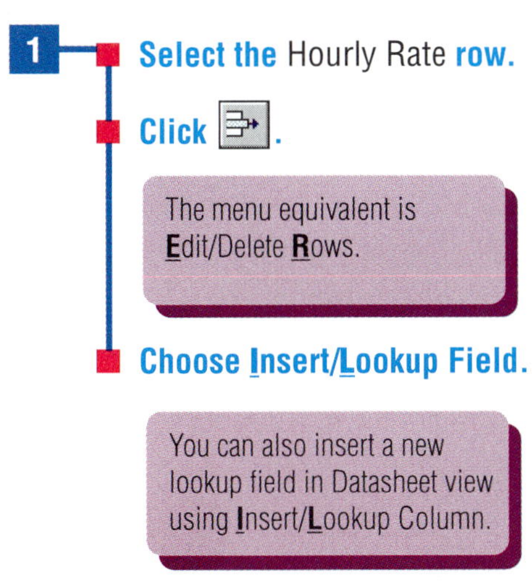.

> The menu equivalent is
> **E**dit/Delete **R**ows.

Choose Insert/Lookup Field.

> You can also insert a new
> lookup field in Datasheet view
> using **I**nsert/**L**ookup Column.

Your screen should look similar to
Figure 4–13.

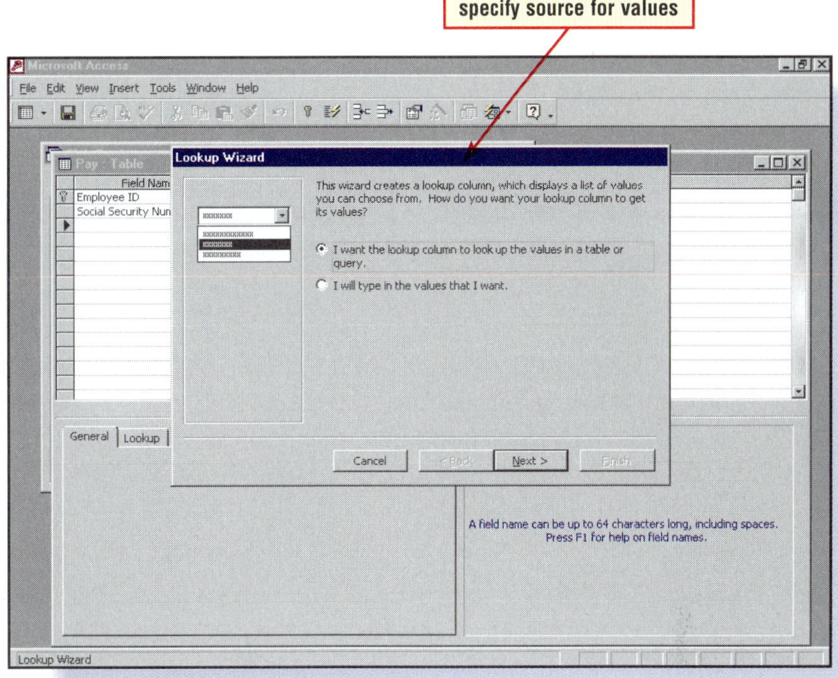

Figure 4–13

In the first Lookup Wizard dialog box you specify the source for the
values for the lookup field. You will enter your own values, the club's pay
rates, for this field.

2 **Select** I will type in the values that
I want**.**

Click 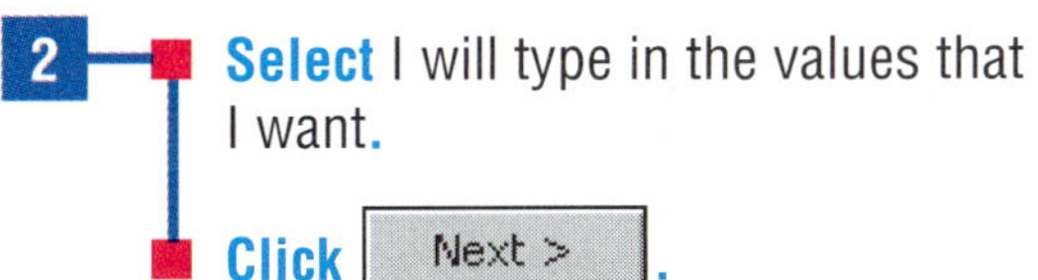 Next > .

Your screen should look similar to
Figure 4–14.

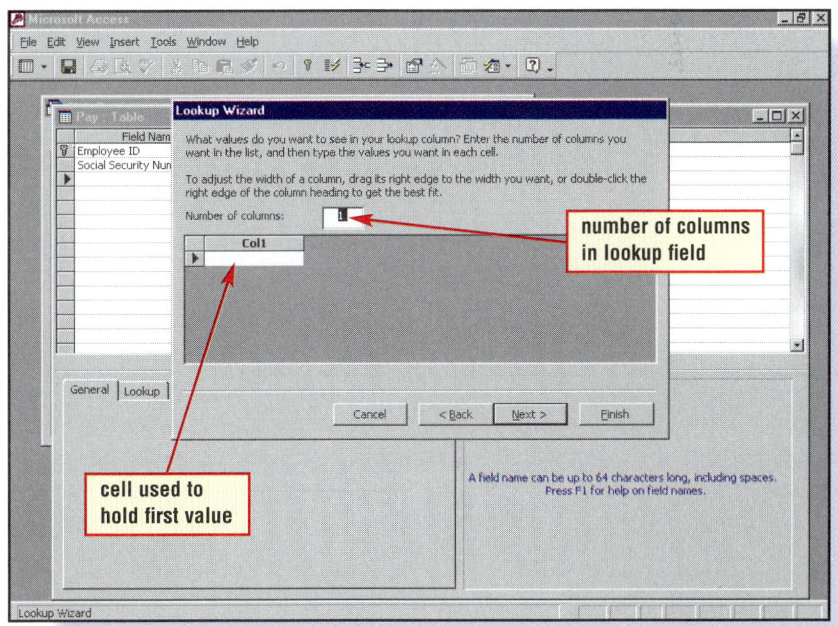

Figure 4–14

The next step in the Lookup Wizard is to enter the values you want listed in the lookup field. You can also add columns and adjust their widths to fit the values you enter, if necessary. You only need one column, and the current width is sufficient for the values you are going to enter. To enter the club's pay rates,

3
- **Click in cell under Col1.**
- **Type $6.00.**
- **Press** Tab.
- **Enter the rest of the pay rates as follows, pressing** Tab **after each to go to the next entry line.**

$6.75
$7.50
$8.25
$9.00
$9.75
$10.50
$11.25
$12.00
Salary

You can correct the entries in the same way you do any other field entry.

Your screen should look similar to Figure 4–15.

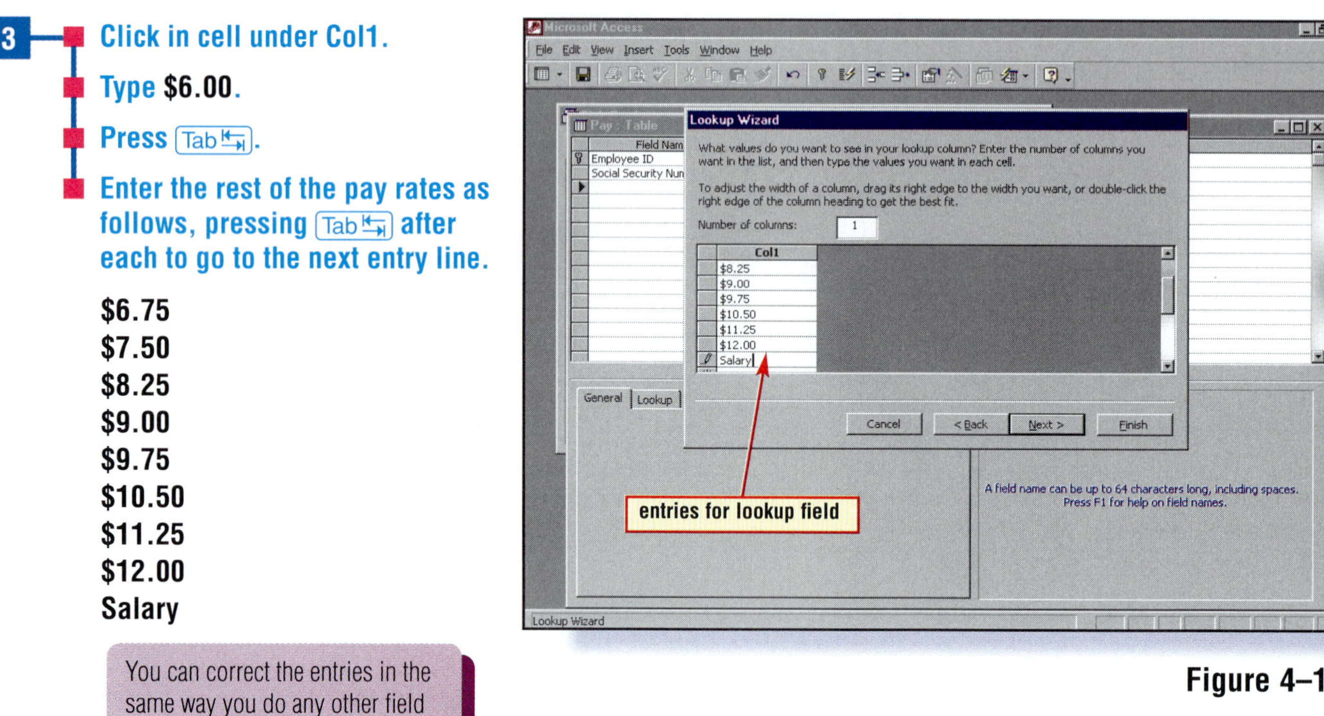

Figure 4–15

You've entered all the pay rates, and you can proceed to the next step in your lookup field creation.

4 ■ **Click** Next > .

Your screen should look similar to Figure 4–16.

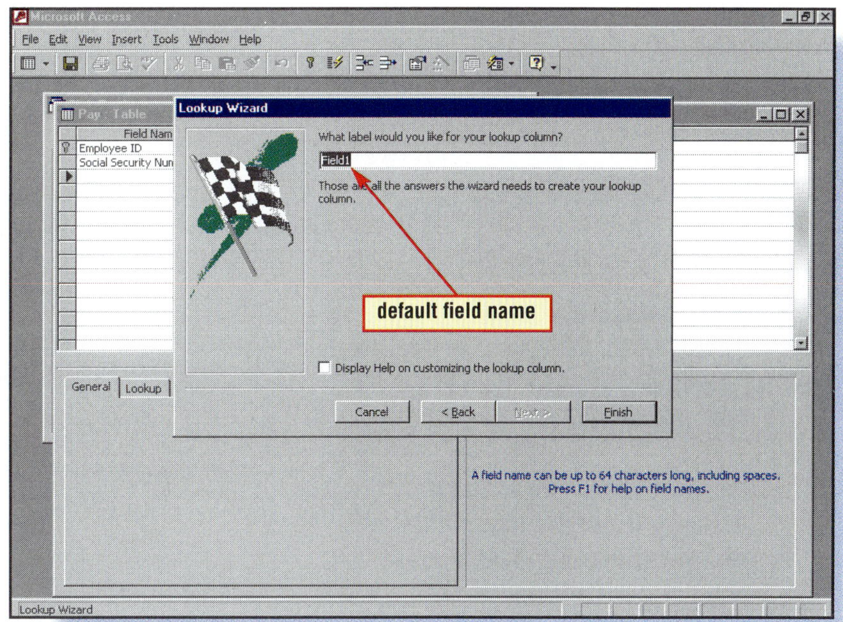

Figure 4–16

The last step is to name the lookup field.

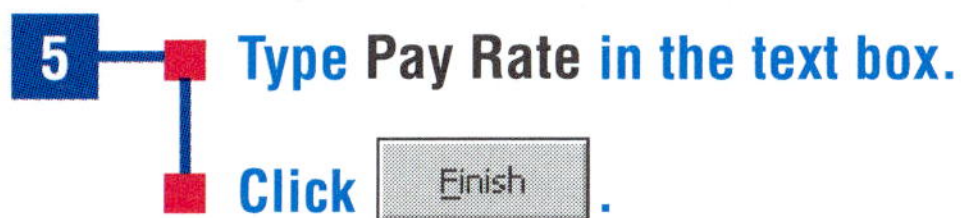

5 ■ **Type Pay Rate in the text box.**

■ **Click** Finish .

The new Pay Rate lookup field has been added to the Pay table design. To see the settings that were established for this field,

6 ■ **Open the Lookup tab.**

Your screen should look similar to Figure 4–17.

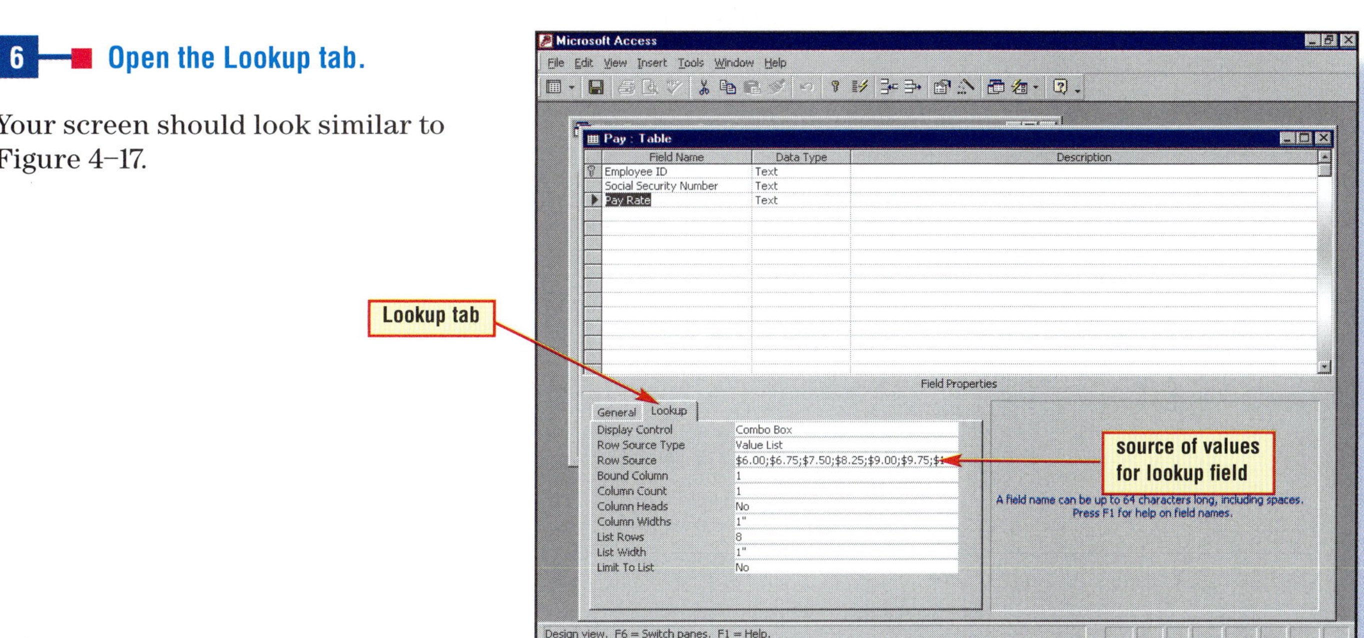

Figure 4–17

The lookup list will appear in a combo box control and gets its list values from the value list containing the values you specified as the source. The other properties are set to the defaults for lookup fields. The only change you want to make is to restrict the data entry in that field to values in the lookup list.

Click ▼ at the end of the box to open the drop-down list of the options.

6 ■ **Change the Limit to List property to** Yes.

You will enter a sample employee pay record to test the table design.

7 ■ **Save the table and switch to Datasheet view.**

■ **Increase the width of the Social Security Number column so the entire field name is displayed.**

■ **Type 1151 in the Employee ID field and press** Tab↹.

■ **Type 123456789 in the Social Security Number field and press** Tab↹.

■ **Type 7.25 in the Pay Rate field and press** ↵Enter.

Your screen should look similar to Figure 4–18.

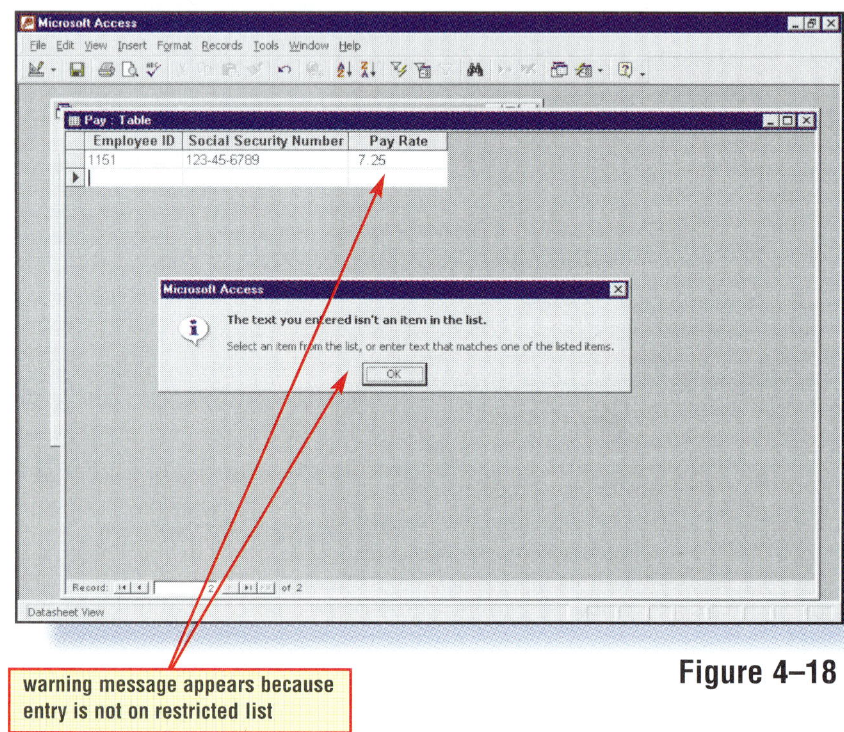

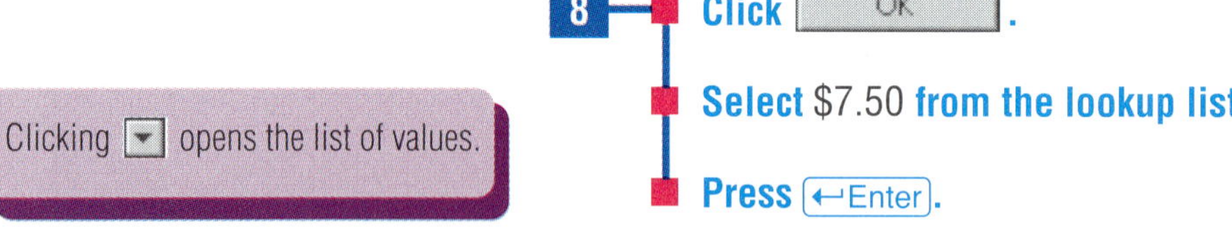

Figure 4–18

A warning box advises you that the entry must match one of the listed items because you restricted field entries in the Pay Rate field to entries on the list.

8 ■ **Click** OK .

■ **Select** $7.50 **from the lookup list.**

■ **Press** ↵Enter.

Clicking ▼ opens the list of values.

You are done designing and testing your Pay table and are ready to add the real employee pay rate information to the table.

9 ■ **Delete the sample record.**

Copying Data

The Employee ID information needed in the Pay table is the same information as in the Employees table. Rather than entering the same information again into the Pay table, you will copy it from the Employees table using the Copy and Paste commands on the Edit menu or their toolbar shortcuts. The copied item is temporarily stored in the Windows Clipboard. Then you move to the new location where you want the contents copied and use the Paste command to insert the Clipboard contents into the selected location. Be careful when pasting to the new location because any existing entries are replaced.

In addition, Access 2000 includes the Office Clipboard feature that allows you to collect multiple items and paste them as needed. The Office Clipboard and the Windows Clipboard are similar, but separate features. The major difference is the Office Clipboard can hold up to 12 items whereas the Windows Clipboard holds only a single item. The last item you copy to the Office Clipboard is always copied to the Windows Clipboard. When you use the Office Clipboard, you can select to paste the items in any order from any of the items stored.

The Office Clipboard is available from all Office 2000 applications. It is accessed through the Clipboard toolbar. Once the Clipboard toolbar is opened, it is available for use in any program including non-Office programs. In some programs, if the Cut, Copy, and Paste commands are not available or in non-Office programs, the toolbar is not visible, however, it is still operational. You can copy from any program that provides copy and cut capabilities, but you can only paste into Word, Excel, Access, PowerPoint, and Outlook.

You will use the Office Clipboard feature to copy the information you need into the Pay table. First you will copy the Employee ID field column to the Office Clipboard.

> You can copy items such as individual field entries, entire records or fields, controls, or even database objects such as entire tables within and between Access databases and to other applications.

1 ▪ **Display the Clipboard toolbar.**

> Right-click the toolbar and select Clipboard from the shortcut menu.

▪ **If necessary, click [icon] Clear Clipboard to remove any items currently stored in Clipboard.**

▪ **Open the Employees table and select the** Employee ID **field column.**

▪ **Click [icon] Copy in the Clipboard toolbar.**

> The menu equivalent is **E**dit/**C**opy and the shortcut key is [Ctrl] + C. Copy is also available on the Shortcut menu.

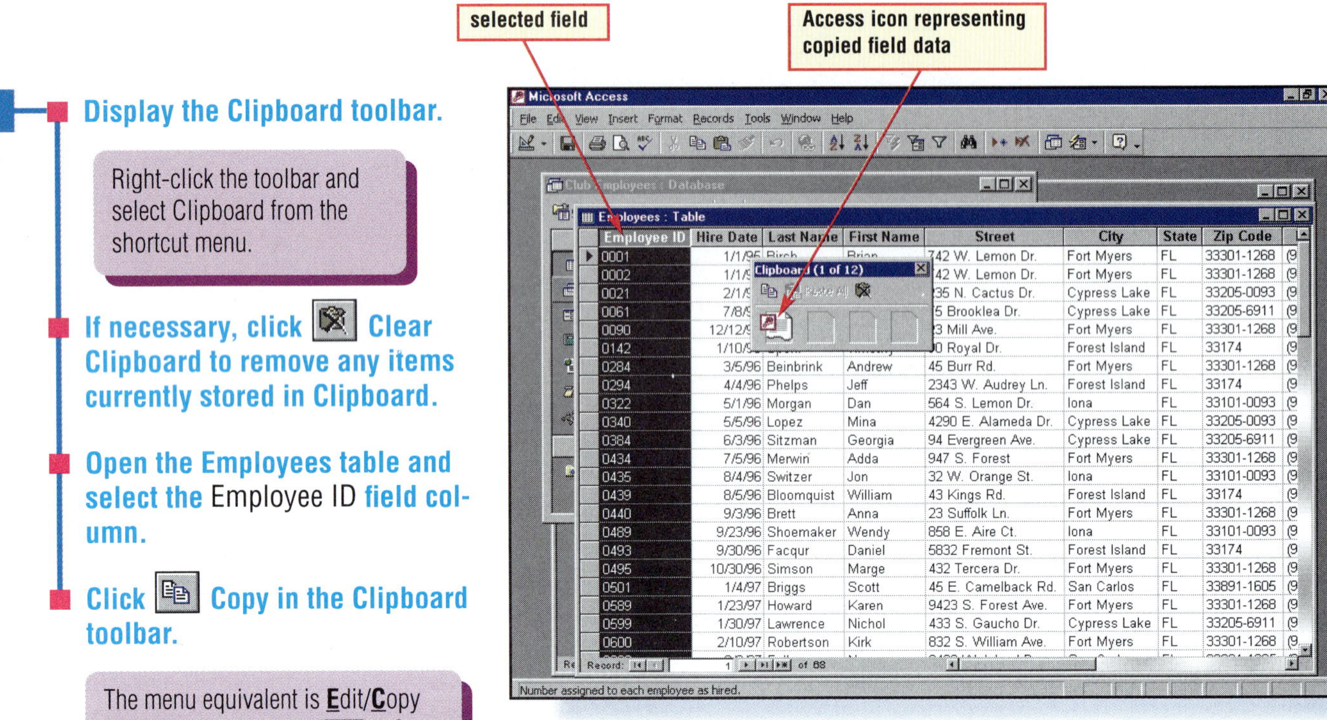

Figure 4–19

Your screen should be similar to Figure 4–19.

You can also use [icon] Copy on the table Datasheet toolbar when the Office Clipboard feature is active and the item will be copied to the Office Clipboard.

The Clipboard toolbar displays an Access icon representing the copied item. While looking at the Employee table, you think that in addition to the Employee ID you may also want to copy the Last Name field into a new field of the Pay table. Since you are currently viewing the table, you will copy the field now and paste it later. Once the Clipboard toolbar is open, as you continue to copy items they are added sequentially to the Office Clipboard.

2 ▪ **Select the** Last Name **field.**

▪ **Click [icon] Copy in the Clipboard toolbar.**

The Clipboard displays two Access icons, one for each copied item. Now you are ready to paste the items into the Pay table. You want to paste the Employee ID field first. You can view the first 50 characters of an item by pointing to the icon on the Clipboard. If the copied item is a drawing object or picture, the label simply displays "Picture" followed by a number that indicates the order in which the item was copied.

3

Close the Employees table.

Switch to the Pay table and se-lect the Employee ID **column.**

Point to the icon representing the Employee ID field in the Office Clipboard.

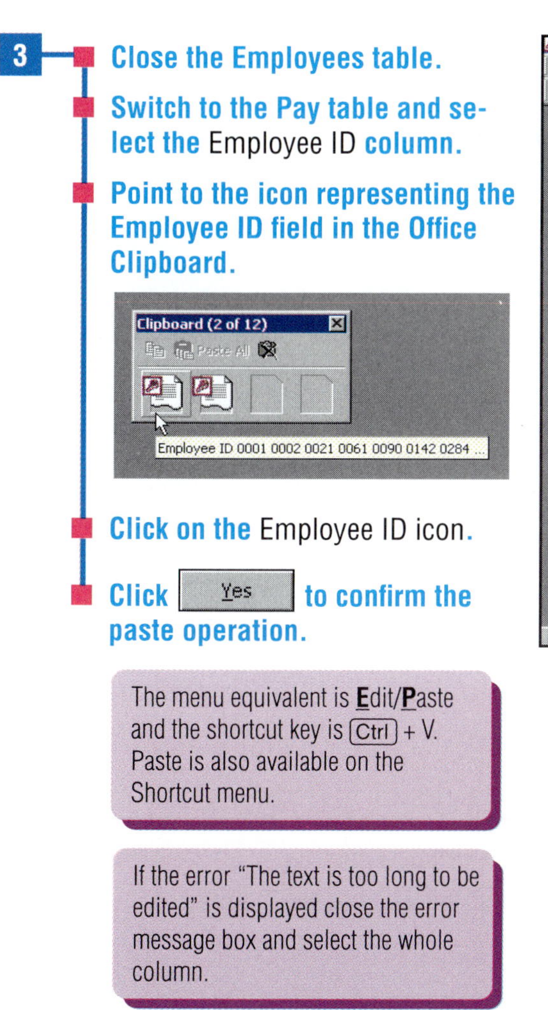

Click on the Employee ID **icon.**

Click Yes **to confirm the paste operation.**

> The menu equivalent is **E**dit/**P**aste and the shortcut key is Ctrl + V. Paste is also available on the Shortcut menu.

> If the error "The text is too long to be edited" is displayed close the error message box and select the whole column.

Your screen should be similar to Figure 4–20.

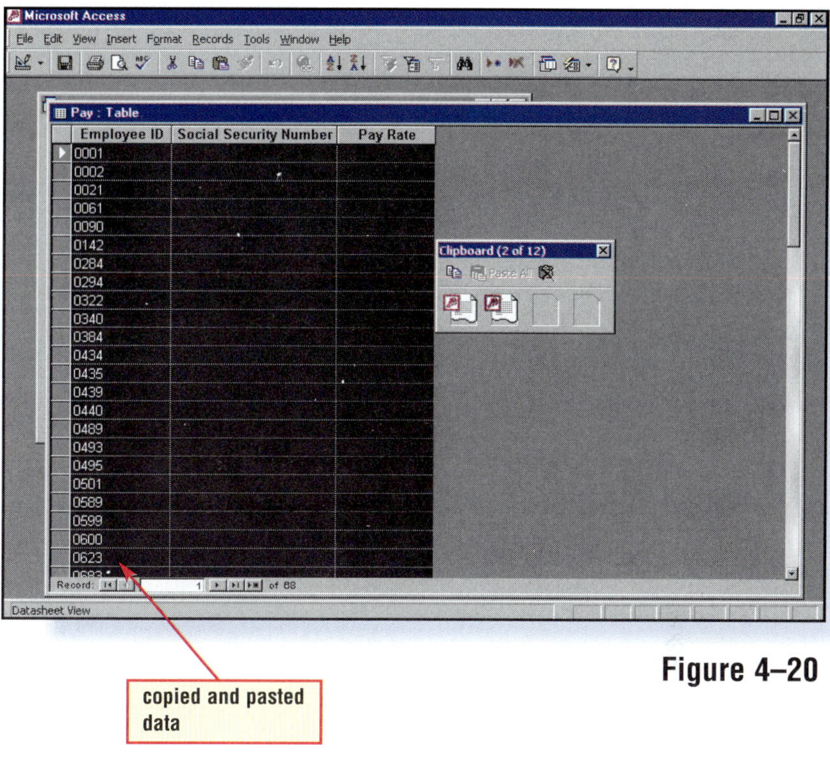

Figure 4–20

Additional Information

The Office Clipboard Paste All op-tion inserts the contents of all copied items in the order in which they were added to the Office Clipboard.

The contents of the copied item are pasted into the selected field column. Next you want to insert the Last Name field information into a new field column in the Pay table.

4 ▪ **Move to the Social Security Number field.**

▪ **Choose** <u>I</u>nsert/<u>C</u>olumn.

▪ **Select the** new blank field column.

▪ **Click on the** Last Name clipboard icon.

▪ **Click** [Yes] **to confirm the paste operation.**

Your screen should be similar to Figure 4–21.

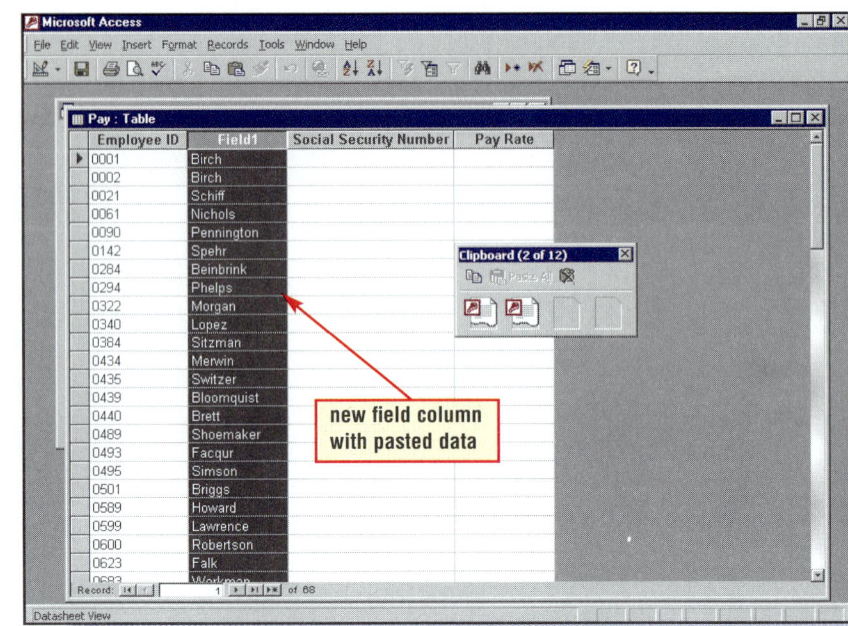

Figure 4–21

Next you will name the new field column and then close the Office Clipboard.

5 ▪ **Right click on the new field heading and choose** Rename Column **from the shortcut menu.**

▪ **Type Last Name in the column heading and press** ⏎Enter.

▪ **Click 🗙 Clear Clipboard and close the Office Clipboard.**

Importing Data

As you were working on the Pay table, you realized that the payroll department must maintain this information already. After checking with payroll, they created an Excel worksheet file for you that includes the employee ID number, social security number, and pay rate information for all employees in sorted order by employee number. After looking at the worksheet, you decide it would be faster and more accurate to copy this information into the Pay table than it would be to enter it manually. To do this, you could open the worksheet file in Excel and select, copy and paste the data into the appropriate location in the Pay table.

An alternative method is to **import** the entire worksheet file contents into the database table. Using this method, you do not need to open the other application and select the information to be copied. However, the worksheet data must be in the same order as needed in the table (Employee ID, Social Security Number, and Pay Rate) and the table must be empty. You will delete the Last Name field and remove all records. Then you will import the worksheet data.

1
- Choose **Edit/Select All Records**.
- Click **Delete Record**.
- Click **Yes** to confirm the delete operation.
- **Select** the Last Name field.
- Choose **Edit/Delete Column**.
- **Close and save the Pay table.**
- Choose **File/Get External Data/Import**.

Your screen should be similar to Figure 4–22.

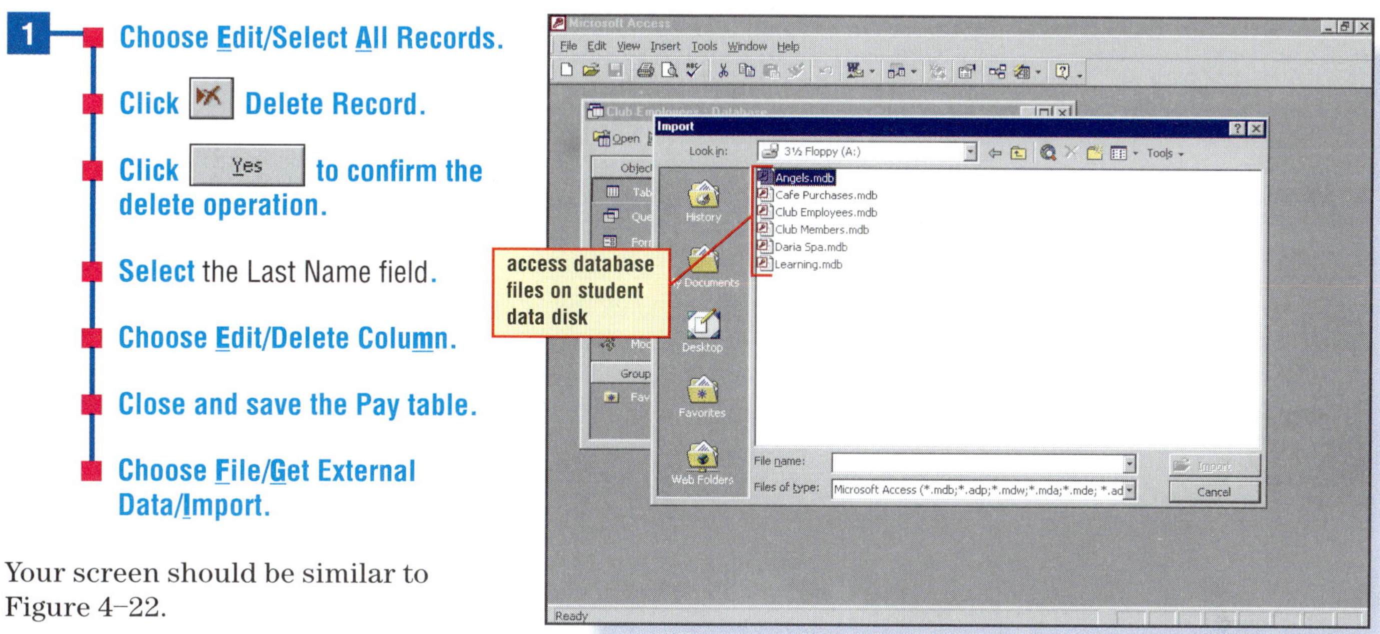

Figure 4–22

The Import dialog box is used to specify the location, type, and name, of the file you want to import.

2
- If necessary, select the drive containing your data disk as the location containing the file you want to import.
- **Open the** Files of type **drop-down list box and select** Microsoft Excel (*.xls).
- **Select the** Pay.xls **file.**
- Click **Import**.

Your screen should be similar to Figure 4–23.

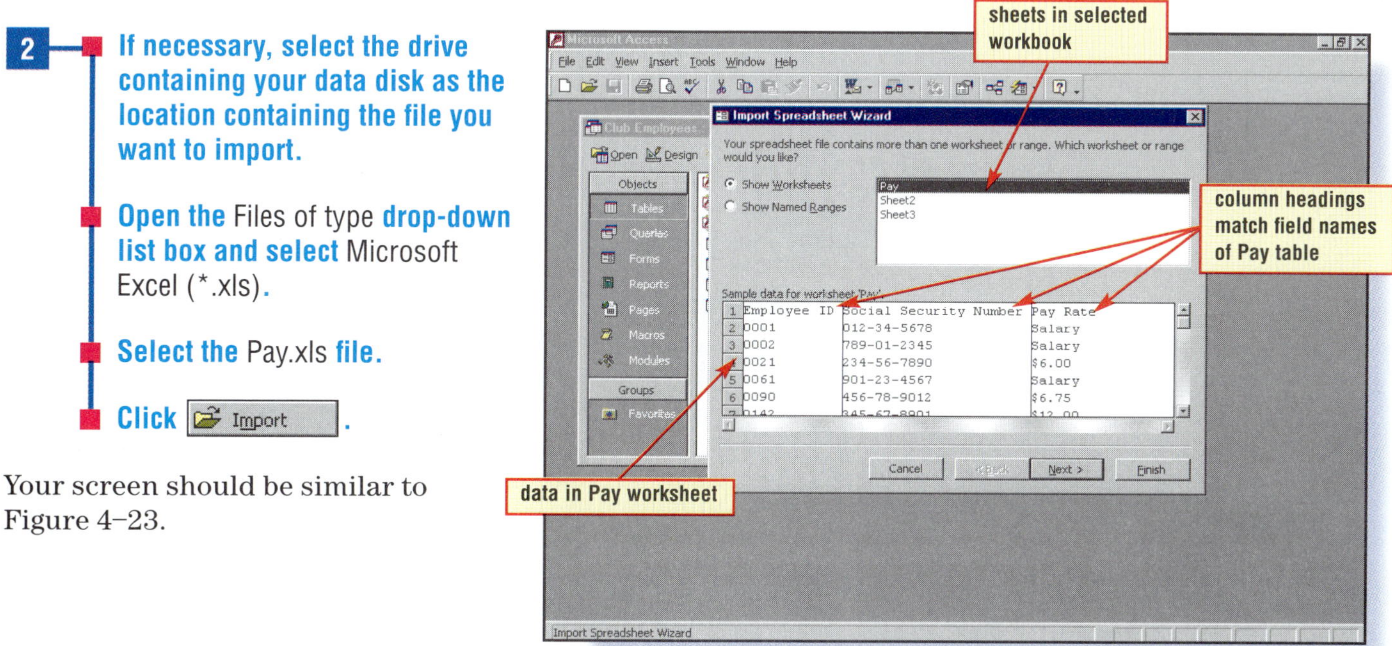

Figure 4–23

The Import Spreadsheet Wizard is started. From the first wizard dialog box you need to select the worksheet or range to import.

3
- If necessary, **select** Pay.
- Click **Next >**.

Next, you can specify whether to use the column headings in the work-sheet as the field names. When importing to an existing table, the column headings in the imported file must match the column headings in the table, as they do here. To identify the first worksheet row as the row containing the column headings to use as field names for the Pay table,

4 ■ **Select** First Row Contains Column Headings.

■ **Click** Next > .

Your screen should be similar to Figure 4–24.

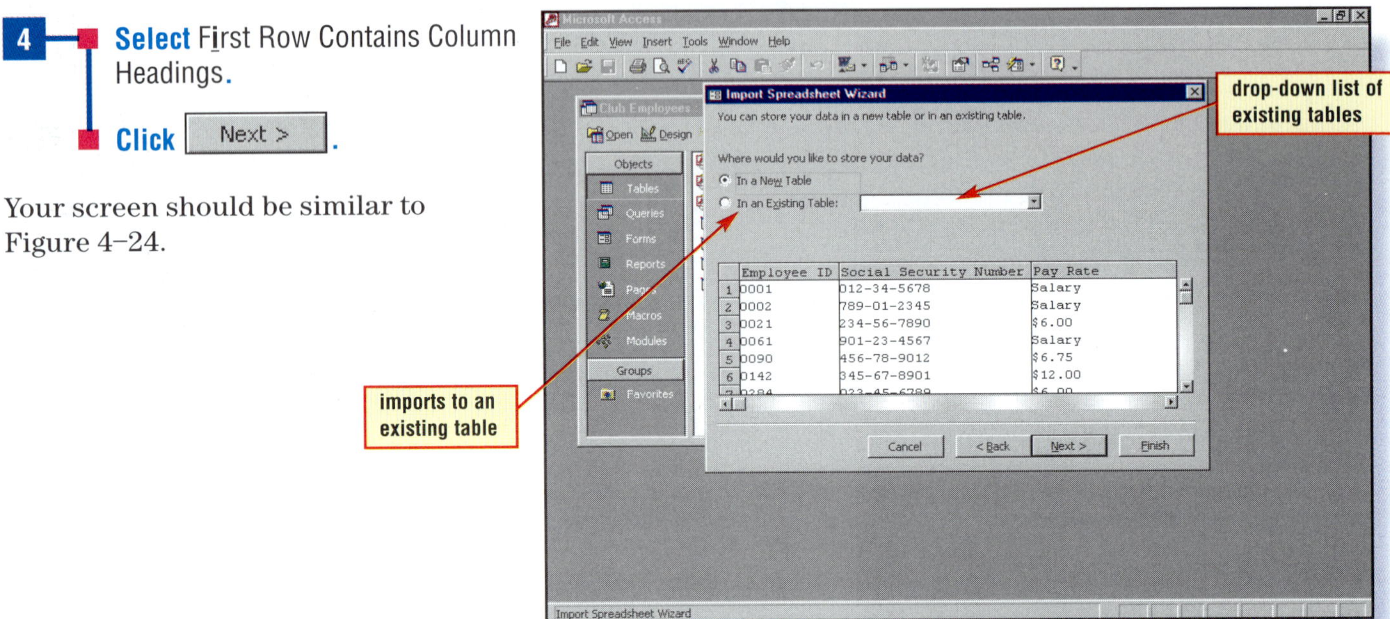

Figure 4–24

The next wizard screen asks if you want to save this data in a new table or an existing table. You want to save it in the existing Pay table.

5 ■ **Select** In an Existing Table.

■ **Select** Pay **from the option's drop-down list.**

■ **Click** Next > .

■ **Click** Finish .

The message box informs you that the data was imported into the Pay table. Now you want to see the data in the table.

6 — **Click** [OK] .

Open the Pay table.

Your screen should be similar to Figure 4–25.

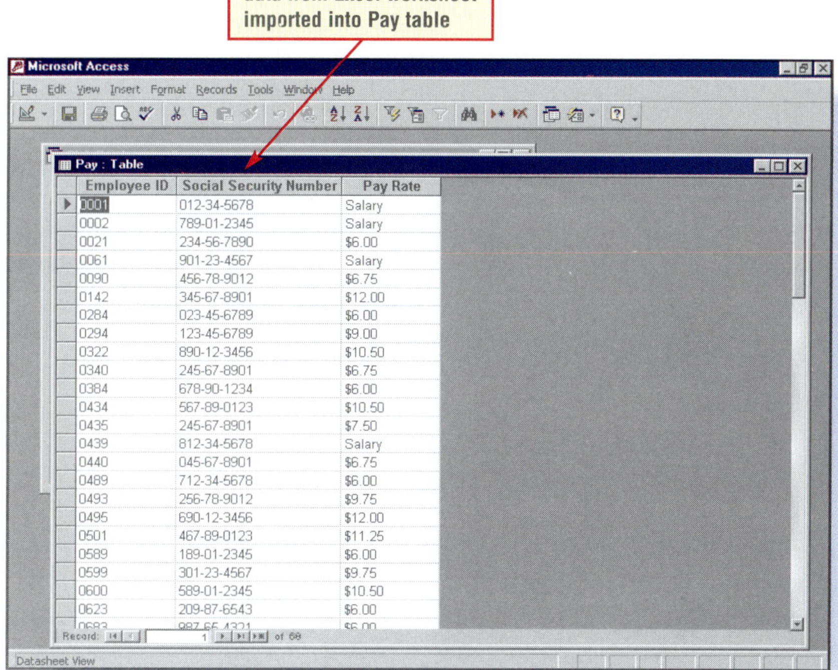

Figure 4–25

The pay data is complete for all records.

Making Fields Required

The final change you want to make to the table is to require that data is entered into all fields. The Pay table includes only three fields, but each of these fields must be filled in for payroll purposes. To ensure that these fields are completed for each club employee, you are going to apply the Required property to them.

Concept ③ Required Property

The **Required property** specifies whether a value is required in a field. If the property is set to Yes for a field, you must enter a value in that field, and the value cannot be null (zero). If you set the Required property to Yes for a field in a table that already contains data, Access gives you the option of checking whether the field has a value in all existing records. The field must have a value in all instances in which data might be entered in the field—in the table itself as well as in forms, queries, reports, and any other data sheets based on the table.

You can set a Required property for any type of field except a field that has the AutoNumber data type assigned to it. A primary key field will not accept null values.

Because a primary key field will not accept null values by default, it automatically requires an entry. Therefore, you do not need to make the Employee ID field required. You set the Required property for a field in the General tab of a field's properties box.

1 ■ **Switch to design view.**

■ **Select** the Social Security Number field.

■ **Change the Required field property to** Yes.

■ **In a similar manner, change the Required property to** Yes **for** the Pay Rate field.

Your screen should look similar to Figure 4–26.

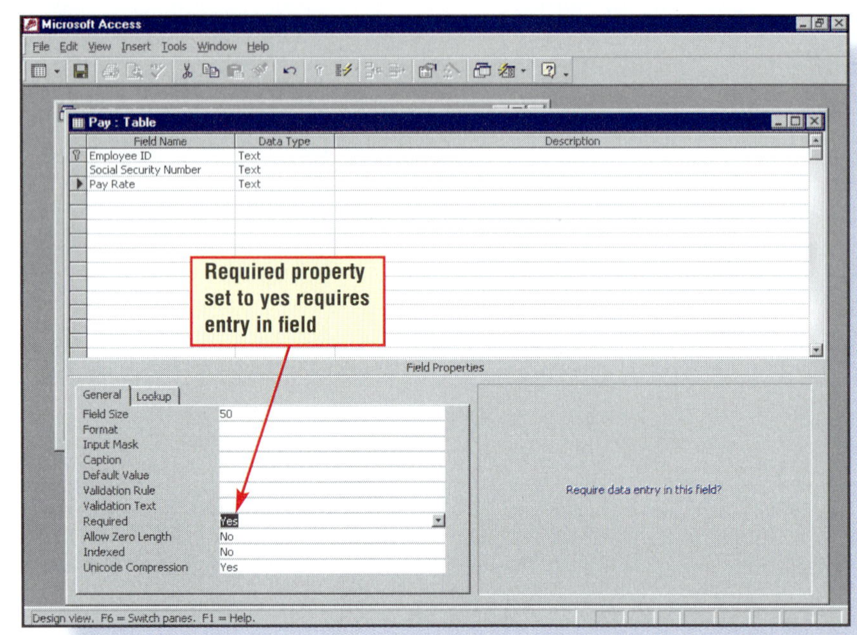

Figure 4–26

The table design is now the way you want it and you will add your record to the table while testing the Required property setting.

2 ■ **Click** 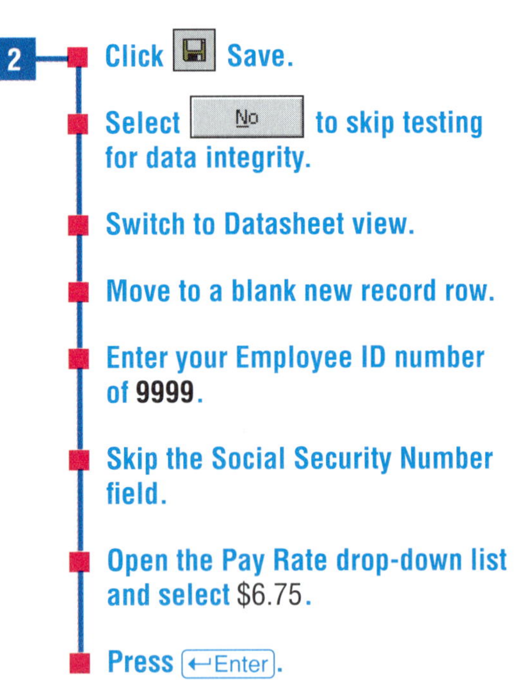 **Save.**

■ **Select** No **to skip testing for data integrity.**

■ **Switch to Datasheet view.**

■ **Move to a blank new record row.**

■ **Enter your Employee ID number of 9999.**

■ **Skip the Social Security Number field.**

■ **Open the Pay Rate drop-down list and select** $6.75.

■ **Press** ←Enter.

Your screen should be similar to Figure 4–27.

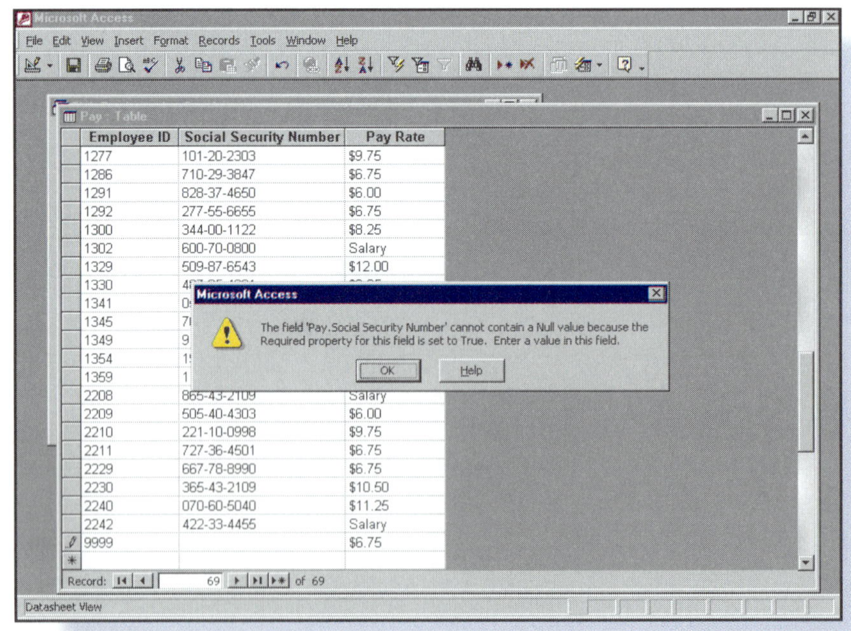

Figure 4–27

The displayed warning message informs you that the Social Security Number field is required and cannot contain a "null value"—in other words, it cannot be empty. To complete the entry in this field,

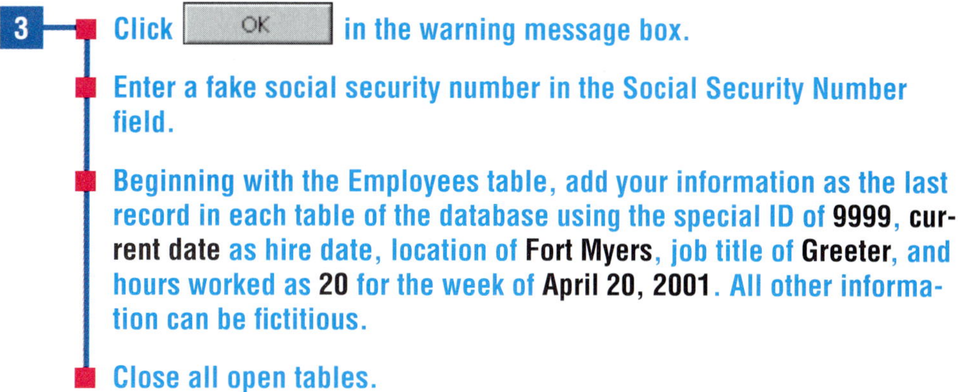

3 ● Click **OK** in the warning message box.

● Enter a fake social security number in the Social Security Number field.

● Beginning with the Employees table, add your information as the last record in each table of the database using the special ID of **9999**, current date as hire date, location of **Fort Myers**, job title of **Greeter**, and hours worked as **20 for the week of April 20, 2001**. All other information can be fictitious.

● Close all open tables.

Creating a Calculated Field

The club owners have asked you for a report showing the gross pay for all employees sorted by location and job title. To create this report, you will need to create a query using all the tables in the Club Employees database: Employees, Location and Position, Pay, and Hours Worked. You will then add a calculated field to the query that calculates the weekly gross pay for each employee.

Concept  **4 Calculated Field**

A **calculated field** displays the results of a calculation in a query. You can perform a variety of calculations in queries. For example, you can calculate the sum of all inventory, the average salary for a department, or the highest sales figures among all sales personnel in the company. You can create your own calculation or use one of Access's seven predefined calculations called **functions**, shown below.

Function	What It Calculates
Sum	Totals values in a field for all records
Average	Averages values in a field for all records
Count	Counts number of values, excluding empty cells, in a field for all records
Minimum	Finds lowest value in a field for all records
Maximum	Finds highest value in a field for all records
Standard Deviation	A measure of the dispersion of a frequency distribution
Variance	Square of the standard deviation

To create a calculated field, you enter an **expression** in the design grid that instructs Access to perform a calculation using the current field values. Then the calculated result is displayed in the calculated field column of the datasheet.

To create the query,

1 • **Select** 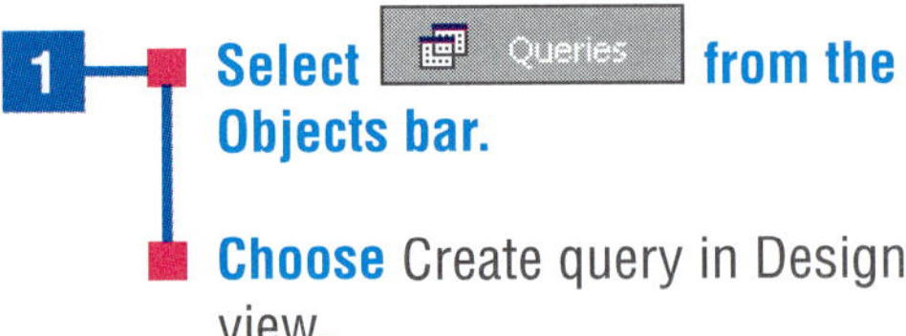 **from the Objects bar.**

• **Choose** Create query in Design view.

Your screen should look similar to Figure 4–28.

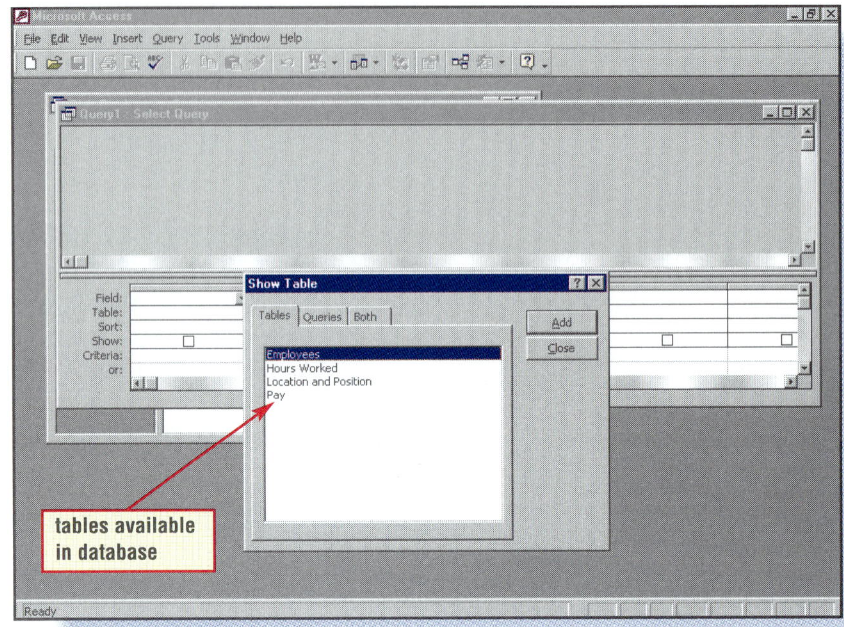

Figure 4–28

A blank query design grid is displayed and the Show Table dialog box is open, ready for you to select the tables in the current database that you want to use in this query. You want to query all four tables to obtain the information you need, but you aren't going to add them to the query in the order they're listed. To select the tables,

2 • **From the Show Table dialog box, add the** Employees, Location and Position, Pay, **and** Hours Worked **tables to the Query Design in that order.**

• **Close the Show Table dialog box.**

• **If necessary, maximize the Select Query window.**

Your screen should look similar to Figure 4–29.

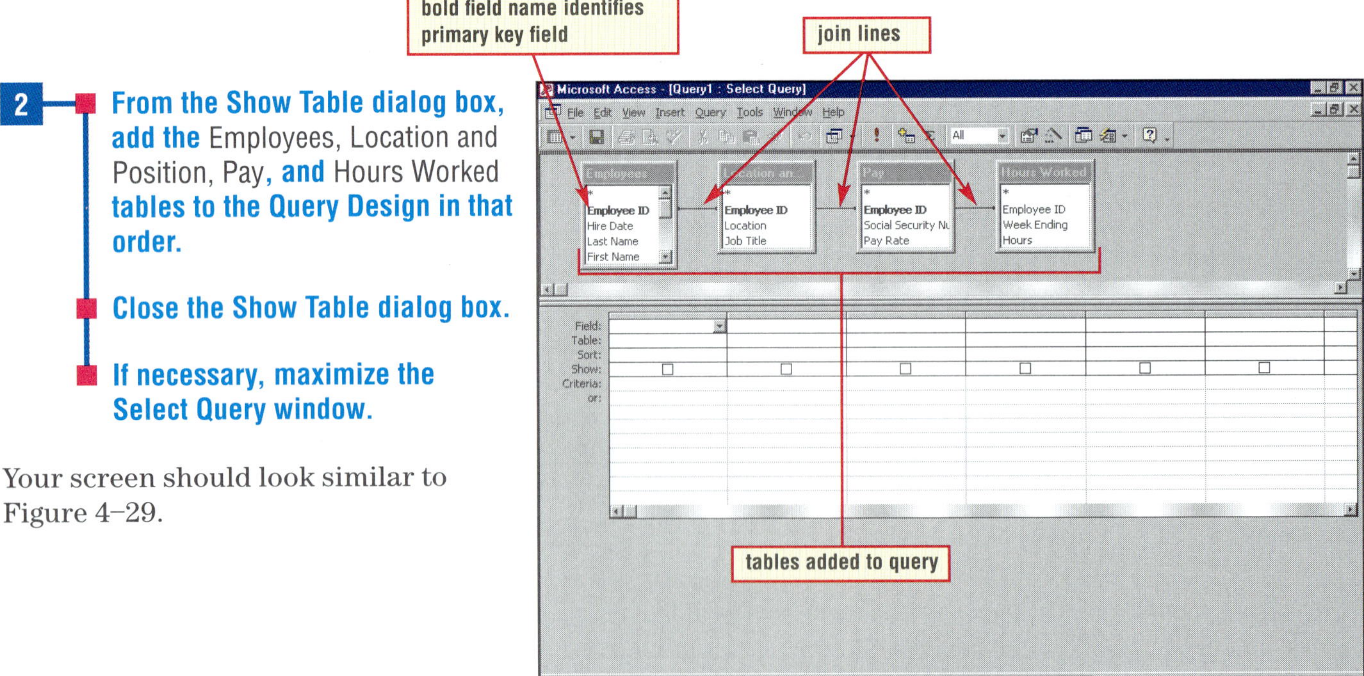

Figure 4–29

The tables are joined and displayed at the top of the design grid. Notice that the Employee ID field in the Hours Worked table is not bold. That is because bold is used to indicate primary key fields, and this field cannot be a primary key in this table because there are multiple entries with the same Employee ID numbers.

Next you will add the fields to be included in the query to the grid and sort them in the order requested by the club owners.

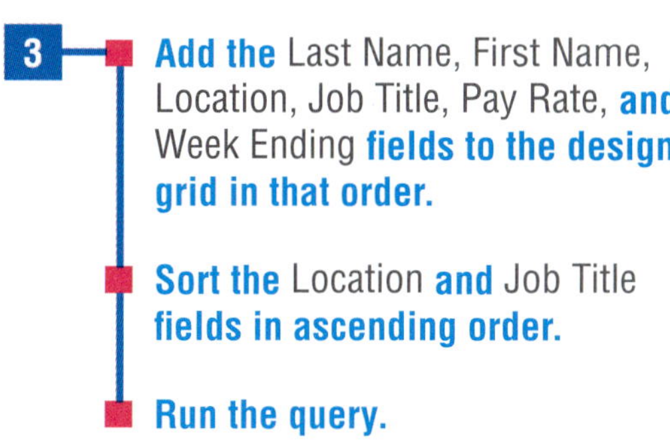

3 ■ **Add the** Last Name, First Name, Location, Job Title, Pay Rate, **and** Week Ending **fields to the design grid in that order.**

■ **Sort the** Location **and** Job Title **fields in ascending order.**

■ **Run the query.**

Your screen should look similar to Figure 4–30.

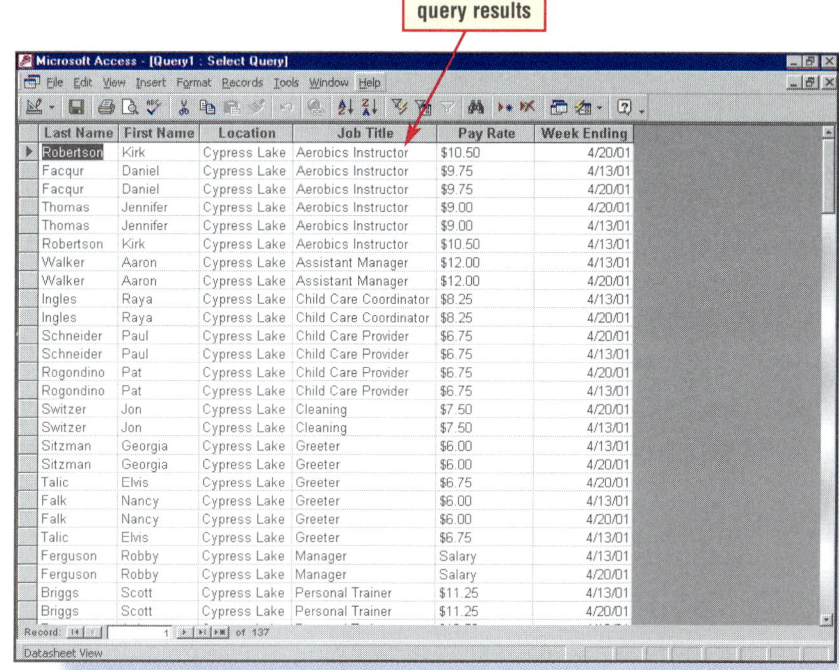

Figure 4–30

The query shows the selected fields for each record. Next you need to refine the query to calculate the gross pay for the week ending 4/20/01 for all employees except those on salary. Also, since the club owners specifically requested the information for this week, you do not need to show it on the query datasheet.

4 ■ **Return to Query Design view.**

■ **Enter the expression =4/20/01 into the Week Ending Criteria cell.**

■ **Clear the Show box for the Week Ending field.**

■ **Enter <>Salary in the Pay Rate field criteria cell and clear the Show box.**

Your screen should look similar to Figure 4–31.

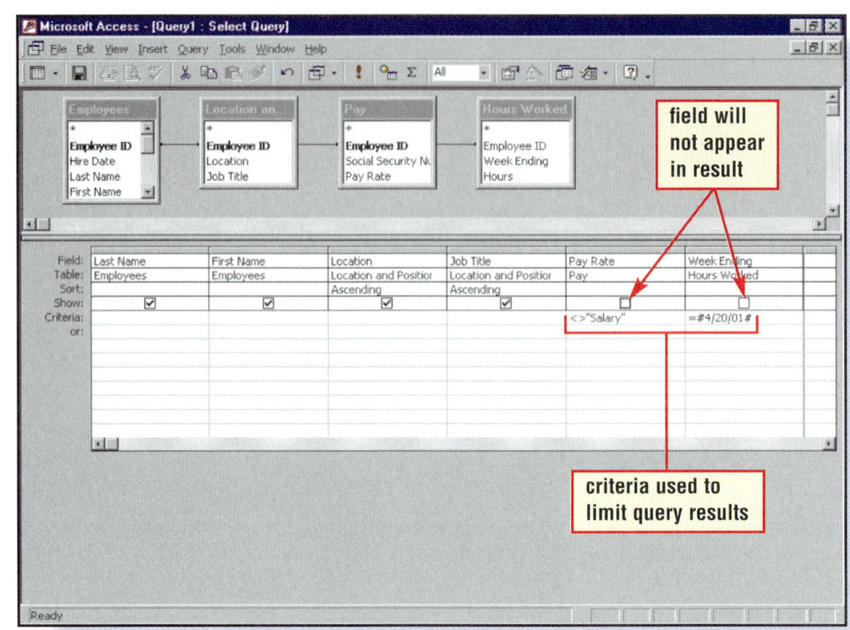

Figure 4–31

Access automatically adds # symbols around the criteria expression in the Week Ending cell indicating that it has been evaluated as a date value that will be used to obtain the specified query data.

Now you can create the calculated field to calculate the gross pay for the week ending 4/20/01. The first part of the calculation formula will name the new calculated field, which in this case will be "Gross Pay." The second part of the formula does the actual calculation. In this case, to calculate the gross pay, the formula will multiply the value in the Hourly Rate field (located in the Pay Rate table) by the value in the Hours field (located in the Hours Worked table).

5 ■ **Move to the field cell of a blank column.**

■ **Type Gross Pay:**

■ **Press** [Spacebar].

■ **Type [Pay Rate]*[Hours].**

> Field names are enclosed in square brackets in a calculation.

■ **Press** [←Enter].

> If you made an error in your calculation entry, a message box will appear advising of the error. Close the message box and correct the error.

■ **Increase the column width to fully display the expression.**

Your screen should look similar to Figure 4–32.

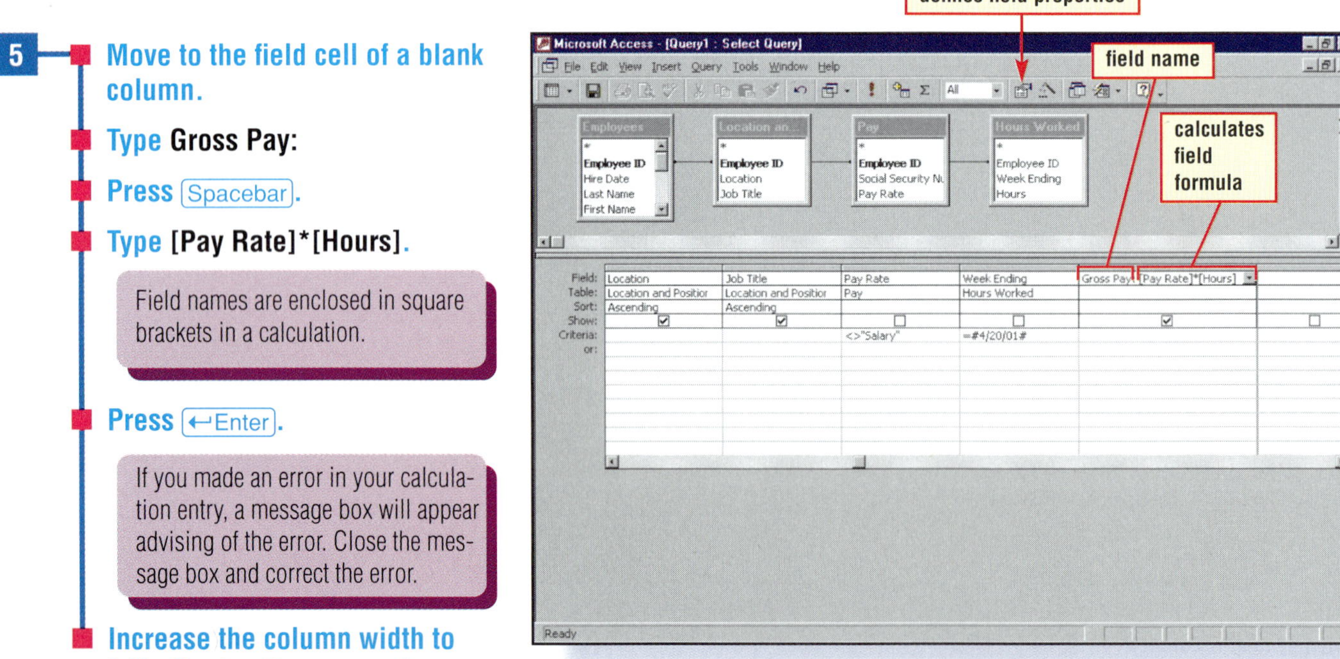

Figure 4–32

Before running the query, you want to change the new field's properties so it will display the calculated values as currency with two decimal places.

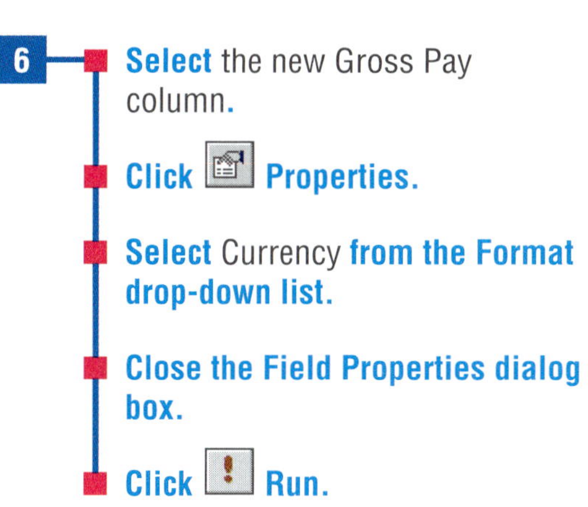

6 — **Select** the new Gross Pay column.

Click Properties.

Select Currency **from the Format drop-down list.**

Close the Field Properties dialog box.

Click **Run.**

Your screen should look similar to Figure 4–33.

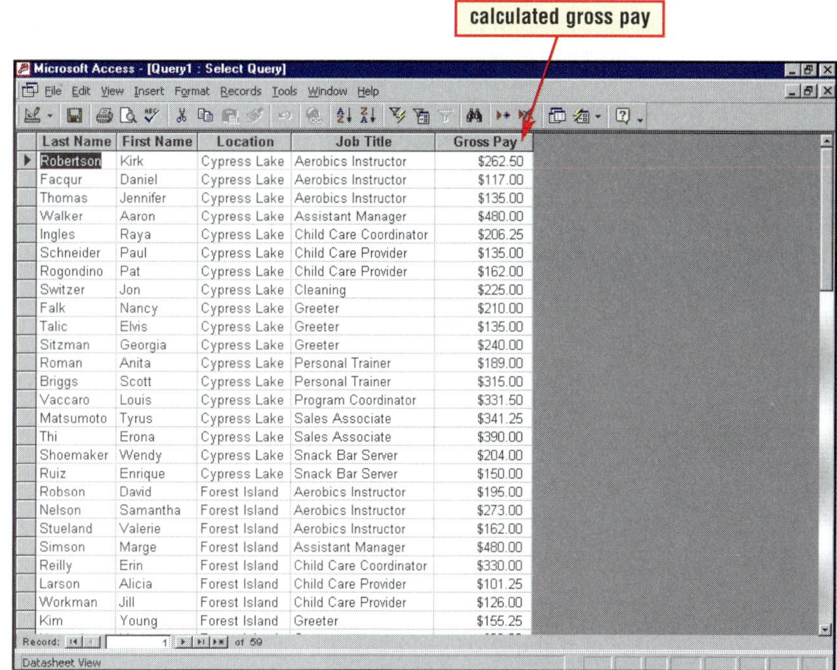

Last Name	First Name	Location	Job Title	Gross Pay
Robertson	Kirk	Cypress Lake	Aerobics Instructor	$262.50
Facqur	Daniel	Cypress Lake	Aerobics Instructor	$117.00
Thomas	Jennifer	Cypress Lake	Aerobics Instructor	$135.00
Walker	Aaron	Cypress Lake	Assistant Manager	$480.00
Ingles	Raya	Cypress Lake	Child Care Coordinator	$206.25
Schneider	Paul	Cypress Lake	Child Care Provider	$135.00
Rogondino	Pat	Cypress Lake	Child Care Provider	$162.00
Switzer	Jon	Cypress Lake	Cleaning	$225.00
Falk	Nancy	Cypress Lake	Greeter	$210.00
Talic	Elvis	Cypress Lake	Greeter	$135.00
Sitzman	Georgia	Cypress Lake	Greeter	$240.00
Roman	Anita	Cypress Lake	Personal Trainer	$189.00
Briggs	Scott	Cypress Lake	Personal Trainer	$315.00
Vaccaro	Louis	Cypress Lake	Program Coordinator	$331.50
Matsumoto	Tyrus	Cypress Lake	Sales Associate	$341.25
Thi	Erona	Cypress Lake	Sales Associate	$390.00
Shoemaker	Wendy	Cypress Lake	Snack Bar Server	$204.00
Ruiz	Enrique	Cypress Lake	Snack Bar Server	$150.00
Robson	David	Forest Island	Aerobics Instructor	$195.00
Nelson	Samantha	Forest Island	Aerobics Instructor	$273.00
Stueland	Valerie	Forest Island	Aerobics Instructor	$162.00
Simson	Marge	Forest Island	Assistant Manager	$480.00
Reilly	Erin	Forest Island	Child Care Coordinator	$330.00
Larson	Alicia	Forest Island	Child Care Provider	$101.25
Workman	Jill	Forest Island	Child Care Provider	$126.00
Kim	Young	Forest Island	Greeter	$155.25

Figure 4–33

The query datasheet displays the gross pay for each employee sorted by location and job title for the week ending 4/20/01.

7 — **Print a copy of the query datasheet for the club owners.**

Save this query as Gross Pay 4/20/01**.**

Close the query datasheet window.

Creating a Crosstab Query

After seeing the gross pay datasheet, the club owners are curious about the number of hours each employee is working. They have asked you for a simple datasheet that shows the average hours per employee for the last two weeks, excluding the employees on salary whose Hours Worked field contains 0. First you will create a simple query to display only those records that do not contain 0 in the Hours Worked field.

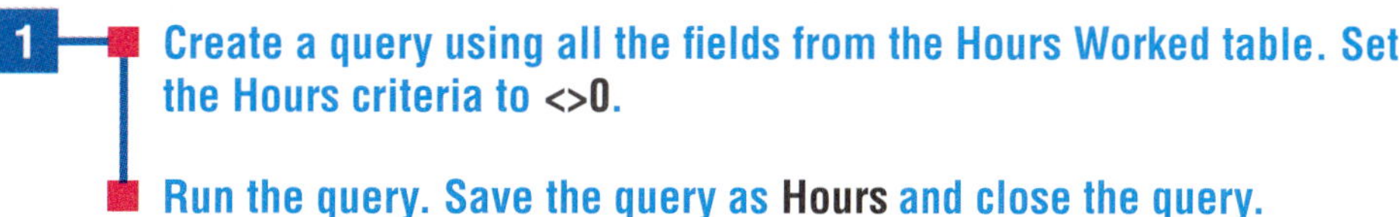

1 — **Create a query using all the fields from the Hours Worked table. Set the Hours criteria to** <>0**.**

Run the query. Save the query as Hours **and close the query.**

Now you will create a crosstab query that will automatically summarize and calculate the data in the Hours query result.

Concept 5   Crosstab Query

A **crosstab query** summarizes table data and displays it in a tabular format. In a crosstab query, field values are calculated by sum, average, and count, and grouped along the left side and across the top of the datasheet in rows and columns. Being able to see table data grouped both horizontally and vertically is particularly helpful for comparing data in large tables where multiple records are entered one after another down the sheet.

Crosstab queries can be created using the Query Wizard. The wizard gives you step-by-step instructions on selecting fields for columns and rows, and for choosing the way you want the data summarized. Although you can only select one table for the original crosstab query, you can open the query in Query Design view and add more tables and fields if needed.

To create the Hours Worked crosstab query,

2 ■ **Click**  **New in the Queries object window.**

   ■ **Select** Crosstab Query Wizard **in the New Query dialog box.**

   ■ **Click** OK .

Your screen should look similar to Figure 4–34.

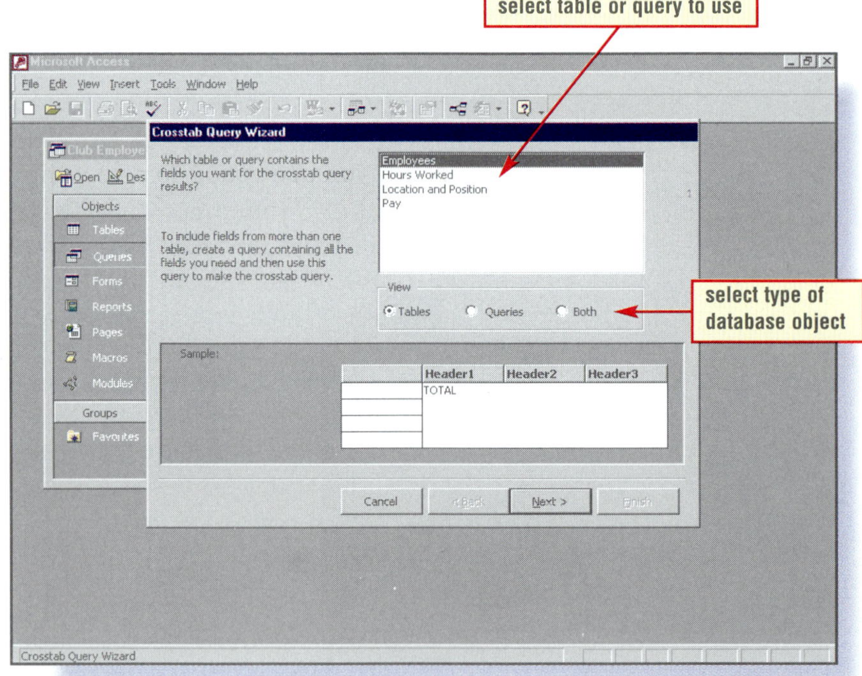

Figure 4–34

The first Crosstab Query Wizard dialog box asks you to select the tables or queries on which you want to base the crosstab query. You will use the Hours query.

3 ■ **Select** Queries **in the View options.**

■ **Select** Hours.

■ **Click** [Next >] .

Your screen should look similar to Figure 4–35.

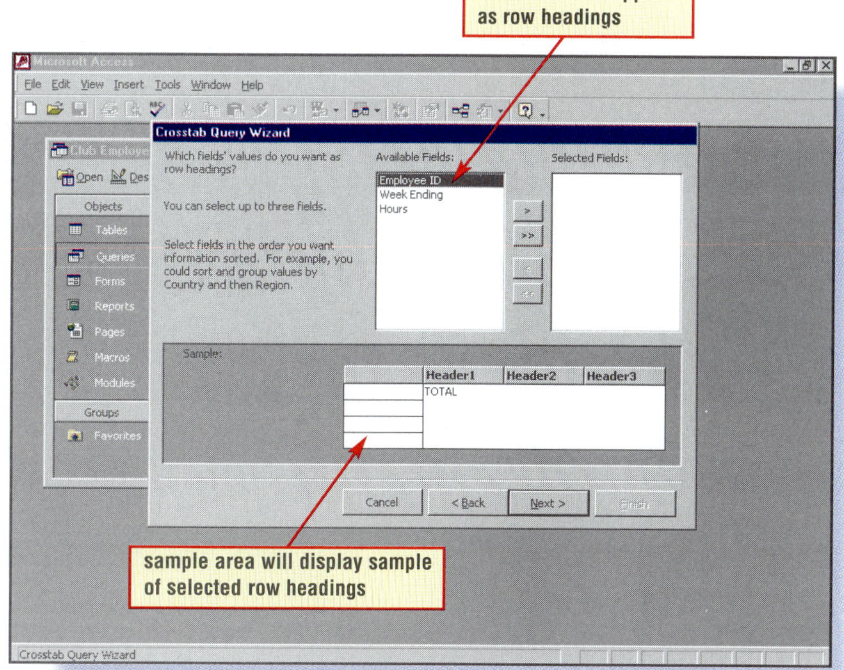

Figure 4–35

Next, you are asked to select the field or fields that you want to use as row headings. These are the fields that will be displayed along the left side of your data sheet. The Sample area shows how your selections will look.

4 ■ **Add the** Employee ID **field to the Selected Fields list.**

■ **Click** [Next >] .

Now you are asked what fields are to be used as column headings (displayed along the top of the data sheet). You want to display the weeks in columns, so the current selection, Week Ending, is acceptable.

5 ■ **Click** Next > .

Your screen should look similar to
Figure 4–36.

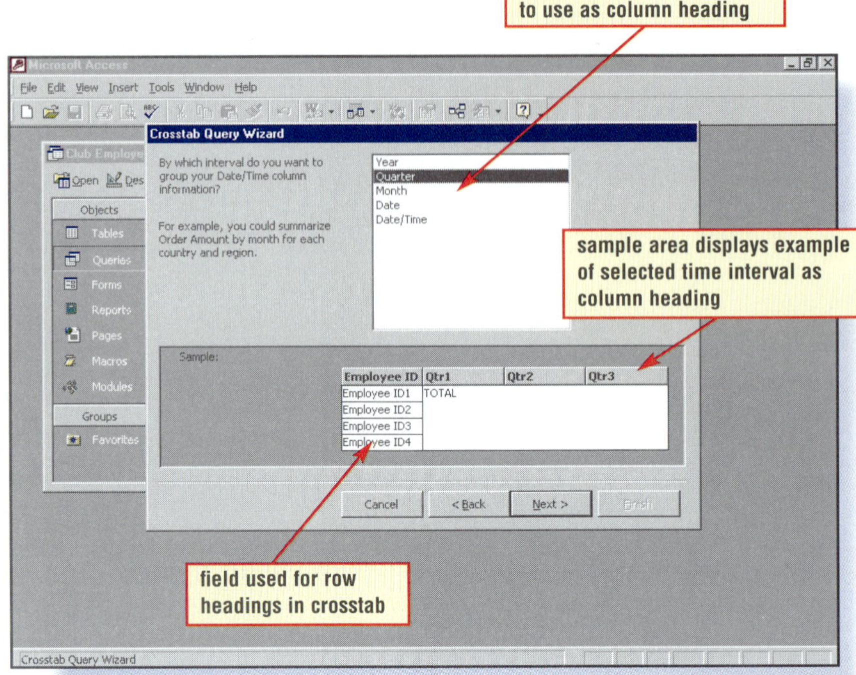

Figure 4–36

Since you selected a date field for the column headings, the wizard asks
you how you want the dates displayed: by year, by quarter, by month, by
exact date, or by date and time. Because the table contains only two dates,
you will use the exact date as the column heading.

6 ■ **Select** Date.

■ **Click** Next > .

Your screen should look similar to
Figure 4–37.

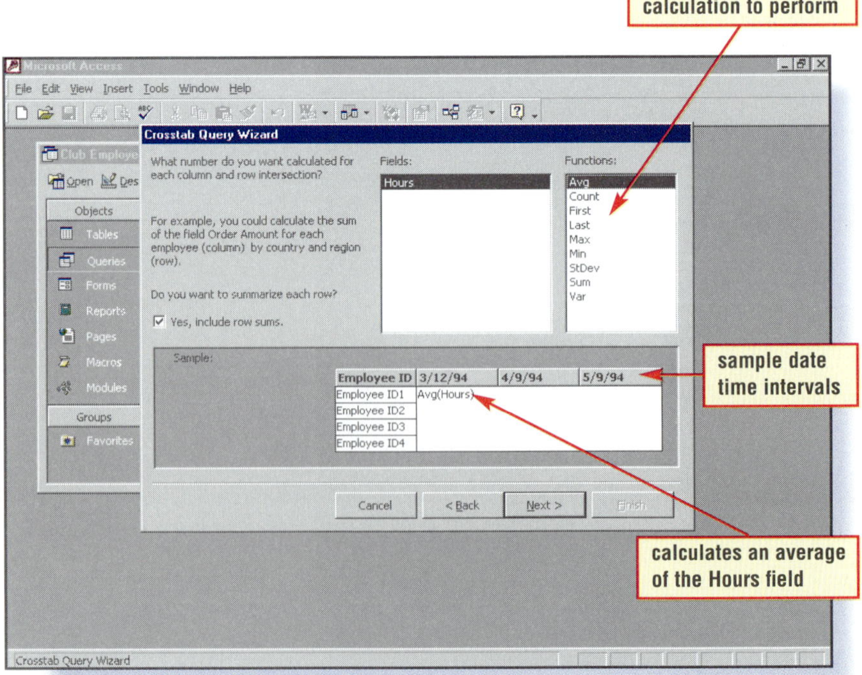

Figure 4–37

The remaining field, Hours, will be the one that is calculated. Since the club owners asked to see an average number of hours for the last two weeks, the current selection is acceptable.

7 — **Click** [Next >] .

The final wizard screen asks you what you want to call this query and if you want to view it right away or go into design view so you can modify it. You like what the wizard has used for the name of this query, and you decide to view the query first to determine whether it will need any modifications.

8 — **Click** [Finish] .

Your screen should look similar to Figure 4–38.

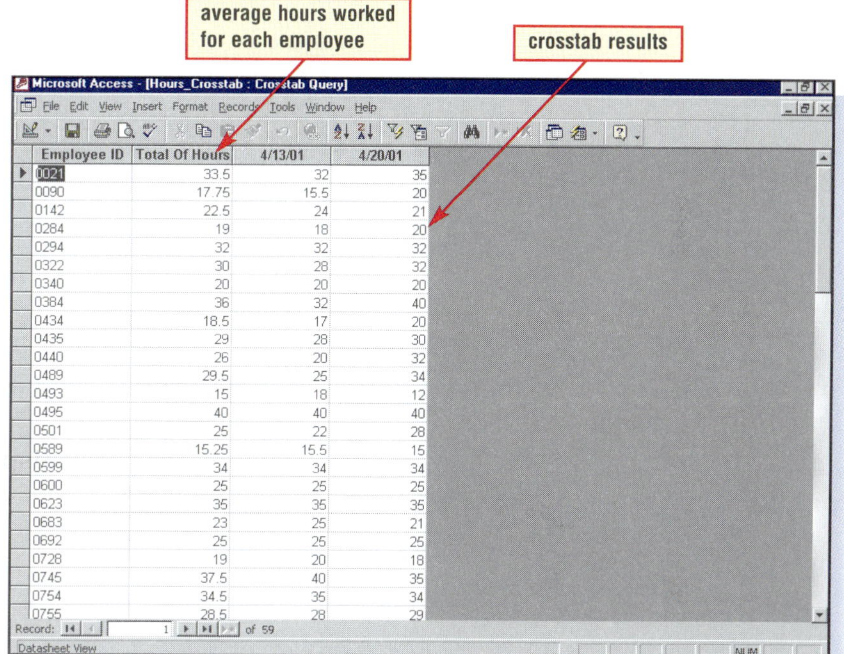

Figure 4–38

The Hours crosstab query automatically calculated the average number of hours per employee per week, which is what the club owners have asked for. However, there are a few things about the query design that you don't like. First of all, you'd like the columns to be in date order, with the average column last. Also, the Total Of Hours column name does not make it clear that this is an average of the hours worked, not the sum. You will move the columns and rename the column name.

9 ■ **Switch to Design view.**

■ **Replace** "Total Of" **in the fourth Field cell with Average.**

■ **Switch to Datasheet view.**

■ **Move** the Average Hours column to the right of the 4/20 column (so it is now the last column).

■ **Expand the Average Hours column to fully display the field name.**

Your screen should be similar to Figure 4–39.

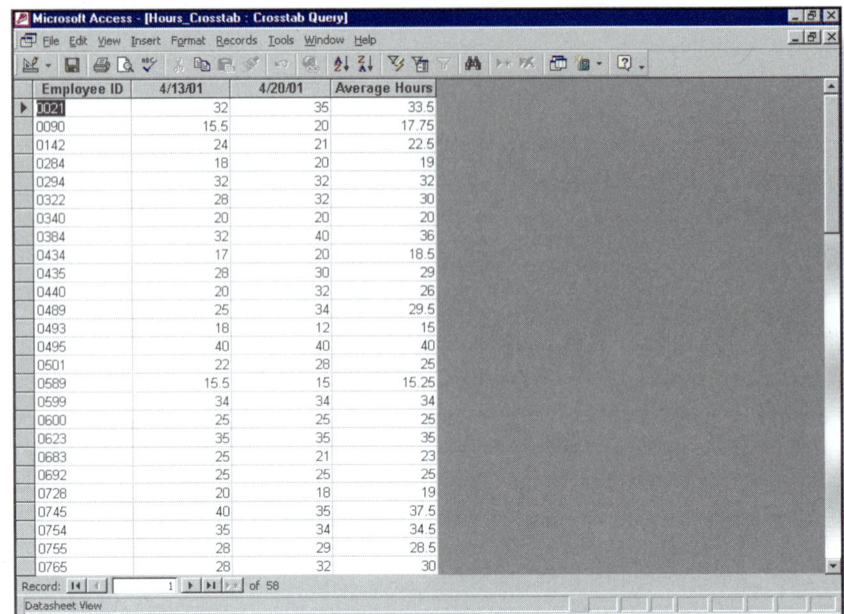

Figure 4–39

The crosstab query is now easier to understand.

10 ■ **Print a copy of the crosstab query for the club owners.**

■ **Save and close the crosstab query.**

Inserting a Subdatasheet

While you've been creating the new data tables and queries, the club owners have been doing some research on standard pay rates for the various positions in other fitness clubs in the area. The club owners want their pay rates to be competitive and have asked you for a list of the club's job titles and current pay rates. You decide to embed the Pay Rates table in the Location and Position table as a subdatasheet in order to get the owners the information they need quickly and easily.

Concept 6 Subdatasheet

A **subdatasheet** is a data table nested in another data table that contains data related or joined to the table where it resides. Creating a subdatasheet allows you to easily view and edit related data. The source of the subdatasheet can be a table or query, and the related or joined data can be viewed and edited in the **master table**, a query, a form, or a subform. The master table is the table that holds the subdatasheet.

When creating a subdatasheet, there must be matching fields between the master datasheet and the subdatasheet. These are called **child fields** and **master fields**. The child fields are one or more fields in the embedded subdatasheet that will be linked to master fields in the master table. These fields don't have to have the same names, but they must contain the same kind of data and have a compatible data type and field size. For example, an AutoNumber field is compatible with a Number field if the Number Field Size property is set to Long Integer.

You are going to use the Location and Position table as the master table, so you need to open it first.

1 ▪ **Open the Location and Position table.**

You decide that it is not necessary to include the Employee IDs in your datasheet, so you will hide this column. However, the club location may be pertinent in deciding what an equitable salary for a person living in that location would be, so you decide to keep the Location column in the datasheet. You will then insert the Pay Rates table as a subdatasheet.

2 ▪ **Hide the Employee ID column.**

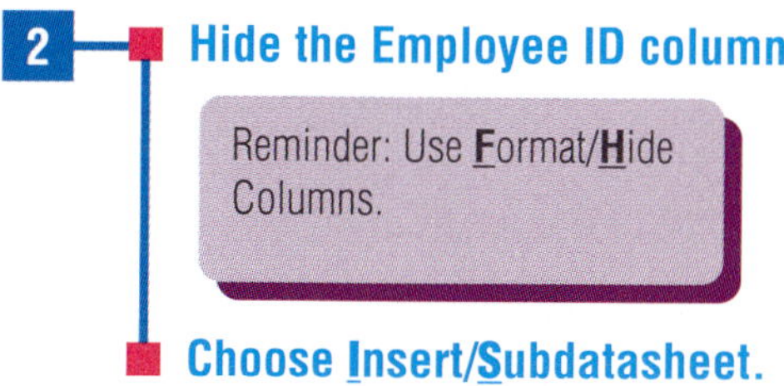

▪ **Choose Insert/Subdatasheet.**

Your screen should look similar to Figure 4–40.

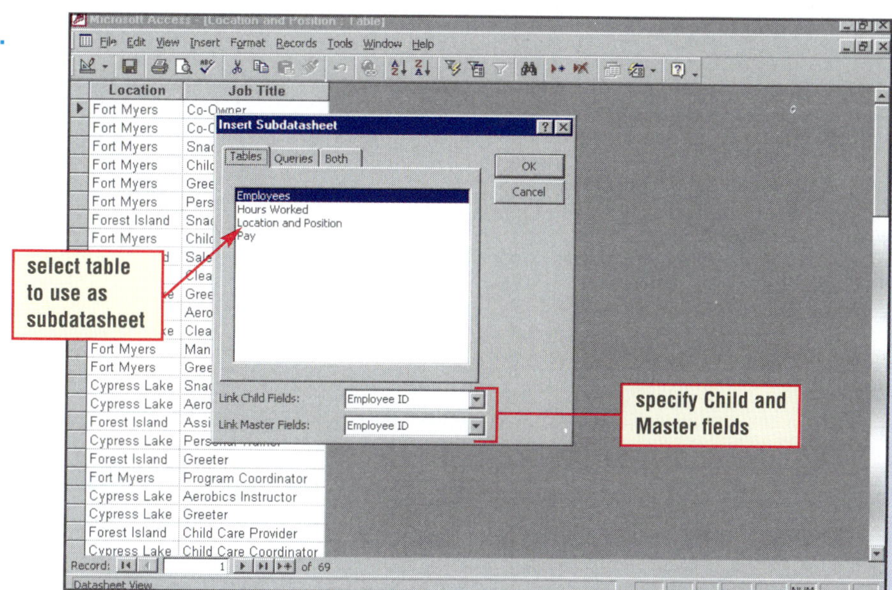

Figure 4–40

You use the Insert Subdatasheet dialog box to select the table from the current database that you want to embed as a subdatasheet in the active table. You also specify the child and master fields in this dialog box.

3 ■ **Select the** Pay **table.**

■ **If necessary, select** Employee ID **from the Link Child Fields drop-down list.**

■ **If necessary, select** Employee ID **from the Link Master Fields drop-down list.**

> Even though the Employee ID field is hidden on the master table itself, it can still be selected as the master field.

■ **Click** OK .

Your screen should be similar to Figure 4–41.

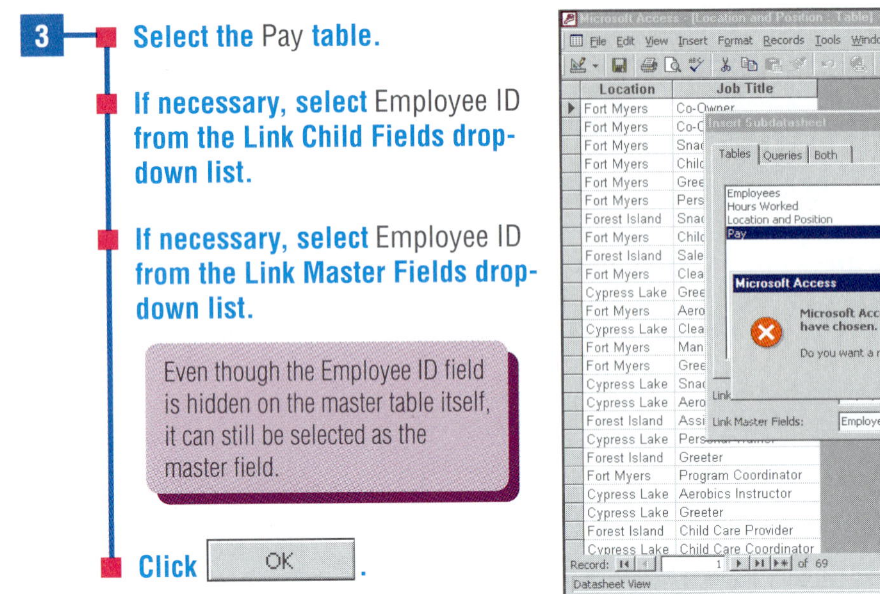

Figure 4–41

An advisory box is displayed asking if you want Access to create a relationship between the selected fields in the tables. A relationship establishes the association between the common fields. It can be a one-way, one-to-many, or many-to-many relationship, just as when you established a relationship when linking tables in a query.

4 ■ **Click** Yes .

Your screen should look similar to Figure 4–42.

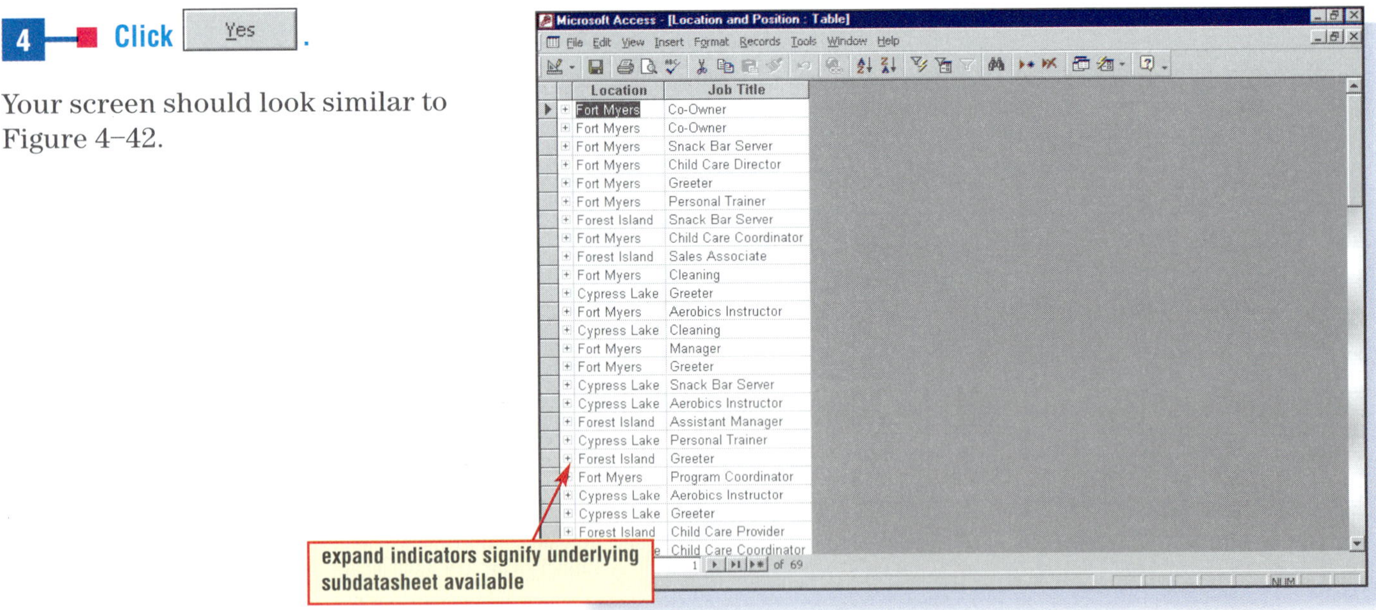

Figure 4–42

The Location and Position table is redisplayed with expand indicators (+) at the beginning of each row. This signifies that there is a subdatasheet linked to the records in this table. You can display the individual subdatasheet record that is linked to a master table record by clicking the expand indicator for each record row, or you can display the entire subdatasheet at once. You need to view the complete subdatasheet in order to modify it, if necessary, and then print it.

5 **Choose Format/Subdatasheet/Expand All.**

Your screen should look similar to Figure 4–43.

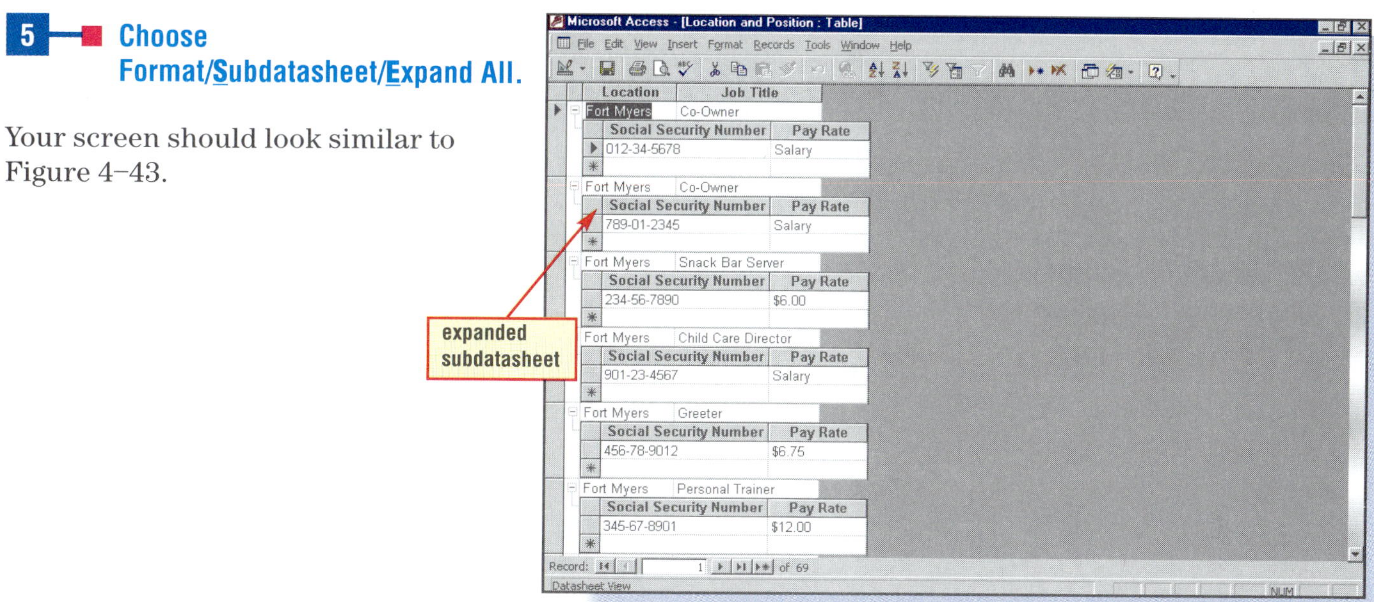

Figure 4–43

The (–) expand indicator means that the underlying subdatasheet information is displayed. Clicking it closes the subdatasheet display.

The Pay Rates subdatasheet is displayed with its records positioned under each related record in the Position and Location table. Like the Position and Location table, you are not interested in seeing the Social Security Number field data. As with any other table, you can hide the columns you don't need in the subdatasheet.

6 **Select the** Social Security Number **field in the first subdatasheet record and hide the column.**

Your screen should look similar to Figure 4–44.

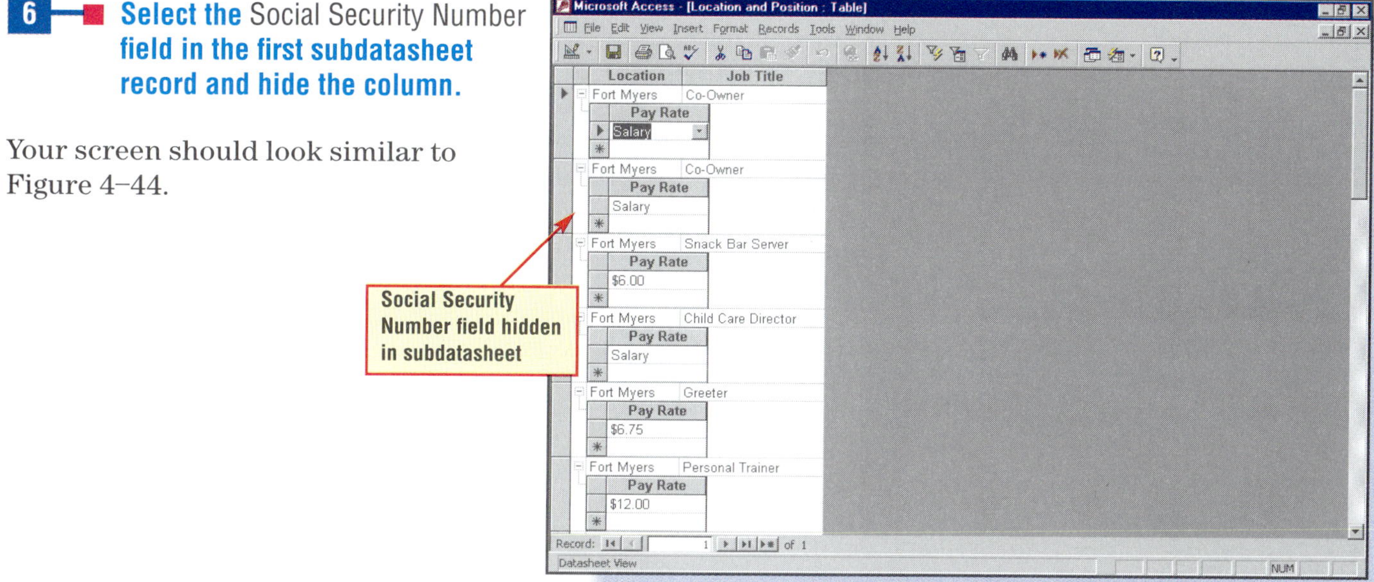

Figure 4–44

The table now shows only the Location, Job Title, and Pay Rate fields, which is what you need.

7

■ **Print the first page of the report.**

■ **Move to the** Pay Rate field **and choose F**o**rmat/U**nhide Columns.

■ **Select** Employee ID **and** Social Security Number **as the columns to redisplay in the Unhide Columns dialog box, and then click** Close .

■ **Click in the first field of the Location and Position table and then choose F**o**rmat/S**ubdatasheet/R**emove.**

■ **Unhide the Employee ID field.**

Your screen should look similar to Figure 4–45.

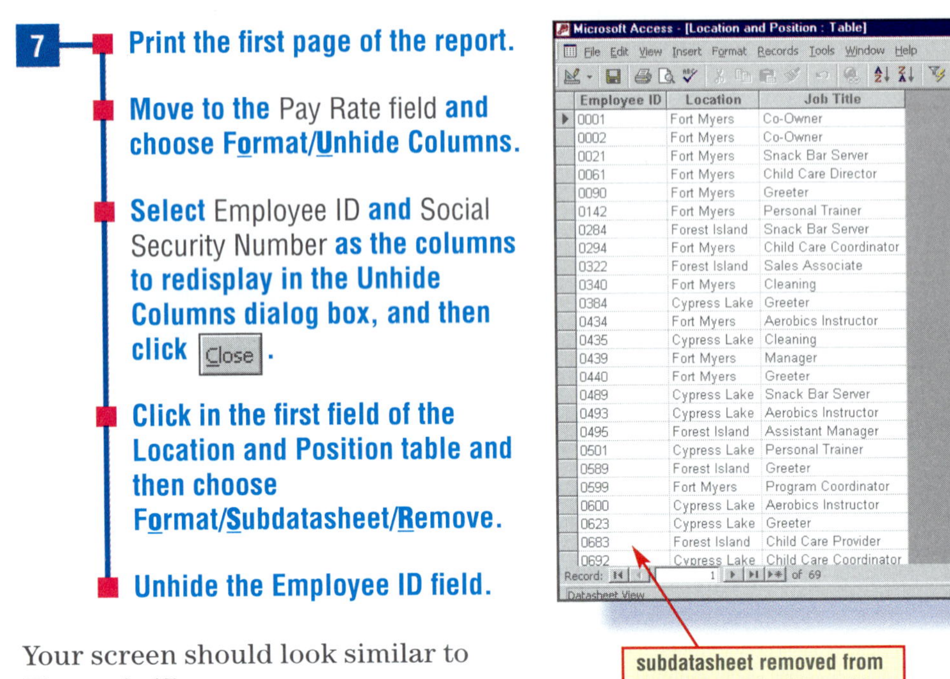

Figure 4–45

The Location and Position table is returned to its original display format, without the subdatasheet. You have given the club owners all the information they requested for now, and you can do a bit of database maintenance.

Defining Relationships and Enforcing Referential Integrity

Refer to the Relationships concept in Tutorial 3 to review this concept.

The first maintenance task you want to complete is to define permanent relationships between tables and ensure that the referential integrity between your joined data tables is enforced during the various data manipulations performed by you or other database users.

Concept ⑦ Referential Integrity

Referential integrity is a set of rules used by Access to ensure that relationships between tables are valid and that related data is not accidentally changed or deleted. The rules include the following:

- A record in a primary table cannot be deleted if matching records exist in a related table. For example, an employee record cannot be deleted from the Employees table if there are hours assigned to this employee in the Hours Worked table.

- A primary key value cannot be changed in the primary table if that record has related records. For example, an employee's ID can't be changed in the Employees table if there are hours assigned to this employee in the Hours Worked table.

Once referential integrity has been set, Access displays a warning message if one of the rules is broken and does not allow you to complete the action you are trying to do.

You will first define permanent table relationships in the Club Employees database. All tables must be closed when you define relationships.

1
- **Close all open tables.**
- **Click 🔲 Relationships.**
- **If necessary, click 🔲 Show Table to open the Show Table dialog box.**

Your screen should look similar to Figure 4–46.

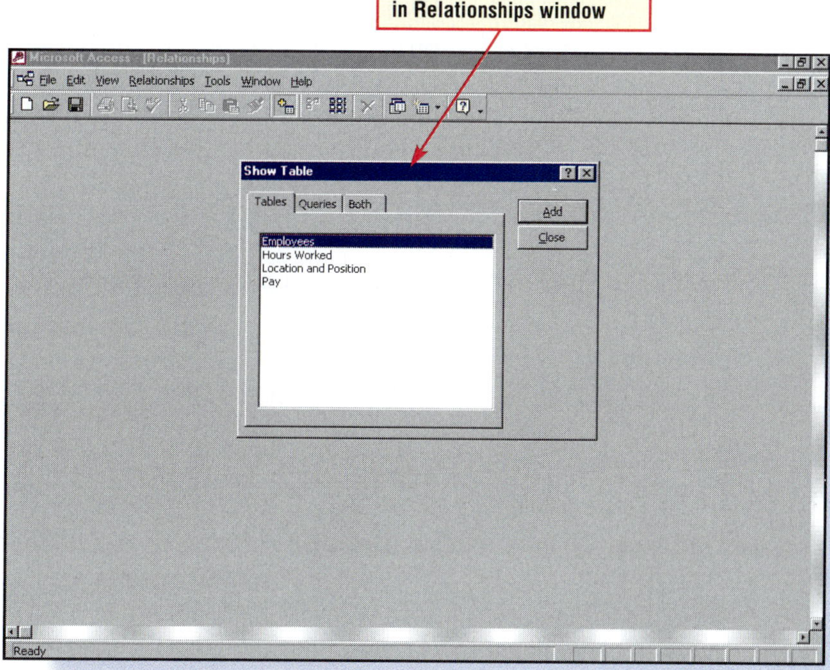

Figure 4–46

Additional Information

If a database already has relationships defined, the existing relationships are displayed. You can add additional tables or queries by opening the Show Table dialog box using 🔲.

The Show Table dialog box is used to specify the tables and queries that you want to define permanent relationships.

2 ■ **Add the four tables to the Relationships window in the following order:** Employees, Location and Position, Pay, **and** Hours Worked.

■ **Close the dialog box.**

Your screen should look similar to Figure 4–47.

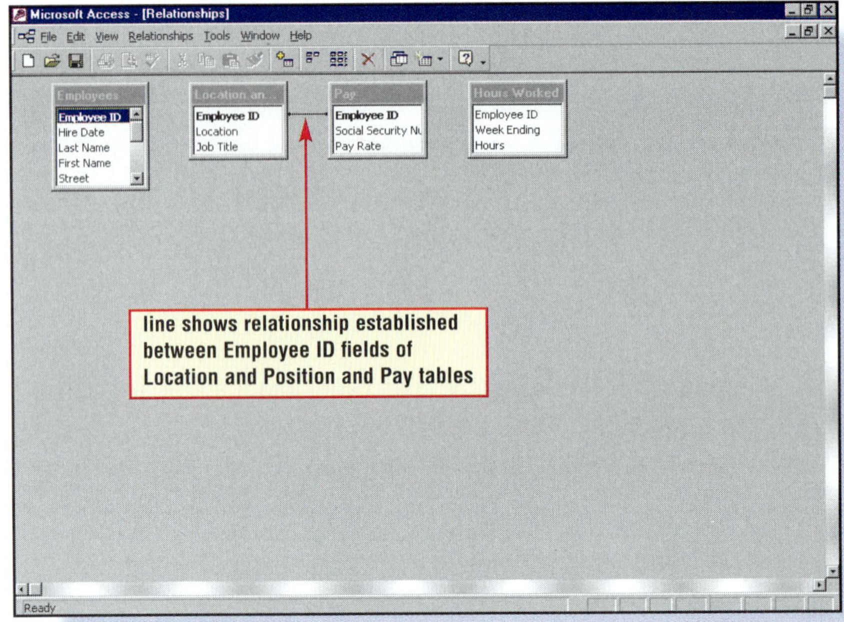

Figure 4–47

The Relationships window displays the selected tables. The four tables will be related on the Employee ID field. The line between the Employee ID fields of the Location and Position table and the Pay table shows the relationship that was established between those tables when creating the subdatasheet. You need to establish relationships between the other tables on the Employee ID field. To do this, you drag the field that you want to relate from one table to the next.

3 ■ **Drag the** Employee ID **field from the Employees table onto the Employee ID field in the table to the right, in this case the Location and Position table.**

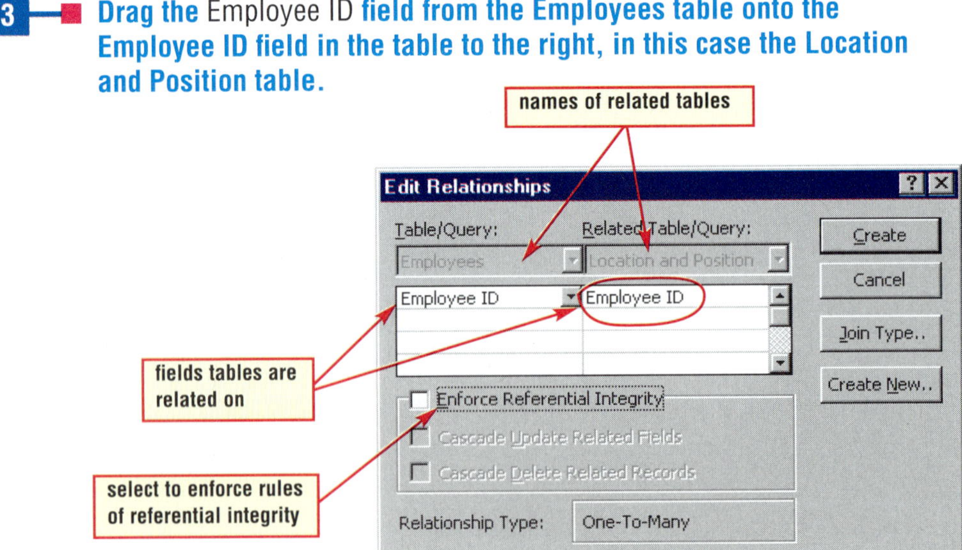

The Edit Relationships dialog box shows the names of the tables to be related and the field names. Then, to also enforce the referential integrity rules,

4 **Select E**nforce Referential Integrity**.**

Click [C̲reate] **.**

Your screen should be similar to Figure 4–48.

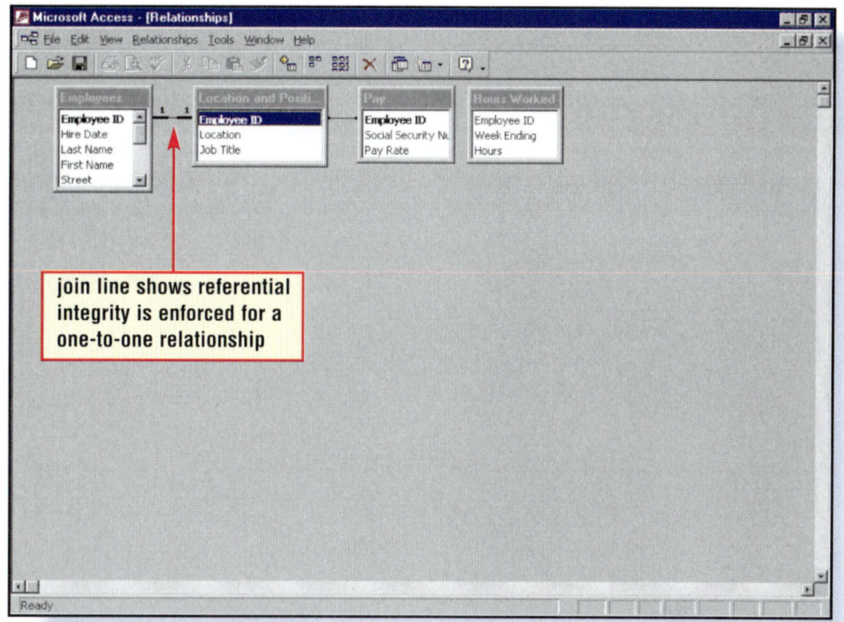

Figure 4–48

> To remove a relationship, click on the relationship line and press [Delete].

The related tables appear with a join line that connects them. The number 1 above the join line shows that referential integrity is enforced for a one-to-one relationship. Next, you need to edit the relationship between the Location and Position table and the Pay table to include referential integrity.

5 **Right click on the relationship line between the Location and Position and the Pay table and choose Edit R̲elationship from the shortcut menu.**

Select E̲nforce Referential Integrity from the Edit Relationships dialog box.

Click [OK] **.**

In the same manner create a relationship between the Pay and Hours Worked tables on the Employee ID field and enforce referential integrity.

Notice the join line between the last two tables displays the ∞ symbol. This indicates the relationship is a one-to-many relationship. Before exiting the Relationships window, you decide to print a report that shows the current relationships between the tables in your database. To produce this report,

6 ■ Choose **F**ile/Print **R**elationships.

Your screen should look similar to Figure 4–49.

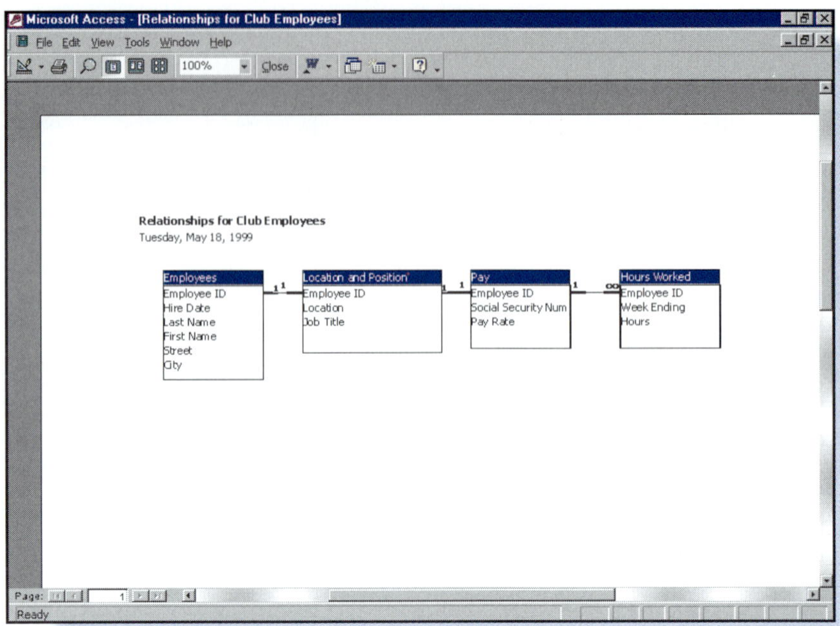

Figure 4–49

A preview of how the report will look when printed is displayed on the screen. The database name and creation date are automatically used as the report header. You can print this report as well as save it for future reference.

7 ■ Print and save the report.

You are finished working with the database relationships, so you can close the relationship report window as well as the Relationships window.

8 ■ Close the Relationship report preview window.

■ Close the Relationships window.

■ Click 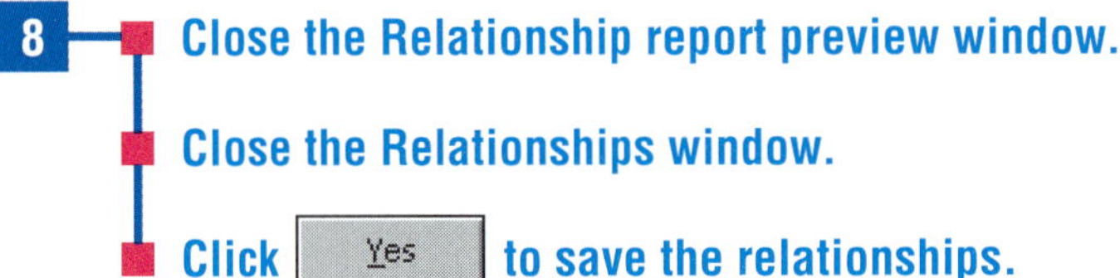 to save the relationships.

Whether you choose to save the relationships or not, they are saved automatically for you.

Defining a new relationship between tables automatically creates subdatasheets in the related tables.

9 ■ Remove the subdatasheets that were created in the Employees and Pay tables, saving your changes.

■ Close all open tables.

Backing Up and Restoring Your Database Files

It is very important that you perform periodic backups of your database files. This ensures that you don't lose too much work if there is a power outage or a system failure. If a database file is lost or corrupted for some reason, you can easily restore the latest file you backed up. It will not include any changes you've made to the file since it was last backed up, but it's better than not having any file at all.

A **backup** operation saves a copy of the database or other type of file to a storage medium other than the computer's hard disk. Backups can be performed using the Windows Explorer, My Computer, Microsoft Backup, the MS-DOS Copy command, or other backup software. Database files can be backed up to any storage medium, such as a tape drive, zip cartridge, or CD. You can also backup files to a floppy disk, but keep in mind that the storage space on this type of disk is limited, and you may have use backup software that will allow you to span several disks to copy your files onto them.

To back up a database file using Windows Explorer or My Computer, you simply insert the storage medium and drag the file you want to back up onto the medium's folder. To use another backup program, follow the instructions provided with that program.

It is a good idea to label the storage medium with the name of the file or files that it contains, the date the backup was done, and the word "Backup."

A **restore** operation copies a backup file from the storage medium back onto the computer's hard drive. You should use the same method to restore the file that you used to back it up (e.g., the Windows Explorer, My Computer, Microsoft Backup, or other backup software). If you used the MS-DOS Copy command, you would use the Restore command to restore the backup copy.

In the same way you performed a backup operation with Windows Explorer or My Computer, you can restore a backup file by dragging it from the storage medium's directory to the database folder (or other folder where you want it to reside). However, keep in mind that if there is an existing file in the database folder with the same name as the backup copy file name, restoring the backup copy may replace the existing database file. If you want to save the existing file, rename it before you copy the backup file.

Since you only have one database to back up at this time, and it is already on a floppy disk, you will not perform any backup or restore operations at this time. However, you should make it a habit of backing up your files once you begin creating your own databases. You will however, compact and repair the database.

1 — Choose **T**ools/**D**atabase Utilities/**C**ompact and Repair Database.

Close the database and exit Access.

Tutorial 4: Controlling Data Input, Using Advanced Queries, and Enforcing Referential Integrity

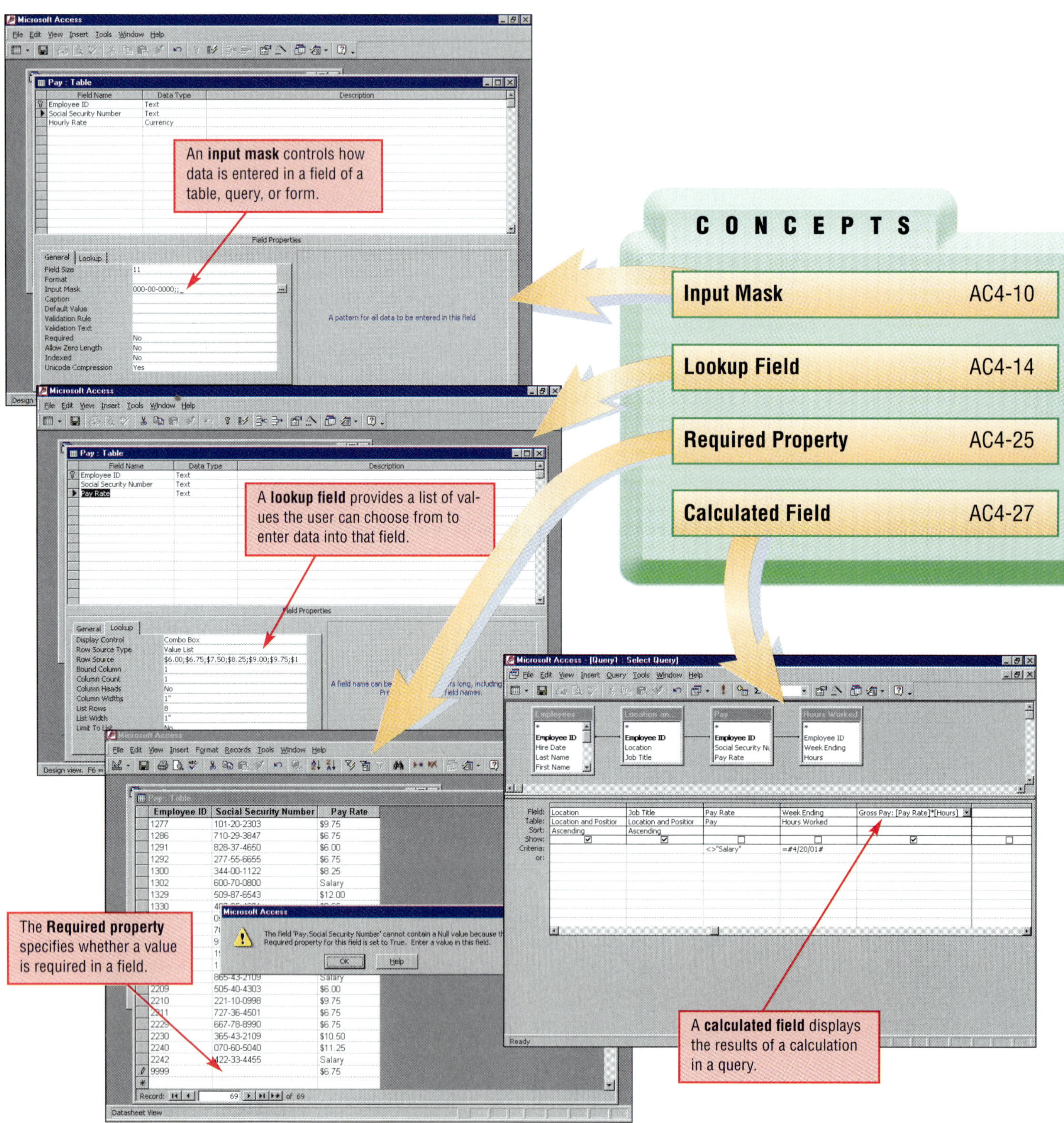

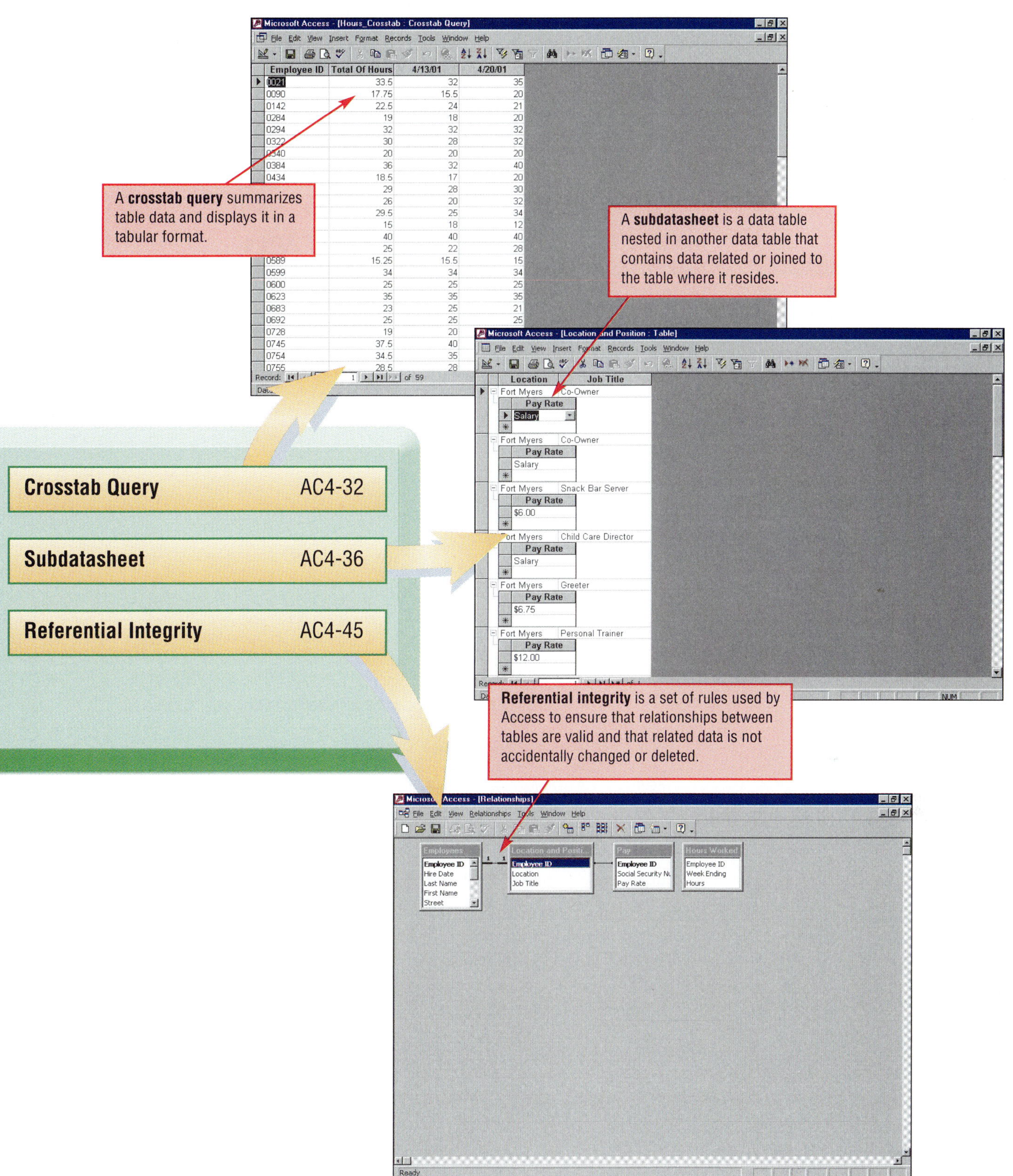

A crosstab query summarizes table data and displays it in a tabular format.

A subdatasheet is a data table nested in another data table that contains data related or joined to the table where it resides.

Crosstab Query   AC4-32

Subdatasheet   AC4-36

Referential Integrity AC4-45

Referential integrity is a set of rules used by Access to ensure that relationships between tables are valid and that related data is not accidentally changed or deleted.

Tutorial Review

Key Terms

backup   AC4-45
calculated field   AC4-27
child field   AC4-36
crosstab query   AC4-32
expression   AC4-27
foreign key field   AC4-14
function   AC4-27
import   AC4-10

input mask   AC4-10
lookup field   AC4-14
lookup list   AC4-14
master field   AC4-36
master table   AC4-36
referential integrity   AC4-41
Required property   AC4-25

restore   AC4-45
subdatasheet   AC4-36
Table Wizard   AC4-4
value list   AC4-14

Command Summary

Command	Shortcut	Toolbar	Action
File/**G**et External Data/**I**mport			Brings data in from another file
File/Print **R**elationships			Creates a report that shows the relationships in the current database
Edit/**C**opy	Ctrl + C		Copies selected text to the clipboard
Edit/**P**aste	Ctrl + V		Pastes text from clipboard to current location
Edit/Select **A**ll Records			Selects all records in table
Edit/Delete **R**ows			Deletes the selected rows.
Edit/Delete Colu**m**n			Removes selected column
Insert/**C**olumn			Adds new column
Insert/**L**ookup Field			Creates a lookup field with specified values from which the user can choose
Insert/**L**ookup Column			Creates a lookup column with specified values from which the user can choose
Insert/**S**ubdatasheet			Inserts a subdatasheet with values from a related table or query into the current datasheet
Format/**H**ide Columns			Removes the selected columns on the datasheet from view
Format/**U**nhide Columns			Displays columns that are currently hidden
Format/**S**ubdatasheet/**E**xpand All			Shows an entire subdatasheet that is embedded in the current datasheet
Format/**S**ubdatasheet/**R**emove			Removes the subdatasheet that is embedded in the current datasheet
Relationships/Edit **R**elationship			Used to change existing relationships or create new relationships in the current database and to enforce referential integrity
Tools/**D**atabase Utilities/**C**ompact and Repair Database			Makes database smaller and repairs errors

Screen Identification

In the following screen, several items are identified by letters. Enter the correct term for each item in the spaces that follow.

a. _______________________

b. _______________________

c. _______________________

d. _______________________

e. _______________________

f. _______________________

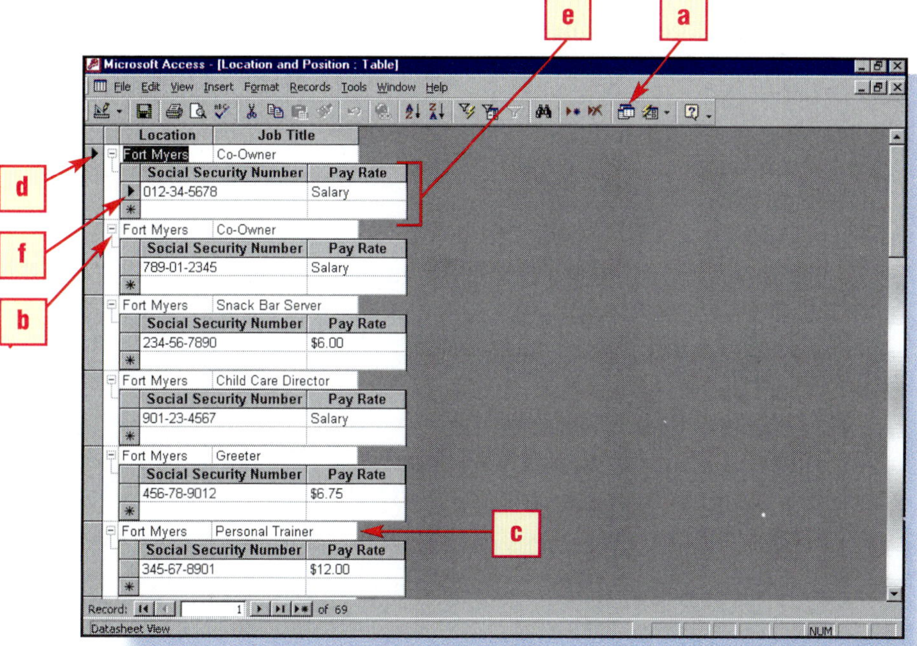

Matching

Match the letter to the correct item in the numbered list.

1. master table	_______	**a.** data that is summarized and displayed in a tabular format
2. backup	_______	**b.** a set of rules that validates table relationships
3. crosstab query	_______	**c.** provides a list of values that can be entered in a field
4. referential integrity	_______	**d.** controls how data is entered into a field
5. master field	_______	**e.** a table that is embedded in another table
6. Required field	_______	**f.** saves a copy of a database file to another location
7. lookup field	_______	**g.** ensures that data is entered into a field
8. subdatasheet	_______	**h.** a datasheet where a subdatasheet is embedded
9. input mask	_______	**i.** used to link a subsdatasheet to the master table

Fill-In

Complete the following statements by filling in the blanks with the correct terms.

a. The _____________________ helps you create a new data table.

b. You set the Required property for a field in the _____________________ tab of a field's properties box.

c. A _____________________ field displays the results of a calculation in a query.

d. A _____________________ displays summarized values in a tabular format.

e. When referential integrity is enforced, a _____________________ value cannot be changed in the primary table if that record has related records.

f. A _____________________ is a data table nested in another data table that contains data related or joined to the table where it resides.

g. The Input Mask Wizard contains 10 _____________________ masks.

h. A _____________________ displays a list of valid field entries.

i. A backup operation places a copy of the selected file onto _____________________.

j. Matching fields between a master datasheet and its subdatasheet are called _____________________ and _____________________.

Multiple-Choice

Circle the letter of the correct answer to the following statements.

1. The following character in an input mask requires a number entry from 0–9:

    a. 0

    b. #

    c. 9

    d. any of the above

2. In a crosstab query, field values are calculated by

    a. count

    b. average

    c. sum

    d. all of the above

3. The _____________________ data type increments the entries in the field.

   a. Increment
   b. AutoNumber
   c. Number
   d. Primary Key

4. When referential integrity is enforced, a primary table record cannot be _____________________ if there are matching records in a related table.

   a. deleted
   b. copied
   c. changed
   d. any of the above

5. The lookup field that uses another table as the source for values is called a _____________.

   a. table list
   b. source list
   c. lookup list
   d. value list

6. Calculated fields are created in a

   a. table
   b. form
   c. report
   d. query

7. A field whose Required property is set to Yes cannot contain a(n) _____________________ value.

   a. alphanumeric
   b. null
   c. existing
   d. any of the above

8. The following symbol indicates that a criteria expression has been interpreted as a date value:

   a. #
   b. /
   c. ?
   d. !

9. Lookup field values are

   a. obtained from another table
   b. entered when the field is created
   c. obtained from the current table
   d. any of the above

10. The source of a subdatasheet is a

   a. master field
   b. child field
   c. table or query
   d. subform

True/False

Circle the correct answer to the following statements.

1. The < input mask symbol converts entries to all uppercase.   True   False

2. Once you have entered a value in a lookup field, you cannot go back . and change it.   True   False

3. The Table Wizard lets you select fields from multiple sample tables.   True   False

4. You can set a Required property for any type of field.   True   False

5. A Count calculation totals values in a field for all records.   True   False

6. You can only select one table in the Crosstab Query Wizard.   True   False

7. Once referential integrity is set, you cannot change the relationship between tables.   True   False

8. Values for a lookup field in one table can be obtained from values in another table.   True   False

9. Database files must be backed up to a tape drive.   True   False

10. When inserting a subdatasheet, Child and Master fields must have the same names.   True   False

Discussion Questions

1. Discuss the differences between using the Table Wizard and the Design View for creating new data tables. When would you use one as opposed to the other?

2. Discuss how input mask and lookup fields can help data entry. To what types of field data could you apply input masks? For what types of data could you create lookup fields?

3. Discuss the purpose of a crosstab query. When would it be better to use this type of query instead of a simple query?

4. Discuss the purpose of enforcing referential integrity. When and why should you enforce it? Are there any situations where this would be a hindrance rather than a help?

Hands-On Practice Exercises

Step-by-Step

Rating System   ☆ Easy
☆☆ Moderate
☆☆☆ Difficult

1. While you've been working on the Club Employees database for the Lifestyle Fitness Club, someone else began designing a Club Members database. Thus far, this database has two tables: one that contains data about the club members and another that contains data about the personal trainers. The reason the club owners requested that these tables be placed in the same database is that they want to be able to track which personal trainers were assigned to which club members. They would also like to see a datasheet that shows the total membership at each club location and the number of members who have personal trainers. Your completed subdatasheet table and crosstab report are shown here.

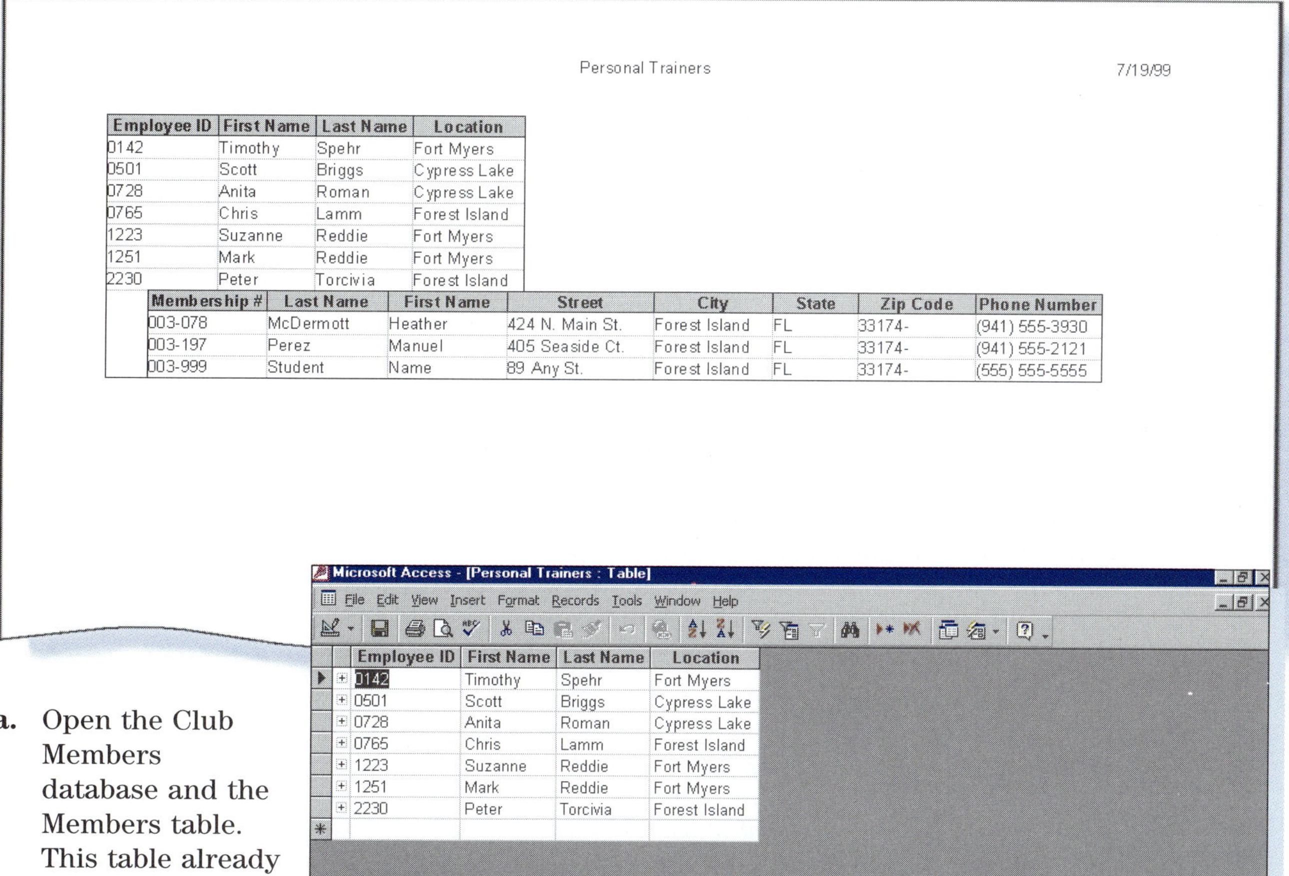

a. Open the Club Members database and the Members table. This table already has one lookup field, the Club Location, but you want to add another lookup field for identifying the club members who have personal trainers.

b. Switch to Design view and insert a lookup field below the Club Location field. In the Lookup Wizard, specify that you want to look up values from another table, accept the Personal Trainers table as the table you want to use, and select all fields from this table as the fields whose values you want to use. Accept the column widths as they are displayed and the default to hide the key column. Name the lookup field **Personal Trainer**. Save the table. Change the new lookup field name (which currently displays "Employee ID") to **Personal Trainer**. Save the new table design.

c. Switch to Datasheet view. Locate the following records and assign the personal trainers as listed below. Adjust the Personal Trainer column width to fit the displayed data when you are finished with your selections.

Member	Personal Trainer
Lauren Menassa	Suzanne Reddie
Rana Jemal	Timothy Spehr
Lynn Michlin	Mark Reddie
George Lombotti	Suzanne Reddie
Karen Collins	Timothy Spehr
Christopher Tamerlin	Suzanne Reddie
Elizabeth Bradley	Mark Reddie
Daniella Choe	Anita Roman
Nicholas Grant	Anita Roman
John Clemett	Scott Briggs
Bianca Ramirez	Scott Briggs
Barbara Dawson	Anita Roman
Heather McDermott	Peter Torcivia
Manuel Perez	Peter Torcivia
Judy Iverson	Chris Lamm
Robert Maxwell	Chris Lamm

d. Add a new record with **003-999** as the Membership # and your **first and last names**. Enter a fictional address and phone number. Select a club location from the lookup list and select a personal trainer from that location.

e. Change the orientation of the table to landscape and then print it. Save and close the table.

f. Next, you will add the Members table as a subdatasheet to the Personal Trainers table to see what members are assigned to each trainer. Open the Personal Trainers table and insert the Members table as a subdatasheet, accepting the default Child and Master field selections. Expand the subdatasheet so you can see all member records that are related to each personal trainer record. Collapse the subdatasheet again once you've viewed the records. Expand the Subdatasheet for the personal trainer you selected for your record and print the table.

g. The final thing the club owners have requested is a datasheet that shows the total membership at each club location and the number of members assigned to each personal trainer at these locations. To produce this datasheet, create a new query using the Crosstab Query Wizard. Select Members as the table on which you want to base the query, Personal Trainer as the row heading, Club Location as the column heading, and Membership # as the field you want calculated with the Count function. Accept the default query name (Members_Crosstab). Adjust the width of the columns to fit the displayed data and print the crosstab query results in portrait orientation.

h. Close the query and the Club Members database, saving the changes.

2. The Animal Angels database has made life much easier for the owners of this charity organization. The three tables it contains—Animals, Fosters, and Adopters—has helped them keep track of the animals that come into and are adopted out of their shelter, as well as the individuals who provide foster care or adopt these animals. To make the database even more helpful, the owners have asked if you could place all the data about the animals placed in foster care or adopted directly under the record that shows who provided this service in the Fosters and Adopters tables (currently these tables only have the ID # of the animal that these individuals provided foster care for or adopted). You inform them that you can do this quite easily by creating a relationship between the tables, which will automatically insert the Animals table as a subdatasheet in both of the other tables. They would also like you to create a new query to show how long the animals that are still being boarded at Animal Angels have been there, which you will accomplish with a calculated field. Your completed Fosters table and Boarded Animals query are shown here.

Boarded Animals   01/24/2001

ID #	Type	Boarded Date	# of Days Boarded
026	Dog	11/15/2001	47
029	Dog	11/30/2001	32
030	Dog	12/12/2001	20
031	Dog	12/23/2001	9
045	Dog	12/01/2001	31
126	Cat	11/15/2001	47
127	Cat	12/21/2001	11
145	Cat	12/01/2001	31
305	Horse	10/07/2001	86
403	Pig	09/01/2001	122
507	Canary	09/02/2001	121
904	Snake	11/24/2001	38

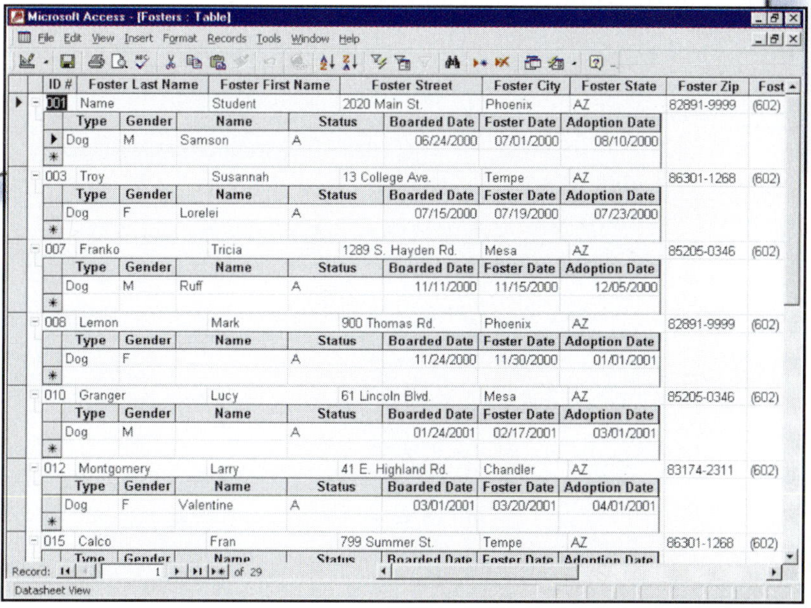

a. Open the database named Angels4.

b. Click [icon] and add the Animals, Fosters, and Adopters tables, in that order.

c. Create a relationship between the Animals and Fosters table, using the ID # field as the common field. Create another relationship between the Animals and Adopters tables, once again using the ID # as the common field. Move the Fosters table down so you can see the join line between the Animals and Adopters tables. Print a

Relationships report. Save the report using the default name, and then close the report. Close the Relationships window, saving the changes.

d. Open the Fosters table and expand the subdatasheet. Change the Foster Last Name and Foster First Name fields in the first record to your first and last name. Change the page layout to landscape and print the first page of the table. Save and close the table.

e. Open the Adopters table and expand the subdatasheet. Change the Adopter Last Name and Adopter First Name fields in the first record to your first and last name. Change the page layout to landscape and print the first page of the table. Save and close the table.

f. Create a query in Design view. Add the Animals table to the design. Add the ID #, Type, Status, and Boarded Date fields to the grid, in that order. You want only the records for animals that are still being boarded to be included in this query, so specify the Status criteria as **B** (for Boarded). Since the status of "boarded" will be assumed in this query, the Status field does not need to be displayed and you can deselect its Show option.

g. In the first blank Field column, enter the following equation to calculate the number of days the animal has been boarded at Animal Angels:

# of Days Boarded: DateDiff("d",[Boarded Date],[Date])

h. Run the query. When you are asked to enter a parameter for the Date, enter 1/1/02.

i. Adjust the column widths as necessary to view all displayed data and print the query in portrait orientation.

j. Save the query as **Boarded Animals** and close it.

k. Close the Angels4 database.

3. Daria O'Dell, the owner of Daria's Day Spa, is quite pleased with the Clients table that you created in the spa's database. She would now like you to create two additional tables: one that contains data about the various spa packages and their costs and another that lists what clients have purchased which package. She would also like you to run a query that shows the spa packages purchased by clients and the total amount spent. When you are finished, you will have created the report shown here.

a. Open the database file Daria Spa 4. Enter your first and last name for Client ID 024

Client Purchases 1/2/99

Last Name	Aromatic	Body Beautiful	Destresser	Fantastic Face	Massage Magic	Sensation	Simple Pleasures	The Ultimate	Total Purchase
Chen		$150.00					$75.00		$225.00
Finch		$150.00							$150.00
Frankson				$75.00					$75.00
Grace								$325.00	$325.00
Griffin	$75.00								$75.00
Grimes				$75.00					$75.00
Kelly							$75.00	$650.00	$725.00
Kendall			$215.00						$215.00
Ky		$150.00						$325.00	$475.00
Michaels	$75.00						$75.00	$325.00	$475.00
Miller				$75.00	$75.00				$150.00
Name								$325.00	$325.00
Pickett				$75.00					$75.00
Richmond		$150.00							$150.00
Riley			$215.00						$215.00
Shoemaker		$150.00							$150.00
Tomano				$75.00		$150.00			$225.00
Townsend						$150.00			$150.00
Tran					$75.00	$150.00			$225.00
Trawe						$150.00			$150.00
Williams	$150.00								$150.00

b. Use the Table Wizard to create a new table using the following fields from the Products sample table, renamed as shown.

Sample Table Field to Add	Rename Field
ProductID	Package ID
ProductName	Package Name
ProductDescription	Package Description
UnitPrice	Package Price

c. Name the table **Spa Packages**, and let Access assign the primary key. Do not assign a relationship between this new table and the existing Clients table. Accept the default to begin entering records right away (without altering the table design) and finish the Wizard.

d. Enter the following records (do not worry about entering a Package ID number—it is an AutoNumber field):

Package Name	Package Description	Package Price
The Ultimate	Deep-tissue massage, aromatherapy, facial, body wrap, and sauna	$325.00
Destresser	Deep-tissue massage, facial, and sauna	$215.00
Sensation	Aromatherapy and facial	$150.00
Body Beautiful	Body wrap and sauna	$150.00
Massage Magic	Deep-tissue massage	$ 75.00
Aromatic	Aromatherapy	$ 75.00
Fantastic Face	Facial	$ 75.00
Simple Pleasures	Sauna	$ 75.00

e. Adjust the column widths to fit the data. Then save and close the table.

f. Create another table in Design view. Name the first field **Client ID** and assign it a Data Type of Text and a Field Size of 3.

g. Insert a lookup field that uses the Package ID and Package Name values from the Spa Packages table. Accept the default Hide key column selection and the displayed column width. Name the lookup column **Package Purchased**, finish the Wizard, and save the table as **Packages Purchased**. If you receive a message asking you whether you want to assign a primary key, do not do so (you will be entering multiple records for each client and package, so they will not be unique).

h. Change the lookup field name from Package ID to **Package Purchased**. Switch to Datasheet view, saving the table design.

i. Use the Office Clipboard to copy the Client ID column from the Clients table to the Packages Purchased table.

j. Select a spa package for each client (assign the Ultimate package to your record) and then add 10 more records for clients that have purchased more than one package. Adjust the column widths as necessary and close the table.

k. Save and close the Packages Purchased table.

l. Create a relationship between the Package Purchases and Clients tables based on the Client ID field. Print and save the Relationship report; then save and close the Relationship window.

m. Create a new query in Design view and include all three tables. Add the Last Name, Package Purchased, Package Name, and Package Price fields to the query design grid. Save the query as **Package Sales**.

n. Use the Crosstab Query Wizard to create a crosstab based on the Package Sales query. Select Last Name as the row heading, Package Name as the column heading, and Package Price as the field you want calculated with the SUM function. Name the crosstab query **Client Purchases**.

o. Adjust the column widths. Rename the Total of Package field **Total Purchases**. Move the field to the last position in the crosstab.

p. Print the crosstab query in landscape orientation with left and right margins set at .6 inch.

q. Close the Daria Spa 4 database.

4. The database you created for the Downtown Internet Cafe contains a table with information about the cafe's inventory and vendors. You've used this table to design a vendor information form, as well as to create queries and reports on items that need to be ordered. The cafe's owner, Evan, has asked you to create another table that lists the costs of the inventory items, the quantity on hand and on order, as well as the vendors who carry these items. Evan would also like you to add a field to the existing To Be Ordered query that will calculate the cost of each order using values from both of the Cafe Purchases database tables. When you are finished, you will have a new database table and a query printout that looks similar to those shown here.

To Be Ordered   1/2/02

Vendor Name	Contact	Phone	Description	# On Hand	# To Order	Unit Price	Order Cost
Best Bakery	Student Name	(909)555-5599	Scones	16	8	$0.75	$6.00
Better Beverages, Inc.	Mae Yung	(415) 555-1122	Earl Grey tea	17	7	$5.95	$41.65
Better Beverages, Inc.	Mae Yung	(415) 555-1122	Orange Pekoe tea	21	3	$5.95	$17.85
Central Ceramics	Dan O'Dell	(602) 555-1924	Coffee mugs	12	12	$4.00	$48.00
Pure Processing	Nancy Young	(650) 555-5689	Decaf Columbian	13	11	$8.25	$90.75
Pure Processing	Nancy Young	(650) 555-5689	Decaf Dark	15	9	$8.25	$74.25
Quality Coffee	Fred Wilmington	(206) 555-9090	Sumatra coffee	14	10	$7.50	$75.00
Quality Coffee	Fred Wilmington	(206) 555-9090	Columbian coffee	19	5	$7.50	$37.50
Quality Coffee	Fred Wilmington	(206) 555-9090	Kenya coffee	24	0	$7.50	$0.00
Quality Coffee	Fred Wilmington	(206) 555-9090	Java coffee	16	8	$7.50	$60.00
Quality Coffee	Fred Wilmington	(206) 555-9090	Kona coffee	15	9	$7.50	$67.50
Quality Coffee	Fred Wilmington	(206) 555-9090	Espresso Roast	10	14	$7.50	$105.00
Quality Coffee	Fred Wilmington	(206) 555-9090	Italian Roast	20	4	$7.50	$30.00
Quality Coffee	Fred Wilmington	(206) 555-9090	French Roast	13	11	$7.50	$82.50
Quality Coffee	Fred Wilmington	(206) 555-9090	Guatamala coffee	23	1	$7.50	$7.50
Restaurant Supply	Manny Smith	(602) 555-0037	Coffee filters	15	9	$10.00	$90.00
Restaurant Supply	Manny Smith	(602) 555-0037	Cups-large	12	12	$11.00	$132.00

a. Open the Cafe Purchases 4 database and enter your name as the content for item# 9999 in the Inventory table. Close the table.

b. Use the Table Wizard to create a new table based on the sample table called Products. Add the following fields from the sample table to your new table field list and rename them to match the corresponding Inventory table fields, as follows:

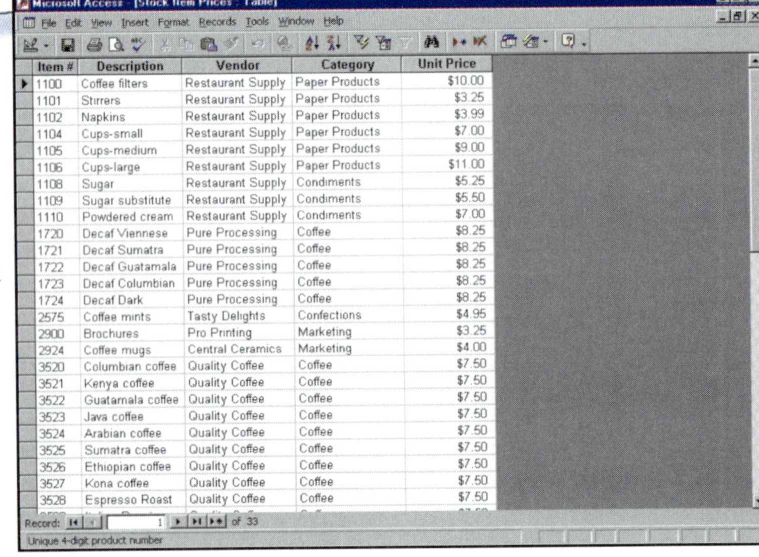

Microsoft Access - [Stock Item Prices : Table]

File Edit View Insert Format Records Tools Window Help

Item #	Description	Vendor	Category	Unit Price
1100	Coffee filters	Restaurant Supply	Paper Products	$10.00
1101	Stirrers	Restaurant Supply	Paper Products	$3.25
1102	Napkins	Restaurant Supply	Paper Products	$3.99
1104	Cups-small	Restaurant Supply	Paper Products	$7.00
1105	Cups-medium	Restaurant Supply	Paper Products	$9.00
1106	Cups-large	Restaurant Supply	Paper Products	$11.00
1108	Sugar	Restaurant Supply	Condiments	$5.25
1109	Sugar substitute	Restaurant Supply	Condiments	$5.50
1110	Powdered cream	Restaurant Supply	Condiments	$7.00
1720	Decaf Viennese	Pure Processing	Coffee	$8.25
1721	Decaf Sumatra	Pure Processing	Coffee	$8.25
1722	Decaf Guatamala	Pure Processing	Coffee	$8.25
1723	Decaf Columbian	Pure Processing	Coffee	$8.25
1724	Decaf Dark	Pure Processing	Coffee	$8.25
2575	Coffee mints	Tasty Delights	Confections	$4.95
2900	Brochures	Pro Printing	Marketing	$3.25
2924	Coffee mugs	Central Ceramics	Marketing	$4.00
3520	Columbian coffee	Quality Coffee	Coffee	$7.50
3521	Kenya coffee	Quality Coffee	Coffee	$7.50
3522	Guatamala coffee	Quality Coffee	Coffee	$7.50
3523	Java coffee	Quality Coffee	Coffee	$7.50
3524	Arabian coffee	Quality Coffee	Coffee	$7.50
3525	Sumatra coffee	Quality Coffee	Coffee	$7.50
3526	Ethiopian coffee	Quality Coffee	Coffee	$7.50
3527	Kona coffee	Quality Coffee	Coffee	$7.50
3528	Espresso Roast	Quality Coffee	Coffee	$7.50

Record: 1 of 33

Unique 4-digit product number

Sample Table Field to Add	Rename Field
ProductID	Item #
ProductDescription	Description
SupplierID	Vendor
UnitPrice	Unit Price

c. Name the table **Stock Item Prices**. Let Access assign the primary key. Do not assign a relationship between this new table and the existing Inventory table. Specify that you want to modify the table design, and then finish the Wizard.

d. Change the properties of the first three fields as follows so they match the corresponding fields in the Inventory table:

Field	Data Type	Description	Field Size
Item #	Text	Unique 4-digit product number	4
Description	Text	Name of product	50
Vendor	Text	Name of supplier	50

e. You decide to add a field that will identify the category of the item, such as coffee, tea, condiments, and so on. Rather than requiring the users of this database table to memorize each category name and enter it consistently, you are going to create a lookup field from which they can choose the appropriate category when entering new item records. To do this, insert a lookup field above the UnitPrice row. In the Lookup Wizard, specify that you want to type in your own lookup values and then enter the following names in the lookup column list and adjust the column width to fit the entries when you're through:

Coffee

Tea

Condiments

Confections

Marketing

Paper Products

f. Name the lookup column **Category** and finish the Wizard.

g. Save the table design and switch to Datasheet view.

h. Rather than having to reenter all the item numbers, descriptions, and vendor names for the cafe's current inventory, you decide to copy this data from the Inventory table. Open the Office Clipboard and then open the Inventory table and use the clipboard to copy the Item #, Description, and Vendor Name columns from this table to the corresponding columns in the Stock Item Prices table. Close the Office Clipboard and adjust the column widths in the Stock Item Prices table to fit the displayed field data.

i. Select the appropriate category and enter a unit price for each table record. When you're finished, adjust these two columns to fit the data you entered.

j. Save and print the table in portrait orientation.

k. You are now ready to update the To Be Ordered query to include costs. Open the To Be Ordered query and add the Stock Item Prices table to the query. Do not show the Special Order column

l.   Next, you need to add a new field that will calculate the number of items that need to be ordered, based on the fact that Evan likes to keep an inventory of 24 units of every item on hand. In the blank field cell to the right of the Phone column, type the following: **# To Order: 24-[# On Hand]**

m.   The next calculation you want to perform is one that will multiply the # To Order value by the Unit Price. Add the Unit Price field from the Stock Item Prices table to the blank field cell to the right of the # To Order calculated field. In the next blank field cell enter: **Order Cost: [# To Order]*[Unit Price]**. Set the format property to currency.

n.   Run the query. Adjust the column widths to fit the displayed data. Change the page orientation to Landscape and print the query. Then save the query as **Order Costs** and close it.

o.   Close the Cafe Purchases 4 database.

5. The database you created for EduSoft Company currently contains a table that lists the educational software titles produced by the company as well as the subject of each package and the designer who is responsible for developing it. You have created several queries and reports based on this table, which has helped the marketing and development managers immensely. After hearing about the success of this database, the sales manager requested that you add tables that contain data about packages that have been purchased so that queries can be run that show how the packages are selling and what the total monthly, quarterly, and annual purchase amounts are. You decide to start this process by creating a simple order table with product name, order date, and quantity purchased data. Then by adding a unit cost field to the existing Software table, you can use both tables to run a query that calculates the total sales per package to date. When you are finished, you will have a new database table and a query printout that looks similar to those shown here.

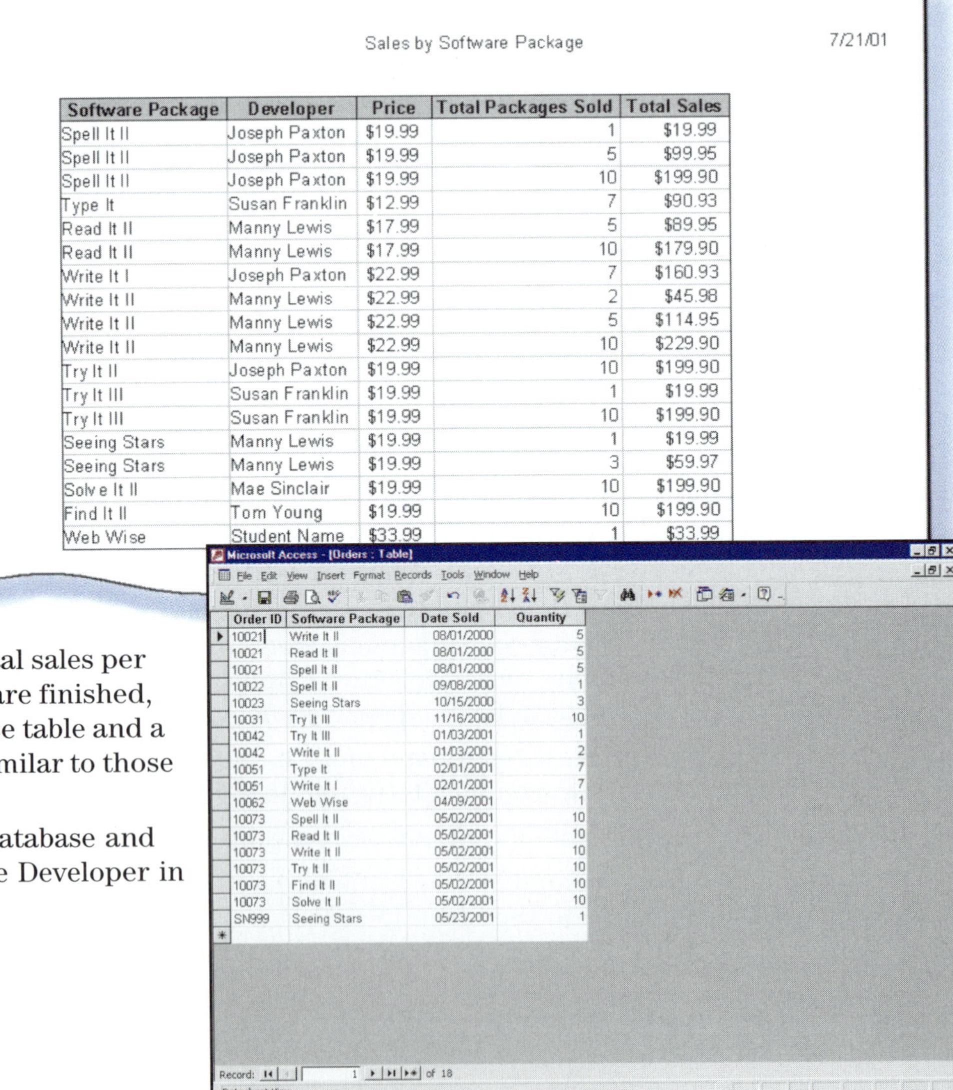

Sales by Software Package   7/21/01

Software Package	Developer	Price	Total Packages Sold	Total Sales
Spell It II	Joseph Paxton	$19.99	1	$19.99
Spell It II	Joseph Paxton	$19.99	5	$99.95
Spell It II	Joseph Paxton	$19.99	10	$199.90
Type It	Susan Franklin	$12.99	7	$90.93
Read It II	Manny Lewis	$17.99	5	$89.95
Read It II	Manny Lewis	$17.99	10	$179.90
Write It I	Joseph Paxton	$22.99	7	$160.93
Write It II	Manny Lewis	$22.99	2	$45.98
Write It II	Manny Lewis	$22.99	5	$114.95
Write It II	Manny Lewis	$22.99	10	$229.90
Try It II	Joseph Paxton	$19.99	10	$199.90
Try It III	Susan Franklin	$19.99	1	$19.99
Try It III	Susan Franklin	$19.99	10	$199.90
Seeing Stars	Manny Lewis	$19.99	1	$19.99
Seeing Stars	Manny Lewis	$19.99	3	$59.97
Solve It II	Mae Sinclair	$19.99	10	$199.90
Find It II	Tom Young	$19.99	10	$199.90
Web Wise	Student Name	$33.99	1	$33.99

Microsoft Access - [Orders : Table]

File   Edit   View   Insert   Format   Records   Tools   Window   Help

Order ID	Software Package	Date Sold	Quantity
10021	Write It II	08/01/2000	5
10021	Read It II	08/01/2000	5
10021	Spell It II	08/01/2000	5
10022	Spell It II	09/08/2000	1
10023	Seeing Stars	10/15/2000	3
10031	Try It III	11/16/2000	10
10042	Try It III	01/03/2001	1
10042	Write It II	01/03/2001	2
10051	Type It	02/01/2001	7
10051	Write It I	02/01/2001	7
10062	Web Wise	04/09/2001	1
10073	Spell It II	05/02/2001	10
10073	Read It II	05/02/2001	10
10073	Write It II	05/02/2001	10
10073	Try It II	05/02/2001	10
10073	Find It II	05/02/2001	10
10073	Solve It II	05/02/2001	10
SN999	Seeing Stars	05/23/2001	1

Record: |◀| ◀ | 1 | ▶ |▶I|▶*| of 18

Datasheet View

a.   Open the Learning 4 database and enter your name as the Developer in the last record

b. Use the Table Wizard to create a new table with the following fields from the Order Details sample table:

OrderID

ProductID

DateSold

Quantity

c. Name the table **Orders**, and let Access assign the primary key. Do not assign a relationship between this new table and the existing Software table. Specify that you want to modify the table design, and then finish the Wizard.

d. Change the Data Type of the OrderID field from AutoNumber to Text and change its Field Size to 5. Because multiple records will be entered for some orders (for multiple software packages purchased on the same order), each record will not necessarily have a unique OrderID, so you also need to remove the primary key from this field.

e. Test the DateSold input mask by selecting the Short Date mask in the Input Mask Wizard and entering numbers both with and without punctuation and of correct and incorrect lengths in the Try It box. Accept the rest of the input mask defaults and exit the Wizard.

f. Delete the ProductID field and insert a lookup field in its place. Specify that you want to use values from another table, select Software as the table you want to use as the source of these values, and select Product Code and Title as the fields containing the values. Accept the default Hide key column selection and the displayed column width. Name the lookup column **Software Package**, finish the Wizard, and save the table when prompted to do so. Change the lookup field name from Product Code to **Software Package**.

g. Make all fields required.

h. Save the table design and switch to Datasheet view.

i. Enter an order number of **10021**, select the Spell It II software package, and enter an order date of **8/1/00** and a quantity of **5**. Since this order was for a school's third grade class computer lab, there were two more software packages purchased on the same order. Therefore, you need to enter two more records with the same order number, one for 5 Read It II packages and another for 5 Write It II packages. Enter the same order date for both.

j. Enter 15 more orders, some with multiple software packages purchased under the same order and on the same date and others purchased as a single order. Use varying quantities for each order. When you're finished, adjust the column widths to fit the displayed data.

k. Add a final record with **your first and last initials** followed by **999** as the Order ID and **today's date** as the Date Sold. (You can select whatever software package and quantity you'd like.) Save and print the table.

l. You are now ready to add a field to the Software table that will contain the cost of each software package. Open this table and switch to Design view. Add a field called **Price** with a Data Type of Currency. Save the design changes and switch back to Datasheet view. Enter prices for each of the software packages that were ordered thus far (the ones you selected in the Orders table). Close the table when you're through.

m. Although you haven't finished entering all the software package prices or orders, you decide to see whether you can use the combined table data to produce the sales-to-date query that the sales manager requested. Use the Simple Query Wizard to create a new query. Include the Software Package and Quantity fields from the Orders table and the Developer and Price fields from the Software table. Select Summary as the type of query you would like to create and in the Summary Options box, select the Sum option for the Quantity field. Name the query **Sales by Software Package**. Specify that you want to modify the query design and finish out of the Wizard.

n.   In the query's Design View, change the Sum of Quantity: Quantity calculated field name to **Total Packages Sold: Quantity**. Then in the blank field column to the right, enter another calculated field: **Total Sales: [Quantity]*[Price]**. Assign the Currency property to the new field. Run the query.

o.   Adjust the column widths to fit the displayed data and then print the query.

p.   Save and close the query. Close the Learning 4 database.

On Your Own

6. As database manager for a dental office, you've been maintaining a database that tracks the patient identification information. The bookkeeper has recently requested that you add a table to this table that will track patient payment information and include this information in the original table as a subdatasheet so that the identification and payment data can be accessed separately or all in one location as necessary. Open the database you updated in Practice Exercise 8 of Tutorial 2 and use the Table Wizard to create a new table. Select the Payments sample table and add the CustomerID, PaymentAmount, and PaymentDate fields, as well as any other payment method fields you want to include in your new table. Rename the CustomerID field to match the field name that you use for patient identification numbers in your existing patient information table (such as Patient ID). Name the table as desired. Change the Data Type of the Patient ID field from AutoNumber to Text, and remove the primary key from it so you can enter more than one record for each patient in this table (which you will do each time they make a payment). Copy the patient IDs from the patient identification table to this new table and enter at least one payment record for each. Print and close the table. Then insert this new table as a subdatasheet in the patient identification table. Print one page of the table with the subdatasheet displayed.

7. The owners of Adventure Travel have been using the database you created to track client information, including the tours that each client has taken. You would now like to add another table to this database that lists the price of each tour package so that you can use both tables in a query that will calculate the total amount of money each package has generated. Open the Adventure database that you updated in Practice Exercise 8 of Tutorial 3 and create a new table that includes one field for the tour package name values and another field for entering the cost of each package. Make both fields required. Copy the names of the packages from the clients table and enter a price for each. Print and close the table. Open the clients table and replace the existing package name fields with lookup fields that use the values from the new tour package table. Reselect the tour(s) for each client record using these new lookup fields; then close the table. Create a query that includes the package name and price fields as well as a calculated field that will display the total income from each package. Run, print, and save the query.

8. Posters Unlimited distributes posters to many different retail outlets. They would like you to create a database to keep track of the posters they have in stock. Design a relational database using the Table Wizard that includes the following.

Product table: Product reference code, supplier ID, description, selling price, wholesale price, and quantity on hand.

Supplier table: Supplier ID, supplier name, street address, city, state, ZIP code, and reorder quantity. Set input mask to the ZIP code and product reference code fields.

Enter at least 20 records into each table. Set the relationship between the supplier ID fields. Create a lookup field for the reorder quantity. Posters come in reorder quantities of 5 to 50 incremented by 5. Query the database for products with a quantity on hand of less than 5. Print the query.

9. You are continuing to work on a database for National Packing. This database currently includes only one table, which contains sales rep data (such as their name and the products they represent). You want to add two more tables to the database: one that shows the products and their prices, and another that contains client information such as client ID, name, address, who their sales rep is, and what products they've purchased. Open the database that you updated in Practice Exercise 7 of Tutorial 2 and create the two new tables using sample tables from the Table Wizard or in Design view. Use input masks where appropriate (such as phone number and ZIP code fields) and lookup fields where applicable (such as the sales rep field in the clients table). Enter records into both tables, copying existing data from one table to another where possible. When the tables are completed, establish relationships between them (if they have not already been established due to the type of data manipulation you've done on them), and print a Relationships report. Then use these tables to create a query that calculates the purchase amounts.

10. Matthew owns an online bookstore. He would like you to create a relational database to help him keep track of items he has for sale. Do some research on the Web about bookstores. With your research, plan and create a relational database with appropriate tables. Enter at least 20 records into each of your tables. Create a crosstab query from your database. Print the crosstab query results. Create a relationship report for your database. Print the relationship report.

Creating Custom Forms

Competencies

After completing this tutorial, you will know how to:

1. Create a multiple-table form.
2. Enhance a form's appearance.
3. Add a title to a form.
4. Create and use a subform.
5. Create a calculated control.
6. Add a header and footer.
7. Add command buttons.

Case Study

Now that all your data tables for the Lifestyle Fitness Club personnel records are complete, the owners would like you to create some tools that will make updating and viewing table data easier and more efficient. For example, they would like a form that will automatically update the Employees, Location and Position, Pay, and Hours Worked tables, rather than requiring each of these tables to be updated separately.

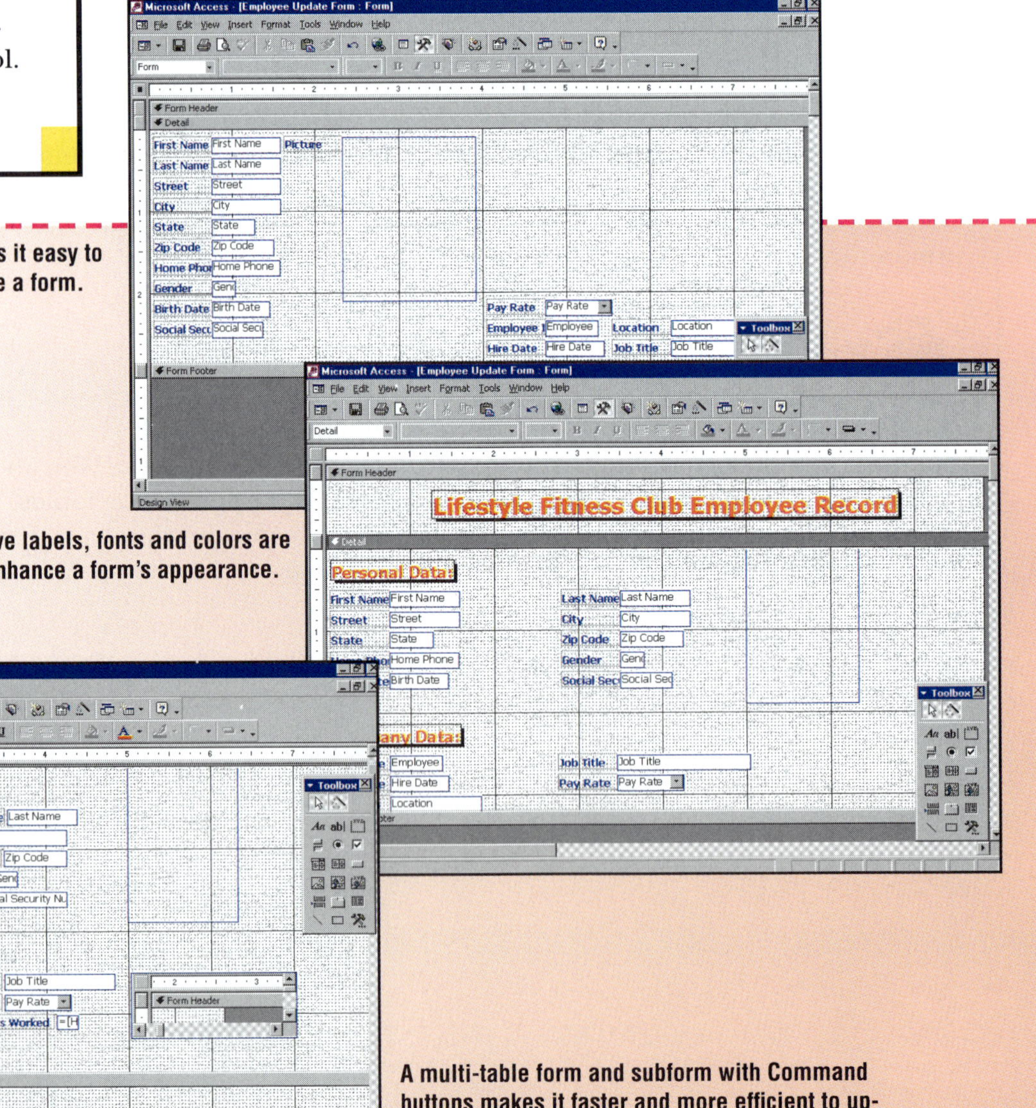

Form design view makes it easy to rearrange and customize a form.

Descriptive labels, fonts and colors are used to enhance a form's appearance.

A multi-table form and subform with Command buttons makes it faster and more efficient to update multiple tables.

To do this, you will create a main form that includes the employee data and add a subform to display the hours worked by each employee. The new form will also have a field that calculates the total number of hours the employee has worked.

When you are finished with the form, you will create command buttons and macros that will enable other database users to add new records and print forms at the touch of a button.

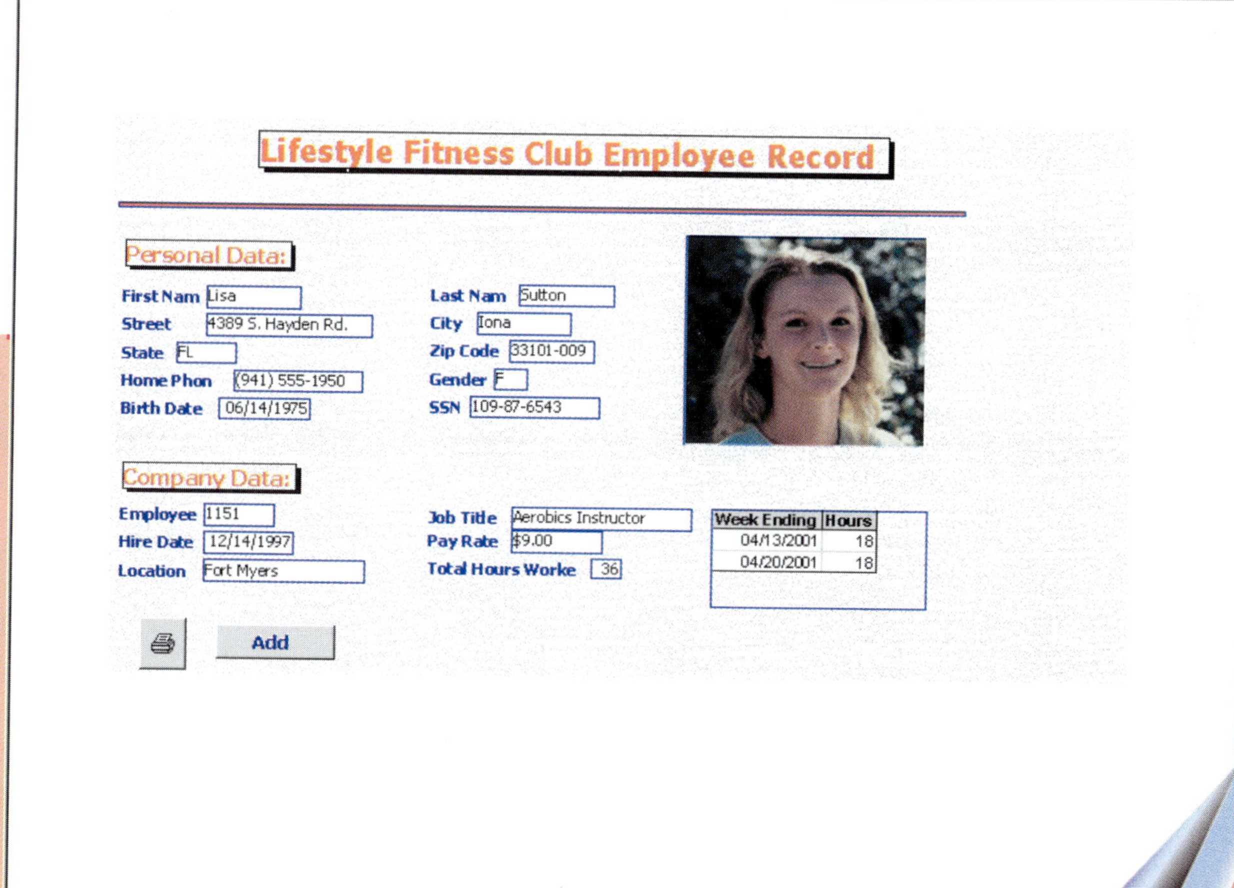

Concept Overview

The following concepts will be introduced in this lab:

1   **Fonts**   Fonts consist of three elements—typeface, size, and style—that can be applied to characters to improve their appearance.

2   **Subform**   A subform is a form that is embedded in another form.

3   **Calculated Control**   A calculated control is used to display data that is calculated from a field in a table or query or from another control in the form.

4   **Command Button**   A command button executes one or more actions on a form.

Creating a Multiple-Table Form

You have been using several tables of employee information that need to be updated each time information changes in an existing record. The Employee Data form you created earlier can only update the records in the Employees table. You want to create a form that will update the Employees, Pay, and Location and Position tables. Because these tables currently have referential integrity enforced (which you did in the previous tutorial), you cannot make any changes to them. Therefore, you must first remove the Enforce Referential Integrity setting.

1

Load Access and open the database file Club Employees.

Click  **Relationships.**

In the Relationships window, right-click on the join line between the first and second tables.

Click on the narrow part of the line.

Choose Edit Relationship.

The menu equivalent is **R**elationships/Edit **R**elationship.

In the Edit Relationships dialog box, clear the Enforce Referential Integrity option.

Click OK **.**

Your screen should be similar to Figure 5–1.

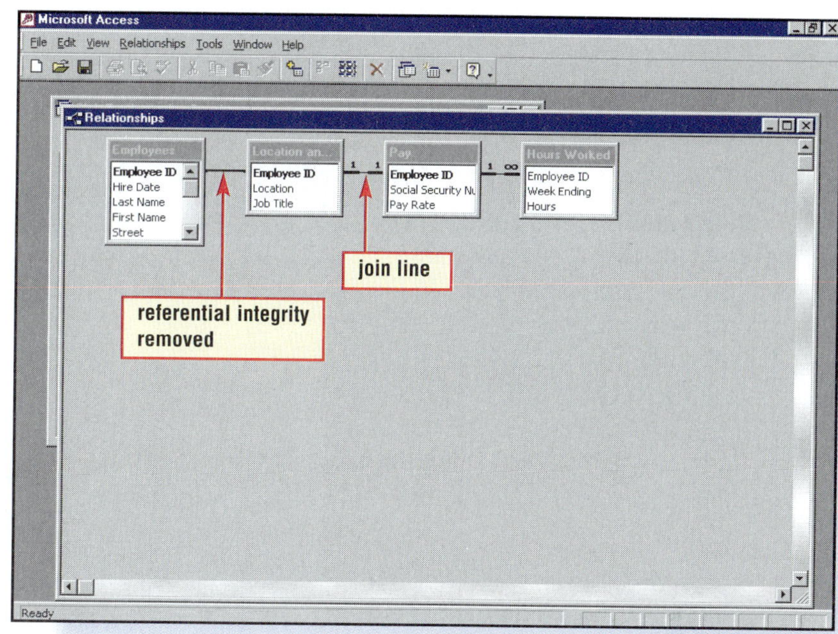

Figure 5–1

2

In a similar manner, clear the Enforce Referential Integrity from the other two relationships.

Close the Relationships window.

Now you can create your multiple-table form. The easiest way to create this form is by using the Form Wizard.

3 ■ **Click** 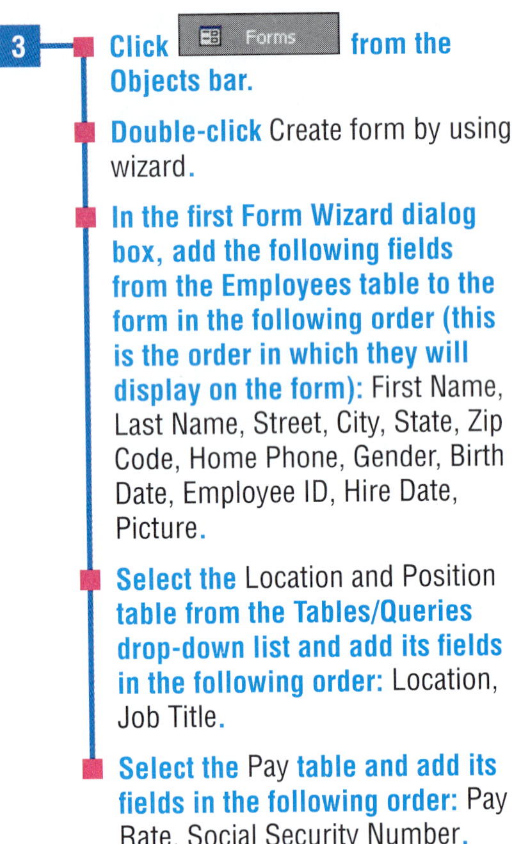 **from the Objects bar.**

■ **Double-click** Create form by using wizard.

■ **In the first Form Wizard dialog box, add the following fields from the Employees table to the form in the following order (this is the order in which they will display on the form):** First Name, Last Name, Street, City, State, Zip Code, Home Phone, Gender, Birth Date, Employee ID, Hire Date, Picture.

■ **Select the** Location and Position **table from the Tables/Queries drop-down list and add its fields in the following order:** Location, Job Title.

■ **Select the** Pay **table and add its fields in the following order:** Pay Rate, Social Security Number.

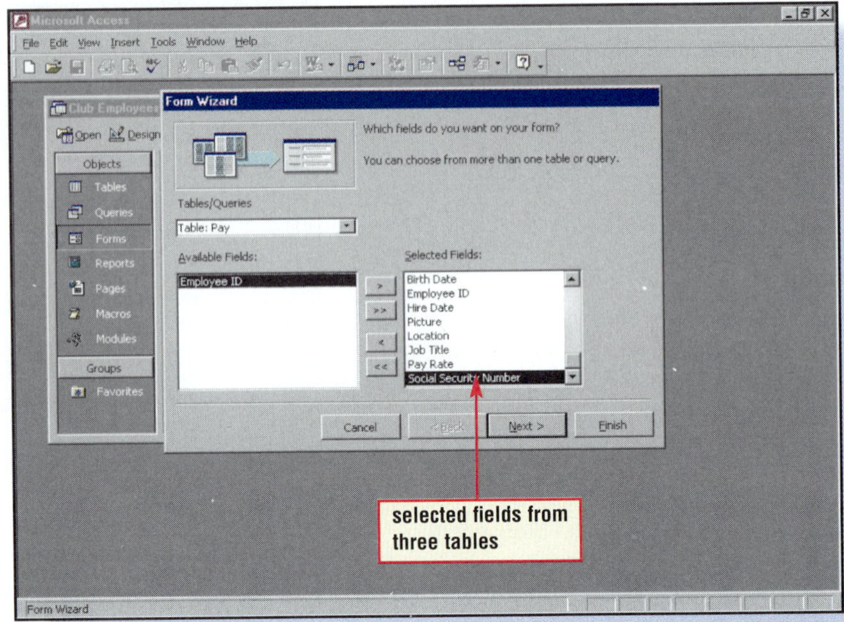

Figure 5–2

Your screen should be similar to Figure 5–2.

4 ■ **Click** Next > .

■ **Click** Next > **again to accept the columnar layout.**

■ **Select the** Sumi Painting **style and click** Next > .

■ **Enter the form title Employee Update Form.**

■ **Click** Finish .

■ **If necessary, maximize the form window.**

Your screen should be similar to Figure 5–3.

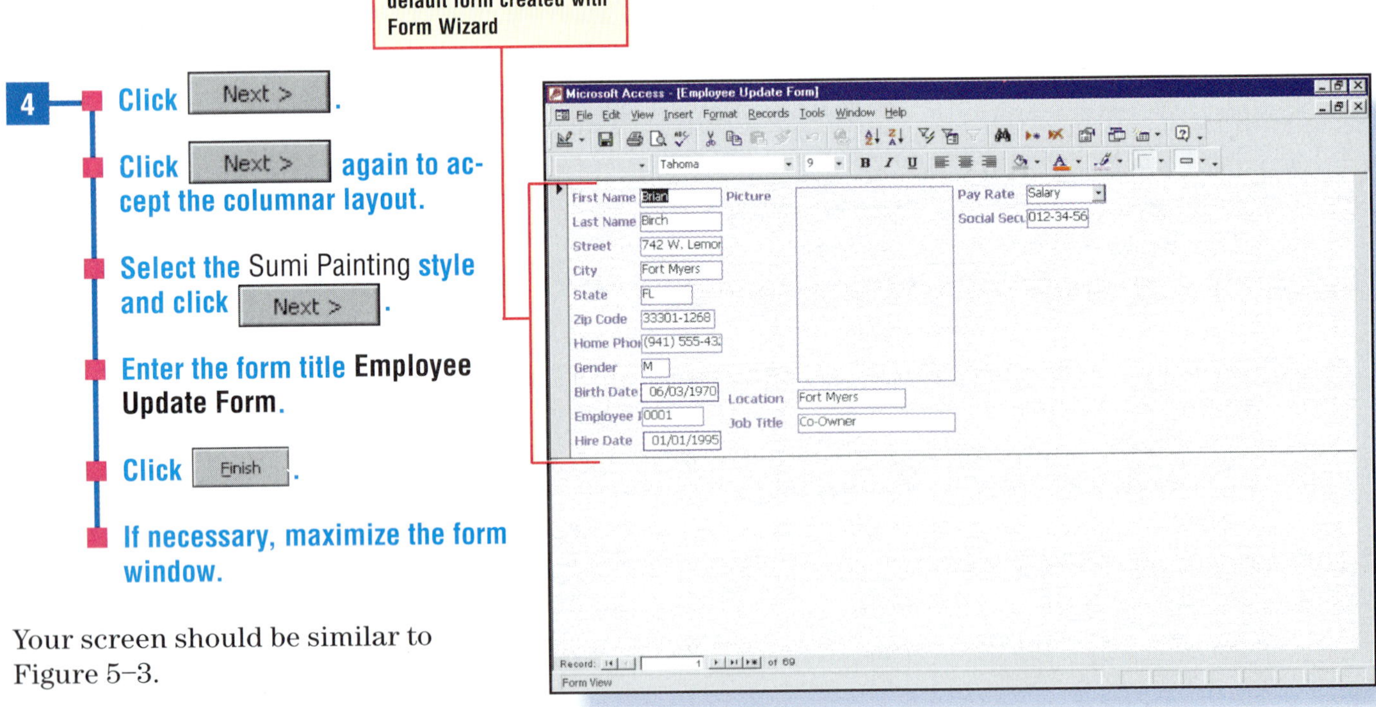

Figure 5–3

The Form window displays the form in the selected style and layout. Each field from the different tables is displayed in the form. You will modify the form's appearance later, but first you want to test the form's ability to update the associated tables. To do this, you will make several changes to your record and then see the effect this has on the related tables.

5 ■ Move to the last record (this should be your record).

■ Change the data in the following fields:

Hire Date	Current date
Location	Cypress Lake
Pay Rate	$7.50

■ Close the form.

■ To confirm that the changes were made to the tables, open the Employees, Location and Position, and Pay tables, go to the last record, and verify the changes.

■ Close all open tables.

As you can see, using a single customized form to update records in all three tables simultaneously is a great time-saving feature. Next, you'll resize the fields so all the data is displayed and do some other cosmetic changes to the form to improve its appearance.

Modifying a Form in Design View

Now that you've created a form for updating multiple employee tables at once, you want to make it easy to use as far as its layout, or the way the fields are displayed and arranged on the form, as well. First of all, you would like the data entries to be completely displayed in each field. You would also like to make it more appealing to the eye by dividing it into sections and adding some different colors and font styles. The form layout you want to create is shown here.

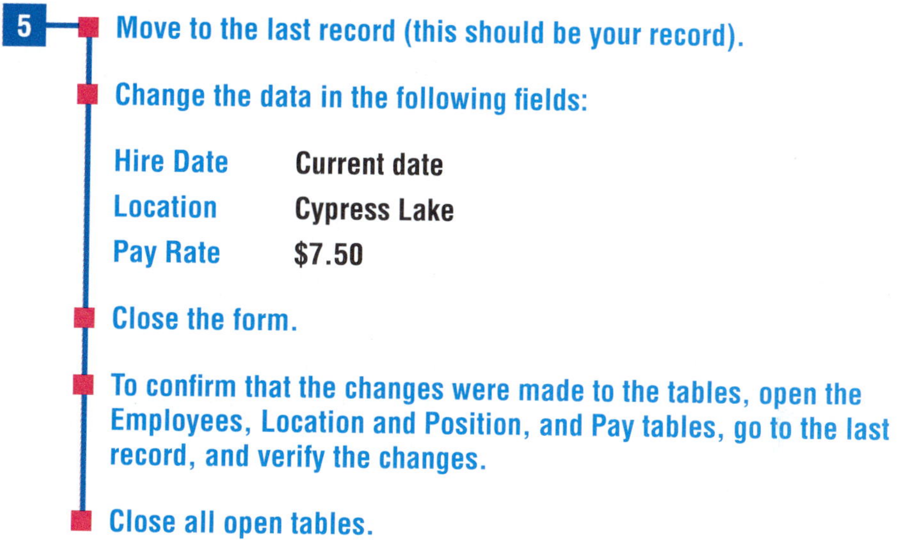

You'll make all these changes in Form Design view.

1

Open the Employee Update Form.

If necessary, maximize the form window.

Click [ ] Design View.

Your screen should be similar to Figure 5-4.

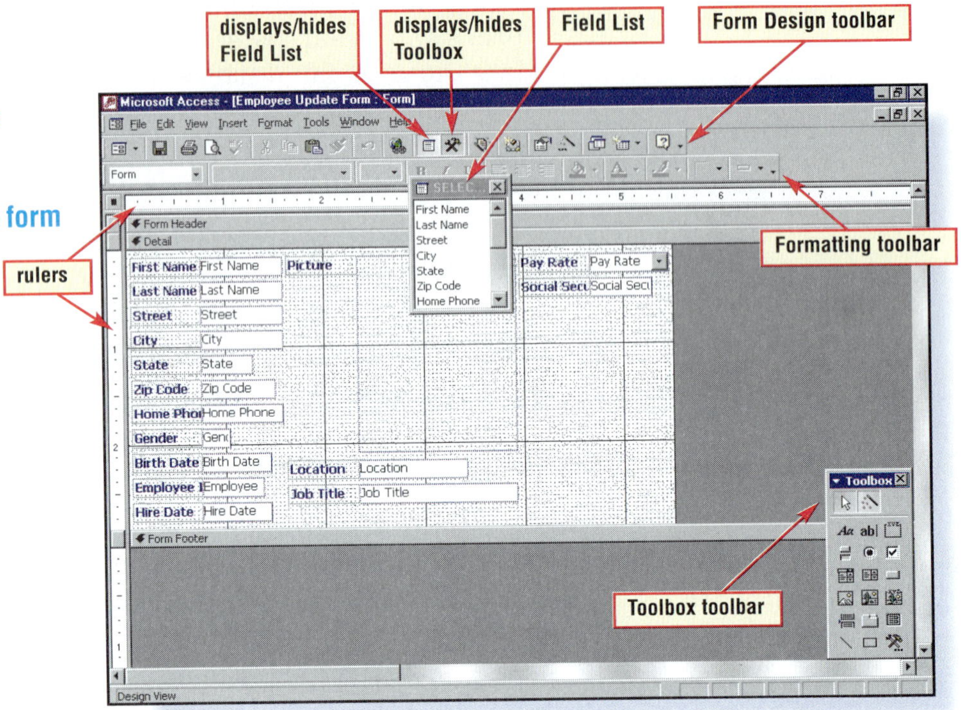

Figure 5-4

The Employee Update Form is displayed in the Form Design view window. Like Report Design view, horizontal and vertical rulers are displayed to help you correctly place items in the Form Design window. The Form Design window is divided into three sections: Form Header, Detail, and Form Footer. The contents of each section appear below the horizontal bar containing the name. The purpose of each of these sections is described in the following table.

Section	Description
Form Header	An optional section that you can include to display information such as the form title, instructions, or graphics. The contents of a Form Header appear at the top of the screen or, if you print the form, at the top of the first page. Form Headers are not visible in Datasheet view, and do not scroll as you scroll through records.
Detail	The area where the table data displays.
Form Footer	Another optional section that can include notes, instructions, or grand totals. Form Footers appear at the bottom of the screen or, if printed, at the end of the last page. Like Form Headers, Form Footers do not display in Datasheet view.

Form Design view also automatically displays three toolbars: Form Design, Formatting, and Toolbox. The **Form Design toolbar** contains the standard buttons as well as buttons that are specific to the Form Design view window, identified below.

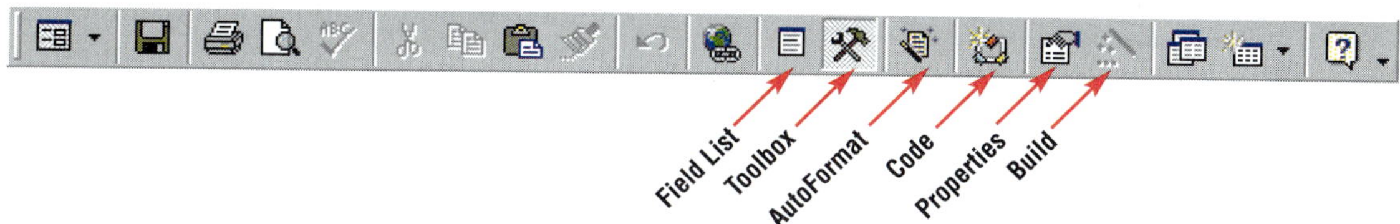

The **Formatting toolbar** contains buttons (identified below) that allow you to make text enhancements.

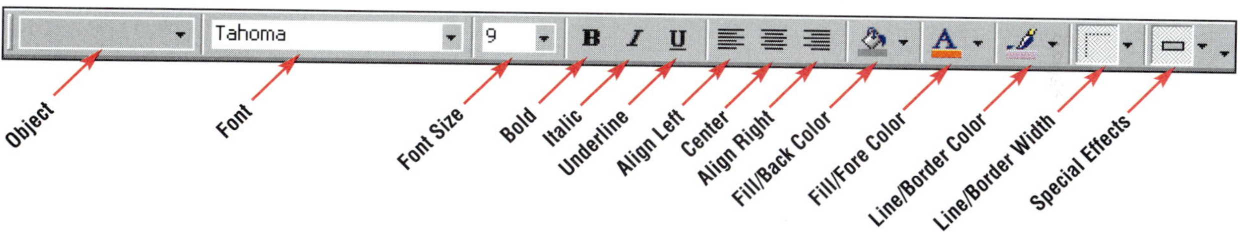

If the Toolbox is not displayed, click on the Form Design toolbar.

The **Toolbox toolbar** contains buttons (identified below) that are used to add and modify controls.

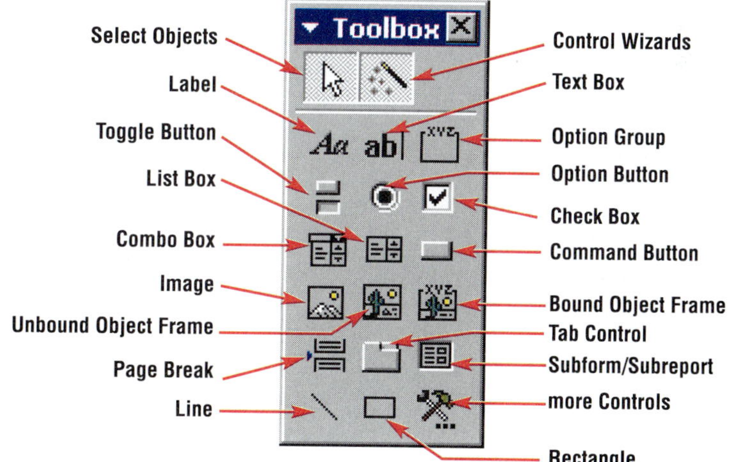

In addition, the Field List may be displayed. It displays a list of all the fields in the record source and can be used to add other fields to the form. The Field List button is used to open and close this list. Since all the fields are already displayed on the form, you can close this list box if it is open.

2 ■ Click 🗏 **Field List to close the Field List dialog box if it is open.**

Refer to Concept 6: Controls in Tutorial 3 to review this feature.

The first design change you want to make is to rearrange the fields on the form by moving the form controls. Many of the controls on the form are compound controls where the label control is displayed on the left and the text control is on the right in each set of controls. When you select a label control, its associated text control is also selected and the two controls will act as one when manipulated.

You want to separate the form fields into two sections: personal data and company data. There is not a lot of room to maneuver on this form, so you are going to move the company data fields out of the way so you can work on the top part of the form, the personal data area, first.

3 ■ **Select and move the** Employee ID, Hire Date, Location, Job Title, **and** Pay Rate **controls to three lines at the bottom right corner of the form (see Figure 5–5).**

Reminder: Hold down ⇧Shift while selecting controls to select multiple controls.

The mouse pointer must be 🖐 in order to move controls.

The form will expand in size as you drag beyond its current edge.

■ **Move the** Social Security Number **control below the Birth Date control.**

■ **Deselect the controls by clicking any blank area of the form.**

Your screen should be similar to Figure 5–5.

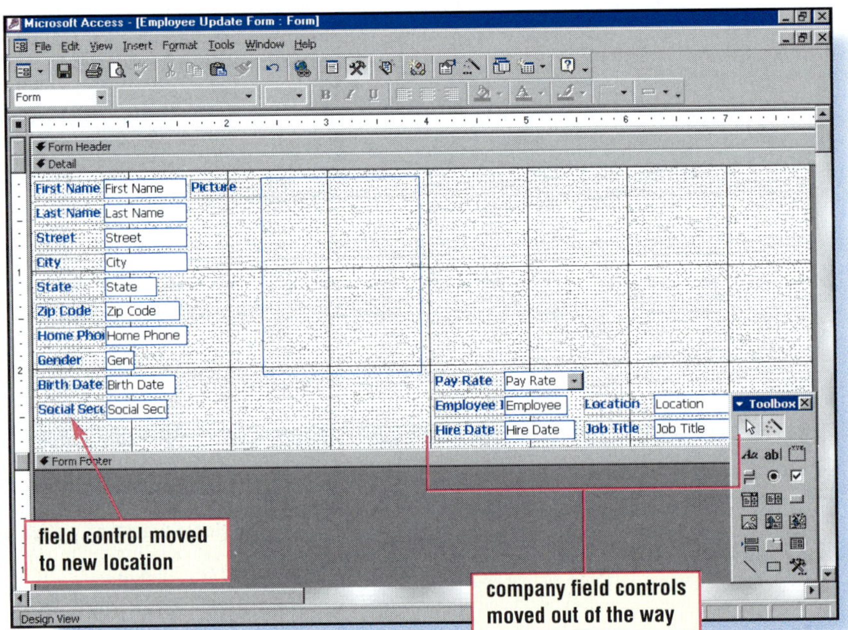

Figure 5–5

You now have some room at the top of the form to start arranging the personal data fields. On the first line of the form, you decide you want the employee's first and last name and their picture. You also decide that, because it will be obvious what the photo is, you don't really need the Picture label, so you'll remove it before moving the picture box.

4

- **Select the** Picture label control **(not the text control, which in this case is the picture box).**

- **Press** `Delete`**.**

- **Select the** picture box **by clicking anywhere on its outside border.**

- **Move the picture box to the 5-inch mark on the horizontal ruler and reduce the size of the box as shown in Figure 5–6.**

- **Select the** Last Name **text and label controls and move them to the right of the** First Name **controls, as shown in Figure 5–6.**

Your screen should be similar to Figure 5–6.

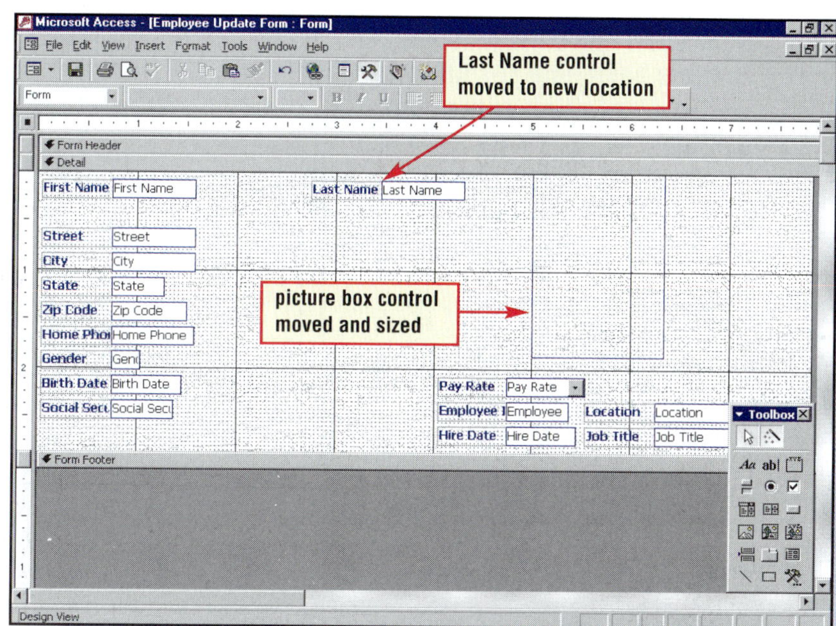

Figure 5–6

You're done with the first row of the form, and you're ready to move the rest of the controls up that you want in the personal data section.

5

- **Select and move the following controls under the First and Last Name controls to create two columns:**

Street	City
State	Zip Code
Home Phone	Gender
Birth Date	Social Security Number

Your screen should be similar to Figure 5–7.

Do not be concerned if your controls are not evenly aligned with the left edge of the form or on the lines. You'll learn how to adjust the alignment and spacing later.

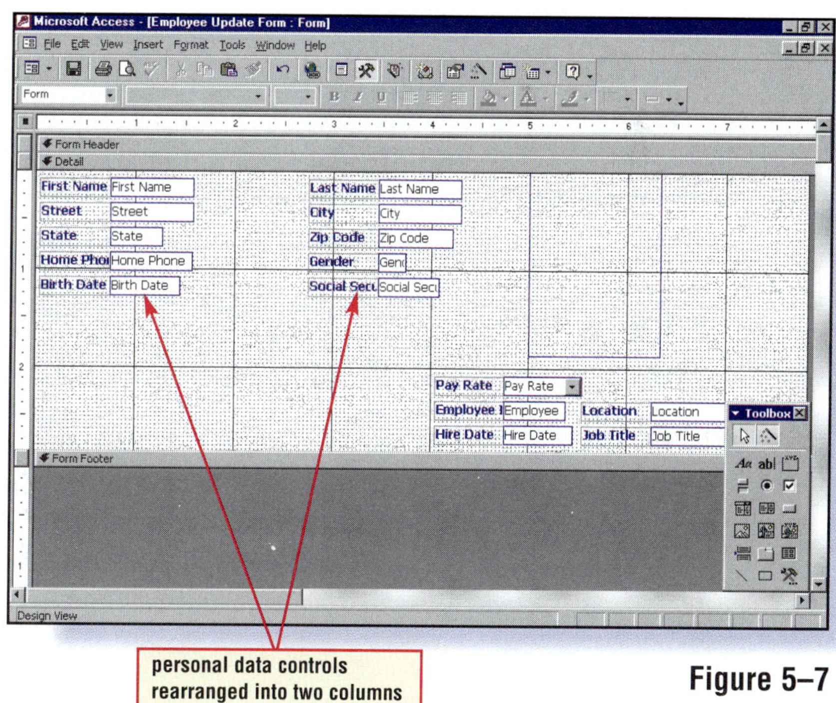

Figure 5–7

Next, you'll rearrange the fields you want to appear at the bottom of the form, in the company data section.

6 ■ **Select and move the following controls beginning slightly below the 2-inch position on the vertical ruler:**

Employee ID	Job Title
Hire Date	Pay Rate
Location	

Your screen should be similar to Figure 5–8.

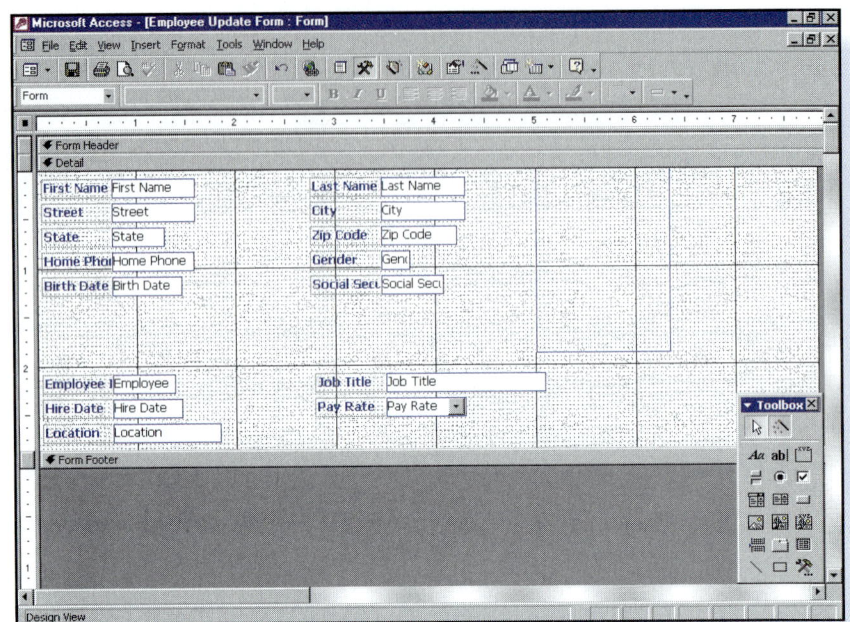

Figure 5–8

Now that you have the controls grouped the way you want, you need to align them and make sure the space between the controls in each group is even.

Aligning Controls

Additional Information

If a control is selected in a group that you do not want selected, you can deselect individual controls by holding down ⇧Shift and clicking on the control.

With all the moving around you've done with the form controls, they are probably not aligned exactly even anymore. Rather than selecting each control individually and moving it, you can select several controls at the same time and align them so they are evenly spaced or in line one below the other. Another way to select a group of adjacent controls is to drag a selection box around the controls. To select the controls using this method, point to a blank area above the first control and drag until the box surrounds the controls you want to select. When you release the mouse button, all the controls inside the box will be selected.

1 **Point to a blank area above the First Name control, click and drag until a box surrounds all the controls on the left side of the form, and then release the mouse button.**

The First Name, Street, State, Home Phone, Birth Date, Employee ID, Hire Date, and Location controls should all be selected.

Choose Format/Align/Left.

When aligning controls, select only controls that are in the same row or column.

Select the controls in the second column of the form (excluding the picture box) and left-align them.

Your screen should be similar to Figure 5–9.

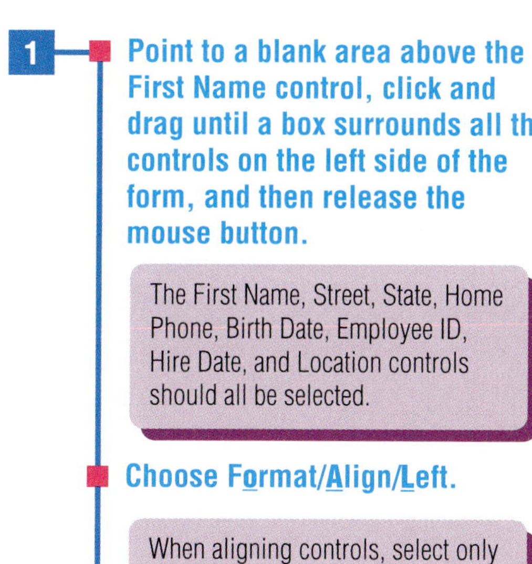

selected fields aligned evenly with left edge of leftmost control

Figure 5–9

The controls in the selected group all shifted to the left and are aligned with the control that was farthest left in the selection.

You now want to adjust the spacing between all the controls in the upper section of the form so that there is an even amount of vertical space between each control. This vertical spacing can be adjusted between any group of three or more selected controls.

When spacing compound controls with attached labels, select the controls, not the labels.

2 ■ **Select** all the controls in the first two columns in the upper part of the form (excluding the picture box).

The First Name, Last Name, Street, City, State, Zip Code, Home Phone, Gender, Birth Date, and Social Security Number controls should all be selected.

■ Choose **F**ormat/**V**ertical Spacing/Make **E**qual.

■ In a similar manner, make the vertical spacing between the three controls in the lower left column of the form equal.

■ Adjust the spacing of the two controls in the lower right column manually.

■ Deselect the controls.

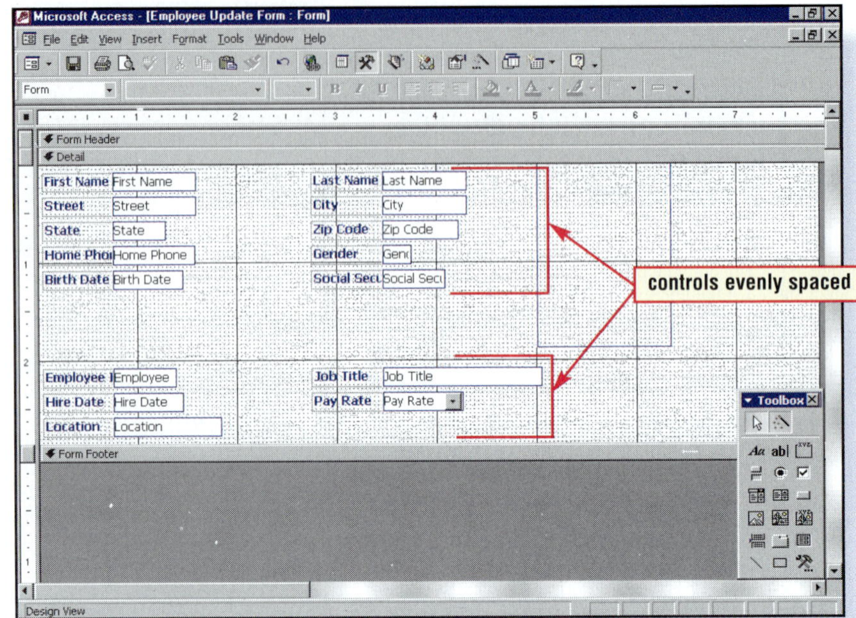

Figure 5–10

Your screen should be similar to Figure 5–10.

The vertical space between controls is adjusted to make the vertical spacing between the selected controls equal. The top and bottom controls do not change locations; only the middle controls in the selection are adjusted to equalize the spacing.

Adding Text to a Form

Next you will add a label control in the form header to display the form title. In addition, you want to add two subheads within the form to identify the personal data and company data areas. The Toolbox buttons let you add text, arrows, boxes, and other design elements to a form. To add the control to the form header, you first need to add a space in the Form Header area.

1

- Point to the top of the Detail section bar.

- When the mouse pointer is a ✛, drag the Detail section bar down approximately 1/2-inch on the vertical ruler.

Your screen should be similar to Figure 5–11.

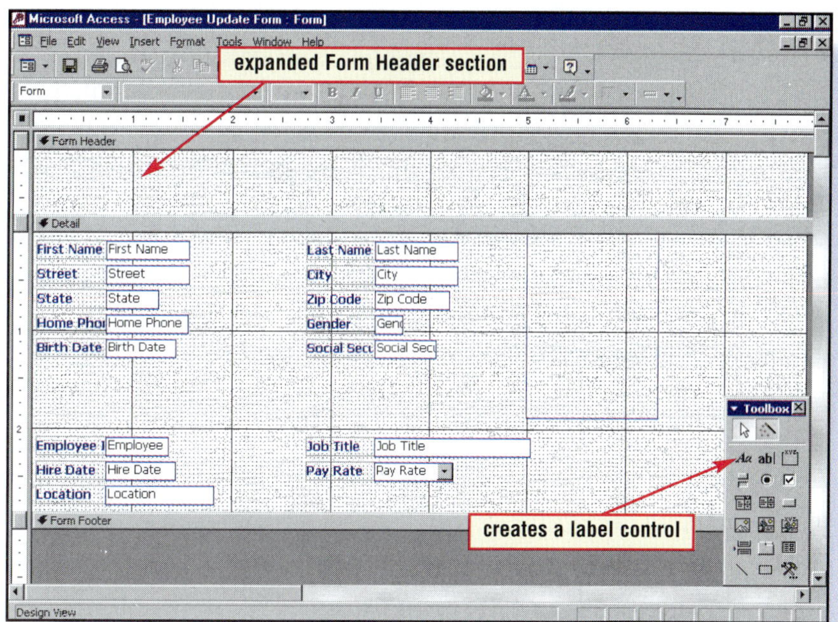

Figure 5–11

The Aa Label on the Toolbox is used to add a label control to a form. The mouse pointer changes to $^+$A when this feature is in use. You indicate where you want the control to appear by clicking on the location in the window. Then an insertion point is displayed indicating that you can begin typing the descriptive label.

2

- Click Aa Label on the Toolbox.

- Click in the Form Header area.

- Type **Lifestyle Fitness Club Employee Record**.

- Press ⏎Enter.

Your screen should be similar to Figure 5–12.

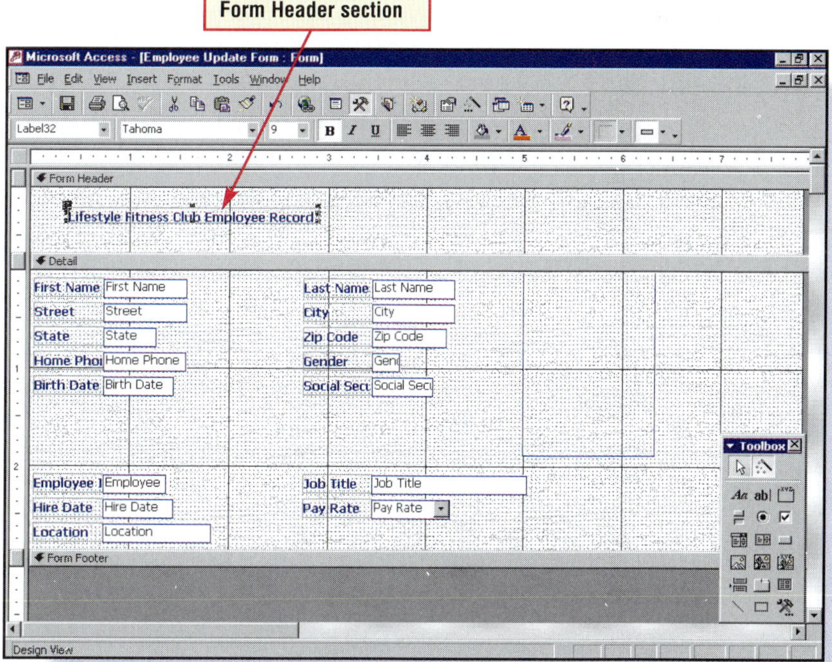

Figure 5–12

The text entry feature is turned off. The form title appears in a label control box and can be sized and moved like any other control. Now you will add two more label controls for the subheads in the Detail section.

3 ■ **Select** all the controls in the top section of the Detail area except the picture box control **and move** the controls **down so that the top row begins at the half-inch mark on the vertical ruler.**

■ **Select** the five controls in the lower section **and move them down to begin at the 2 1/2-inch mark on the vertical ruler.**

■ **Add a label control containing the text Personal Data: in the space above the First Name control in the Detail section.**

■ **In a similar manner, enter the subhead Company Data: in the space above the Employee ID control.**

■ **Align the two subhead controls along the left edge.**

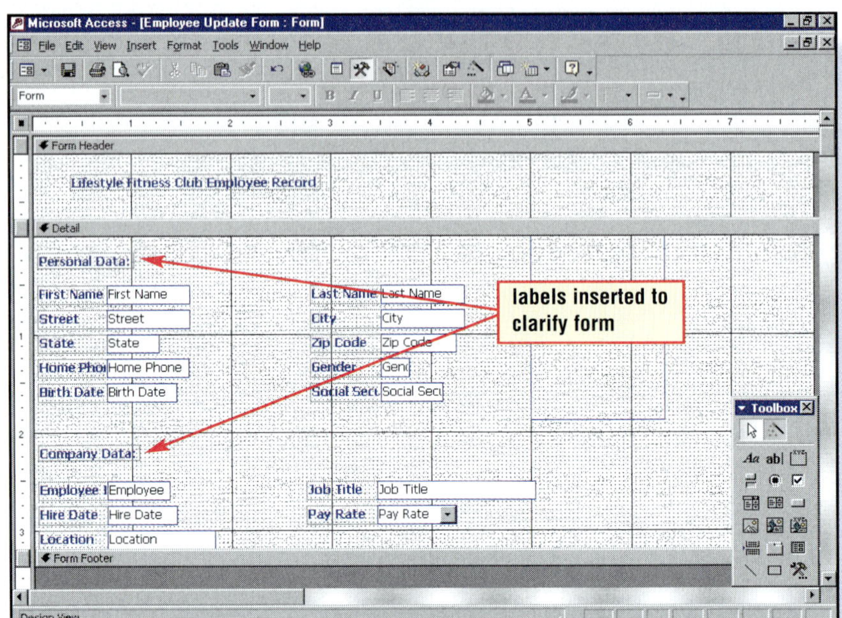

Figure 5–13

Your screen should be similar to Figure 5–13.

The two sections of the form are clearly identified.

Changing Fonts

Although the form contains everything you want on it now, all the text looks the same. To make the form more attractive, you decide to change some of the font settings.

Concept  Fonts

Fonts consist of three elements—typeface, size, and style—that can be applied to characters to improve their appearance. A **typeface** is the design and shape of characters. Two common typefaces are Times New Roman and Courier. **Type size** refers to the size of the printed characters and is commonly measured in **points**. A 72-point character is I-inch tall. The most common type sizes for text are 10 and 12 points.

   Type style refers to the special attributes you assign to characters, such as bold or italic. You can also add special effects such as underlines and color to the characters.

   Several common fonts in different sizes and styles are shown in the table below.

Font Name	Font Size	Font Style
Arial	This is 12 pt. This is 18 pt.	**Bold 18 pt.**
Courier New	This is 12 pt. This is 18 pt.	**Bold 18 pt**
Times New Roman	This is 12 pt. This is 18 pt.	**Bold 18 pt.**

Although you must apply font changes to entire controls rather than changing individual characters or words, you can apply multiple font changes to a table, form, or report by selecting and changing fonts for individual controls. You should be careful, however, not to combine too many different fonts and colors or to use fancy fonts that might make it difficult to read the screen or are distracting to use for long periods of time.

   The Formatting toolbar buttons are used to make text enhancements, such as changing the font type, font size, font style, or font color.

The first text enhancement you want to make is to increase the font size of the text controls in the Detail section of the form. Larger fonts make it easier to read the data that is displayed in the form.

1 **Select** all of the text controls in the Detail section.

Notice that the Font Size box currently displays "9" as the point size of all text in the selected controls.

Click `9 ▼` **Font Size** and select 10 from the drop-down list.

The menu equivalent is **F**ormat/**F**ont/**S**ize

Your screen should be similar to Figure 5–14.

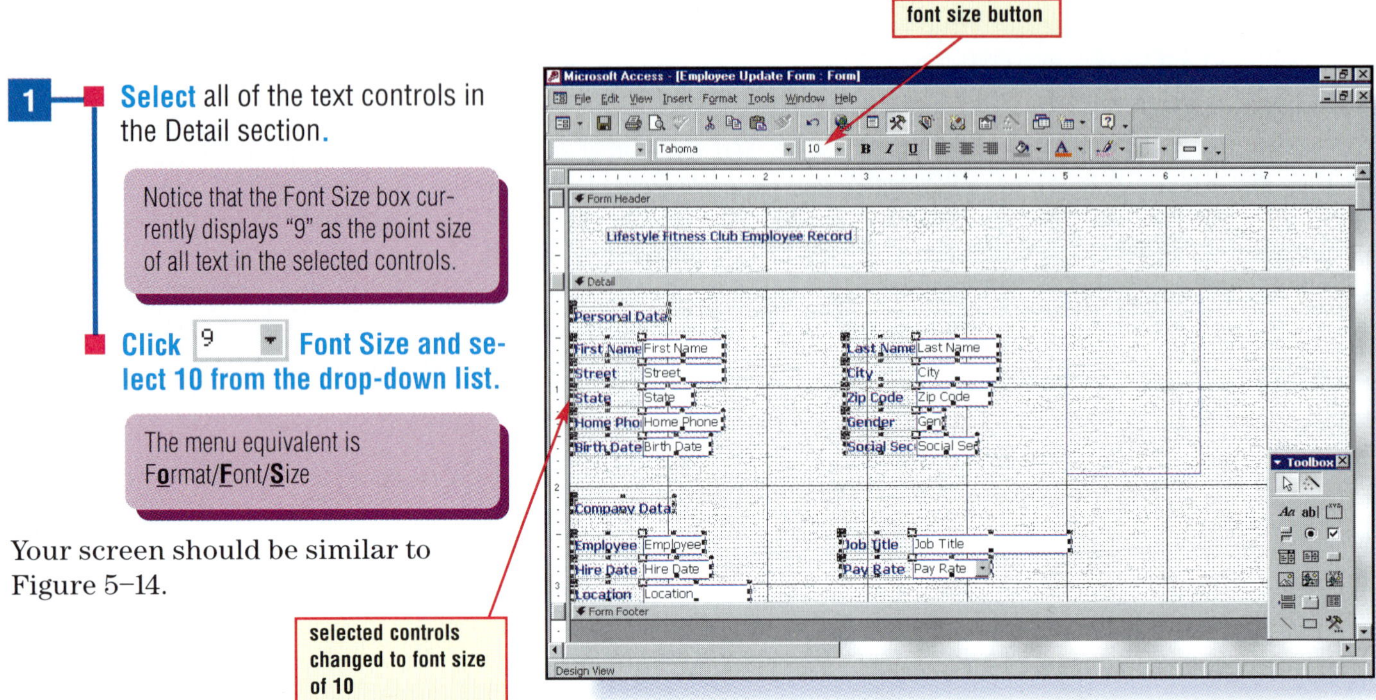

Figure 5–14

The point size of all text in the selected text controls changes to 10 points and is now much easier to read. Next you want to make the form title a larger font size.

2 **Select** the label control in Form Header section **and change the font size to 20.**

Your screen should be similar to Figure 5–15.

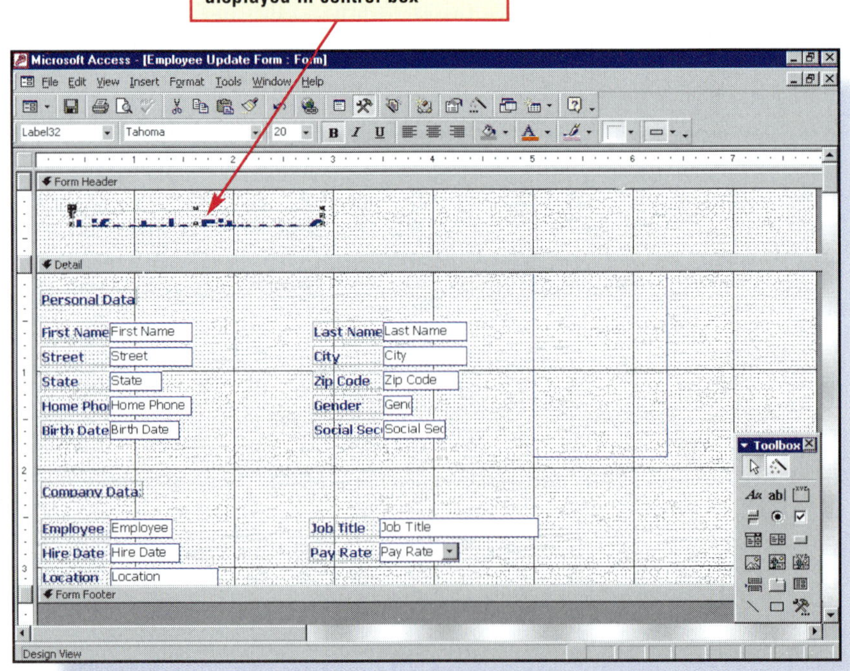

Figure 5–15

Now the title is too large to be fully displayed in the control box. You can size the control to fully display the label by dragging on the sizing handles, or you can allow Access to automatically size the control to fit the contents. To automatically resize the control,

3 Choose F**o**rmat/**S**ize/To **F**it.

Move the label control **to the location shown in Figure 5–16.**

Your screen should be similar to Figure 5–16.

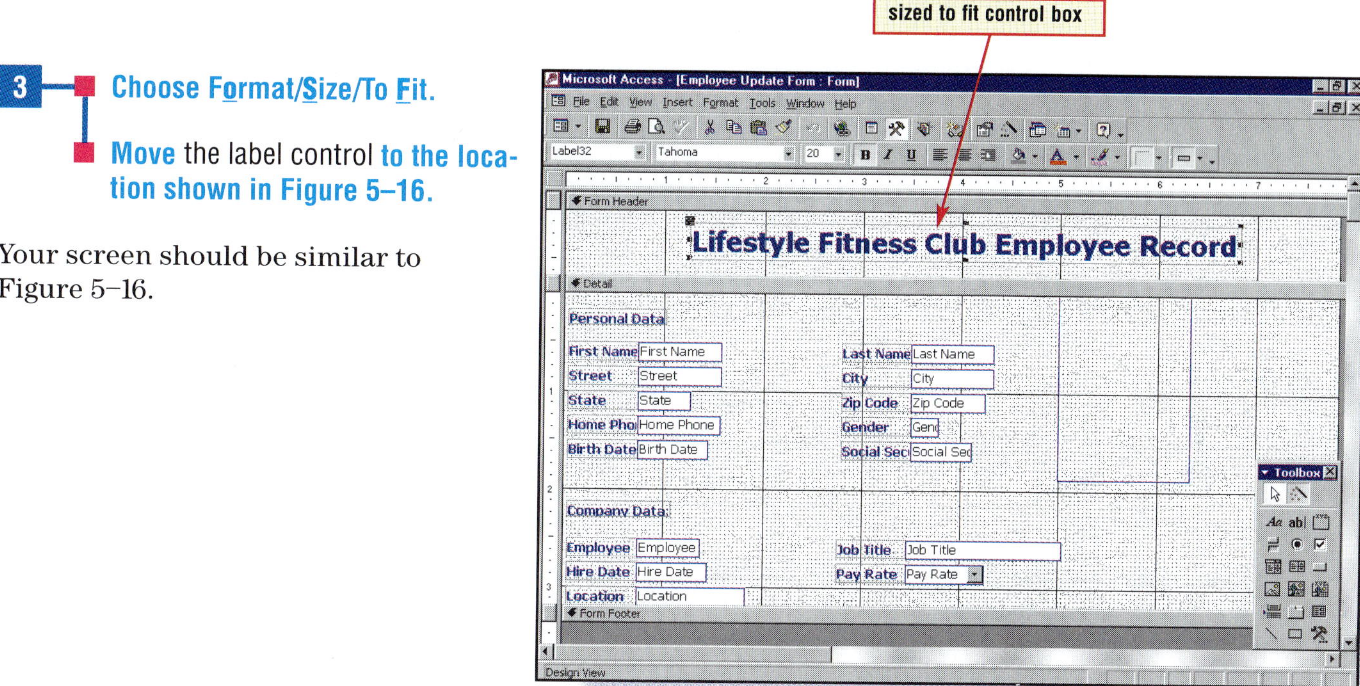

Figure 5–16

You also want to size the text controls of the subheads to make them stand out from the rest of the text.

4 **Select the** Personal Data and Company Data label controls **and change the font size to 14.**

Size the labels to fit and position them appropriately above the other controls.

Your screen should be similar to Figure 5–17.

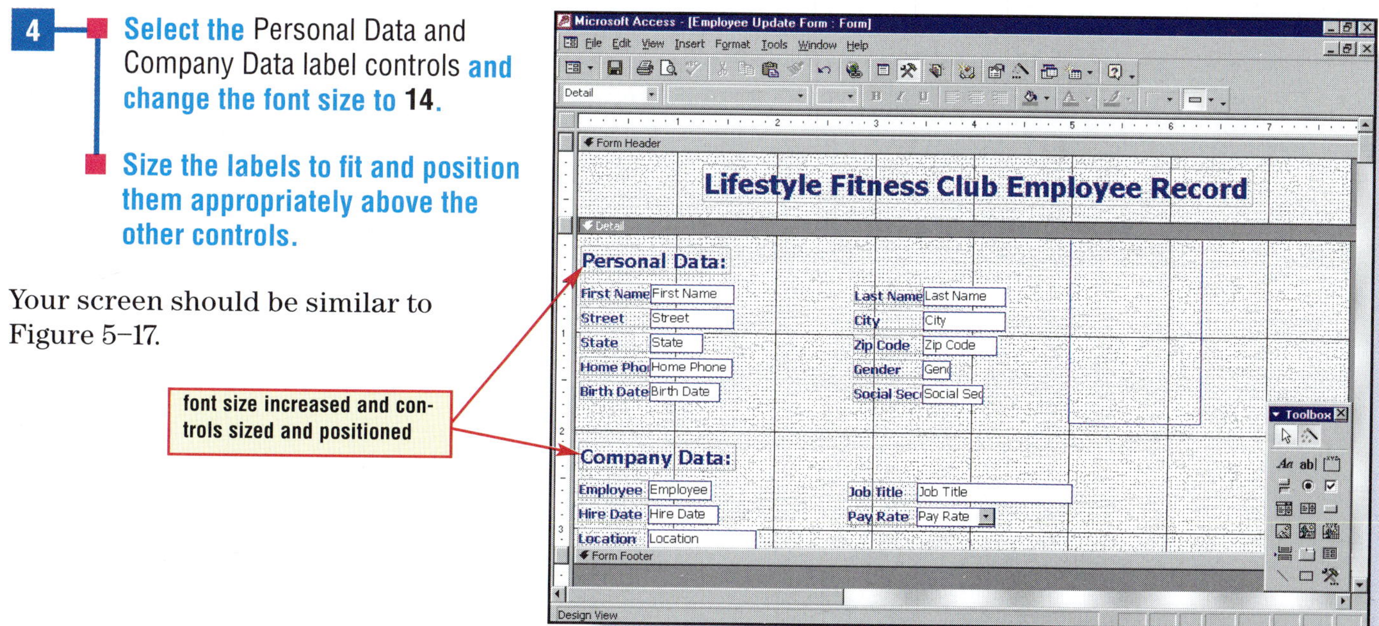

Figure 5–17

Adding Text Color

The final text enhancement you want to make to your form is to add some color. You can make controls more noticeable by adding color to their background, text, or borders. In addition, you can use special effects such as shadows to enhance the control border. You will make the text in the form header label red and add a shadow box to the control.

1

- Select the label control in the Form Header.

- Click **A** Font/Fore Color and select ■ Red from the color palette.

- Click ▭ Special Effects and select ▭ Shadowed from the drop-down list.

- Add the same color and shadow effect to the form subheads.

You can quickly apply the last used font color and shadow effect selection simply by clicking the button without opening the drop-down menu.

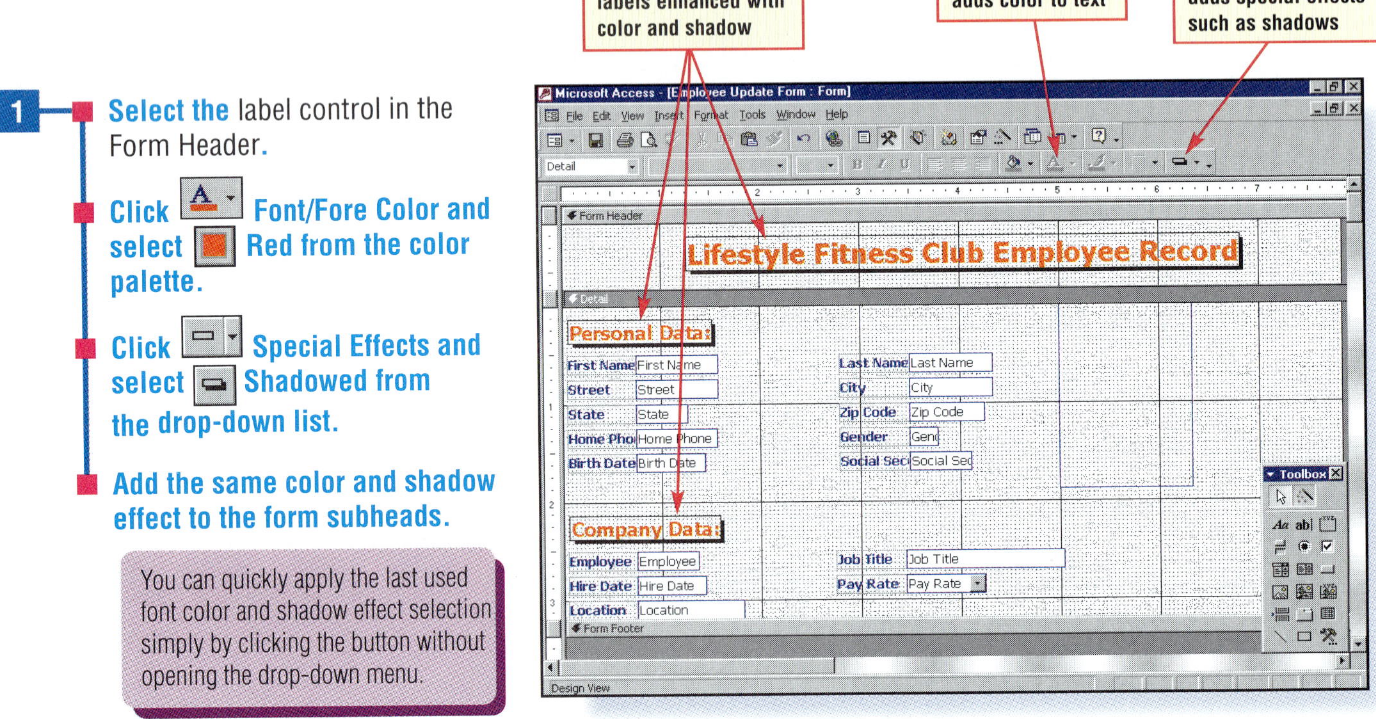

Figure 5–18

Your screen should be similar to Figure 5–18.

The color and shadow settings have been applied to the form title. To see how the form looks onscreen, you will switch back to Form view.

The menu equivalent is **V**iew/**F**orm View.

Your screen should be similar to Figure 5–19.

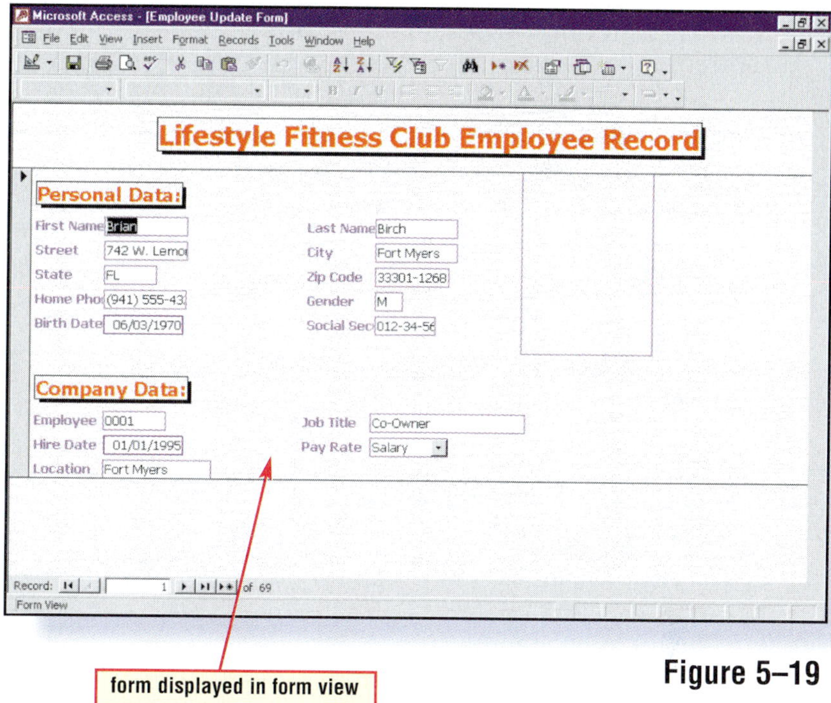

form displayed in form view

Figure 5–19

The layout and design changes greatly enhance the appearance of the form. However, now you can also see that the Street and Home Phone text box controls are not wide enough to display the data in the fields. You also notice that some of the text box controls are separated by too much space from the label controls whereas others overlap the text box control.

Resizing Controls

After viewing several records in your form, you realize that some of the fields need to be resized in order to display all the data and that there are some spacing problems between the labels and the data. To correct these problems, you will return to Form Design view and increase the size of some of the label controls and adjust the spacing between compound controls.

1

- **Switch back to Form Design view.**

- **Increase the size of the** Street, Home Phone, **and** Location **text box controls.**

- **Select** the State label box control **and reduce the size of the label box to fit the text.**

- **Point to the move handle of the State text box control.**

- **When the mouse pointer is a** 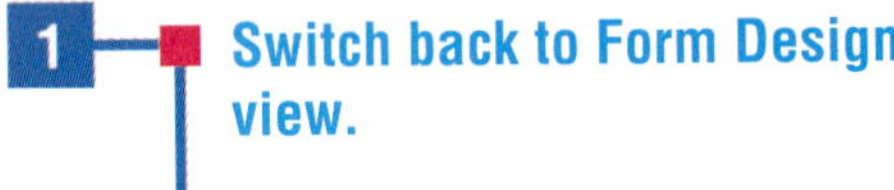**, drag the control closer to the State label control.**

Your screen should be similar to Figure 5–20.

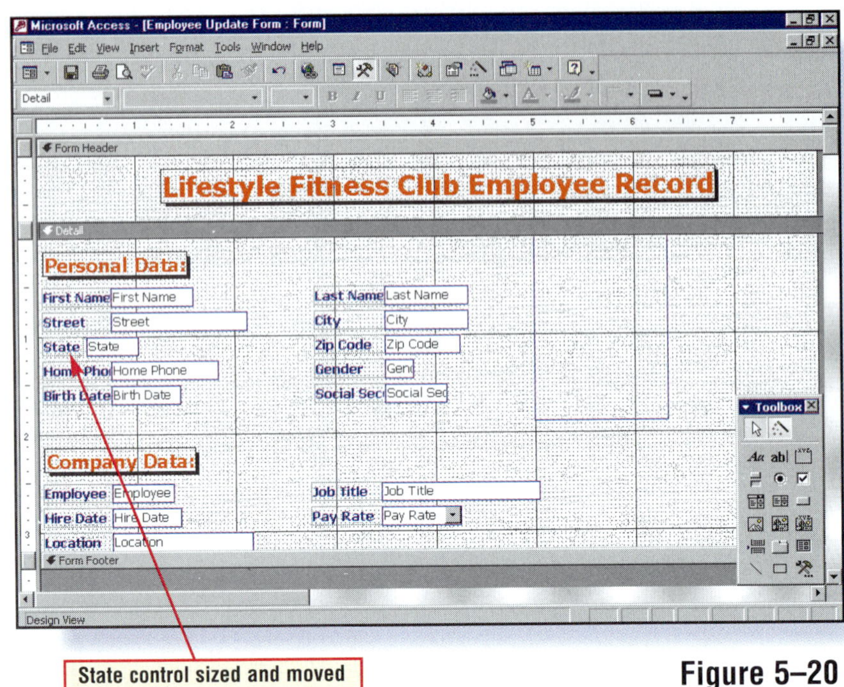

Figure 5–20

2

- **In a similar manner, adjust the size and spacing of all other controls as needed except the Social Security Number control.**

Your screen should be similar to Figure 5–21.

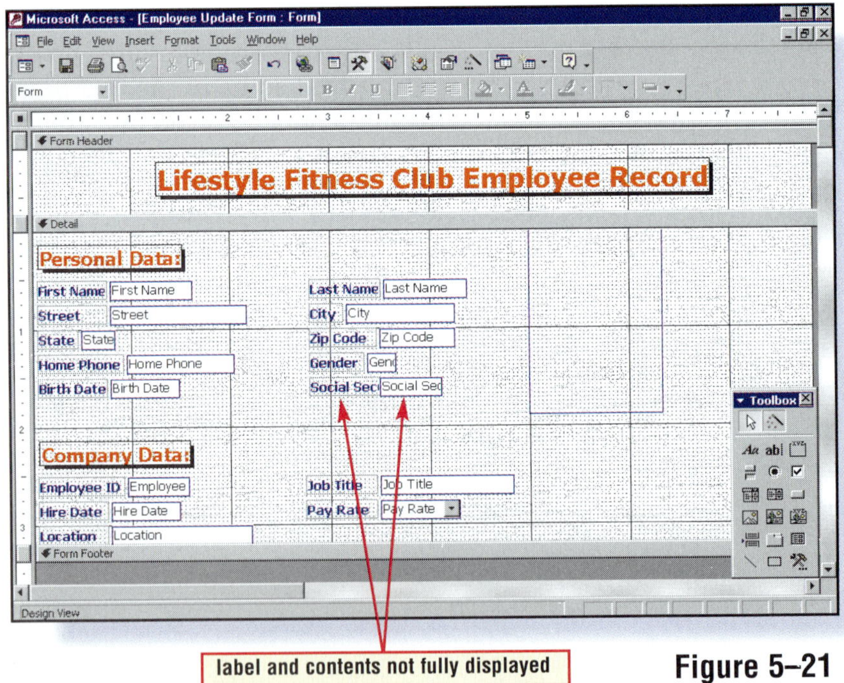

Figure 5–21

The Social Security Number field does not show all the entered data and the field label does not fully display either. Rather than having to extend both the label and the field controls, you decide to change the label to SSN.

3 — **Double-click the** Social Security Number **label control.**

> The menu equivalent is **V**iew/**P**roperties and the toolbar short cut is [icon].

Your screen should be similar to Figure 5–22.

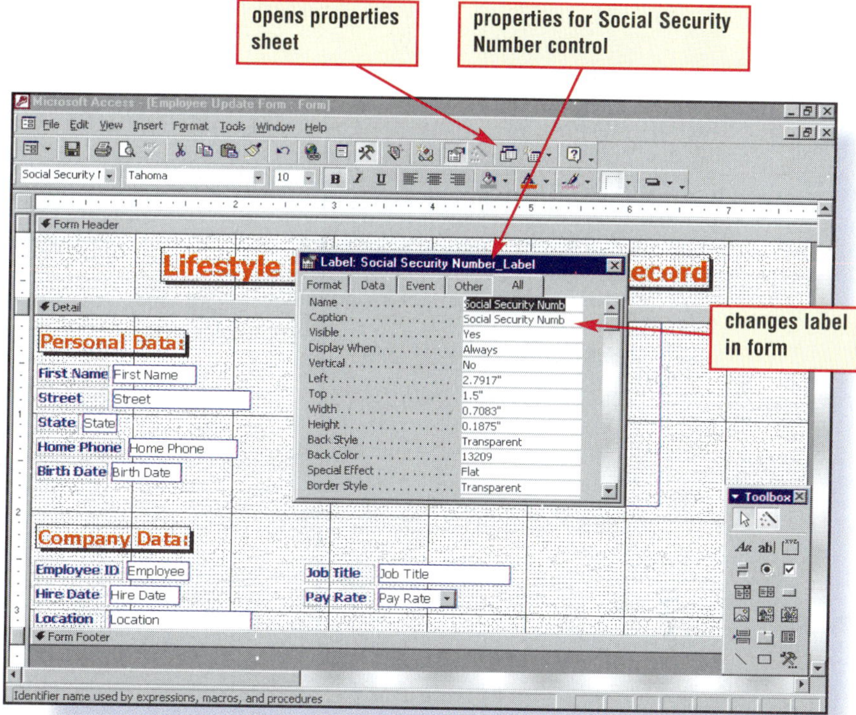

Figure 5–22

The Label properties sheet window enables you to change the way a label is displayed on the screen. The Name is the actual field name, which is the way the field is identified in all related tables. You do not want to change this. You do, however, want to change the Caption, or the way the field is labeled on the form.

4 — **Replace the current entry, Social Security Number, in the Caption field with SSN.**

■ **Close the Label properties sheet.**

■ **Appropriately size and adjust the spacing between the text box and label controls of the Social Security Number control.**

Your screen should be similar to Figure 5–23.

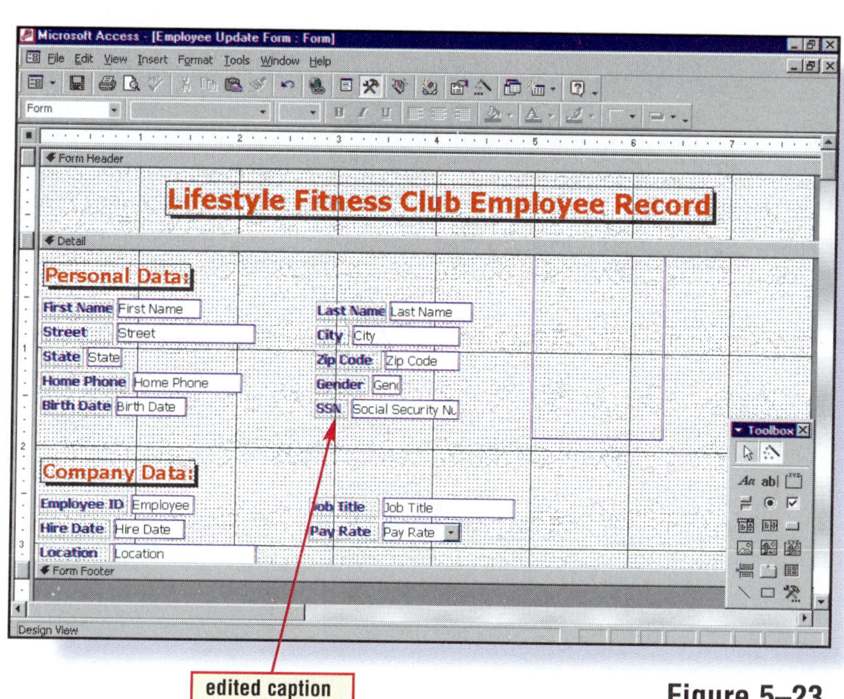

Figure 5–23

You've resized all the controls and are ready to see how your form looks now.

5 ■ **Return to Form view.**

Your screen should be similar to Figure 5–24.

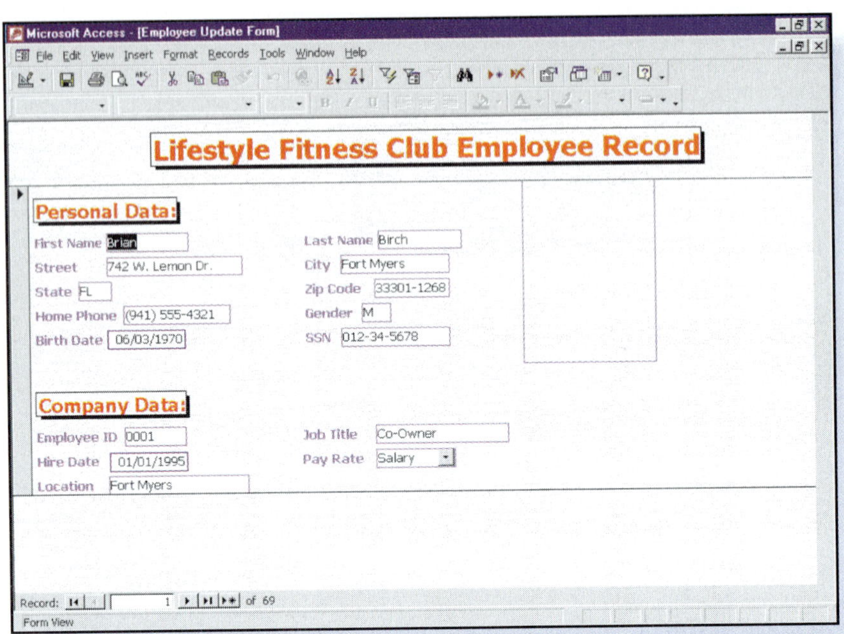

Figure 5–24

Creating a Subform

The appearance of the form is much improved. However, as you are thinking about the use of the form, you realize that the form does not include the Hours Worked table data. You will add this table as a subform to the form.

Concept ❷ **Subform**

A **subform** is a form that is embedded in another form. The primary form is called the **main form**, and the form/subform combination is also referred to as a **hierarchical form**, a **master/detail form**, or a **parent/child form**.

Subforms can be used to show data from tables or queries that have a **one-to-many relationship**. For example, the main form could show the sales representative data (the "one" side of the relationship) and the subform could show all the products the sales representative is responsible for selling (the "many" side of the relationship).

A main form can have multiple subforms. You can also embed a subform within another subform. This means you can have a subform within a main form, and you can have another subform within that subform, and so on, up to 10 levels deep. For example, you could have a main form that displays sales reps, a subform that displays products, another subform that displays product orders, and another subform that displays order details.

When creating a subform, there must be a pre-existing relationship between the main form and subform. This relationship has already been established when you specified table relationships for the database. Therefore, you are ready to add the subform to the main form.

1 **Switch to Design view.**

Click   Subform/Subreport.

The mouse pointer is a   after selecting   to show that the program is ready to create the button.

Click in the detail section of the form below the picture box control to create a subform box object.

Your screen should be similar to Figure 5–25.

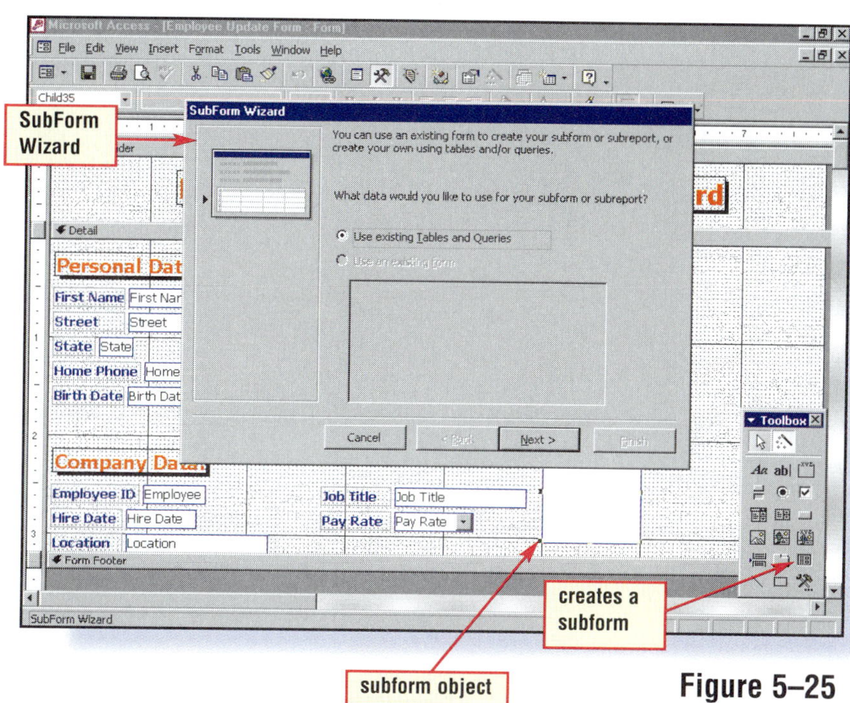

Figure 5–25

The first SubForm Wizard dialog box appears in which you specify the source of data for the subform. You will use an existing table.

2 **If necessary, select** Use existing Tables and Queries.

Click   Next > .

Your screen should be similar to Figure 5–26.

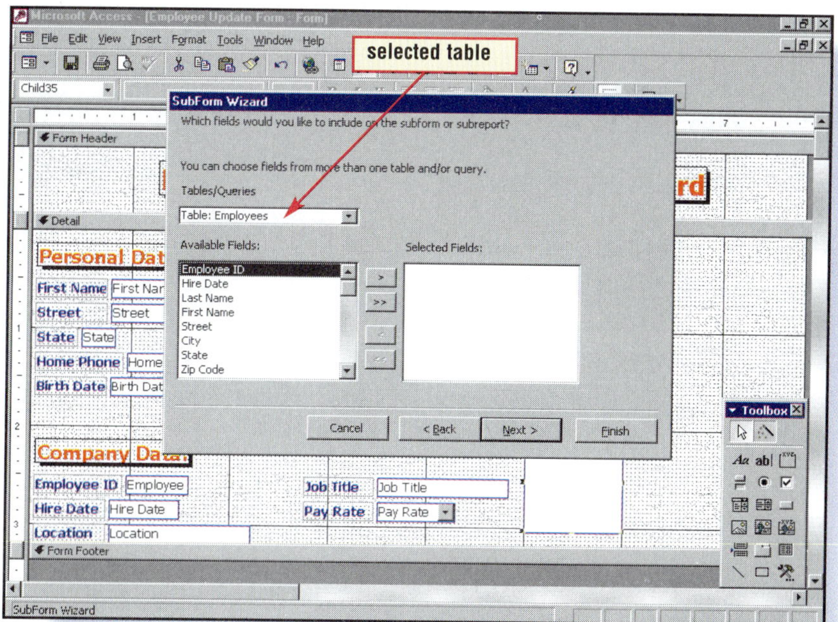

Figure 5–26

In the second wizard dialog box, you specify the table to use as the data source and the fields from the selected table to display in the form.

3   Select the Hours Worked **table from the** Tables/Queries **drop-down menu.**

   Add the Week Ending **and** Hours **fields to the selected fields list.**

   Click   Next > .

Your screen should be similar to Figure 5–27.

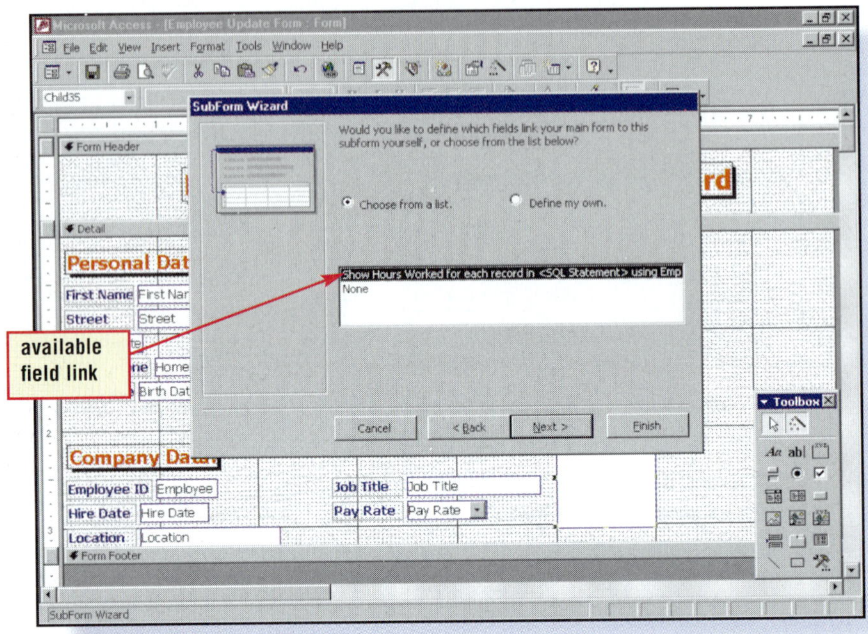

Figure 5–27

In the next wizard screen, you are asked to specify the field in the subform that will link it to the main form. The list box correctly suggests using the Employee ID field. To accept the suggestion,

4   Click   Next > .

The final wizard screen asks you to name the subform. To accept the default name and display the subform in the main form in Design view,

5   Click   Finish .

   Maximize the window.

Your screen should be similar to Figure 5–28.

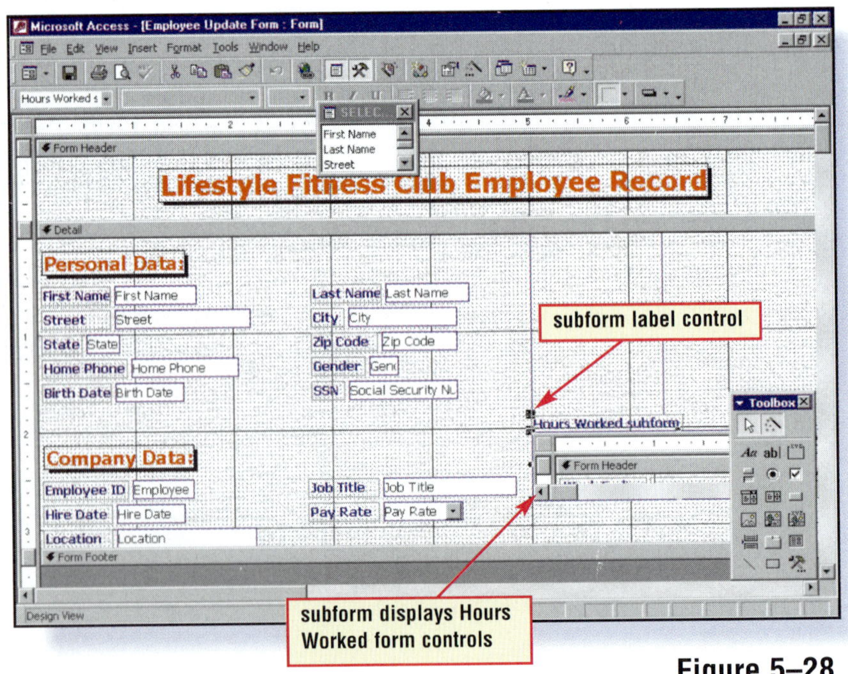

Figure 5–28

The subform displays the Hours Worked form controls.

6

- **If necessary, move the Toolbox up so that it does not cover the subform and close the Field List.**

- **Delete the subform label control.**

- **Expand the subform object until the Form Footer bar is visible.**

> Do not be concerned if you cover other controls you will size the subform again.

- **Reduce the size of the Hours label and text control.**

- **Switch to Form view.**

- **Using the scroll bar in the form window, scroll two records forward to see a record with hours in the subform.**

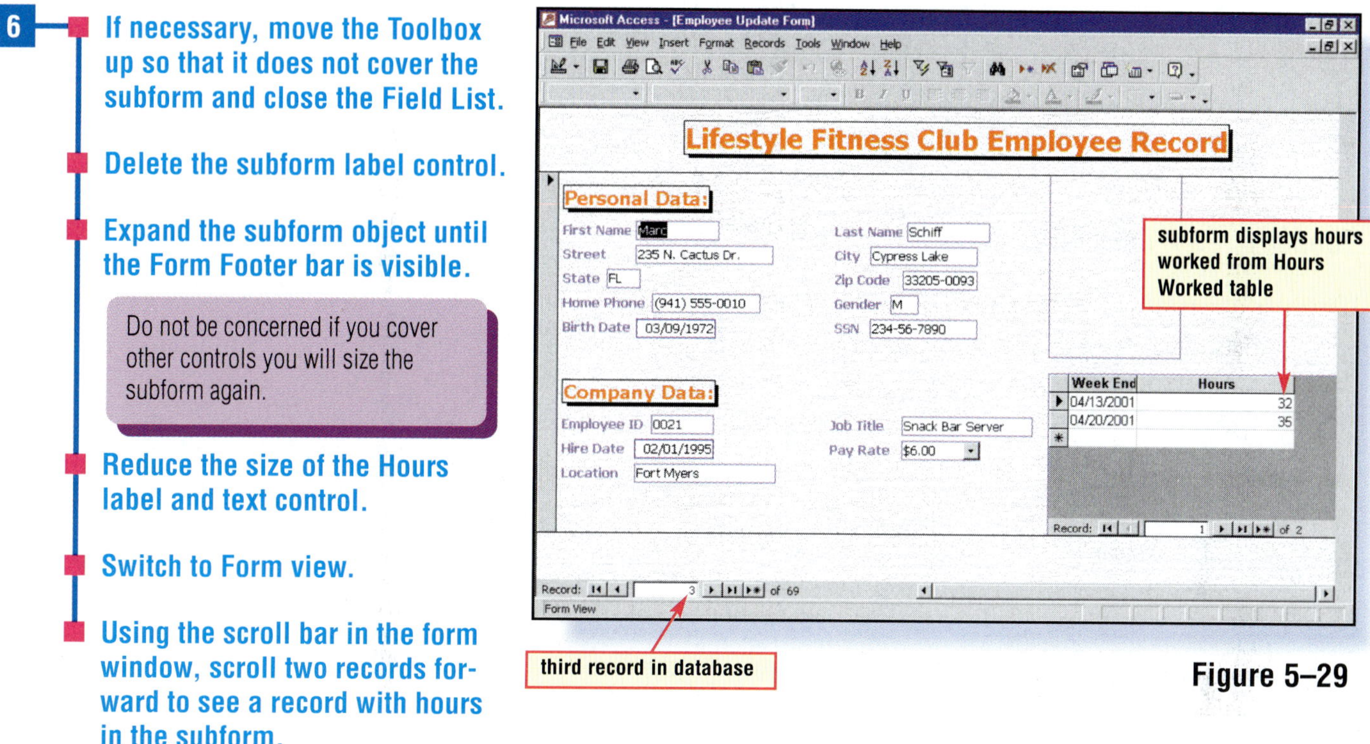

Figure 5–29

Your screen should be similar to Figure 5–29.

The first two employees' records did not display hours worked in the subform because they are paid on salary. The third record shows the hours worked for both weeks recorded in the table for that record.

7

- **Display your record in the form and enter last Friday's date in a new row of the Week Ending field and 20 in the Hours field.**

- **Just like in a standard table, drag the outside border of the Hours column to the left to decrease its width and best fit the Week Ending column.**

- **Save the form.**

> You do not need to go into Design view to make this kind of change. However, if you want to make any changes to the subform design, such as the width of the subform border, you must do this in Design view.

Creating a Calculated Control

Next, you want to add a control that will calculate the total hours worked for each record.

Concept  **3   Calculated Control**

A **calculated control** is used to display data that is calculated from a field in a table or query or from another control in the form. A calculated control is typically created from a text box, with the calculation entered in the text control. You can, however, create a calculated control from any type of control that has a ControlSource property.

A calculated-control expression should always begin with an equal sign (=). For example, a calculated control in an Employee Discount field would be =[Price]*.50 if the employees get a 50% discount off the merchandise selling price. The **identifier** is the element that refers to the value of a field, control, or property.

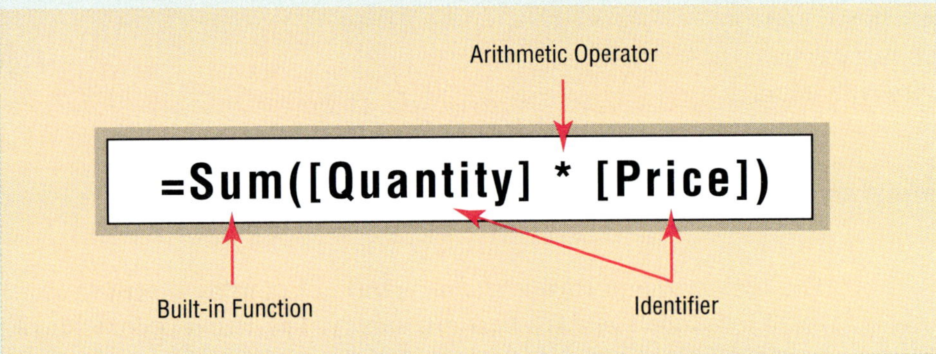

You can enter the expression yourself or you can have Access help you by using the Expression builder feature.

Refer to Concept 4: Validity Checks in Tutorial 2 to review expressions and Concept 4: Calculated Field in Tutorial 4.

You need to add the calculated control to the subform. Because it calculates a subtotal, it is entered in the form footer area of the subform.

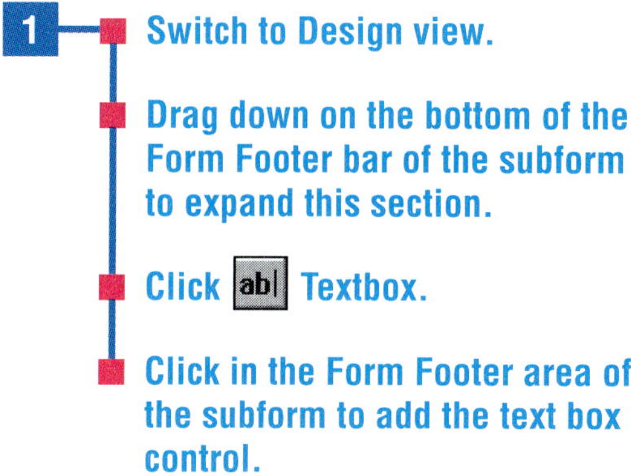

1

- Switch to Design view.

- Drag down on the bottom of the Form Footer bar of the subform to expand this section.

- Click **ab|** Textbox.

- Click in the Form Footer area of the subform to add the text box control.

Your screen should be similar to Figure 5–30.

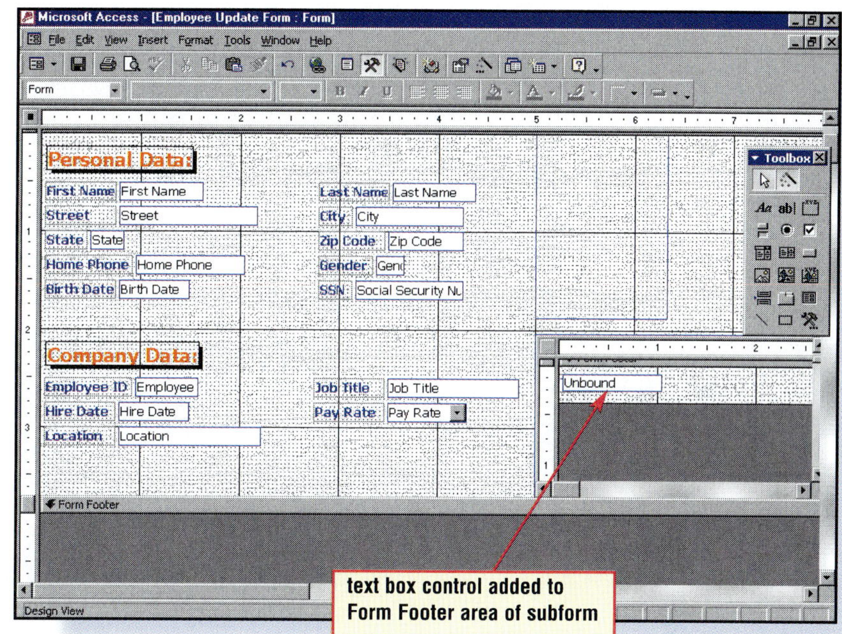

Figure 5–30

Changing Control Properties

Text and label controls for a new text box have been added to the form. Next you will rename the label control and enter the expression to perform the calculation in the text control.

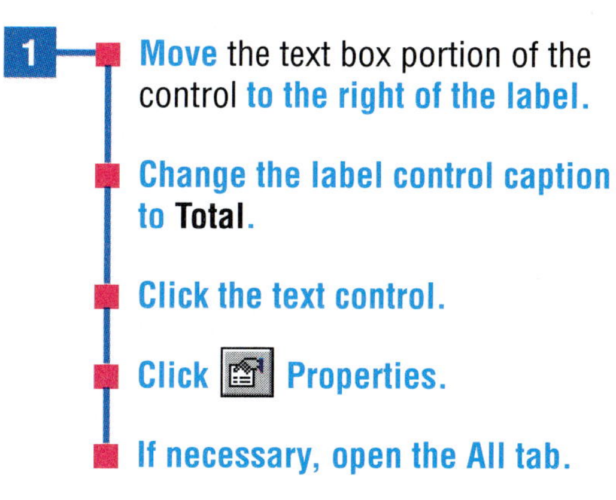

1

- **Move** the text box portion of the control **to the right of the label.**

- **Change the label control caption to Total.**

- **Click the text control.**

- **Click** Properties.

- **If necessary, open the All tab.**

Your screen should be similar to Figure 5–31.

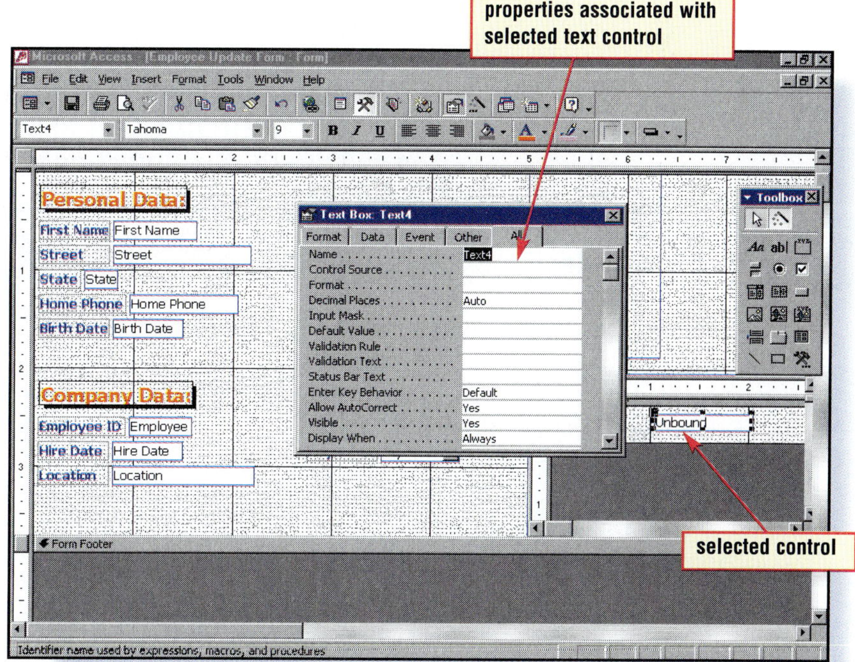

Figure 5–32

Each control has **property** settings that affect how the control looks and acts. The All tab of the Property sheet for the Text Box control lists the default property settings associated with the selected control. The Name, Text4, displayed in the Name text box is the default name assigned to the text control. Each text control is named Text followed by a number that identifies the order in which it was added to the form. This was the fourth text control added to the subform. In the Control Source text box, you enter the expression to perform the calculation. You will enter the expression using the Expression Builder.

2 Click in the Control Source text box and click [...] to open the Expression Builder.

Your screen should be similar to Figure 5-32.

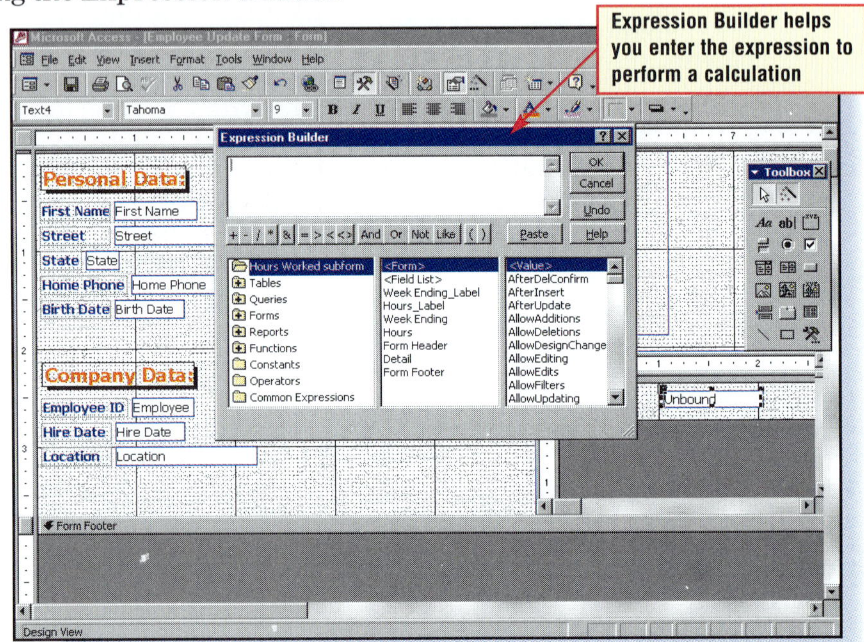

Figure 5-32

The Expression Builder helps you enter the expression by allowing you to select the type of function to use and the identifiers for the expression. You will use the Sum function to total the values in the Hours field.

3 Double-click  to expand the Functions folder.

Select Built-In Functions to open the folder.

Scroll the list of functions and double-click Sum.

Your screen should be similar to Figure 5-33.

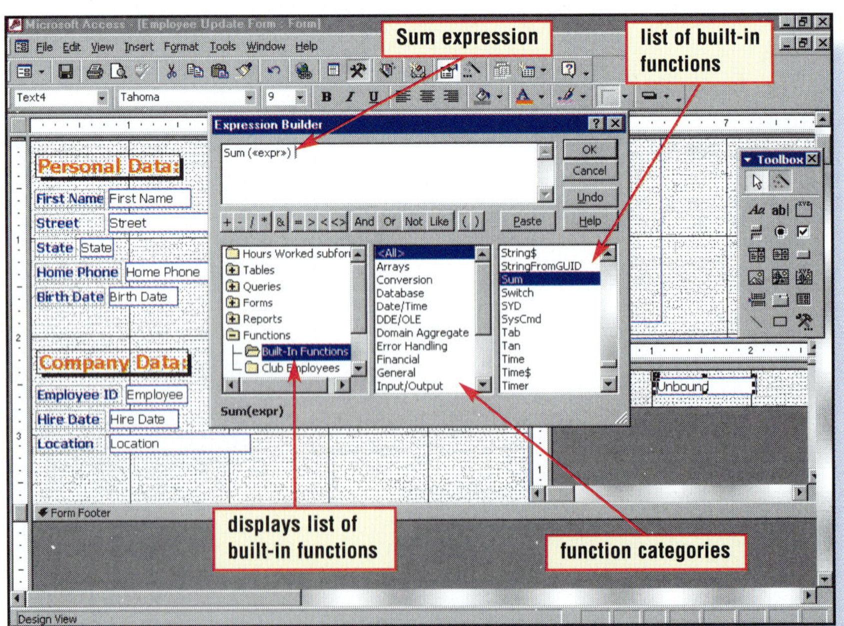

Figure 5-33

The identifier is always enclosed in parentheses after the function name.

The Expression box shows the selected function. Next you need to replace the text in the parentheses (<expr> the expression placeholder) with the identifier to use. In this case the identifier is the Hours field.

4 ■ **Select** <expr>.

■ **Open the Hours Worked subform folder.**

■ **Double-click Hours from the middle box.**

Your screen should be similar to Figure 5–34.

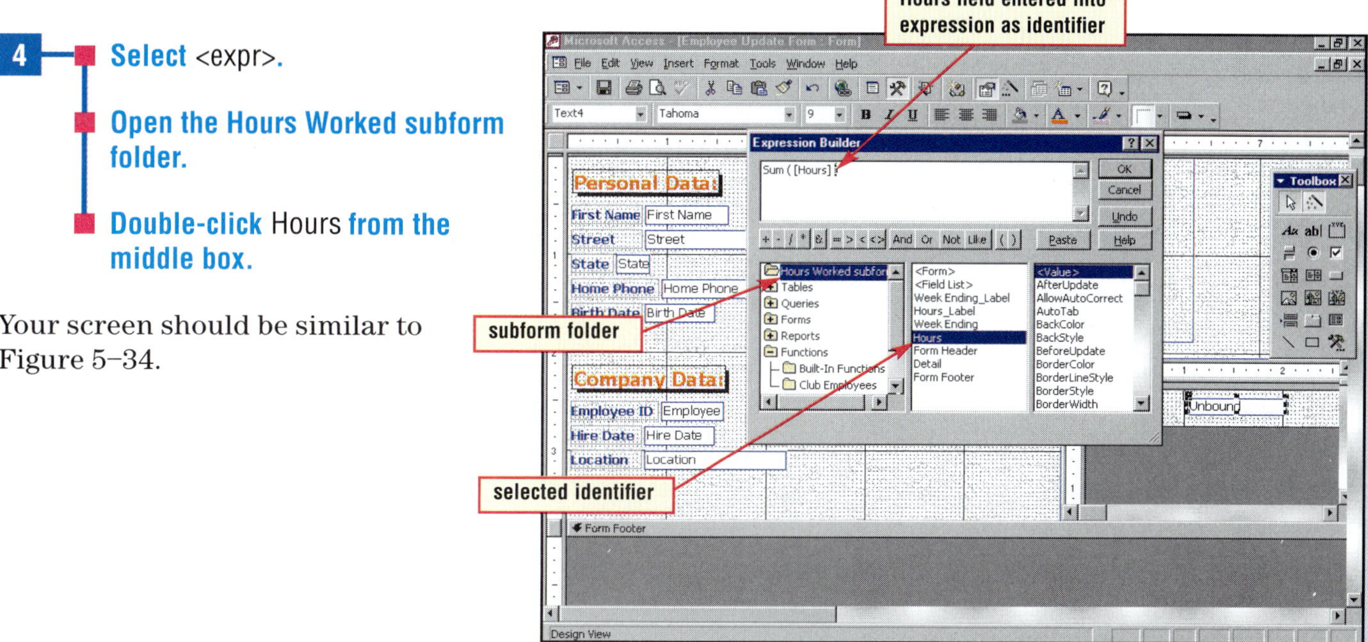

Figure 5–34

The expression box displays the selected identifier that will be used by the Sum function. To complete the expression,

5 ■ **Click**  OK .

■ **Close the Property sheet.**

Your screen should be similar to Figure 5–35.

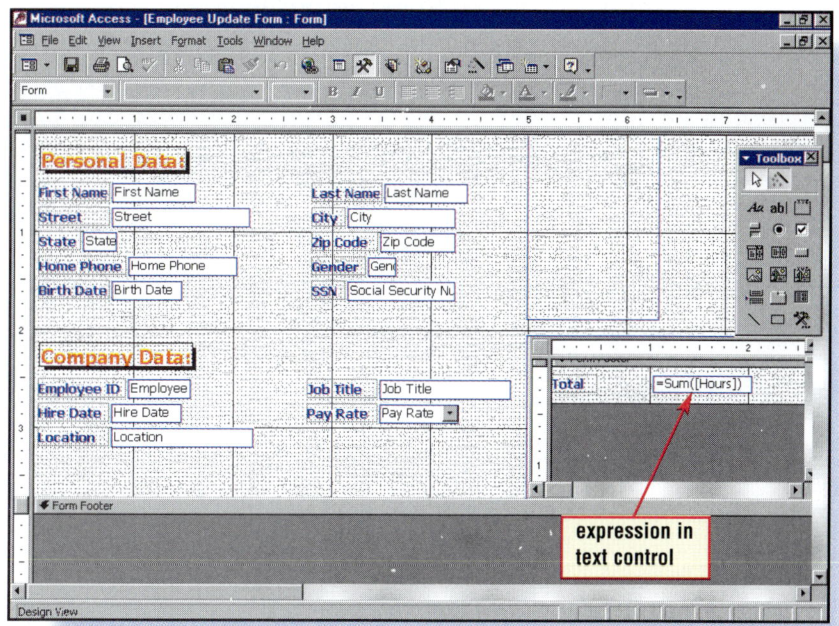

Figure 5–35

You could also have typed the expression directly in the text control box.

The text control displays the expression. Because the calculated control is entered in the subform, it will calculate the sum for the record information displayed in the subform only.

6 Reduce the size of the subform until it is just large enough to display the two label controls in the subform Form Header.

Switch to Form view.

Save the changes you have made to the form so far.

Additional Information

You must save the form after adding a new control so that the new controls will be available in the Expression Builder for selection.

Your screen should be similar to Figure 5–36

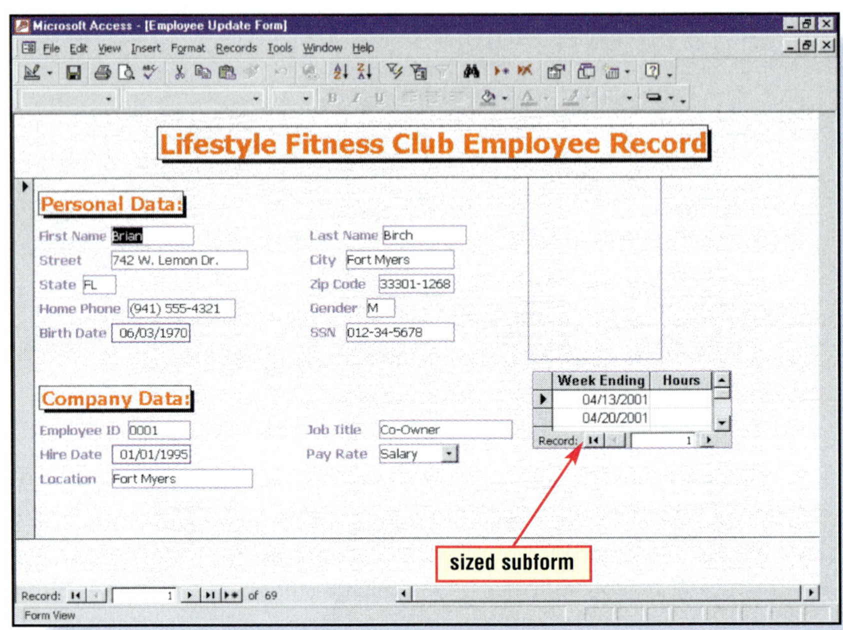

Figure 5–36

Next, to display the calculated value in the form, you need to add a second calculated control in the main form that references the calculated control in the subform.

7

- **Switch back to Design view.**

- **Click** abl **Textbox and click in the blank space under the Pay Rate field in the main form to add the text box control.**

- **Change the label control text to Total Hours Worked.**

- **Display the Property sheet for the text control.**

- **Click in the Control Source text box and click** **...** **to open the Expression Builder.**

- **Click** = **to enter the type of numeric operation to perform.**

> Entering = instructs the control to perform a calculation.

- **Double-click** ⊞ **to expand the Employee Update Form folder.**

- **Click the** Hours Worked subform **to open the folder.**

- **Double-click** Text4 **in the middle box to specify the control in the subform to reference.**

- **Click** OK **.**

- **Close the Property sheet.**

> You could also have typed = [Hours Worked subform].Form![Text4] directly in the text control.

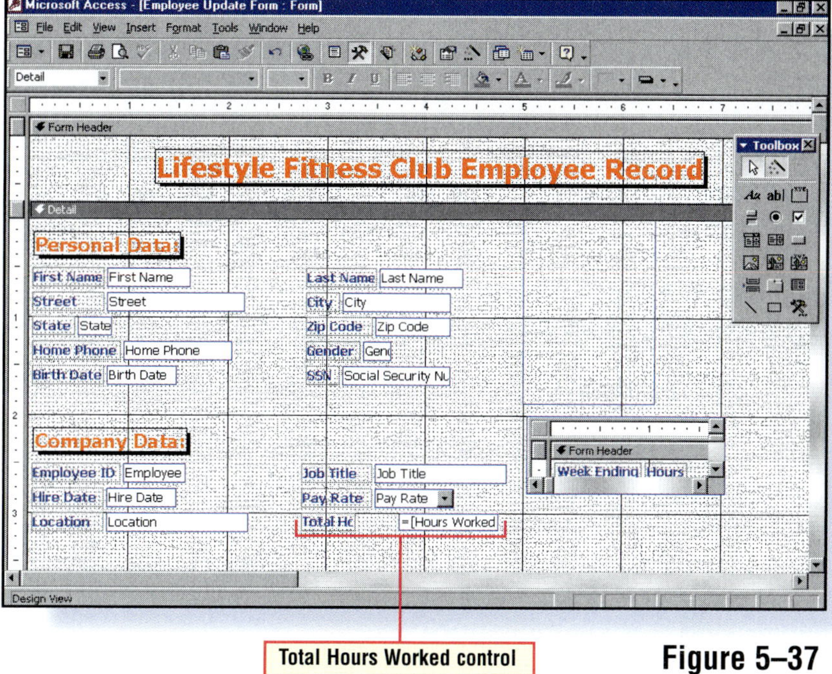

Figure 5–37

Your screen should be similar to Figure 5–37.

Next you will size and position the control, then you will see if and how your new calculated control works.

8 ■ **Appropriately size and position the controls.**

■ **Adjust the placement of the sub-form to top align with the other controls in the Company Data section.**

■ **Save the form changes and switch to Form view.**

■ **Display** record 3.

If necessary, return to Design view and adjust the size of the subform and text box control to fully display the data.

Your screen should be similar to Figure 5–38.

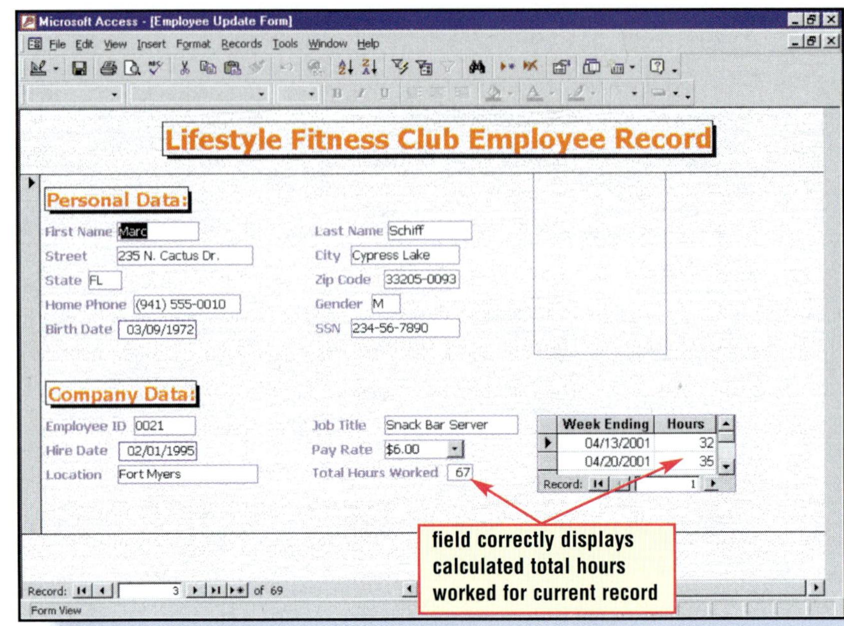

Figure 5–38

The calculated control in the main form displays the calculated value from the calculated field for that record from the subform. Now as the hours table is updated, the total hours will be updated to reflect the change. You will add another pay week to your record to test the calculation.

9 ■ **Display your record.**

■ **Enter the current date for the WeekEnding date and 20 for the hours worked.**

The total hours worked reflects the total for the three weeks of hours recorded.

Adding Command Buttons

The last element you want to add to the form is a command button that will make it easy for those who are using the form to access the underlying tables if needed to filter the table or view it in a datasheet format and to access the saved queries.

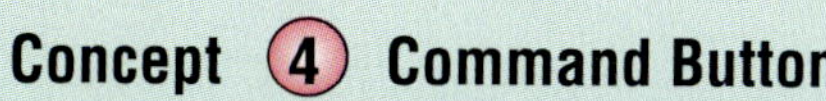

Concept ④ Command Button

A **command button** executes one or more actions on a form. For example, you can create command buttons that perform actions within a form, such as moving from record to record and adding, copying, saving, printing, and deleting a record. You can also create a command button that opens another form.

You can create a command button on your own by writing an event procedure in the Properties dialog box, or you can select from over 30 types of predefined procedures to create a command button using the Command Button Wizard.

You will add two command buttons to your form: one that prints the current record and another that displays a blank form. You will place them in the form footer section, which is a typical location for command buttons or other instructions on using a form. This way they do not appear at the bottom of every record when you print the form; however, they are visible when viewing each form. To add the first command button,

1

Switch to Form Design view.

Expand the form footer section to make room for the button.

Click Command Button.

To use the Command Button Wizard, the Control Wizard button must be activated (the button must be pressed in). If it is not, click the button to activate it.

The mouse pointer is a ⁺□ after selecting to show that the program is ready to create the button.

Click on the left side in the form footer section to add the command button.

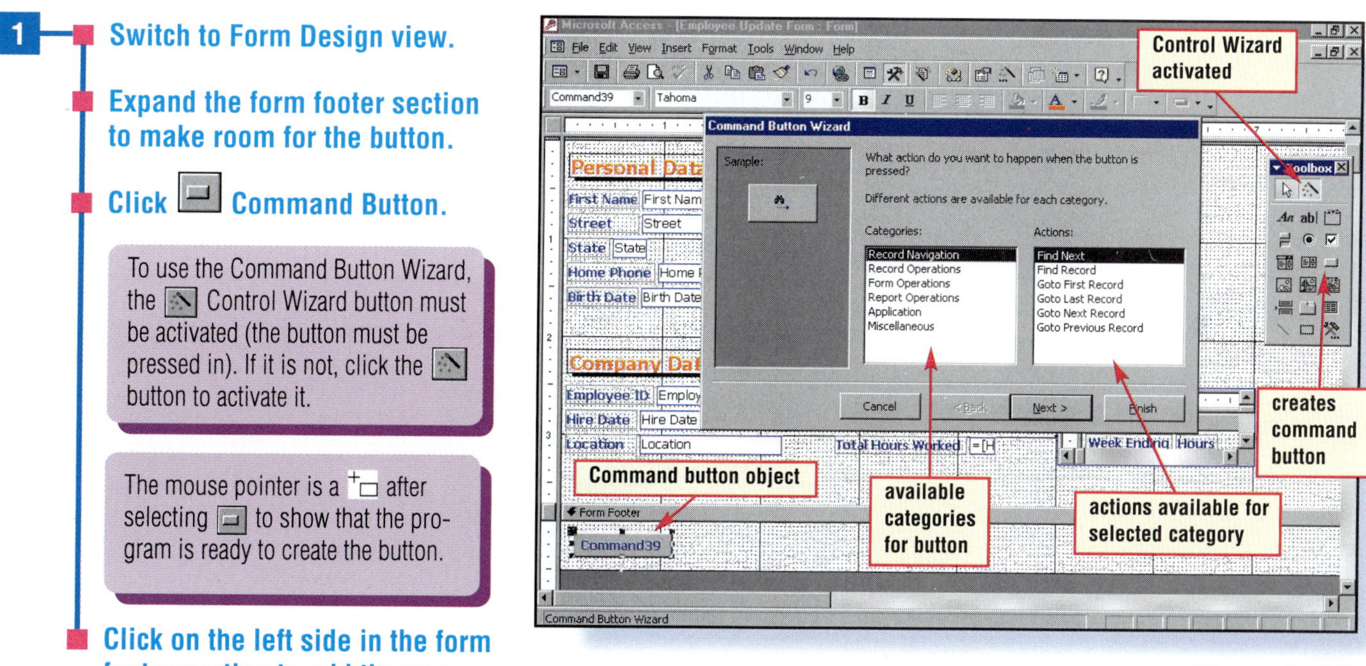

Figure 5–39

Your screen should be similar to Figure 5–39.

The Command Button Wizard dialog box displays a list of predefined categories and actions that can be assigned to the button. The Record Navigation category is selected and displays six record navigation actions that can be assigned to a button. The action you will use to print the current record is in the Record Operations category, but, first, you'll take a look at what's available in all categories before selecting the command button category and action for your form.

2 Select each category in the list and review the actions available in that category.

Select the Record Operations category.

Select the Print Record action.

Click Next > .

Your screen should be similar to Figure 5–40.

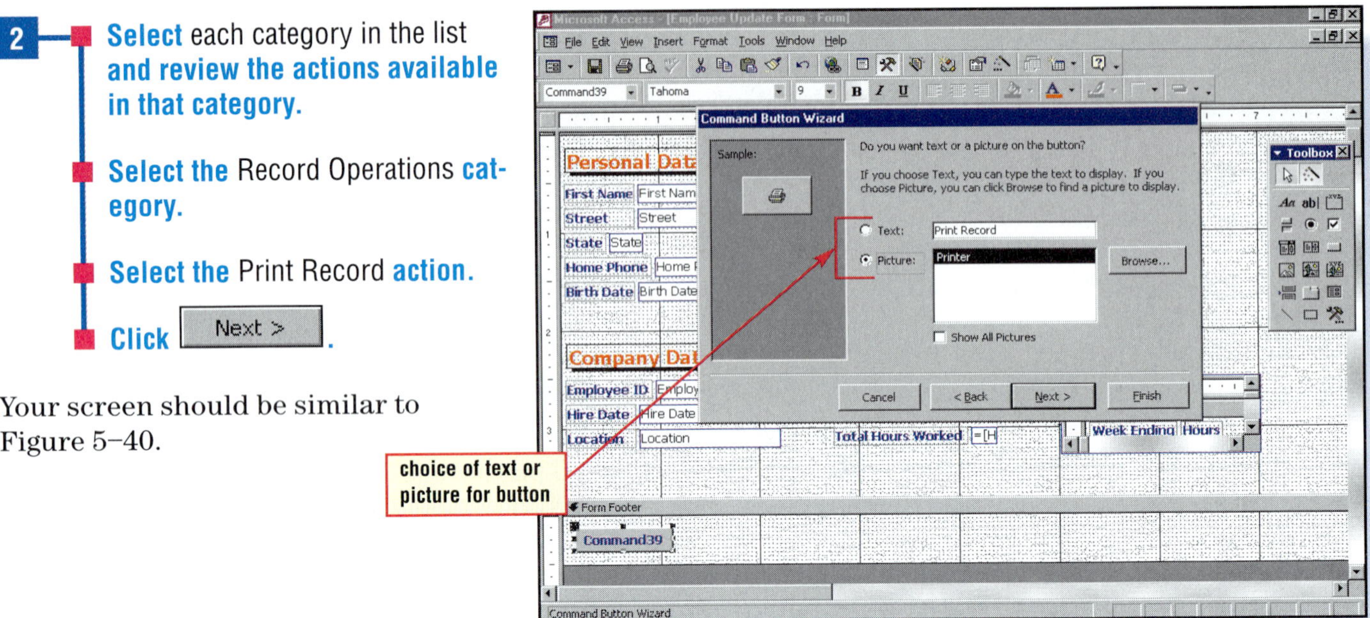

Figure 5–40

The second Wizard box gives you a choice of displaying a picture or text on the command button. You will use the default picture of a printer to indicate the action it will perform.

3 If necessary, select Picture.

Click Next > .

Your screen should be similar to Figure 5–41.

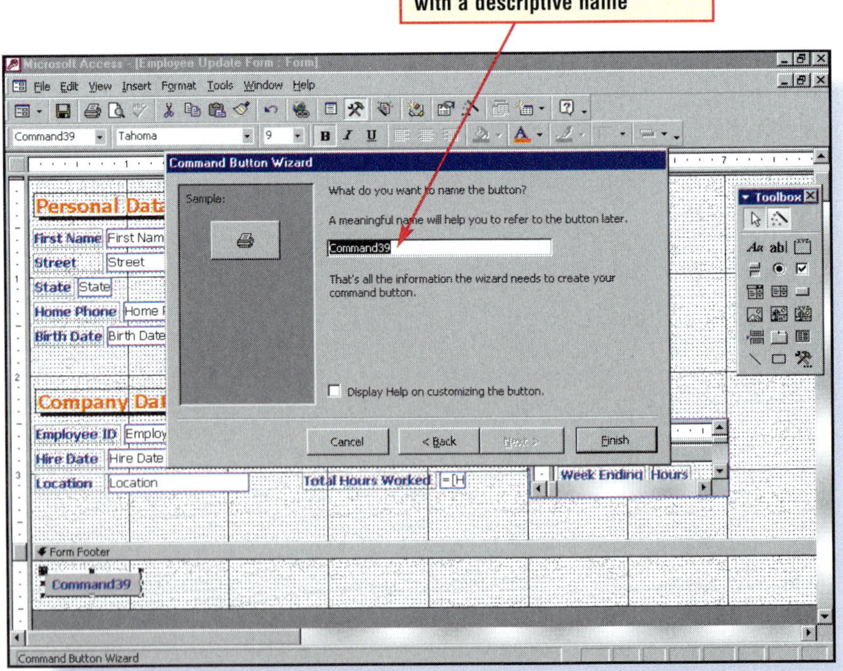

Figure 5–41

The final wizard screen asks you what you want to name the button.

4 ■ Type **Print**.

■ Click [Finish].

Your screen should be similar to Figure 5–42.

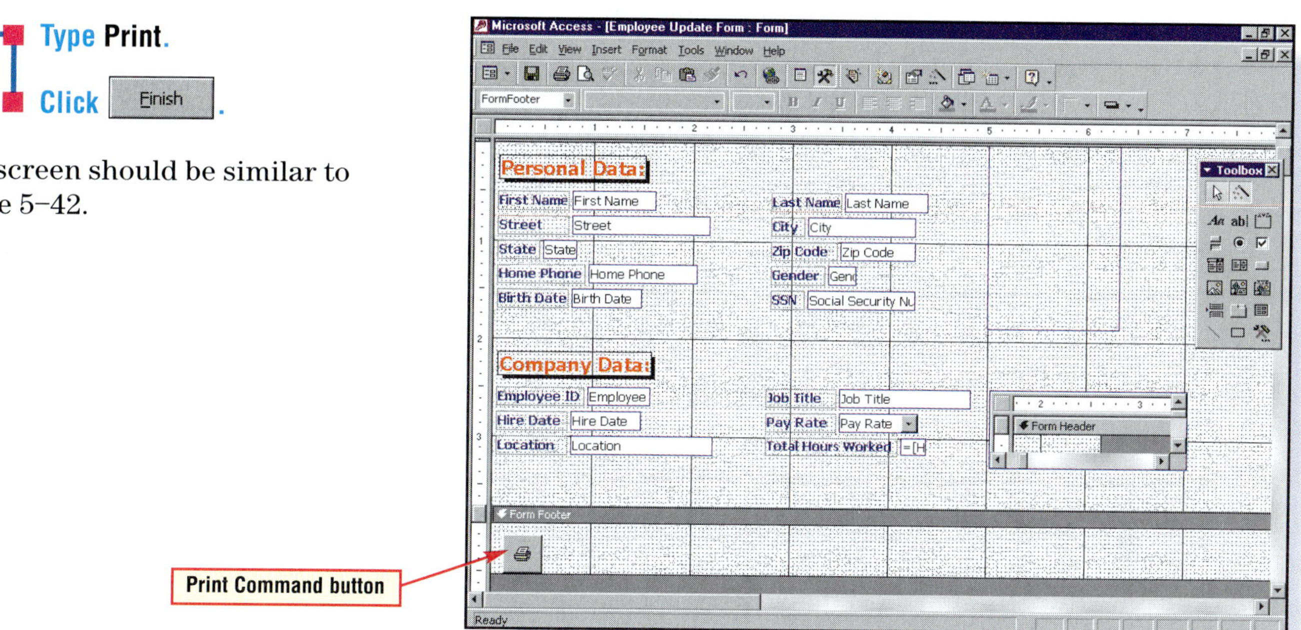

Figure 5–42

The Print button is now ready to use. The second button you want to add is to display a blank new record for adding a new employee to the database.

5 ■ Click ▣ **Command Button**.

■ **Place the button to the right of the Print button.**

■ **From the** Record Operations **category, select** Add New Record.

■ **Select the option to** display text on the button using the default text suggestion.

■ **Name the button New Record.**

■ **If needed, adjust the position of the button.**

Your screen should be similar to Figure 5–43.

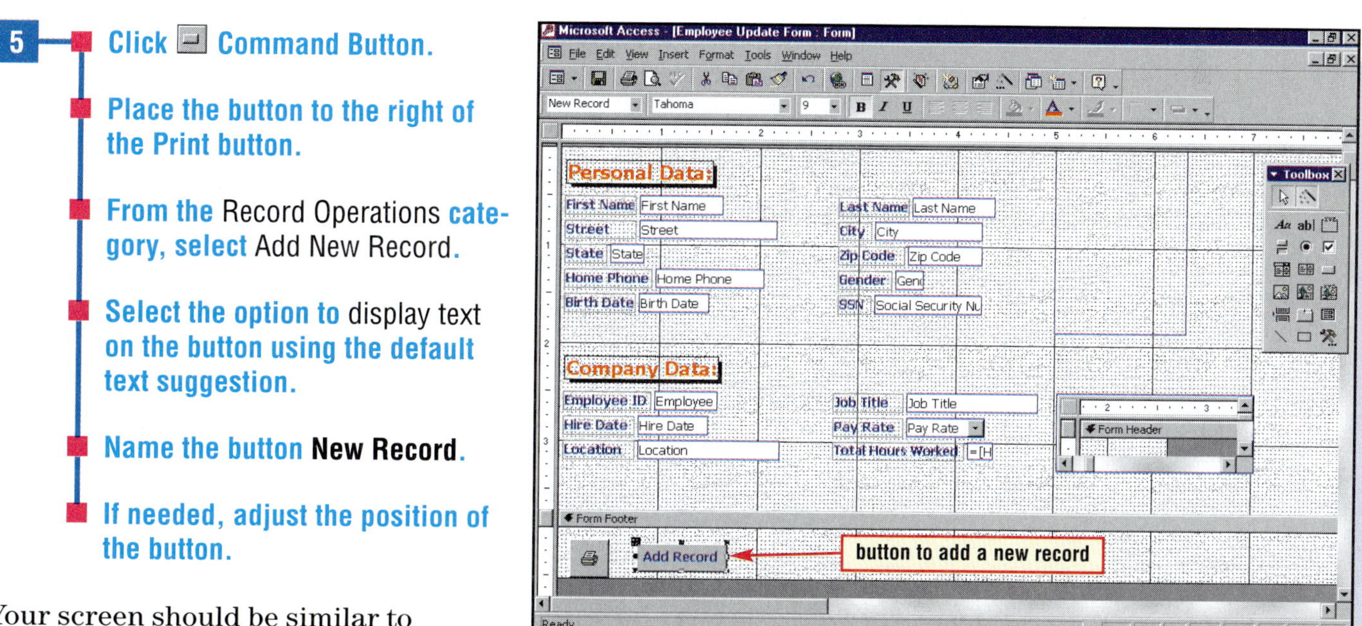

Figure 5–43

The second command button has been added to your form. You will test this button next and use the Print button shortly when you print the form.

6 — Switch to Form view.

Click  **Add Record** .

A blank form is displayed and ready for entry of a new record.

Finally, you need to check the record that contains an employee picture to make sure it displays correctly.

7 — Display record 35.

You can see that the picture control needs to be larger to fully display the picture.

8 — Return to Form Design view.

Widen the picture box control to the 7 inch position.

Adding Page Headers and Footers

The final changes to the form that you want to make are changes that will affect the printed form. You want the form to be printed in landscape layout, with a thick borderline at the top and the page number at the bottom of every page. To do this, you'll create a page header and footer for your form. Unlike form headers and footers, which print only on the first and last page of a form, page headers and footers print on every page.

To change the form to landscape layout,

1. — Choose **F**ile/**P**age Set**u**p

Open the Page tab and select **L**andscape.

Click 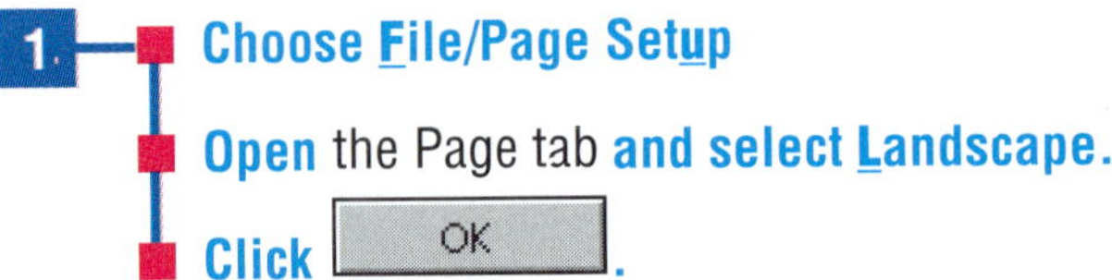 OK .

To create the page header and footer sections of the form,

2 — Choose **V**iew/**P**age Header/Footer.

You can only add a header and footer as a pair.

Your screen should be similar to Figure 5–44.

Page Header section opened

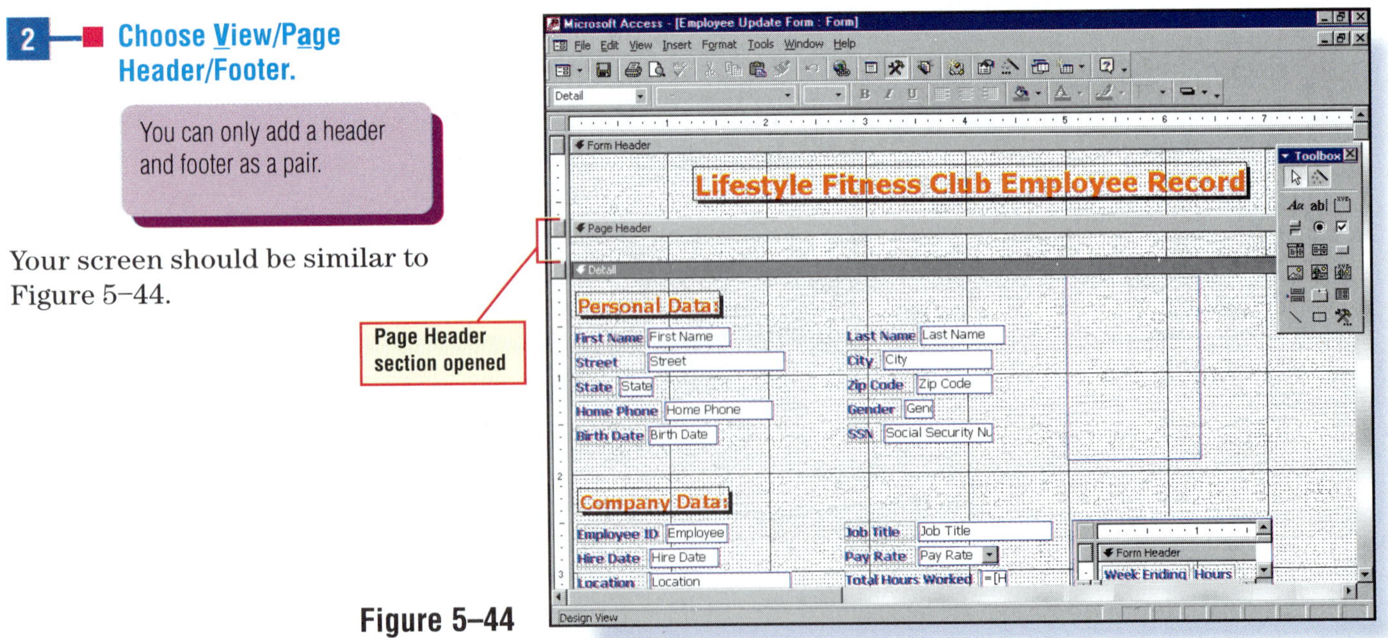

Figure 5–44

A Page Header and Page Footer section are added to the form. You can now adjust the size of these sections and add controls and objects to them just as you can in the other form sections. To add the border line in the page header,

3 • **Click** 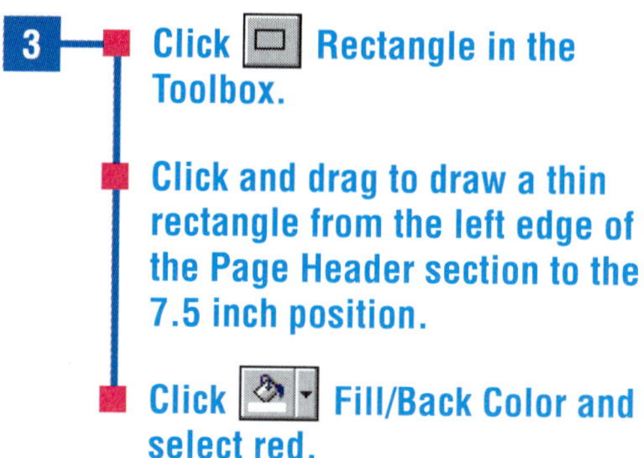 **Rectangle in the Toolbox.**

• **Click and drag to draw a thin rectangle from the left edge of the Page Header section to the 7.5 inch position.**

• **Click** **Fill/Back Color and select red.**

Your screen should be similar to Figure 5–45.

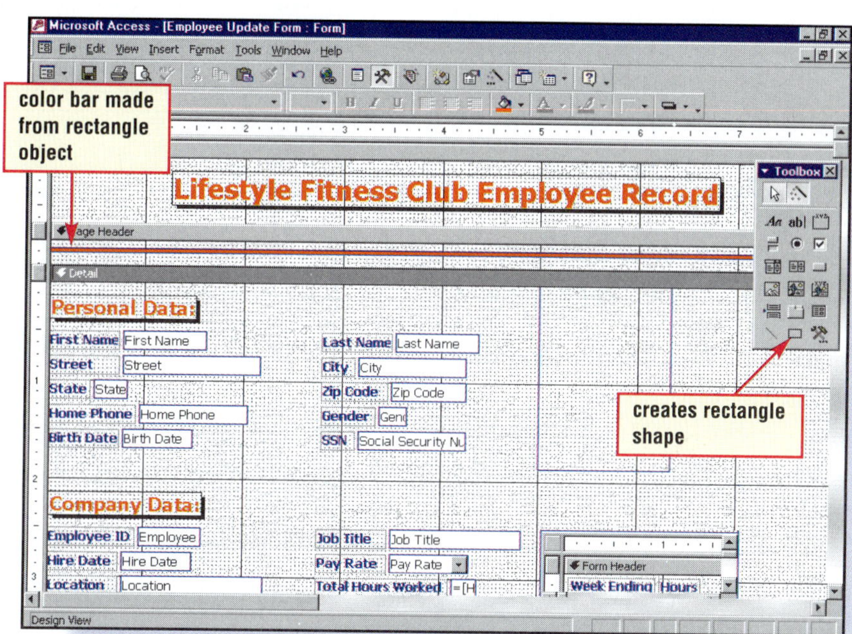

Figure 5–45

Next you will add the page number in the Page Footer section.

4 • **Choose Insert/Page Numbers.**

Your screen should be similar to Figure 5–46.

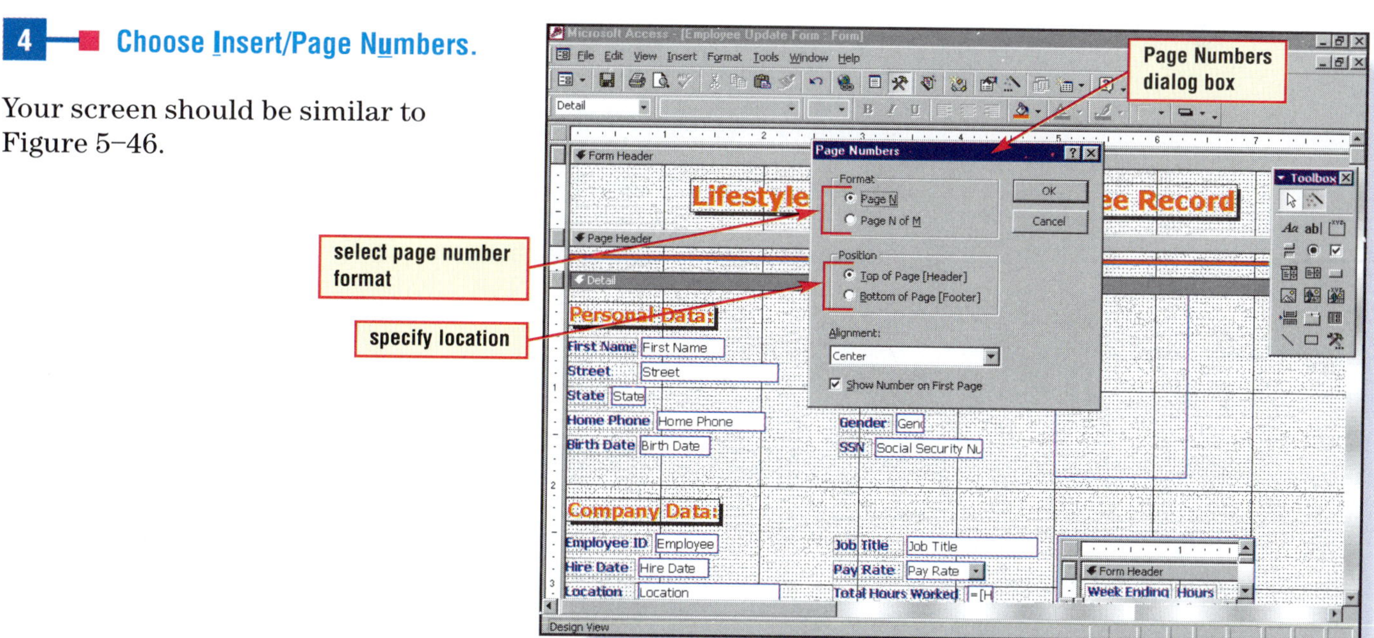

Figure 5–46

The Page Numbers dialog box lets you insert page numbers in your form in either the header or footer in the format "Page N" (such as Page 2) or "Page N of M" (such as Page 2 of 5). You can also choose the alignment of the page number (centered, left, or right) and whether you want the page number printed on the first page or not. You want the single page number centered in the footer and printed on the first and all pages.

5 — If necessary, select Page <u>N</u>, <u>B</u>ottom of Page [Footer], Alignment/Center, and <u>S</u>how number on First Page.

■ Click   OK .

■ Scroll to the bottom of the form to see the Page Footer section.

Your screen should be similar to Figure 5–47.

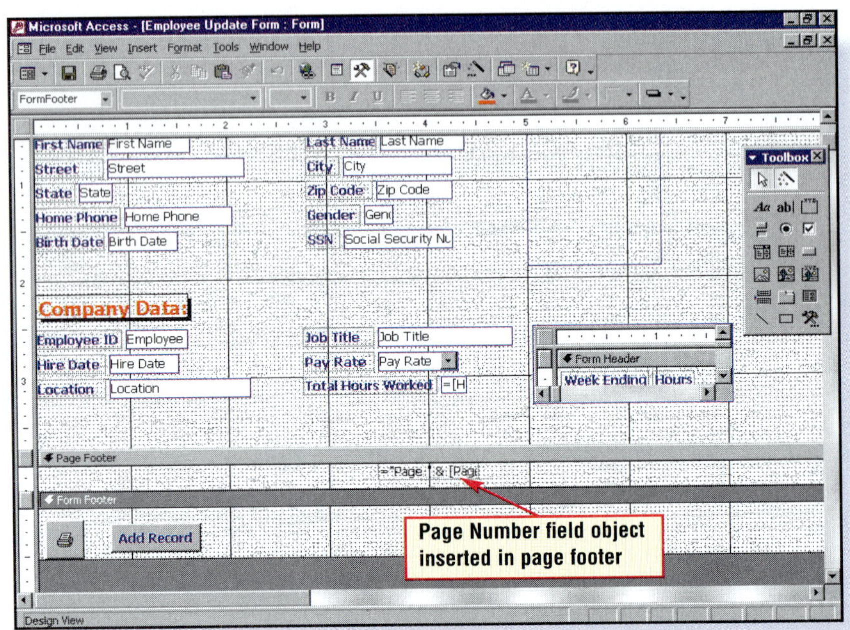

Figure 5–47

Your header and footer are all set, and you're ready to print, save, and close the form.

6 — Return to Form view.

■ Display your record in the form.

■ Print your record using the Print command button.

■ Close the form, saving the changes.

Deleting a Form

Since you have a new form that will update multiple tables in the database, you no longer need the original form you created to update the Employee table. All types of objects can be easily deleted from the database.

1 — **Select** Employee Data Form.

Click 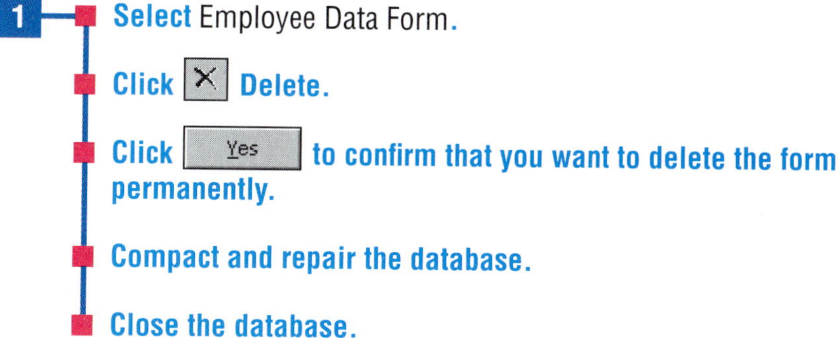 **Delete.**

Click Yes **to confirm that you want to delete the form permanently.**

Compact and repair the database.

Close the database.

Tutorial 5: Creating Custom Forms

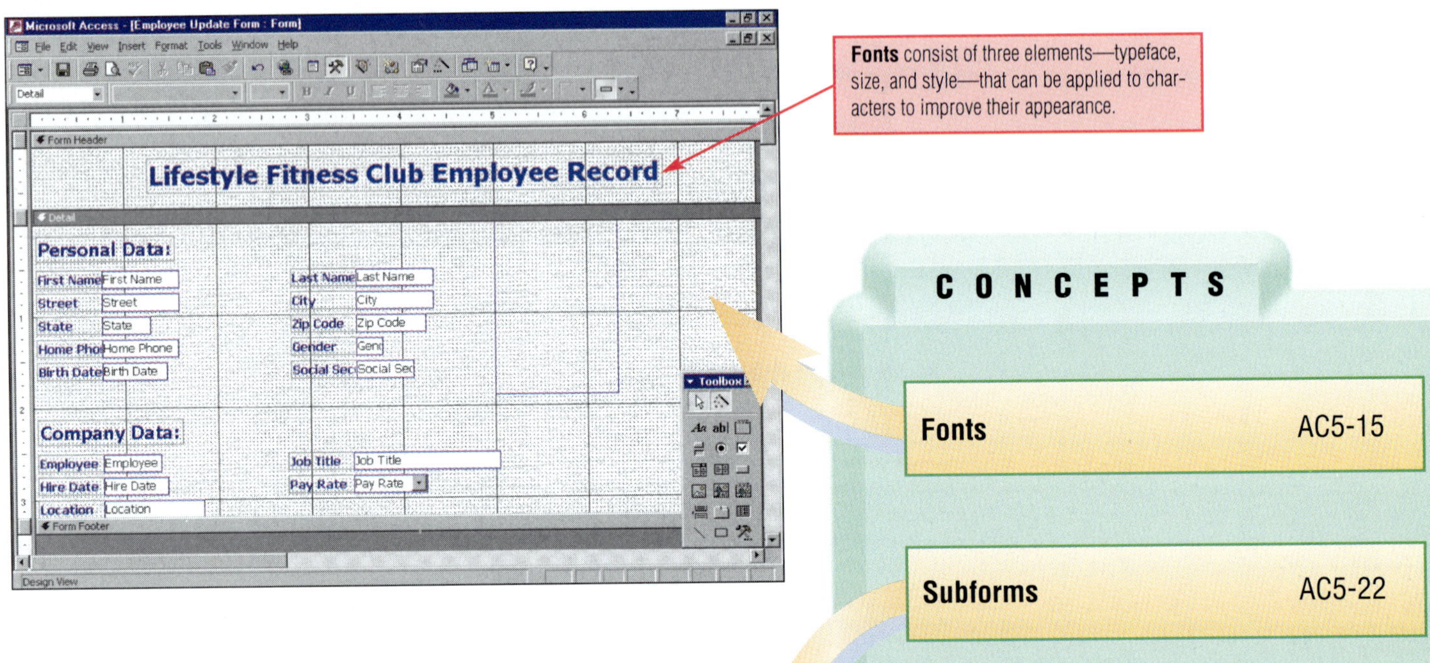

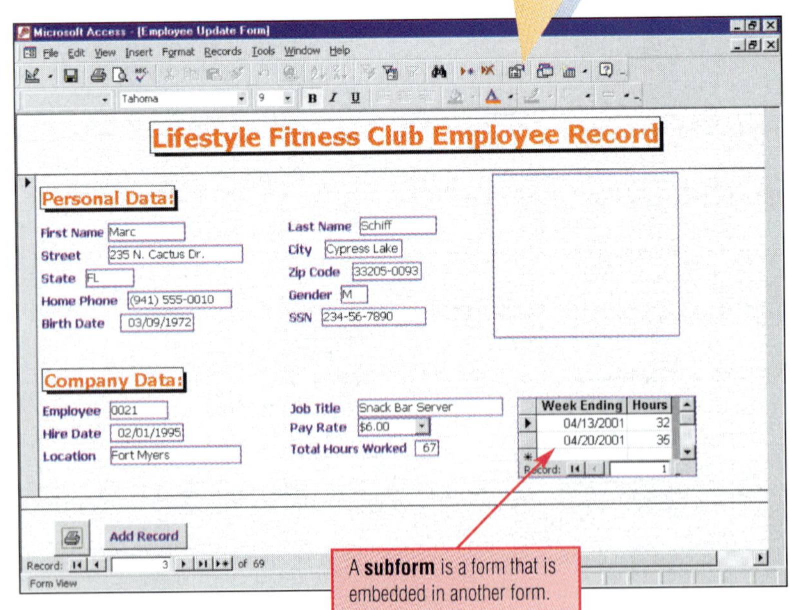

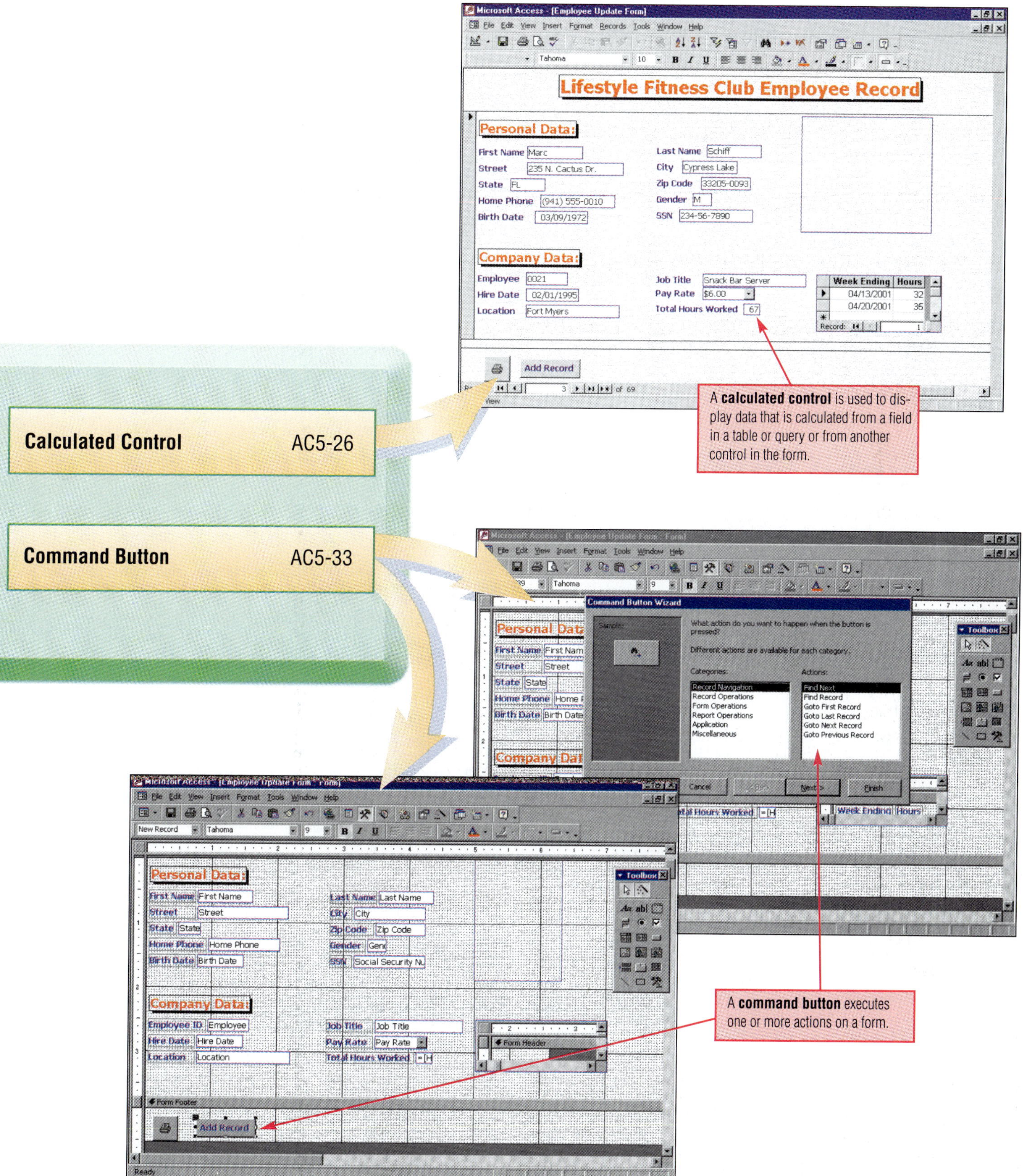

Calculated Control   AC5-26
Command Button   AC5-33
A **calculated control** is used to display data that is calculated from a field in a table or query or from another control in the form.
A **command button** executes one or more actions on a form.
Lifestyle Fitness Club Employee Record

Tutorial Review

Key Terms

calculated control   AC5-26
command button   AC5-33
fonts   AC5-15
Formatting toolbar   AC5-7
Form Design toolbar   AC5-7
hierarchical form   AC5-22
identifier   AC5-26
main form   AC5-22

master/detail form   AC5-22
one-to-many relationship   AC5-22
parent/child form   AC5-22
points   AC5-15
property   AC5-28
subform   AC5-22
Toolbox toolbar   AC5-7

typeface   AC5-15
type size   AC5-15
type style   AC5-15

Command Summary

Command	Shortcut	Toolbar	Action
View/**Pa**ge Header/Footer			Adds or removes the page header and footer section in a form
View/Properties		🖼	Displays properties associated with selection
Insert/Page N**u**mbers			Inserts a page number text box in the page header or footer of a form
F**o**rmat/**F**ont/**S**ize		9 ▾	Sets font size of selection
F**o**rmat/**A**lign/**L**eft			Aligns the left edges of the selected form controls
F**o**rmat/**S**ize/To **F**it			Automatically resizes the selected control to fit its contents
F**o**rmat/**V**ertical Spacing/Make **E**qual			Equalizes the vertical space between selected controls

Screen Identification

In the following worksheet, several items are identified by letters. Enter the correct term for each item in the spaces that follow.

a. ______________________

b. ______________________

c. ______________________

d. ______________________

e. ______________________

f. ______________________

g. ______________________

Matching

Match the letter to the correct item in the numbered list.

1. identifier   ______   **a.** the design and shape of characters

2. property   ______   **b.** appear at the bottom of the form

3. [Aa]   ______   **c.** form that is embedded in another form

4. main form   ______   **d.** executes an action in a form

5. calculated control   ______   **e.** adds a label control to a form

6. typeface   ______   **f.** form that can hold other forms

7. subform   ______   **g.** settings that affect how the control looks and acts

8. [ab]   ______   **h.** element that refers to the value of a field, control, or property

9. command button   ______   **i.** displays the result of an expression in a form

10. Form Footers   ______   **j.** adds a text box to a form

Fill-In

Complete the following statements by filling in the blanks with the correct terms.

1. A _______________________ appears at the top of the screen or, if you print the form, at the top of the first page.

2. The _________________ spacing can be adjusted between any group of three or more selected controls.

3. Type size is commonly measured in _________________.

4. A _________________ is the design and shape of characters.

5. A _________________ is a form that is embedded in another form.

6. Controls can be made more noticeable by adding _________________ to their background, text, or borders.

7. A command button is created from _________________ that you write yourself or select in the Command Button Wizard.

8. Unlike form headers and footers, ___________ headers and footers print on every page.

9. You can build a calculated control in the _________________ dialog box.

10. A _________________ control refers to two controls that act as one.

Multiple-Choice

Circle the letter of the correct answer to the following statements.

1. The _________________ toolbar contains buttons used to add and modify controls.

    a. Formatting
    b. Toolbox
    c. Form Design
    d. Form View

2. A calculated-control expression must begin with

    a. =
    b. /
    c. "
    d. +

3. _________________refers to the special attributes you assign to characters, such as bold or italic.

   a. Type style
   b. Point size
   c. Typeface
   d. Font

4. The primary form in a form/subform relationship is called the

   a. hierarchical form
   b. source form
   c. main form
   d. destination form

5. To select more than one control on a form, hold down the ______________ key while you click the control.

   a. ⇧Shift
   b. Tab
   c. Alt
   d. ←Enter

6. A form/subform combination is also called a:

   a. hierarchical form
   b. master/detail form
   c. parent/child form
   d. all of the above

7. A calculated control displays data that is calculated from a

   a. table
   b. query
   c. form
   d. any of the above

8. _________________appear at the top of the screen or, if you print the form, at the top of the first page.

   a. Form headers
   b. Form footers
   c. Page headers
   d. Page footers

9. The ______________ button must be activated in order to use the Command Button Wizard.

   a. [Aa]
   b. [ab|]
   c. [▢]
   d. [⚒]

10. The area on a form that contains the table data is called the _________________ section.

   a. Detail
   b. Main
   c. Table
   d. Format

True/False

Circle the correct answer to the following statements.

1. Page headers and footers print only on the first and last page of a form.   True   False

2. Typeface refers to the special attributes you can apply to characters.   True   False

3. To select both a text control and its associated label control, you click the label control.   True   False

4. You can left-align controls from any row or column.   True   False

5. You cannot apply font changes to individual characters or words.   True   False

6. Subforms can be used to show data from tables or queries that have a one-to-many relationship.   True   False

7. Vertical spacing can be adjusted between two or more selected controls.   True   False

8. The identifier is the element that refers to the value of a field, control, or property.   True   False

9. A calculated-control expression should always begin with an equal sign (=).   True   False

10. A form can have more than one subform.   True   False

Discussion Questions

1. Discuss how multiple-form tables are used. When would it be more appropriate to use a subform as opposed to a multiple-form table?

2. Discuss the way a form's appearance can be enhanced. Why would you use these enhancements? What drawbacks are there to using too many enhancements?

3. Discuss the purpose of a calculated control. Give examples of the types of form fields where this feature would be most useful.

4. Discuss how command buttons can be used. What are some form functions that can be automated with a command button?

Hands-On Practice Exercises

Step-by-Step

1. You've set up a Club Members database for the Lifestyle Fitness Club, with tables that contain data on the club members and personal trainers at each club location. Next, you need to create a form that will make entering data into these tables easier. As you did when you inserted the Members table within the Personal Trainers table as a subdatasheet, you want the form to display the member data on the records of the personal trainers assigned to them. To do this, you will create a personal trainers form with a members subform. You are also going to customize this form by including different font sizes and colors as well as a form header and footer to make it more attractive. When you are finished, your form will look like the form shown here.

To create the form, follow these steps:

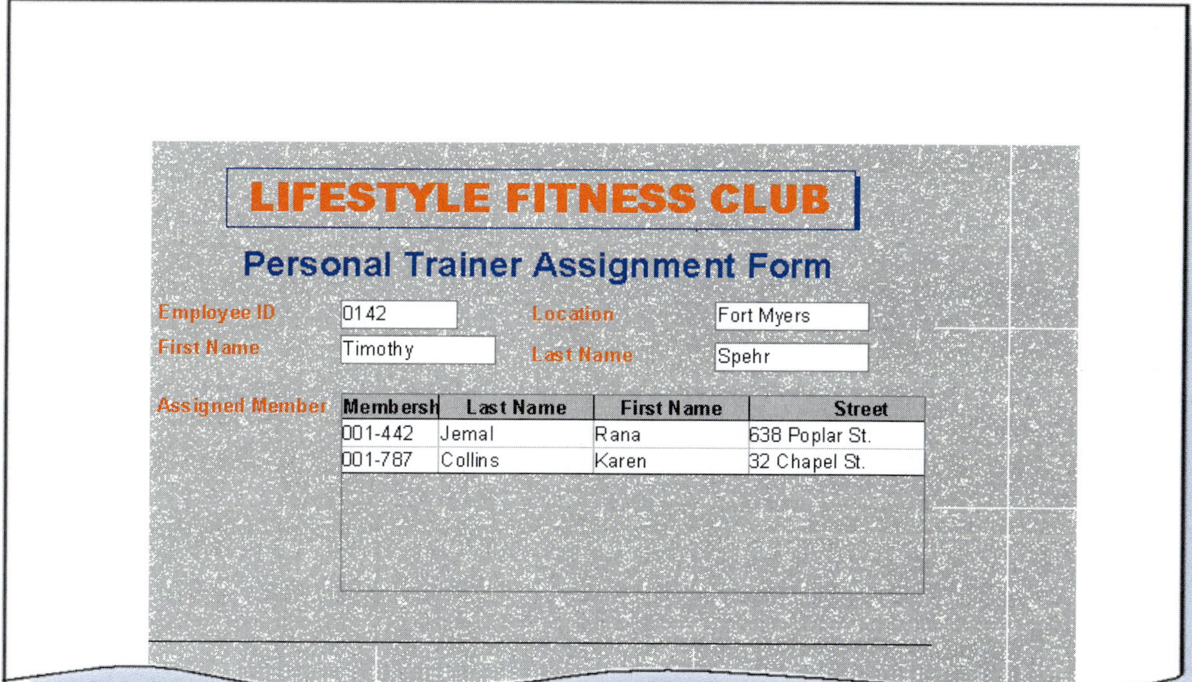

a. Open the Club Members database (which you worked on in Practice Exercise 1 of Tutorial 4).

b. Use the Form Wizard to create a new form using all of the fields in the Personal Trainers table as well as all of the fields in the Members table (in that order). Specify that you want to view the data with the Personal Trainers table as the main form and the Members table as the subform. Use the Datasheet layout for the subform and the SandStone style. Keep the form and subform names as Personal Trainers and Members, and specify that you want to open the form in Design view. Finish the Wizard.

c. Maximize the Form Design window, if necessary. Move the Location label and text controls so they are on the same line and to the right of the Employee ID controls. Then move the Last Name controls so they are on the same line and to the right of the First Name controls. Adjust the alignment and spacing of the controls as needed.

d. Change the Members label to **Assigned Members**, and move the label and subform up so they are about 1/4 inch from the First and Last Name line.

e. Change the font size of all labels and text from 9 to 10. Assign a font color of your choice to the labels.

f. Add a label in the Form Header section for the form title that reads **LIFESTYLE FITNESS CLUB**. Change the font to Arial Black and the font size to 20. Size the label to fit, and center it at the top of the form. Assign a font color, border weight and color, background color, and special effect of your choice.

g. Add a label in the Form Footer section that reads **Created by [Your Name]**. Center the label at the bottom of the form.

h. Display the Page Header and Footer. In the Page Header, add a label that reads **Personal Trainer Assignment Form**. Change the font to 18-point Arial with a font color of your choice. Size the label to fit and center it on the form.

i. In the Page Footer, insert an automatic page number control.

j. Return to Form view and adjust the column widths in the subform so the entire contents are displayed. (You will need to scroll the form horizontally to access all the columns.) Display the personal trainer you selected for your record and print the form for the record only, and then save and close it.

k. Close the Club Members database.

2. The owners of the Animal Angels organization like the way the Fosters and Adopters tables show the corresponding animal data from the Animals table; however, they have asked if you can create a form that contains the animal, foster care, and adoption data in one place to make it easier to view and update. To do this, you will create a main animal data form with two subforms for the foster and adoption data. Your completed form will look similar to that shown here.

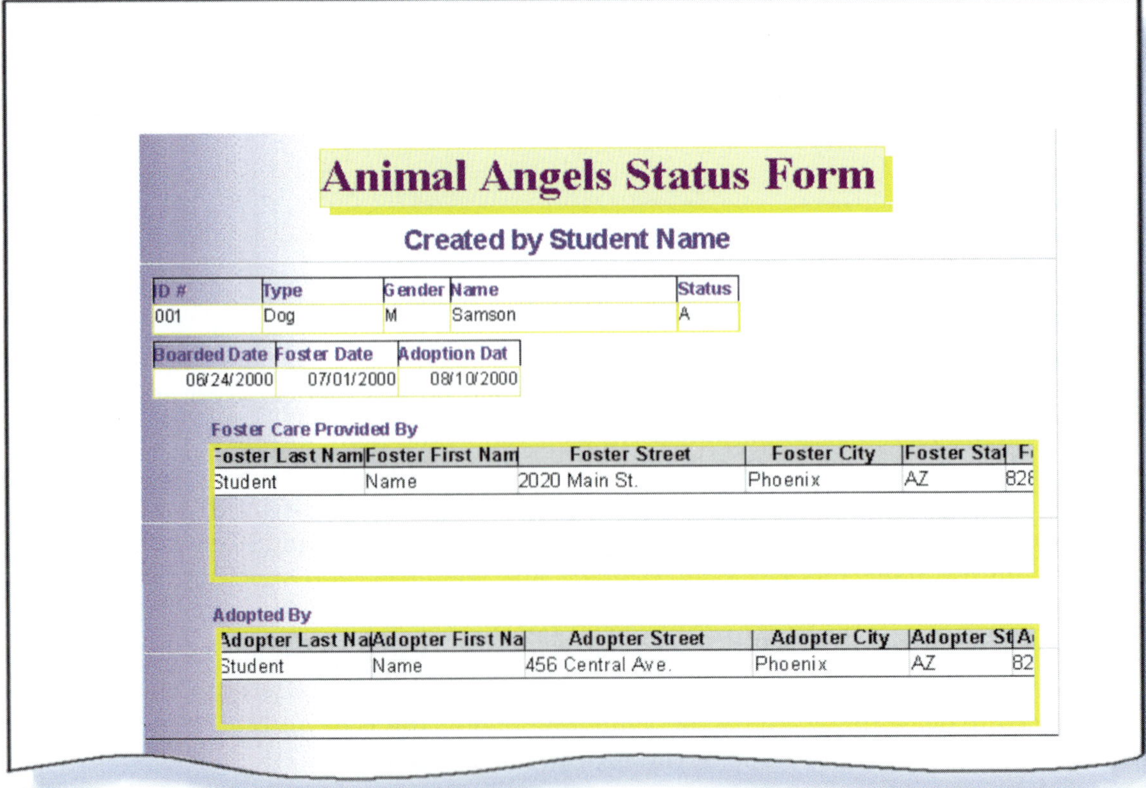

ID #	Type	Gender	Name	Status
001	Dog	M	Samson	A

Boarded Date	Foster Date	Adoption Dat
06/24/2000	07/01/2000	08/10/2000

Foster Last Nam	Foster First Nam	Foster Street	Foster City	Foster Stat	F
Student	Name	2020 Main St.	Phoenix	AZ	828

Adopter Last Na	Adopter First Na	Adopter Street	Adopter City	Adopter St	A
Student	Name	456 Central Ave.	Phoenix	AZ	82

To create the form, follow these steps:

a. Open the database named Angels 4 (which you last worked on in Practice Exercise 2 of Tutorial 4).

b. Use the Form Wizard to create a new form and add all of the fields from the Animals table. Use the Justified layout and Blends style. Name the form **Animal Status Form** and open it in Design view.

c. Change the Boarded Date and Foster Date label and text control box sizes so they are equivalent to the Adoption Date control boxes. (*Hint:* You will have to temporarily move the Adoption Date control boxes out of the way to resize the Foster Date boxes; then move them back.) Move the Boarded Date control boxes to the second line, to the left of the Foster Date and Adoption Date control boxes. (*Hint:* You'll have to move the Foster Date and Adoption Date control boxes first to make room for the Boarded Date.) Realign the control boxes as necessary after you have completed the move.

d. Increase the size of the Detail section and insert a subform at the bottom. Use the Fosters table as the source of the subform and add all fields except the ID # field from this table. Accept the default link option and name the subform **Foster Care Provided By**. Resize and realign the subform as necessary so you can see it in its entirety.

e. Repeat the previous step to create another subform using the Adopters table and all of its fields except the ID #. Name the subform **Adopted By** and adjust the subform size and placement as necessary.

f. In the Form Header section, add a form title that reads **Animal Angels Status Form** in an 24-point Times New Roman font. Assign a font color, border, background color, and special effect of your choice. Resize and center the title as necessary.

g. Add a label that reads **Created by [Your Name]** in the Page Header in 14 pt. Center it below the title. Add an automatic page numbering in the Page Footer.

h. Return to Form view and adjust the column widths in the subforms so each column's contents are displayed.

i. Print the form for ID# 001 in portrait orientation.

j. Save and close the form.

k. Close the Angels 4 database.

3. After reviewing the tables that you created for Daria's Day Spa, the owner has asked you to create a form that will enable users of the database to update information about the spa packages as well as the clients who have purchased each package. This will require you to create a multiple-table form using fields from all three tables in the Daria's Spa database. Ms. O'Dell would also like this new form to enable users to quickly access the existing Client Information form so they can update it when necessary. You will provide this access via a command button that links the two forms. The completed form will look similar to the form shown here.

DARIA'S DAY SPA

Spa Package Purchases

Package ID   1

Package Name   The Ultimate

Package Description   Deep-tissue massage, aromatherapy, facial, body wrap, and sauna

Package Price $325.00

Package Purchasers

Client ID	First Name	Last Name
001	Elaine	Grace
005	Huye	Ky
008	Lisa	Michaels
024	Student	Name
017	Pauline	Kelly
017	Pauline	Kelly

To create the form, follow these steps:

a. Open the database called Daria Spa 4 (which you last worked on in Practice Exercise 3 of Tutorial 4).

b. Use the Form Wizard to create a new form using all fields from the Spa Packages table; the Client ID, First Name, and Last Name fields from the Clients table; and the Package Purchased field from the Packages Purchased table. Specify that you want to view the data by Spa Packages. Use the Datasheet layout for the subform and the Blueprint style. Name the form **Spa Package Purchases** and the subform **Package Purchasers**. Open the form in Form view.

c. Maximize the Form window, if necessary. Since the Package Name is already displayed on the main form, and the only clients that will display on a package's record will be the ones who purchased that package, you don't need the Package Name column to appear in the subform as well. Use the same technique for hiding any table or form column to hide the Package Purchased column in the subform. Adjust the column widths to fit the displayed data.

d. Switch to Design view. Decrease the size of the subform to show only the first three columns (excluding the Package Purchased column). Make its right margin the same as the Package Description text control box (approximately 4.5 on the horizontal ruler).

e. Select the Detail section and assign a light blue background fill color to it.

f. Add **DARIA'S DAY SPA** to the Form Header. Apply a font type, font size, color, background, border, and special effect as desired. Adjust its size to display the entire title, and center it at the top of the form.

g. Add a command button in the Form Footer section to open the Client Information form and show all the records. Specify that you want text to appear on the button and enter **Open Client Information Form** as the button label. Name the button **Client Information Form**. Center the button as necessary.

h. Display the Page Header and Footer. In the Page Header, add a label that reads **Spa Package Purchases**. Assign a font size of 14 and a color, border, background color, and special effect of your choice. Resize and center the title as necessary.

i. In the Page Footer, insert an automatic page number control.

j. Return to Form view and try out the command button. Close the Client Information form to return to the Spa Package Purchases form.

k. Print the form for package ID 1 in portrait orientation. Save and close the form.

l. Close the Daria Spa 4 database.

4. The database you created for the Downtown Internet Cafe contains two tables: one with data regarding the cafe's inventory and vendors and another with inventory item costs and order information. To make it as easy as possible to review and update all of this data, the owner of the cafe would like you to create a form that combines both tables. He would also like you to include the same order calculations on this form as in the To Be Ordered query you created previously. The completed multi-table form will look similar to the form shown here.

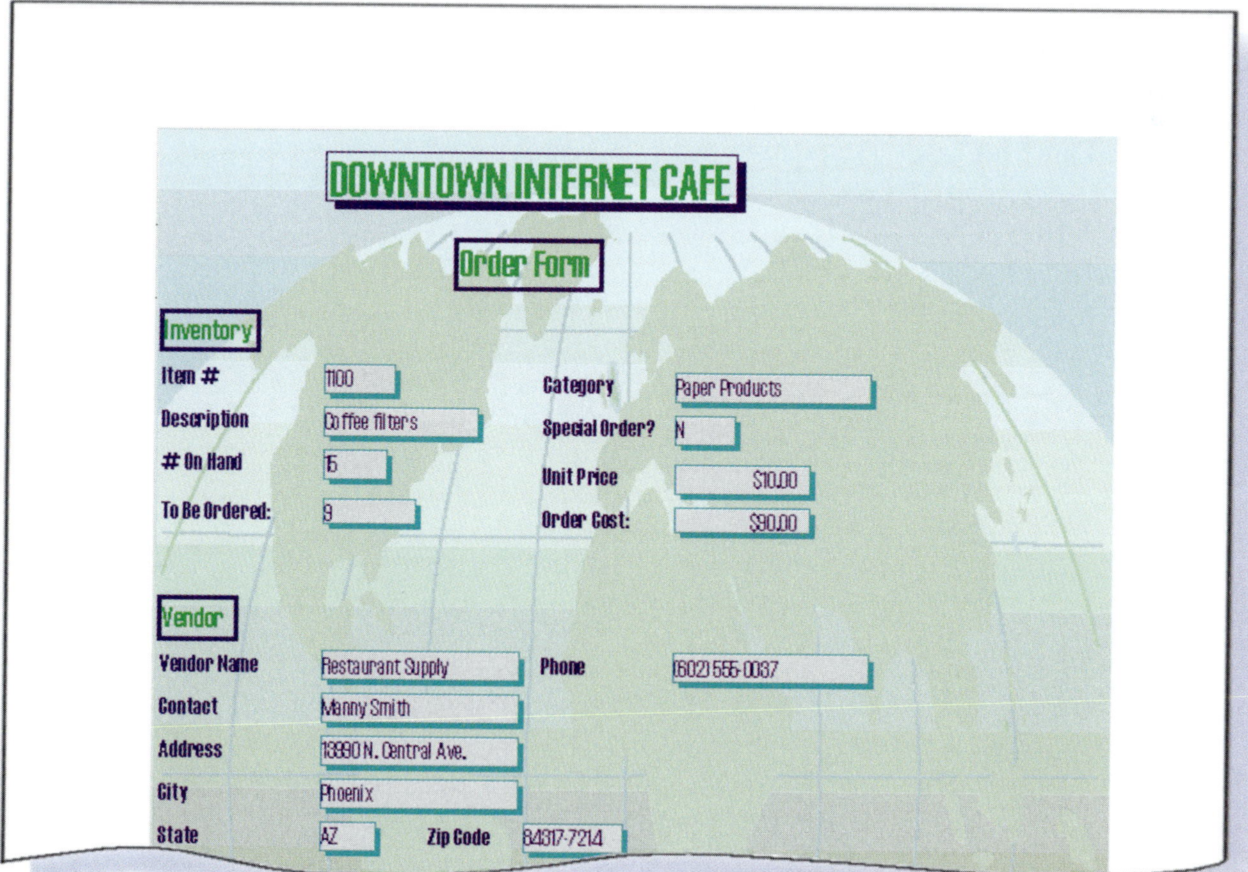

To create the new table and query, follow these steps:

a. Open the Cafe Purchases 4 database (which you last worked on in Practice Exercise 4 of Tutorial 4).

b. Establish a one-to-one relationship between the Inventory and Stock Item Prices tables.

c. Use the Form Wizard to create a multiple table form with all of the fields from the Inventory table and the Category and Unit Price fields from the Stock Item Prices table. Use the columnar format and a style of your choice. Name the form **Stock Item Orders**. Open the form in Design view.

d. Divide the form into two separate parts: the top part for information pertaining to the inventory items and costs and the bottom part for vendor information. Begin by expanding the Detail section moving controls and adding **Inventory** and **Vendor** labels to the top and middle of the sections. Then resize the controls as needed. (Use the figure at the beginning of this exercise for reference.)

e. Insert a calculated control between the Inventory and Vendor parts with the label **To Be Ordered:**. Use the Expression Builder to calculate the number of items to be ordered by subtracting the # On Hand from 24 (the amount of stock the owner likes to keep on hand). (*Hint:* Begin with an equal sign, followed by the calculation.) Name the text box **Control Order**. Save the form so the new calculated control will be available for the next calculation. Display the form in Form view to check that your calculated field works correctly.

f. Insert another calculated control next to the first with the label **Order Cost** and a calculation that multiplies the number of items to be ordered by the unit price. Name the text box **Control Cost**. Apply the Currency format property to the new calculated control.

g. Position, align, vertically space and size all controls appropriately. Add an appropriate Form Header and Footer as well as a Page Header and Page Footer. Add enhancements of your choice to the form.

h. Switch to Form view and locate the record with your name as the vendor contact. Select and print that record, and then save and close the form.

i. Close the Cafe Purchases 4 database.

5. You are still working on the EduSoft Company's database. The database currently contains two tables—Software and Orders—which you want to combine into one easy-to-use form. The owners have also requested that you include a calculation that shows the total sales to date as you did in the query you created previously. The completed form is shown here.

To create the new figure, follow these steps:

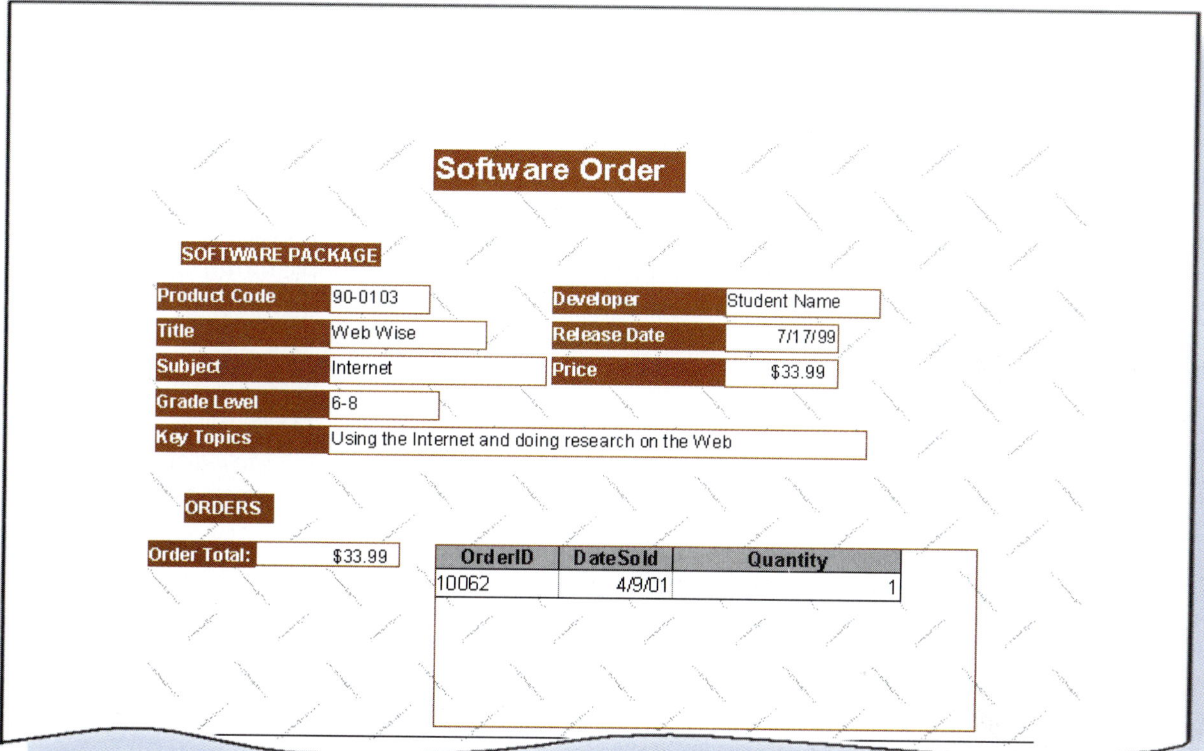

a. Open the Learning 4 database (which you last worked on in Practice Exercise 5 of Tutorial 4).

b. Create a multiple-table form with all of the fields from the Software table and the Order ID, Date Sold, and Quantity fields from the Orders table. View the data by Software, use the Datasheet format, and select a style of your choice. Name the form **Software Orders** and open it in Form view.

c. The Key Topics text field is too short, the Price text field is too long, and the subform is too large and too close to the main form. Switch to Design view and fix these problems.

d. Insert a control in the subform's Form Footer called **Total** that will add the Quantity values. Name the text **Control Total**. Save the form.

e. Then insert another calculated control on the main form, to the left of the subform, that is called **Order Total** and that multiplies the subform total quantity calculation by the Price. (You may need to move the subform to the right to fit the new calculated field next to it.) Name the text control **Order Total** and apply the Currency format property to the new calculated control.

f. Reduce the size of the subform so the Form Footer is no longer displayed.

g. Divide the form into two parts by moving all controls down, adding a label above the product information called **SOFTWARE PACKAGE**, and changing the existing Orders label to all uppercase and sized to fit. Move the subform so it is aligned with the top of the Order Total control. (See the figure at the beginning of this exercise for reference.)

h. Insert a command button in the Form Footer that will add a new record to the form.

i. Add appropriate Page and Form Headers and automatic page numbers in the Page Footer.

j. Switch to Form view and display the record with your name as the developer. If this record does not have any orders associated with it, add some. Select and print the record and then save and close the form. Close the Learning 4 database.

On Your Own

6. You want to enhance the database you developed for the dental office where you work by creating a form that combines both of its tables. This way, anyone (including yourself) who has to access or update a patient's contact, insurance, or payment information can do so in one central location. Open the database you updated in Practice Exercise 6 of Tutorial 4 and use the Form Wizard to create a multiple-table form. Reformat the form to divide it into patient contact information and patient billing information. Add a Form Header with the company name, a Page Header with the form name, a Form Footer with **Created by [Your Name]**, and a Page Footer with automatic page numbering. Print the first page of the form and then save and close it.

7. The Posters Unlimited database you created in Practice Exercise 8 in Tutorial 4 needs a data entry form. Create a form that can be used to enter all the data into the underlying tables. Use subform(s) where necessary. Add a calculated control to total the number of prints you have from different suppliers. Use the features you learned in these tutorials to enhance the appearance of the form. Create command buttons to print the form and any others that enhance the use of the form. Enter your name as one of the suppliers and print the form that displays your name.

8. The database you created for Adventure Travel includes client and tour data in separate tables. However, you just found out that the same person will be entering information into these tables, so you decide to make this task much simpler by combining the tables into one multi-table form. Because the clients table contains so much data, you decide to include only certain client fields and add a command button to enable the data entry person to switch to the full clients form you created previously as necessary to update the complete client records. When you present this plan to the owners, they heartily approve but request that you also include a calculation that shows the total amount of money each package has generated, much like you did for the query you ran for them earlier. To create the new form, open the Adventure database that you updated in Practice Exercise 7 of Tutorial 4 and create a multi-table form that lists tour package data in the main form and the name of the clients who have purchased each package in a subform. Format the form to add different font types, sizes, and colors. Create a calculated control that will display the total income generated from each package. Insert a command button in the Form Footer that will open the clients form. Add an appropriate Page Header and insert the page numbers in the Page Footer. Locate the record that has your name as the client (or create one if none exists) and then select and print that record. Save and close the form.

9. As database manager for National Packing, you have created a database with sales rep, product, and client data—all in separate tables (Practice exercise 9 in Tutorial 4). You now decide that it would be much more efficient to have all this data in one form. Create a form from the product table and add the sales rep and clients tables as subforms. Include a calculated field that displays the total purchase amount for each product. Reformat the table as desired. Include your name in the Form Footer and automatic page numbers in the Page Footer. Print one page of this form and then save and close it.

10. Mathew likes the database you created for the online bookstore (Practice Exercise 10 in Tutorial 4). He has asked you to do some additonal work on the database to make entering data more efficent. Create a data entry form for the tables in the database. Use subform(s) where necessary. Add a calculated control for an appropriate field in the database. Use the features you learned in these tutorials to enhance the appearance of the form. Create command buttons to print the form and any others that enhance the use of the form. Enter your name as one of the book authors and print the form that displays your name.

6

Creating Custom Reports, Mailing Labels, Macros, and Switchboards

Competencies

After completing this tutorial, you will know how to:

1. Group report records.
2. Calculate group totals.
3. Customize a report's layout.
4. Enhance a report's appearance.
5. Add a calculated control to a report.
6. Create mailing labels.
7. Create macros to automate database tasks.
8. Use a switchboard to navigate a database.

Reports can group and summarize data to provide meaningful information.

Switchboards help quickly navigate through objects in the database.

Case Study

The owners of the Lifestyle Fitness Club are impressed with your ability to use Access to locate and analyze the employee data. You have used the program to automate the updates and changes that occur to the employee tables and to quickly find answers to many different types of queries. Thus far, you've created simple reports from these queries that are quite acceptable for many informal uses. However, the club owners would like you to create a more formal status report to be distributed to managers and

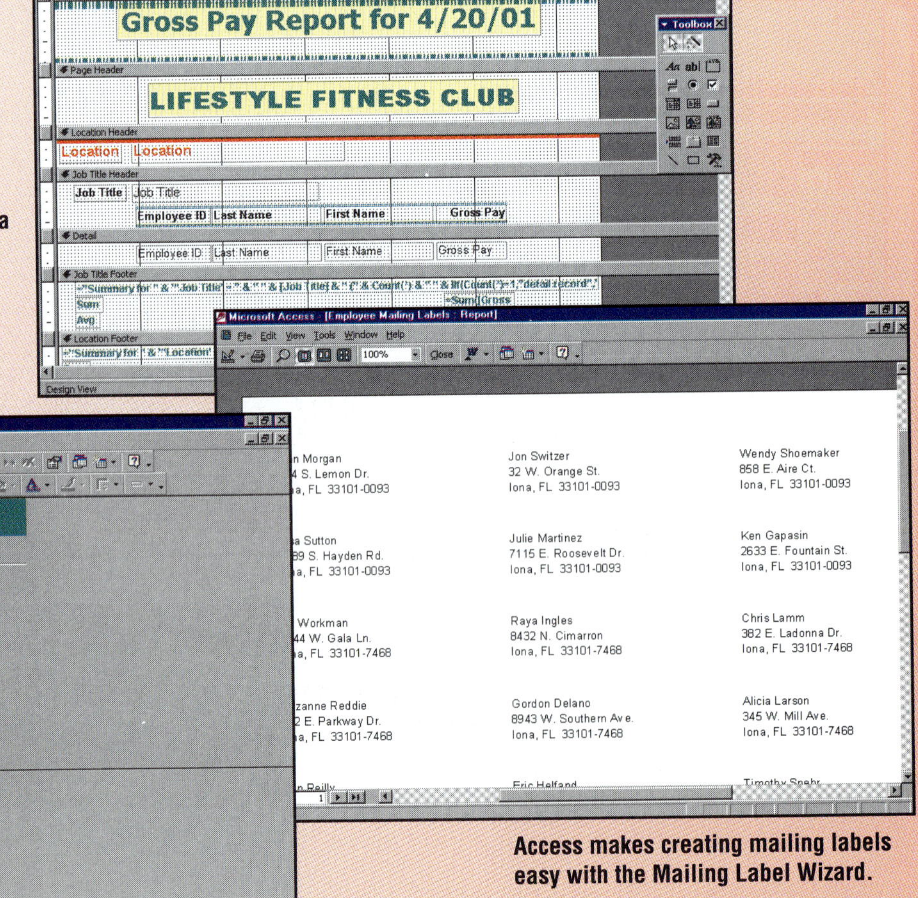

Access makes creating mailing labels easy with the Mailing Label Wizard.

accountants at the various club locations. This report will group and summarize the payroll data in an organized and attractive manner, as shown in the report example below.

You have also been asked to use the employee database to create mailing labels.

Finally, the owners would like you to develop macros and a switchboard system that will help the users of the Employee database quickly navigate through its forms and reports to work with them as necessary and then close the database when through.

Gross Pay Report for 4/20/01

LIFESTYLE FITNESS CLUB

Location Cypress Lake

Job Title Aerobics Instructor

Employee ID	Last Name	First Name	Gross Pay
0493	Facqur	Danial	$117.00
0600	Robertson	Kirk	$262.50
1238	Thomas	Jennifer	$135.00

Summary for 'Job Title' = Aerobics Instructor (3 detail records)

Sum	$514.50
Avg	$171.50

Job Title Assistant Manager

Employee ID	Last Name	First Name	Gross Pay
1235	Walker	Aaron	$480.00

Summary for 'Job Title' = Assistant Manager (1 detail record)

Sum	$480.00
Avg	$480.00

Job Title Child Care Coordinator

Employee ID	Last Name	First Name	Gross Pay
0692	Ingles	Raya	$206.25

Summary for 'Job Title' = Child Care Coordinator (1 detail record)

Sum	$206.25
Avg	$206.25

Job Title Child Care Provider

Employee ID	Last Name	First Name	Gross Pay
2229	Rogondino	Pat	$162.00
2211	Schneider	Paul	$135.00

Summary for 'Job Title' = Child Care Provider (2 detail records)

Sum	$297.00
Avg	$148.50

5/26/99

Page 1 of 8

Concept Overview

The following concepts will be introduced in this lab:

1 **Grouping Records**   Records in a report can be grouped into categories to allow you to better analyze the data.

2 **Group Calculations**   If you group data in your report, you can perform group calculations on values, such as a group total, an average, a minimum value, and a maximum value.

3 **Macro**   A macro automates common Access database tasks, such as opening and printing tables, forms, and reports.

4 **Switchboard**   A switchboard is an Access form that contains buttons for performing a variety of actions in a database, such as viewing and printing tables, forms, and reports.

Creating a Grouped Report

The first report you want to create will display the employees' gross pay grouped by location and job title. You have sketched out the report to look like the one shown below.

```
                      Gross Pay Report for xx/xx/xx

Location:           XXXXXX
Job Title:          XXXXXX
Employee ID         Last Name      First Name      Gross Pay
XXXX                XXXXXX         XXXXXX          $XXXX.XX
XXXX                XXXXXX         XXXXXX          $XXXX.XX


Sum by Location                                    $XXXX.XX
Avg by Location                                    $XXXX.XX
Sum by Job Title:                                  $XXXX.XX
Avg by Job Title                                   $XXXX.XX
```

To create this report, you will use the query you created in Tutorial 4 and saved as Gross Pay for 4/20/01. It is usually helpful to run the query first to remind you of the data that the query gathers.

1 Start Access 2000.

Open the Club Employees database file from your data disk.

Open the Gross Pay for 4/20/01 query.

Maximize the window.

Your screen should be similar to Figure 6–1.

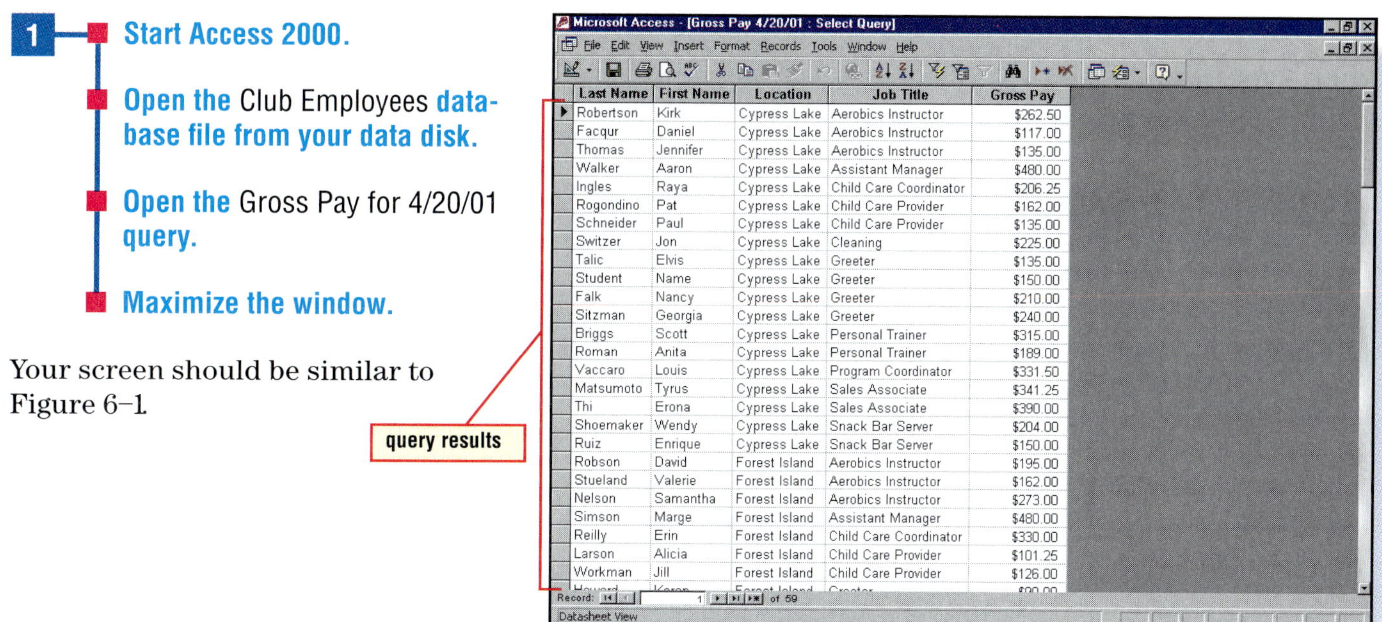

Figure 6–1

The query datasheet displays the Last Name, First Name, Location, Job Title, and Gross Pay fields. In addition, you need the report to display the Employee ID field. To include this field in the report, you need to add it to the query design grid.

2 Switch to Query Design view.

Double-click the Employee ID field to add it from the Employees table to the design grid.

Run the query.

Your screen should be similar to Figure 6–2.

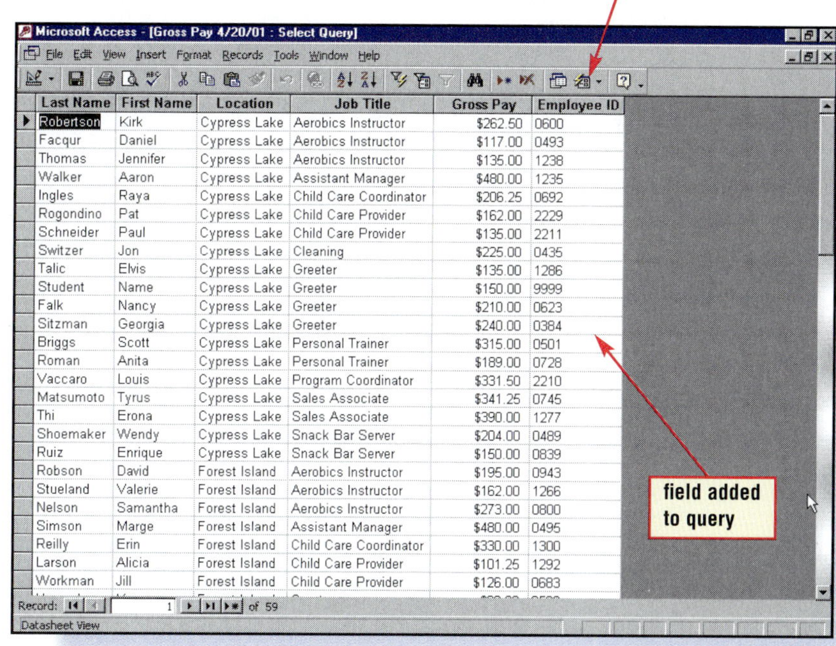

Figure 6–2

Now you are ready to create a report using the data from the query. Rather than switching to the Report tab of the Database window and choosing New, you can use the 　 New Object button to create a new object of any type.

3 ■ Open the 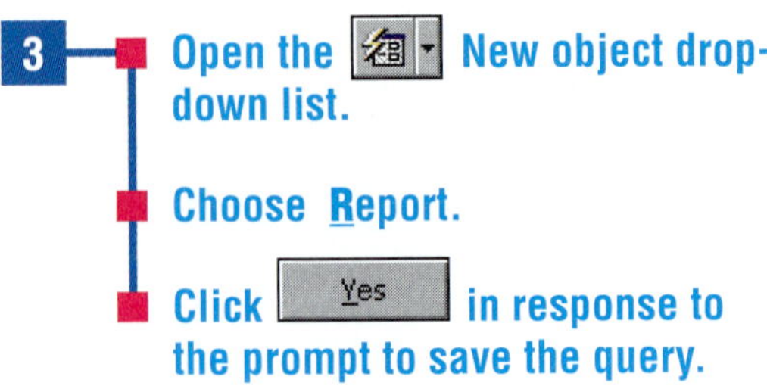 New object drop-
down list.

■ Choose **R**eport.

■ Click **Yes** in response to
the prompt to save the query.

Your screen should be similar to
Figure 6–3.

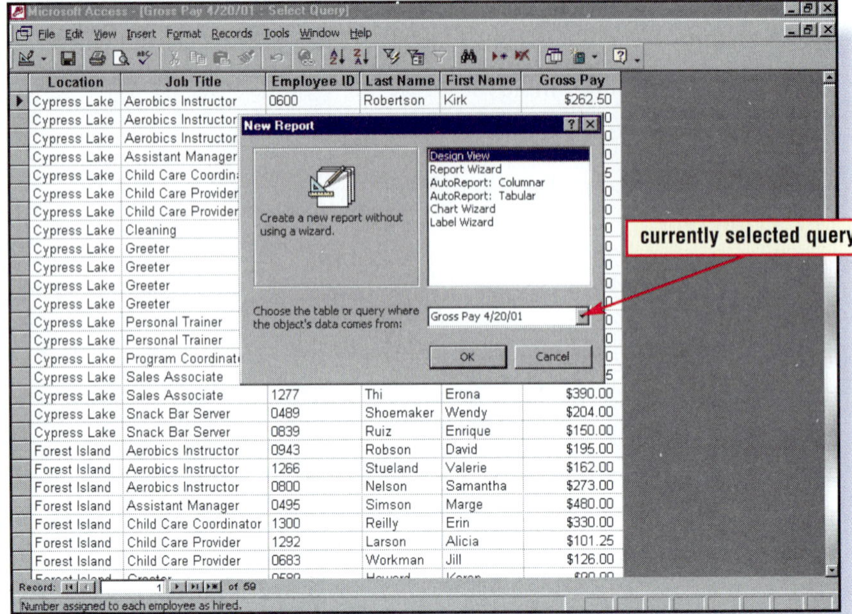

Figure 6–3

You will use the Report Wizard to create the new report. The New Report
dialog box correctly displays the name of the selected query as the object
on which the report will be based.

4 ■ **Select** Report Wizard.

■ Click **OK**.

Your screen should be similar to
Figure 6–4.

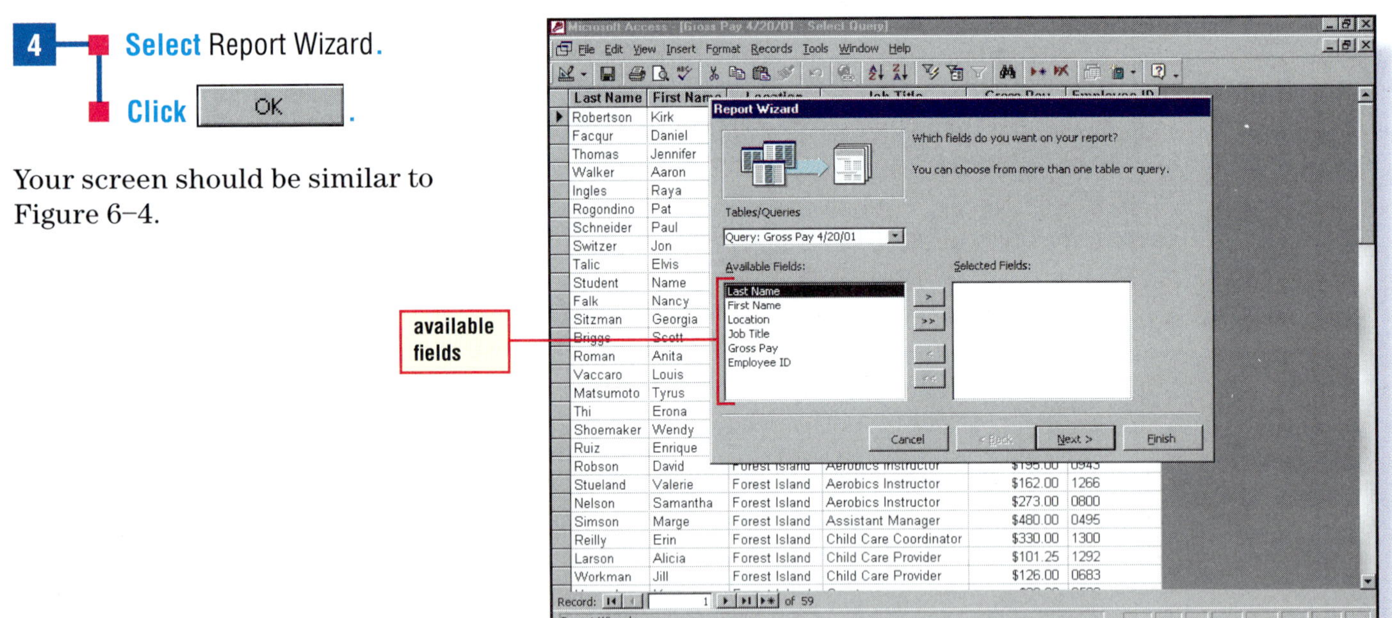

Figure 6–4

The Available Fields list box displays the fields that are included in the design grid in the Gross Pay for 4/20/01 query. You want to include all the
fields in the report.

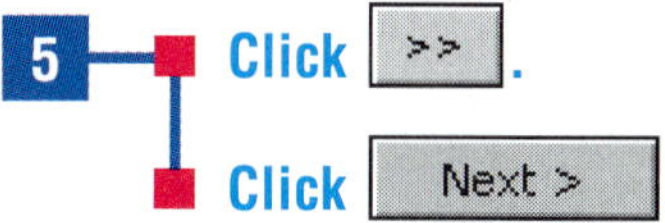

In the next dialog box, you need to select the fields on which you want to group the report.

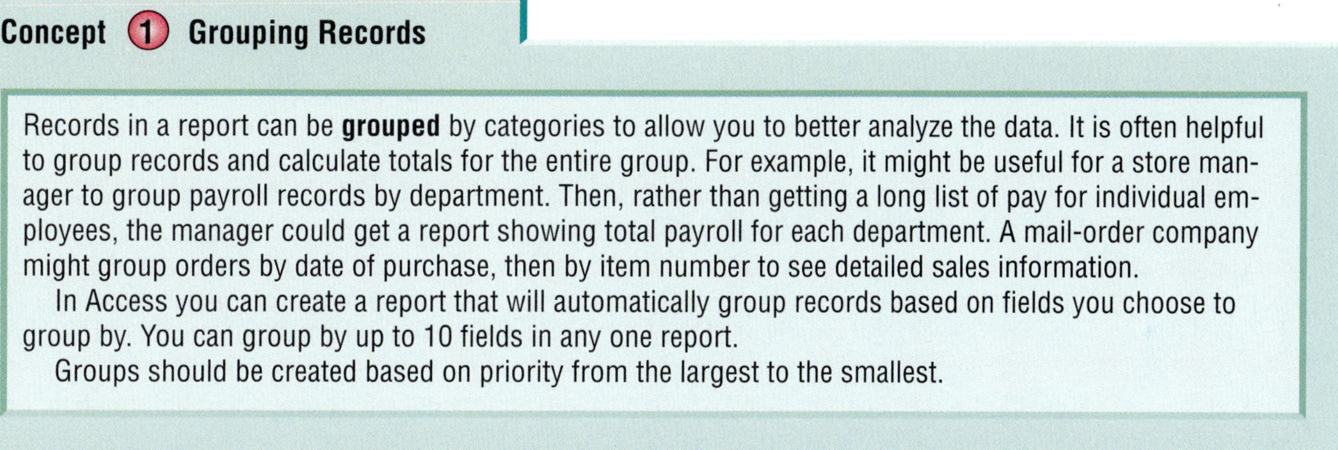

Concept 1 Grouping Records

Records in a report can be **grouped** by categories to allow you to better analyze the data. It is often helpful to group records and calculate totals for the entire group. For example, it might be useful for a store manager to group payroll records by department. Then, rather than getting a long list of pay for individual employees, the manager could get a report showing total payroll for each department. A mail-order company might group orders by date of purchase, then by item number to see detailed sales information.

In Access you can create a report that will automatically group records based on fields you choose to group by. You can group by up to 10 fields in any one report.

Groups should be created based on priority from the largest to the smallest.

To group the report by location and then by job titles within each location,

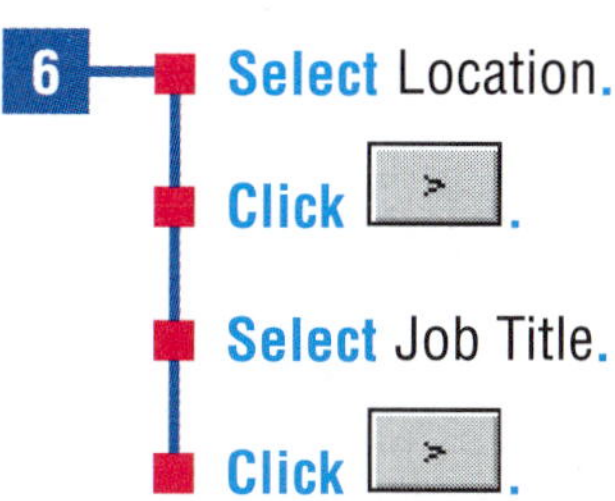

Your screen should be similar to Figure 6–5.

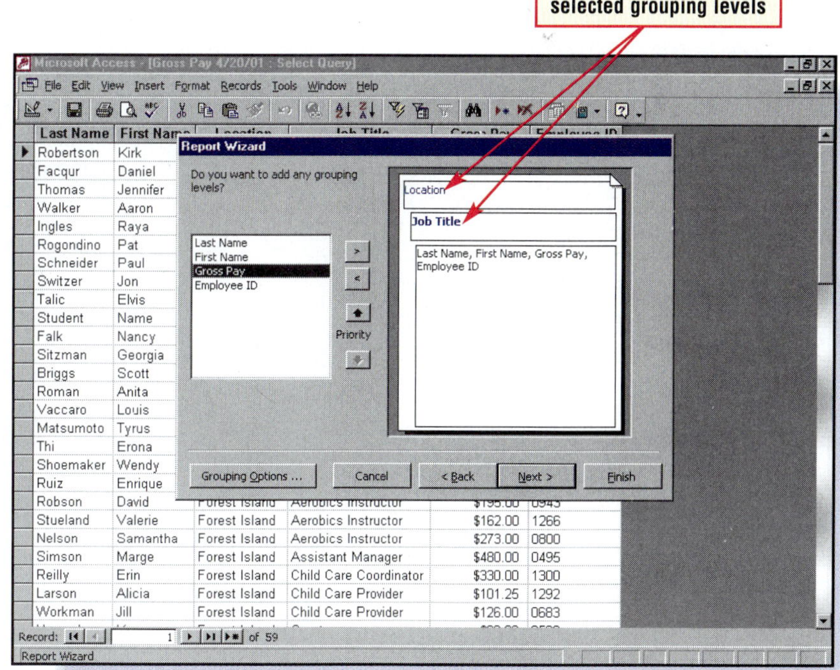

Figure 6–5

The report will group the data first by location and then by job title within the location.

The data is sorted by field within the specified groups.

In addition, because you have specified groups, you can also include calculations to summarize the grouped data.

Concept (2) Group Calculations

If you group data in your report, you can perform one or more of the following **group calculations** on values: **Sum** (adds all values by group), **Avg** (calculates the average value for the group), **Min** (calculates the lowest value for the group), and **Max** (calculates the highest value for the group).

You can select multiple calculations to complete different analyses of the data. For example, a mail order company might calculate the sum of different products sold on each day of the month and the average sale for each day. You can also calculate the percent of total for the sums. For example, the mail order company might want to know what percentage of total sales were made on a specific product for June 15.

You can further customize the report to display both detailed information and the summary information, or just the summary information while hiding the details about the individual items.

You would like the report to display a total and average for each location and job title.

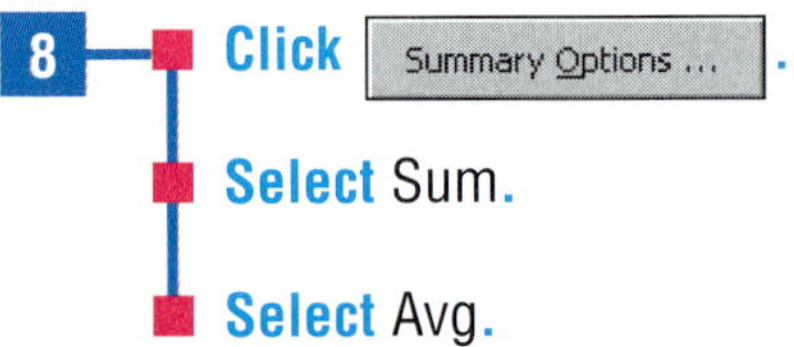

Your screen should be similar to Figure 6–6.

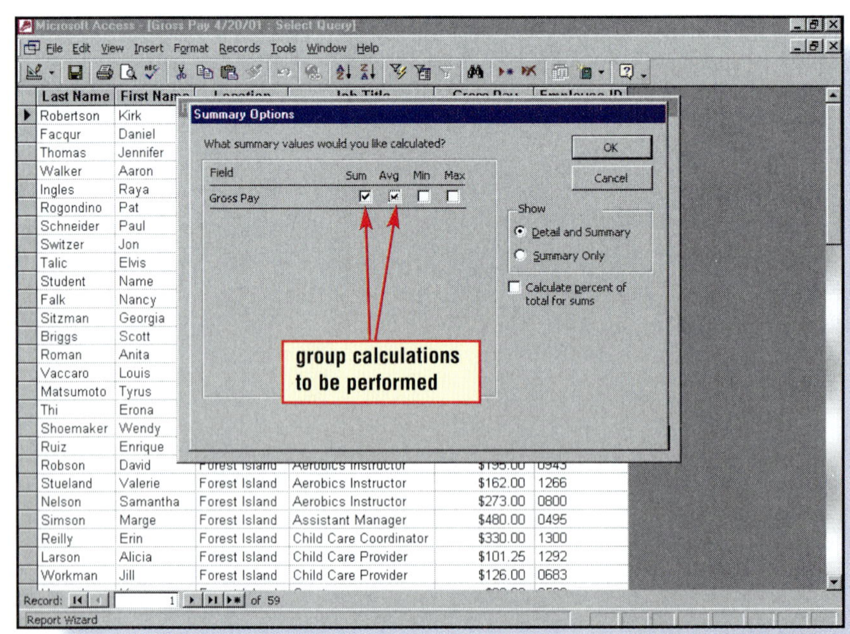

Figure 6–6

The report will display a total and average for the gross pay field for each group.

9

Click OK .

Click Next > .

Your screen should be similar to Figure 6–7.

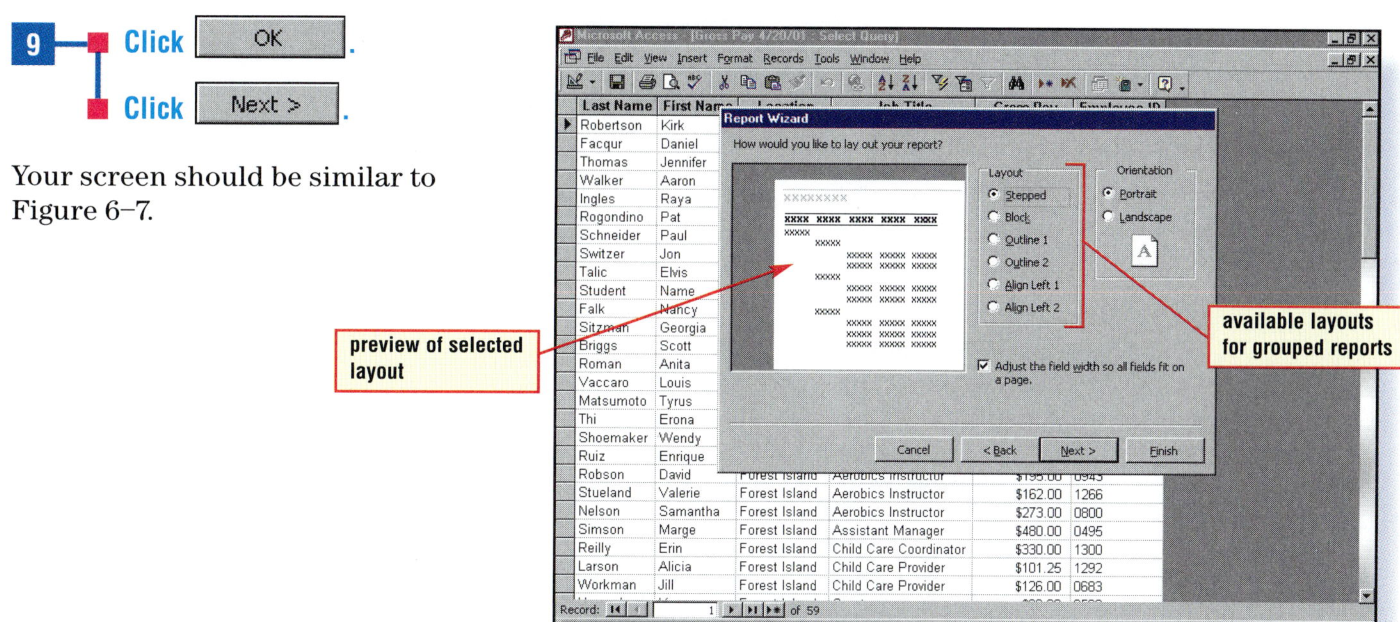

Figure 6–7

In this dialog box you are asked to select from six different layout options for a grouped report. You will use the Outline 1 layout.

10

Select each layout option and look at the sample previews.

Select Outline 1.

Click Next > .

Select the report style of Casual.

Click Next > .

Enter the report title of **Gross Pay Report for 4/20/01**.

Click Finish .

Your screen should be similar to Figure 6–8.

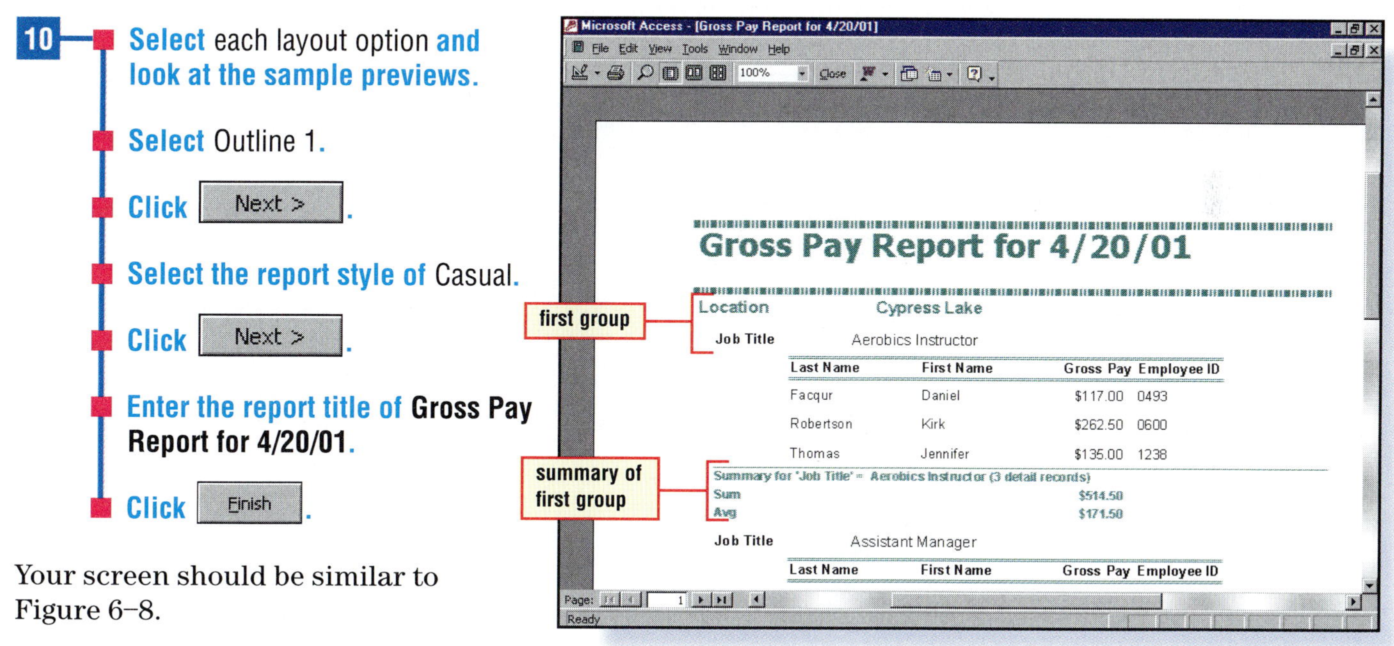

Figure 6–8

The data in the report is grouped by location and job title, and the records are alphabetized by last name within groups. The information for the Cypress Lake club is the first location group, and Aerobics Instructor is the first job title group within that location group. In addition, each location group displays a count of employees and the sum and average values for that job title.

11 ▪ **Display page 3 and look at the summary information at the end of the Cypress Lake group and the beginning of the Forest Island group.**

Your screen should be similar to Figure 6–9.

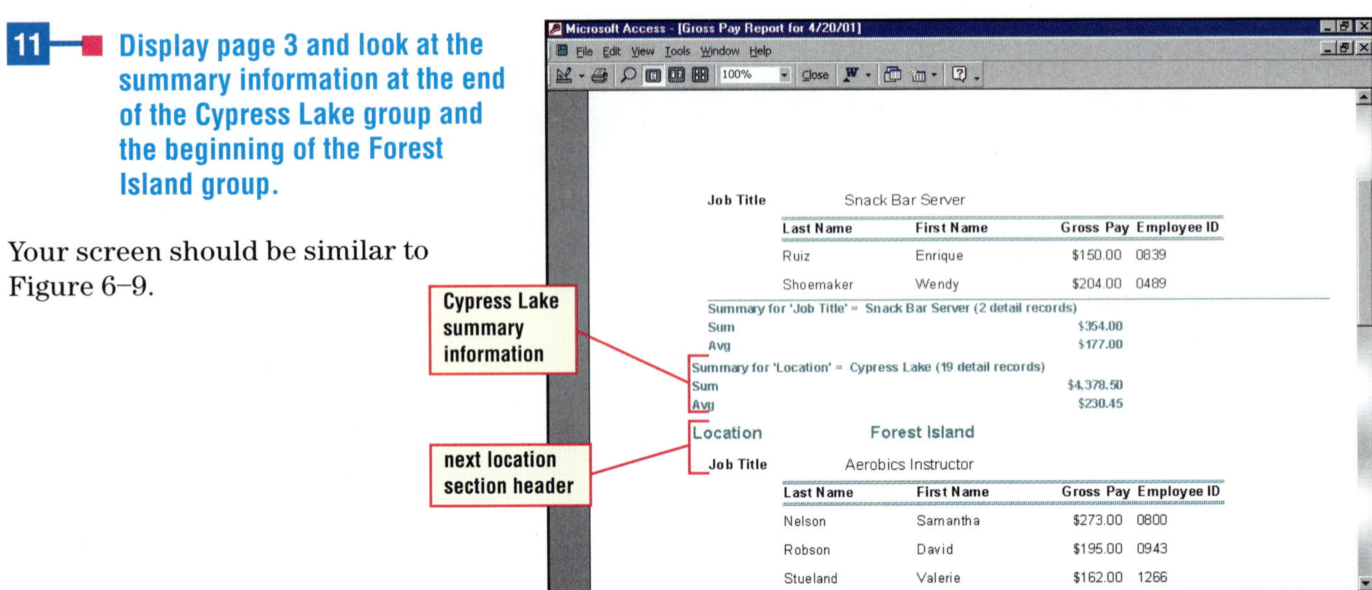

Figure 6–9

The summary information for Cypress Lake appears above the Forest Island group head. It includes a count value, and the total and average gross pay values for the club location.

12 ▪ **Display the end of the last page of the report.**

Your screen should be similar to Figure 6–10.

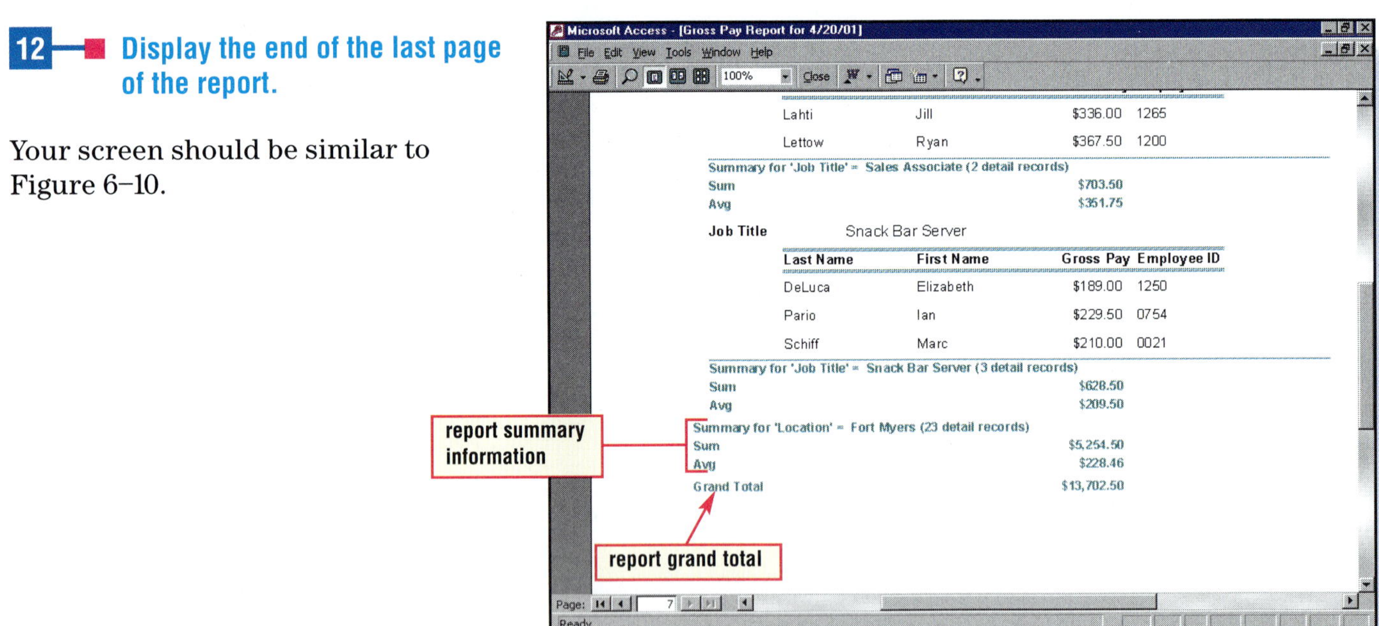

Figure 6–10

A grand total value for all clubs appears at the end of the report.

13 ▪ **Display the top of page 1 again.**

The report has all the data you requested, but you are not totally pleased with the way the report looks. You would like to move some things around to improve the report's appearance.

Customizing the Report Layout

As you looked through the report, you saw several changes you wanted to make. The first change is to rearrange the order of the fields in the report and to size the fields appropriately. In addition, you want to make the location group head more noticeable, to change the display of the date in the footer to exclude the day of the week, and to center the title over the report. As you recall from your previous work with reports, these changes are made in Report Design view.

1 ■ **Switch to Report Design view.**

   ■ **If necessary, close the Field List.**

Your screen should be similar to Figure 6–11.

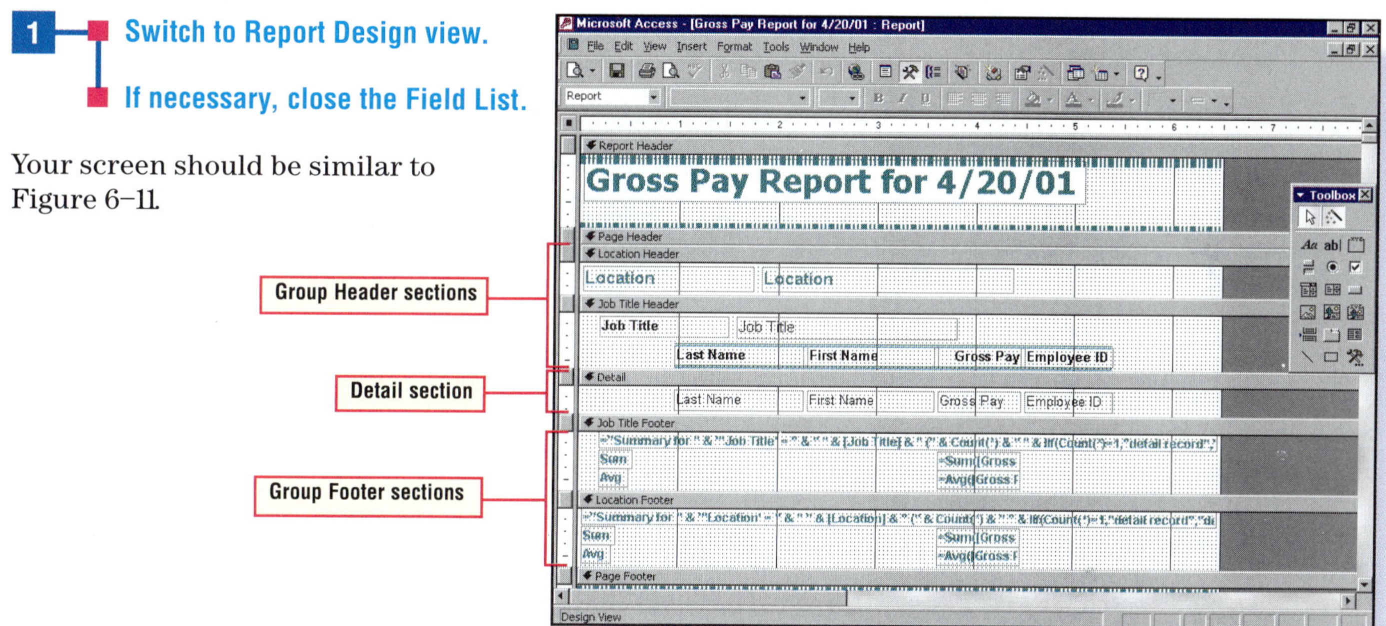

Figure 6–11

Notice that the Report Design view is slightly different for grouped reports than for the reports you've created previously. Besides the standard Report Header, Page Header, Detail, Page Footer, and Report Footer sections, there are also sections called Location Header and Job Title Footer. These are called **Group Header and Footer sections** and display group identification information on the report each time the group changes. Notice that the Job Title section displays the label control for each field column, while the Detail section contains the text box controls. You will first move and resize several of the report controls.

2 ■ **Resize and adjust the placement of the** Job Title **and** Location **label controls to fit their contents as necessary.**

Use **F**ormat/**S**ize/To **F**it to automatically resize the selected control to fit its contents.

■ **Select** the Employee ID controls **and move them to the left of the Last Name controls.**

■ **Select** all eight controls **and position them as a group so they are within the column title borders (use the double green bars in the Job Title Header section as a guide), as shown in Figure 6–10.**

■ **Select** the five Gross Pay summary text controls **in the Job Title Footer, Location Footer, and Report Footer sections and move them to the right to align with the Gross Pay text control in the Detail section.**

Align the right border of the controls.

■ **Clear the selection.**

Your screen should look similar to Figure 6–12.

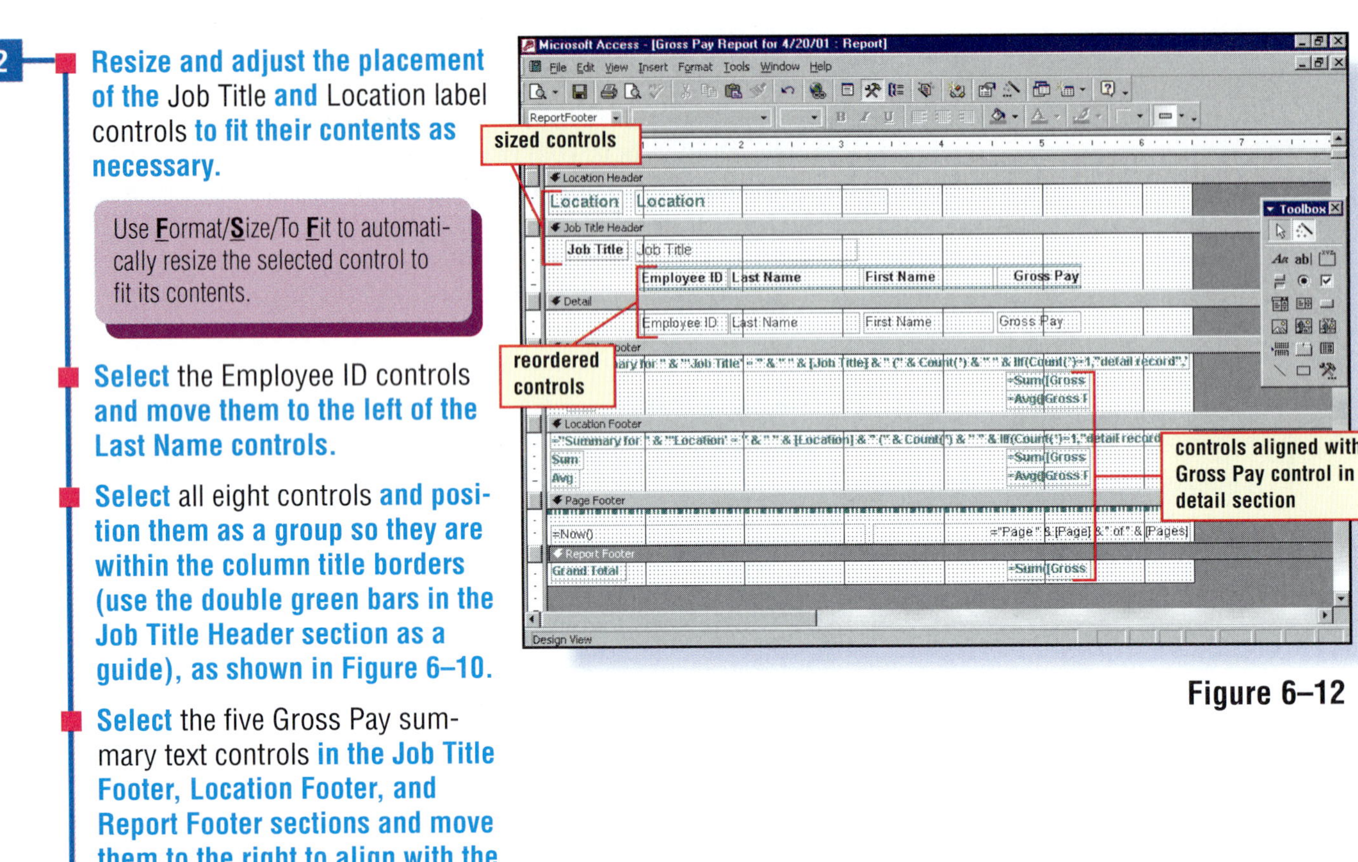

Figure 6–12

The next change you will make is to modify how the date is displayed in the Page Footer. To do this, you will change the date's control property.

Changing Control Properties

Notice that the date control in the Page Footer is =Now(). This is an expression that directs Access to enter the current date maintained on your computer into the report. Each control has property settings that affect how the control looks and acts. By default, the property setting associated with the date control displays the date in the Long Date format. To change the date control properties,

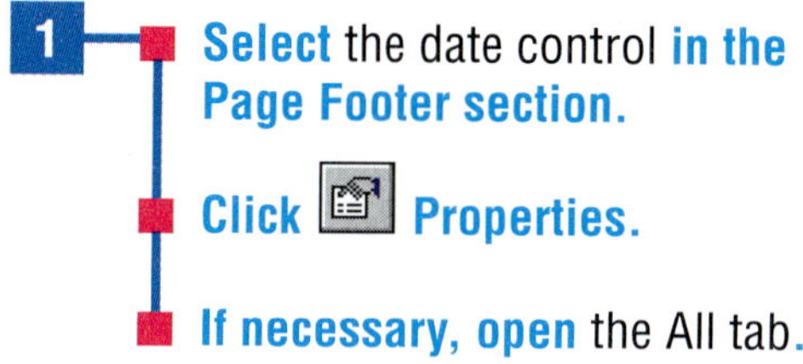

1   **Select** the date control **in the Page Footer section.**

■ **Click** 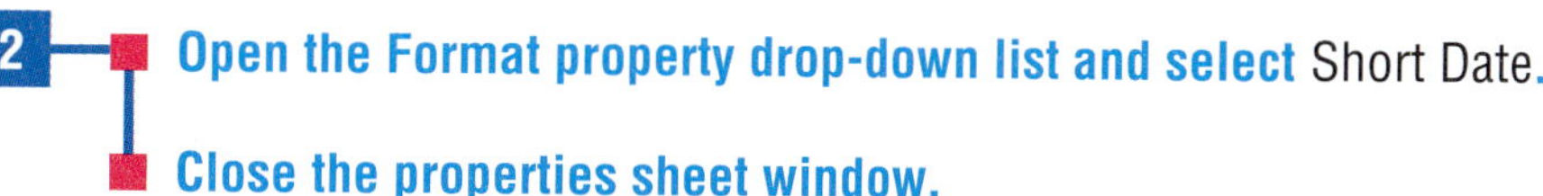 **Properties.**

■ **If necessary, open** the All tab.

Your screen should be similar to Figure 6–13.

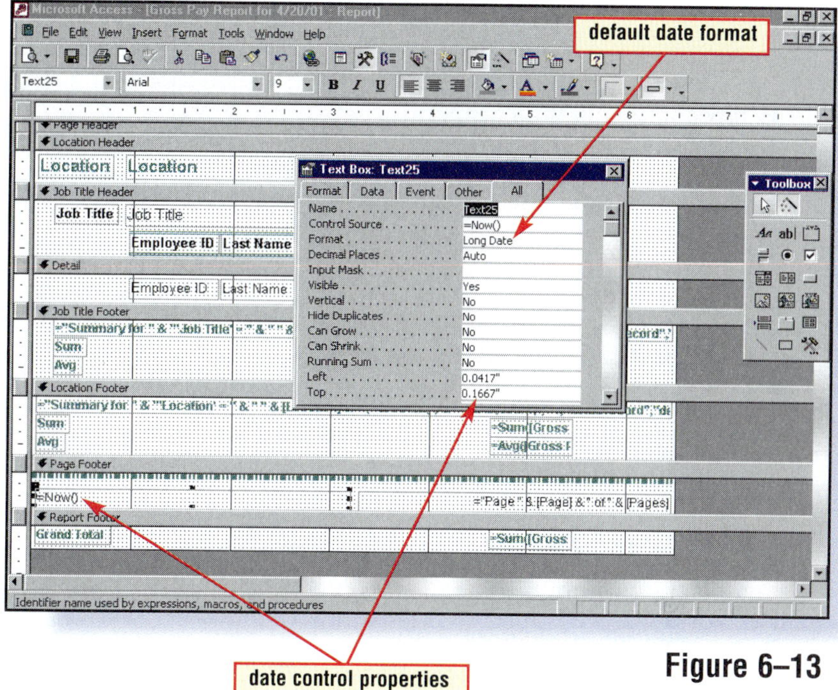

Figure 6–13

The properties sheet for the date control is displayed. The All tab displays a list of all properties associated with the selected control. The Format properties contain the same options as in Table Design and vary with the data type of the field. The Format text box displays "Long Date." This date format displays the date as Day, Month xx, 19xx. You want to display the date in the Short Date format of mm/dd/yy.

> Scroll the drop-down list to the right to see the examples of different date formats.

2   **Open the Format property drop-down list and select** Short Date.

■ **Close the properties sheet window.**

Next, you'll make some cosmetic changes to your report to enhance its appearance.

Adding Font, Color, and Line Enhancements

To make the Location heading stand out more and visually separate the report areas, you decide to change the text color and add a heavy colored horizontal line above the controls.

1

Select the Location label and text box controls **in the Location Header section.**

> Even though this is a compound control, you need to select each control individually to apply font color changes to each.

Select a color of your choice **from the** 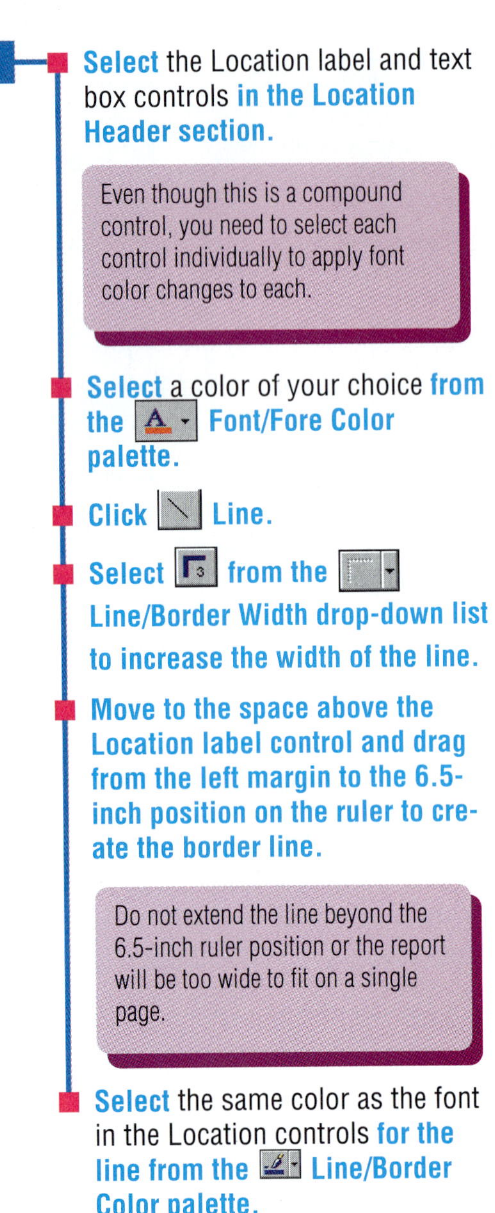 **Font/Fore Color palette.**

Click Line.

Select from the **Line/Border Width drop-down list to increase the width of the line.**

Move to the space above the Location label control and drag from the left margin to the 6.5-inch position on the ruler to create the border line.

> Do not extend the line beyond the 6.5-inch ruler position or the report will be too wide to fit on a single page.

Select the same color as the font in the Location controls **for the line from the** **Line/Border Color palette.**

Your screen should be similar to Figure 6–14.

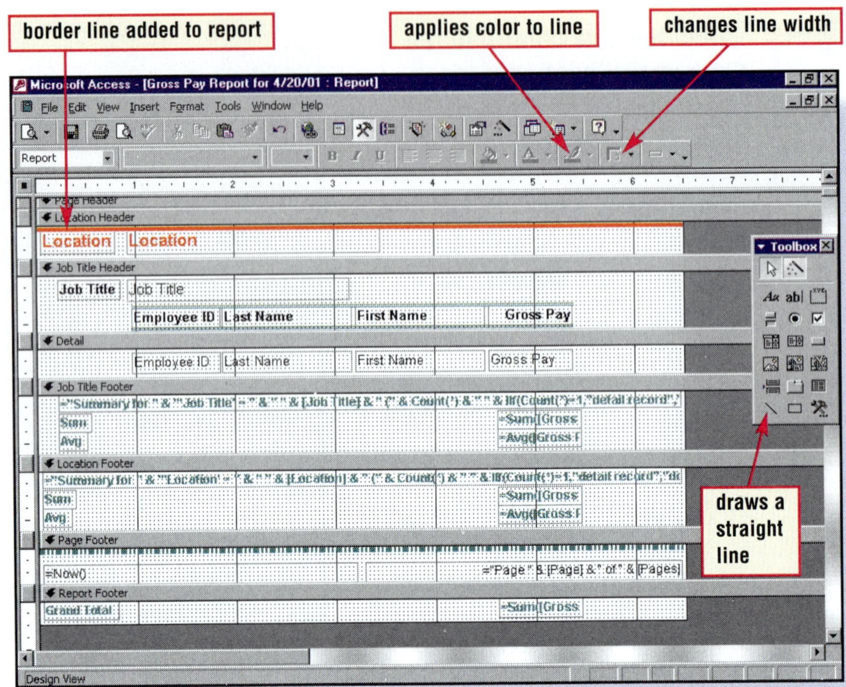

Figure 6–14

You also want to center the title over the report and change the background shading color of the Report Header control.

2

Select the report title control in the Report Header section.

Move the title until the left border of the box aligns with the .75-inch ruler mark and the control is centered vertically in the Report Header section (see Figure 6–15).

Select a color of your choice from the 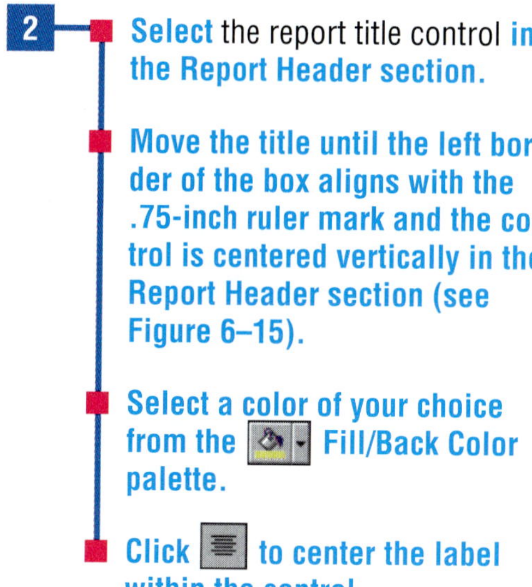 Fill/Back Color palette.

Click to center the label within the control.

Your screen should be similar to Figure 6–15.

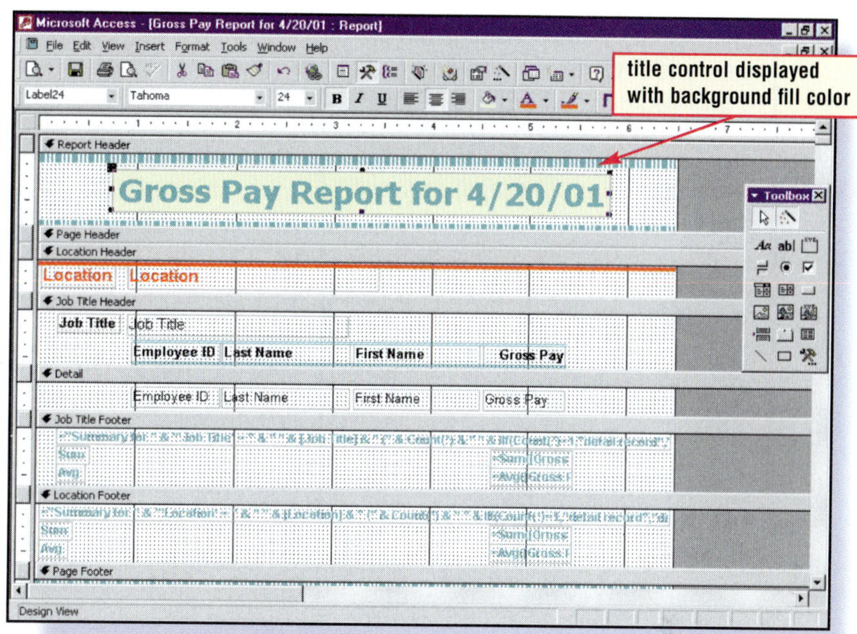

Figure 6–15

Next, you'd like the name of the club to appear on every page of the report, so you will add it to the Page Header section.

Adding a Page Header to the Report

Unlike a report header, which prints only on the first page of a report, a page header will print at the top of every page. You want the header to display the name of the club.

1

- **Drag** the Location Header bar down to increase the size of the Page Header section.

- **Click** 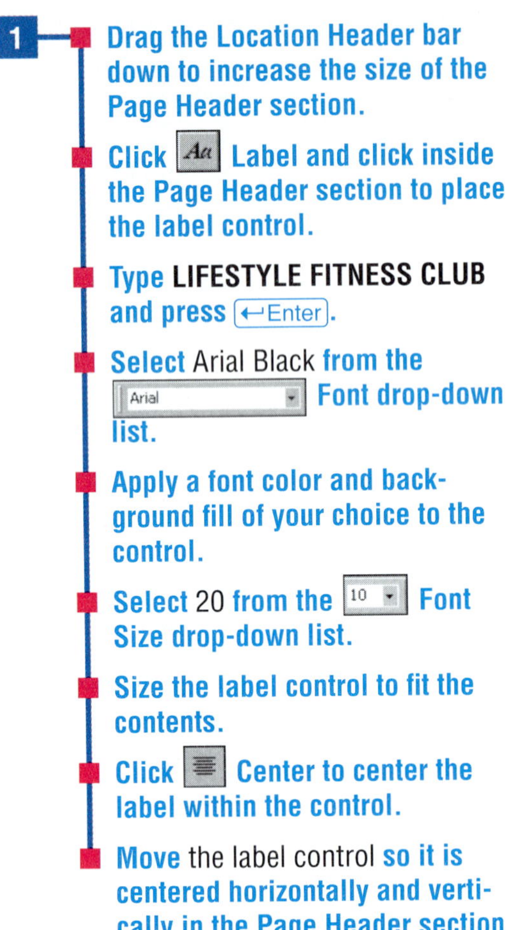 **Label** and click inside the Page Header section to place the label control.

- **Type** LIFESTYLE FITNESS CLUB and press ←Enter.

- **Select** Arial Black **from the** Arial **Font drop-down list.**

- **Apply** a font color and background fill of your choice to the control.

- **Select** 20 **from the** 10 **Font Size drop-down list.**

- **Size** the label control to fit the contents.

- **Click** Center **to center the** label within the control.

- **Move** the label control so it is centered horizontally and vertically in the Page Header section.

Your screen should be similar to Figure 6–16.

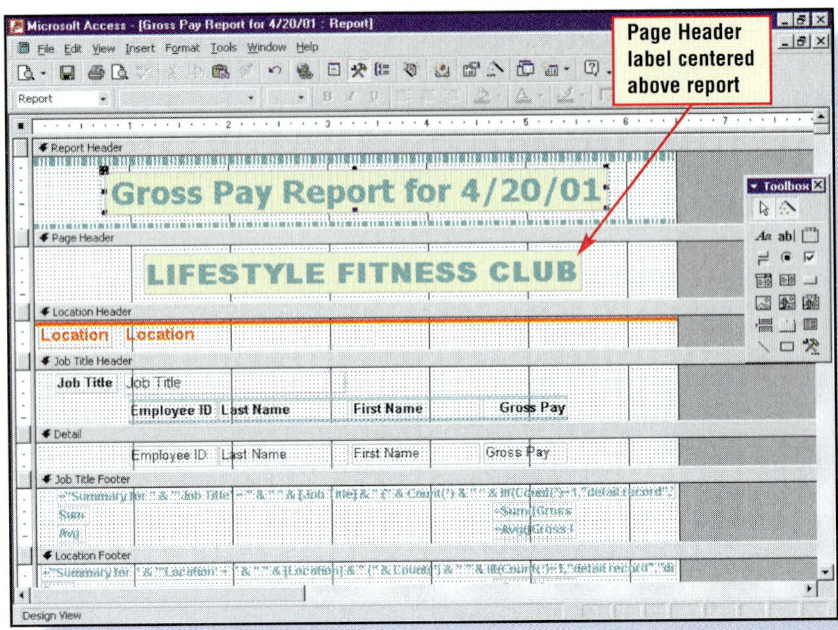

Figure 6–16

This is the last change you want to make to the report's layout and appearance. Now you need to see how the report data looks with all these enhancements.

2 ■ **Switch to Print Preview.**

Your screen should be similar to
Figure 6–17.

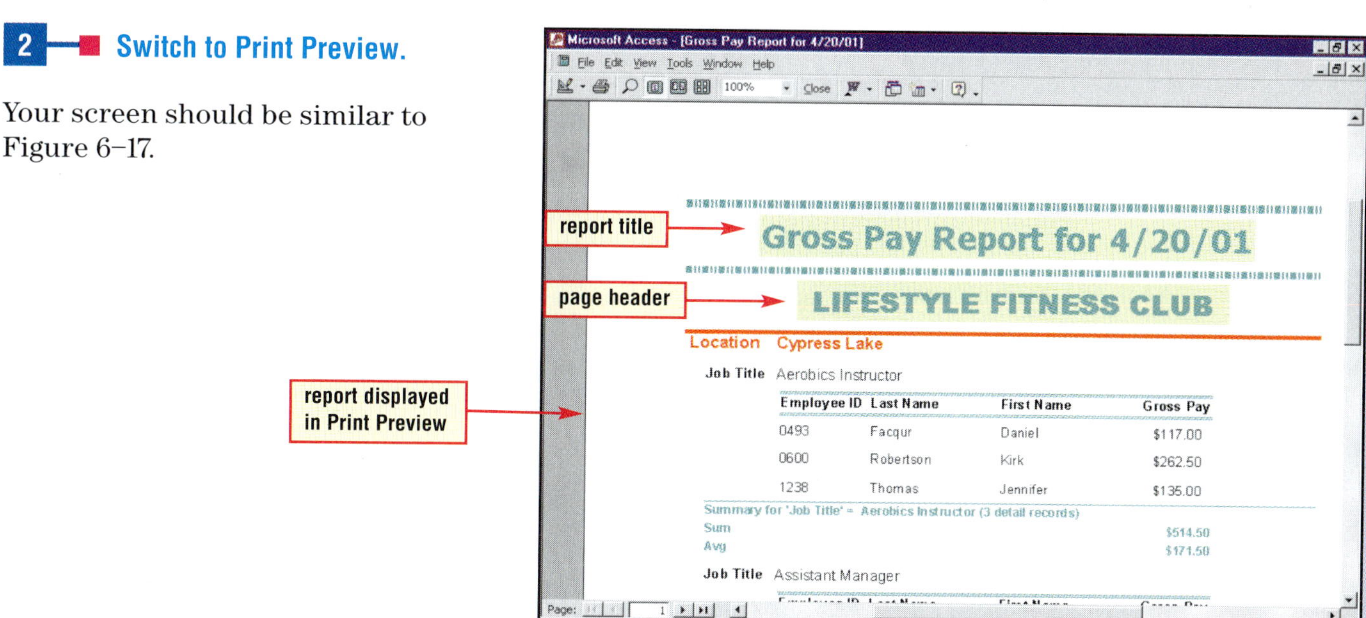

Figure 6–17

The title appears centered and with the background color you selected,
and the club name is displayed under it. The color change you made to the
Location controls and the addition of the colored horizontal line make it
much easier to locate the beginning of a new section.

There is only one more thing you want to add to your report before
you print it out. The club owners have asked that the report include the
annual gross pay to date. To provide this information, you will add a control to the end of the report that will calculate this value.

Adding a Calculated Control to a Report

A **calculated control** works the same way in a report as it does in a form—
you enter an expression into it that calculates values from other controls
in the report or its underlying table or query, and it displays the results of
that expression. Since you want the calculated control to display the to-
date gross pay at the end of the report, you will add it below the Grand
Total field in the Report Footer section of the report.

1   **Switch to Report Design view.**

Increase the size of the Report Footer section by dragging the bottom border of the report down.

Your screen should be similar to Figure 6-18.

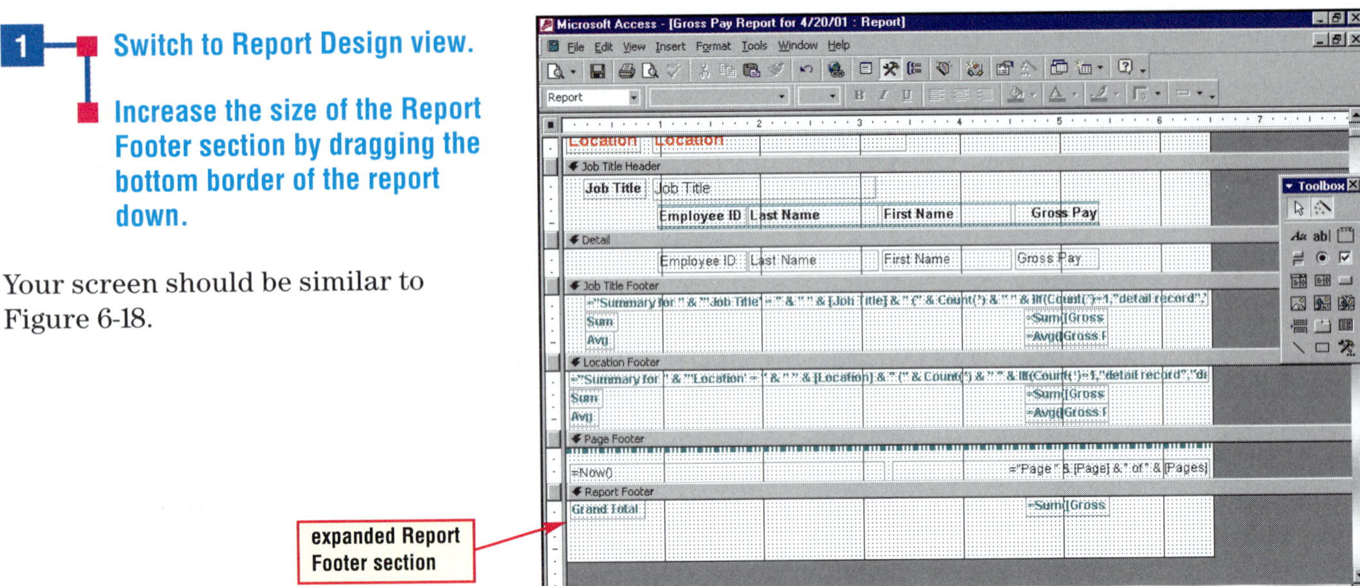

Figure 6–18

Next, you'll add a text box under the Grand Total and use it for your calculated control. The calculation you will enter in this control will add the total gross pay for this pay period to the gross pay for the previous pay periods, which the accounting department has reported was $33,198.92.

2   **Click** abl **Text Box and place the new control under the Grand Total label control.**

Move the new text control so it is right-aligned with the Grand Total text control above it.

Click inside the new text control and type =Sum([Gross Pay])+33198.92.

Press ←Enter.

Move the new label control so it is left-aligned with the Grand Total label control above it.

Change the label to Gross Pay To-Date

Change the font size of the label and text control to 9pt and select a font color of your choice. Bold both parts of the control.

Your screen should be similar to Figure 6–19.

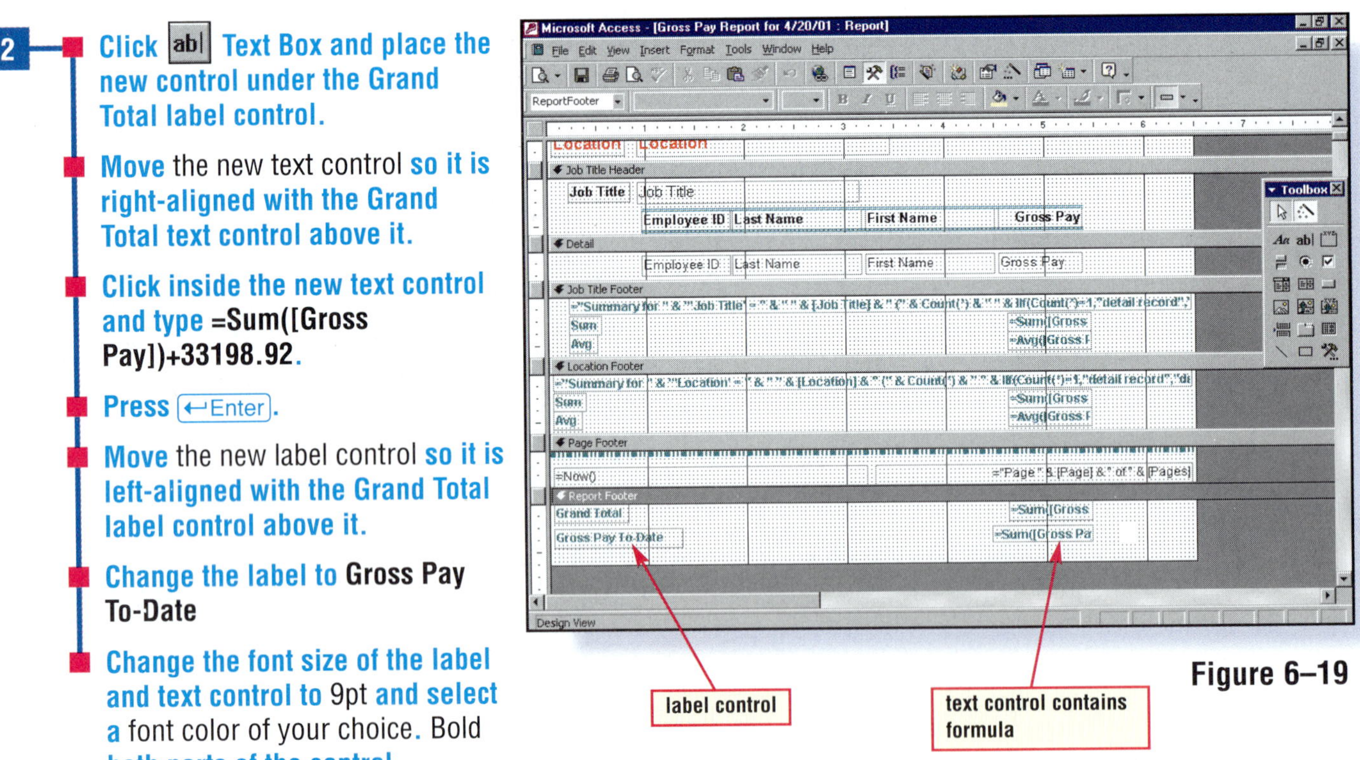

Figure 6–19

To see if and how your new calculated control works in the report,

3 **Switch to Print Preview.**

Go to the last page of the report. If necessary, scroll down until you can see the Grand Total and Gross Pay To-Date fields.

Your screen should be similar to Figure 6–20.

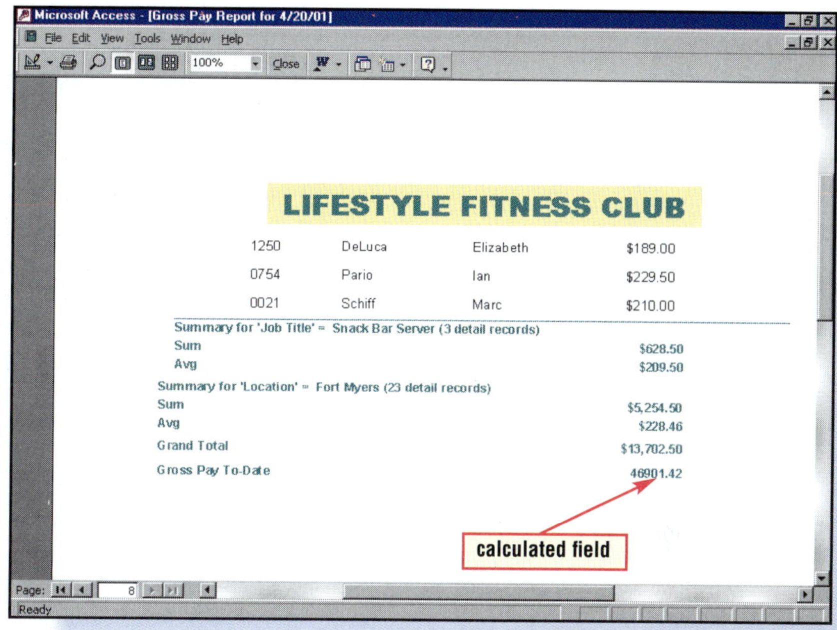

Figure 6–20

It looks like the calculated control has calculated the to-date amount just fine. However, it isn't displayed as currency. To fix this problem:

4 **Switch back to Report Design view.**

Select the Gross Pay to-date calculated control **in the Report Footer section.**

Click **Properties.**

Select Currency **from the Format drop-down list.**

Your screen should be similar to Figure 6–21

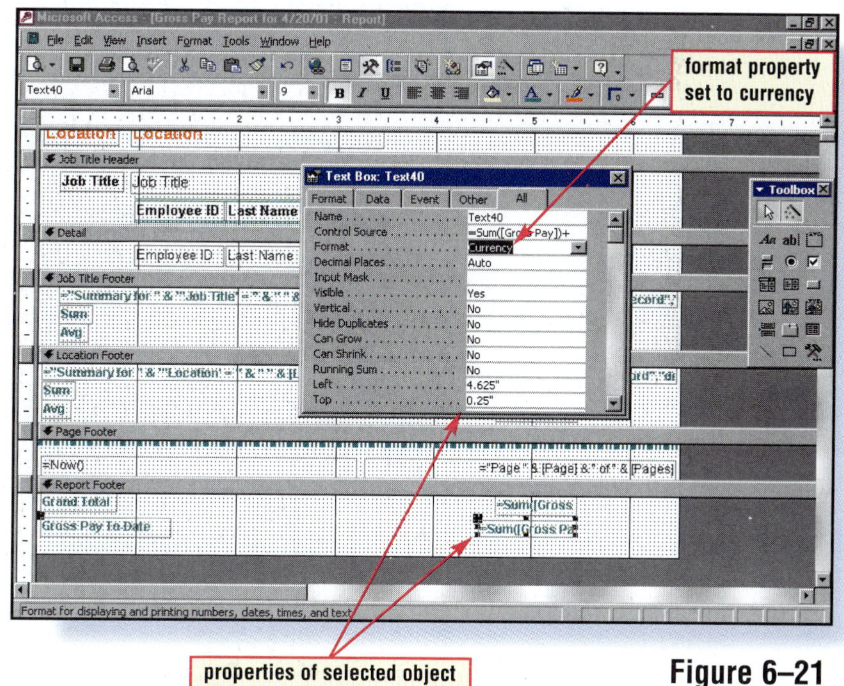

Figure 6–21

You are now ready to view your report as it will look when you print it.

5 • **Close the properties window.**

• **View the report.**

• **Click 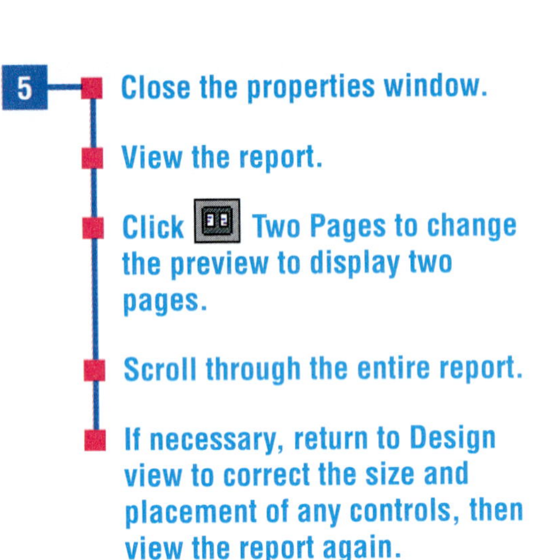 Two Pages to change the preview to display two pages.**

• **Scroll through the entire report.**

• **If necessary, return to Design view to correct the size and placement of any controls, then view the report again.**

Your screen should be similar to Figure 6–22.

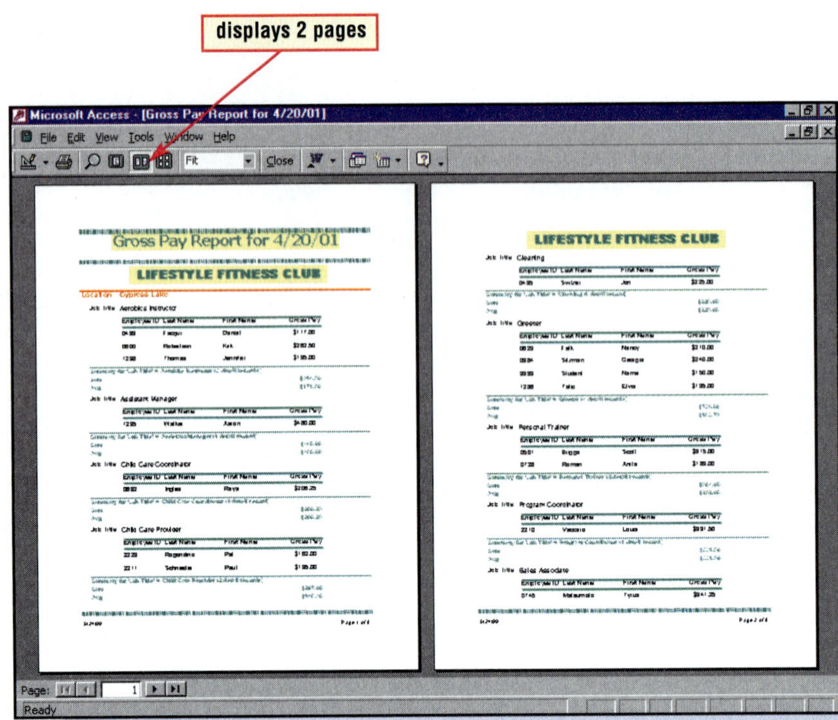

Figure 6–22

You are satisfied with the way the report looks, so you will print and then close it.

6 • **Print pages 1–3 and page 8 of the report.**

• **Close the report, saving any changes.**

• **Close the Gross Pay query.**

Creating Mailing Labels

The final report that the club owners have requested is one that will print mailing labels for every employee in the Employees table. A sample of a mailing label appears below:

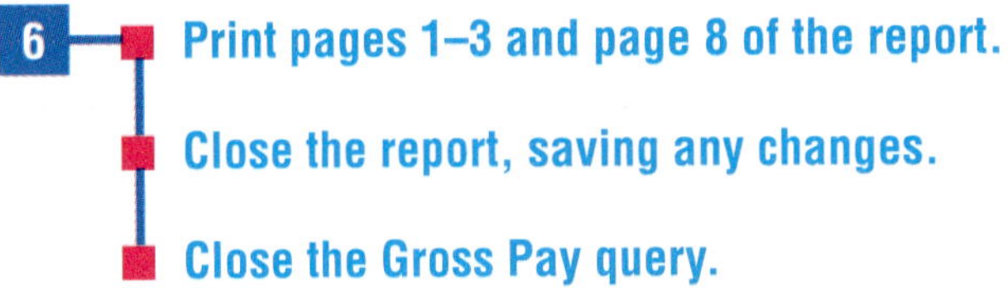

The Report Wizard includes a **Label Wizard** that will create mailing labels. To use this feature,

1
- **Open the** 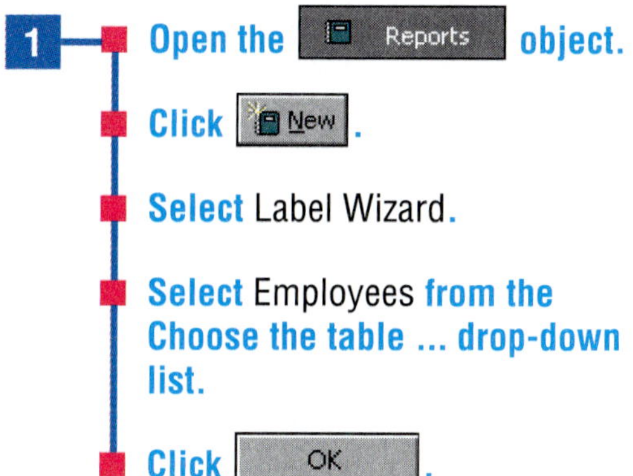 **object.**
- **Click** New .
- **Select** Label Wizard.
- **Select** Employees **from the Choose the table ... drop-down list.**
- **Click** OK .

Your screen should be similar to Figure 6–23.

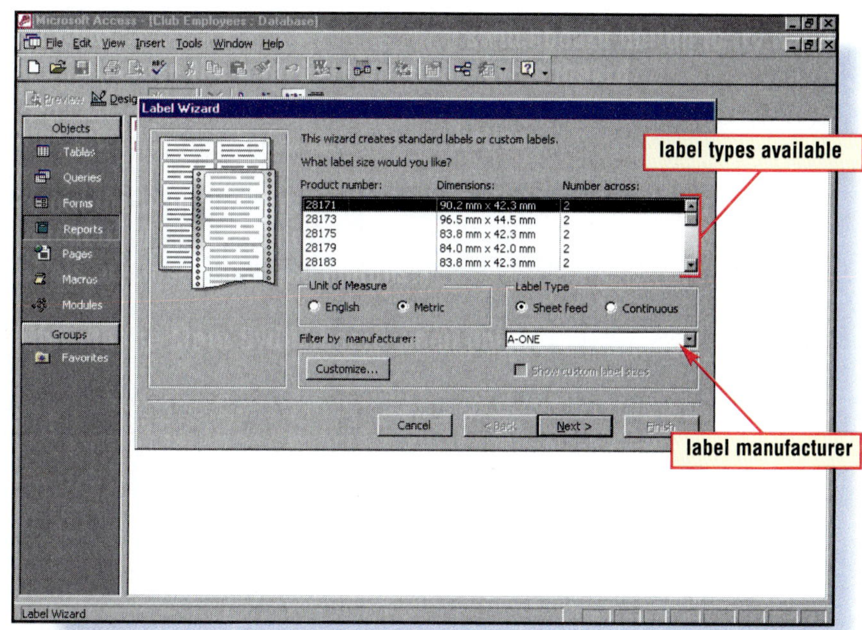

Figure 6–23

In the first LabelWizard dialog box, you specify the type of label you want to create. You can either use a predefined label or create a custom label. The Lifestyle Fitness Club uses mailing labels made by Avery, number 5160. These labels appear three across the width of the paper.

2
- **Select** English **as Unit of Measure.**
- **Select** Avery **from the Filter by manufacturer drop-down list.**
- **Select** 5160 **under the Product number.**
- **Click** Next > .

Your screen should be similar to Figure 6–24.

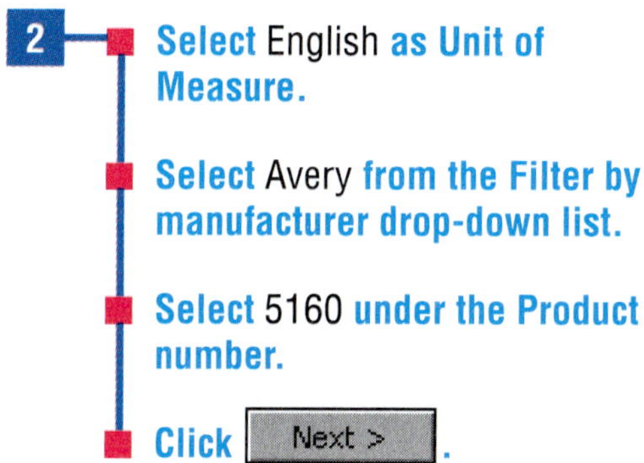

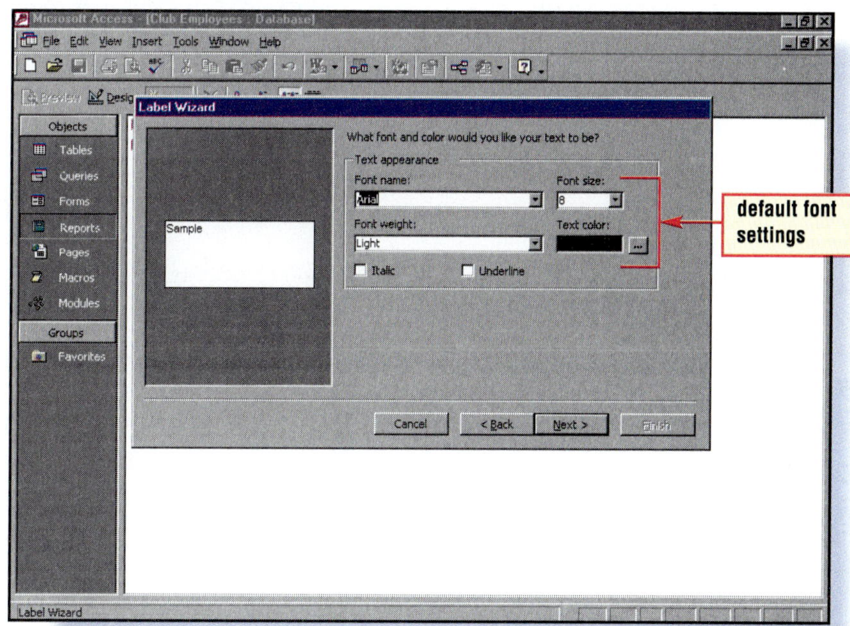

Figure 6–24

In this dialog box, you specify the font and text color settings for the labels. The default font is Arial and the default font size is 8. Because the Label Wizard remembers previous selections, your font size may already be set to 10.

3 **If necessary, change the font size to 10 point.**

Click Next > .

Just as with other reports, you select the fields from the table to include in the labels. Unlike other reports, however, as you select the fields, you also design the label layout in the Prototype Label box. You may type any additional text, such as punctuation or a holiday message, directly onto the prototype.

4 **Select the** First Name **field and click** > **to add it to the Prototype label box.**

Your screen should be similar to Figure 6–25.

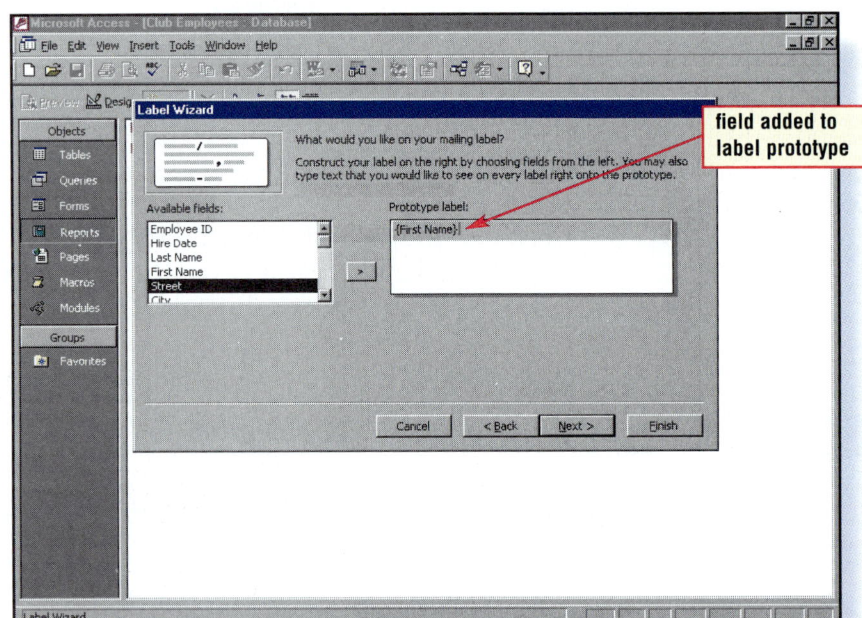

Figure 6–25

The First Name field is displayed in the Prototype label box. You want the last name to be on the same line as the first name, separated from the first name by a space. The address will then be entered on the next line.

5 Press Spacebar.

 Add the Last Name field to the label prototype.

> You can double click the field name to add it to the label prototype.

 Press ←Enter.

 Add the Street field to the prototype and press ←Enter.

 Add the City followed by a comma and a space, the State followed by two spaces, and the Zip Code.

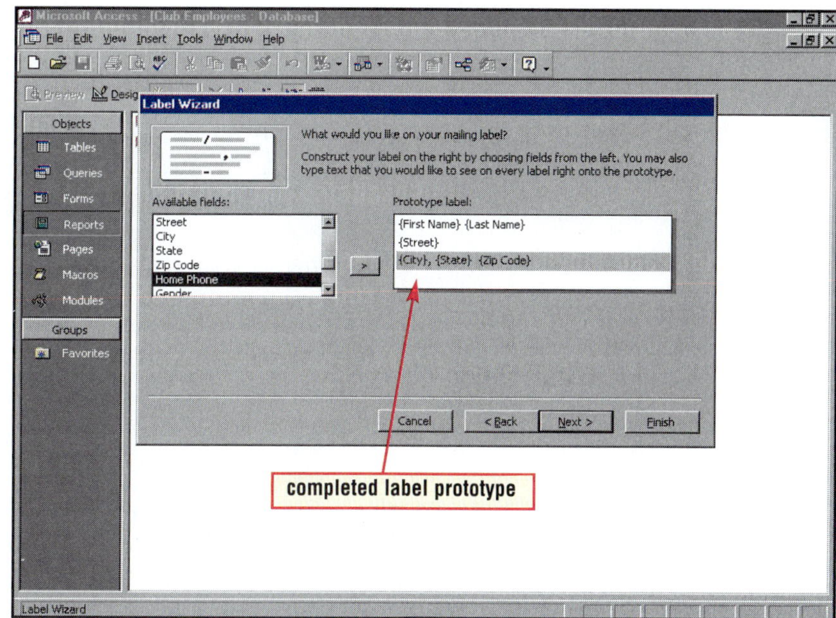

Your screen should be similar to Figure 6–26.

Figure 6–26

You are finished designing the label prototype and are ready to proceed with the label creation.

6 Click Next > .

Your screen should be similar to Figure 6–27.

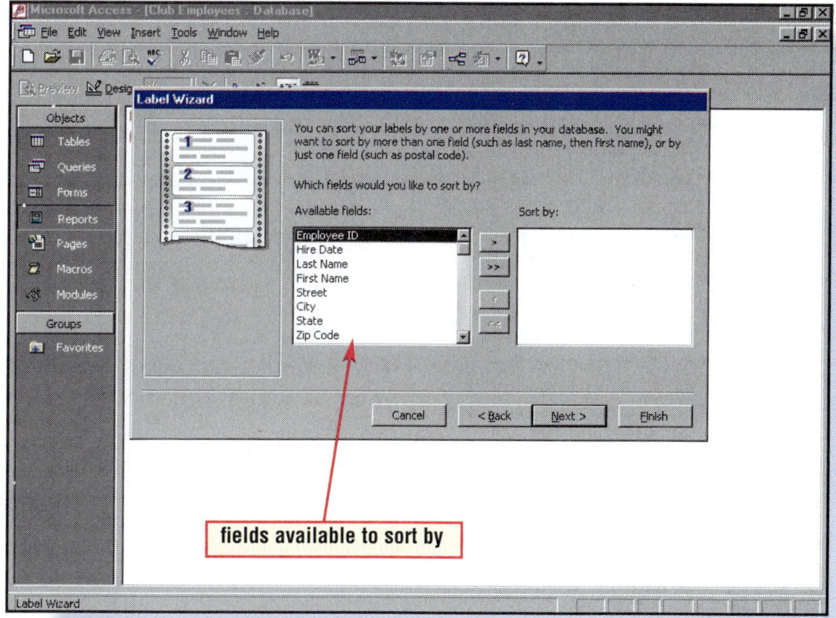

Figure 6–27

In this dialog box you can specify a field on which to sort the labels. You want to take advantage of postal discounts resulting from mailings that are sorted by zip code.

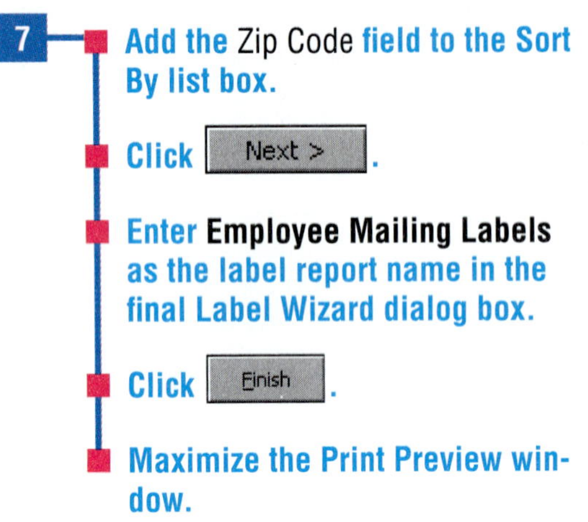

7

Add the Zip Code field to the Sort By list box.

Click   Next >   .

Enter **Employee Mailing Labels** as the label report name in the final Label Wizard dialog box.

Click   Finish   .

Maximize the Print Preview window.

Your screen should be similar to Figure 6–28.

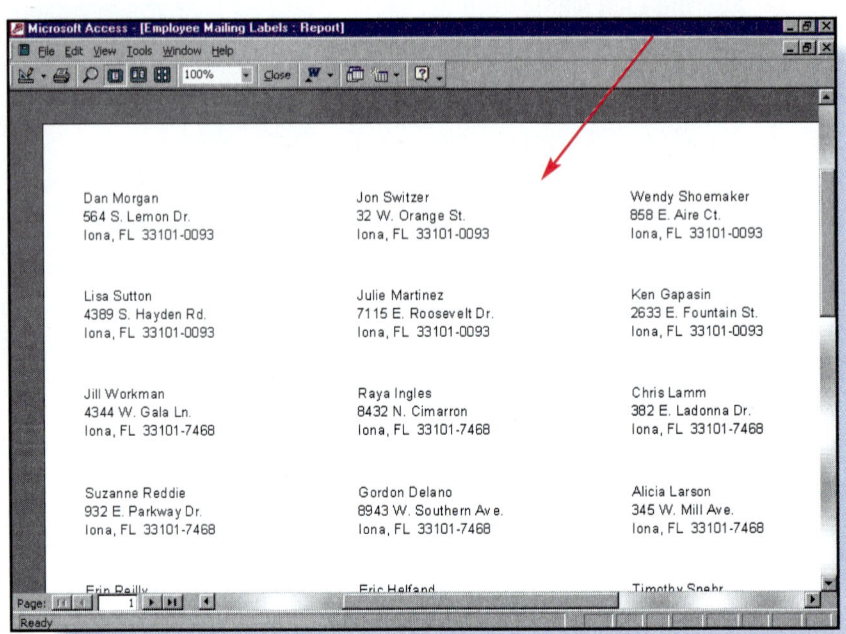

Figure 6–28

Three columns of mailing labels appear across the width of the page. The placement of the labels on the page corresponds to the 5160 Avery labels you selected using the Label Wizard. The labels are also sorted by zip code, from left to right across the rows, then down the page from top to bottom.

8

Print the page of labels that displays your name.

Close the mailing labels report.

Creating and Using Macros

By now, you have created database tables, forms, and reports that contain various types of data about the Lifestyle Fitness Club employees. You want to make it as easy as possible for users of this database to access the objects they need and view or print them as necessary, so you decide to create a few macros.

Concept ③ Macro

A **macro** automates common Access database tasks, such as opening and printing tables, forms, and reports. To create a macro, you enter a series of **actions** that you want Access to perform. An action is a self contained instruction that can be combined with other actions to automate tasks. In addition, you specify the **arguments** associated with the action. Arguments provide additional information on how the action is to be carried out.

Once a macro is created, you can run it from the Macros section of the database window. You can also attach a macro to a command button on a form or create a custom menu command or toolbar button that will execute the macro.

When a macro is run, Access starts at the beginning of the macro and performs all the specified actions in order until it reaches the end of the macro or, if the macro is part of a group of macros, the next macro in the group.

The first macro you will create is one that will open the Employee Update Form and maximize its view window.

1 ■ Click  on the Object bar.

■ Click **New**.

Your screen should be similar to Figure 6–29.

Macro window is empty because the macro does not contain any actions yet

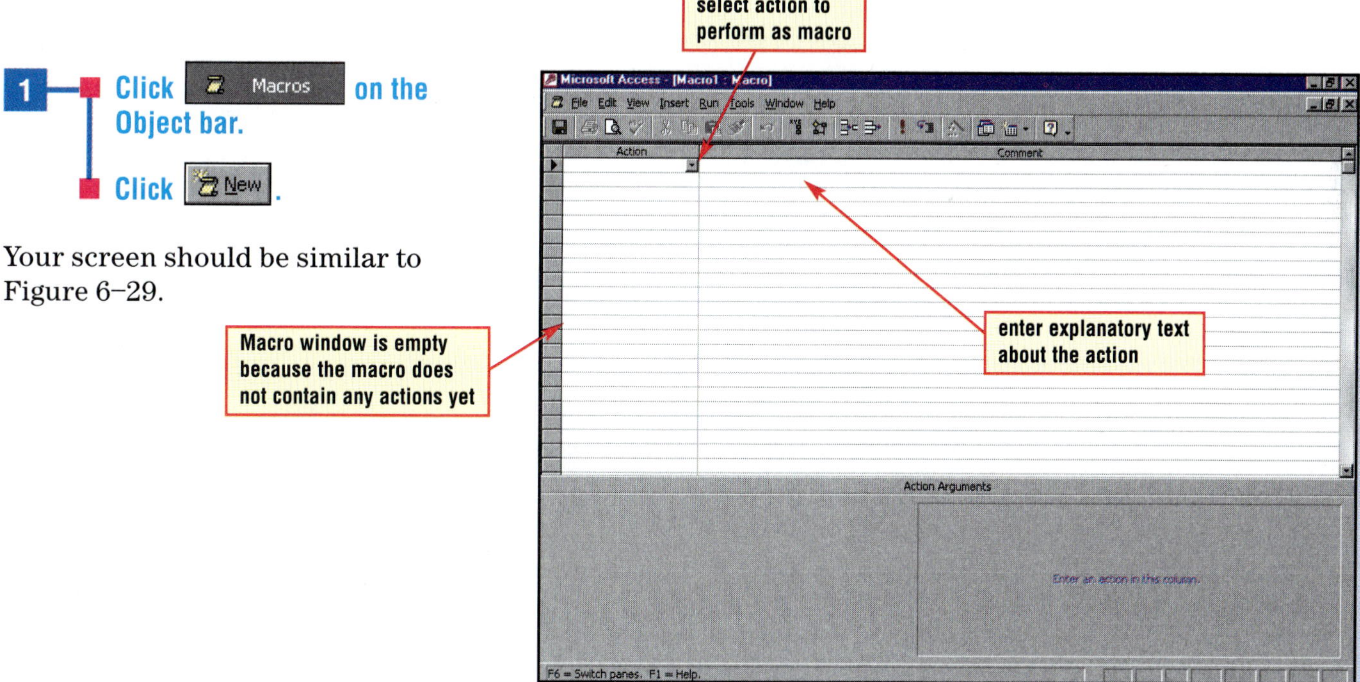

Figure 6–29

The Macro Design view window is used to specify the action you want the macro to perform. Because you have not defined the macro actions yet, the table is blank. To create a new macro, you select the actions you want it to perform from the pull-down list in the Action column and enter any explanatory information you want to include about each action (such as its purpose) in the Comment column. If there are any arguments associated with the selected action (such as the name of the form you want the macro to open), they are entered in the bottom portion of the Macro window.

To specify the first action you want this macro to perform,

2 **Open the Action column drop-down menu.**

Select OpenForm **from the Action list.**

You will have to scroll down the list to locate and select this action.

Type Open Employee Update Form in the Comment column of the same row.

Your screen should be similar to Figure 6–30.

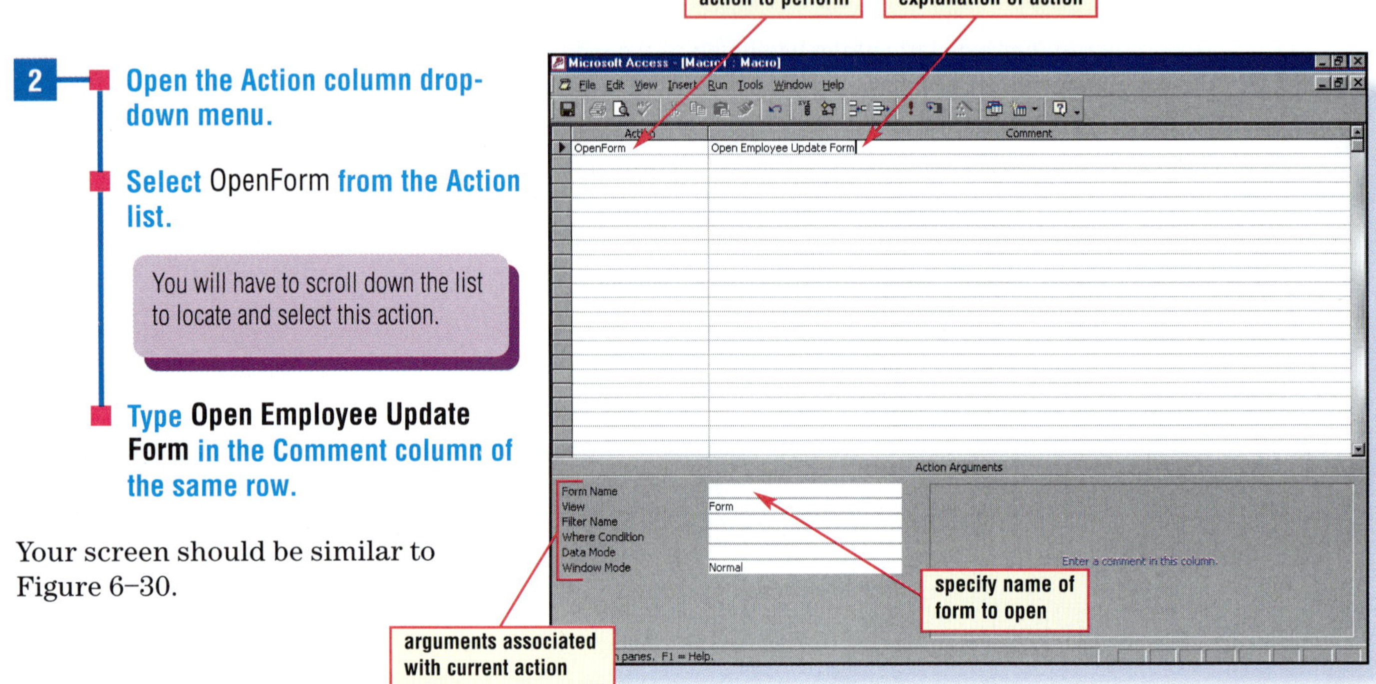

Figure 6–30

The arguments for the selected action are displayed at the bottom of the window. For this action, you need to specify the name of the form you want to open in the Form Name argument field.

3   **Click in the Form Name field.**

The comments box on the right changes to a description of how to use the Form Name field.

Open the Form Name drop-down menu and select Employee Update Form **from the list.**

Your screen should be similar to Figure 6–31.

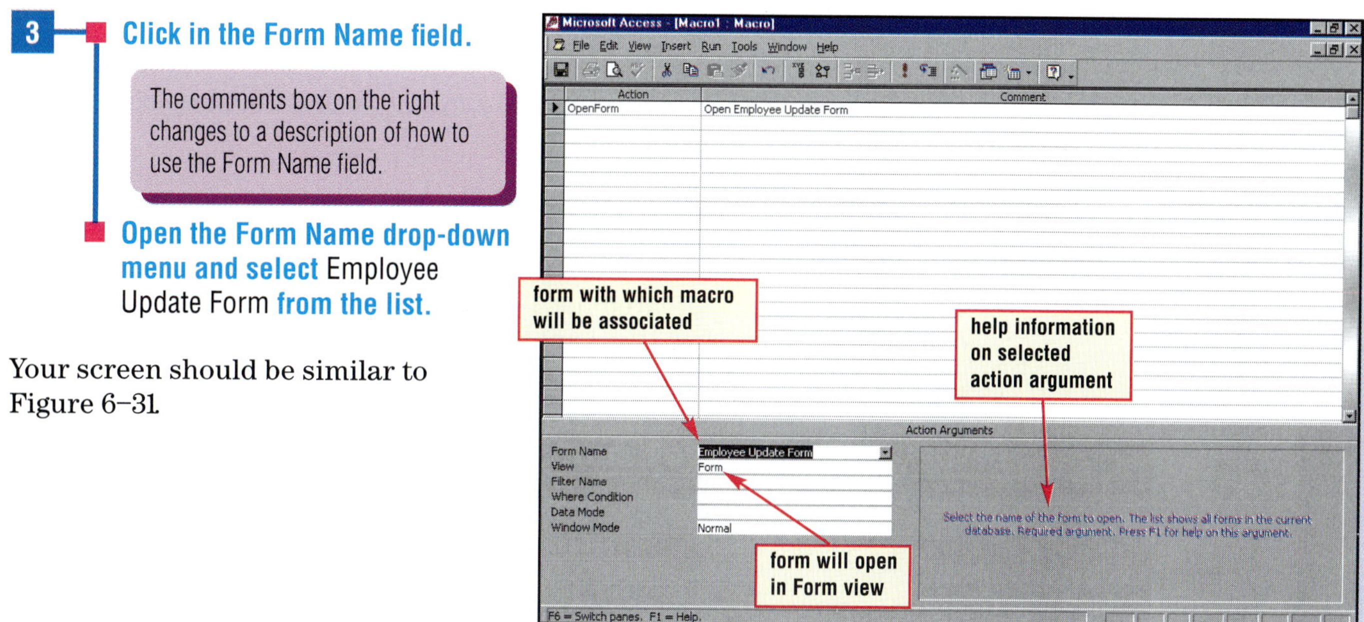

Figure 6–31

The next action you want this macro to perform is to maximize the table window.

4   **In the second row of the Action column, select** Maximize **from the drop-down list.**

Type Maximize window in the Comment column.

There are no arguments for this action.

Your screen should be similar to Figure 6–32.

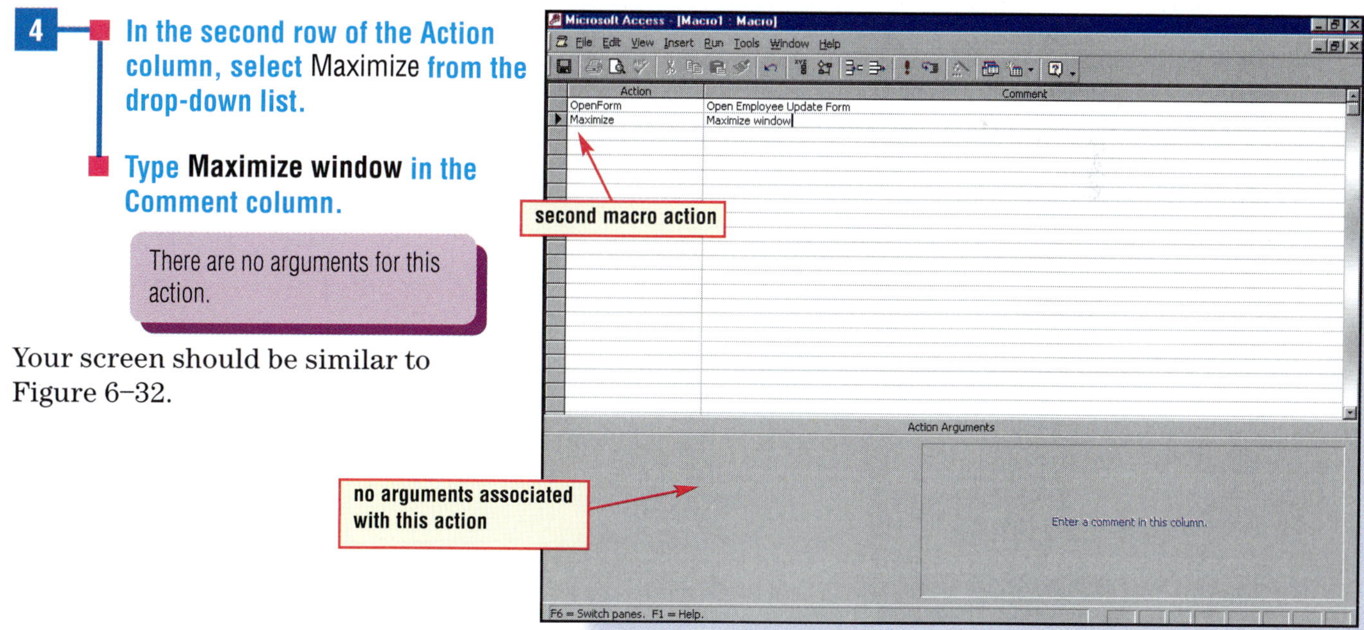

Figure 6–32

Those are all the actions you want to include in this first simple macro, so you can save and close it.

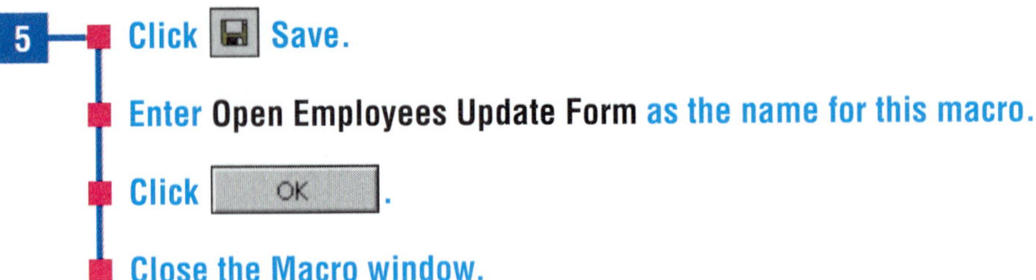

The macro you just created has been added to the Macros section of the database window. Now you want to run the macro.

The Employee Update Form is opened in Form view and maximized.

Next, you'll create a macro to preview the form. Since the only difference in the macros is the specification for the action, you will copy and then edit the macro.

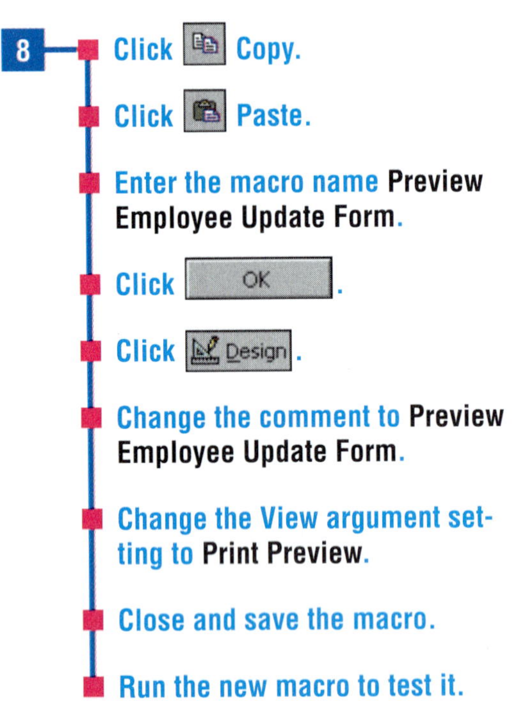

Your screen should be similar to Figure 6–33.

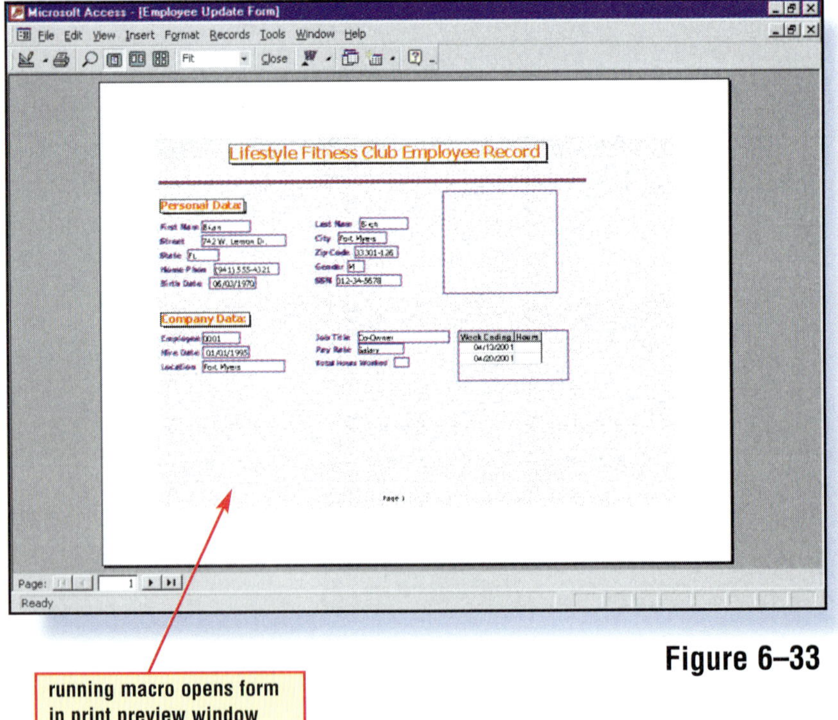

Figure 6–33

9 ■ Click ❌ to close the preview window.

The third macro you'll create will automatically print the mailing labels, without the user even having to open the report. To create this print report macro,

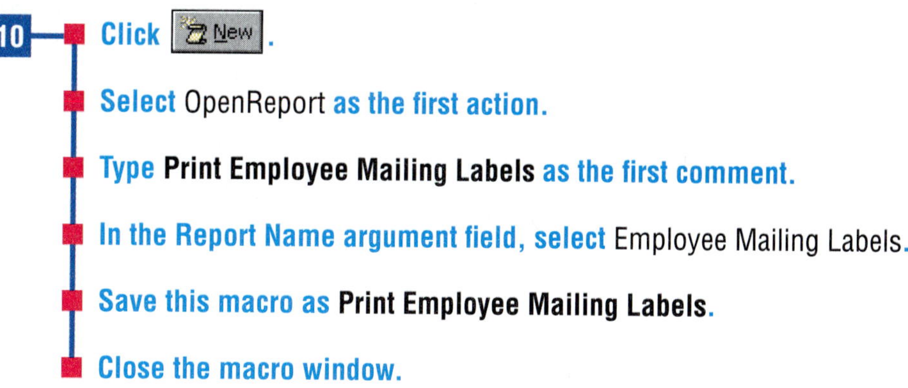

10 ■ Click 📄 New .

■ **Select** OpenReport **as the first action.**

■ **Type Print Employee Mailing Labels as the first comment.**

■ **In the Report Name argument field, select** Employee Mailing Labels.

■ **Save this macro as Print Employee Mailing Labels.**

■ **Close the macro window.**

You will not test this macro as it will automatically print a copy of the entire Employee Mailing Labels Report.

Users of this database can now open and preview the update form, and print mailing labels by running the appropriate macros from the Macro section of the Objects bar. You would like to simplify this process even further by creating a switchboard system.

Creating a Switchboard

You want to provide the users of the Club Employees database with a way to easily navigate through the database objects, selecting what they want from one central switchboard "menu." You also want to restrict access to the tables so that records are only entered through the form.

Concept ④ Switchboard

A **switchboard** contains buttons for performing a variety of actions in a database, such as viewing forms and reports. A switchboard can also include buttons that run macros, buttons that open other switchboards, and a button to exit the application.

Each switchboard in a database is called a **switchboard page**. You use the **Switchboard Manager** to create and modify switchboard pages. When you first use the Switchboard Manager, Access automatically creates a Main Switchboard page. You can put all the buttons for the database on this one page, or you can create individual switchboard pages that divide the buttons by category and then use the Main Switchboard to access these pages. For example, you could create a switchboard page called View Tables that contain buttons for opening the tables in the database, and then place a View Tables button on the Main Switchboard that would take you to this page. You could use View Forms and View Reports switchboard pages in the same way.

> Each switchboard page can contain up to eight buttons.

You decide to create separate switchboard pages for your table, form, and report macros and then add buttons to the Main Switchboard for each page. This will enable the database user to select the category wanted and switch to the page that contains the macros for that category. To begin creating these switchboard pages, you need to open the Switchboard Manager.

1 ■ Choose **T**ools/**D**atabase Utilities/**S**witchboard Manager.

■ Click [Yes] in response to the advisory message that informs you that no switchboards were found in this database and to confirm that you want to create one.

Your screen should be similar to Figure 6–34.

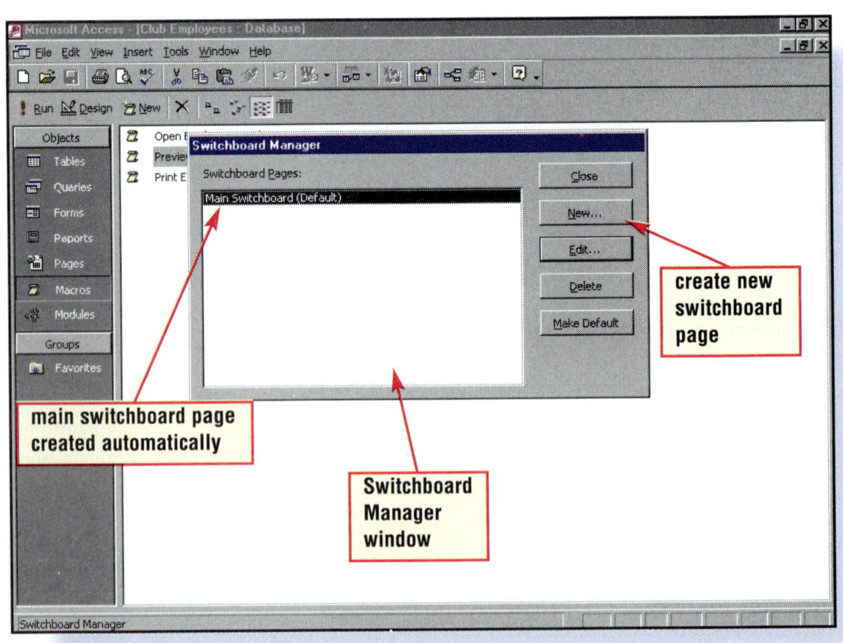

Figure 6–34

Access initially creates a Main Switchboard page as the default. You will edit this switchboard to contain the buttons for the individual switchboard pages after you create them. To create the first switchboard page,

2   ■ **Click** New... **.**

■ **Type Employee Form as the new switchboard page name.**

■ **Click** OK **.**

■ **In the same manner, create another new switchboard page called Employee Reports.**

Your screen should be similar to Figure 6–35.

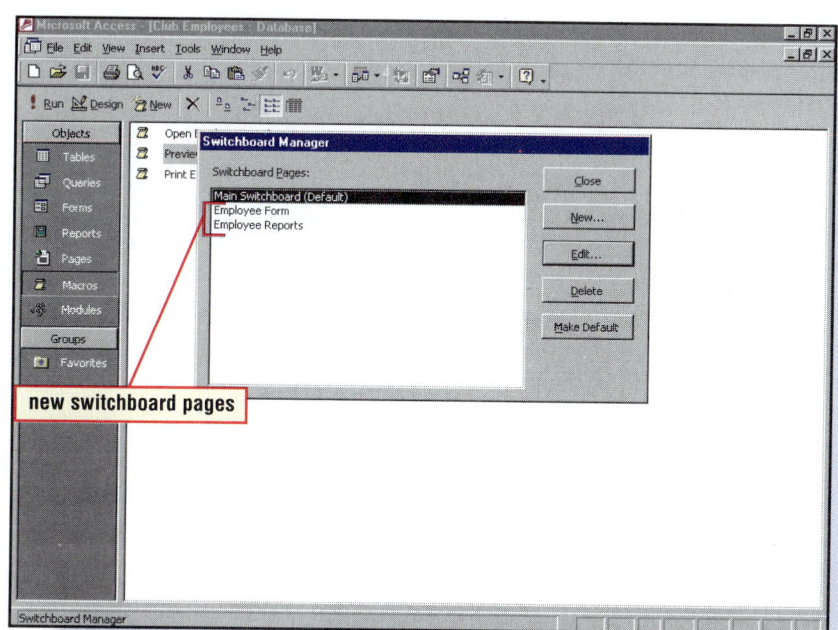

Figure 6–35

The new switchboard pages are displayed in the Switchboard Manager dialog box. Next, you will add the buttons you want each switchboard page to contain.

3 ■ **Select the** Employee Form **switch-board page.**

■ **Click** Edit... .

Your screen should be similar to
Figure 6–36.

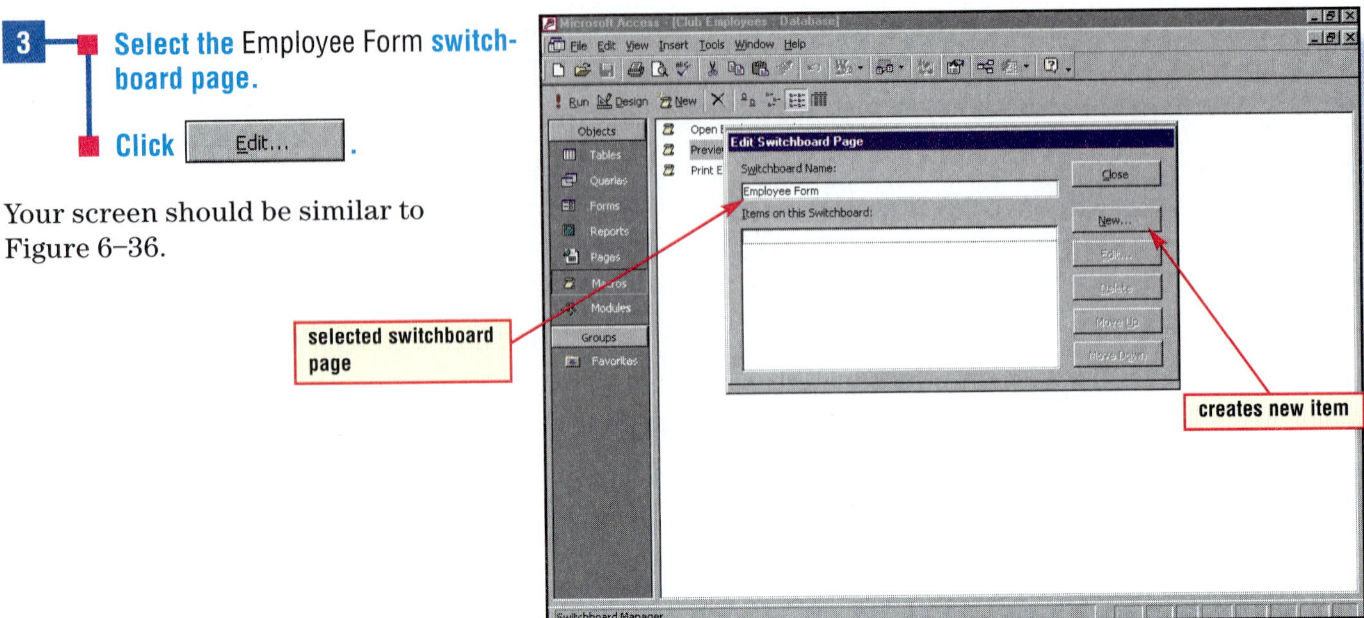

Figure 6–36

The Edit Switchboard Page dialog box is used to add new buttons to a
switchboard page or edit existing items on the page. You will add three
new items to this switchboard page.

4 ■ **Click** New... .

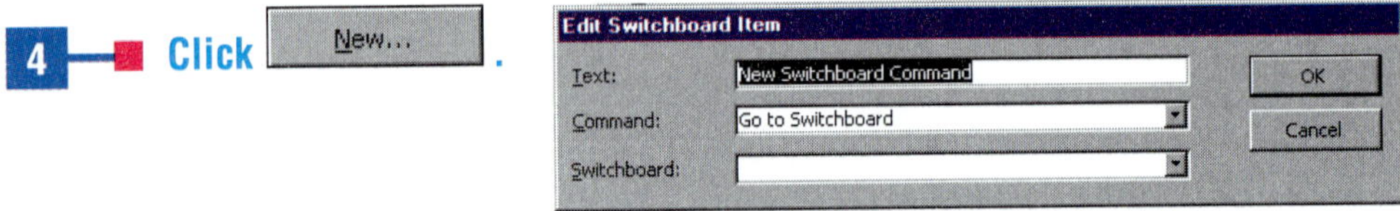

You use the Edit Switchboard Item dialog box to name your new item and
select the action you want it to perform, or change the name or action of
an existing switchboard item. Since you already created macros to open
the database tables, you will use these as the items in your switchboard.
This way, when the user selects one of these items, the corresponding
macro will be executed automatically.

5   Type **Open Employee Update Form** in the Text box.

Select Run Macro **from the Command drop-down list.**

Select Open Employee Update Form **from the Macro drop-down list.**

Click   OK   .

Your screen should be similar to Figure 6–37.

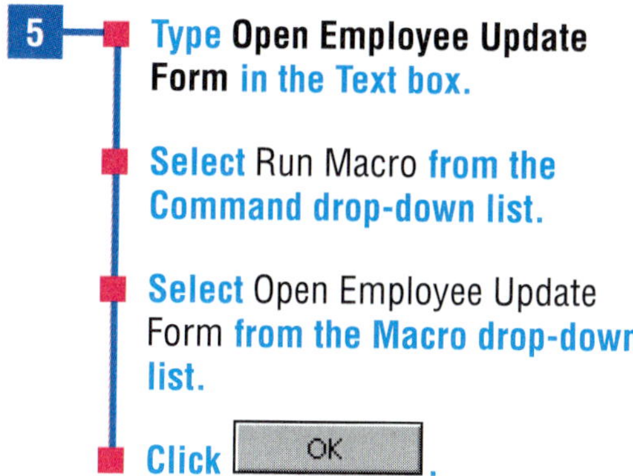
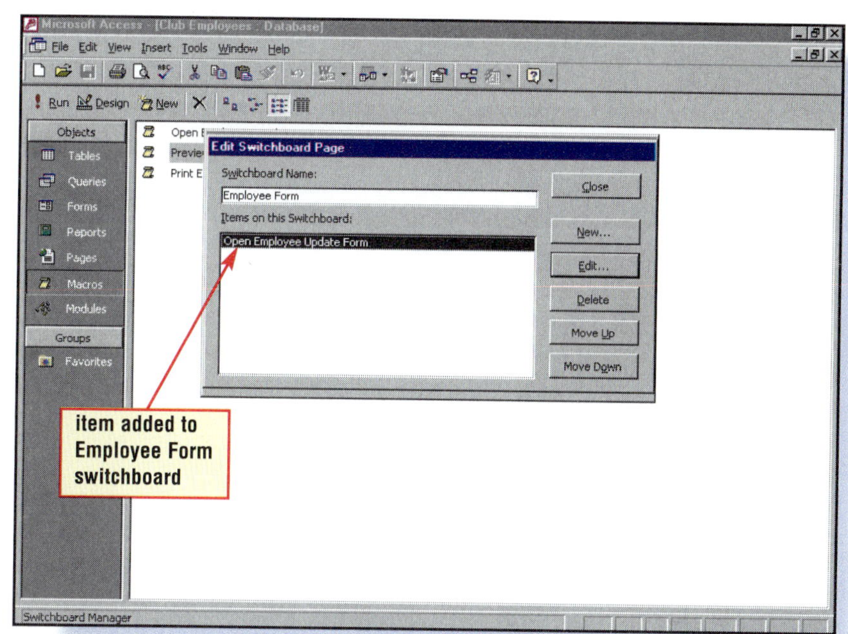

Figure 6–37

You have created your first switchboard item. Next, you will add the Preview Employee Update Form macro as a second item on this switchboard page.

6   Repeat the same procedure to create a second item to Preview Employee Update Form using the appropriate macro.

Your switchboard should now contain two items that will run the macros. You also want to include an item that will enable the user to return to the Main Switchboard from this switchboard page.

7   Click   New...   .

Name the switchboard item **Return to Main Switchboard.**

Leave the default Command selection, Go To Switchboard, as is.

Select Main Switchboard **from the Switchboard drop-down list.**

Click   OK   .

Your screen should be similar to Figure 6–38.

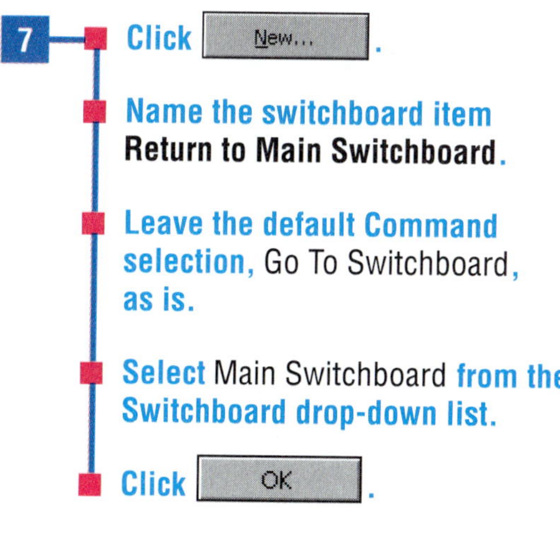
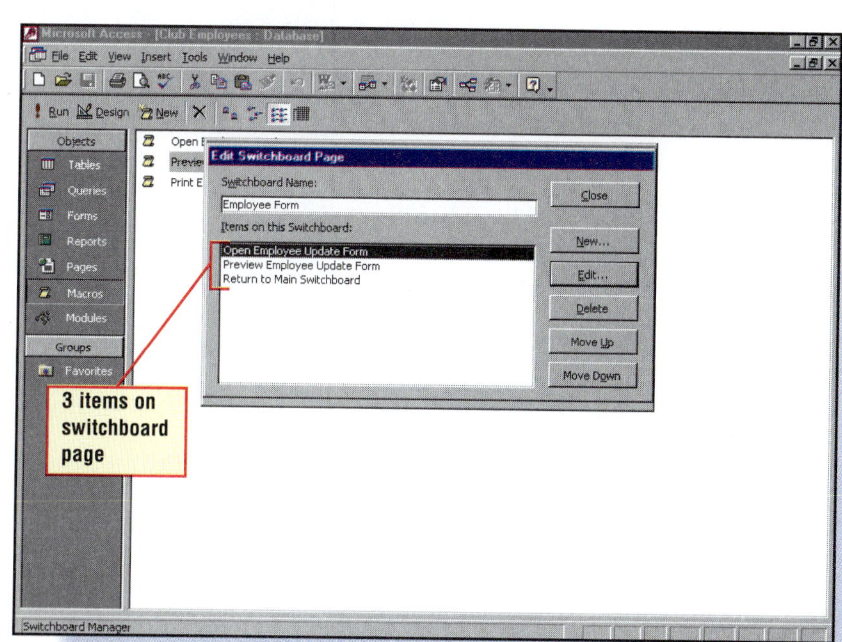

Figure 6–38

8 ■ Click [Close] to close the Edit Switchboard Page dialog box.

Next, you will add items to the Employee Reports switchboard page. First, you will add the report macros as you have done on the previous switchboard page.

9 ■ Select the Employee Reports switchboard page.

■ Click [Edit...].

■ Click [New...] to create the first item.

■ Name the switchboard item **Print Employee Mailing Labels**.

■ Select Run Macro from the Command drop-down list.

■ Select Print Employee Mailing Labels from the Macro drop-down list.

■ Click [OK].

In addition you want the users to be able to open the address labels report from this page as well. This item does not have a macro associated with it. To add this item,

10 ■ Click [New...].

■ Name the switchboard item **Open Employee Mailing Labels**.

■ Select Open Report from the Command drop-down list.

■ Select Employee Mailing Labels from the Report drop-down list.

■ Click [OK].

■ Add a last item to return to the Main Switchboard to the Employee Reports page.

■ Click [Close] to close the Edit dialog box for the Employee Reports switchboard page.

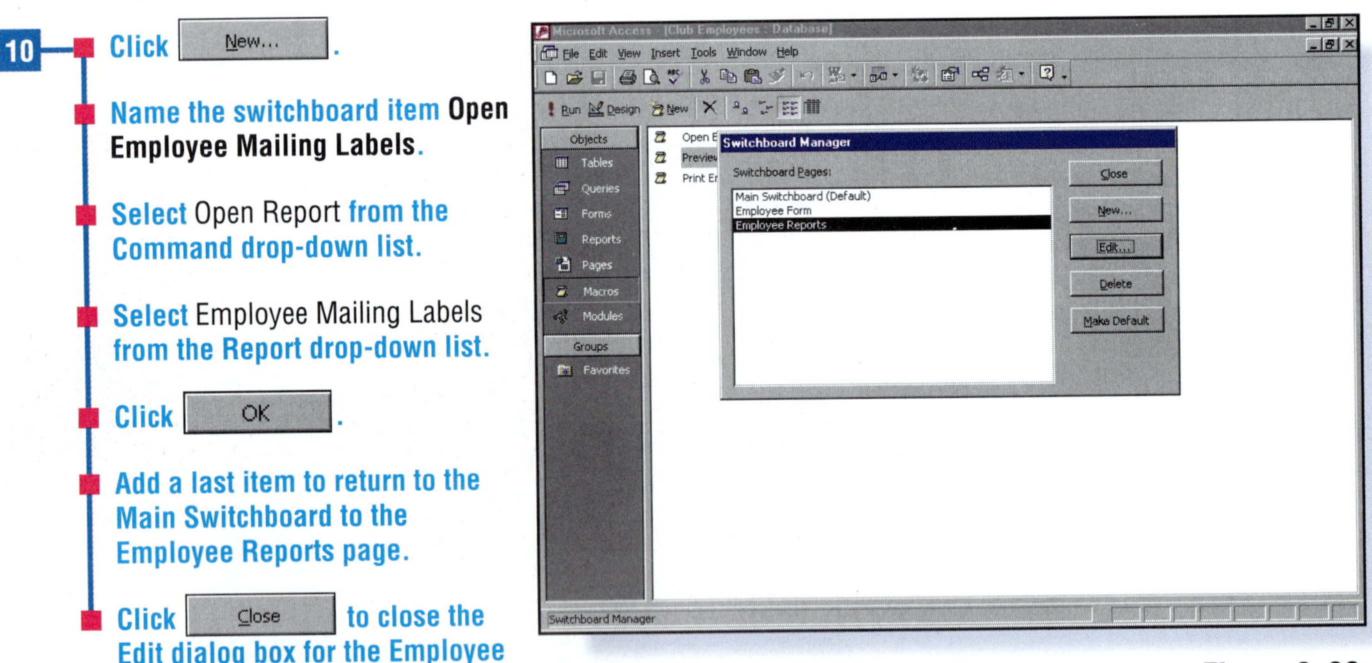

Figure 6–39

Your screen should be similar to Figure 6–39.

You are now ready to add items to the Main Switchboard that will enable the user to switch to the pages you just created.

11
- **Select the** Main Switchboard (Default) **page.**
- **Click** [Edit...] **.**
- **Click** [New...] **on the Edit Switchboard Page dialog box.**
- **Name the switchboard item Open Employee Forms.**
- **Leave the current Command se-lection,** Go To Switchboard, **as is.**
- **Select** Employee Form **from the Switchboard drop-down list.**
- **Click** [OK] **.**
- **Add another item** Open and Preview Employee Reports **to the Main Switchboard that will go to the Employee Reports switch-board page.**
- **Click** [OK] **.**

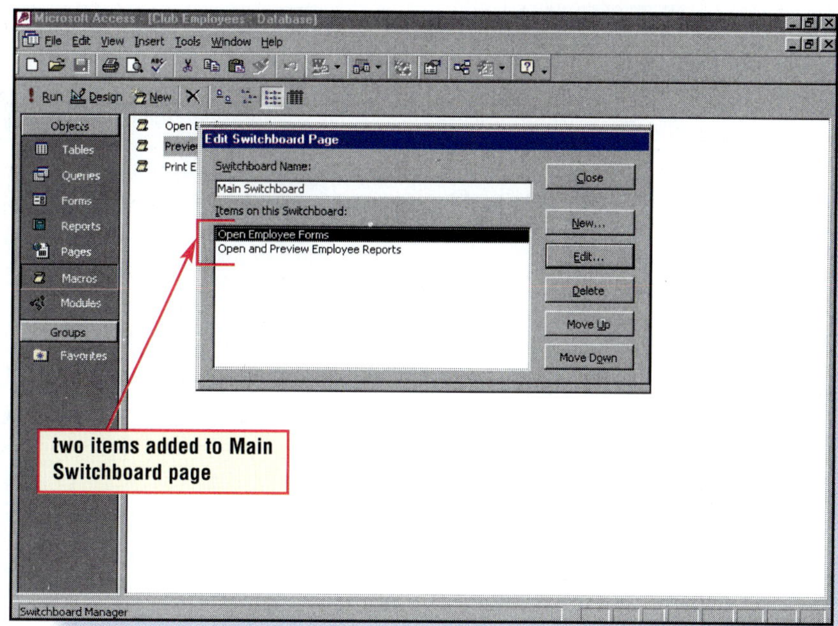

Figure 6–40

Your screen should be similar to Figure 6–40.

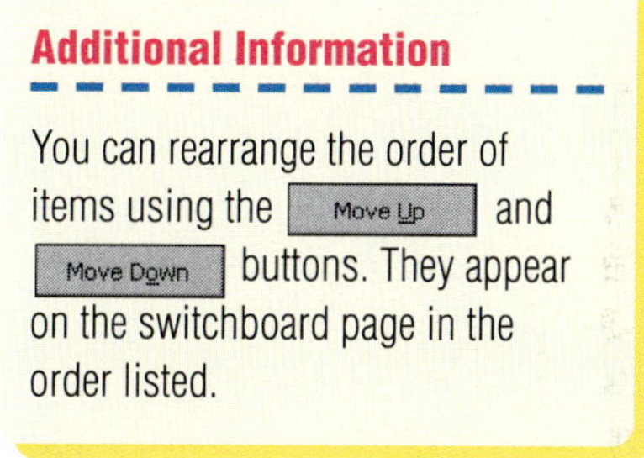

There are now two items on the Main Switchboard. You want to add a final item to this switchboard—one that will close the switchboard and the current database.

12
- **Click** [New...] **.**
- **Name the switchboard item Close Database.**
- **Select** Exit Application **from the Command drop-down list.**
- **Click** [OK] **.**
- **Click** [Close] **to close the Edit Switchboard Page dialog box.**
- **Click** [Close] **to exit the Switchboard Manager.**

Using a Switchboard

You now have a Main Switchboard that will enable users to access the forms and reports in the database from one central location and then close the database when they are through. Access also automatically created a **Switchboard Items table** that includes all the items on the Main Switchboard. You will now use your new switchboard to view the database items and exit Access.

1 • **Click** 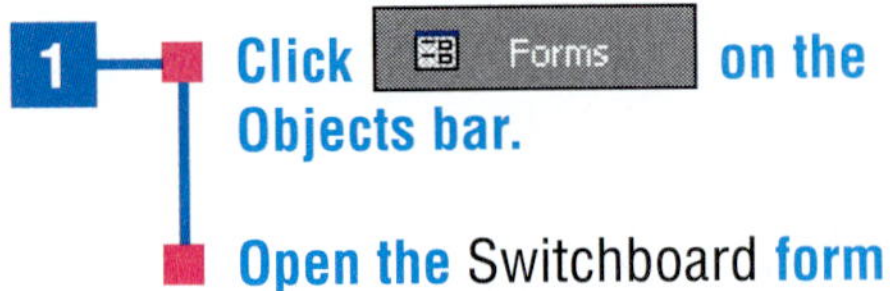 **on the Objects bar.**

• **Open the** Switchboard **form.**

Your screen should be similar to Figure 6–41.

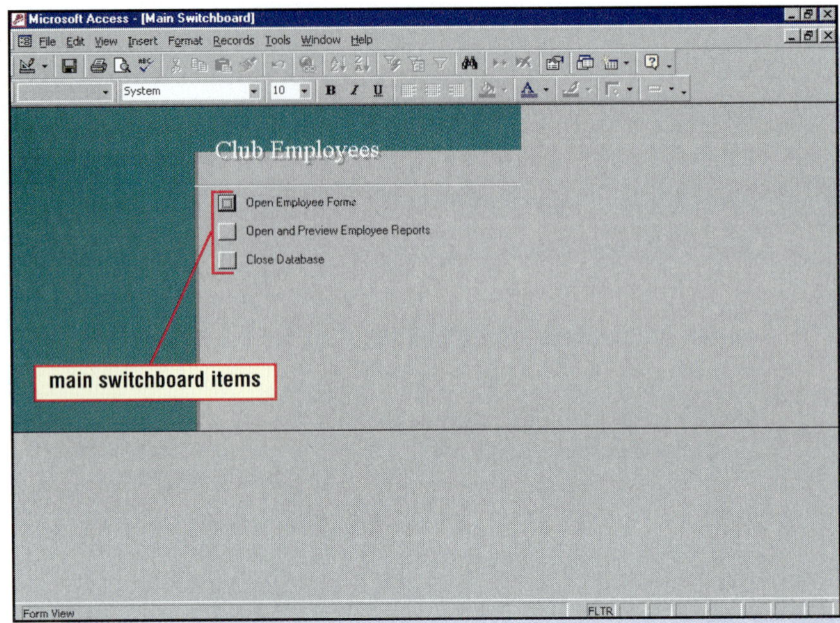

Figure 6–41

The Main Switchboard is displayed with buttons for all the items it contains.

2 • **Click the first button,** Open Employee Forms.

Your screen should be similar to Figure 6–42.

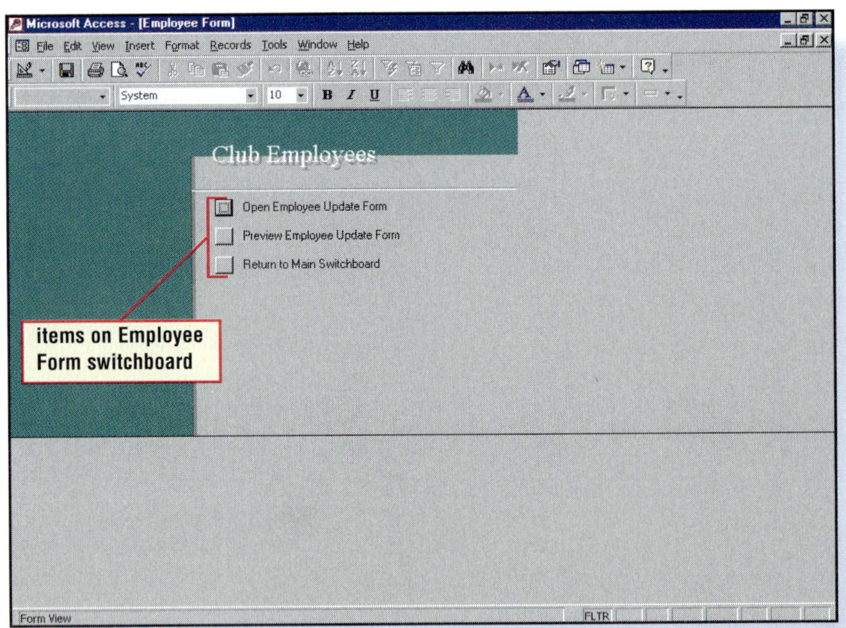

Figure 6–42

The Employee Form switchboard is displayed with buttons to the Employee Update Form and a final button to return to the Main Switchboard. When the user clicks one of the buttons, the corresponding macro will be executed. The user can then work with this form as usual (changing the form design; adding, editing, and deleting records; printing the form; and so on) and close the form when finished to return to the switchboard.

3 Click the Open Employee Update Form switchboard button to try it out, and then close the form to return to the switchboard.

Click the Return to Main Switchboard button.

Try out the other buttons on the Main Switchboard and corresponding switchboard pages as desired. (Do not use the Print Employee Mailing Labels or Close Database buttons.)

Return to the Main Switchboard when finished.

The final adjustment to the switchboard you want to make is to have the Main Switchboard page open automatically when the database is opened rather than the Database window. Access allows you to customize how a database looks and acts when opened, including what menus and toolbars are displayed, what window features are displayed, and how various features act.

4 Choose **T**ools/Start**u**p.

Select Switchboard from the Display F**o**rm/Page drop-down menu.

Select Display **D**atabase Window to clear the checkmark.

Your screen should be similar to Figure 6–43.

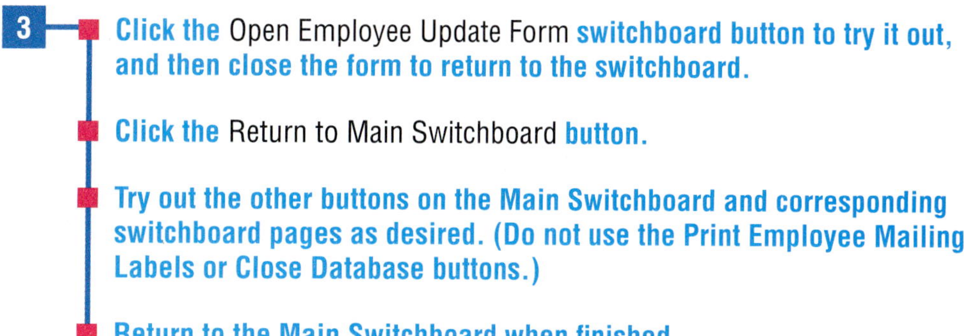
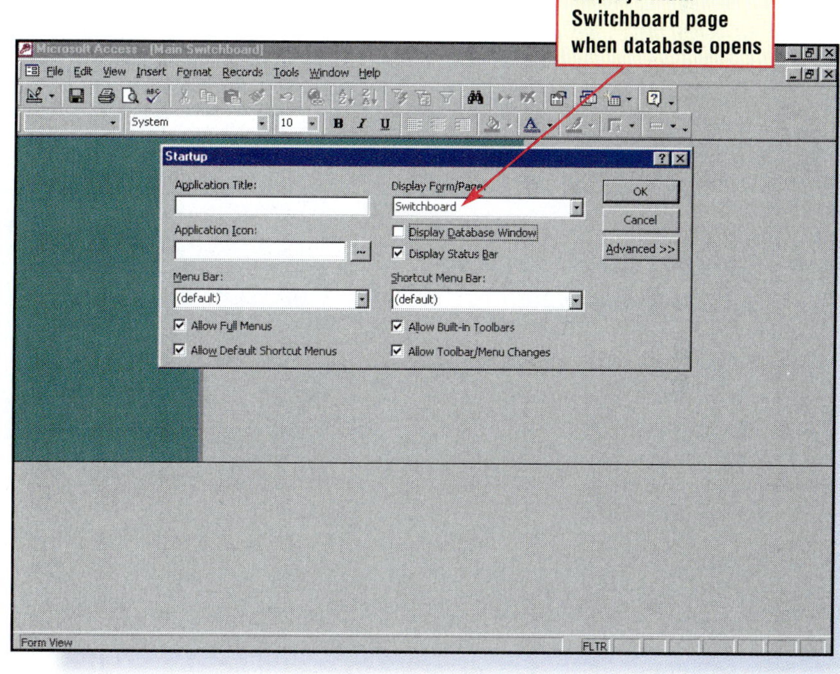

Figure 6–43

The Main Switchboard page will display automatically when the database is opened and the Database Window will not display.

5 Click  OK .

Click the Close Database button on the Main Switchboard.

The Club Employee database is closed.

Securing a Database

Additional Information

Before password protecting a database, it is a good idea to make a copy of the unprotected database and store it in a secure place. This way, in case you forget the password, you have a backup database file that you can access.

Because much of the information in the Club Employee database is confidential in nature, you also want to prevent unauthorized users from opening the database. To do this, you can restrict access to the database by requiring that a password be entered in order to open the database. You can also set the database to **exclusive** access to prevent others in a multiuser environment from opening the database while you are accessing it. A **multiuser** database allows multiple users to access and modify the same database at the same time.

First you will change the mode of use to exclusive then you will add a password to protect the database.

1 ■ Choose **File/Open** and select the Club Employees **database file**.

■ From the 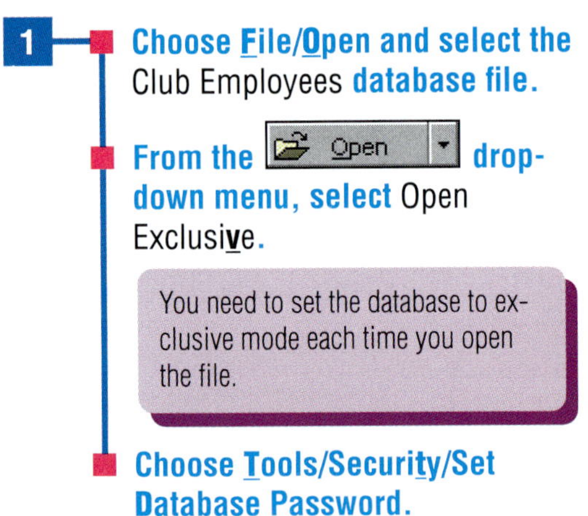 **drop-down menu, select** Open Exclusive.

You need to set the database to exclusive mode each time you open the file.

■ Choose **Tools/Security/Set Database Password.**

Your screen should be similar to Figure 6–44.

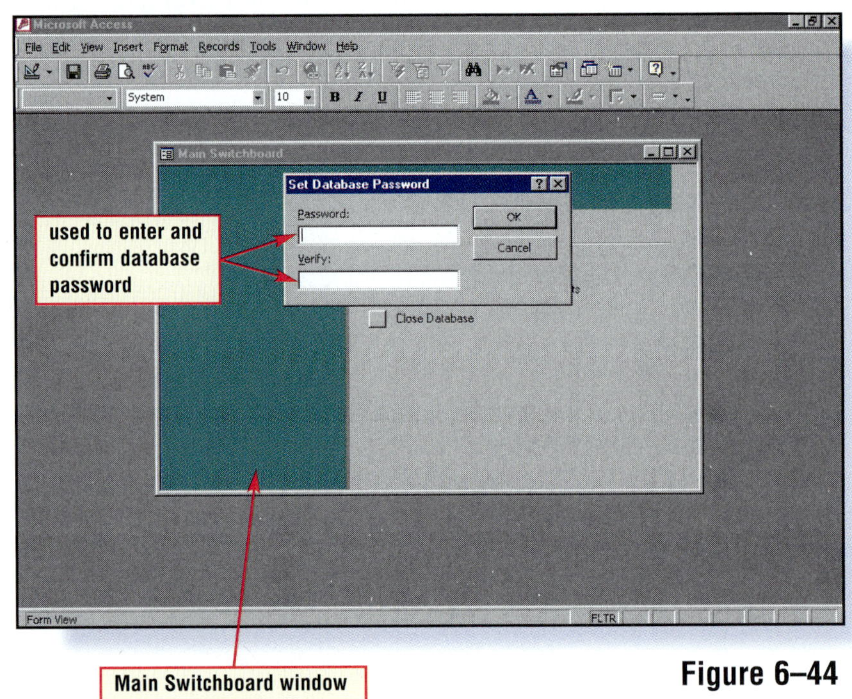

Figure 6–44

To remove a password, open the Database in Exclusive use and use the **T**ools/Securi**t**y/Unset **D**atabase Password command.

You enter your password in the Password box and then confirm the password by entering it again in the Verify box. Because passwords are case sensitive, you must enter it using exactly the same capitalization each time. As you enter the password, asterisks are displayed instead of the characters you type to further ensure the privacy of your password.

2 ▪ **Enter and then verify your first name as the password for the database file.**

▪ **Click 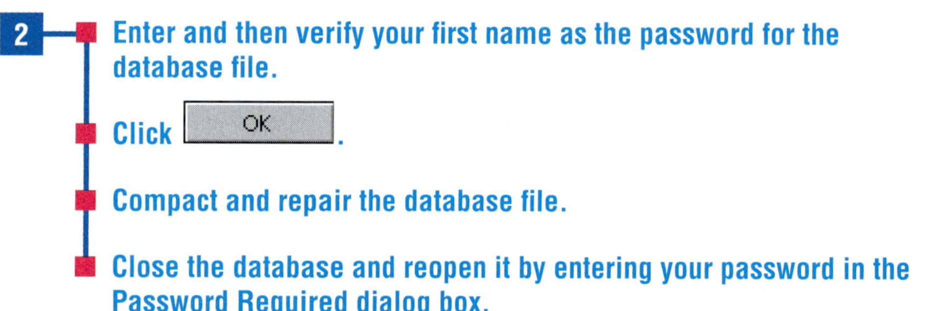 .**

▪ **Compact and repair the database file.**

▪ **Close the database and reopen it by entering your password in the Password Required dialog box.**

The database opens with the Main Switchboard window open automatically.

3 ▪ **Exit the Access application.**

Concept Summary

Tutorial 6: Creating Custom Reports, Mailing Labels, Macros, and Switchboards

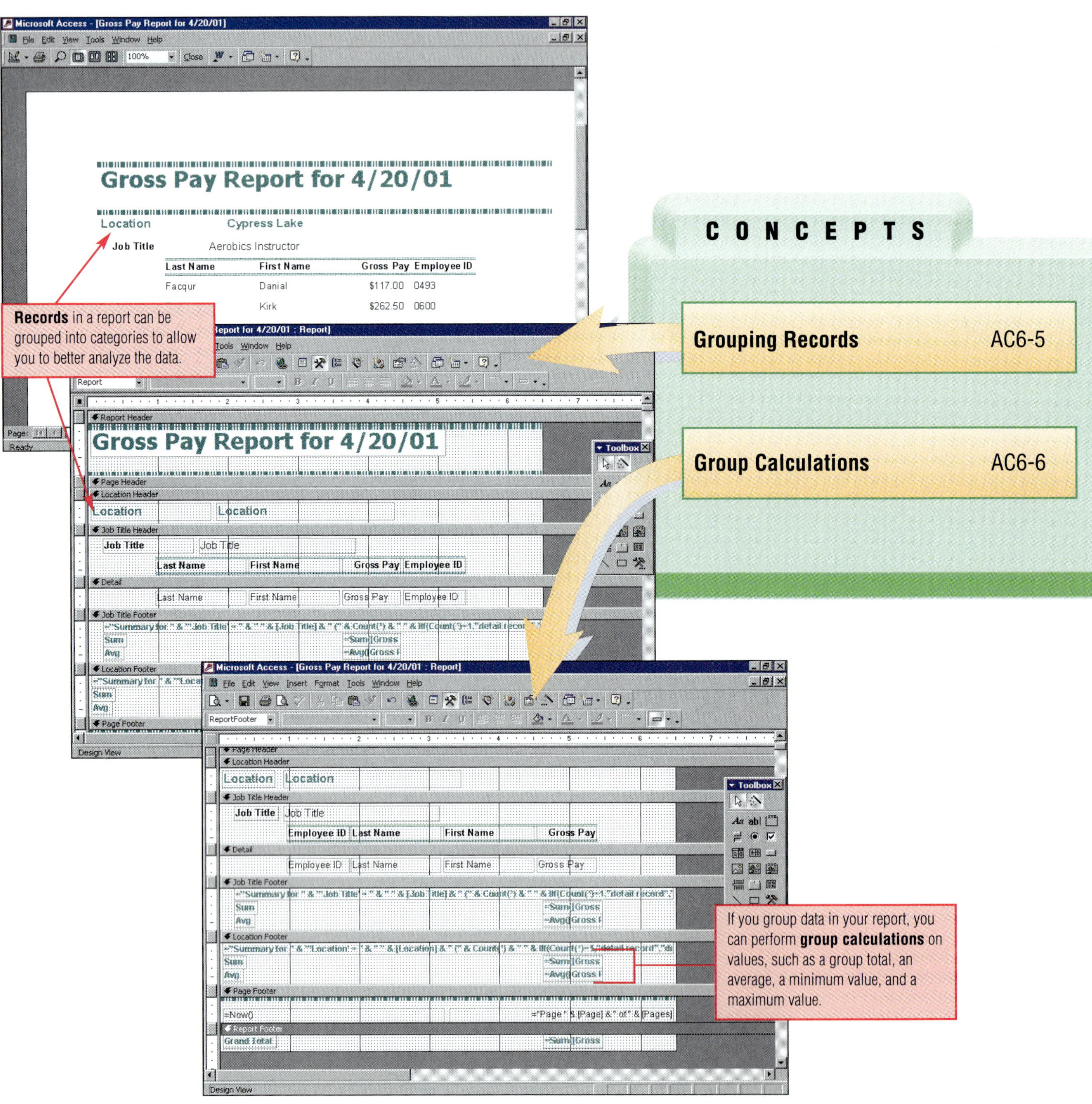

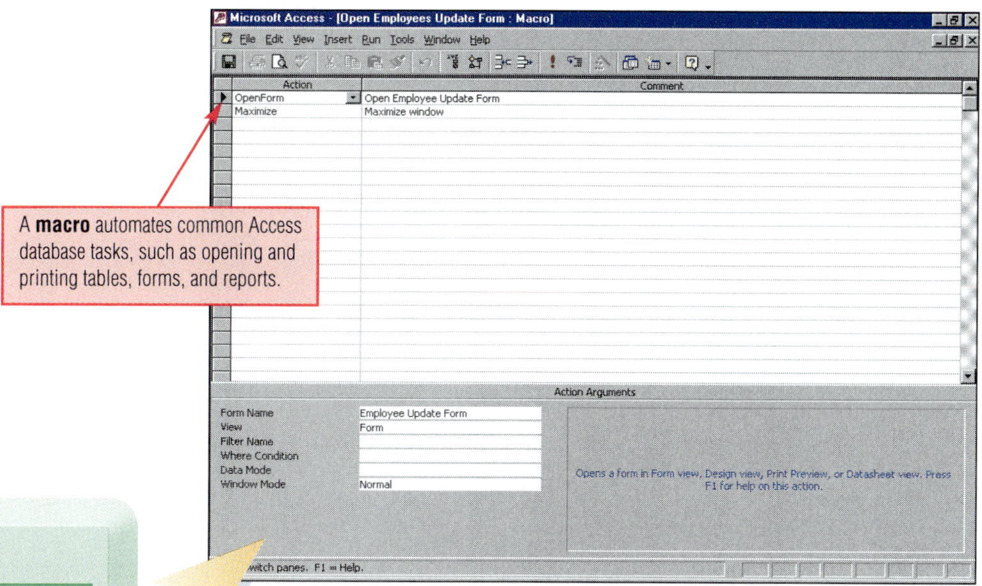

A **macro** automates common Access database tasks, such as opening and printing tables, forms, and reports.

Macro   AC6-23

Switchboard   AC6-28

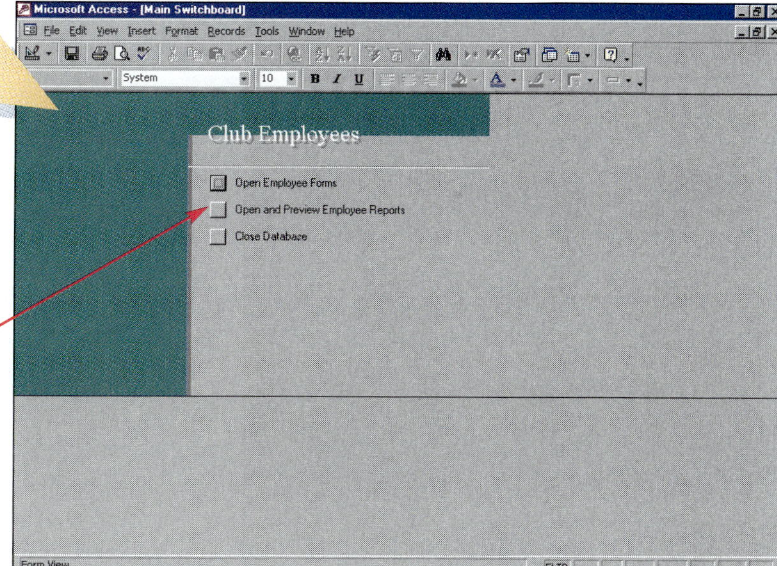

A **switchboard** is an Access form that contains buttons for performing a variety of actions in a database, such as viewing and printing tables, forms, and reports

Tutorial Review

Key Terms

actions   AC6-23
argument   AC6-23
Avg   AC6-6
calculated control   AC6-15
exclusive   AC6-36
group   AC6-5
group calculations   AC6-6
Group Header and Footer sections   AC6-9
Label Wizard   AC6-18
macro   AC6-23

Macro design view window   AC6-24
Max   AC6-6
Min   AC6-6
Multiuser   AC6-36
sum   AC6-6
switchboard   AC6-28
Switchboard Items table   AC6-33
Switchboard Manager   AC6-28
Switchboard page   AC6-28

Command Summary

Command	Shortcut	Toolbar	Action
Format/**S**ize/To **F**it			Automatically resizes the selected control to fit its contents
View/**P**roperties			Displays the current properties for the selected control
Tools/**D**atabase Utilities/ **S**witchboard Manager			Opens the Switchboard Manager for creating and editing switchboards

Screen Identification

In the following database report, several items are identified by letters. Enter the correct term for each item in the spaces that follow.

a. _______________________

b. _______________________

c. _______________________

d. _______________________

e. _______________________

f. _______________________

g. _______________________

h. _______________________

i. _______________________

j. _______________________

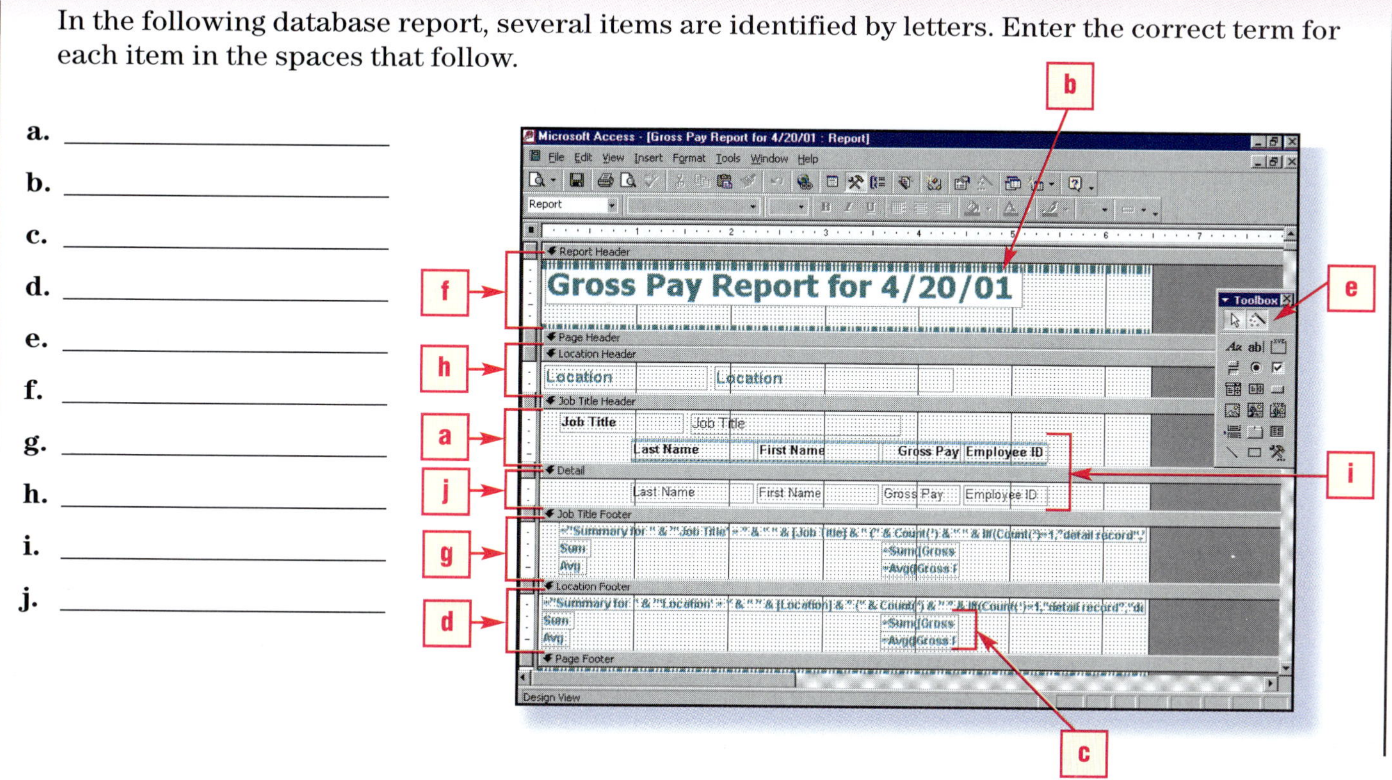

Matching

Match the letter to the correct item in the numbered list.

1. [Summary Options …]   _______   **a.** creates a new database item from anywhere within the database

2. group records   _______   **b.** contains information that prints at the top of every report page

3. calculated control   _______   **c.** performs predefined calculations in grouped reports

4. Group Header section   _______   **d.** executes a macro

5. label prototype   _______   **e.** contains buttons for performing database actions

6. [! Run]   _______   **f.** contains group identification information

7. Page Header section   _______   **g.** separates table records by categories

8. switchboard   _______   **h.** displays the results of an expression

9. [icon]   _______   **i.** used to design a label layout

10. group calculations   _______   **j.** arranges table data by major categories for clarity and ease of understanding

Fill-In

Complete the following statements by filling in the blanks with the correct terms.

1. Records can be _________________ by categories to allow better analysis of data.

2. The _________________ calculation computes the average value for a group.

3. The _________________ section of Report Design view contains information to be printed at the top of each page.

4. _________________ and _________________ can be added to the design of a report to enhance the report's appearance.

5. The _________________ tab in the Properties dialog box displays a complete list of the properties associated with the selected control.

6. You enter a(n) _________________ into a calculated control box to calculate values and display the results.

7. You use the _________________ _________________ to create mailing labels.

8. To create a macro, you enter a series of _________________ that you want Access to perform.

9. The Switchboard Manager creates a default switchboard called the _________________ _________________.

10. You can edit a switchboard in the _________________ _________________ or the _________________ _________________.

Multiple-Choice

Circle the letter of the correct answer to the following statements.

1. In a grouped report, records are separated by

    a. rows
    b. columns
    c. categories
    d. values

2. You can group by up to _________________ fields in any one report.

    a. 20
    b. 5
    c. 10
    d. 8

3. The ________________ calculation adds all values by group.

   a. Sum

   b. Count

   c. Add

   d. Avg

4. The ________________ section in a grouped report displays the label control for each field column.

   a. Detail

   b. Group

   c. Header

   d. Footer

5. The ________________ expression displays the system date on the report.

   a. =Date()

   b. =Time()

   c. =System()

   d. =Now()

6. Report layout changes are made in ________________ view.

   a. Design

   b. Layout

   c. Report

   d. Form

7. A control's ________________ affect how the control looks and acts.

   a. control settings

   b. property settings

   c. property attributes

   d. control attributes

8. To change the color of text on a report, you use

   a.

   b. Times New Roman

   c.

   d.

9. Some macro actions require additional information called

   a. parameters

   b. arguments

   c. options

   d. comments

10. A switchboard can contain up to ________________ items.

   a. 20

   b. 5

   c. 10

   d. 8

True/False

Circle the correct answer to the following statements.

1. Groups should be created based on priority from largest to smallest.   True   False

2. A grouped report always displays both detailed information and the summary information.   True   False

3. By default, a date is displayed in a report using the Short Date format.   True   False

4. A report header prints at the top of every report page.   True   False

5. You can add text and punctuation to a label in the Prototype Label box.   True   False

6. A calculated control automatically displays the result of an expression in Number format.   True   False

7. The Group Header section contains information that changes every time the group changes.   True   False

8. You must select one of the predefined labels in the Label Wizard to create a label prototype for a report.   True   False

9. You must enter a comment for every macro action that you select.   True   False

10. A switchboard can be used to execute macros.   True   False

Discussion Questions

1. Discuss how grouping records in a report makes the report more meaningful.

2. Discuss how group calculations can be used in a report. Give examples of the kinds of information that could benefit from summary data.

3. Discuss how calculated controls can be used in a report. What types of calculations could you perform?

4. Discuss how macros and switchboards can help automate database operations. Give examples of some operations that could be automated with these tools.

Hands-On Practice Exercises

Step by Step

Rating System 

1. The Club Members database that you created for the Lifestyle Fitness Club contains all the tables and forms the owners requested, and they would now like you to use this data to create some reports. The first report they requested is one that groups the records by location and lists the personal trainer and club members at each location. They would also like you to create a report that contains mailing labels for the club members so they can use them when necessary to send out promotional materials. When you are finished, your grouped report and mailing label report will be similar to those shown here.

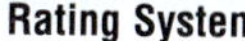

a. Open the Club Members database (which you last updated in Practice Exercise 1 of Tutorial 5).

b. Use the Report Wizard to create a new report. Add the Location,

Employee ID, First Name, and Last Name fields (in that order) from the Personal Trainers table, and then add the Membership #, First Name, and Last Name fields from the Members table. Accept the default to view the data by Personal Trainers. Group the report by Location, and sort the Member records by Last Name and then by First Name. Use the Outline 1 layout in Portrait orientation. Use the Casual style and accept the default report name, Personal Trainers. Finish the Wizard. Upon previewing the report, you decide that you don't like how the personal trainer and member names are displayed or how close the records are to each other. Switch to Report Design view.

c. You will fix these problems and make some other cosmetic changes so the form is more attractive and easier to read. Change the Personal Trainers_First Name label to **First Name** and the Personal Trainers_Last Name label to **Last Name**. Decrease the sizes of the Location, Employee ID, First Name, and Last Name label and text boxes, and then move the Last Name controls so they are on the same line and to the right of the First Name controls.

d. Add a label above the Members labels that reads **Assigned Members**. Align it with the left margin of the Employee ID and First Name labels above it. Change the Members_Last Name label to **Last Name** and the Members_First Name label to **First Name**.

e. Increase the size of the Detail section slightly so the records are not so close together.

f. Change the font color of the Location label and text so it is not the same as the form title and border. To make it more obvious where a new record begins, apply a fill/background color to the Employee ID label that is the same as the form title color and change the font color to white.

g. Next, you decide to move the Personal Trainers title so that it is displayed on every page rather than on the first page only. Expand the Page Header section and move the Personal Trainers label from the Report Header into this section instead. Change the font style to Arial, the font size to 22, and the font color to black. Size the label to fit its new text size, and adjust the height of the Page Header appropriately.

h. Add a new label in the Report Header that reads **LIFESTYLE FITNESS CLUB**. Change the font size to 20. Adjust the label control box size to display the entire title, and then center it. Assign a font color to it that matches the form border color.

i. Change the control property of the Now date control in the Page Footer so it displays in Short Date format rather than Long Date.

j. Expand the Report Footer section and add a label to it that reads **Created by [Your Name]**. Center the label box as necessary.

k. Print the report, and then save and close it.

l. To create the second report that the club owners requested, use the Label Wizard to create mailing labels from the Members table. Use the Avery 5160 labels. (*Hint:* If you don't see these labels in the product list, check the Unit of Measure and make sure English is selected.) Accept the default font and color. Create a prototype by adding the name and address fields in the order they would normally appear in an address, including spacing and punctuation where necessary (for example, enter a space between the first and last names and a comma and space after the city). Sort the labels by Zip Code, and name the report **Club Members Mailing Labels**. Finish out of the Wizard. Print the first page of labels and then close the report.

m. Close the Club Members database.

2. You are finished creating the tables and forms for the Animal Angels database, and you've asked the owners if there's anything in particular they would like to see. In response, they ask if it would be possible to get a report of all animals grouped by current status so they can have a record of what animals are still being boarded and since when, what animals are still in foster care, and what animals were adopted and by whom. They would also like to know if you can create mailing labels from the foster care and adopter data so they can use them to send thank you notes and other correspondence. You tell them you can easily create a grouped report that shows exactly what they want, as well as mailing label reports from the Adopters and Fosters tables. They are quite pleased and ask you to get right on it. When you're finished, your customized grouped report and two mailing label reports should be similar to those shown here.

Animal Status Report

Status	A
Type	Cat

Boarded Date	Foster Date	Foster Last Name	Adoption Date	Adopter Last Name
2/17/01			3/1/01	Smith
11/15/01	12/3/01	McMurphy	1/7/02	Ehmann
10/30/01			11/30/01	Snider
9/19/01	10/1/01	Bromley	12/1/01	Dodd
8/29/01			9/11/01	Klinger
8/3/01	8/17/01	Fox	9/30/01	Castillo
7/11/01			7/21/01	Herrera
6/26/01	7/3/01	Olsen	8/4/01	Falano
5/14/01	5/20/01	Young	6/1/01	Watson
5/1/01			5/20/01	Lewis
12/16/01	12/24/01	Zito	2/25/02	
3/23/01	4/18/01	Valdez	5/15/01	Wendale
12/6/00	12/23/00	Hawkins	1/7/00	Smalley
1/21/01	2/4/01	Franko	4/5/01	Richards
1/9/01	1/25/00	Ryan	2/12/01	Samuals
11/14/00			12/24/00	Richards
9/15/00			9/23/00	Fulton
9/10/00			9/20/00	Falk
8/20/00	9/1/00	Gold	10/15/00	Fadaro
7/18/00	7/30/00	Smithson	9/1/00	Ehmann
7/1/00			7/15/00	Dodd
6/15/00	6/20/00	Summerset	7/1/00	Candelari
4/12/01			4/22/01	Herrington
10/23/00	10/25/00	Burke	11/8/00	Granger

7/22/99   Page 1 of 5

Mark Lemon
900 Thomas Rd.
Phoenix, AZ 82891-9999

Mark Lemon
900 Thomas Rd.
Phoenix, AZ 82891-9999

Calvin Summerset
912 N. Central Ave.
Phoenix, AZ 82891-9999

Kurt Valdez
44 Franklin Dr.
Phoenix, AZ 82891-9999

Allyn McMurphy
111 S. Central Rd.
Phoenix, AZ 82891-9999

Ned Young
387 Rawhide Rd.
Chandler, AZ 83174-2311

Larry Montgomery
41 E. Highland Rd.
Chandler, AZ 83174-2311

Larry Montgomery
41 E. Highland Rd.
Chandler, AZ 83174-2311

Theresa Fox
959 Price Rd.
Tempe, AZ 85201-1268

Bradley Hawkins
789 University Ave.
Tempe, AZ 85201-1268

Tony Olsen
1003 Fifth Ave.
Scottsdale, AZ 85201-6760

Judith Gold
663 Alameda Dr.
Scottsdale, AZ 85201-6760

Lucy Granger
61 Lincoln Blvd.
Mesa, AZ 85205-0346

Jennifer Shane
22 Mill Ave.
Mesa, AZ 85205-0346

Gloria Atherton
808 McDonald Rd.
Mesa, AZ 85205-0346

Katherine Burke
834 Forest Ln.
Mesa, AZ 85205-0346

Susannah Troy
13 College Ave.
Tempe, AZ 86301-1268

Fran Calco
799 Summer St.
Tempe, AZ 86301-1268

1289 S. Hayden Rd.
Mesa, AZ 85205-0346

Susannah Troy
13 College Ave.
Tempe, AZ 86301-1268

Bonnie Brookfield
7 N. Williams Ave.
Tempe, AZ 86301-1268

a.   Open the database named Angels 4 (which you last worked on in Practice Exercise 2 of Tutorial 5).

b.   Check the current table relationships and edit the links so that all records in the Animals table are included, but only those records with matching fields in the Fosters and Adopters tables are included (option 2 in the Join Properties dialog box).

c.   Use the Report Wizard to create a new report. From the Animals table add the Status, Type, Boarded Date, and Foster Date field first. Then from the Fosters table add the Foster Last Name field. Select the Animals table again and add the Adoption Date field, and then select the Adopters table and add the Adopter Last Name field. Group the report by Status and then by Type. Do not select any sort fields for this report. Use the Align Left 1 layout in Portrait orientation. Use the Bold style and name the report **Animal Status Report**. Finish the Wizard.

d.   When you see the report preview, you decide that it needs several layout changes, such as increasing the font size of the boarded, foster, and adopter data, as well as increasing the space between categories so it is easier to read. Switch to Report Design view and move the label and text controls as shown in the figure at the beginning of this exercise. Increase the font size of the labels and text from 9 to 10, and make all the text left-justified. Size the labels to fit, and extend the horizontal lines above and below the label controls to accommodate these changes.

e.   The next enhancement you would like to make to this layout is changing the Status and Type font attributes so they are more prevalent. Increase the font size of the text in both Status control boxes to 12. Apply a maroon fill/background and white font color to the Status label box, and decrease the width of the Status text box. Then increase the font size of the text in both Type control boxes to 12, apply a light gray fill background and maroon text color to the label Type box, and decrease the width of the Type text box.

f.   Change the control property of the Now date control in the Page Footer so it displays in Short Date format rather than Long Date.

g.   Expand the Report Footer section and add a label to it that reads **Created by [Your Name]**. Center the label box as necessary.

h.   Make any other layout changes you desire and then return to Print Preview. Print the report, and then save and close it.

i.   You are now ready to create the two mailing label reports that were requested. Use the Label Wizard to create each report, one with name and address fields from the Fosters table and the other with name and address fields from the Adopters table. Use the Avery 5160 label and create a standard mailing label prototype for each. Sort the labels by Zip Code, and name the first report **Foster Care Mailing Labels** and the second report **Adopters Mailing Labels**. Print the first page of labels in each report and then close it.

j.   Close the Angels 4 database.

3. Daria O'Dell, the owner of Daria's Day Spa, is quite pleased with how the database you created for her has automated what used to be quite time-consuming manual record-keeping tasks. She is particularly pleased with how the data can be used to track the sales of massage packages offered at the spa. Her most recent request is for a report that shows the spa packages that were purchased and by whom as well as the sales total for each package and the total income generated from these sales. The report will include group calculations as well as a calculated control that will generate the grand total. The completed grouped report is shown here.

To create the report, follow these steps:

a. Open the database called Daria Spa 4.

b. Use the Report Wizard to create a new report that contains the Package ID, Package Name, Package Description, and Package Price fields from the Spa Packages table; the Client ID from the Package Purchased table, and the First Name and Last Name fields from the Clients table. Specify that you want to view the data "by Package Purchases" and group the report by Package Name. Do not sort on any fields. Open the Summary Options and select the Sum option for the Package Price field. Use the Outline 1 layout and the Casual style. Name the report **Spa Package Purchases** and finish out of the Wizard.

c. Switch to Report Design view and fix the spacing problems. For example, to make more room, you can rename the Package ID label to **ID**, Package Price to **Price**, and Client ID controls to **Client**; move the ID controls to the left margin to extend the amount of space you have to work with; and increase the width of the Package Description controls so more of the text can be displayed. Size the other controls appropriately and left align the text controls. (See the figure at the beginning of the exercise for an example of how the layout can be modified.) Extend the horizontal lines above and below the labels to accommodate your changes as necessary.

Spa Package Purchases

Package Name   Aromatic

ID	Package Description	Price	Client	First Name	Last Name
6	Aromatherapy	$75.00	00	Barbara	Williams
6	Aromatherapy	$75.00	00	Barbara	Williams
6	Aromatherapy	$75.00	00	Lisa	Michaels
6	Aromatherapy	$75.00	01	Patsy	Griffin

Summary for 'Package Name' = Aromatic (4 detail records)
Sum $300.00

Package Name   Body Beautiful

ID	Package Description	Price	Client	First Name	Last Name
4	Body wrap and sauna	$150.00	00	Bonnie	Shoemaker
4	Body wrap and sauna	$150.00	00	Huye	Ky
4	Body wrap and sauna	$150.00	02	Lin	Chen
4	Body wrap and sauna	$150.00	01	Marcellus	Finch

Summary for 'Package Name' = Body Beautiful (5 detail records)
Sum $750.00

Package Name   Destresser

ID	Package Description	Price	Client	First Name	Last Name
2	Deep-tissue massage, facial, an	$215.00	01	Charlene	Riley
2	Deep-tissue massage, facial, an	$215.00	02	Georgia	Kendall

Summary for 'Package Name' = Destresser (2 detail records)
Sum $430.00

Package Name   Fantastic Face

ID	Package Description	Price	Client	First Name	Last Name
7	Facial	$75.00	00	Denise	Pickett
7	Facial	$75.00	00	Bobbi	Miller

7/23/99   Page 1 of 3

  d. Expand the Package Name Footer to .5 inch to add more space between the record groups, and change the format property of the date control to Short Date.

  e. You are now going to add a calculated control to count the number of packages sold. Expand the Report Footer section and move the Grand Total label and text controls down to make room for the new control. Insert a text box above the Grand Total. Align the new label control with the Grand Total label control box, change its name to **Packages Sold**, and resize the box to fit the contents. Align the new Unbound text control with the Grand Total text control box and make both control boxes the same size. Access the Unbound text control's property settings and use the Expression Builder to create a Count expression that will calculate the number of packages that were sold. (*Hint:* You can use any of the fields in the Details section of the report, such as Package ID or Package Description, as the Count expression to produce the desired results.) Select the Packages Sold and Grand Total labels and text controls and apply a font size of 12 point, red font color, and shadowed special effect for emphasis. Make all four control boxes the same size. Center the text in the Packages Sold and Grand Total text boxes to take care of any alignment problems that may be caused by the results of the calculations being two different types of values (number and currency). Bold the Packages Sold text box control.

  f. Make further enhancements to the report layout as desired (text color, font size and style, special effects). When you are finished, return to Report view and print the report. Then save and close it.

  g. Close the Daria Spa 4 database.

4. As database manager for the EduSoft Company, you get many requests for reports on software titles, development, sales, and so on from the company's department heads and marketing personnel. For example, you just received a request from the product sales manager to create a report that is grouped by software package number, summarizes the sales of each package, and includes a calculated total of all packages sold. The completed report will look similar to that shown here. There has also been some concern about unauthorized use of the database, so you are going to assign a password that will be given out upon management approval only.

a. Open the Learning 4 database.

b. Open the Sales By Software Package query that you created in Practice Exercise 5 of Tutorial 4. Create a new report using the Report Wizard and all fields from this query. Group the report by Software Package. (Don't select any sort fields.) Select the Sum for all three fields in the Summary Options. Select the layout and style of your choice. Name the report **Software Sales**, and finish out of the Wizard.

c. Change the Total Packages Sold label to read **# Sold**. Resize the control boxes for this field as well as any others that are too large or small. Move the Detail text controls and their corresponding label controls so they are equidistant from each other between the horizontal border lines. Resize and move the control boxes in the Software Package Footer and Report Footer so they are in line with their corresponding Detail controls.

Software Sales

Software Package	Developer	Price	# Sold	Total Sales
15-0202				
	Joseph Paxton	$19.99	1	$19.99
	Joseph Paxton	$19.99	5	$99.95
	Joseph Paxton	$19.99	10	$199.90
Summary for 'Software Package' = 15-0202 (3 detail records)				
Sum		$59.97	16	$319.84
15-0301				
	Susan Franklin	$12.99	7	$90.93
Summary for 'Software Package' = 15-0301 (1 detail record)				
Sum		$12.99	7	$90.93
15-0502				
	Manny Lewis	$17.99	5	$89.95
	Manny Lewis	$17.99	10	$179.90
Summary for 'Software Package' = 15-0502 (2 detail records)				
Sum		$35.98	15	$269.85
15-0601				
	Joseph Paxton	$22.99	7	$160.93
Summary for 'Software Package' = 15-0601 (1 detail record)				
Sum		$22.99	7	$160.93
15-0602				
	Manny Lewis	$22.99	2	$45.98
	Manny Lewis	$22.99	5	$114.95
	Manny Lewis	$22.99	10	$229.90
Summary for 'Software Package' = 15-0602 (3 detail records)				
Sum		$68.97	17	$390.83
24-0102				
	Joseph Paxton	$19.99	10	$199.90
Summary for 'Software Package' = 24-0102 (1 detail record)				
Sum		$19.99	10	$199.90
24-0103				

7/23/02 — Page 1 of 2

d. Change the date format in the Page Footer to Short Date and apply a red font color to the Grand Total label and text controls for emphasis. Align these controls with their corresponding Detail controls. Make any other layout changes you'd like and then print, save, and close the report.

e. Secure the Learning 4 database by assigning a password to it.

5. Evan, the owner of the Downtown Internet Cafe, is finding the database and its tables, forms, queries, and reports that you created quite useful for keeping track of inventory items and order details. In fact, he would like you to create another report that groups orders by vendor, includes product pricing information, and calculates the order costs. You have also been thinking about automating the database even further by creating macros to access its various tables, forms, and so on, as well as a switchboard to centralize the database operations, which you will do after creating the grouped report. Your completed report will be similar to the one shown here.

a. Open the Cafe Purchases 4 database.

b. Open the Order Costs query that you created in Practice Exercise 4 of Tutorial 4. In Query Design view, hide the # On Hand field (you won't need it for the report). Run and save the query.

c. Create a new Report object from the Query window using the Report Wizard and all fields from this query. Group the report by Vendor Name. (Don't select any sort fields.) Open the Summary Options and select the Sum option for the Order Cost field. Select the layout and style of your choice. Name the report **Cafe Orders**, and finish out of the Wizard.

d. Fix the spacing in the report Details section so that all data is fully displayed. Add other enhancements of your choice to the report.

Cafe Orders

Vendor	**Best Bakery**					
	Description	Contact	Phone	# To Order	Unit Price	Order Cost
	Scones	Student Name	(909) 555-5599	8	$0.75	$6.00

Summary for 'Vendor Name' = Best Bakery (1 detail record)

Sum $6.00

Vendor	**Better Beverages, Inc.**					
	Description	Contact	Phone	# To Order	Unit Price	Order Cost
	Earl Grey tea	Mae Yung	(415) 555-1122	7	$5.95	$41.65
	Orange Pekoe tea	Mae Yung	(415) 555-1122	3	$5.95	$17.85

Summary for 'Vendor Name' = Better Beverages, Inc. (2 detail records)

Sum $59.50

Vendor	**Central Ceramics**					
	Description	Contact	Phone	# To Order	Unit Price	Order Cost
	Coffee mugs	Dan O'Dell	(602) 555-1924	12	$4.00	$48.00

Summary for 'Vendor Name' = Central Ceramics (1 detail record)

Sum $48.00

Vendor	**Pure Processing**					
	Description	Contact	Phone	# To Order	Unit Price	Order Cost
	Decaf Columbian	Nancy Young	(650) 555-5689	11	$8.25	$90.75
	Decaf Dark	Nancy Young	(650) 555-5689	9	$8.25	$74.25

Summary for 'Vendor Name' = Pure Processing (2 detail records)

Sum $165.00

Vendor	**Quality Coffee**					
	Description	Contact	Phone	# To Order	Unit Price	Order Cost
	Sumatra coffee	Fred Wilmington	(206) 555-9090	10	$7.50	$75.00
	Columbian coffee	Fred Wilmington	(206) 555-9090	5	$7.50	$37.50
	Kenya coffee	Fred Wilmington	(206) 555-9090	0	$7.50	$0.00
	Java coffee	Fred Wilmington	(206) 555-9090	8	$7.50	$60.00
	Kona coffee	Fred Wilmington	(206) 555-9090	9	$7.50	$67.50
	Espresso Roast	Fred Wilmington	(206) 555-9090	14	$7.50	$105.00

01/27/2001 Page 1 of 2

e. Enter a calculated control above the Grand Total in the Report Footer with a label that reads **Number of Orders to Be Placed** and an expression that counts the number of orders by Vendor Name. Add emphasis to the Grand Total and Number of Orders to Be Placed data by enlarging the font size and applying a fill background color and text color to both the labels and text. Make the label control boxes the same size and do the same with the corresponding text control boxes. Center the text in the text control boxes.

f. Change the date format in the Page Footer to Short Date, and make any other layout changes you'd like. Then print, save, and close the report.

g. Create macros that will open each database object. Test the macros after you create them.

h. Create a switchboard page for each object category (tables, forms, etc.) and create a switchboard item that will run each macro in that category. Also include an item on each page that will return to the Main Switchboard page. Edit the Main Switchboard page to include items that will access the other switchboard pages as well as a final item that will close the Main Switchboard and current database. Change the database startup options so the Main Switchboard page is displayed automatically when you open this database.

i. Test each switchboard, ending with the Main Switchboard button that closes the Cafe Purchases database.

On Your Own

6. The Posters Unlimited database you created in Practice Exercise 7 in Tutorial 5 would be more useful if it also contained a table with contact information for the suppliers. Create a new table that uses the Supplier ID as the key field and address and phone information of each supplier. Enter data into the table. Create a query that can be used to create mailing labels. Create mailing labels for the suppliers. Print the mailing label report.

7. Part of your job at the dental office where you work is to maintain the patient database. You have already created several tables, a data-input form, as well as queries and reports upon request by one of the dentists or the office bookkeeper. You just received a request for a report that groups records by dentist and includes the contact and billing information for the patients assigned to each dentist. You also need to create patient mailing labels for appointment reminders. Open the database you updated in Practice Exercise 6 of Tutorial 5 and use the Report Wizard to create a report that includes the dentist name field; the patient name, address, and phone fields; and patient billing fields from the appropriate tables. Group the report by dentist name and sort it by patient last and first names. Make any changes necessary to the report layout to make it easier to read or enhance its appearance. Add a Report Header with the dental office name and a Form Footer with **Created by [Your Name]**. Change the format property of the date control in the Page Footer to Short Date. Print the first page of the report and then save and close it. Create the mailing label report using the Label Wizard and the patient contact information table. Print the first page of labels and then close the report.

8. The owners of Adventure Travel have asked you to use the database you created for them to produce a report that groups records by tour package and clients who've used each package. They would also like this report to calculate the income that each package has generated as well as the total package sales. Open the database that you last updated in Practice Exercise 8 of Tutorial 3. Open the package pricing query and add the client name fields from the clients table. From within the query, create a new report using Report Wizard to generate a report that is based on this query, is grouped by tour package, and calculates the sum of the package sales. Once the report is generated and displayed, reformat it as necessary to fix any spacing or font sizing problems and enhance its appearance. Add a calculated control above the grand total at the end of the report that displays the number (count) of packages sold. When you have finished refining the report layout, print, save, and close the report.

9. Your job as database manager at National Packing includes updating product and client database records as well as generating reports based on these records. You have recently received a request from the regional sales manager for a report grouped by product that calculates the total sales for each product and the grand total for all products. Open the database that you updated in Practice Exercise 9 of Tutorial 5 and the purchase amount query you created earlier. Create a report based on this query that is grouped by product and includes associated pricing, sales rep, and customer information, as well as a summary option that calculates the sales totals. Reformat the report as necessary and/or desired and then print, save, and close the report. Before closing the database, create macros that will open its various tables, forms, queries, and reports. Also, create a switchboard that contains these macros as well as a button to close the database. Change the database startup options to automatically display the Main Switchboard when the database is opened.

10. Mathew is happy with the form you created in Practice Exercise 10 in Tutorial 5. He would like you to create a grouped report on the books in the database. He has asked you to group the books by category. If necessary, add a field to the appropriate table that contains categories for the books (i.e., children, adult, adult fiction, autobiography, etc). Create a query with appropriate fields from the database to show the books in each category. Create a report based on this query that is grouped by category. Reformat the report as necessary and then print and save the report. Create a switchboard that contains options to open, print, and preview the objects in the database. Set the switchboard to open automatically and password protect the database.

Working Together 2: Exporting and Importing, Creating Web Pages, and Using Hyperlinks

Case Study The Lifestyle Fitness Club accountants have reviewed the gross pay query datasheet you created and would like to do some further data manipulation on it. However, they are more used to working in Excel and would like you to export the Access query so it can be opened in Excel. Once they are done with their data manipulations, they plan to send the file back to you so you can import it back into Access.

The club has also just established an intranet to share internal information among employees who are authorized to use it, such as the club managers. The owners would like you to save the

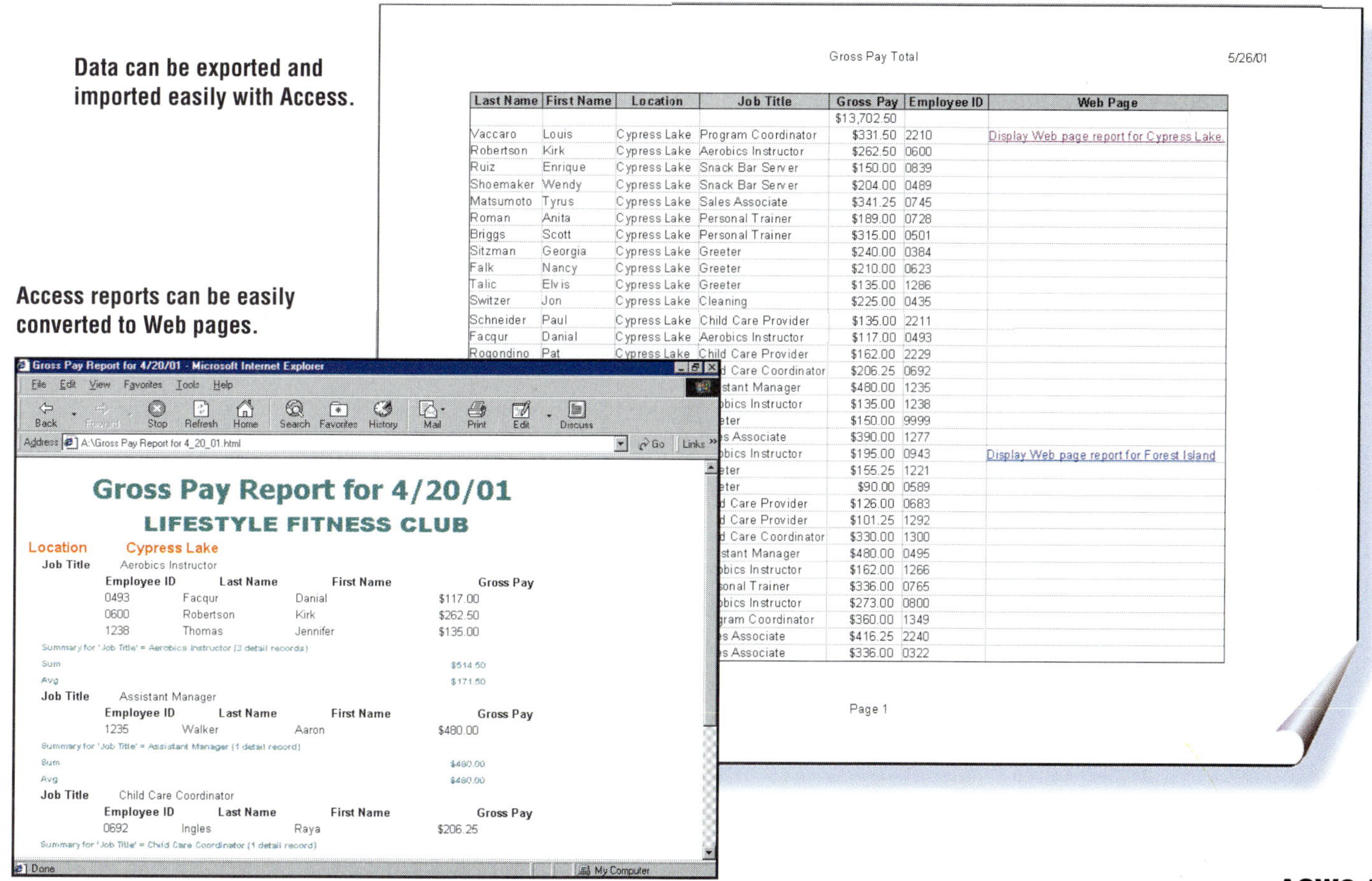

Data can be exported and imported easily with Access.

Access reports can be easily converted to Web pages.

gross pay report as a Web page so it can be viewed and discussed during the next management meeting conference call.

Note: This tutorial assumes that you already know how to use Excel 2000 and that you have completed all of the Access tutorials.

Exporting and Importing

Exporting saves data created using Access in another format to be inserted into a document created in a different application. **Importing**, as you have learned, retrieves data that has been saved in another format into an Access table. There are many different types of file formats. Access will import and export data in the following formats.

- Text files (.asc, .txt, .csv, .tab) — These include delimited text and fixed-width text. **Delimited text** is a file containing values separated by commas, tabs, semicolons, or other characters as in the following example: 3/2/98 0:00:00,/"Reddie","Suzanne". **Fixed-width text** is a file containing values arranged so that each field has a certain width, as in the following example: 3/2/98 0:00:00 Reddie Suzanne.

- Rich text format (.rtf) — This file format retains all the format settings, such as font, alignment, and number formatting for column heads and data, as shown below:

Hire Date	Last Name	First Name
9/23/96	Shoemaker	Wendy
8/4/96	Switzer	Jon
3/2/98	Reddie	Suzanne

- Excel versions 3.0, 4.0, 5.0, 7.0/95, 8.0/97, and 9.0/2000 (.xls)

- Lotus 1-2-3 .wkl and .wk3 formats

- Paradox releases 3.x, 4.x, and 5.0 (.pdx)

- Visual FoxPro versions 3.0, 5.0, and 6.x (.dbf)

- dBase III, III+, IV, and 5 (.dbf)

- HTML versions 1.1, 2.0., 3.x., and 4.x

Access can import files saved in any of these formats and converts the information into an Access table. Access files that are exported to any of these formats can be read and used by any programs that use these formats. The Export command on the File menu is used to convert database objects into the different file formats that can be used in other applications.

First, you need to export the Gross Pay for 4/20/01 query datasheet to an Excel workbook so that the club accountants can perform additional mathematical analysis on the data. Rather than opening the query, you can simply select the query object name from the Queries tab and export it to an Excel file format.

1

- **Start Access 2000.**

- **Open the Club Employees database from your data disk.**

- **When prompted, enter the password to open the database (this should be your first name).**

- **Click** 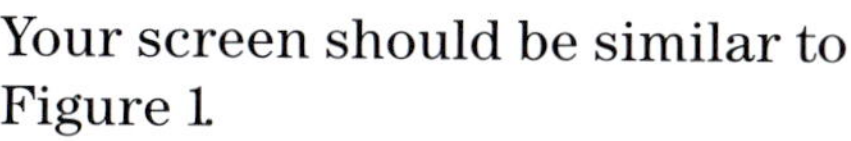 **Database Window to display the Database window.**

- **Select** the Gross Pay 4/20/01 query object.

- **Choose** **F**ile/**E**xport.

- **If necessary, select the drive containing your data disk as the location to save the file.**

Your screen should be similar to Figure 1.

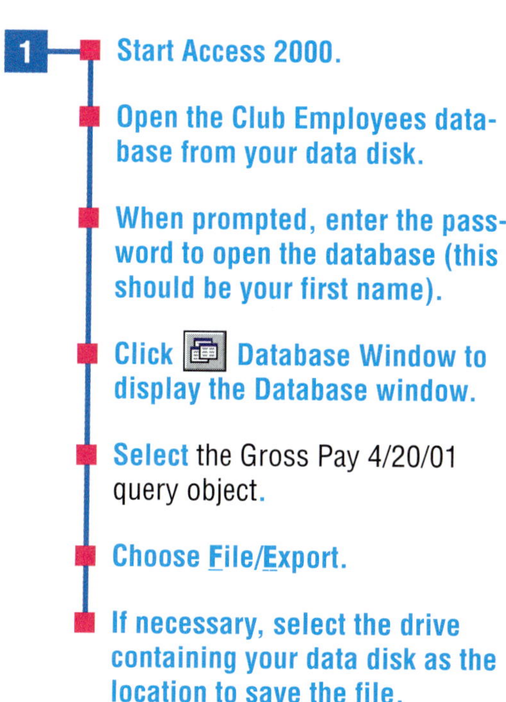
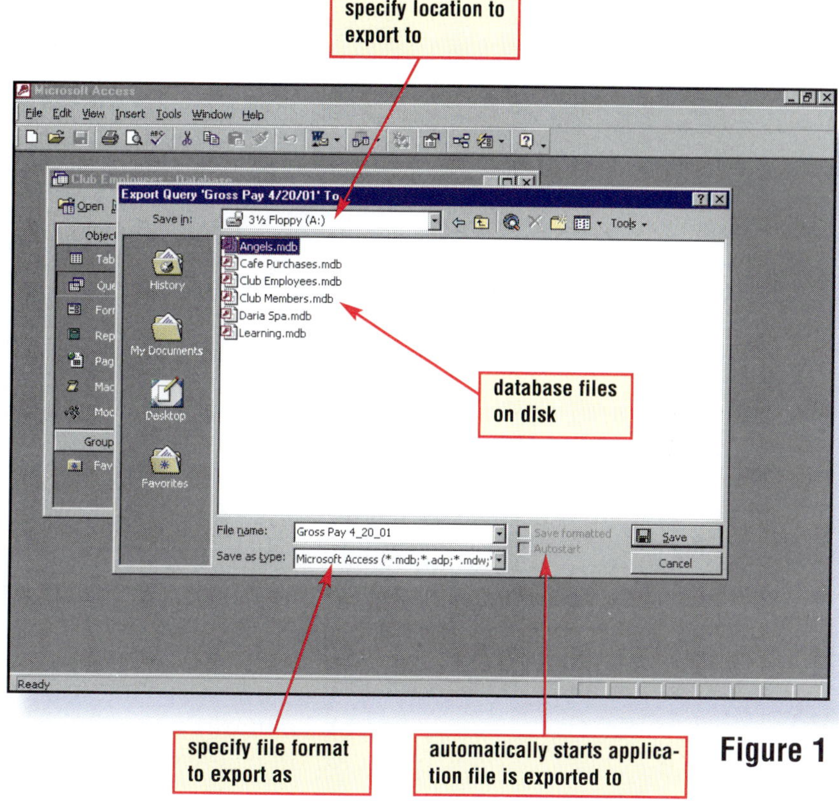

Figure 1

You use the Export Query dialog box to specify where and in what format you want to export the selected query. In addition, you can specify whether you want to include the original file formatting in the new file and if you want to have the exported file automatically opened in the selected application. You will save the query as an Excel 2000 file format to your data disk preserving the original table formats such as fonts and field widths. You will also have the new application load automatically and display the new file.

Figure 4

2 From the Save as Type drop-down list box, select Microsoft Excel 97–2000.

Select Save **F**ormatted.

Select A**u**tostart.

Click 💾 **S**ave .

Your screen should be similar to Figure 2.

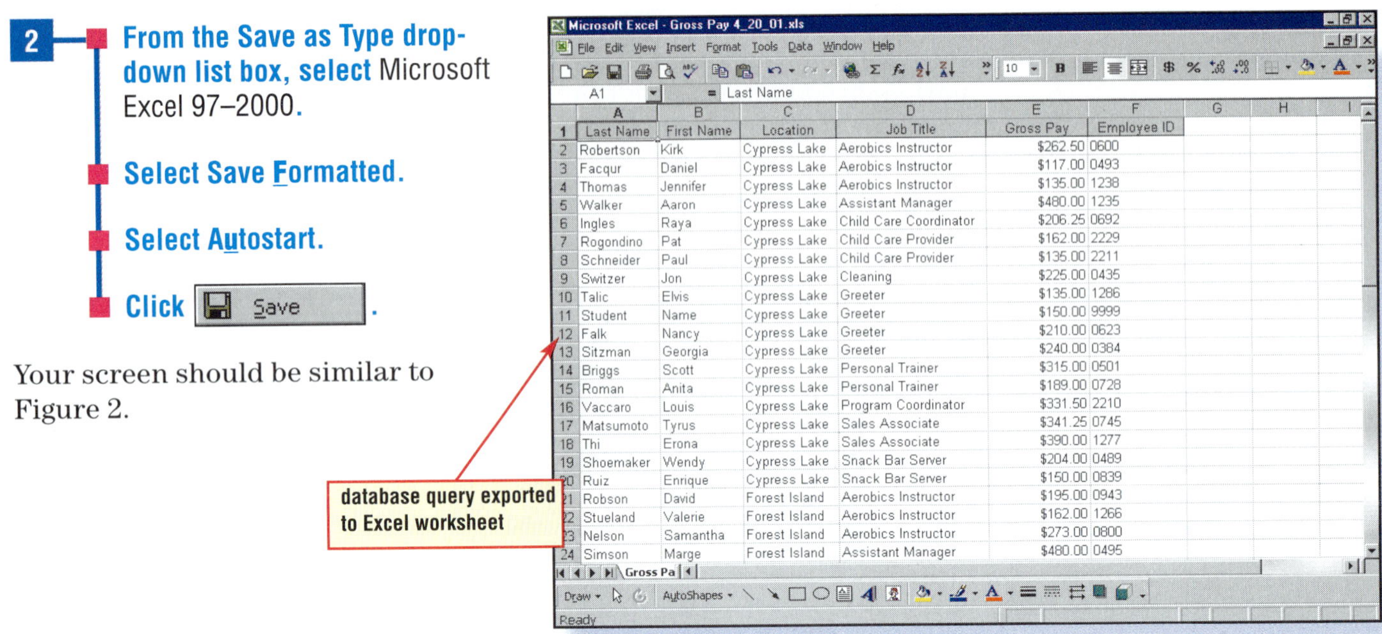

	A	B	C	D	E	F
1	Last Name	First Name	Location	Job Title	Gross Pay	Employee ID
2	Robertson	Kirk	Cypress Lake	Aerobics Instructor	$262.50	0600
3	Facqur	Daniel	Cypress Lake	Aerobics Instructor	$117.00	0493
4	Thomas	Jennifer	Cypress Lake	Aerobics Instructor	$135.00	1238
5	Walker	Aaron	Cypress Lake	Assistant Manager	$480.00	1235
6	Ingles	Raya	Cypress Lake	Child Care Coordinator	$206.25	0692
7	Rogondino	Pat	Cypress Lake	Child Care Provider	$162.00	2229
8	Schneider	Paul	Cypress Lake	Child Care Provider	$135.00	2211
9	Switzer	Jon	Cypress Lake	Cleaning	$225.00	0435
10	Talic	Elvis	Cypress Lake	Greeter	$135.00	1286
11	Student	Name	Cypress Lake	Greeter	$150.00	9999
12	Falk	Nancy	Cypress Lake	Greeter	$210.00	0623
13	Sitzman	Georgia	Cypress Lake	Greeter	$240.00	0384
14	Briggs	Scott	Cypress Lake	Personal Trainer	$315.00	0501
15	Roman	Anita	Cypress Lake	Personal Trainer	$189.00	0728
16	Vaccaro	Louis	Cypress Lake	Program Coordinator	$331.50	2210
17	Matsumoto	Tyrus	Cypress Lake	Sales Associate	$341.25	0745
18	Thi	Erona	Cypress Lake	Sales Associate	$390.00	1277
19	Shoemaker	Wendy	Cypress Lake	Snack Bar Server	$204.00	0489
20	Ruiz	Enrique	Cypress Lake	Snack Bar Server	$150.00	0839
21	Robson	David	Forest Island	Aerobics Instructor	$195.00	0943
22	Stueland	Valerie	Forest Island	Aerobics Instructor	$162.00	1266
23	Nelson	Samantha	Forest Island	Aerobics Instructor	$273.00	0800
24	Simson	Marge	Forest Island	Assistant Manager	$480.00	0495

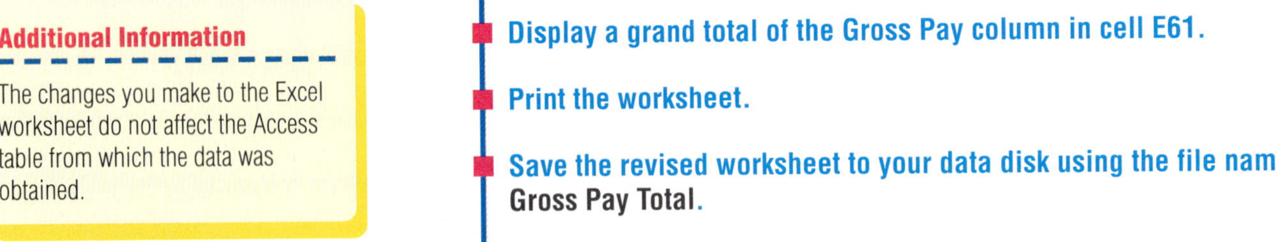

Figure 2

The database query is saved to a file in an Excel file format and Excel 2000 is loaded. The new workbook file is open with the information from the query displayed in it. The field names are placed in the first row of the spreadsheet, and the data begins in row 2. The column heads and column widths are formatted as they appeared in the query datasheet. Now the data can be manipulated using Excel commands and features. For example, it would be easy to calculate total and average values by departments.

3 If necessary, maximize the Excel worksheet window.

Display a grand total of the Gross Pay column in cell E61.

Print the worksheet.

Save the revised worksheet to your data disk using the file name **Gross Pay Total**.

Exit Excel.

Additional Information

The changes you make to the Excel worksheet do not affect the Access table from which the data was obtained.

Importing to a New Table

You will now import this new Excel file back into the Access database as a new table.

1 ■ **Choose** **F**ile/**G**et External Data/**I**mport.

■ **If necessary, select the drive containing your data disk as the location containing the file you want to import.**

■ **Open the Files of Type drop-down list box and select** Microsoft Excel (.xls)**.**

■ **Select the** Gross Pay Total.xls **file.**

■ **Click** [📂 Import] **.**

The Import Spreadsheet Wizard is started. Make the following selections from the wizard dialog boxes to create a new table.

2 ■ **Click the** First Row contains column headings **box to select it.**

■ **Click** [Next >] **.**

■ **Click** [Next >] **to accept the default selection of** In a New Table**.**

Your screen should be similar to Figure 3.

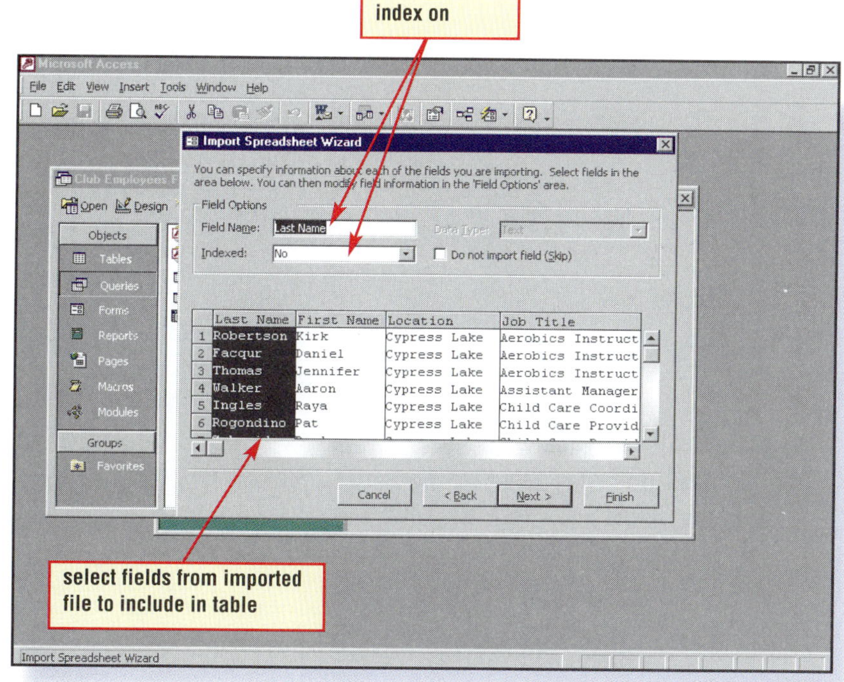

Figure 3

Next, you select the fields from the imported file that you want to include in your table and which fields should be indexed. You can exclude fields from the imported file so they are not part of your new table. You want to include all fields and index the Employee ID field.

3
- **Click the Employee ID column heading.**
- **Select Yes (No Duplicates) from the Indexed drop-down list.**
- **Click** Next > .

Your screen should be similar to Figure 4.

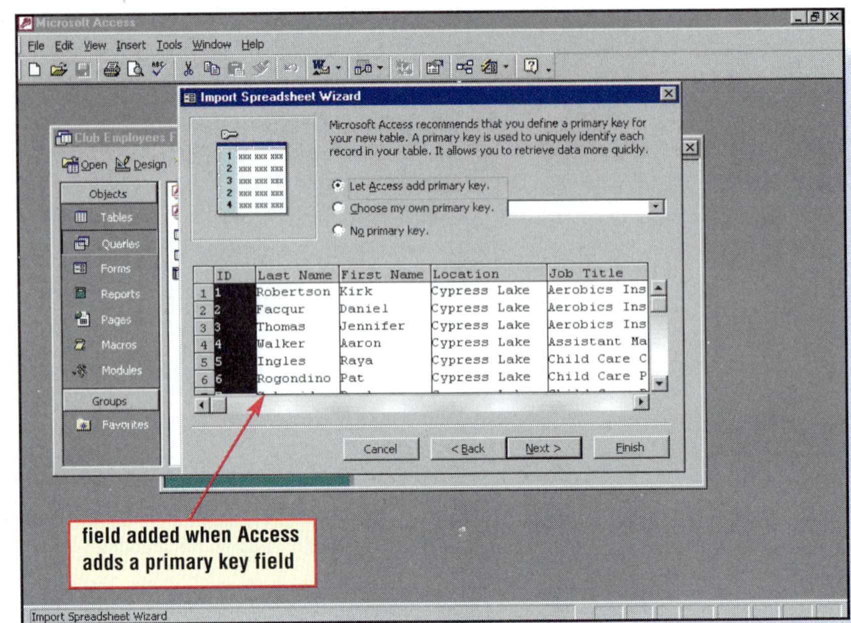

Figure 4

You can have Access automatically apply a primary key to a field or you can choose your own primary key field. You can also choose to omit a primary key, which is the option you will choose because the Grand Total row does not contain all the fields and will therefore cause a "blank primary key" error message to display when the new table is created.

4
- **Select No primary key.**
- **Click** Next > .
- **Enter Gross Pay Total as the new table name.**
- **Click** Finish .
- **Click** OK .
- **Open the new Gross Pay Total table.**
- **If necessary, maximize the window.**

Your screen should be similar to Figure 5.

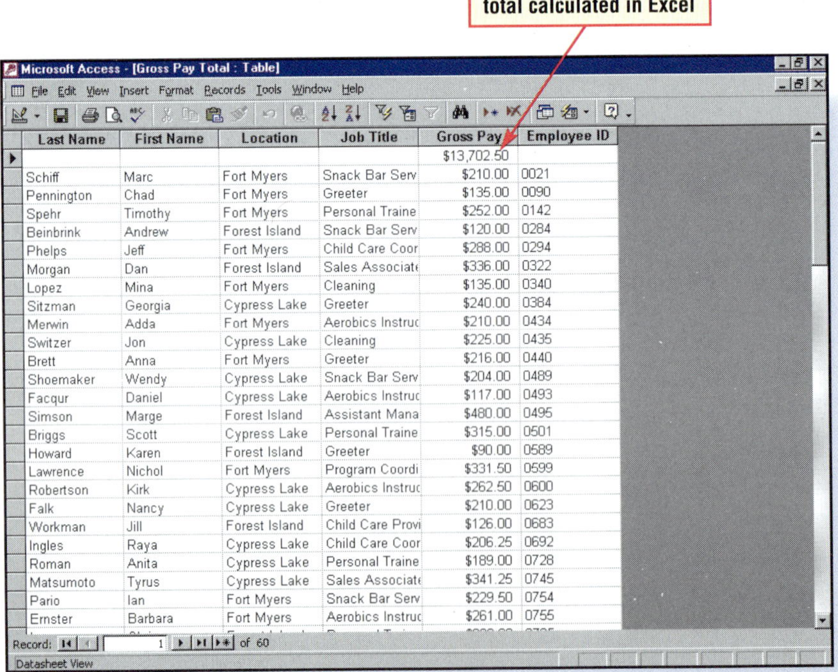

Figure 5

Notice the first record row displays the Gross Pay Total value. You can now work with this table as you would any other Access table. For example, you might want to widen columns to fit the contents, add fields to the table design, or add, modify, or delete records.

5 **Best Fit the field columns.**

Change the column order to Employee ID, Last Name, First Name, Job Title, Location, and Gross Pay.

Close the table, saving any changes.

Saving a Database Object as a Web Page

You have been asked to save the Gross Pay Report as a Web page for viewing on the club's **intranet** (an internal network set up by a company to share data online). A **Web page** is a document that can be used on the World Wide Web (WWW) and displayed in your browser application. The **browser** is a program that connects you to the remote computers and displays the Web pages you request.

In order to save a database object (a table, form, report, or query) as a Web page, Access converts the object to HTML file format by adding **HTML (Hypertext Markup Language)** coding to the document. All Web pages are written using a programming language called HTML. HTML commands are interpreted by the browser software you are using and control how the information on a page is displayed, such as font colors and size, and how an item will be processed, such as a form. HTML also allows users to click on **hyperlinks** that jump to other locations on the same page, other pages in the same site, or to other sites and locations on the WWW altogether.

You can export the file directly as a **static HTML** page that can only be viewed, not modified, on the Web. A separate Web page is created for each page in the table, form, report, or query. If you want the Web pages to be **dynamic**—allowing viewers to edit, update, delete, filter, and group live data — you need to create a **data access page** that contains a shortcut to the location of the corresponding HTML file, publish this page to a Web folder or server, and make the source database available to users of the page.

Since the club owners want this report available only for viewing and discussion, you will export it as a static HTML file.

This portion of the tutorial assumes that a Web browser application is installed on the computer you are using.

1 ● **From the Reports Object group, select** the Gross Pay Report for 4/20/01.

● **Choose File/Export.**

● **Open the Save as Type drop-down list box and select** HTML Documents.

Selecting Autostart when you are exporting to HTML will automatically open the Web pages in the browser that is installed on your system. You will not be selecting this option at this time, but will view the Web pages from your data disk later.

● **Click**  Save.

Your screen should be similar to Figure 6.

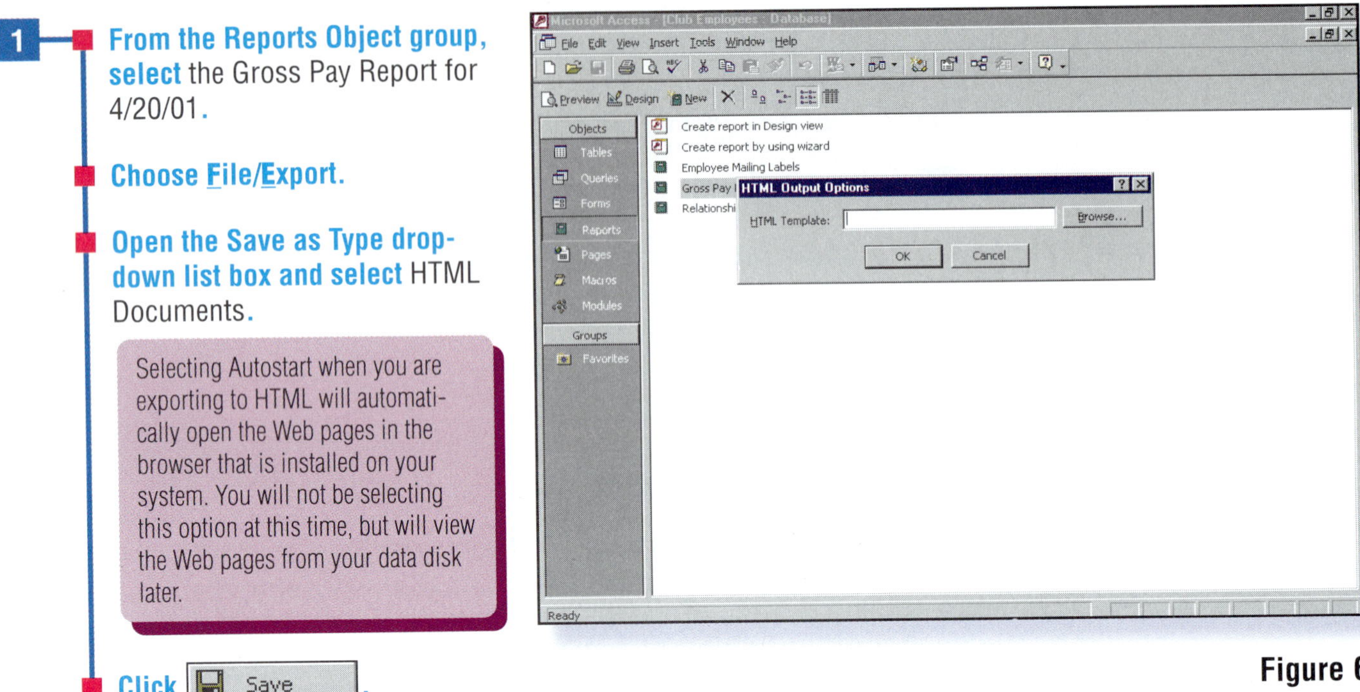

Figure 6

This HTML Output Options dialog box enables you to apply a current HTML document as a template for these Web pages. You do not have a document that you want to apply, so you can proceed without naming a template. Access will use the default navigations scheme.

2 ● **Click** OK.

A dialog box briefly appears while the report is being exported. When the export process is finished, you can open the Web pages from the Web toolbar in Access.

3 ━ ■ **Choose <u>V</u>iew/<u>T</u>oolbars/Web to display the Web toolbar.**

The Web toolbar buttons are identified below.

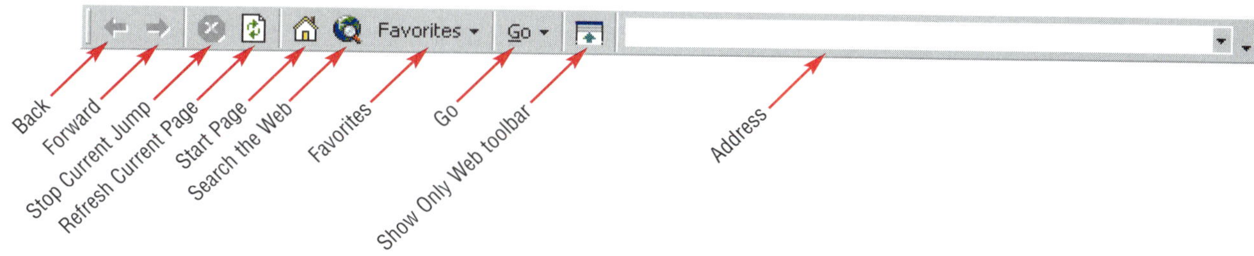

To open the Web page,

4 ━ ■ **Click** Go ▾ **and select <u>O</u>pen from the drop-down menu.**

■ **Click** Browse... **.**

■ **If necessary, select the** Look in location that contains the Web page **file you just created.**

Your screen should be similar to Figure 7.

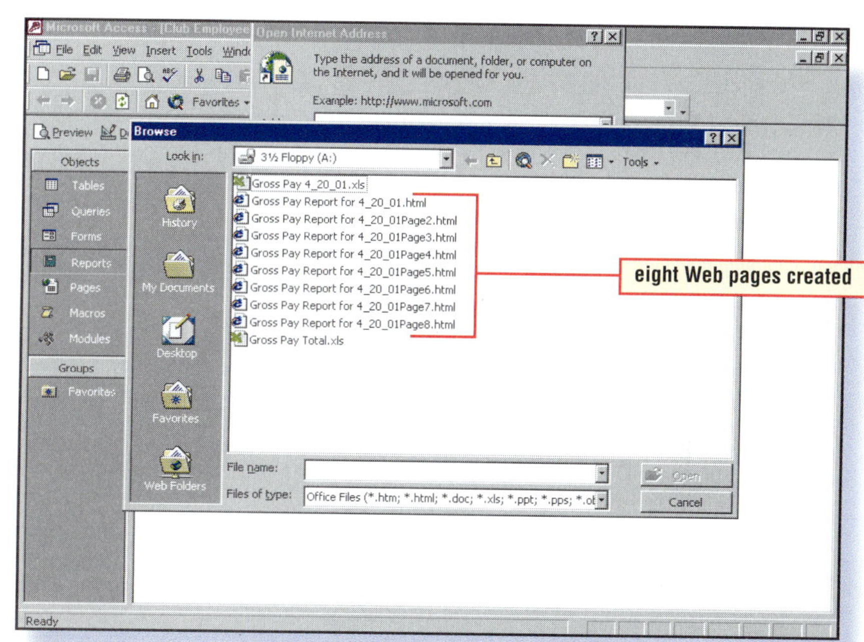

Figure 7

Each page of the Gross Pay Report was saved as a separate Web page. To open the first page of the report,

4 ▪ **Select** Gross Pay Report for 4_20_01.html.

▪ **Click** Open .

▪ **Click** OK .

You could also type the path to the Web page you want to display directly in the Address text box of the Web toolbar. For example, A:\Gross Pay Report for 4_20_01.html.

▪ **If necessary, maximize your browser window.**

Your screen should be similar to Figure 8.

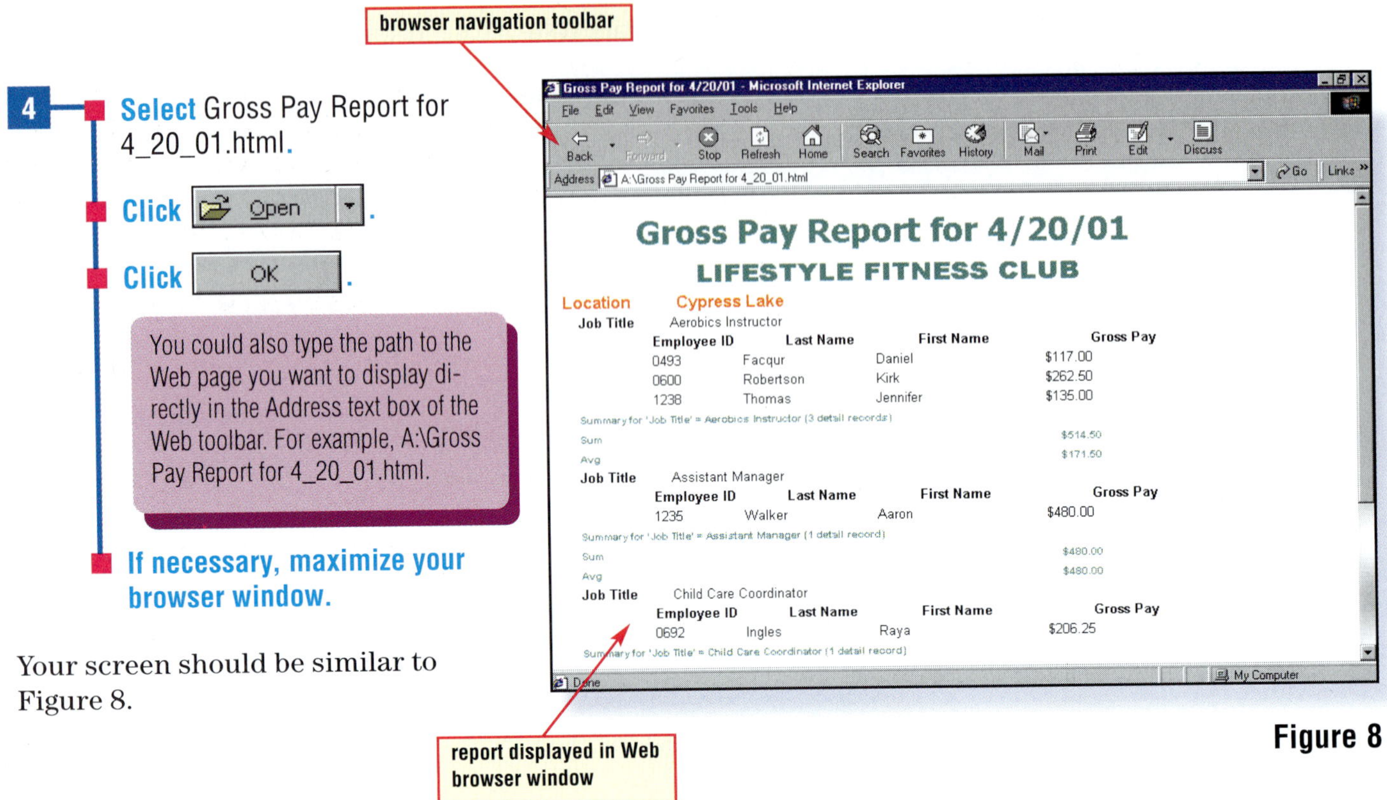

Figure 8

The Web browser on your system opens and displays the first Gross Pay Report Web page. The appearance of the navigation buttons on the browser toolbar may vary depending on what browser you are using. At the bottom of the page are hyperlinks that allow you to move through the report.

5 — Scroll to the bottom of the page.

Your screen should be similar to Figure 9.

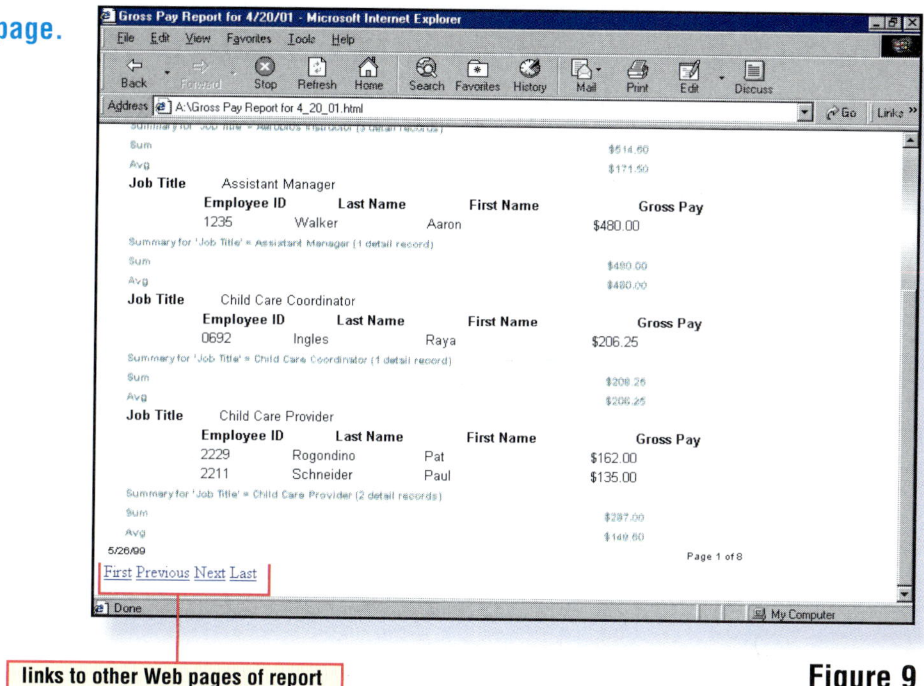

Figure 9

6 — Click **Next.**

The second page of the report is displayed. To exit the browser,

7 — Click ☒ (in the browser window title bar.)

Finally, you decide to create hyperlinks from the Gross Pay Total table to the Gross Pay Report Web page. This way, those who view the table can jump from a record to the related report Web page whenever they'd like.

Adding a Hyperlink to a Database Object

As you have seen, a hyperlink creates a shortcut or jump to another location in the same or different database table, form, report, or query; to a document in a different application; or to a Web page. You want to add a hyperlink in the Gross Pay Totals database table to the Web page.

1
- **Open the** Gross Pay Total **table.**
- **Switch to Design view.**
- **Add a field called Web Page.**
- **Select** Hyperlink **from the Data Type drop-down list.**
- **Save the design changes.**

Your screen should be similar to Figure 10.

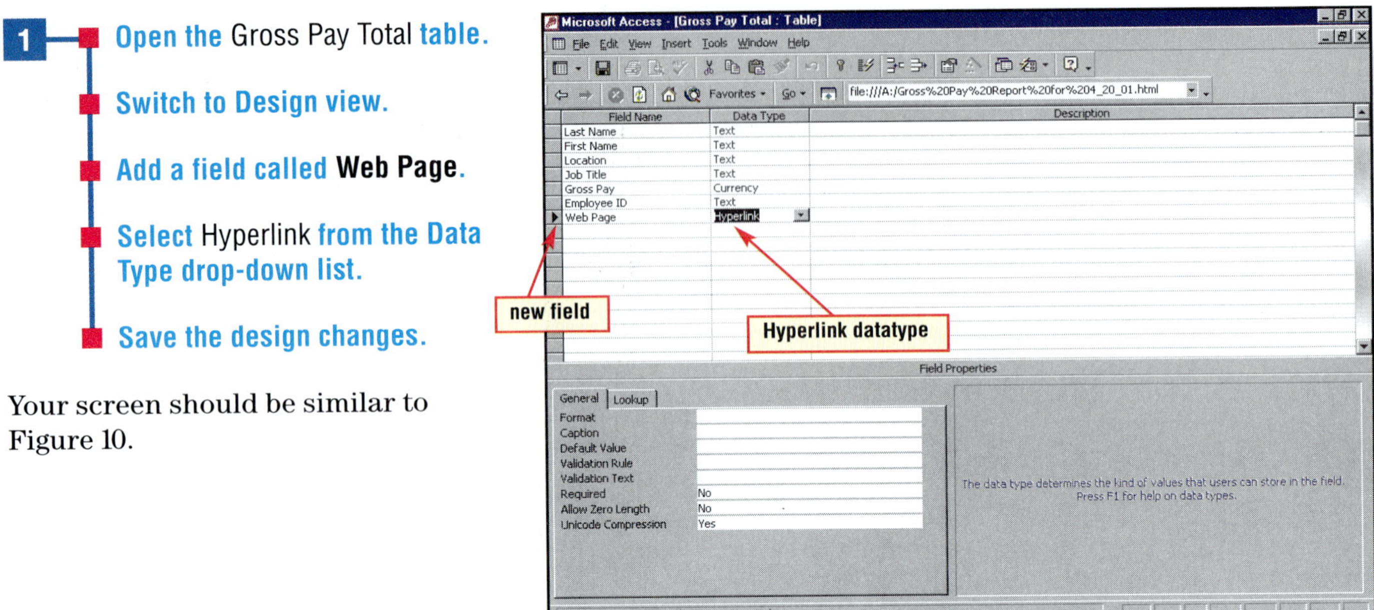

Figure 10

Next, you'll start adding the Web page hyperlinks to the table records.

2
- **Switch to Datasheet view.**
- **If necessary, maximize the window.**
- **Sort the table by Location in ascending order, if it is not already.**
- **Move to the Web page field for the first record in Cypress Lake.**
- **Click** Insert Hyperlink.

The menu equivalent is Insert/Hyperlink. You can also right-click to display a shortcut menu for this field and then select Hyperlink/Edit Hyperlink to enter a new or edit an existing hyperlink.

Your screen should be similar to Figure 11.

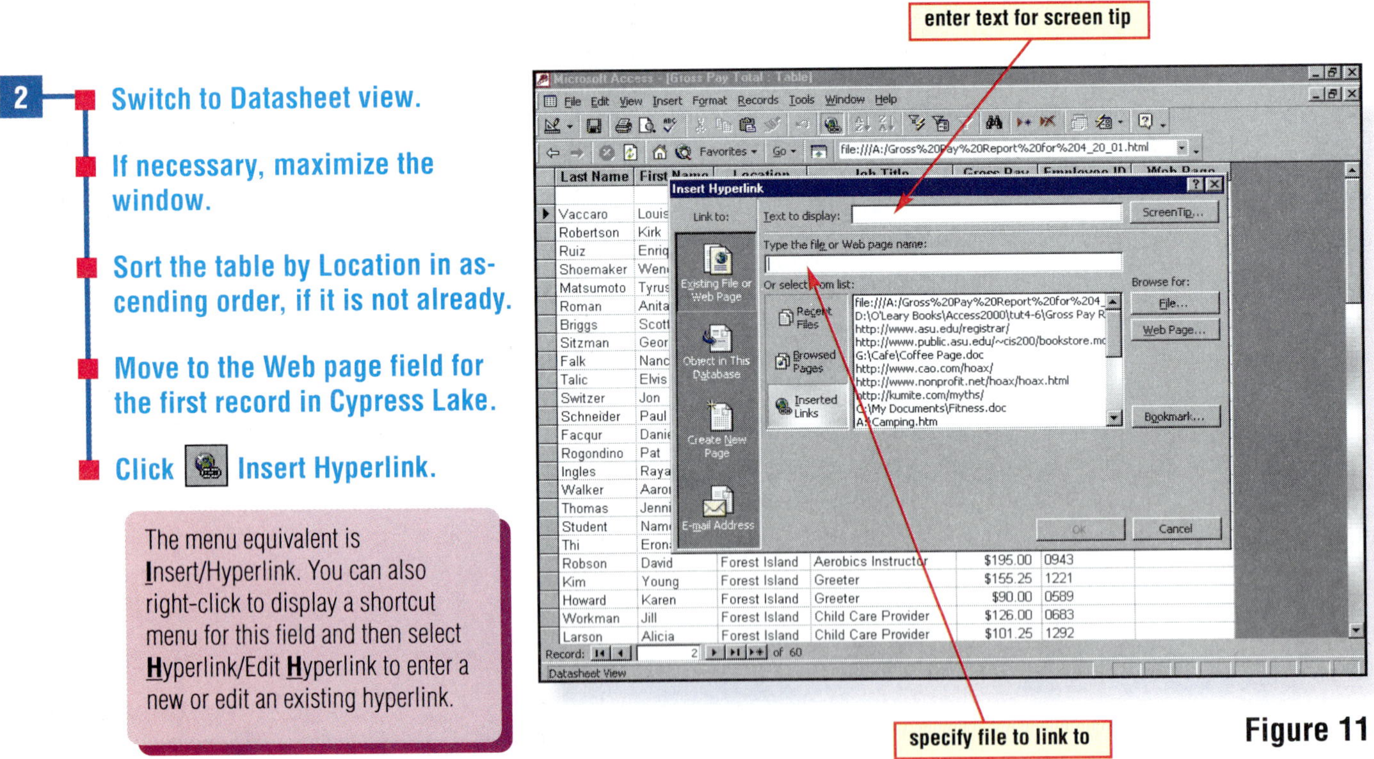

Figure 11

You use the Insert Hyperlink dialog box to specify the file to which you want the hyperlink to jump. You can also specify whether you want the hyperlink field to display the address of the linked file or a text message. You can also add a screen tip that will display whenever the mouse pointer rests on the hyperlink field. For this record, you want to link to the first page of the Web page report (which contains the Cypress Lake data).

3

- In the Text to display text box, type **Display Web page report for Cypress Lake**.

- In the Type the file or Web page name text box, type **A:\Gross Pay Report for 4_20_01.html**.

  You can also use [File...] to locate and select the file.

- Click [OK].

- Increase the width of the Web Page field column so you can see the entire hyperlink text.

Your screen should be similar to Figure 12.

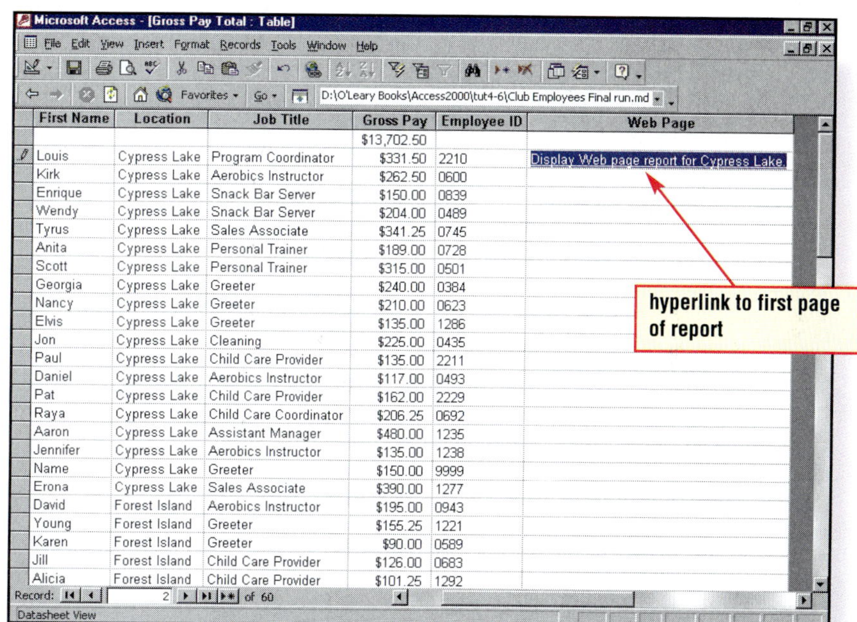

Figure 12

To test this hyperlink,

4

- Click the hyperlink text.

Your screen should be similar to Figure 13.

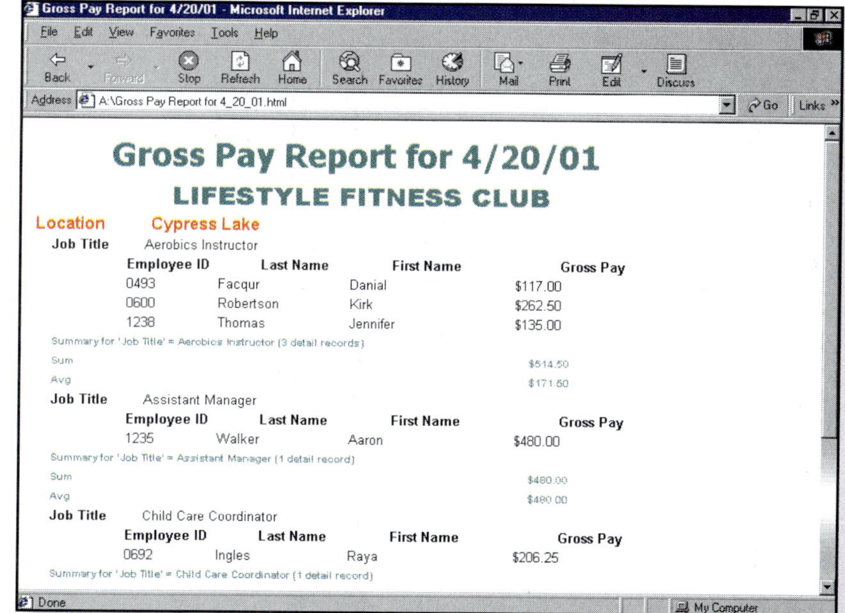

Figure 13

Your Web browser is started and displays the first page of the Web page report that contains the information for Cypress Lake. You will now enter hyperlinks in the table to other pages of this report.

5 — ■ **Close the browser window.**

■ **Move to the Web Page field of the first Forest Island record.**

> You could enter a hyperlink in every record to the appropriate report Web page. However, for the purposes of this tutorial, you will only enter a hyperlink for each new location.

■ **Click 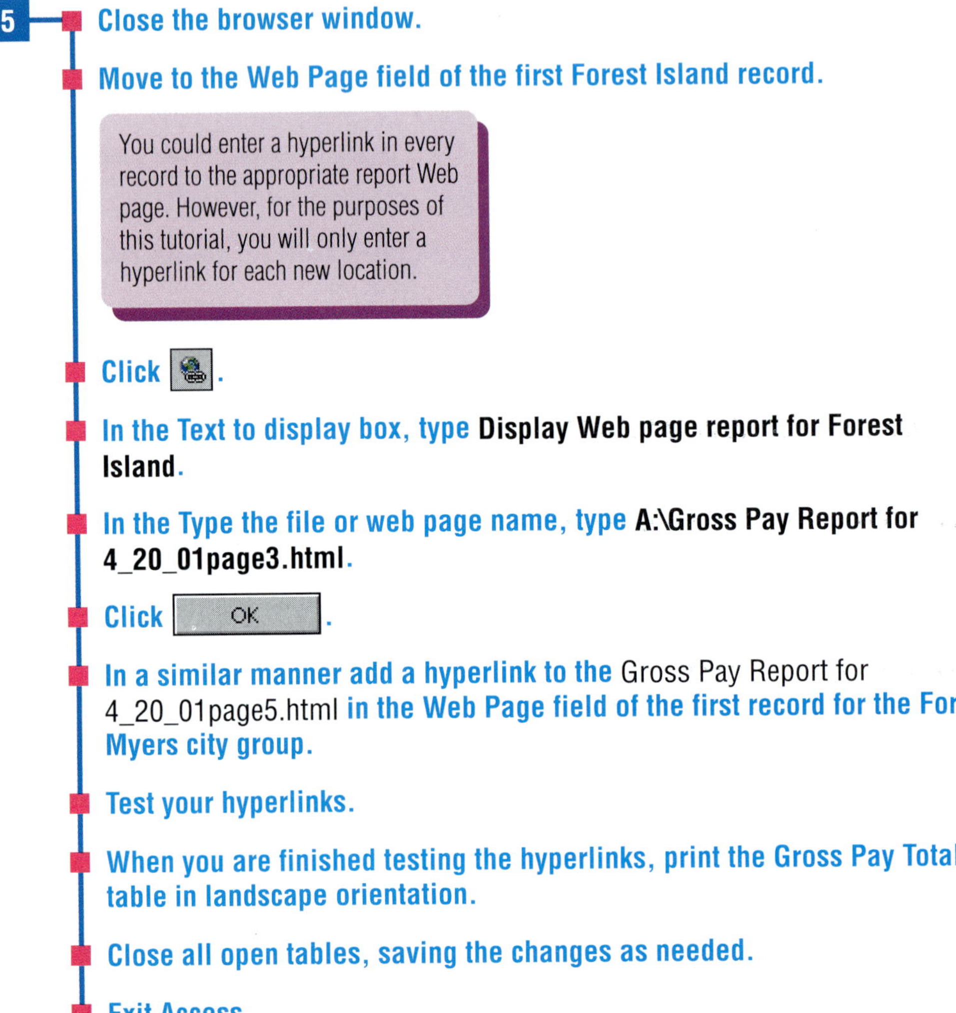 .**

■ **In the Text to display box, type Display Web page report for Forest Island.**

■ **In the Type the file or web page name, type A:\Gross Pay Report for 4_20_01page3.html.**

■ **Click** OK **.**

■ **In a similar manner add a hyperlink to the** Gross Pay Report for 4_20_01page5.html **in the Web Page field of the first record for the Fort Myers city group.**

■ **Test your hyperlinks.**

■ **When you are finished testing the hyperlinks, print the Gross Pay Total table in landscape orientation.**

■ **Close all open tables, saving the changes as needed.**

■ **Exit Access.**

Key Terms

browser   ACW2-7
data access page   ACW2-7
delimited text   ACW2-2
dynamic HTML   ACW2-7
export   ACW2-2
fixed-width text   ACW2-2
HTML (Hypertext Markup Language)   ACW2-7
hyperlink   ACW2-7
import   ACW2-2
intranet   ACW2-7
static HTML   ACW2-7
Web page   ACW2-7

Command Summary

Command	Action
File/**E**xport	Saves an Access database object in another file format so it can be used in a different application or as a Web page.
File/**G**et External Data/**I**mport	Copies data from a file saved in another format into an Access database.
Insert/Hyper**l**ink	Inserts a new hyperlink or modifies the selected hyperlink.
View/**T**oolbars/Web	Displays the Web toolbar.

Hands-On Practice Exercises

Step-by-Step

1. The Downtown Internet Cafe has just hired an accountant, and she would like to use the Stock Item Costs database table you created to set up her own pricing spreadsheet in Excel. You are more than happy to provide this, and, what's more, you'll export it in Excel for her. In return, she will send you the customer contact information sheet that she created in Excel so that you can import it into Access and use it as necessary. Your completed customers table is shown here.

a. Open the Cafe Purchases 4 database (which you last worked on in Practice Exercise 5 of Tutorial 5).

b. Select the Stock Item Prices table and export it. Save it as a formatted Excel 97–2000 document to your data disk. Select AutoStart so you can view the document to make sure it's okay before you give it to the accountant.

c. Review the file in Excel and then close the file and exit the Excel application.

d. Import the Excel file called Cafe Customers.xls from your data disk. Select the Customers worksheet as the one you want to import in the first Import Wizard dialog box. The column headings that you want to use as field names in your Access database table are contained in row 2, not row 1, so don't select the "First Row Contains Column Headings" option. Accept the default to store the data in a new table. Do not index any of the fields. Specify that you do not want a primary key defined. Accept the "Customers" default name for the new table and finish out of the Wizard.

Customers   7/23/02

Last Name	First Name	Street	City	State	Zip	Phone
Amlin	Francis	6698 Chestnut St.	Joliet	IL	60790	(815) 555-2468
Beinbrink	Andrew	45 Burr Rd.	Hartford	CT	31922	(860) 555-4456
Bloomquist	William	43 Kings Rd.	Little Silver	NJ	07739	(941) 555-3333
Brett	Anna	23 Suffolk Ln.	Holmdel	NJ	07734	(941) 555-1038
Briggs	Scott	45 E. Camelback Rd.	Scottsdale	AZ	85230	(602) 555-3908
Brown	Jill	4344 W. Gala Ln.	Rochester	NY	14892	(518) 555-1234
Brown	Kurt	124 Main St.	Guilford	CT	31002	(860) 555-5446
Brown	Sara	1005 First Ave.	Albany	NY	20203	(518) 555-1234
Chaplin	Lon	91 Monmouth Ave.	Long Branch	NJ	07735	(732) 555-3993
Dryer	Jack	21 N. Navesink River Rd.	Red Bank	NJ	07730	(732) 555-0202
Facqur	Daniel	5832 Fremont St.	Long Branch	NJ	07735	(732) 555-3993
Falk	Nancy	9483 W. Island Dr.	Long Branch	NJ	07735	(732) 555-6032
Hamlin	Rose	7 Church St.	Dayton	OH	73904	(937) 555-7982
Howard	Karen	9423 S. Forest Ave.	Hartford	CT	31922	(860) 555-4600
Ingles	Raya	8432 N. Cimarron	Scottsdale	AZ	85230	(480) 555-2011
Lawrence	Nichol	433 S. Gaucho Dr.	Holmdel	NJ	07734	(732) 555-4494
Liston	Frank	3021 Ash St.	St. Paul	MN	47089	(612) 555-3017
Lopez	Mina	4290 E. Alameda Dr.	Long Branch	NJ	07735	(732) 555-3003
Marino	Timothy	90 E. Royal Dr.	Red Bank	NJ	07730	(732) 555-9388
Matsumoto	Tyrus	34 S. Onza Ave.	Mesa	AZ	85202	(602) 555-8778
Merwin	Adda	947 S. Forest	St. Paul	MN	47089	(612) 555-7664
Morgan	Dan	564 S. Lemon Dr.	Red Bank	NJ	07730	(732) 555-8399
Nichols	Cathy	75 Brooklea Dr.	Red Bank	NJ	07730	(732) 555-8243
Pennington	Chad	23 Mill Ave.	Albany	NY	20203	(518) 555-2334
Phelps	Jeff	2343 W. Audrey Ln.	Red Bank	NJ	07730	(732) 555-7112
Robertson	Kirk	832 S. William Ave.	Poughkipsie	NY	12590	(914) 555-6699
Roman	Anita	2348 S. Bala Dr.	St. Paul	MN	47089	(612) 555-6455
Shoemaker	Wendy	858 E. Mt. Aire Ct.	Poughkipsie	NY	12590	(914) 555-4522
Simson	Marge	432 Tercera Dr.	E. Aurora	NY	14052	(716) 555-9421
Sitzman	Georgia	94 Evergreen Ave.	Albany	NY	20203	(518) 555-5009
Switzer	Jon	32 W. Orange St.	Winfield	IL	60790	(815) 555-6855
Thomas	Grant	214 White Rd.	Red Bank	NJ	07730	(732) 555-0893
Trent	Maria	525 E. Palm Dr.	Mesa	AZ	85215	(602) 555-3618
Student	Name	89 Any St.	Little Silver	NJ	07739	(732) 555-1133

Page 1

e. Open the newly imported Customers table and delete the first 16 records ("Criteria" through "Last Name"). Switch to Design view and delete Fields 8 through 19. Name the remaining fields **Last Name, First Name, Street, City, State, Zip, and Phone.** Change the Field Size property for each of these fields to a lower, more appropriate number. Save the table design and switch back to Datasheet view. Appropriately adjust the column widths. Add a new record that contains your first and last name and a fictional address and phone number. Print the table and then close the table and the Cafe Purchases database.

2. You have received a request from the Orders Department at EduSoft Company for a copy of the orders database table that you created in Excel format so they can check it against their department's product order records. After you are finished with this, you need to take care of a request from the marketing manager. Based on how much the reports you've produced have helped target potential clients for the company's educational software, she would like to see what kind of response they get if they are put on the company's Web site. To give the Web site designer an idea of what he will be working with, you will save one of these reports as a Web page so you can send it to him for review and redesign, if necessary. When you are finished, you will have a Web page that looks like the page shown here.

a. Open the Learning 4 database (which you last worked on in Practice Exercise 4 of Tutorial 6).

b. Export the Orders table in Excel format to your data disk. AutoStart the Excel application so you can check the exported document. Exit the Excel application when you're finished reviewing the file.

c. Export the EduSoft Programs for Grades 3–8 report in HTML format to your data disk. (When the dialog box appears asking you for a template name, leave it blank and just click OK to proceed.)

d. To view the Web pages you just created (if you have a Web browser on your system), enter the location and file name in the Address box on the Web toolbar. You'll see that there are some text

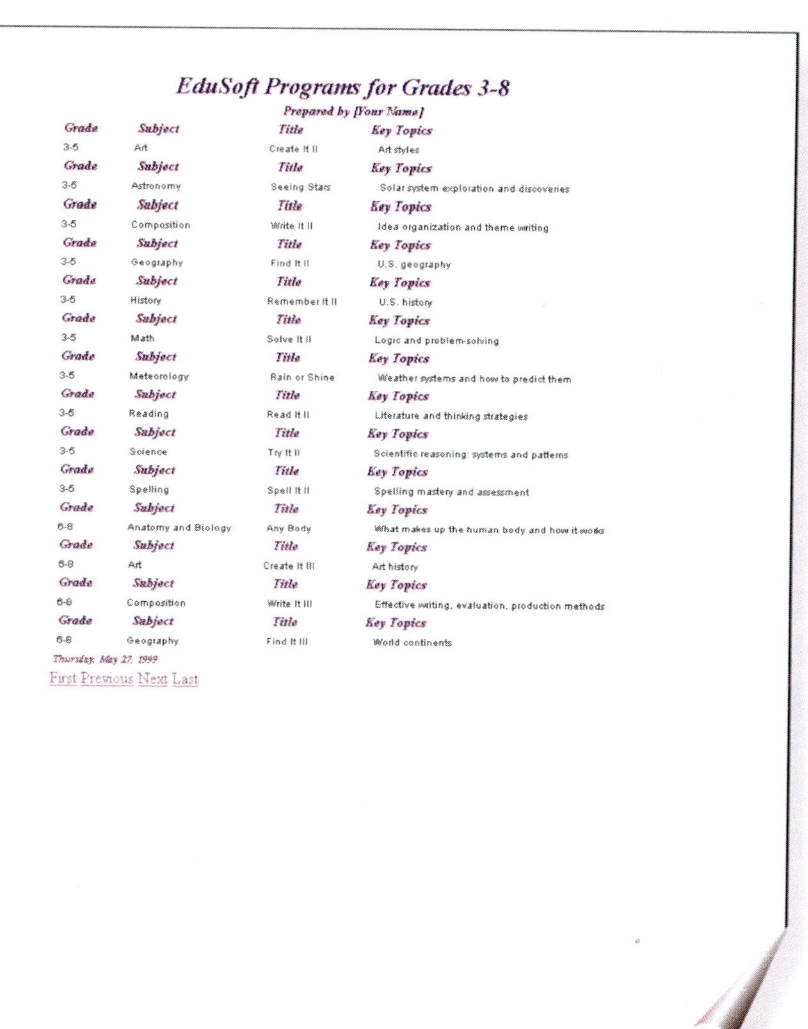

EduSoft Programs for Grades 3-8
Prepared by [Your Name]

Grade	Subject	Title	Key Topics
3-5	Art	Create It II	Art styles
Grade	*Subject*	*Title*	*Key Topics*
3-5	Astronomy	Seeing Stars	Solar system exploration and discoveries
Grade	*Subject*	*Title*	*Key Topics*
3-5	Composition	Write It II	Idea organization and theme writing
Grade	*Subject*	*Title*	*Key Topics*
3-5	Geography	Find It II	U.S. geography
Grade	*Subject*	*Title*	*Key Topics*
3-5	History	Remember It II	U.S. history
Grade	*Subject*	*Title*	*Key Topics*
3-5	Math	Solve It II	Logic and problem-solving
Grade	*Subject*	*Title*	*Key Topics*
3-5	Meteorology	Rain or Shine	Weather systems and how to predict them
Grade	*Subject*	*Title*	*Key Topics*
3-5	Reading	Read It II	Literature and thinking strategies
Grade	*Subject*	*Title*	*Key Topics*
3-5	Science	Try It II	Scientific reasoning: systems and patterns
Grade	*Subject*	*Title*	*Key Topics*
3-5	Spelling	Spell It II	Spelling mastery and assessment
Grade	*Subject*	*Title*	*Key Topics*
6-8	Anatomy and Biology	Any Body	What makes up the human body and how it works
Grade	*Subject*	*Title*	*Key Topics*
6-8	Art	Create It III	Art history
Grade	*Subject*	*Title*	*Key Topics*
6-8	Composition	Write It III	Effective writing, evaluation, production methods
Grade	*Subject*	*Title*	*Key Topics*
6-8	Geography	Find It III	World continents

Thursday, May 27, 1999

First Previous Next Last

alignment problems, but the Web designer will take care of these. For now, just print the first page and exit the browser.

  e. Close the Learning 4 database.

3. Daria O'Dell, the owner of Daria's Day Spa, is very impressed with the spa package database table that you created. In fact, she would like you to save it as a Web page so she can use it on the Web site she is having developed for the spa. She would also like you to add hyperlinks to the Web page in the Package Purchases table so those who are entering purchase information can view the package descriptions on the Web if they so choose. Your completed Web page is shown here.

  a. Open the database called Daria Spa 4 (which you last worked on in Practice Exercise 3 of Tutorial 6).

  b. Export the Spa Packages table in HTML format to your data disk. If you have a Browser on your system, view the Web page you just created. Print the page and exit the browser.

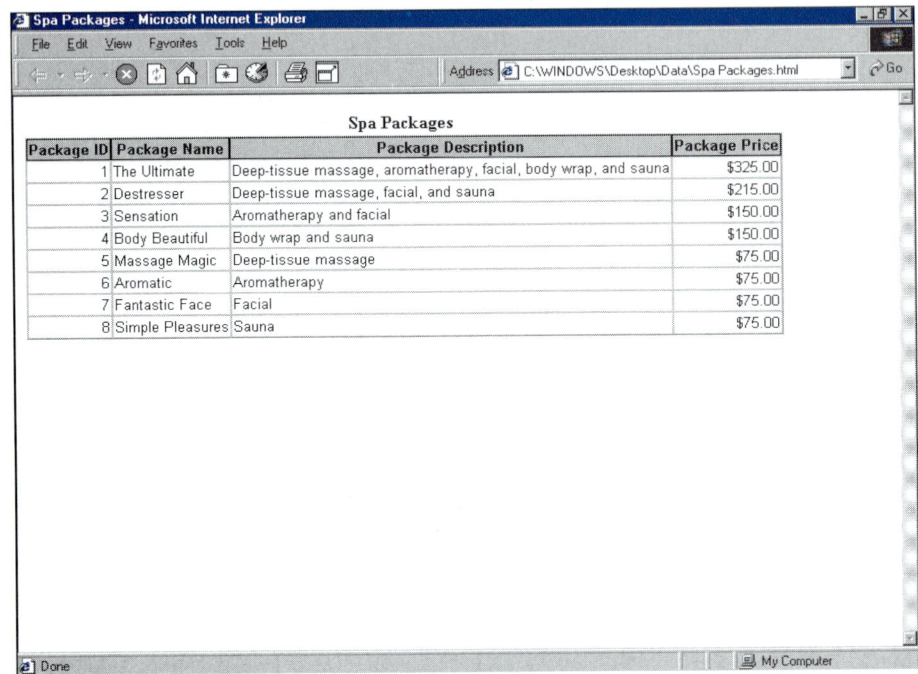

Spa Packages

Package ID	Package Name	Package Description	Package Price
1	The Ultimate	Deep-tissue massage, aromatherapy, facial, body wrap, and sauna	$325.00
2	Destresser	Deep-tissue massage, facial, and sauna	$215.00
3	Sensation	Aromatherapy and facial	$150.00
4	Body Beautiful	Body wrap and sauna	$150.00
5	Massage Magic	Deep-tissue massage	$75.00
6	Aromatic	Aromatherapy	$75.00
7	Fantastic Face	Facial	$75.00
8	Simple Pleasures	Sauna	$75.00

  c. Open the Packages Purchased table and add a field called **Web Page** with a Data Type of Hyperlink. Insert hyperlinks in the Web Page field of each record to the Web page you just created (Spa Packages.html). If you have a Web browser, test one of the hyperlinks by clicking on it; then exit the browser.

  d. Save and close the table. Close the Daria's Spa database.

Glossary of Key Terms

Best Fit: A feature that automatically adjusts column width to fit the longest entry.

Bound control: A control that is tied to a field in an underlying table.

Calculated control: Displays the results of a calculation in the form or report.

Cell: The space created by the intersection of a vertical column and a horizontal row.

Clip art: A collection of graphics that is usually bundled with a software application.

Column selector bar: In Query Design view, the thin gray bar just above the field name in the grid. It is used to select an entire column.

Column width: The number of characters that are displayed in a column in Datasheet view.

Comparison operator: A symbol used in expressions to compare two values. The > (greater than) and < (less than) symbols are examples of comparison operators.

Compound control: Text box and label controls that are connected and act as one when manipulated.

Control: In Form and Report Design views, graphical objects that can be selected and modified.

Criteria expression: An expression that will select only the records that meet certain limiting criteria.

Character string: A sequence of characters (letters, numbers, or symbols) that must be handled as text, not as numeric data.

Current record: The record, containing the insertion point, that will be affected by the next action.

Database: An organized collection of related information.

Data type: Attribute for a field that determines what type of data it can contain.

Design grid: The part of the Design window which displays settings that are used to define a table design or define a query.

Design view: Used to create new database objects and modify the design of existing objects.

Destination file: The document in which a linked object is inserted.

Drawing object: A graphic consisting of shapes, such as lines and boxes, that can be created using a drawing program such as Paint.

Edit mode: Used to enter and edit data in a field.

Expression: A combination of symbols that produces specific results.

Field: The smallest unit of information about a record, the values of which appear in a column of the database.

Field list: A small window that lists all fields in an underlying table.

Field name: Label used to identify the data stored in a field.

Field property: A character associated with a field that affects its appearance or behavior.

Field selector: A small gray box or bar in datasheets and queries that can be clicked to select an entire column. The field selector usually contains the field names.

Field size: Field property that limits a text data type to a certain size or limits numeric data to values within a specific range.

Filter: A restriction placed on records in an open datasheet or form to temporarily isolate a subset of records.

Form: A database object used primarily for onscreen display of records, to make it easier to enter data and to make changes to existing records.

Graphic: A non-text element or object, such as a drawing or picture, that can be added to a database.

Identifier: A part of an expression that refers to the value of a field, a graphical object, or property.

Inner join: The default Access join that joins tables based on the common fields if one of the common fields is a primary key.

Input mask: Used in fields and text boxes to format data and provide control over what values can be entered into a field.

Join: An association that tells Access how data between tables is related.

Label control: Displays descriptive text associated with the text box control.

Landscape: Printing orientation that prints a report across the length of the page.

Linked object: An object that is pasted into another application. The data is stored in the source document, and a graphic representation of the data is displayed in the destination document.

Live link: When a source document is edited, the changes are automatically reflected in the linked object in the destination document.

Many-to-many relationship: Records in both tables can have many matching records in the other table.

Move handle: A large box that is used to move a selected control.

Multitable query: A query that uses more than one table.

Navigation buttons: Used to move through records with a mouse.

Navigation mode: Used to move from field to field and to delete a field entry.

Object: An item such as a table, form, or report that can be selected and manipulated as a unit.

Object bar: Used to quickly access the different database objects.

Object list box: Displays a list of objects associated with the selected object type.

One-to-many relationship: Records in one table can have many matching records in a second table, but the second table can only have one match in the first table.

One-to-one relationship: Records in both tables only have one matching record.

Operator: A symbol or word that indicates that an operation is to be performed.

Orientation: The direction text prints on a page, either landscape or portrait.

Picture: An illustration such as a scanned photograph.

Portrait: Printing orientation that prints the report across the width of a page.

Primary key: One or more fields in a table that uniquely identify a record.

Query: A question you ask of the data contained in a database. Used to view data in different ways, to analyze data, and to change data.

Query datasheet: Where the result or answer to a query is displayed.

Record: A row of a table, consisting of all the information about one person, thing, or place.

Record number indicator: Displays the current record number and total number of records in the lower left corner of most views.

Record selector: Displayed to the left of the first column; it indicates which record is the current record.

Relational database: A database containing multiple tables linked by a common field.

Relationship: A link made between tables, usually through at least one common field.

Report: Printed output generated from queries or tables.

Sizing handles: Small boxes surrounding a selected control that are used to size the control.

Sort: A temporary record order in the datasheet that reorders records in a table.

Source file: The document in which a linked object is created.

Tab order: The order in which Access moves through a form or table when the Tab key is pressed.

Table: Consists of vertical columns and horizontal rows of information about a particular category of things.

Text box control: Creates a link to the underlying source, usually a field from a table, and displays the field entry in the report or form.

Unbound control: A control that is not connected to a field in an underlying table.

Validation text: Text that is displayed when a validation rule is violated.

Validity check: Process of checking to see whether data meets certain criteria.

Value: A part of an expression that is a number, date, or character.

View: An Access window format for viewing objects in a database.

Command	Shortcut Key	Button	Action
File/**N**ew	Ctrl + N	☐	Creates a new database
File/**O**pen	Ctrl + O	☐	Opens an existing database
File/**G**et External Data/**I**mport			Copies data from a file saved in another format into an Access database
File/**C**lose		☒	Closes open window
File/**S**ave	Ctrl + S	☐	Saves table
File/**E**xport			Saves an Access database object in another file format so it can be used in a different application or as a Web page
File/Page Set**u**p/Page/**L**andscape			Changes page orientation to landscape
File/**P**rint/Pa**g**es/**F**rom			Prints selected pages
File/Print Pre**v**iew		☐	Displays file as it will appear when printed
File/Print **R**elationships			Creates a report that shows the relationships in the current database
File/**P**rint	Ctrl + P	☐	Prints contents of file
File/**E**xit		☒	Closes Access
Edit/**U**ndo	Ctrl + Z	☐	Cancels last action
Edit/Cu**t**	Ctrl + X or Delete	☐ or ☒	Deletes selected record
Edit/**C**opy	Ctrl + C	☐	Copies selected text to the clipboard
Edit/**P**aste	Ctrl + V	☐	Pastes text from clipboard to current location
Edit/Delete Colu**m**n			Removes selected column
Edit/Se**l**ect Record	Shift + Spacebar		Selects current record
Edit/Select **A**ll Records	Ctrl + A		Selects all controls on a form in
Edit/**F**ind	Ctrl + F	☐	Locates specified data
Edit/R**e**place	Ctrl + H		Locates and replaces specified data
Edit/Delete **R**ows			Deletes selected field in Design view

Command	Shortcut Key	Button	Action
Edit/Primary **K**ey			Defines a field as a primary key field
Edit/Cle**a**r Grid			Clears query grid
View/**D**esign View			Displays form in Design view
View/**F**orm View			Displays form in Form view
View/**D**atasheet View			Display a form in Datasheet view
View/**P**roperties			Displays the current properties for the selected control
View/P**a**ge Header/Footer			Adds or removes the page header and footer section in a form
View/**T**oolbars/Web			Displays the Web toolbar
View/**Z**oom/%.			Displays previewed document at set percentage
View/**Z**oom/**F**it to Window			Displays entire previewed document page
View/**P**ages			Displays specified number of pages of previewed document
Relationships/Edit **R**elationship			Used to change existing relationships or create new relationships in the current database and to enforce referential integrity
Insert/**R**ows			Inserts a new field in table in Design view
Insert/Page Nu**m**bers			Inserts a page number text box in the page header or footer of a form
Insert/**C**olumn			Adds new column
Insert/**L**ookup Field			Creates a lookup field with specified values from which the user can choose from
Insert/**L**ookup Column			Creates a lookup column with specified values from which the user can choose
Insert/**O**bject			Inserts object into database
Insert/**R**eport			Creates a new report object
Insert/**S**ubdatasheet			Inserts a subdatasheet with values from a related table or query into the current datasheet
Insert/Hyper**li**nk			Inserts a new hyperlink or modifies the selected hyperlink
Filte**r**/Appl**y** Filter/Sort			Applies filter to table
Query/**R**un			Displays query results in Query Datasheet view
Query/Show **T**able			Displays Show Table dialog box
F**o**rmat/**F**ont/**S**ize		9	Applies font settings to selection
F**o**rmat/**C**olumn Width			Changes width of table columns in Datasheet view

Index

Notes